MICRO
COMPUTER
APPLICATIONS
FOR BUSINESS

MICRO
COMPUTER
APPLICATIONS
FOR BUSINESS

DOS

WordPerfect® 5.1

Lotus 1-2-3 Release 2.2

dBASE III PLUS®

■   ■   ■

Roy Ageloff University of Rhode Island
Scott Zimmerman Brigham Young University
Beverly Zimmerman Brigham Young University

Course Technology, Inc. One Main Street, Cambridge, MA 02142

Microcomputer Applications for Business is published by Course Technology, Inc.

Publisher	Joseph B. Dougherty	
Editor	Susan Solomon Communications	
Production Manager	Josh Bernoff	
Production Coordinator	Paddy Marcotte	
Desktop Publishing Group	Debbie Crane	Kim Munsell
Cover Design	Janet Bollow and Associates	
Designers	Andy Giammarco	Darci Mehall
Artists	Stacey Alickman	Mark Valentine
	Darrell Judd	
Copy Editor	Nancy Wirtes	
Proofreader	Darlene Bordwell	
Indexer	Barbara Hagerty	
Word Processor	Denise Nerahoo	
Manufacturing, Package Design	Mark Dec	
Quality Assurance Specialist	Rob Spadoni	
Quality Assurance Group	Peter Came	Betsy Paquelet
	David Crocco	Jeremy Parker
	John Harvie	Katherine Pinard
	Nicole Jones	Mark Valentine
	Marjorie Osterhout	Mark Vodnik

Microcomputer Applications for Business © 1992 Course Technology, Inc.

Trademarks

Course Technology and the open book logo are registered trademarks of Course Technology, Inc.
dBASE and dBASE III PLUS are registered trademarks of Borland International.
Lotus and 1-2-3 are registered trademarks of Lotus Development Corporation.
WordPerfect is a registered trademark of WordPerfect Corporation.
Some of the product names used in this book have been used for identification purposes only and may be trademarks or registered trademarks of their respective manufacturers and sellers.

Disclaimer

Course Technology, Inc., reserves the right to revise this publication and from time to time make changes in its content without notice.

ISBN 1-878748-76-9 (text)
ISBN 1-878748-77-7 (text and 5¼-inch disk, Lotus 1-2-3 Release 2.2, and dBASE III PLUS)
ISBN 1-878748-78-5 (text and 3½-inch disk, Lotus 1-2-3 Release 2.2, and dBASE III PLUS)

Printed in the United States of America

10 9 8

From Lotus Development Corporation

Today's global businesses require a workforce that knows how to use personal computers and other information tecnology for communication, analysis, and decision making. Thus, today's business professional must be adept at using software tools, such as 1-2-3, to communicate, analyze, and solve complex problems.

Lotus is helping students and instructors with tools that help them accomplish this goal. We are delighted to be working with Course Technology in bringing you *Microcomputer Applications for Business*, a high-quality text and software combination that offers, for the first time ever, a full-function, full-capacity version of 1-2-3 Release 2.2 specifically for the microcomputer applications course. We hope this text and accompanying software help prepare students for challenging careers in the business world.

■   ■   ■

From the Publisher

At Course Technology, Inc., we are very excited about bringing you, college professors and students, the most practical and affordable technology-related products available.

The Course Technology Development Process

Our development process is unparalleled in the higher education publishing industry. Every product we create goes through an exacting process of design, development, review, and testing.

Reviewers give us direction and insight that shape our manuscripts and bring them up to the latest standards. Every manuscript is quality tested. Students whose background matches the intended audience work through every keystroke, carefully checking for clarity, and pointing out errors in logic and sequence. Together with our own technical reviewers, these testers help us ensure that everything that carries our name is error-free and easy to use.

Course Technology Products

We show both **how** and **why** technology is critical to solving problems in college and in whatever field you choose to teach or pursue. Our time-tested, step-by-step instructions provide unparalleled clarity. Examples and applications are chosen and crafted to motivate students.

The Course Technology Team

This book will suit your needs because it was delivered quickly, efficiently, and affordably. In every aspect of our business, we rely on a commitment to quality and the use of technology. Every employee contributes to this process. The names of all of our employees, each equity holders in the company, are listed below:

Stephen M. Bayle, Josh Bernoff, Jan Boni, Irene Brennan, Susan Collins, John M. Connolly, Rebecca Costello, Debbie Crane, David Crocco, Tracy Day, Mark Dec, Yvette Delgado, Katie Donovan, Joseph B. Dougherty, Susan Feinberg, Lori Glass, Suzanne Goguen, David Haar, Deanne Hart, Peter Jakobs, Nicole Jones, Matt Kenslea, Peter Lester, Paddy Marcotte, Laurie Michelangelo, Kim Munsell, Paul Murphy, Amy Oliver, Debbie Parlee, George J. Pilla, Katherine Pinard, Diana Simeon, Rob Spadoni, Kathy Sutherland, Mark Valentine

■   ■   ■

Preface

Microcomputer Applications for Business represents a new approach to microcomputer applications education by combining a carefully developed text with fully functional software. It is designed for any first course on how word processing, spreadsheets, and database management are used in business.

THE TEXTBOOK

This textbook presents a unique approach to teaching how to use DOS, WordPerfect, Lotus 1-2-3, and dBASE III PLUS. Students learn to plan before they press keys. They learn to analyze the business problem and design their solution — whether it be a memo or letter, a worksheet or graphic, a query or a report. Then they solve the problem by following a distinctive step-by-step methodology, frequently referring back to their original plan. From this process students learn that word processing, spreadsheets, and database management are valuable tools to help make informed business decisions.

ORGANIZATION

The textbook consist of four parts:

Part I   *Essential Computer Concepts and DOS Tutorials*
Part II   *WordPerfect 5.1 Tutorials*
Part III   *Lotus 1-2-3 Release 2.2 Tutorials*
Part IV   *dBASE III PLUS Tutorials*

Part I acclimates students to the microcomputer environment. *Essential Computer Concepts* presents an overview of computers and includes only those concepts that students need before they go into the lab. The two DOS tutorials give students step-by-step instructions on how to use DOS for file management in both diskette and hard-disk environments. Both the concepts chapters and the DOS tutorials are unique in their approach. They motivate all of the concepts and skills they teach by explaining *why* students need to learn them.

Parts II, III, and IV contain hands-on tutorials with step-by-step instructions on how to use today's most popular microcomputer applications.

APPROACH

The *Microcomputer Applications for Business* textbook employs a problem-solving approach to teach students how to use WordPerfect 5.1, Lotus 1-2-3 Release 2.2, and dBASE III PLUS. This approach is achieved by including the following features in each tutorial:

Objectives A list of objectives orients students to the goals of each tutorial.

Tutorial Case This case presents the business problem that students will solve in the tutorial and that they could reasonably encounter in an entry-level job. Moreover, each business problem is geared to what the typical student taking this course is likely to know about business. Thus, the process of solving the problem using the microcomputer tool will be meaningful to the student. All of the key business areas — accounting, finance, marketing, production, and management — are represented.

Planning Section Each tutorial's case also includes discussion about planning the document, the worksheet, or the database management activity. Students learn to analyze the business problem and then set clear goals for the solution before they press keys. Outlines, planning sheets, worksheet sketches, and record layout sheets are introduced as basic tools.

Step-by-Step Methodology The unique CTI methodology integrates concepts and keystrokes. Students are asked to press keys always within the context of solving the problem. The text constantly guides students, letting them know where they are in the problem-solving process and referring them back to their original plan.

Page Design Each page is designed to help students easily differentiate between what they are to *do* and what they are to *read*. In addition, the numerous screen shots include labels that direct students' attention to what they should look at on the screen.

Exercises Each tutorial concludes with meaningful, conceptual questions that test students' understanding of what they learned in the tutorial.

Tutorial Assignments These assignments provide students with additional practice on the particular skills that they learned in the tutorial. Students practice these skills by modifying the business problem that they solved in the tutorial.

Case Problems Each tutorial concludes with several additional business problems that have approximately the same scope as the Tutorial Case. Students are asked to use the skills they learned in the tutorial to solve these case problems.

Additional Cases The progression from Exercises to Tutorial Assignments to Case Problems culminates in the Additional Cases. These are located after the last tutorial in each of Parts II, III, and IV. They range from relatively simple to challenging, and they require students to *integrate* the skills they learned in more than one of the tutorials. A list of the skills required to solve each Additional Case appears at the beginning of each case.

THE SOFTWARE — Lotus 1-2-3 Release 2.2 and dBASE III PLUS

Microcomputer Applications for Business is available with a full-sized (256 columns by 8,192 rows) and fully functional version of the Lotus 1-2-3 spreadsheet software. All the 1-2-3 features are included, with the exception of Allways. Installation instructions accompany the software.

   Also available is a fully functional version of dBASE III PLUS limited to 31 records.

   Both Lotus 1-2-3 and dBASE III PLUS are available in 3½-inch and 5¼-inch formats.

CTI Pocket Reference Cards These invaluable reference guides are included in every book and provide lists of functions, menu trees, and summaries of commonly used commands for all of the software covered in the text.

CTI Keyboard Template This useful aid is a laminated strip with WordPerfect 5.1 keyboard commands on one side and Lotus 1-2-3 function keys and commands on the other.

Coupon Students who buy this textbook packaged without Lotus 1-2-3 software can purchase their own copy of the software for a nominal price. Look for the valuable upgrade coupon included with this textbook. Students who buy this textbook with the software can use this coupon to upgrade to *Essentials of 1-2-3, Release 2.3* at a low price. The *Essentials* package contains an updated version of 1-2-3 with the powerful WYSIWYG spreadsheet publishing add-in and a textbook that introduces the software.

THE SUPPLEMENTS

Sample Files Disk The Sample files disk includes all of the documents, worksheets, and database files needed to complete all of the Tutorial Cases, Tutorial Assignments, Case Problems, and Additional Cases.

Instructor's Manual The Instructor's Manual is written by the authors and is quality assured. It includes:
- Answers and solutions to the all of the text's Exercises, Tutorial Assignments, Case Problems, and Additional Cases
- A diskette (3½-inch or 5¼-inch) containing solutions to all of the text's Tutorial Assignments, Case Problems, and Additional Cases
- Transparency Masters of key illustrations in the text
- A trouble-shooting guide for Lotus 1-2-3
- Hardware driver information for Lotus 1-2-3
- Tips on customizing installation of Lotus 1-2-3

Test Bank This supplement contains 50 questions per tutorial in true/false, multiple choice, and fill-in-the-blank formats. Each question has been quality-assurance tested by students for accuracy and clarity.

Electronic Test Bank This Electronic Test Bank allows professors to edit individual test questions, select questions individually or at random, and print out scrambled versions of the same test to any supported printer. In addition, technical support is available from Publishing Innovations at (508) 741-8010.

ACKNOWLEDGMENTS

Many people provided their special contributions to the successful completion of this book. While "thank you" never seems enough, this our thanks to each of them.

We want to thank the many reviewers of this text, in particular:

Hilda Allred, ADE Corporation; Carol Jeffries, University of North Carolina at Charlotte; Jon E. Juarez, New Mexico State University - Dona Ana Branch Community College; Lo-Ping Esther Ling, University of Rhode Island; Mel Martin, ETON Technical Institute; Marilyn Meyers, California State University at Fresno; June A. Parsons, Northern Michigan University; Thomas Pollack, Duquesne University; Leonard Presby, Patterson State University; Dennis Shafer, Cuyahoga Community College; B. J. Sineath, Forsyth Technical Institute; Sandy Stalker, North Shore Community College; David Stephan, Baruch College - CUNY; Marco Urbano, University of Rhode Island; Barry Walker, Monroe Community College; and Stuart Westin, University of Rhode Island.

Our appreciation goes to the Course Technology staff for their energetic quality assurance and for working tirelessly under tight deadlines to produce a quality, professional product. Rob Spadoni's attention to detail and Darlene Bordwell's eagle eye were invaluable to us. Debbie Crane and Kim Munsell worked magic with desktop publishing. David Haar's and Deanne Hart's marketing savvy were comforting. We especially thank Paddy Marcotte for her serene patience and her production expertise.

Thanks to Lotus Development Corporation, in particular, Alan Minard, for his support and encouragement.

We truly appreciate Joe Dougherty's unfailing support and willingness to make things work and we prized Steve Bayle's knowledge of software publishing and Josh Bernoff's production know-how. To John Connolly goes our admiration and thanks for creating an exciting, innovative company that will have a significant impact on the education of college students for years to come.

Last, but certainly not least, we give special thanks to editor Susan Solomon for her advice, counsel, and suggestions that have significantly shaped and improved this text. Without her expertise and leadership, this project would have never come to fruition.

Roy Ageloff
Scott Zimmerman
Beverly Zimmerman

Brief Contents

Contents

Part One
Essential Computer Concepts and DOS Tutorials

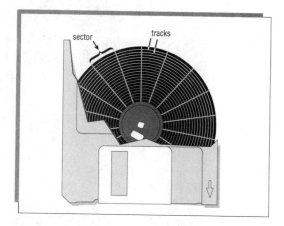

Part Two
WordPerfect 5.1 Tutorials

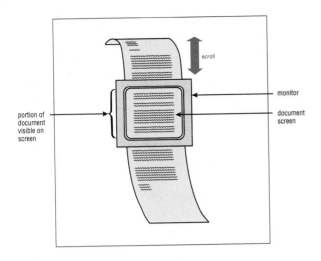

Tutorial 2   Formatting and Editing a Document   129

Writing a Product Information Memo for an Ad Launch

Tutorial 3   Using Additional Editing Features   177

Writing an Inventory Observation Memo

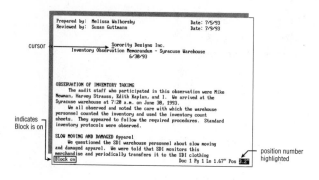

cursor

indicates
Block is on

position number
highlighted

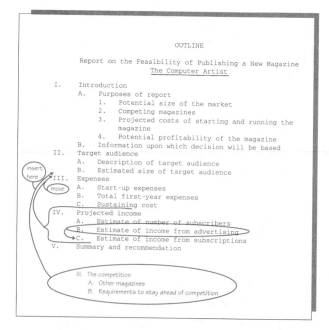

My Goal:

Calculate Net Asset Value for Balboa Equity Fund each day

What results do I want to see?

Net Asset Value (Price/Share) of Balboa Equity Fund

Breakdown of companies that make up the fund along with the market value of companies' stock

What information do I need?

For each company stock owned by the fund:

Name of the company

Number of shares of the company's stock owned by fund

Current price company's stock is selling for

What calculations will I perform?

Calculate market value of each stock in the fund

Calculate total value for all stock in the fund

Calculate Net Asset Value

```
A40: "CUST #                                              MENU
Input Criteria Output Find Extract Unique Delete Reset Quit
Specify the range to which extracted records are copied
                      Query Settings
   Input range:    A10..I32 (DATABASE)

   Criteria range: A35..I36 (SEARCH)

   Output range:   A40..I40 (HIGH_BALANCE)  <--

27      10 Landmark Medical Center  H   RI   3    23000   22,630.79
28       4 Oaklawn Pharmacy         P   RI   4     6000    4,513.21
29      19 Depasquale Pharmacy      P   RI   1     5000    4,214.50
30      17 De Bellis Pharmacy       P   RI   1     4000    2,715.35
31       1 Bristol Pharmacy         P   RI   4     3000    2,647.10
32      11 Lypho_Med Laboratory     L   RI   2     1000      538.62
33
34 Criteria Range
35   CUST # CUSTOMER NAME        TYPE ST  REP   CRD LMIT   BAL OWED
                                                           +G11>6000
36
37
38
39 Output Range
40   CUST # CUSTOMER NAME        TYPE ST  REP   CRD LMIT   BAL OWED
C6FILE1.WK1
```

output range now part of settings

Tutorial 7 Creating and Using Macros 557

Lotus 1-2-3 Additional Cases 585

Part Four
dBASE III PLUS Tutorials

Tutorial 1 An Introduction to Database Concepts and dBASE III PLUS 597

Tutorial 2 Creating a Database File Structure 615

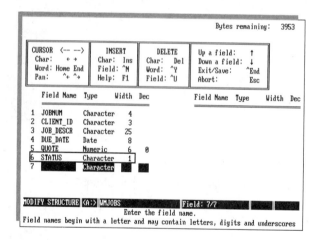

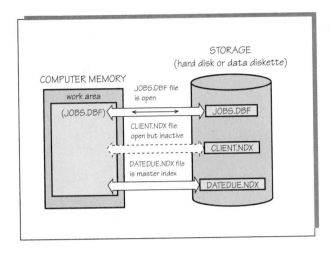

Part One

. . .

Essential Computer
Concepts and DOS Tutorials

- **Essential Computer Concepts**

- **Tutorial 1   Introduction to DOS**

- **Tutorial 2   Working with Directories**

- **Creating Your Data Diskettes for the WordPerfect, Lotus 1-2-3, and dBASE III PLUS Tutorials**

Essential Computer Concepts

What Is a Computer?

Computers have become prominent tools in almost every type of activity in virtually every type of business (Figure 1). What exactly is this important business tool? By definition, a **computer** is an electronic device that can perform operations — such as mathematical calculations or comparisons of numbers and characters — at extremely high speeds. But this definition fails to convey the power and the influence of computers in today's society. Computers can organize and process **data** (information of any kind — numbers, words, formulas, and so forth), manage financial information, create and manipulate graphics, and perform many other tasks to help business personnel be more efficient and productive.

Figure 1: Office workers at their computers

Types of Computers

Figure 2: A microcomputer

Computers are often classified by their size, speed, and cost. **Microcomputers**, also called **personal computers**, are inexpensive enough — $500 to $15,000 — for individuals to own and small enough to fit on an office desk (Figure 2). Some microcomputers are so small they can fit comfortably on your lap; appropriately they are called **laptop computers** (Figure 3). Other microcomputers, called **notebook computers**, are small enough to fit easily into a briefcase (Figure 4).

You'll probably use microcomputers throughout college and throughout your business career. Microcomputers are used extensively in small and large businesses. But some large businesses, government agencies, and other institutions also use larger and faster types of computers. One of these larger and faster computers is the **minicomputer** (Figure 5). Minicomputers are too large and too heavy for desktops, run three to 25 times faster than microcomputers, and cost anywhere from $15,000 to $500,000.

Figure 3: A laptop computer

Figure 4: A notebook computer

Figure 5: A minicomputer

A still larger and more powerful computer is the **mainframe computer** (Figure 6). Mainframes have large capacities for storing and manipulating data, run 10 to 100 times faster than a microcomputer, and cost anywhere from $100,000 to $2 million.

Figure 6: A mainframe computer

Figure 7:   A Cray supercomputer

The largest and fastest computers, called **supercomputers**, are so large and expend so much energy that they require their own internal cooling systems to dissipate the heat generated during their operation (Figure 7). Supercomputers are so expensive, often costing several million dollars, that only the largest companies, government agencies, and universities can afford them. Typically supercomputers run 50 to 10,000 times faster than a microcomputer.

With the accelerated development of new and better computers, the guidelines for classifying types of computers have become fuzzy. For example, some recently developed microcomputers run at higher speeds than some minicomputers. Since this book focuses on microcomputers, subsequent discussions will deal primarily with microcomputers. Most of the concepts, however, apply equally well to larger, more powerful computers.

Computer Hardware

The components of a computer that you can see and touch are often collectively called **hardware**. They include the monitor (the TV-like screen), the keyboard, the disk drives, the printer, and the part of the computer that does most of the work.

Computer hardware typically is divided into four categories: input devices, processing hardware, output devices, and storage media (Figure 8). These categories reflect the activities that the computer hardware performs. Suppose, for example, that you wanted to use the computer to write a letter. You would use the keyboard (an input device) to put the words of your letter into the processing hardware, which is found inside the main computer. Once inside the processing hardware, your words would be manipulated to form lines of the appropriate width and pages of the appropriate length and be centered, underlined, or italicized according to your instructions. After you finished your letter, you would use the printer (an output device) to reproduce the letter on paper. Finally, you would save a copy of your letter on a disk (a storage medium) for future reference.

Since you have to use input devices, processing hardware, and output devices for every task you want to perform on a computer, let's discuss each of these components in more detail.

Input Devices

Data entered into the computer are called **input**. The hardware involved in sending input to the computer is called an **input device**. The two most common microcomputer input devices are a **keyboard** and a **mouse**.

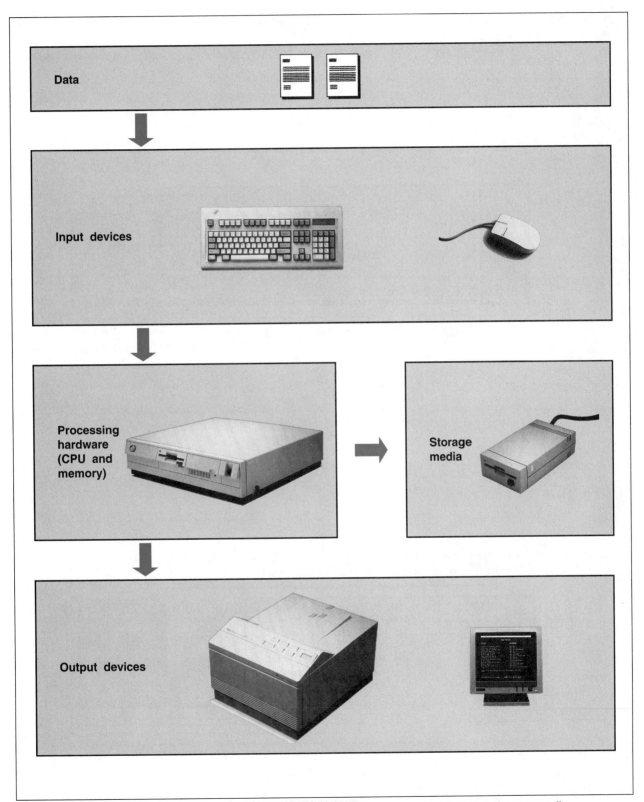

Figure 8: The relationship among input devices, processing hardware, output devices, and storage media

Most of the keys on your computer keyboard work just like the keys on a typewriter. Some features of a computer keyboard, however, are unique to computers. Figure 9 shows the standard 83-key IBM PC-style keyboard, and Figure 10 shows the enhanced 101-key IBM PS/2-style keyboard.

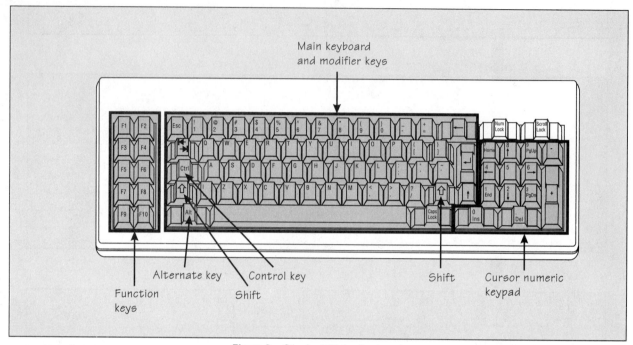

Figure 9:   Standard 83-key keyboard

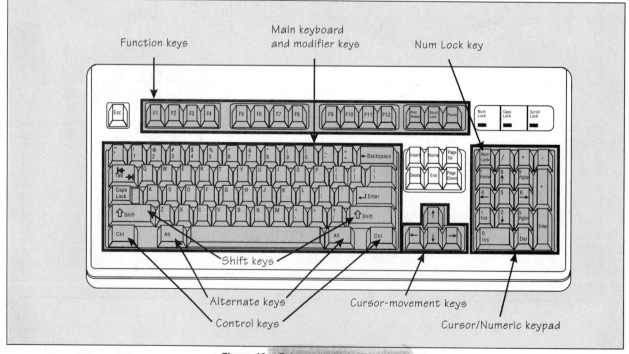

Figure 10:   Enhanced 101-key keyboard

The computer keyboards in Figures 9 and 10 consist of three major parts:

- Main keyboard and modifier keys
- Cursor/numeric keypad
- Function keys

The **main keyboard** works like the keys on an electric typewriter. To type text, you just press the keys. To type uppercase letters or symbols such as ~, !, @, #, and $, you press the [Shift] key (a modifier key) and while holding it down, press the desired keyboard letter or symbol key, then release both keys. In addition, you can combine the [Shift] key, the alternate key, [Alt], and the control key, [Ctrl], with other keystrokes to accomplish special tasks, such as saving or printing data.

The **cursor/numeric keypad** on both the standard and the enhanced keyboards is located to the right of the main keyboard. Turn [Num Lock] off (the [Num Lock] key is located just above the numeric keypad), and you can use the keypad to move the **cursor**, a blinking underscore character (_) or a rectangle that marks where the next character that you type will appear on the screen. Turn [Num Lock] on, and you can use the keypad to type numbers and other special symbols, such as the decimal point, the plus sign, and the minus sign.

Enhanced keyboards contain a separate set of cursor-movement keys between the main keyboard and the keypad. Thus, you can leave [Num Lock] on and use the numeric keypad to enter numbers and the cursor-movement keys to move the cursor.

The **function keys** are located to the left of the main keyboard on a standard keyboard and above the main keyboard on an enhanced keyboard. You use the function keys alone or with the modifier keys ([Shift], [Alt], and [Ctrl]) to execute special tasks, such as saving or printing data.

Your computer system may also be equipped with a **mouse** (Figure 11). As you push or pull the mouse along a surface, such as your desk, a **mouse pointer** moves on the monitor screen. A mouse allows you to position the cursor anywhere on the screen and to execute certain commands. Sometimes you can accomplish tasks more efficiently by using a mouse than by using a keyboard.

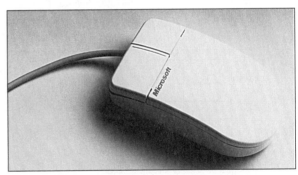

Figure 11: A mouse

Processing Hardware

The most important hardware elements within a computer are the **central processing unit** (**CPU**), or **microprocessor** — sometimes called the "brains" of the computer — and the **memory**, which stores instructions and data in the computer. Although you usually don't have to think consciously about the CPU and the memory while you are using a computer, you should be aware of the different types and speeds of microprocessors. Knowing about the different memory capacities of computers is helpful in case you want to buy your own computer or have to help decide what computers to buy in your business.

Figure 12: An Intel 80386 microprocessor, the CPU found in many IBM-compatible computers

The most popular microprocessors in IBM personal computers and IBM-compatible computers — those that run like IBM computers — are the Intel 8088, 8086, 80286, 80386, and 80486 (Figure 12). The numbers are simply model numbers designated by the manufacturer. Generally speaking the higher the number, the more powerful the microprocessor, meaning the microprocessor can handle more data at a time and faster.

The speed of a microprocessor is determined by its **clock rate**. The computer clock is part of a group of circuits associated with the CPU. Think of the clock rate as the "heartbeat" or "pulse" of the computer. The higher the clock rate, the faster the computer. Clock rate is measured in millions of cycles per second, or **megahertz (MHz)**. The Intel 8088 microprocessor on the first IBM PC ran at only 4.77 MHz; the Intel 80486 microprocessor on some current machines runs at 50 MHz.

The computer memory is a set of storage locations in the main part of the computer. Computers store instructions and data by using microscopic electronic switches, which can be either on or off. By associating an on switch with the number 1 and an off switch with the number 0, we can represent computer data with **binary** or **base-2** numbers, which consist of binary digits (called **bits**) with the value 0 or 1.

Computers generally store data in groups of eight bits, called **bytes**. A byte representing the integer value 0 is 00000000, with all eight bits set to 0; a byte representing the integer value 1 is 00000001; and a byte representing the integer value 2 is 00000010. Figure 13 shows the binary representation of some of the integer numbers from 0 through 255.

Each byte can also represent a character, such as A or @. For example, in IBM-compatible microcomputers an A is represented by the byte 01000001, B by 01000010, and C by 01000011. The characters ! (exclamation point), . (period), and + (plus sign) are represented by 00100001, 00101110, and 00101011, respectively.

Byte values can represent not only integers and characters, but also other types of data or instructions. A computer can determine the difference between the various types of data or instructions based on the context of the byte value, just as you can tell, based on the context, the difference between the two meanings of the word "hit" in the sentences "He hit me in the arm" and "The movie was a big hit."

As a computer user, you don't have to know the binary representation of numbers, characters, and instructions, since the computer handles all the necessary conversions internally. However, because the amount of memory in a computer and the storage capacity of disks are expressed in bytes, you should be aware of how data are stored so you will understand the capacity and the limitations of your computer.

Number	Binary representation
0	00000000
1	00000001
2	00000010
3	00000011
4	00000100
5	00000101
6	00000110
7	00000111
8	00001000
⋮	⋮
14	00001110
15	00001111
16	00010000
17	00010001
⋮	⋮
253	11111101
254	11111110
255	11111111

Figure 13: Binary representation of the numbers 0 through 255

For example, most IBM-compatible microcomputers have 640K (K means **kilobytes**) or 1MB (MB means **megabytes**) of memory. The prefix *kilo-* means one thousand, but for historical and technical reasons, a kilobyte is actually 1,024 bytes. The prefix *mega-* usually means one million, but in computer terms it literally means 1,024 x 1,024, or 1,048,576. A 640K computer can hold the equivalent of 640 x 1,024, or 655,360, characters. A 1MB computer can hold the equivalent of 1,048,576 characters, which approximately equals the amount of text in a 400-page book.

Memory comprises two types: read-only memory and random access memory. **Read-only memory**, or **ROM**, is the part of memory reserved for special data that are required for the internal workings of the computer. The microprocessor can read these data,

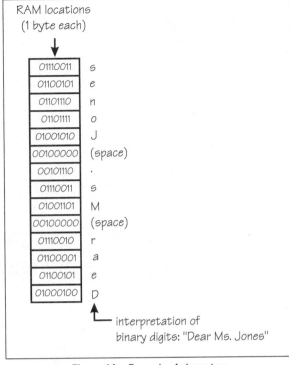

Figure 14: Example of characters stored in RAM

but it cannot erase or change the data. When you turn off your computer, the data in ROM remain intact, ready for use when you turn the computer back on.

Random-access memory, or **RAM**, is memory that is available to store input and processed information. A computer's microprocessor can read data from and write data to any location in RAM at any time. For example, when you type a report on your computer, the microprocessor stores the characters (letters, numbers, and so forth) of your report in RAM (Figure 14). When you modify the report, the microprocessor saves the new version in RAM. When you turn off your computer, the information in RAM is lost. Therefore, before turning off your computer, you need to save your work to a more permanent data storage medium.

Computer hardware also consists of ports and slots. **Ports** are the electronic pathways that pass data between the computer's CPU and its peripherals. **Peripherals** are hardware components, such as printers and monitors, that are connected to the main part of the computer. Microcomputers have two types of ports: serial and parallel (Figure 15). **Serial ports** send information between the CPU and other computer components one bit at a time. **Parallel ports** send information as multiple bits,

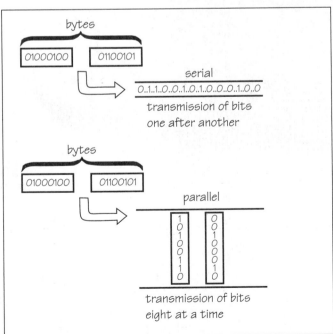

Figure 15: Comparison of serial and parallel ports

usually eight bits (one byte) at a time. Computer printers are often designated as serial or parallel to indicate the type of port to which they connect. Serial printers are usually connected to the port called **COM1** or **COM2** (for COMmunications port 1 or 2), and parallel printers are usually connected to the port called **LPT1** or **LPT2** (for Line PrinTer port 1 or 2). You need to know about these ports if you ever have to set up your own computer.

When you buy a printer or any other peripheral, make sure your computer has the right kind of port to match the peripheral. For example, if a new laser printer requires a serial port, make sure your computer has an available serial port to which you can connect the printer. If it doesn't, you can buy and install a board (or add-in card) that contains one or more additional ports. A **board**, or an **add-in card**, is a rectangular plate with electronic circuitry that you can insert into a slot. **Slots** are electrical connectors inside the computer (Figure 16). For example, one slot might contain a board that provides a serial port for a printer, as shown in Figure 16.

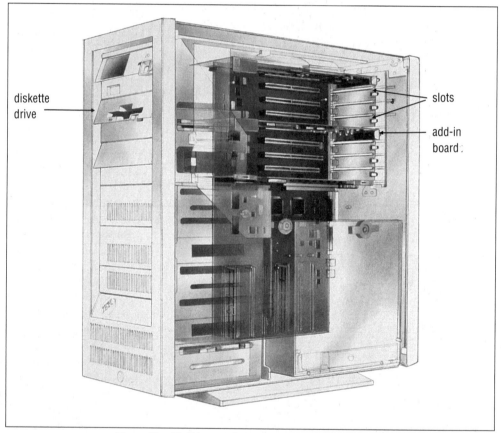

Figure 16: Slots in a vertically-configured microcomputer

Another slot might contain a board that allows the computer to communicate with other computers through a telephone line.

Output Devices

After you send data to the computer through an input device and after the CPU processes the data, the computer sends the processed data to a peripheral for storage or display. Data sent from the computer to the peripheral are called **output**, and the storage or display peripheral is called an **output device**. The most commonly used output devices are monitors and printers.

A **monitor** is the TV-like video screen that displays the output from a computer (Figure 17). Most micro-computers use a **CRT** (cathode ray tube) as the monitor screen. Most laptop computers use a flat-panel display, such as an **LCD** (liquid crystal display).

The text and graphics displayed on computer monitors are created with little dots of light called **pixels** (short for "picture elements") (Figure 18). Each pixel on a monochrome monitor has only one color (green, amber, or white) when the pixel is on and no color (black) when the pixel is off. Each pixel on a color monitor, on the other hand, can appear in any of several colors.

Figure 17: A color monitor

The entire monitor screen is a grid of pixels that combine to create the illusion of a continuous image. For example, a **CGA** (color graphics adaptor) monitor has a 320 x 200 grid, that is, 320 pixels horizontally and 200 pixels vertically. A **VGA** (video graphics array) monitor has a 640 x 480 grid. The higher the number of pixels on a monitor, the clearer and sharper the graphics images it can display.

IBM-compatible monitors have two modes: text and graphics. In **text mode**, the monitor can display only text — letters, digits, and special characters. In **graphics mode**, the monitor can display graphic images as well as text. All monitors have a text mode, but not all monitors have a graphics mode.

A **printer** produces a paper copy of the text or graphics processed by the computer. A paper copy of computer output is called **hard copy**, because it is more tangible and permanent than the electronic or magnetic copies found on a disk, in the computer memory, or on the monitor.

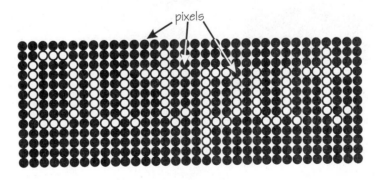

Figure 18

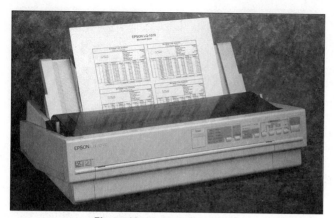

Figure 19: A dot-matrix printer

This is sample output from a
24-pin dot-matrix printer
in DRAFT mode

This is sample output from a
24-pin dot-matrix printer
in NLQ mode

Figure 20:   Sample output from a dot-matrix printer

The three most popular types of printers are dot-matrix, ink-jet, and laser printers. **Dot-matrix printers** form images by producing tiny dots of ink on the printer paper (Figure 19). The dots are formed when pins strike an inked ribbon. Less expensive dot-matrix printers have nine pins. More expensive models have 24 pins and produce higher-quality output. Figure 20 shows the text output from a 24-pin dot-matrix printer in draft mode. **Draft mode** prints very quickly but produces relatively low-quality output. Figure 20 also shows text printed in **near letter-quality mode** (**NLQ**), which prints more slowly but produces higher-quality output.

Figure 21: An ink-jet printer

Ink-jet printers spurt tiny dots of ink onto the paper to form text or graphics (Figure 21). Most ink-jet printers are faster than dot-matrix printers. They produce graphics of reasonable quality and text of high quality.

Laser printers use a laser beam to bond a black powdery substance, called **toner**, to the paper. This produces the highest-quality text and graphics of any type of printer (Figure 22). Moreover, laser printers are faster and quieter than dot-matrix and ink-jet printers. Laser printers can usually create output in several type styles (the appearance of the characters; for example, italics) and type sizes (the size of the characters) (Figure 23). For these reasons, laser printers are becoming the standard type of printer in the business world.

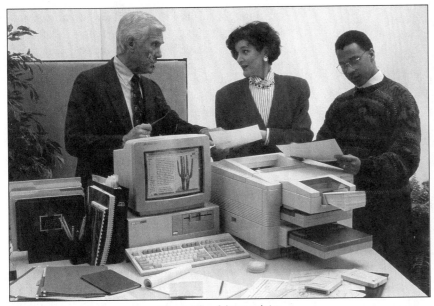

Figure 22: A laser printer

This is Courier.

This is Times Roman.

This is Helvetica.

This is Bookman.

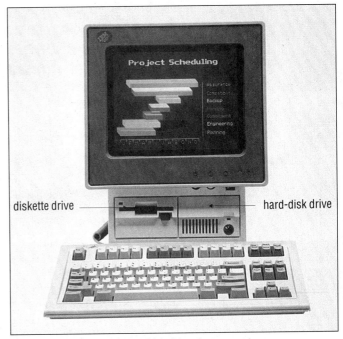

Figure 23: Sample output from a laser printer showing four typefaces in different font sizes

A **disk drive** is actually classified as both an input and an output device because it can send data to and receive data from the CPU (Figure 24). A disk drive helps the computer store data. Think of a disk drive as storing data in a manner similar to a tape recorder storing sound, except that instead of winding a tape, the disk drive spins a disk.

Storage Media

When you turn off your computer, you lose the information in the computer's RAM. For example, suppose you were typing the names, addresses, and other relevant data of the clients for a large company. As you typed, the computer would store this data in RAM. But how would you save these data for future use? You would store the data on a more permanent storage medium (Figure 25 on the next page). The most common storage media for microcomputers are diskettes and hard disks.

Figure 24: Disk drives in a computer

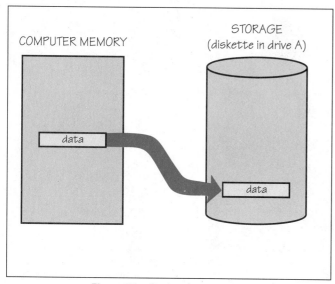

Figure 25:   Storing data on a disk

Sometimes called **floppy disks**, **diskettes** are made of flat, circular, oxide-coated plastic enclosed in a square case called a **disk jacket**. The most common sizes of diskettes for microcomputers are 5¼ inches and 3½ inches (Figure 26). The 5¼-inch diskettes have soft, flexible disk jackets and are usually stored in paper sleeves for protection. The 3½-inch diskettes have hard plastic cases and don't require sleeves.

The most common types of diskettes are double-sided, double-density (DS/DD) and double-sided, high-density (DS/HD). The 5¼-inch DS/DD diskettes have a capacity of 360K, and the 3½-inch DS/DD diskettes have a capacity of 720K. The 5¼-inch DS/HD diskettes have a capacity of 1.2MB. The 3½-inch DS/HD diskettes have a capacity of 1.44MB.

Diskette drives are also available in double-density and high-density types. A high-density diskette drive can read from both high-density and double-density diskettes. A double-density diskette drive, on the other hand, can read only double-density diskettes. Before you purchase diskettes, make sure they match your diskette drive. For example, if you have a 3½-inch high-density diskette drive, you should generally buy and use only 3½-inch DS/HD diskettes. Usually you cannot distinguish between DD and HD diskettes just by looking at them. High-density diskettes sometimes have "HD" written on their cases; usually, however, you have to rely on the information printed on the packaging.

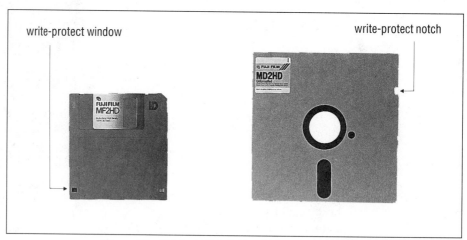

Figure 26:   3½-inch disk *(left)* and 5¼-inch disk *(right)*

Sometimes after you store information on a diskette, you may want to make sure that no one writes more information onto the diskette or erases the information from the diskette. For this purpose, diskettes provide **write protection**, which serves as a safeguard against losing valuable information. To write-protect a 5¼-inch diskette, you attach a write-protect tab across the write-protect notch; to write-protect a 3½-inch diskette, you open the write-protect window (Figure 27).

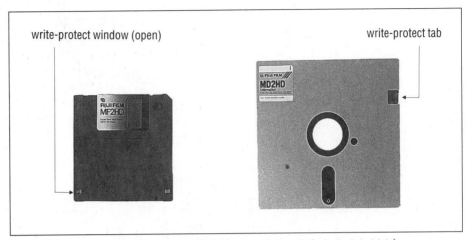

write-protect window (open)   write-protect tab

Figure 27: Write-protected 3½-inch disk *(left)* and 5¼-inch disk *(right)*

Hard disks, also called **fixed disks**, are nonremovable, oxide-covered metal disks, usually mounted permanently within the computer. Hard disks have two advantages over diskettes: speed and capacity. The speed of a hard disk is measured by its **access time**, that is, the time required to read or write a byte of data. A typical hard disk has access times one-third to one-tenth those of a floppy disk; therefore, a hard disk is 3 to 10 times faster at accessing data.

The capacity of a hard disk is measured in megabytes (MB). A small hard disk with a capacity of 20MB can store the equivalent of about 8,000 pages of text, compared to only about 150 pages of text on a 360K 5¼-inch floppy disk. Most microcomputer hard disks have capacities in the range of 20MB to 400MB. These high capacities are more than just conveniences; much of the work currently performed by businesses using microcomputers requires these higher-capacity hard disks.

Networks

In the business world you usually don't work alone but rather as part of a team. As a team member, you'll probably use a **network**, a collection of connected computers and peripherals. A network allows you to share data and equipment with other members of the team.

Typically one of the computers on a network is equipped with a high-capacity hard drive and is designated as the **file server**, that is, it "serves" the data to the other computers and peripherals on the network. The most common type of network involving microcomputers is a local-area network. In a **local-area network** (**LAN**), computers are joined by direct cable links and are located relatively close to each other, for example, in the same building (Figure 28 on the next page). Each computer in the LAN has a special network board inserted into one of its slots, and each board is joined by an electrical cable to the file server. Other computer equipment, such as laser printers, may similarly be joined to the LAN. Many businesses use a LAN so groups of workers can share resources.

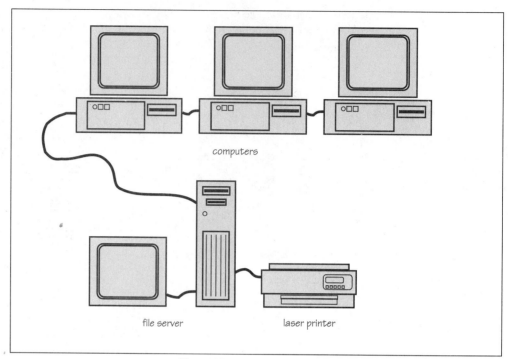

computers

file server   laser printer

Figure 28:   A local-area network

Computer Software

Just as a tape recorder or a compact disc player would be worthless without tapes or compact discs, computer hardware would be worthless without computer software. Software, also called **computer programs**, is sets of instructions that tell the computer what to do (Figure 29). The types of software that you use determine what you can do with your computer. For example, word processing software lets you use a computer to prepare documents, and graphics software lets you use a computer to create graphs and illustrations. Software can be divided into two general types: systems software and applications software.

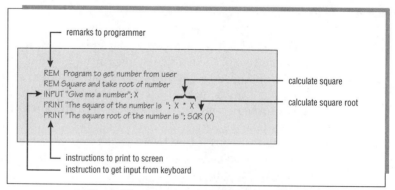

remarks to programmer

REM Program to get number from user
REM Square and take root of number
INPUT "Give me a number"; X
PRINT "The square of the number is "; X * X
PRINT "The square root of the number is "; SQR (X)

calculate square

calculate square root

instructions to print to screen
instruction to get input from keyboard

Figure 29:   A computer program written in the
BASIC programming language

Systems Software

Systems software includes the programs that run the fundamental operations within your computer, such as starting the computer, loading programs and data into memory, executing programs, saving data to a disk, displaying information on the monitor screen, sending information through a port to a peripheral, and performing many other basic functions.

A special type of systems software is the **operating system**, which works like an air-traffic controller to coordinate the activities within a computer, including all the input and output operations to and from the peripherals. The most popular operating system for IBM-compatible microcomputers is **DOS** (rhymes with "boss"), for Disk Operating System. PC-DOS is marketed by IBM; the PC stands for Personal Computer. MS-DOS is marketed by Microsoft Corporation; hence, the abbreviation MS. Both systems were developed primarily by Microsoft Corporation and work in essentially the same way. Another systems software program developed by Microsoft is **Windows**, a graphics-based operating environment designed for ease of learning and ease of use.

Applications Software

A wide variety of software exists to help you accomplish many tasks on your computer. This type of software is called **applications software** because it allows you to *apply* your computer to accomplish specific goals. The four major types of applications software for business are word processing, spreadsheets, database management, and graphics.

Word processing software allows you to electronically create, edit, format, and print documents (Figure 30). The advantages of a word processor over a typewriter are numerous. With a word processor, you can move and delete text, check spelling, create tables and columns, modify margins, draw lines, change the appearance of text (to boldfaced or underlined, for example), and view how a document will appear *before* you print it. A word processor

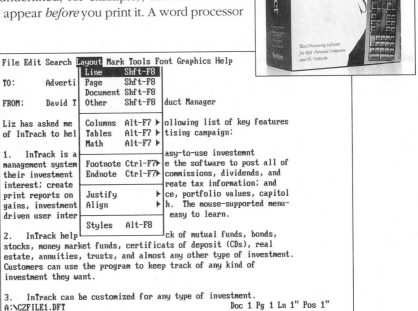

Figure 30: Example of a memo being produced with WordPerfect software and its pull-down menus

simplifies the process of printing headers, footers, page numbers, footnotes, endnotes, and line numbers. With a word processor, you don't have to worry about lines of text running into the margin, footnotes running off the bottom of the page, or titles being off-center. Word processing software takes care of these problems almost automatically.

An **electronic spreadsheet** allows you to perform calculations on numbers arranged in a grid of rows and columns on the computer screen (Figure 31). You can enter numbers, labels, formulas, and other kinds of information into the spreadsheet and automatically calculate the results. By using appropriate data and formulas, you can use an electronic spreadsheet to prepare financial reports and statements, analyze investment portfolios, calculate amortization tables, project income, and prepare a payroll, as well as perform many other tasks involved in making informed business decisions.

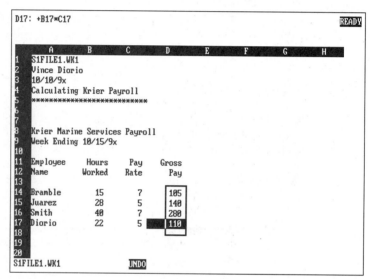

Figure 31:   Example of a spreadsheet created with Lotus 1-2-3 software

Database software helps you manage and manipulate information in the form of records, for example, information about employees, clients, schedules, supplies, equipment, or catalog entries (Figure 32). Database software allows you to easily retrieve, search, sort, select, delete, organize, and update a collection of data.

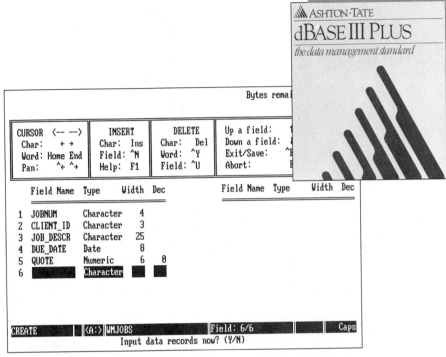

Figure 32: Example of a database file created with dBASE III PLUS software

Graphics software allows you to create illustrations, diagrams, graphs, and charts (Figure 33). For example, you could use graphics software to create a pie chart showing the major categories of expenses in your monthly budget. Most graphics software allows you to draw lines, boxes, circles, arrows, and other images; mix text and graphics; and enter raw data to create charts and graphs, as well as perform other operations to help prepare graphics as part of your business presentations, reports, and newsletters.

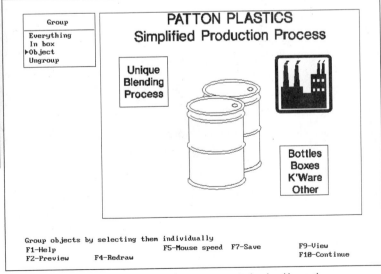

Figure 33: Example of a screen created using Harvard Graphics from Software Publishing Corporation

■   ■   ■

Exercises

1. Define or describe the following:
   a. hardware
   b. software
   c. cursor
   d. clock rate
   e. pixel

2. List and describe the four major classifications of computers based on their cost and speed.

3. What is the difference between a serial port and a parallel port?

4. Fill in the empty boxes in the following table with the storage capacities in kilobytes (K) or megabytes (MB) of each size of computer diskette:

	5¼-inch diskettes	3½-inch diskettes
DS/DD		
DS/HD		

5. Describe the two types of memory used by microcomputers.

6. Name the four major types of applications software used in business.

7. Describe each of the following hardware items:
   a. microprocessor
   b. slot
   c. port
   d. keyboard
   e. mouse
   f. monitor
   g. diskette drive

8. How would you write-protect a 5¼-inch diskette? A 3½-inch diskette? What is the purpose of write-protecting a diskette?

9. List the three most popular types of printers.

10. What is a network? What is the advantage of networking computers in business?

11. What is a network file server?

Tutorial 1

Introduction to DOS

Before You Begin

Before you begin this tutorial, make sure you have the following items:

- **A blank, unformatted diskette**. This should be either a 5¼-inch or 3½-inch diskette, to match the size of the diskette drive(s) on your computer.

- **A blank diskette label and a felt-tip pen**.

- **A diskette known as the Systems Disk**. This diskette is prepared in a special way and contains the DOS software. If your computer has a hard disk, the hard disk will serve as your Systems Disk, and you won't need a separate Systems Disk. If your computer has one or two diskette drives and no hard drive, you'll need a Systems Disk that matches the size of drive A of your computer. Check with your technical support person about the Systems Disk.

- **The Sample Files Disk that came with this textbook**.

After you collect these items, you are ready to prepare the DOS data diskette. You will use this diskette to help you work through DOS Tutorials 1 and 2.

OBJECTIVES

In this tutorial you will learn to:

- Start your computer and the disk operating system (DOS)

- Recognize the DOS prompt and execute DOS commands

- Set the date and time of the computer clock

- Clear the screen

- Check the DOS version

- Change the default drive

- List the names of the files on a diskette and recognize correct DOS filenames and common filename extensions

- Name, copy, rename, and delete files

- Format and write-protect a diskette

- Copy and check an entire diskette

- Use wildcard characters in DOS commands

- Turn off your computer

Carefully follow these steps to create your DOS data diskette:

❶ Using a felt-tip pen, write the words "DOS data diskette" on the label of the blank, formatted diskette.

❷ Start your computer. If you need help see your technical support person or follow the instructions on pages 25 and 26.

If you have *two diskette drives*, the drives are called drive A and drive B. If your drives are next to each other, drive A is on the left and drive B is on the right. If the drives are stacked, drive A is on the top and drive B is on the bottom.

If you have *one diskette drive*, the drive is called drive A.

❸ If there is a diskette in drive A remove it. Then insert the Disk Maker Program Disk in drive A (Figures 1-1a and 1-1b).

If your Disk Maker Program Disk doesn't match drive A but does match drive B, insert it in drive B instead. Then use drive B instead of drive A in the following instructions.

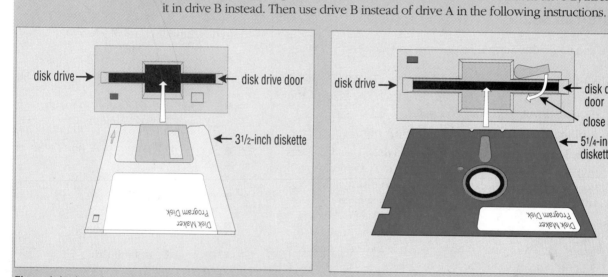

Figure 1-1a: Inserting a diskette into a 3½-inch drive

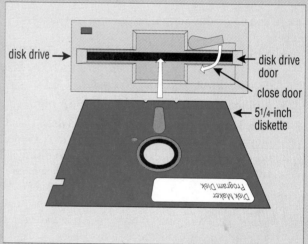

Figure 1-1b: Inserting a diskette into a 5¼-inch drive

❹ Type **a:** and press **[Enter]**. (If you inserted the Disk Maker Program Disk in drive B, type **b:** and press **[Enter]**.)

❺ Type **diskmake** and press **[Enter]**. The Disk Maker Main Menu screen appears. The *menu* is a list of five options: Exit to DOS, Make a DOS Data Diskette, Make a WordPerfect 5.1 Data Diskette, Make a Lotus 1-2-3 Release 2.2 Data Diskette, and Make a dBASE III PLUS Data Diskette. The highlight (a solid rectangle) is currently on "Exit to DOS."

❻ Press **[↓]** (down-arrow key) once. This moves the highlight to "Make a DOS Data Diskette." If you cannot find the down-arrow key, or if pressing it does not move the highlight, try pressing [Num Lock]. If this fails, ask your instructor or technical support person for help.

❼ Make sure the highlight is on "Make a DOS Data Diskette." Press **[Enter]**.

Messages appear on the screen and then you see another menu with three options: Continue, Exit to DOS, and Return to Menu.

8. Remove the Disk Maker Program Disk and put it away. Replace it with the DOS data diskette (the blank, formatted diskette you labeled in Step 1.)

9. Be sure the highlight is on the option "Continue," then press **[Enter]**.

10. Messages again appear on your screen. Eventually, you see the message "DOS data diskette created." Remove the diskette from the disk drive.

Now that you have created your DOS data diskette, you're ready to begin learning about DOS.

What Is DOS?

Often likened to an air-traffic controller, the **disk operating system**, usually called **DOS** (rhymes with *boss*), is a set of programs that controls the fundamental activities of your computer. For example, DOS starts the computer, prepares the diskettes so they can store data, copies the contents of one diskette to another, and manages the flow of data from the keyboard into the CPU, from the CPU to the monitor, from the CPU through the ports to the printer, and so forth.

Some of these activities — such as managing the flow of data from the CPU to the monitor — occur automatically. Other activities — such as preparing and copying diskettes — occur only when *you* instruct DOS to perform those activities. Whether you use a computer to write letters, prepare financial reports, manage client information, or perform any other type of task, you need to know how to use DOS.

Starting Your Computer and DOS

The procedure of turning on your computer and starting DOS is commonly referred to as **booting** the computer or booting the system. You can't boot your system unless you use a hard disk or diskette that contains DOS. Such a disk is called the **Systems Disk** because it contains the systems software essential for your computer to work.

Now let's see how to boot a computer. If you're using a computer in a classroom laboratory, consult with your technical support person before starting the following procedure. Complete this procedure only if you are using your own computer or your instructor or technical support person tells you to do so.

In the procedures in this and subsequent tutorials, a word or symbol within brackets refers to a key on the keyboard. For example, [Enter] refers to the Enter key on the right side of the main keyboard.

To boot a computer:

1. If you have a *two-diskette system*, insert the Systems Disk in drive A.

   If you have a *hard-disk system* or if your computer is part of a network, make sure no diskette is in drive A and the door, if any, to drive A is open.

2. Be sure to turn on the monitor and any other peripherals you are going to use.

For example, if you are going to print a file, turn on your printer as well as your monitor.

❸ If your computer is off, turn it on.

Usually the switch has a 0 or a circle for "off" and 1 or a line for "on" and is often found on the right side of your computer. Flip the switch to 1. You'll see the disk drive light go on while DOS and perhaps other programs are loaded into the computer.

If your computer has a built-in clock/calendar, the booting process is complete. If your computer doesn't have a clock/calendar, the screen displays two messages similar to those shown in Figure 1-2. The first line usually is the date 01-01-1980 (January 1, 1980). The second line is a **prompt**, that is, a message that requests information and waits for you to type that information into the computer. In this particular case the prompt requests you to type in a new date.

Figure 1-2
Prompt for the
new date

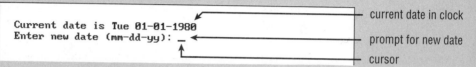

```
Current date is Tue 01-01-1980                     current date in clock
Enter new date (mm-dd-yy): _                        prompt for new date
                                                    cursor
```

❹ Enter today's date and press **[Enter]**.

You must type the date as numbers, with hyphens separating the month, day, and year. For example, if today were March 16, 1992, you would type 3-16-92.

If you make a mistake while typing the date, press [Backspace] (the key marked with a left arrow and located in the upper right corner of the main keyboard) to delete the mistake, then type the correct information.

After you enter today's date, you'll see two additional messages, as shown in Figure 1-3. The first message is the time, given in hours, minutes, and seconds (to the nearest one-hundredth of a second), that has elapsed since you turned on your computer. The second message is a prompt asking you to enter the current time.

Figure 1-3
Prompt for the
new time

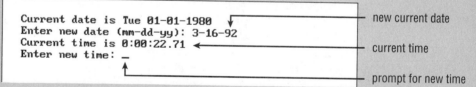

```
Current date is Tue 01-01-1980                     new current date
Enter new date (mm-dd-yy): 3-16-92
Current time is 0:00:22.71                          current time
Enter new time: _
                                                    prompt for new time
```

❺ Enter the current time and press **[Enter]**.

You must enter the time in 24-hour format. For example, if the time were 10:12 a.m., you would type 10:12; if the time were 3:36 p.m., you would type 15:36. You can enter the time to the nearest second or even to the nearest one-hundredth of a second, but usually the nearest minute is sufficient.

This completes the procedure for booting your computer. You will probably see a message telling you what version of DOS you are using, similar to what you see in Figure 1-4. The **version** is a number (such as 2.1, 3.0, 3.3, or 5.0) that indicates a particular variation from the original DOS. Each update of DOS is assigned a new version number. The higher the number, the later the release date, and the newer and more improved the features.

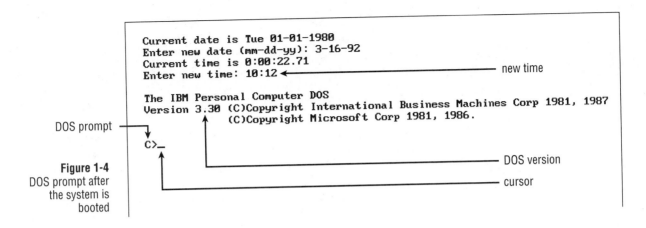

Figure 1-4
DOS prompt after the system is booted

The DOS Prompt

After you have booted your computer, the DOS prompt appears on the screen. The DOS prompt is a letter such as C or A, usually followed by a greater-than sign (>), similar to the prompt in Figure 1-4. When the DOS prompt first appears, the letter indicates the drive that contains the Systems Disk. For example, if you booted your computer using a hard disk, the DOS prompt is probably C>. If you booted your computer using a diskette in drive A, the DOS prompt is A>. If you booted your computer and logged into a network, the DOS prompt may be F> or something else. On some computers the DOS prompt may appear as C:\> or A:\>.

Immediately to the right of the DOS prompt is the **cursor**, usually a blinking underscore (_) character, which shows where the next character you type will appear on the screen. The DOS prompt and the cursor indicate that the computer is ready for you to give it instructions.

If your computer is not part of a network, go to the section "DOS Commands" on the next page.

Logging into a Network

If the computer you use is part of a network, you may have to log into the network. To **log in** or **log on** means to identify yourself as an authorized user and to gain access to the network resources. The following procedure describes how to log into a Novell network. You would follow similar steps for other commonly used networks. Consult your technical support person for your procedure.

To log into a Novell network:

❶ At the DOS prompt type the log-in command and your group name or user name (if required) and press **[Enter]**.

For example, if your group name is simply your course title and section, you might type something like LOGIN BUS101-12. Type the log-in command and the group name supplied by your instructor or your technical support person.

The network software now prompts you to type the **password**, a secret code or word that you must know to log into the network.

❷ Type the password supplied by your instructor or technical support person and press **[Enter]**.

The monitor usually doesn't display a password as you type it. This keeps other people from seeing the password on the screen and gaining illegal access to the network. If you see a message such as "Access denied," you may have made a mistake in typing the password. If this happens, retype the password. If you still are denied access, check with your instructor or technical support person.

If you have used the correct group name and password, you will be able to use the DOS programs and the applications software to which your group name (or user name) and password give you access. As you follow the steps in this and the next tutorial, some DOS commands might not be available on your network. Consult your technical support person if you have questions about access to DOS commands.

If your computer is part of a network, follow the steps in this book identified as those for a hard-disk system. Whenever this book refers to drive C or DOS prompt C>, substitute drive F or DOS prompt F> or whatever prompt is on your network.

DOS Commands

Once you have booted your computer, you can issue DOS commands. A **command** is an instruction that you enter into the computer to accomplish a specific task. Figure 1-5 lists the most commonly used DOS commands. "Internal" and "External" are explained in a later section. As you work through this tutorial and DOS Tutorial 2, you will learn how to execute these commands.

DOS Command	Description	Type
CHDIR (CD)	Change default directory	Internal
CHKDSK	Check disk	External
CLS	Clear the screen	Internal
COPY	Copy file(s)	Internal
DATE	Set or change date of DOS calendar	Internal
DEL	Delete file(s) (see also ERASE)	Internal
DIR	List the contents of a directory	Internal
DISKCOPY	Copy an entire disk	External
ERASE	Erase file(s) (see also DEL)	Internal
FORMAT	Format a disk	External
MKDIR (MD)	Make a new directory	Internal
PROMPT	Change appearance of DOS prompt	Internal
RENAME (REN)	Rename a file	Internal
RMDIR (RD)	Remove (erase) a directory	Internal
TIME	Set or change time of DOS clock	Internal
VER	Display the DOS version number	Internal

Figure 1-5
Commonly used
DOS commands

To execute a DOS command, you must first be sure that the DOS prompt (C>, A>, or F>, for example) appears on the screen and that the cursor is to the right of the prompt. If you don't see the DOS prompt, consult your technical support person.

If you make a mistake while typing a command and have not yet pressed [Enter], you can press [Backspace] to delete the mistake and then type the correct information. If you make a mistake and then press [Enter], DOS displays the error message "Bad command or file name." If this occurs, retype the DOS command correctly.

Setting the Date and Time (DATE, TIME)

Let's execute a DOS command by using the commands DATE and TIME. Some computers have an internal clock run by a battery. If the clock's battery runs down or the clock is not set to the correct time, these commands let you set the correct date and time. Having the correct date and time in the computer is important because DOS records the date and time whenever you save your computer work to a disk. Knowing the date and time of your work helps you, for example, keep track of which draft of a report you did first or when you wrote a certain letter.

First let's use the DATE command to set the correct date on your computer.

To execute the DATE command:

❶ Make sure the DOS prompt and the cursor appear on your screen.

❷ Type **date** and press **[Enter]**.

You can type the name of this or any DOS command in uppercase or lowercase letters or a mixture of both. DOS displays the message "Current date is" followed by a date (such as 1-01-1980) and then displays a prompt for you to enter the new date, as shown in Figure 1-6.

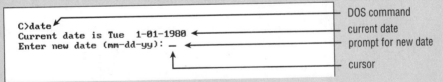

Figure 1-6
The DATE command

```
C>date
Current date is Tue  1-01-1980
Enter new date (mm-dd-yy): _
```
— DOS command
— current date
— prompt for new date
— cursor

❸ Type today's date and press **[Enter]**.

You must type the date as numbers, with hyphens separating the month, day, and year. For example, if today were March 16, 1992, you would type 3-16-92.

Next let's use the TIME command to set the correct time on your computer.

To execute the TIME command:

❶ Type **time** and press **[Enter]**.

DOS displays the messages shown in Figure 1-7 on the next page.

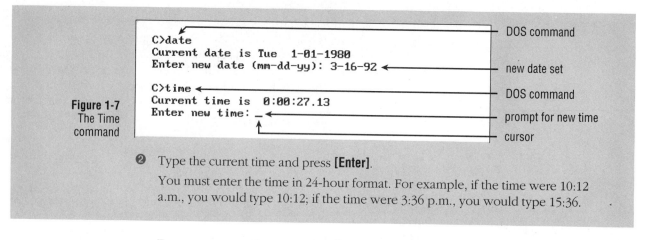

Figure 1-7
The Time
command

```
C>date
Current date is Tue  1-01-1980
Enter new date (mm-dd-yy): 3-16-92  ◄————————  new date set

C>time  ◄————————  DOS command
Current time is  0:00:27.13
Enter new time: _  ◄————————  prompt for new time
                  ↑
                  └————————  cursor
```
DOS command

❷ Type the current time and press **[Enter]**.

You must enter the time in 24-hour format. For example, if the time were 10:12 a.m., you would type 10:12; if the time were 3:36 p.m., you would type 15:36.

From now on until you turn it off, your computer will keep the correct date and time. You might have to reset the date and time whenever you turn on your computer.

Clearing the Screen (CLS)

Another commonly used DOS command is **CLS**, which stands for **cl**ear **s**creen. You use this command to clear your screen of unwanted output, such as you now have. Let's clear the screen.

To clear the screen:

❶ Make sure the DOS prompt and the cursor appear on your screen.

❷ Type **cls** and press **[Enter]**.

Remember, you can type a command in uppercase or lowercase letters or both.

DOS clears the screen and then displays the DOS prompt and the cursor in the upper left corner.

Checking the DOS Version (VER)

Another DOS command is **VER**, which checks the version of your DOS. You should know which version of DOS you are using, since some versions of DOS have commands not found in earlier versions.

To check the DOS version:

❶ Make sure the DOS prompt and the cursor appear on your screen.

❷ Type **ver** and press **[Enter]**. The version of DOS running on your computer appears on the screen (Figure 1-8). Instead of version number 3.30, you may see the number 2.10, 3.20, 5.00, or some other number. If the number is less than 2.1, consult your technical support person. Some of the DOS commands explained in this book require version 2.1 or higher.

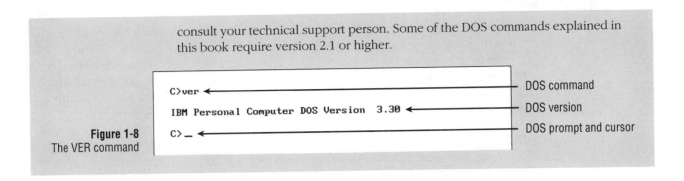

Figure 1-8
The VER command

C>ver ←	DOS command
IBM Personal Computer DOS Version 3.30 ←	DOS version
C> _ ←	DOS prompt and cursor

Changing the Default Drive

When you boot your computer, the DOS prompt displays the letter of the boot drive, for example, A, C, or F. This letter designates the **default drive**, which is the disk drive that DOS will use for any DOS command you issue, unless you specifically designate a different drive. You can change the default drive by typing the letter of the disk drive that you want to be the default drive, typing a colon (:), and then pressing [Enter]. In the following steps, you'll change the default drive so you can work with the DOS data diskette you created at the beginning of this tutorial.

To change the default drive using a *two-diskette system*:

❶ Insert the DOS data diskette into drive B.

❷ Type **b**: and press **[Enter]**.

Notice that the DOS prompt now indicates that the new default disk drive is B.

To change the default drive using a *hard-disk system*:

❶ Insert the DOS data diskette into drive A.

❷ Type **a**: and press **[Enter]**.

Notice that the DOS prompt now indicates that the new default disk drive is A.

You'll now be able to check the contents of the DOS data diskette by executing the appropriate DOS command.

Listing the Files on a Disk (DIR)

The contents of a disk are collected into groups of data or into sets of instructions called **files**. Each file contains the data from a particular application or the instructions for a particular computer program. For example, suppose you were writing a letter to a customer. The word processing program that you would use to write the letter would be in one or more files. The data (in this case, the words and punctuation marks) for the letter would be in another file. If you then wrote a second letter, the data for that letter would be stored in still another file.

To distinguish among the various files, DOS uses a different filename for each file. A **filename** is a unique name, composed of up to eight characters, that identifies a particular file on a diskette. A filename may also include a **filename extension**, which is composed of up to three characters. Filename extensions are described in more detail later.

You can obtain a list of the filenames and other information about the files by using the **DIR** command, which stands for "directory listing." A **directory listing** is a list of information about the files on a diskette. The information in the directory listing usually includes the filename, the size of the file, and the date and time that the file was created or last modified.

Listing the Files on the Default Drive

We'll first list the files on the default drive, which should be drive B if you're using a two-diskette system or drive A if you're using a hard-disk system.

To list the files on the default drive:

Make sure that the DOS prompt indicates the default disk drive letter where the DOS data diskette is located.

If you're using a *two-diskette system*, the DOS prompt should be B, indicated by B> or B:\>.

If you're using a *hard-disk system*, the DOS prompt should be A, indicated by A> or A:\>.

Type **dir** and press **[Enter]**.

Your screen should look similar to Figure 1-9. The DOS data diskette actually has more files than can fit on one screen.

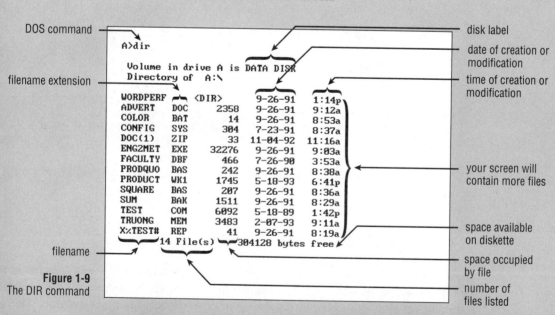

Figure 1-9
The DIR command

DOS first lists the volume label or tells you that the disk has no label. If you have DOS version 5.0 or later, DOS also indicates the volume serial number. Then DOS provides information about each file on the default drive: the filename and filename extension, the size of the file in bytes, and the date and time that the file was created or last modified. At the end of the directory, DOS lists the number of files on the disk, displays the amount of free storage space on the disk (in bytes), and redisplays the DOS prompt and cursor at the end of the directory listing.

Listing the Files on Another Drive

Suppose you want to list the files on a drive other than the default drive. You can do this by using the DIR command with the drive designation. In the following steps, you'll leave the default drive, where the DOS data diskette is located, and list the directory of the boot drive.

To list the files on a disk other than the default drive on a *two-diskette system*:

❶ Make sure the DOS data diskette is still in drive B and the default drive is drive B.

❷ Make sure the Systems Disk is still in drive A.

❸ Type **dir a**: and press **[Enter]**.

In this DOS command *a:* is a **parameter**, that is, it specifies the object of the DIR command. In this case, the object of the DIR command is the disk drive for which you want a directory listing. Be sure to type a space between *dir* and its parameter, *a:*. A listing of the files on the diskette in your drive A appears on the screen.

To list the files on a disk other than the default drive using a *hard-disk system*:

❶ Make sure the DOS data diskette is still in drive A and the default drive is drive A.

❷ Type **dir c**: and press **[Enter]**.

In this DOS command *c:* is a **parameter**, that is, it specifies the object of the DIR command. In this case, the object of the DIR command is the drive for which you want a directory listing. Be sure to type a space between *dir* and its parameter, *c:*. A listing of the files on your hard disk appears on the screen.

The directory listing you see is in the same format as Figure 1-9, but the actual filenames listed will be different.

Pausing the Directory Listing (/P)

You probably noticed that when you used DIR to get a directory listing of the files on the DOS data diskette not all the file information fit on the screen at once. Those files at the beginning of the listing disappeared from the screen before you could read the information. To solve this problem, you can use the **/P** (pause) option with the DIR command. An **option** specifies how you want DOS to carry out a command and is usually represented by a slash (/) and a letter. In this case, the /P option, when used with the DIR command, instructs DOS to pause the directory listing after each screenful. This pause allows you to look at the screen;

when you're ready, you press a key to view the next and any subsequent screenfuls one at a time. Let's see how the /P option works.

To pause the directory listing using the /P option:

❶ Make sure the DOS data diskette is still in drive B if you're using a *two-diskette system* or in drive A if you're using a *hard-disk system*.

❷ Make sure the default drive is where the DOS data diskette is located.

❸ Type **dir/p** and press **[Enter]**.

In this DOS command, */p* is the option. You can type the /P option with an uppercase or a lowercase P. You may include a space between *dir* and the option, but you don't need one. DOS displays one screenful of files and then displays a message such as "Strike a key when ready . . ." at the bottom of the screen. See Figure 1-10.

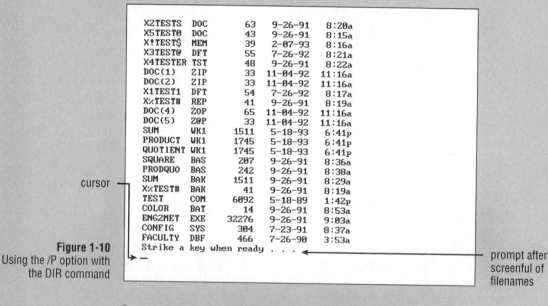

cursor

Figure 1-10
Using the /P option with the DIR command

prompt after
screenful of
filenames

❹ Press a key when you are ready to continue the listing.

You may press a key such as [Enter], [Space] (the Spacebar), a letter, or a number, but *not* [Shift], [Ctrl], or [Alt], to have the listing continue.

Repeat Step 4 as often as necessary to view the entire listing of files.

Displaying Only Filenames (/W)

Another way to display a long directory listing is to use the **/W** (wide) option. When you include this option in the DIR command, DOS lists only the filenames (including the filename extensions) across the width of the screen, five filenames per line. The file size and other information about the file are not listed. Let's use the /W option to get a directory listing of the DOS data diskette.

To use the /W option:

❶ Make sure the DOS data diskette is in the default drive, as before.

❷ Type **dir/w** and press **[Enter]**. A listing like the one in Figure 1-11 appears on the screen.

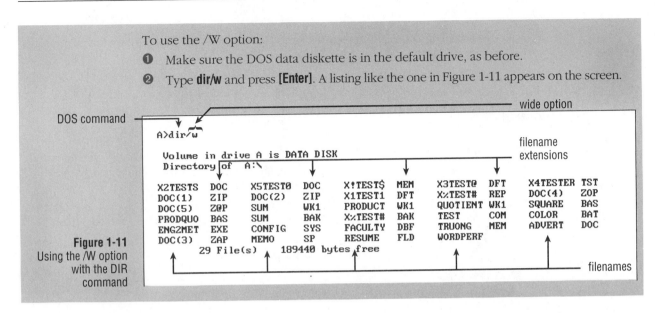

Figure 1-11
Using the /W option
with the DIR
command

For extremely long listings, you can combine the /P and /W options. If you typed *dir/p/w*, for example, DOS would display five filenames per line and pause after each screen. You can also combine parameters and options. For example, by typing *dir b:/p/w*, you would get a directory listing of the diskette in drive B that displays five filenames per line and pauses after each screen.

Filenames and Filename Extensions

As mentioned earlier, each file has a name by which you can identify the file on the disk. The name of a file usually has two parts: the **filename**, which should reflect the specific contents of the file, and the **filename extension**, which often reflects the general type of file. For example, the file that contains the WordPerfect word processing program has the name WP.EXE, where WP is the filename and EXE is the filename extension. The filename WP is an easy-to-remember abbreviation for WordPerfect, the contents of the file. The filename extension EXE indicates that this file is an executable file, in other words, a file that contains instructions the computer can execute.

Rules for Naming Files

You should know the DOS rules for naming files, because you'll have to name the files that you create when you use applications programs. Whenever you name a file, follow these rules:

- The filename must consist of one to eight characters.
- The filename may (but doesn't have to) include a filename extension, with a period separating the filename from the filename extension. A filename extension consists of one to three characters.
- A filename or filename extension may contain any of the letters A through Z in uppercase (although you may enter the letters in either uppercase or lowercase), the digits 0 through 9, and any of the following keyboard characters:

$$\$ \ \& \ \# \ @ \ ! \ \% \ ' \ ` \ \sim \ (\ ) \ \{ \ \} \ \_ \ \wedge$$

These letters, numbers, and characters are said to be *valid*.

- A filename or filename extension may *not* contain any of the following characters:

$$? . " / \setminus [\ ] : | < > + = ; , *$$

These characters are said to be *invalid;* a space is also invalid. A period (.) is valid only to separate the filename and the filename extension.

The following examples of filenames follow these naming rules. Such filenames are said to be *legal.*

LETTER.2	The filename has eight or fewer characters, the filename extension has three or fewer characters, and all the characters are valid.
93REPORT.{3}	The filename consists of eight valid characters, and the filename extension consists of three valid characters.
W63&9%	The filename consists of six valid characters; using no filename extension is legal.

The following examples of filenames do *not* follow the DOS naming rules. Such filenames are said to be *illegal.*

JONESLETTER.2	The filename contains more than eight characters. If you tried give a file this name, DOS would automatically shorten the filename to eight characters: JONESLET.2
REPORT.1993	The filename extension contains more than three letters. DOS would automatically shorten the filename extension to three characters: REPORT.199
MY REP.[5]	The filename contains an invalid character (a space), and the filename extension contains two invalid characters, [and]. DOS would not allow this filename.

Common Filename Extensions

Although files may have *any* filename extension that follows the above rules, some filename extensions are used more frequently because they have special meanings. Figure 1-12 lists some of these common filename extensions and their usual meanings. Some of these filename extensions are required; for example, all execution files must have the extension EXE or COM. Others are not required; for example, your backup files don't have to have the extension BAK. They could have the extension OLD or something else.

Filename Extension	Usual Meaning
BAK	Backup file — contains a copy of another file
BAS	BASIC file — contains instructions in the BASIC programming language
BAT	Batch file — contains multiple DOS commands
COM	Command file — contains computer instructions
DBF	Database file — contains data from dBASE
EXE	Execution file — contains computer instructions
SYS	System file — provides information for DOS
WK1	Spreadsheet file — contains data from Lotus 1-2-3

Figure 1-12
Common filename extensions

Renaming a File (RENAME or REN)

Choosing meaningful, descriptive names for your files is not easy. Sometimes you'll find that your choice of a filename is not the best, and you want to change it. For example, suppose you created a file that contained a memo to your coworker Sergio Pelota, and you named the file MEMO.SP. You then realized that the name of the file was not as descriptive as it could be, because after a week or two you might forget what MEMO.SP contains. You could solve the problem by changing the filename from MEMO.SP to PELOTA.MEM, a more descriptive name. Let's try this now.

To rename a file:

❶ Make sure the DOS data diskette is still in drive A or B, as before, and the default drive is the drive that contains the DOS data diskette.

❷ Type **dir/w** and press **[Enter]** to get a directory listing. Then verify the file MEMO.SP is on the diskette.

❸ Type **rename memo.sp pelota.mem** and press **[Enter]**.

Instead of typing *rename*, you could type *ren*, the shortened version of the command to rename a file.

The RENAME command always requires two parameters, the first one specifying the original filename and the second one specifying the new filename. See Figure 1-13.

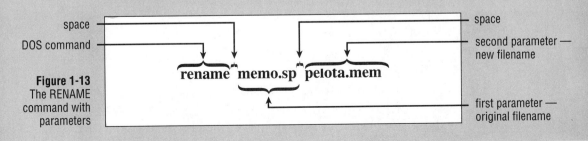

Figure 1-13
The RENAME command with parameters

space — DOS command — rename memo.sp pelota.mem — space — second parameter — new filename — first parameter — original filename

If the file has been renamed successfully, DOS displays no message; it simply displays the DOS prompt. Usually DOS displays a message only when an error occurs.

❹ Type **dir/w** again to view the directory listing to see that the filename has been changed from MEMO.SP to PELOTA.MEM. See Figure 1-14.

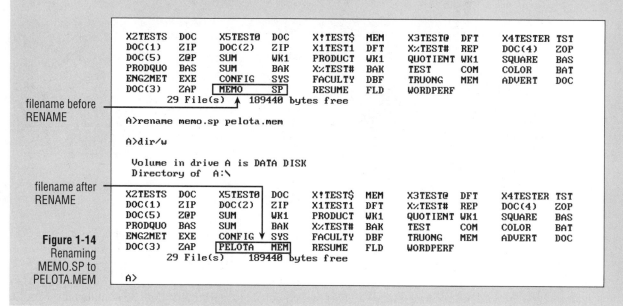

filename before RENAME

filename after RENAME

Figure 1-14
Renaming
MEMO.SP to
PELOTA.MEM

The RENAME (or REN) command changes the filename but does not modify the contents of the file.

Deleting a File (ERASE or DEL)

Suppose that a month after writing your memo to Sergio you no longer needed to keep the file on your disk. You could use the DOS command **ERASE** or **DEL** (delete) to remove the file from the disk. In fact, it is good practice to periodically erase files that you no longer need. This maximizes your disk capacity and keeps your disk from becoming cluttered. To see how ERASE and DEL work, you'll now erase the file PELOTA.MEM from your DOS data diskette.

If you are working on a network system, do not do the following steps unless your instructor tells you to do so.

To erase a file from the diskette:

❶ Make sure the DOS data diskette is in drive A or B, as before, and the default drive is the drive that contains the DOS data diskette.

❷ Type **erase pelota.mem** and press **[Enter]**.

Instead of typing *erase*, you could type del (for "delete"). The functions of ERASE and DEL are identical, so it doesn't matter which of the two commands you use. Both commands require one parameter, the filename of the file you want to delete.

③ Type **dir/w** to view the directory listing and to verify that PELOTA.MEM is no longer on the diskette. See Figure 1-15.

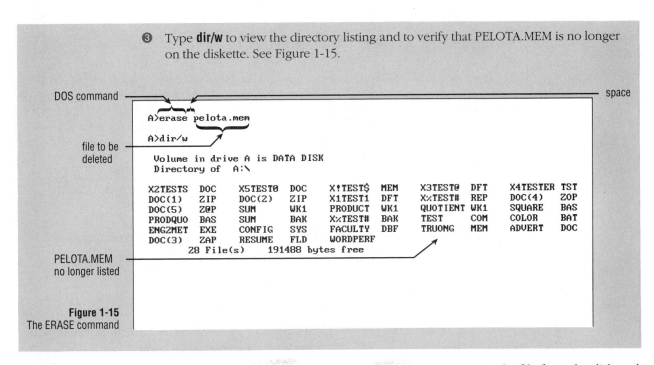

DOS command ——————————————————————————————— space

file to be
deleted

PELOTA.MEM
no longer listed

Figure 1-15
The ERASE command

```
A>erase pelota.mem

A>dir/w

 Volume in drive A is DATA DISK
 Directory of  A:\

X2TESTS   DOC    X5TEST0   DOC    X!TEST$   MEM    X3TEST@  DFT    X4TESTER TST
DOC(1)    ZIP    DOC(2)    ZIP    X1TEST1   DFT    X%TEST#  REP    DOC(4)   ZOP
DOC(5)    Z@P    SUM       WK1    PRODUCT   WK1    QUOTIENT WK1    SQUARE   BAS
PRODQUO   BAS    SUM       BAK    X%TEST#   BAK    TEST     COM    COLOR    BAT
ENG2MET   EXE    CONFIG    SYS    FACULTY   DBF    TRUONG   MEM    ADVERT   DOC
DOC(3)    ZAP    RESUME    FLD    WORDPERF
         28 File(s)      191488 bytes free
```

When you use the ERASE or DEL command, DOS removes the file from the disk and frees up the space on the disk. Files that you subsequently save to the disk can use the space previously occupied by the deleted file.

Be careful when you use ERASE or DEL. Once you delete a file, you *cannot* restore it, unless you have access to a specialized "undelete" program. Always double-check the name of the file you use with ERASE or DEL before you press [Enter].

Internal vs. External DOS Commands

Up to this point in the tutorial, all the commands you've used have been internal DOS commands. An **internal command** is built into DOS and can be executed without the Systems Disk in a disk drive. You can execute an internal command any time after you boot your computer, regardless of what diskettes are in a drive.

In the next section, you'll use an external DOS command. An **external command** is a program file that resides on the DOS Systems Disk. The program file has a filename that corresponds to the name of the command and a filename extension of COM or EXE. For example, in the next section, you'll use the FORMAT command. This is an external DOS command that uses the program file FORMAT.COM. This file, therefore, must be on your hard drive or on the Systems Disk in a diskette drive for you to use the FORMAT command. If you try to execute this or any other external command without the Systems Disk, DOS will give you the error message "Bad command or file name." To avoid this error or to correct it, make sure the file corresponding to the command is on a diskette and then try to execute the command again. If you're not certain about the availability of an external command, consult your technical support person.

Figure 1-5 shows the command type, internal or external, of the most commonly used DOS commands.

Formatting a Diskette (FORMAT)

A new diskette is like a phonograph record with no grooves; it can't receive or store any files. Before you can use a new diskette, you must **format** it, that is, prepare the diskette to receive files. If you were to use the DIR command, for example, with an unformatted diskette, DOS would display the error message shown in Figure 1-16. If you ever encounter such an error message, replace the unformatted diskette with a formatted one and then press *A* (abort) to stop the action and return to the DOS prompt.

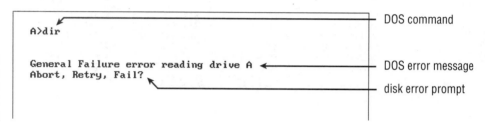

Figure 1-16
DOS error message
when you execute the
DIR command on an
unformatted diskette

You can think of a formatted diskette as having magnetic grooves called **tracks** on which DOS can store files. Formatting creates tracks in concentric circles around the center of the diskette and divides each track into **sectors**. Each side of a 1.44M 3½-inch diskette, for example, contains 80 tracks divided into 18 sectors (Figure 1-17). Diskettes of lower capacity have fewer tracks and fewer sectors. For example, each side of a 360K 5¼-inch diskette contains 40 tracks divided into nine sectors.

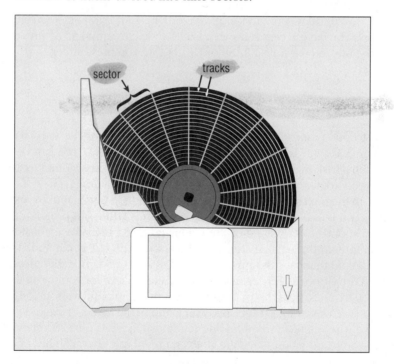

Figure 1-17
Tracks and sectors
on a formatted
3½-inch diskette

Before you continue, ask your instructor or technical support person for permission to format diskettes.

In the following steps, you'll use the FORMAT command to format a diskette. *Be sure you do not format your hard disk or any diskette that contains important information.* Formatting a used diskette destroys all data on that diskette. To avoid problems, check with your technical support person, then carefully perform the following steps.

To format a diskette on a *two-diskette system*:

❶ Make sure the Systems Disk is in drive A, then type **a:** and press **[Enter]** to make drive A the default drive.

❷ Type **format b:** and press **[Enter]**.

This command instructs DOS to format a diskette in drive B. The message shown in Figure 1-18 appears on the screen. If you see any other message on the screen, consult your technical support person immediately.

Figure 1-18
Prompt after you execute the FORMAT command on a two-diskette system

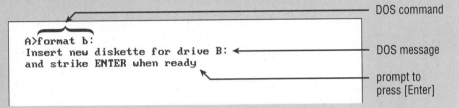

DOS command

DOS message

prompt to press [Enter]

```
A>format b:
Insert new diskette for drive B:
and strike ENTER when ready
```

❸ Insert a *blank* diskette into drive B.

Make sure the blank diskette matches the size and the capacity of the disk drive.

Now go to Step 5 on the next page.

To format a diskette using a *hard-disk system*:

❶ Remove the DOS data diskette from drive A.

❷ Type **c:** and press **[Enter]** to make drive C the default drive.

❸ Type **format a:** and press **[Enter]**.

This command instructs DOS to format a diskette in drive A. A message similar to the one in Figure 1-19 appears on the screen. If you see any other message on the screen, consult your technical support person immediately.

Figure 1-19
Prompt after you execute the FORMAT command on a hard-disk system

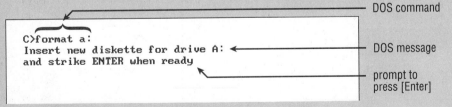

DOS command

DOS message

prompt to press [Enter]

```
C>format a:
Insert new diskette for drive A:
and strike ENTER when ready
```

❹ Insert a blank diskette into drive A.

Make sure the blank diskette matches the size and the capacity of the disk drive.

For either a *two-diskette system* or a *hard-disk system*:

⑤ Press **[Enter]** to initiate the formatting process.

While the diskette is formatting, a DOS message tells you what is happening. The particular message you see depends on the version of DOS you're using.

After the formatting is complete, DOS displays the message "Format complete." Depending on which version of DOS you are using, DOS may then display the message "Volume label (11 characters, ENTER for none)?" A **volume label** is a name recorded electronically on a diskette. Whenever you use DIR to view the contents of your diskette, the volume label will appear. Using a volume label helps you identify and manage your diskettes.

⑥ If you see the volume label prompt, type a volume name (such as WP FILES or your own last name) and press **[Enter]** or just press [Enter] without typing a volume name.

DOS now displays a message giving you the disk space and the technical information about how DOS uses that space. See Figure 1-20. It then displays a final message asking if you want to format another diskette.

Figure 1-20
Screen after you format a diskette

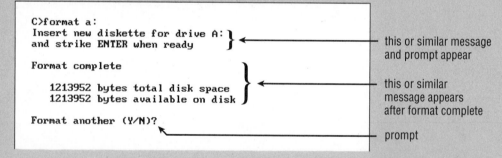

```
C>format a:
Insert new diskette for drive A:  }
and strike ENTER when ready       }      ← this or similar message
                                           and prompt appear
Format complete                    }
                                   }
    1213952 bytes total disk space }     ← this or similar
    1213952 bytes available on disk}       message appears
                                           after format complete
Format another (Y/N)?              ←       prompt
```

⑦ Press **n** (*no*) and press **[Enter]** to indicate that you don't want to format another diskette.

⑧ Remove the newly formatted diskette from the disk drive. If it is a 5¼-inch diskette, place it into a diskette sleeve.

⑨ On an adhesive diskette label, write a description of what you plan to store on the diskette, such as "WP Data diskette," and the date. Attach the label in the upper left corner of the diskette. See Figure 1-21.

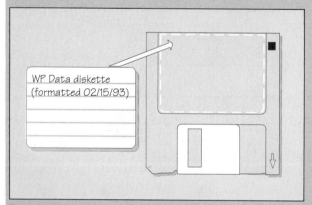

Figure 1-21a: Applying an adhesive label to a 3½-inch diskette

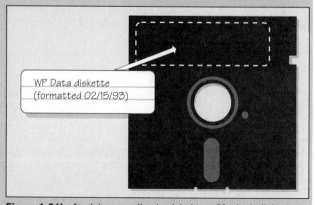

Figure 1-21b: Applying an adhesive label to a 5¼-inch diskette

Be sure to write the description on the label *before* you attach it to the diskette to avoid damaging the diskette.

This completes the steps for formatting a diskette. You can now store information on the diskette.

Write-Protecting a Diskette

When you save important files or store valuable programs on a diskette, you may want to ensure that no one can alter these data or programs. You can **write-protect** the diskette, which means you can prevent anyone from writing more information onto the diskette, renaming the files on the diskette, or erasing information from the diskette. You can load files from a write-protected diskette into your computer's memory so you can use the files, but you can't modify the contents of the diskette in any way.

To write-protect a 5¼-inch diskette, you attach a write-protect tab — a piece of plastic tape — across the write-protect notch. To write-protect a 3½-inch diskette, you open the write-protect window. See the chapter *Essential Computer Concepts* for more information on write-protection notches and windows.

If you try to erase a file from a write-protected diskette, DOS displays the error message shown in Figure 1-22. If you still want to erase the file, you have to take the diskette out of the drive, remove the write-protect tab or close the write-protect window, reinsert the diskette into the drive, and press *R* (*retry*). If you decide not to erase the file from the diskette, you press *A* (*abort*) to cancel the command.

Figure 1-22
DOS error message
when you try to erase
a file from a
write-protected
diskette

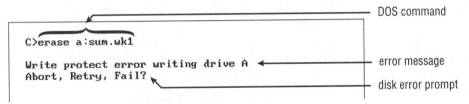

Even though write-protection helps safeguard files, you shouldn't write-protect a diskette as soon as you save information to it. For example, if you're in the middle of writing a report, you don't want to write-protect the diskette, because you'd have to remove the write-protection to save an updated version of the report.

Copying Files (COPY)

You can also safeguard files by making backups. A **backup** file is a copy of a file that you can keep as a safeguard against accidental deletion, damage, or loss of the original file. Having a backup when something goes wrong saves you considerable time, effort, and anguish.

Another reason to copy files is to create different versions of similar files. For example, suppose you're looking for a job in sales and have decided to apply for positions in field sales and telemarketing. You might want to create two versions of your résumé, each one emphasizing different skills. After using a word processor to create the first version, called RESUME.FLD (the résumé emphasizing field sales skills), you could copy it using a different filename, such as RESUME.TEL, then modify the copy to create a new version that emphasizes telemarketing skills.

Copying a File from One Disk to Another

In the following steps, you'll copy the file RESUME.FLD from drive A to drive B if you're using a two-diskette system, or from drive A to drive C if you're using a hard-disk system. Follow the steps appropriate for your computer system.

To copy a file from one drive to another on a *two-diskette system*:

❶ Insert the DOS data diskette into drive A, then type **a:** and press **[Enter]** to set the default drive to drive A.

❷ Insert a blank, formatted diskette, such as the one you formatted earlier in this tutorial, into drive B.

❸ Type **copy a:resume.fld b:** and press **[Enter]**.

This command says, "Copy the file RESUME.FLD from drive A to drive B." In this command the first parameter, *a:resume.fld*, specifies the **source**, which is the file you're going to copy. The second parameter, *b:*, specifies the **target**, which is the diskette onto which the copy will be made. See Figure 1-23.

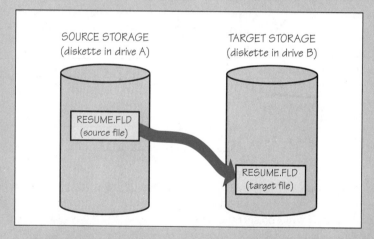

Figure 1-23
Copying a file from a diskette in drive A to a diskette in drive B

Make sure you do not type a space between the disk designation, *a:*, and the filename, *resume.fld*. You must, however, type a space between the source filename and the target drives. In this example, you could also type *copy resume.fld b:* without specifying the drive of the source file, since the source file is on a diskette in the default drive. Your screen should now look similar to Figure 1-24. A message indicates that DOS has copied one file.

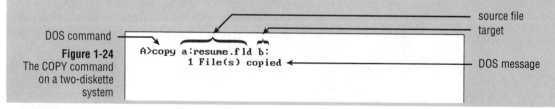

Figure 1-24
The COPY command on a two-diskette system

④ Type **dir b:/p** and press **[Enter]** to verify that RESUME.FLD was in fact copied to drive B.

To copy a file from one drive to another on a *hard-disk system*:

① Insert the DOS data diskette into drive A.

② Type **copy a:resume.fld c:** and press **[Enter]**.

This command says, "Copy the file RESUME.FLD from drive A to drive C." In this command, the first parameter, *a:resume.fld*, specifies the **source**, that is, the file that you're going to copy. The second parameter, *c:*, specifies the **target**, which is the disk onto which the copy will be made. See Figure 1-25.

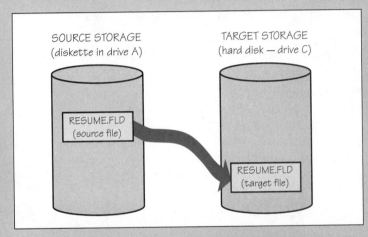

Figure 1-25
Copying a file from a diskette in drive A to a hard disk

Make sure you do not type a space between the disk designation, *a:*, and the filename, *resume.fld*. You must, however, type a space between the source filename and the target drive. In this example, you could also type *copy a:resume.fld* without specifying the target drive, since in this case the target drive is the default drive. Your screen should now look similar to Figure 1-26. A message indicates that DOS has copied one file.

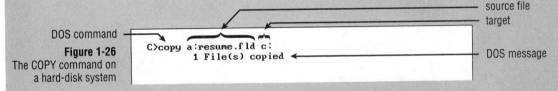

Figure 1-26
The COPY command on a hard-disk system

③ Type **dir c:/w/p** and press **[Enter]** to verify that RESUME.FLD was in fact copied to drive C.

In these steps, you have made a backup copy of the file RESUME.FLD on a disk other than the DOS data diskette. It is always a good idea to keep backup files of important files.

Copying a File Using a New Filename

Besides using the COPY command to make backups of important files, you can also use COPY to help create two versions of a file on the same disk. In the following steps, you'll copy the file RESUME.FLD, the field sales résumé, to the file RESUME.TEL, which you can then modify to create a telemarketing résumé.

To copy a file using a new filename on a *two-diskette system*:

❶ Make sure your formatted diskette containing RESUME.FLD is still in drive B.

❷ Type **b:** and press **[Enter]** to change the default drive to drive B.

❸ Type **copy resume.fld resume.tel** and press **[Enter]**. See Figure 1-27.

This command says, "Make a copy of the file RESUME.FLD on the same diskette but name the copy RESUME.TEL." The first parameter of the command is the source file, that is, the file that you want to copy. The second parameter is the target file, that is, the file that you want to create. See Figure 1-28. Since you haven't specified a drive with either the source file or the target file, DOS uses the default drive (in this case, drive B) to find the source file RESUME.FLD and to copy the target file RESUME.TEL.

❹ Type **dir/w/p** and press **[Enter]** to verify that RESUME.TEL is now on the diskette in drive B.

To copy a file using a new filename on a *hard-disk system*:

❶ Type **c:** and press **[Enter]** to change the default drive to the hard disk, where a copy of the file RESUME.FLD is located.

❷ Type **copy resume.fld resume.tel** and press **[Enter]**. See Figure 1-27.

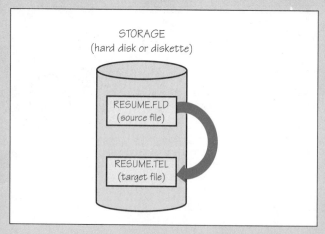

Figure 1-27
Copying a file to
the same diskette
with a new filename

STORAGE
(hard disk or diskette)

RESUME.FLD
(source file)

RESUME.TEL
(target file)

This command says, "Make a copy of the file RESUME.FLD on the same disk but name the copy RESUME.TEL." The first parameter of the command is the source file, that is, the file you want to copy. The second parameter is the target file, that is, the file you want to create. See Figure 1-28. Since you haven't specified a drive with either the source file or the target file, DOS uses the default drive (in this case, drive C) to find the source file RESUME.FLD and to copy the target file RESUME.TEL.

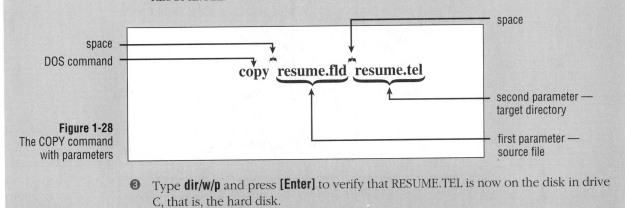

Figure 1-28
The COPY command
with parameters

❸ Type **dir/w/p** and press **[Enter]** to verify that RESUME.TEL is now on the disk in drive C, that is, the hard disk.

After you make a copy of the original field sales résumé, you can use your word processor to modify the copy to emphasize your telemarketing skills.

Copying a Diskette (DISKCOPY)

Sometimes you want to copy an entire diskette, not just one or two files, to another diskette. For example, when you purchase applications software, such as WordPerfect, you should copy all the original diskettes to backup diskettes and then use the backups in your day-to-day computer work. If you have a diskette with extremely important data, you should make a backup of the entire diskette to safeguard against accidental deletions, damage, or loss. If you need to give a colleague all your files on a particular diskette, you could copy the entire diskette.

To copy an entire diskette, you use the **DISKCOPY** command. The diskette you want to copy is called the **source diskette**, and the diskette that will be the copy is called the **target diskette** (Figure 1-29 on the next page). In the following steps, you'll copy the DOS data diskette to a blank diskette.

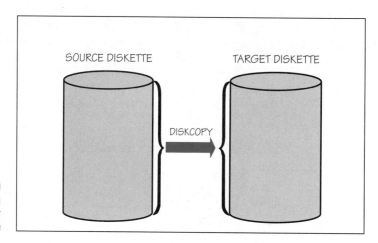

Figure 1-29
Copying an entire
diskette to another
diskette

Follow the appropriate steps for your system. If you have a two-diskette system with drives of equal size, that is, both are 5¼-inch drives or both are 3½-inch drives, and you use diskettes of equal capacity, you can copy from drive A to drive B. If you have a two-diskette system with drives of unequal size, that is, one is a 5¼-inch drive and one is a 3½-inch drive, you will have to use just drive A or just drive B to make diskette copies. If you have questions about your disk drive capacities or the method for using DISKCOPY, consult your technical support person.

To copy a diskette using a *two-diskette system* with drives of *equal* size:

❶ Insert a Systems Disk that contains the file DISKCOPY.COM into drive A and make drive A the default drive.

Since DISKCOPY is an external DOS command, you need the program file available to execute the command. If you have questions about the availability of DISKCOPY.COM, consult your technical support person.

❷ Type **diskcopy a: b:** and press **[Enter]**.

Make sure you type a space between the *a:* and the *b:*. This command says, "Copy a source diskette in drive A to a target diskette in drive B." The first parameter of DISKCOPY specifies the drive that contains the source diskette and the second parameter specifies the drive containing the target diskette. The DOS messages instruct you to insert the source diskette into drive A and the target diskette into drive B. See Figure 1-30.

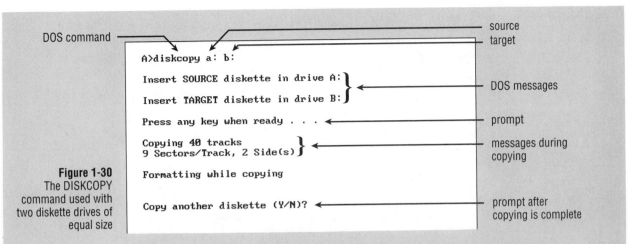

Figure 1-30
The DISKCOPY
command used with
two diskette drives of
equal size

③ Remove the Systems Disk and insert the source diskette — in this case, the DOS data diskette — into drive A.

④ Insert the target diskette — a blank diskette — into drive B.

Make sure that your target diskette is blank or that you no longer need the information on it. Any data currently on the target diskette will be destroyed when you execute the DISKCOPY command. DOS prompts you to press any key when you are ready.

⑤ Press **[Enter]** to start the copying process.

If soon after you start the copy process, DOS displays the error message "Drive types or diskette types not compatible," follow the steps below for copying with drives of unequal size.

While copying is occurring, messages similar to those in Figure 1-30 appear on the screen. If your blank diskette was already formatted, you won't see the message "Formatting while copying."

After the source diskette has been copied, DOS asks if you want to copy another diskette.

⑥ Press **n** (*no*) to instruct DOS that you don't want to copy another diskette.

To copy a diskette using a *two-diskette system* with drives of *unequal* size:

❶ Insert a Systems Disk that contains the file DISKCOPY.COM into drive A and make drive A the default drive.

Because DISKCOPY is an external DOS command, you need the program file available to execute the command. If you have questions about the availability of DISKCOPY.COM, consult your technical support person.

❷ Type **diskcopy a: a:** and press **[Enter]**.

Make sure you type a space between the first *a:* and the second *a:*. This command says, "Copy a source diskette in drive A to a target diskette also in drive A." The first parameter of DISKCOPY specifies the drive that contains the source diskette, and the second parameter specifies the drive that contains the target diskette. You could also type *diskcopy b: b:* and press [Enter].

Assuming that you're using drive A, DOS next prompts you to insert the source diskette into drive A. You will use the same drive for both the source diskette and the target diskette since DISKCOPY does not allow you to copy using two drives of unequal size or capacity.

❸ Remove the Systems Disk and insert the source diskette — that is, the DOS data diskette — into drive A.

DOS prompts you to press any key when ready.

❹ Press **[Enter]** to start the copying process.

❺ When prompted to do so, remove the source diskette from drive A and insert the target diskette — that is, a blank diskette — in drive A.

Make sure that your target diskette is blank or that you no longer need the information on the diskette. Any data currently on the target diskette will be destroyed when you execute the DISKCOPY command. DOS again prompts you to press any key when ready.

❻ Press **[Enter]** to continue the copy process.

❼ Continue to respond to the DOS prompts to insert the source diskette or the target diskette until the copying process is complete.

While copying is taking place, messages similar to those in Figure 1-31 appear on the screen. If you are using an unformatted diskette as the target diskette, you'll also see the message "Formatting while copying."

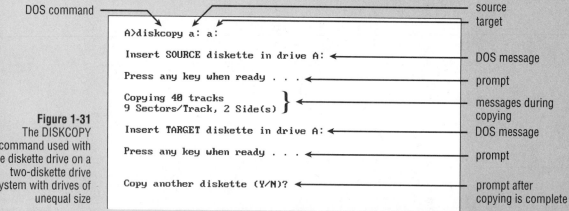

Figure 1-31
The DISKCOPY command used with one diskette drive on a two-diskette drive system with drives of unequal size

After the source diskette has been copied, DOS asks if you want to copy another diskette.

❽ Press **n** (*no*) to tell DOS that you don't want to copy another diskette.

To copy a diskette on a *hard-disk system*:

❶ Make sure drive C is the default drive.

Since DISKCOPY is an external DOS command, you need the program file available to execute the command. If you have questions about the availability of DISKCOPY.COM, consult your technical support person.

❷ Type **diskcopy a: a:** and press **[Enter]**.

This command says, "Copy a source diskette in drive A to a target diskette also in drive A." The first parameter of DISKCOPY specifies the drive that contains the source diskette, and the second parameter specifies the drive that contains the target diskette. See Figure 1-32.

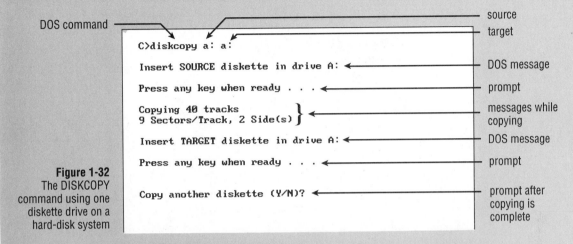

DOS command

source
target

```
C>diskcopy a: a:

Insert SOURCE diskette in drive A:    ← DOS message

Press any key when ready . . .    ← prompt

Copying 40 tracks          ⎫
9 Sectors/Track, 2 Side(s) ⎬    ← messages while copying

Insert TARGET diskette in drive A:    ← DOS message

Press any key when ready . . .    ← prompt

Copy another diskette (Y/N)?    ← prompt after copying is complete
```

Figure 1-32
The DISKCOPY command using one diskette drive on a hard-disk system

DOS then prompts you to insert the source diskette into drive A.

❸ Insert the source diskette — that is, the DOS data diskette — into drive A.

DOS prompts you to press any key when ready.

❹ Press **[Enter]** to start the copying process.

❺ When prompted to do so, remove the source diskette from drive A and insert the target diskette — that is, a blank diskette — into drive A.

Make sure that your target diskette is blank or that you no longer need the information on the diskette. Any data currently on the target diskette will be destroyed when you execute the DISKCOPY command. DOS again prompts you to press any key when ready.

❻ Press **[Enter]** to continue the copying process.

❼ Continue to respond to the DOS prompts to insert the source diskette or the target diskette until the copying process is complete.

While copying is taking place, messages similar to those in Figure 1-32 appear on the screen. If you are using an unformatted diskette as the target diskette, you'll also see the message "Formatting while copying."

After the source diskette has been copied, DOS asks if you want to copy another diskette.

❽ Press **n** (*no*) to tell DOS that you don't want to copy another diskette.

Now you have two exact copies of the same diskette. Be sure to write a brief description of the diskette, in this case, "Backup DOS data diskette," and the date on an adhesive label. Then attach the label to the backup diskette.

Checking a Disk (CHKDSK)

After you format or copy a diskette, it is a good idea to use the **CHKDSK** (check disk) command to check the diskette for possible problems and to get a report on the status of your diskette and your computer's memory. The CHKDSK command tells you if the files on the diskette are properly stored. It also tells you the capacity of the diskette, the amount of free space available on the diskette, the capacity of your computer's memory, and the amount of free space available in memory.

To use the CHKDSK command on a *two-diskette system*:

❶ Insert a Systems Disk that contains the file CHKDSK.COM or CHKDSK.EXE into drive A and make drive A the default drive.

Because CHKDSK is an external DOS command, you need the program file available to execute the command. If you have questions about the availability of CHKDSK, consult your technical support person.

❷ Insert the diskette that you want to check into drive B. In this case, insert your backup DOS data diskette into drive B.

❸ Type **chkdsk b:** and press **[Enter]**.

The parameter *b:* specifies the diskette that you want to check. DOS produces messages similar to those in Figure 1-33.

DOS command ──────┐

```
A>chkdsk b:
Volume DATA DISK    created Sep 26, 1991 9:38a

  362496 bytes total disk space
       0 bytes in 1 hidden files
    1024 bytes in 1 directories
  167936 bytes in 55 user files
  193536 bytes available on disk

  655360 bytes total memory
  468976 bytes free
```

information about diskette

information about computer memory

Figure 1-33
The CHKDSK command to check the diskette in drive B on a two-diskette system

To use the CHKDSK command on a *hard-disk system*:

❶ Make drive C the default drive.

Because CHKDSK is an external DOS command, you need the program file available to execute the command. If you have questions about the availability of CHKDSK, consult your technical support person.

❷ Insert the diskette that you want to check into drive A. In this case, insert your backup DOS data diskette into drive A.

❸ Type **chkdsk a:** and press **[Enter]**.

The parameter *a:* specifies the disk that you want to check. DOS produces messages similar to those shown in Figure 1-34.

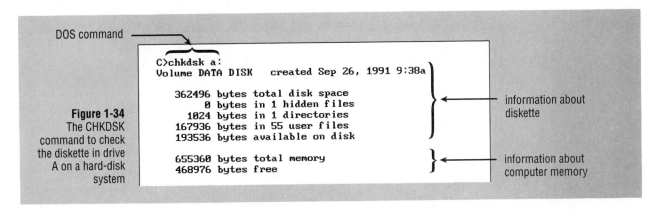

Figure 1-34
The CHKDSK command to check the diskette in drive A on a hard-disk system

```
C>chkdsk a:
Volume DATA DISK     created Sep 26, 1991 9:38a

   362496 bytes total disk space
        0 bytes in 1 hidden files
     1024 bytes in 1 directories
   167936 bytes in 55 user files
   193536 bytes available on disk

   655360 bytes total memory
   468976 bytes free
```

DOS command

information about diskette

information about computer memory

As you can see, CHKDSK gives you helpful information about your diskettes and your computer's memory.

Using Wildcards in DOS Commands

Sometimes you might want to use the same DOS command on more than one file. For example, suppose you want to delete all the files on a disk. Or suppose you want to copy several files on one disk to another disk. You can use the ERASE (DEL) or COPY command to perform this task on one file at a time—or you can use wildcards. **Wildcards** are symbols that represent characters common to the filenames of a group of files. The two DOS wildcards are the asterisk (*) and the question mark (?). In a DOS command the asterisk means "match any number of characters," and the question mark means "match any single character." Because a wildcard tells DOS to act on several files at once, you must exercise extreme caution in using wildcards with ERASE or DEL, since you could easily delete valuable files by accident.

First let's see how to use wildcards with the DIR command. Suppose you had 27 files on a diskette and three of them had the filename extension WK1, the standard filename extension for Lotus 1-2-3 worksheet files. Suppose also that you wanted to view a listing of only the worksheet files and you didn't have time to search through the entire list of 27 files. You could use the * wildcard in your DIR command to create a directory listing of only those files with the extension WK1. Let's try this now.

To use the * wildcard:

❶ Make sure the DOS data diskette is in drive A, then type **a:** and press **[Enter]** to make A the default drive.

❷ Type **dir *.wk1** and press **[Enter]**.

This command means, "Give a directory listing of all files that have any filename and that have the filename extension WK1." DIR can take a parameter that specifies the filename or set of filenames for which you want a listing.

DOS lists the files that satisfy the command's requirements. See Figure 1-35. As you can see, the DOS data diskette has three files with the filename extension WK1, which indicates that each file is a Lotus 1-2-3 spreadsheet file.

wildcard matches
any filename

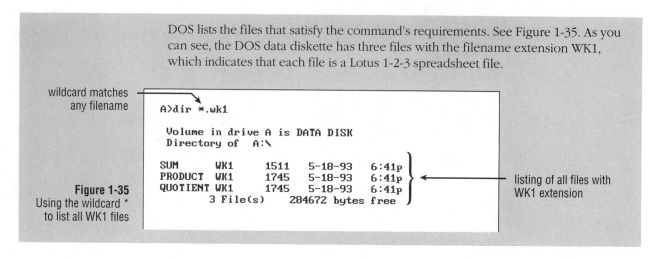

listing of all files with
WK1 extension

Figure 1-35
Using the wildcard *
to list all WK1 files

Now suppose that among the 27 files on your diskette, several files had the closely related filenames X1TEST1, X5TEST0, X!TEST$, and so forth, and had different filename extensions, such as DFT and DOC. You could use the ? wildcard to get a listing of only this particular group of files without having to look through all the other files on your diskette.

To use the ? wildcard:

❶   Make sure the DOS data diskette is in drive A and drive A is the default drive.

❷   Type **dir x?test?.*** and press **[Enter]**.

This command means, "Give a directory listing of all the files that begin with an X, have any character (letter, digit, or special character) after the X, then have the word TEST followed by any character, and then have any filename extension." DOS lists the files X1TEST1.DFT, X5TEST0.DOC, X!TEST$.MEM, and so forth. See Figure 1-36.

wildcard matches
any character

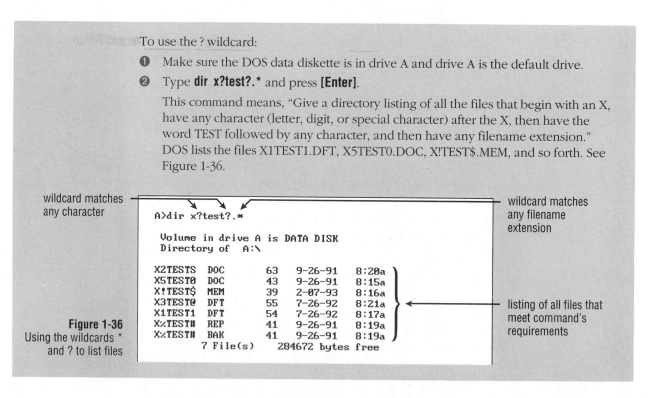

wildcard matches
any filename
extension

listing of all files that
meet command's
requirements

Figure 1-36
Using the wildcards *
and ? to list files

Wildcards are especially valuable when you are copying a group of files from one diskette to another, because usually you want to make backup copies of several files on a diskette at one time. Rather than copying 20 files by executing 20 COPY commands, you can save time and effort by executing just one COPY command with wildcards.

Let's copy a group of files. In the next steps you will copy a group of related files that have the filenames DOC(1), DOC(2), DOC(3), and so forth, and that have filename extensions that begin with Z and end with P, such as ZIP, ZAP, and ZOP. We'll use the wildcards * and ? to copy all the related files at one time.

To copy a group of files from one diskette to another using a *two-diskette system:*

1. Make sure your DOS data diskette is still in drive A and a formatted diskette is in drive B.
2. Make sure drive A is the default drive.
3. Type **copy doc*.z?p b:** and press **[Enter]**.

   This command instructs DOS to copy onto the diskette in drive B all the files on the diskette in drive A whose filenames begin with DOC, that have any set of letters, digits, and other characters after DOC, and that have a filename extension of ZIP, ZAP, ZOP, and so forth. As the command is executed, DOS lists the filename of each file it copies. See Figure 1-37.

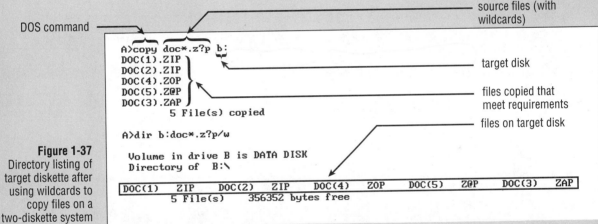

Figure 1-37
Directory listing of target diskette after using wildcards to copy files on a two-diskette system

4. Type **dir b:doc*.z?p/w** to confirm that the files have been copied to the diskette in drive B. See Figure 1-37.

   This command instructs DOS to list only those files whose names meet the specified requirements and to use the /W (wide) option.

To copy a group of files from one disk to another using a *hard-disk system:*

1. Make sure your DOS data diskette is still in drive A.
2. Make sure drive A is the default drive.
3. Type **copy doc*.z?p c:** and press **[Enter]**.

   This command instructs DOS to copy onto drive C all the files on the diskette in drive A whose filenames begin with DOC, that have any set of letters, digits, and other characters after DOC, and that have a filename extension of ZIP, ZAP, ZOP, and so forth. As the command is executed, DOS lists the filename of each file it copies. See Figure 1-38.

❹ Type **dir c:doc*.z?p/w** to see a directory listing of the newly copied files on the disk in drive C. See Figure 1-38.

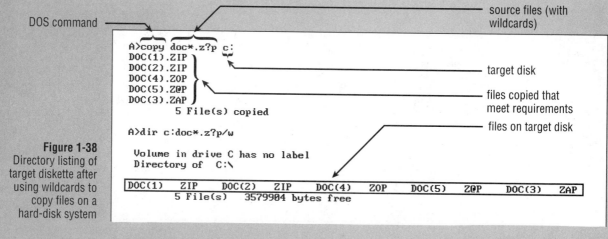

DOS command ──────

source files (with wildcards)

```
A>copy doc*.z?p c:
DOC(1).ZIP
DOC(2).ZIP
DOC(4).ZOP
DOC(5).Z@P
DOC(3).ZAP
         5 File(s) copied

A>dir c:doc*.z?p/w

 Volume in drive C has no label
 Directory of  C:\

DOC(1)   ZIP    DOC(2)   ZIP    DOC(4)    ZOP    DOC(5)   Z@P    DOC(3)   ZAP
         5 File(s)   3579904 bytes free
```

target disk

files copied that meet requirements

files on target disk

Figure 1-38
Directory listing of target diskette after using wildcards to copy files on a hard-disk system

This command instructs DOS to list only those files whose names meet the specified requirements and to use the /W (wide) option.

You can also use wildcards to delete a group of files. For example, suppose you no longer wanted the TEST*.Z?P files on the disk to which they were just copied. You could use ERASE or DEL with wildcards to delete only those files and no others.

To delete a group of files using a *two-diskette system*:

❶ Make sure your formatted diskette from the previous steps is still in drive B.

❷ Type **del b:doc*.z?p** and press **[Enter]**.

DOS deletes all the files on drive B that meet the requirements. If the deletions are successful, DOS gives no message. You can use the DIR command to verify that DOS has in fact deleted the files.

To delete a group of files using a *hard-disk system*:

❶ Make sure drive A is still the default drive.

❷ Type **del c:doc*.z?p** and press **[Enter]**.

DOS deletes all the files on drive C that meet the requirements. If the deletions are successful, DOS gives no message. You can use the DIR command to verify that DOS has in fact deleted the files.

Remember to be especially cautious about using wildcards to delete files, since you can easily delete valuable files by accident.

Turning Off Your Computer

If you are in a computer lab, check with your instructor or technical support person before proceeding.

After you have finished a session on your computer or at the end of a day's work, you may want to turn it off. The following guidelines will help you to know when and how to turn off your computer:

- Before you turn off your computer, make sure the cursor is at the DOS prompt. In general, don't turn off your computer from within an applications program, such as WordPerfect or Lotus 1-2-3. Exit the application first.

- If you're going to be away from your computer for a short time — less than two hours, for example — just leave your computer on. In these situations, it causes more wear on your computer system to turn it off and then back on than it does just to leave it on.

- Never flip the computer back on immediately after you have turned it off. If you turn off your computer and then decide to turn it back on, wait about 30 seconds. This gives the circuitry time to discharge properly and avoids damage to the computer chips. Some computers have a delay mechanism that prevents you from turning them back on without a short waiting period.

- Never turn off a computer connected to a network unless instructed to do so by your technical support person.

If appropriate, turn off your computer now. Make sure that the peripherals — the monitor, the printer, and so forth — are also turned off. Remove any diskettes that might be in the drives.

Exercises

1. What is the purpose of the disk operating system (DOS)?

2. List five tasks that you can instruct DOS to do.

3. What is the DOS prompt? Why is it important?

4. What is the difference between an internal and an external DOS command? Why is it important to know this difference?

5. What keys would you press to change the default drive from C to A? Why would you want to change the default drive from C to A?

6. Why do you have to format a diskette before you use it the first time?

7. Explain the purpose of each of the following DOS commands and write the keys you would press (including parameters, if necessary) to execute each command.
   a. VER
   b. CLS
   c. DATE
   d. DIR
   e. DEL
   f. TIME

8. What is another name for each of the following commands?
   a. RENAME
   b. ERASE

9. Explain each of the following terms:
   a. boot
   b. logging in
   c. password
   d. filename extension
   e. tracks
   f. sectors
   g. source disk
   h. target disk
   i. write-protect
   j. wildcards
   k. parameter
   l. option

10. What is the function of the following DIR options?
    a. /W
    b. /P

11. What are the two DOS wildcards? Why would you use them?

12. Explain how you would perform the following tasks, including the keys you would press:
    a. Format a diskette.
    b. Copy a file named INFO.FIL from drive A to drive B.
    c. Copy all the files with the filename extension LET from drive A to drive B.
    d. Get a listing of all the files on a disk that have the filename extension EXE.
    e. Check the capacity and the free space on a disk and in the computer's memory.
    f. Copy the entire contents of a diskette.

13. Which of the following characters are valid for a DOS filename? Which are invalid?
    a. /
    b. &
    c. +
    d. {
    e. [
    f. *
    g. @
    h. space

14. Which of the following filenames are legal? Which are illegal? For each illegal filename, state why it is illegal.
    a. MYFILE.001
    b. BOB CALL.LET
    c. 1993REP.Q2
    d. CHPT_02.DOC
    e. WP{FIL}.%%%
    f. PARKCITY.FILE
    g. QUARTER-2.REP
    h. $HAPPY$
    i. MOM+DAD.LET

Tutorial Assignments

Perform the following activities and answer the following questions while at your computer. You may have to use one or more DOS commands to answer a question.

1. Immediately after you boot your system and get to the DOS prompt, what does your DOS prompt look like?

2. What version of DOS is your computer running?

3. Clear your computer screen.

Get a directory listing of your DOS data diskette, then answer the following questions.

4.   How many files are on the diskette?

5.   Which file is the oldest, that is, has the earliest date and time of creation or modification? What is the date and time of that file?

6.   Which file is the largest, that is, takes up the greatest amount of space in bytes? What is the size (in bytes) of that file?

7.   How many files on the DOS data diskette have the filename extension WK1? *Hint:* Use a wildcard with DIR to answer this question.

Use the DOS data diskette to perform the following exercises and to answer the following questions:

8.   Check the DOS data diskette using the CHKDSK command.
    a.   What is its capacity (in bytes)?
    b.   How much free space (in bytes) is available?
    c.   What is the memory capacity of the computer you're using?
    d.   How much free memory is available in your computer at this time?

9.   Copy the file SUM.WK1 with the new filename ADD.WK1 so that both files reside on the DOS data diskette.

10. Delete all the files with the filename extension BAK.

Tutorial 2

Working with Directories

Before You Begin

Before you begin this tutorial, make sure you have the following items:

- **The diskette that you formatted in DOS Tutorial 1 or any other newly formatted diskette**. We'll call this the "work diskette" because you will work with it in learning and using the DOS commands explained in this tutorial. Using a felt-tip pen, write "WORK DISKETTE" on the diskette label.

- **The Systems Disk**. If you have a two-diskette system, the Systems Disk is the diskette that contains DOS. If you have a hard-disk system, the hard disk is the Systems Disk, so you don't need a separate Systems Disk.

- **The DOS data diskette**, which you created at the beginning of DOS Tutorial 1.

What Is a Directory?

Suppose you worked in an office and wanted to find the 1992 annual sales report that you wrote several weeks ago. You'd go to your file cabinet, open the appropriate file drawer, and find the hanging folder labeled "REPORTS." You'd then take out the manila folder labeled "SALES," open the folder, and remove the document titled "1992 Annual Sales Report." The document wouldn't be hard to find if you had filed it away in the correct file drawer, the correct hanging folder, and the correct manila folder. But imagine how hard the report would be to find if you had filed it randomly in the file drawer among dozens or even hundreds of other documents.

OBJECTIVES

In this tutorial you will learn to:

- Use directories to organize files

- Use paths to access files within a directory

- Make a new directory or subdirectory

- Name a directory

- Remove a directory from a disk

- Change the information in the DOS prompt

- Change the default directory

Managing your computer files works the same way, but instead of using a file cabinet, you store your computer files on a disk (Figure 2-1). Instead of using hanging folders and manila folders, you use directories. A **directory** is a division of a disk in which a group of files can be stored.

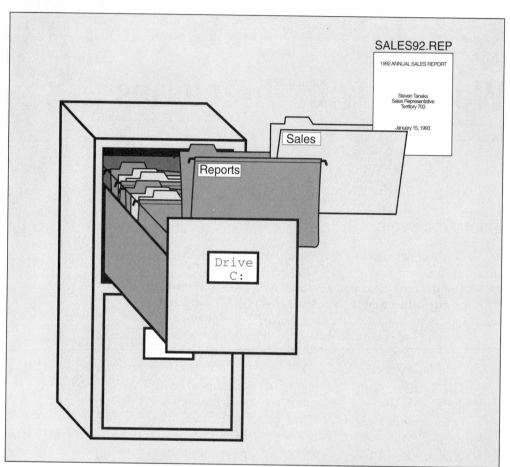

SALES92.REP

1992 ANNUAL SALES REPORT

Steven Tanaka
Sales Representative
Territory 703

January 15, 1993

Sales

Reports

Drive
C:

Figure 2-1
Directories and
subdirectories

DOS allows you to have directories within directories within other directories and so forth, enabling you to have a complete **tree** of directories (Figure 2-2). The directory tree begins with the **root directory**, which is the disk itself and which is usually represented by the disk letter followed by a colon and a backslash (\), for example, C:\ or A:\. All the other directories on the disk branch from the root directory. Directories found within other directories are sometimes called **subdirectories**. Actually DOS commands don't differentiate between directories and subdirectories — they treat all levels of branches on the directory tree as directories. Although we use the term *subdirectories*, keep in mind that subdirectories are simply directories within other directories.

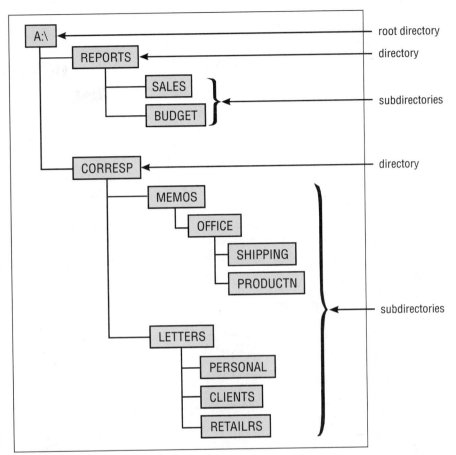

Figure 2-2
A sample
directory tree

What Is a Path?

Suppose you had to tell a colleague how to find the 1992 Annual Sales Report shown in Figure 2-1. You'd say, "Open drawer C, get out the hanging folder named REPORTS, remove the manila folder named SALES from the REPORTS hanging folder. There you'll find the Annual Sales Report."

Similarly, when you want to access a file on a disk — so you can copy the file, delete it, rename it, or do something else with it — you have to tell DOS where the file is located. The complete specification of a file — including disk, directories (if any), and filename — is called the complete **path** to the file. For example, the complete path to the file SALES92.REP in Figure 2-1 is C:\REPORTS\SALES\SALES92.REP. In this path, "C:\" is the root directory on drive C, "REPORTS" is the directory REPORTS within the root directory, "SALES" is the subdirectory SALES within REPORTS, and "SALES92.REP" is the file that contains the annual sales report. Backslashes separate directories and subdirectories within a path.

Besides complete paths, you can use partial paths. For example, if the default drive were C, you could leave off the C: and just use the path \REPORTS\SALES\SALES92.REP to access the file SALES92.REP. In this case, the initial backslash takes the place of "C:\."

You can also specify paths to directories and subdirectories. For example, if you wanted to get a directory listing of the files within the directory REPORTS, you would type the DIR command and then use the path A:\REPORTS (or just \REPORTS if A were the default drive) to indicate the directory you wanted to list.

Making a Directory (MKDIR or MD) *Make Directory*

Suppose you wanted to use your computer to prepare quarterly, annual, and special reports. Rather than saving all the files of your reports in the root directory of a disk, you could create a directory called REPORTS as in Figure 2-2. Furthermore, suppose that you also used your computer to write letters and other types of correspondence. Rather than saving all those files in the root directory or mixing them with the report files, you could create a separate directory called CORRESP (for "correspondence"). Finally, you could create another separate directory called MEMOS, in which you would save your memo files. By creating those three directories within the root directory and saving your files within the appropriate directory, you could keep your reports, letters (correspondence), and memos well organized.

You can create a directory within the root directory or within another directory by using the DOS command MKDIR, or MD for short. Let's use the MD command to create the three directories — REPORTS, CORRESP, and MEMOS — on the diskette that you formatted in DOS Tutorial 1 or on some other newly formatted diskette. MD and all the other DOS commands used in this tutorial are *internal* commands, so you don't have to have the Systems Disk to execute the commands.

To make a new directory:

❶ If you have a *two-diskette system*, insert the Systems Disk into drive A, turn on your computer, and get to the DOS prompt A>. After the DOS prompt appears on the screen, remove the Systems Disk from the drive.

If you have a *hard-disk system*, turn on your computer and get to the DOS prompt C>.

If you're using a computer on a network, make sure the computer is on, that you are logged into the network, and that the DOS prompt (for example, F>) is on the screen.

❷ Insert the work diskette, the diskette you formatted in DOS Tutorial 1 or some other newly formatted diskette, into drive A.

❸ Make sure drive A is the default drive.

If necessary type **a:** and press **[Enter]** to make A the default drive.

❹ Type **md reports** and press **[Enter]**.

The DOS command MD requires one parameter, the name of the new directory you want to create. DOS makes the new directory REPORTS, which in this case is a subdirectory of the root directory.

❺ Type **md corresp** and press **[Enter]** to create a directory for holding letters and other correspondence.

DOS creates a second directory within the root directory.

❻ Type **md memos** and press **[Enter]** to create a directory for holding memo files.

DOS creates a third subdirectory of the root directory. Now REPORTS, CORRESP, and MEMOS are all subdirectories within the root directory (Figure 2-3).

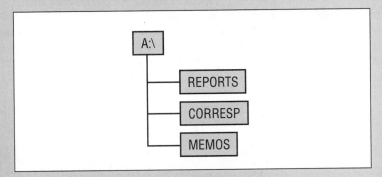

Figure 2-3
A directory tree with the three new directories

❼ To verify that the directories have been created, type **dir** and press **[Enter]**. Your screen should look similar to Figure 2-4.

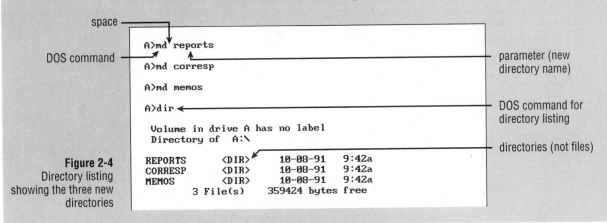

Figure 2-4
Directory listing showing the three new directories

Notice that in the directory listing, "<DIR>" appears to the right of the names of the directories REPORTS, CORRESP, and MEMOS to indicate that these are directory names, not filenames.

Naming a Directory

Since you'll have to create directories on your own disks to keep your personal and business files organized, you must learn the rules for naming directories. Fortunately the rules for naming a directory are the same as those for naming a file. A directory name consists of one to eight characters, and may have an extension of up to three characters. Most computer users, however, don't use extensions in directory names. The characters in directory names may be the letters A through Z, the digits 0 through 9, and any other keyboard characters *except* the symbols ? . " / \ [ ] : | < > + = ; , and *. A space is not allowed in a directory name.

Removing a Directory (RMDIR or RD)

Once you no longer need a directory, you can use the DOS command RMDIR or RD to remove it from the disk. Suppose, for example, you realized that memos are actually a type of correspondence and thus decided to remove the MEMOS directory. (Later you'll see how to make it a subdirectory in CORRESP.) In the following steps, you'll remove the MEMOS directory using the RD command.

To remove a directory:

❶ Make sure the work diskette is still in drive A and A is the default drive.

❷ Type **rd memos** and press **[Enter]**.

DOS deletes the directory from the diskette.

❸ Type **dir** and press **[Enter]** to verify that MEMOS is no longer on the diskette. See Figure 2-5.

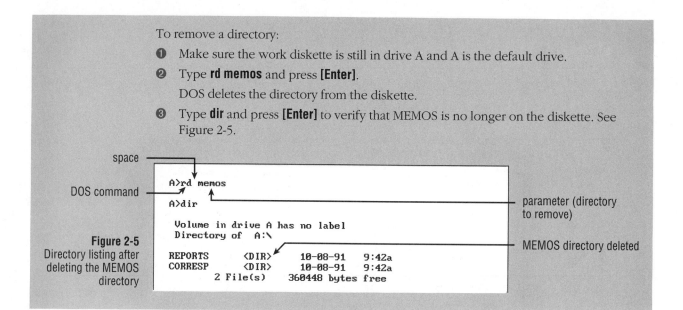

space

DOS command

parameter (directory to remove)

Figure 2-5
Directory listing after deleting the MEMOS directory

MEMOS directory deleted

```
A>rd memos

A>dir

    Volume in drive A has no label
    Directory of  A:\

REPORTS       <DIR>      10-08-91    9:42a
CORRESP       <DIR>      10-08-91    9:42a
        2 File(s)     360448 bytes free
```

A directory must be completely empty before you can delete it. Usually you will have to use the ERASE or DEL command to erase all the files in the directory before you remove the directory. Let's see what happens if you try to remove a directory that isn't empty.

To try to remove a directory that isn't empty:

❶ Remove the work diskette from drive A and insert the DOS data diskette into drive A. Make sure drive A is still the default drive.

❷ Type **dir *.** and press **[Enter]**.

Notice that this command uses the wildcard * for the filename but no wildcard for the filename extension. This tells DOS to list only those files or directories with no extension in their names. Since most filenames but few directory names have extensions, this command gives you a listing of only the subdirectories of the A drive root directory. In this case, you'll see the directory listing similar to the one in Figure 2-6.

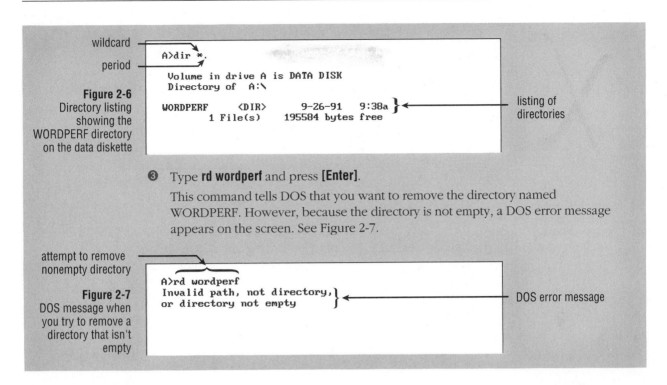

Figure 2-6
Directory listing
showing the
WORDPERF directory
on the data diskette

wildcard
period
listing of
directories

```
A>dir *.

Volume in drive A is DATA DISK
Directory of   A:\

WORDPERF      <DIR>       9-26-91    9:38a
       1 File(s)      195584 bytes free
```

❸ Type **rd wordperf** and press **[Enter]**.

This command tells DOS that you want to remove the directory named WORDPERF. However, because the directory is not empty, a DOS error message appears on the screen. See Figure 2-7.

attempt to remove
nonempty directory

Figure 2-7
DOS message when
you try to remove a
directory that isn't
empty

```
A>rd wordperf
Invalid path, not directory,
or directory not empty
```

DOS error message

In these steps, you didn't really want to remove the WORDPERF directory, of course. When you actually do want to remove a directory that isn't empty you should then use the ERASE or DEL command to erase all the files in the directory and then use the RD command again to remove the directory. As always, be extremely careful not to delete any file that might be valuable.

Changing the Information in the DOS Prompt (PROMPT)

If immediately after you boot your computer, your DOS prompt appears as C:\> rather than C> or as A:\> rather than A>, you don't need to use the DOS command PROMPT. Consult your instructor or technical support person on whether you need to read this section.

The usual DOS prompt, such as A> or C>, indicates the default drive but not the default directory. The **default directory** is the directory, such as C:\REPORTS, that DOS uses when you issue any DOS command, unless you specifically instruct DOS to use a different directory. The default directory includes not only the default root directory, such as C:\ or A:\, but also the directory or subdirectory, such as REPORTS. When you issue the DIR command, for example, without specifying a drive or a directory, DOS gives you a listing of files and directories within the default directory. Thus, if you execute the DIR command when A:\REPORTS is the default directory, you'll see a listing of the files within the directory REPORTS. The next section explains how to change the default directory.

The DOS command PROMPT PG lets you modify the DOS prompt so it includes not only the default drive but also the default directory (Figure 2-8 on the next page). With the name of the default directory path as part of the DOS prompt, you'll always know where DOS is in the directory tree and whether you have to change the default directory or specify the path to access a file or another directory. Let's use the PROMPT PG command to change the DOS prompt so that it shows the default directory.

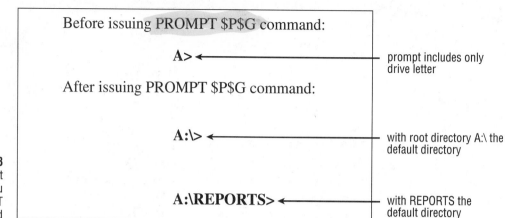

Figure 2-8
The DOS prompt before and after you issue the PROMPT command

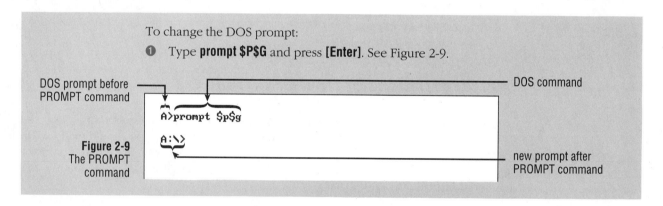

Figure 2-9
The PROMPT command

In the parameter PG of the PROMPT command, $P instructs DOS to include the path in the prompt, and $G tells DOS to include a greater-than sign (>). If the default directory is the root directory in drive A, then the DOS prompt will look like this: A:\>. If you changed the default directory to REPORTS, for example, the DOS prompt would look like this: A:\REPORTS>.

Changing the Default Directory (CD)

Suppose you wanted to view a listing of the files in a subdirectory, delete a file within that subdirectory, and perform other activities with files in the subdirectory. The simplest way to work with files in a subdirectory is to change the default directory to that subdirectory. This allows you to use only filenames as parameters to DOS commands, rather than having to use complete paths.

To change the default directory, you use the CHDIR or CD command. Let's practice this command by first changing the default directory from the root directory A:\ on the DOS data diskette to the WORDPERF directory.

To change the default directory:

❶ Make sure the DOS data diskette is still in drive A and A is the default drive.

❷ Type **cd \wordperf** and press **[Enter]**. See Figure 2-10.

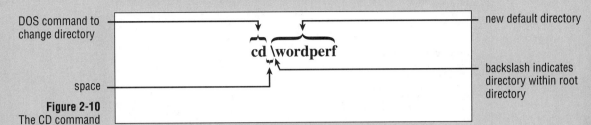

DOS command to change directory — new default directory

space — backslash indicates directory within root directory

Figure 2-10
The CD command

When a backslash (\) begins a path name, it takes the place of the root directory name, in this case, A:\. Therefore, "cd \wordperf" means, "Change the default directory to WORDPERF, a subdirectory of the root directory." The DOS prompt now appears as A:\WORDPERF>.

❸ Type **dir/w** and press **[Enter]** to get a directory listing, with the wide option, of the contents of WORDPERF. See Figure 2-11.

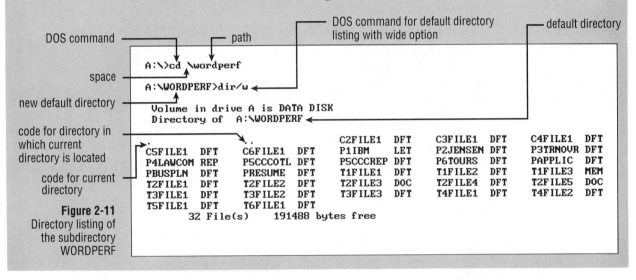

Figure 2-11
Directory listing of the subdirectory WORDPERF

Because WORDPERF is now the default directory and because the DIR command doesn't specify a path to another directory, DOS gives a directory listing of only those files within the WORDPERF directory, not a listing of all the files on the diskette. The file listing in Figure 2-11 includes two codes: one period (.) means the current directory; two periods (..) mean the directory in which the current subdirectory is located. In this case, therefore, the single-period code stands for WORDPERF, and the double-period code stands for the root directory A:\.

Now let's use the CD command to change the default directory on the work diskette.

To change the default directory:

❶ Remove the DOS data diskette from drive A and insert the work diskette.

❷ Type **cd \reports** and press **[Enter]** to change the default directory to REPORTS. Now the default directory is REPORTS, and the DOS prompt is A:\REPORTS>.

❸ Type **dir** and press **[Enter]** to get a directory listing of the contents of REPORTS. See Figure 2-12.

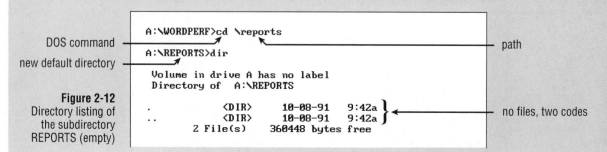

DOS command ————

new default directory ————

Figure 2-12
Directory listing of
the subdirectory
REPORTS (empty)

```
A:\WORDPERF>cd \reports

A:\REPORTS>dir

Volume in drive A has no label
Directory of   A:\REPORTS
.               <DIR>       10-08-91    9:42a
..              <DIR>       10-08-91    9:42a
         2 File(s)     360448 bytes free
```

———— path

———— no files, two codes

Since REPORTS is currently empty, no filenames appear in the directory listing; only the single-period and double-period codes appear.

❹ Type **cd \corresp** and press **[Enter]** to change the default directory to CORRESP. The DOS prompt is now A:\CORRESP>.

❺ Type **cd ** and press **[Enter]** to change the default directory back to the root directory. By typing a backslash (\) without a directory name in the CD command, you instruct DOS to make the root directory the default directory. The DOS prompt now appears as A:\>.

As you can see from these examples, you can go from any directory, such as the root directory A:\, to any other directory or subdirectory, such as REPORTS, by typing the command CD, a space, a backslash (\), and then the name of the directory.

Making a Subdirectory within a Directory

Up until now, the only directories you've made are subdirectories of the root directory. Now let's see how to make a subdirectory within another directory or subdirectory. In this case, we'll change the default directory to CORRESP and then make the subdirectories MEMOS and LETTERS within CORRESP. Furthermore, we'll create three subdirectories within the subdirectory LETTERS (Figure 2-13).

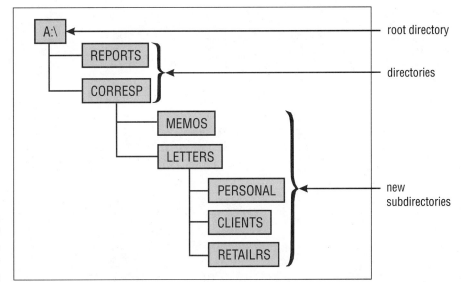

Figure 2-13
Directory tree of
the work diskette
with the new
subdirectories

To make a subdirectory within a directory:

❶ Make sure the work diskette is still in drive A.

❷ Type **cd \corresp** and press **[Enter]** to change the default directory to CORRESP.

The DOS prompt should now appear as A:\CORRESP>, indicating that the default directory is CORRESP, which is a subdirectory of the root directory A:\.

❸ Type **md memos** and press **[Enter]**.

The command MD makes a subdirectory within the current default directory. The default directory in this case is CORRESP. Therefore, the command **md memos** creates the subdirectory MEMOS within the directory CORRESP.

❹ Type **md letters** and press **[Enter]**.

This command creates the subdirectory LETTERS within the directory CORRESP.

❺ Type **dir** and press **[Enter]** to get a directory listing of the files and subdirectories within the directory CORRESP. See Figure 2-14.

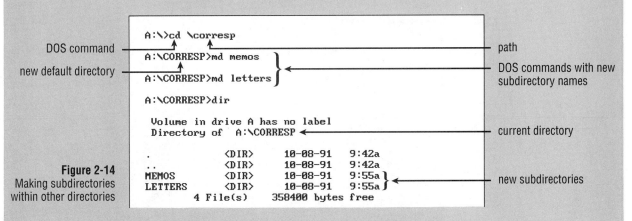

Figure 2-14
Making subdirectories
within other directories

⑥ Type **cd \corresp\letters** and press **[Enter]**.

This changes the default directory to the subdirectory LETTERS within the subdirectory CORRESP.

If you use your computer to type a lot of letters, you'll want to keep them organized on your disk. Suppose, for example, that you write three types of letters: personal letters to friends and relatives, letters to clients, and letters to retailers. It makes sense, therefore, to create a subdirectory of \CORRESP\LETTERS for each of these three types of letters. Let's create the three subdirectories PERSONAL, CLIENTS, and RETAILRS.

To create new subdirectories:

❶ Type **md personal** and press **[Enter]**.
❷ Type **md clients** and press **[Enter]**.
❸ Type **md retailrs** and press **[Enter]**.

You can't use the word *retailers* for a directory name because it has nine letters. Instead, you have to use the shortened name *retailrs*.

The commands in these steps created the subdirectories PERSONAL, CLIENTS, and RETAILRS within the LETTERS directory. Now your work diskette has the directory tree shown in Figure 2-13.

Using Paths with DOS Commands

You can use paths with any DOS command that accepts a drive letter or a filename as a parameter. For example, you can get a directory listing of all the files in the WORDPERF subdirectory of the DOS data diskette even when the default directory is the root directory A:\ by including the path \WORDPERF as the parameter of DIR. Using a path with DIR saves you time when you want to see what is in a directory but you don't necessarily want to work with the files in that directory.

Using a Path with DIR

First let's see how to use a path to get a directory listing of the files in a directory other than the default directory.

To use a path to get a directory listing:

❶ Remove the work diskette and insert the DOS data diskette into drive A.
❷ Type **cd ** and press **[Enter]** so the root directory becomes the default directory.

The DOS prompt should appear as A:\>.

❸ Type **dir a:\wordperf/w** and press **[Enter]**.

DOS gives you a directory listing similar to Figure 2-15.

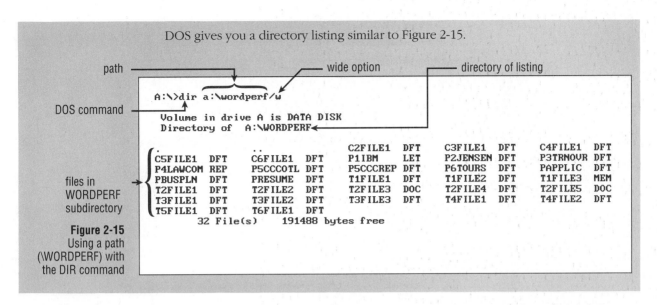

path ——————— wide option ——— directory of listing

```
A:\>dir a:\wordperf/w

Volume in drive A is DATA DISK
Directory of  A:\WORDPERF

                            C2FILE1   DFT   C3FILE1   DFT   C4FILE1   DFT
C5FILE1   DFT      ..       C6FILE1   DFT   P1IBM     LET   P2JENSEN  DFT   P3TRNOVR  DFT
P4LAWCOM  REP   P5CCCOTL  DFT   P5CCCREP  DFT   P6TOURS   DFT   PAPPLIC   DFT
PBUSPLN   DFT   PRESUME   DFT   T1FILE1   DFT   T1FILE2   DFT   T1FILE3   MEM
T2FILE1   DFT   T2FILE2   DFT   T2FILE3   DOC   T2FILE4   DFT   T2FILE5   DOC
T3FILE1   DFT   T3FILE2   DFT   T3FILE3   DFT   T4FILE1   DFT   T4FILE2   DFT
T5FILE1   DFT   T6FILE1   DFT
          32 File(s)     191488 bytes free
```

Figure 2-15
Using a path
(\WORDPERF) with
the DIR command

files in
WORDPERF
subdirectory

As this example demonstrates, you can list the files in a directory other than the default directory.

Using Paths to Copy Files

You can also use paths to copy files from one subdirectory to another. For example, suppose you wanted to save all your Lotus 1-2-3 spreadsheet files in a separate subdirectory called 123FILES, but they were currently stored in the root directory. You would then create a new subdirectory named 123FILES, copy the spreadsheet files from the root directory into the subdirectory, and then delete the copy of the files from the root directory. Recall from Tutorial 1 that Lotus 1-2-3 files have the filename extension WK1. Let's perform these commands on the DOS data diskette.

To use paths to copy files from one directory to another:

❶ Make sure the DOS data diskette is still in drive A and the root directory A:\ is the default directory.

❷ Type **md 123files** and press **[Enter]**.

This creates a new directory on the DOS data diskette where you can save your Lotus 1-2-3 spreadsheet files.

❸ Type **copy *.wk1 \123files** and press **[Enter]** to copy the WK1 files into the directory 123FILES. See Figure 2-16.

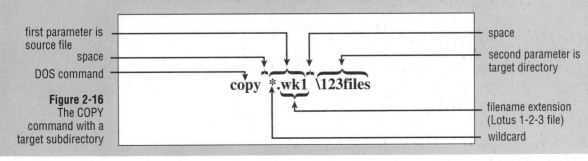

first parameter is source file — space — second parameter is target directory

space

DOS command

Figure 2-16
The COPY
command with a
target subdirectory

```
copy *.wk1 \123files
```

filename extension (Lotus 1-2-3 file)

wildcard

In this command, the parameter *.WK1 specifies that the target files are all the files within the default directory (in this case, the root directory) that have the filename extension WK1. The parameter \123FILES specifies that the target directory is 123FILES.

❹ Type **dir\123files** and press **[Enter]** to verify that the WK1 files were copied. See Figure 2-17.

new directory name

DOS command

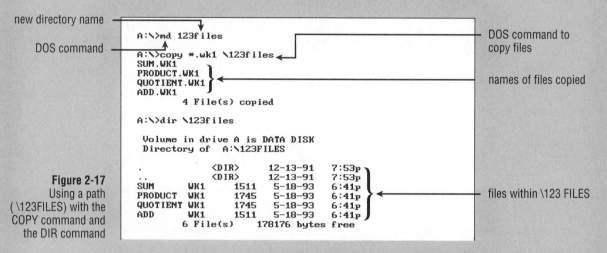

Figure 2-17
Using a path
(\123FILES) with the
COPY command and
the DIR command

DOS command to
copy files

names of files copied

files within \123 FILES

❺ Type **del *.wk1** and press **[Enter]** to delete the WK1 files from the root directory.

❻ Type **dir/w** and press **[Enter]** to verify that the WK1 files were deleted. See Figure 2-18.

DOS command

WK1 files deleted

Figure 2-18
Directory listing
after you delete
the WK1 files

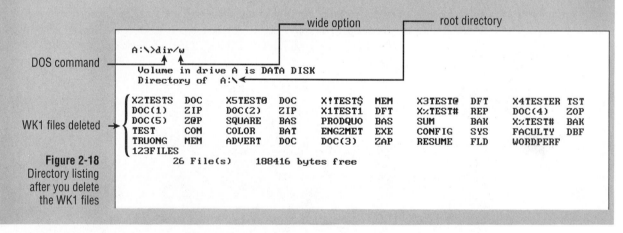

You can also copy files from one subdirectory to another subdirectory when neither subdirectory is the default directory. Suppose, for example, that the root directory A:\ were the default directory and you wanted to copy a file from the subdirectory 123FILES into the subdirectory WORDPERF using a new filename. In the following steps, you'll copy the file QUOTIENT.WK1 from the subdirectory 123FILES into the subdirectory WORDPERF using the new filename DIV.WK1.

To copy a file from one subdirectory to another:

① Make sure the DOS data diskette is still in drive A and the root directory A:\ is the default directory.

② Type **copy \123files\quotient.wk1 \wordperf\div.wk1** and press **[Enter]**. See Figure 2-19.

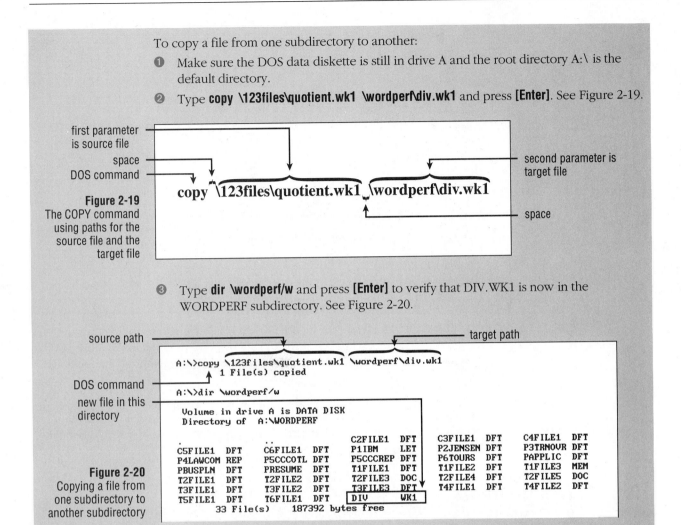

first parameter is source file

space

DOS command

Figure 2-19
The COPY command using paths for the source file and the target file

second parameter is target file

space

③ Type **dir \wordperf/w** and press **[Enter]** to verify that DIV.WK1 is now in the WORDPERF subdirectory. See Figure 2-20.

source path

target path

DOS command

new file in this directory

Figure 2-20
Copying a file from one subdirectory to another subdirectory

```
A:\>copy \123files\quotient.wk1 \wordperf\div.wk1
         1 File(s) copied

A:\>dir \wordperf/w

 Volume in drive A is DATA DISK
 Directory of  A:\WORDPERF

.                  ..                 C2FILE1  DFT    C3FILE1  DFT    C4FILE1  DFT
C5FILE1  DFT    C6FILE1  DFT    P1IBM    LET    P2JENSEN DFT    P3TRNOVR DFT
P4LAWCOM REP    P5CCCOTL DFT    P5CCCREP DFT    P6TOURS  DFT    PAPPLIC  DFT
PBUSPLN  DFT    PRESUME  DFT    T1FILE1  DFT    T1FILE2  DFT    T1FILE3  MEM
T2FILE1  DFT    T2FILE2  DFT    T2FILE3  DOC    T2FILE4  DFT    T2FILE5  DOC
T3FILE1  DFT    T3FILE2  DFT    T3FILE3  DFT    T4FILE1  DFT    T4FILE2  DFT
T5FILE1  DFT    T6FILE1  DFT    DIV      WK1
         33 File(s)     187392 bytes free
```

In this command, the source file is specified by the path \123FILES\QUOTIENT.WK1, and the target file is specified by the path \WORDPERF\DIV.WK1. Because you have included a filename in the second parameter and not just a directory name, DOS knows that you want to use a new filename for the copy of the source file. Notice that in these examples, you don't have to include "A:" because drive A is the default. You could, however, include the entire paths — A:\123FILES\QUOTIENT.WK1 and A:\WORDPERF\DIV.WK1.

These steps have demonstrated the power of paths. Using paths, you can access any directory or any file from within any other directory.

■   ■   ■

Exercises

1. Define or describe the following:
   a. directory
   b. subdirectory
   c. default directory
   d. root directory
   e. directory tree

2. List and explain the step(s) to make a directory.

3. What are the rules for naming a directory?

4. List and explain the step(s) to change the default directory.

5. List and explain the step(s) to remove a directory from a disk.

6. What is the purpose of the DOS command PROMPT PG?

7. What is a path? What is a pathname?

8. Suppose you wanted to delete the file CHECKING.WK1 from the subdirectory 123FILES on the diskette in drive A when A:\ is the default directory. List the instructions you would issue to DOS to delete CHECKING.WK1 from 123FILES without changing the default directory.

9. Suppose you wanted to copy the file JONES.LET from the subdirectory COMPANY within the directory LETTERS on drive C to the subdirectory CORRESP within the directory WPFILES on the diskette in drive A. List the instructions you would issue to DOS to perform this operation.

Tutorial Assignments

Perform the following activities using the work diskette from this tutorial.

1. Within the directory REPORTS, make the subdirectories SALES and BUDGET.

2. Within the directory MEMOS, which is found within the directory CORRESP, make the subdirectory OFFICE.

3. Within the directory OFFICE from Assignment 2, make the subdirectories SHIPPING and PRODUCTN.

4. Draw a directory tree of the organization of the directories and subdirectories on the work diskette.

Perform the following activities using the DOS data diskette (not the work diskette):

5. From the root directory, make a subdirectory named WPFILES in which you will store your WordPerfect document files.

6. Copy the document files that have the filename extension DOC from the root directory into the WPFILES subdirectory. Delete the DOC files in the root directory.

7. From the root directory, get a directory listing of the files in the WPFILES subdirectory.

8. Change the default directory to WPFILES and get a directory listing of the files in that directory.

9. Change the default directory back to the root directory.

10. From the root directory, rename the file ADVERT.DOC in the directory WPFILES with the new name INVEST.DOC. *Hint:* Use the path to the file ADVERT.DOC in the first parameter of the RENAME command, but use only the new filename in the second parameter.

Creating Your Data Diskettes for the WordPerfect, Lotus 1-2-3, and dBASE III PLUS Tutorials

Before you do the tutorials in *Microcomputer Applications for Business*, you must create data diskettes for each of the applications you plan to learn. The Disk Maker Program Disk included with this textbook contains the data files you will need. Do not use the Disk Maker Program Disk to work through the steps in the Tutorials. You must make data diskettes.

Before you begin, make sure you have the following items:

- Four blank, formatted 5¼-inch or 3½-inch diskettes. The size of the disks should match the size of the Disk Maker Program Disk that came with this book. If you don't know how to format a diskette, see your instructor or technical support person, or follow the instructions on pages 41 and 42.
- Three blank diskette labels and a felt-tip pen.
- The Disk Maker Program Disk that came with this book.

After you collect these items, you are ready to create your data diskettes.

Carefully follow these steps to create your data diskettes:

❶ Using a felt-tip pen, write the words "WordPerfect 5.1 data diskette" on the first blank, formatted diskette; write "Lotus 1-2-3 data diskette" on the second blank, formatted diskette; and write "dBASE III PLUS data diskette" on the third blank, formatted diskette.

❷ Start your computer. If you need help see your technical support person or follow the instructions on pages 25 and 26.

❸ If there is a diskette in drive A remove it. Then insert the Disk Maker Program Disk in drive A.

If your Disk Maker Program Disk doesn't match drive A but does match drive B, insert it in drive B instead. Then substitute drive B instead of drive A in the following instructions.

If you don't know how to determine which diskette drive is drive A and which is drive B, or if you don't know how to insert a disk into a diskette drive, see page 24.

❹ Type **a:** and press **[Enter]**. (If you inserted the Disk Maker Program Disk in drive B, type **b:** and press **[Enter]**.)

❺ Type **diskmake** and press **[Enter]**. The screen shown in Figure 1 appears.

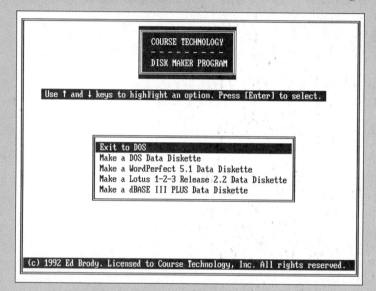

Figure 1
Disk Maker
Program Main
Menu

This is the Disk Maker Main Menu screen. The highlight (a solid rectangle) is currently on the words "Exit to DOS."

❻ Press **[↓]** (down-arrow key) until you have moved the highlight to the type of data diskette you are creating. For example, to create your WordPerfect data diskette, move the highlight to the words "Make a WordPerfect 5.1 Data Diskette." If you cannot find the down-arrow key, or if pressing it does not move the highlighted bar, try pressing [Num Lock]. If this fails, ask your instructor or technical support person for help.

❼ Make sure the highlight is on the correct option. For example, if you are creating your WordPerfect data diskette, make sure the highlight is on "Make a WordPerfect 5.1 Data Diskette." Press **[Enter]**. Messages appear on the screen and then the screen shown in Figure 2 appears.

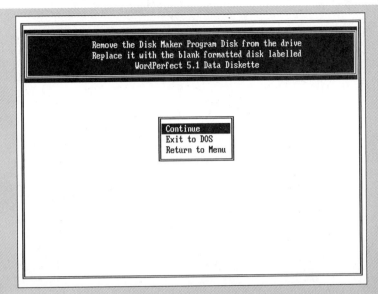

```
Remove the Disk Maker Program Disk from the drive
Replace it with the blank formatted disk labelled
         WordPerfect 5.1 Data Diskette




                    ┌─────────────────┐
                    │ Continue        │
                    │ Exit to DOS     │
                    │ Return to Menu  │
                    └─────────────────┘
```

Figure 2
Disk Maker asks
you to insert a
new diskette

⑧ Remove the Disk Maker Program Disk. Replace it with the data diskette you are creating (one of the blank, formatted diskettes you labeled in Step 1). For example, if you are creating your WordPerfect data diskette, replace the Disk Maker Program Disk with your WordPerfect data diskette.

⑨ Be sure the highlight bar is on the option "Continue," and press **[Enter]**.

⑩ Messages again appear on your screen. Eventually, you see the message telling you that your data diskette has been created. For example, if you are creating your WordPerfect data diskette, you will see the message "WordPerfect 5.1 data diskette created." Remove your data diskette from the disk drive.

After you have created the first data diskette, repeat Steps 3 through 10 to create each of your data diskettes. After you have created all three of your data diskettes, put your Disk Maker Program Disk in a safe place. If any of your data diskettes becomes damaged, you can create a replacement using the Disk Maker Program Disk.

Part Two

■   ■   ■

WordPerfect 5.1 Tutorials

Tutorial 1

Creating a Document
Requesting Information on Training Materials

Case: Clearwater Valve Company

Andrea Simone recently received a degree in business management with a specialty in operations and production. She has just been hired as the executive assistant to Steve Morgan, the operations manager for Clearwater Valve Company. Clearwater designs and manufactures specialty valves for industrial sprinkler, cooling, and plumbing systems.

One of Steve's responsibilities as operations manager is to train employees at Clearwater's production plant on safety procedures. He decides to purchase training videos so he can conduct safety training easily and inexpensively. After looking through several catalogs, Steve determines that Learning Videos Inc., of Pecos, Texas, publishes a video that seems appropriate, but he has several questions about the video. Steve asks Andrea to write a letter to request further information. He gives her a handwritten note with his questions.

In this tutorial you'll complete Andrea's assignment. You'll learn how to plan a letter and then how to use WordPerfect to write the letter to Learning Videos Inc.

OBJECTIVES

In this tutorial you will learn to:

■ Start WordPerfect

■ Use the pull-down menus, the function keys, and the function-key template

■ Get help on WordPerfect features

■ Clear the document screen

■ Delete text

■ Use word wrap

■ Move the cursor

■ Save and retrieve a document

■ Preview and print a document

■ Exit WordPerfect

Writing with WordPerfect

Before you begin you need to learn three key terms that WordPerfect users frequently use: document, document screen, and document file. In WordPerfect terminology, the letter that you'll write is called a document. A **document** is any written item, such as a memo, letter, or report. You use the document screen to create and edit documents. The **document screen** is the visual display on the computer monitor where you see the text you type and the changes you make to the document that you are creating and editing. You save your WordPerfect documents in a **document file**, which is stored on a hard disk or a diskette and which contains the text and formatting information about your document. You'll then print the document (Figure 1-1).

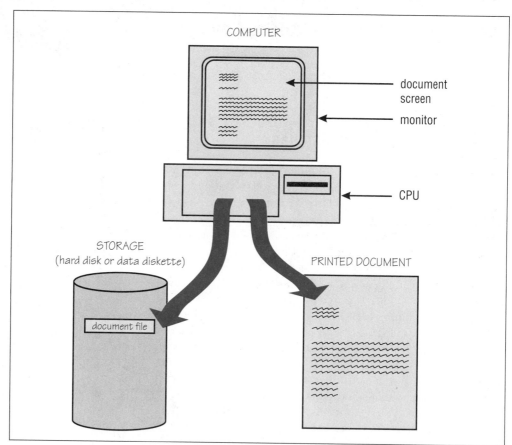

Figure 1-1
Document screen
on the monitor,
document file on
disk, and printed
document

Let's now begin with the first step in writing with WordPerfect — planning a document.

Planning a Document

Planning a document before you write it increases the quality of your writing, makes your document more attractive and readable, and, in the long run, saves you time and effort. You can divide your planning into four parts: content, organization, style, and format.

Content

Begin your planning by first determining what you want to say in the document, that is, the content. The content should clearly convey your purpose and should be appropriate for your reader(s). Are you writing to obtain information, to persuade, to inform, or to motivate? If you don't have all the information necessary to accomplish your purpose, gather additional details from such sources as notes, memos, letters, reports, and colleagues.

After you have assembled the necessary information, you should determine the scope of the document. Usually you won't use all the information you've gathered. Include enough information to achieve your objective but not so much that your reader may become overwhelmed or bored. Keep your message simple, yet complete.

As Andrea considers her purpose and her reader, she focuses on the handwritten note from Steve Morgan (Figure 1-2). The note lists Steve's questions and contains the catalog information about the training video. Andrea decides that the questions will be the primary content of her letter and that the catalog information will help her reader identify the correct video. She knows that this is all the information she needs to plan the content and that she should keep the letter to a few short paragraphs.

Figure 1-2
Handwritten note
from Steve Morgan
to Andrea Simone

> Andrea, please write and find out the following:
>
> Does the video cover the most recent OSHA, HAZCOM, and EPA regulations on chemical safety?
>
> What instructor materials are available?
>
> The video is catalog number LV18427, "Safety in the Work Place." Our customer service rep is Peter Argyle. His address is Learning Videos Inc., 862 Pinewood Road, Suite #210, Pecos, TX 79772.

Organization

After you have determined the content of your document, you should decide how to organize the information so that your ideas appear in a logical and coherent sequence. For example, if you're telling a story, you might want to recount the events in chronological order. If you're giving instructions on a procedure, you should give step-by-step directions. If you're sending a message that might upset your reader, you could begin with an explanation or with positive or neutral statements before you deliver the bad news.

For a short letter or memo, you can organize the information in your head; for a longer document, you should create a complete outline before you begin writing.

How should Andrea organize her letter? She decides to use the standard organization for a business letter, which begins with the date, the inside address, and the salutation, then presents the body or text of the letter, and concludes with a complimentary closing and the writer's name and title. For the body of the letter, Andrea decides to include four paragraphs. The first paragraph will identify the video and express Clearwater's interest in the video. The second and third paragraphs will include Steve's questions about the video, and the fourth paragraph will close the letter and request a prompt reply.

Style

After you have settled on the content and the organization of your document, you should next begin writing, using an appropriate style that satisfies your purpose and meets the needs of your audience. In business documents the style should be simple and direct. You can achieve this style by using simple words, direct sentences, and short paragraphs so your reader can easily grasp the meaning of the text and read at a brisk, natural pace. Simplicity and directness are the hallmarks of a good business writing style.

Your style can be simple and direct yet still have variety in writing tones. A report to your company's board of directors, for example, might be formal and reserved. A memo to a colleague, on the other hand, might be informal and conversational. In all documents, however, you should avoid trite expressions, overstatements, euphemisms, inappropriate jargon, and sexist language. Make your ideas concrete, specific, and exact.

In the case of Andrea's letter to request information, her style should be clear, simple, and direct. She should also make the tone of her letter positive and pleasant, to encourage a quick response from Learning Videos.

Format

Finally you should make your documents visually appealing. An attractive document is a readable document. Such formatting features as ample white space, sufficient line spacing, and appropriate headings make your document readable and your message clear. Your reader will spend less time trying to understand your message and more time acting on it. Usually the longer and more complex a document is, the more attention you'll need to pay to its format.

Since Andrea's letter to Learning Videos is short and simple, she decides to use the standard business letter format provided by WordPerfect. This format includes single-spaced lines and one-inch margins around all four edges of the page.

■   ■   ■

Having planned what she's going to write, Andrea is ready to use WordPerfect to write the letter to Learning Videos Inc. In this tutorial, you'll create Andrea's letter as shown in Figure 1-3.

Before you start this tutorial, make sure WordPerfect is installed on your computer system. If you're using a computer in a lab, check with your instructor or technical support person. If you're using your own computer, install WordPerfect by following the installation instructions that came with your copy of the software.

November 2, 1992

Mr. Peter Argyle
Learning Videos Inc.
862 Pinewood Road, Suite #210
Pecos, TX 79772

Dear Mr. Argyle:

I have read the catalog description of your training video number LV18427, entitled "Safety in the Work Place." The video seems appropriate for our training needs at Clearwater Valve Company, but I would like additional information.

Specifically, please answer these questions:

1. Does the video cover the most recent OSHA, HAZCOM, and EPA regulations on handling hazardous chemicals?

2. What instructor materials are available for testing and documenting student performance?

Your attention to this matter is appreciated. I hope to hear from you soon.

Sincerely yours,

Andrea Simone

Andrea Simone
Executive Assistant

Figure 1-3
Letter from Andrea
Simone to Learning
Videos Inc.

Starting WordPerfect

To use WordPerfect to create documents, you have to start the WordPerfect software. Let's start WordPerfect now.

To start WordPerfect:

❶ Make sure you have the WordPerfect data diskette ready. If you haven't already created the WordPerfect data diskette, follow the instructions on page 79.

❷ If necessary, turn on your computer.

If a menu of programs appears on the screen and WordPerfect is listed as one of those programs, you can run WordPerfect simply by selecting that menu item. If the menu doesn't list WordPerfect, exit from the menu. If you don't know how to exit the menu or how to select WordPerfect, consult your technical support person. Steps 3 through 6 assume that your computer can't start WordPerfect directly from a menu program.

③ Make sure the DOS prompt and the cursor appear on the screen.

④ If necessary, change the default disk drive to the drive where WordPerfect is installed by typing the letter of the disk drive and a colon (:) and then pressing **[Enter]**.

For example, if WordPerfect is installed on disk drive C, type **C:** and press **[Enter]**. If WordPerfect is installed on disk drive F, type **F:** and press **[Enter]**. Check with your technical support person if you are not sure how to change drives.

⑤ Change the default directory to where WordPerfect is installed. For example, if your WordPerfect program was installed in the subdirectory WP51, you would type **cd\wp51** and press **[Enter]**. This changes the current default directory to the subdirectory called WP51.

If the message "Invalid directory" appears on the screen, WordPerfect is probably installed in a different directory, in which case you have to change the default directory to the one on which WordPerfect is located. If necessary, check with your technical support person for the directory containing WordPerfect.

⑥ Type **wp** and press **[Enter]**.

This starts WordPerfect. You'll first see the WordPerfect title screen, then after another moment or two, the WordPerfect document screen. See Figure 1-4.

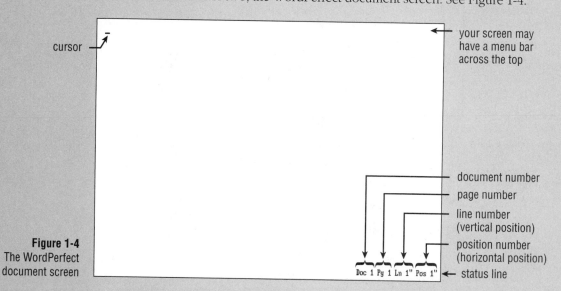

cursor

your screen may have a menu bar across the top

document number
page number
line number (vertical position)
position number (horizontal position)

Figure 1-4
The WordPerfect
document screen

Doc 1 Pg 1 Ln 1" Pos 1"   status line

Sometimes when you start WordPerfect, you may see the message "Are other copies of WordPerfect currently running?" This message indicates that you may be running WordPerfect from a network and using the same directory as other users. If you see this message and you are on a network, ask your technical support person how to proceed. If you see this message and you're not on a network, press **n** ("no").

WordPerfect may then display the message "Old backup file exists. 1 Rename; 2 Delete." Press **2** to delete the old backup file.

You have now completed the procedure for starting WordPerfect.

The Document Screen and the Status Line

Figure 1-4 shows the blank WordPerfect document screen on which you create and edit WordPerfect documents. As you type words and phrases, they become part of the document that appears on the document screen. Notice the blinking cursor in the upper left corner. The cursor marks the spot where the next character that you type will appear in the document.

The bottom line of the screen is called the **status line**. It tells you the document number, the page number, the line number, and the position number where the cursor is located.

Document Number

WordPerfect allows you to have two documents in your computer memory at a time. *Doc 1* on the status line means that the cursor is currently in document 1; *Doc 2* would mean that the cursor is currently in document 2. (You'll see how to use the second document screen in WordPerfect Tutorial 5.)

Page Number

Pg 1 means that the cursor is currently on page 1 — the first printed page — of your document. If your document has more than one page, this message will change as you move the cursor to other pages of the document.

Line Number

The line number is the distance from the top of the page to the current location of the cursor. *Ln 1″* means that the text you type will be one inch from the top of the page when you print the document. As you add lines of text to the document, the cursor moves farther down on the screen and the line number increases.

Unless you specify otherwise, your document will automatically have a one-inch margin at the top and the bottom of each page.

Position Number

The position number is the distance from the left edge of the page to the current location of the cursor. *Pos 1″* means that the text that you type at Pos 1″ will be one inch from the left edge of the printed page when you print the document. As you type each character along a line of text, the cursor moves to the right and the position number increases.

Unless you specify otherwise, your document will automatically have a one-inch margin along the left and right edges of the page.

The word "Pos" on the status line also gives information about the keyboard and the appearance of the characters at the cursor. For example, if Caps Lock is on (so that typed letters appear in uppercase), "Pos" appears as "POS." If Num Lock is on, "Pos" first appears as blinking characters. These characters stop blinking once you start to use WordPerfect or you press [Num Lock]. You'll learn the other features of the status line later.

The Default Settings

Part of planning a document is deciding the document format, including the width of the margins, the line spacing, and the justification (how the text is aligned along the left and right margins). WordPerfect provides a set of standard format settings that you can use with most documents. These standard settings are called the **default** format settings because they automatically specify a format for your document unless you specifically change them. Figure 1-5 lists common WordPerfect default format settings. Your setup of WordPerfect may have different default settings. Some of these settings may not make sense to you now, but they will become clear as you work through the tutorials. You won't change any format settings in this tutorial.

Default Format Settings	
Left margin	1 inch
Right margin	1 inch
Top margin	1 inch
Bottom margin	1 inch
Justification	Full
Line spacing	1 (single)
Paper size	8.5 x 11 inches
Tabs	Every 0.5 inch
Page numbering	None
Hyphenation	Off
Repeat value	8
Date format	Month Day, Year
Widow/orphan	Off
Units of measure	" (inches)

Figure 1-5
Some WordPerfect default format settings

Executing WordPerfect Commands

Now that you have started WordPerfect, you are ready to use it by executing WordPerfect commands. A **command** is an instruction you issue to WordPerfect to perform a specific task, such as set the size of the margins, change the line spacing, or underline text.

You can issue a command using two general methods: pull-down menus or function-key commands. A **pull-down menu** is a list of commands that appears to be "pulled down" from the top of the document screen. You can then select the command you want from the list. A **function-key command** is a command you issue by pressing a function key, sometimes alone and sometimes in combination with a modifier key ([Shift], [Ctrl], or [Alt]).

In the steps that follow, you'll use a pull-down menu, with and without a mouse, and a function-key command to insert the date into the text.

Using the Keyboard with Pull-Down Menus

First let's see how to use the keyboard with the pull-down menus.

To use the keyboard to pull down a menu:

❶ Press **[Alt][=]**

This key combination means that you press [Alt] and hold it down; while you are holding it down, press [=] (the equal sign). Then release both keys.

This key combination causes the WordPerfect menu bar to appear across the top of the screen. See Figure 1-6. You'll learn the meaning of each of the nine items in the menu bar later.

menu bar ➔

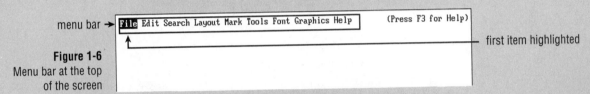

Figure 1-6
Menu bar at the top
of the screen

first item highlighted

With the menu bar on the screen, you can press [→] to move the cursor to the right and [←] to move it to the left to highlight the menu items.

❷ Press **[→]** five times to move the cursor to Tools.

Notice that each time you press [→], the cursor moves and highlights the next item to the right.

❸ Press **[↓]** or **[Enter]** to pull down the Tools menu.

This menu lists the various Tools options. See Figure 1-7.

Tools highlighted

first option highlighted

menu of options
and their equivalent
function-key
commands

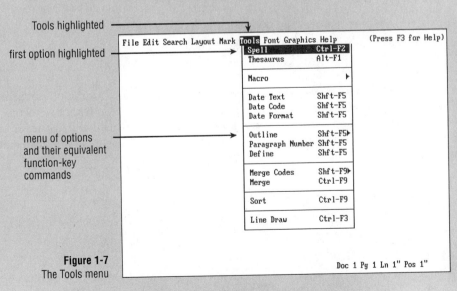

Figure 1-7
The Tools menu

❹ Press [→] to pull down the Font menu, then press [←] to return to the Tools menu. This step demonstrates how you can move from one pull-down menu to another by pressing the arrow keys.

❺ Press **[Esc]** twice to close the menu bar.

Pressing [Esc] once closes the Tools pull-down menu; pressing [Esc] a second time closes the menu bar. You also could have pressed [F1] or [Space] (the spacebar), but don't do so now — you have already closed the pull-down menu and the menu bar. All three keys work the same in closing menus.

Now that you know how to pull down a menu, move from one menu to another, and close a pull-down menu and the menu bar, you are ready to execute a WordPerfect command. In the following steps, you will use the Date Text command, which automatically inserts the current date into the document. Using the Date Text command saves you the keystrokes of typing the date and ensures that the date is accurate. Let's execute the Date Text command using the keyboard and the pull-down menu.

To execute the Date Text command from a pull-down menu:

❶ Press **[Alt][=]** to display the menu bar.

❷ Press **[→]** five times to highlight Tools, then press **[Enter]**. The Tools menu appears on your screen.

❸ Press **[↓]** three times to highlight Date Text and press **[Enter]**.

The menu bar disappears from the screen, and the current date appears on the document screen. See Figure 1-8. The document you are creating now contains the current date.

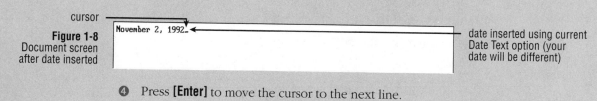

cursor

Figure 1-8
Document screen
after date inserted

November 2, 1992.

date inserted using current
Date Text option (your
date will be different)

❹ Press **[Enter]** to move the cursor to the next line.

You can use an alternative keyboard method to select an option from a pull-down menu. In this method, you press the highlighted letter of the command you want to execute. The highlighted letter is called the **mnemonic letter** because it is usually the first letter of the command and is easy to remember. In the following steps, you'll use this alternative method to insert the date again into the document. Later you'll erase the extra date.

To use the mnemonic letters to pull down a menu and execute a command:

❶ Press **[Alt][=]** to display the menu bar.

❷ Press **T** or **t** to select Tools.

Notice that the *T* in the word *Tools* on the menu bar is highlighted. This means you can select the menu item simply by pressing that letter. You can use either an uppercase or a lowercase letter to select a menu item. *In this book, we'll show the letter that you should press in uppercase, but you can press an uppercase or lowercase letter to execute the command.*

❸ Press **T** again to select Date Text.

The *T* in *Date Text* in the pull-down menu is highlighted and thus is the mnemonic letter. Now the current date appears again on the screen.

❹ Press **[Enter]** to move the cursor to the next line.

Using the mnemonic-letter method of selecting an option rather than pressing [↓] to highlight the option and then pressing [Enter] almost always requires fewer keystrokes. With mnemonic letters you had to use only four keystrokes to insert today's date: [Alt][=], T, and T. With the cursor keys, you had to use 12 keystrokes.

Using the Mouse with Pull-Down Menus

WordPerfect also allows you to use the mouse pointer and the mouse button to select items on the pull-down menu. If your computer doesn't have a mouse, go to the next section.

Using a mouse involves moving the mouse pointer, clicking a button, and dragging the mouse. To move the mouse pointer, which in WordPerfect appears as a rectangular box on the screen, move the mouse along a hard surface until the mouse pointer is at the desired location. To **click** on an item means to move the mouse pointer to the desired location and then to press and immediately release either the left mouse button (found on the left side of the mouse) or the right mouse button (located on the right side of the mouse). To **drag** the mouse means to move the mouse pointer to the desired location on the screen; press the left button and hold it down; while still holding down the button, move the mouse pointer to a new location on the screen; then release the mouse button.

Now that you know how to use a mouse, let's use it to insert the date once again into the document.

To use the mouse to pull down a menu:

❶ Press the right mouse button. This displays the menu bar at the top of the screen, just as if you'd pressed [Alt][=]. (If you accidentally press the right mouse button while working in WordPerfect — that is, you don't want the menu bar to appear — just press [Esc] or the right mouse button again to close the menu bar.)

❷ Click on Tools in the menu bar.

This means move the mouse pointer to any letter in the word Tools and then press and immediately release the *left* mouse button. The Tools menu appears on the screen.

❸ Click on Date Text.

This means move the pointer to any letter in Date Text; then press and immediately release the left mouse button. This operation selects Date Text, and inserts today's date again into the document.

❹ Press **[Enter]** to move the cursor to the next line.

In this book, we assume that you are using the keyboard to pull down menus and to select menu options. Feel free, however, to use the mouse if you have one.

Using the Function Keys and the Template

In addition to using the menu bar and pull-down menus, you can execute WordPerfect commands by pressing function keys. The commands available with the function keys are listed on the function-key templates (Figure 1-9).

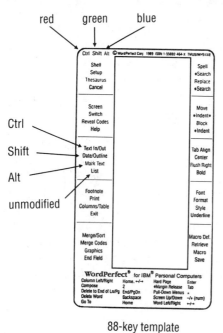

88-key template

The **template** is a plastic sheet that sits on the keyboard over the function keys and lists the names of the WordPerfect function-key commands, also called simply **WordPerfect keys**. The names of the WordPerfect keys are color coded to indicate which modifier key, if any, you have to press with the function key to issue the command. A command name in black indicates no modifier key; green indicates [Shift]; blue indicates [Alt]; and red indicates [Ctrl]. Thus, to execute the command for Date/Outline, which appears in green next to the function key [F5], you would press [Shift][F5]. In these tutorials, when you are to issue any WordPerfect command using the function keys, the modifier and the function key will be in boldface and in separate brackets, for example, [Shift][F5]. Following the modifier and the function key will be the name of the WordPerfect key in parentheses, for example, (Date/Outline). In the following steps you'll use the template and the function keys to insert the current date into the document for the third time.

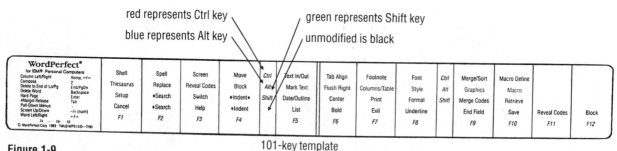

Figure 1-9
The WordPerfect function-key templates

To insert today's date using the function keys:

❶ Press **[Shift][F5]** (Date/Outline). The Date/Outline menu appears on the status line. See Figure 1-10.

• Date/Outline menu
on status line

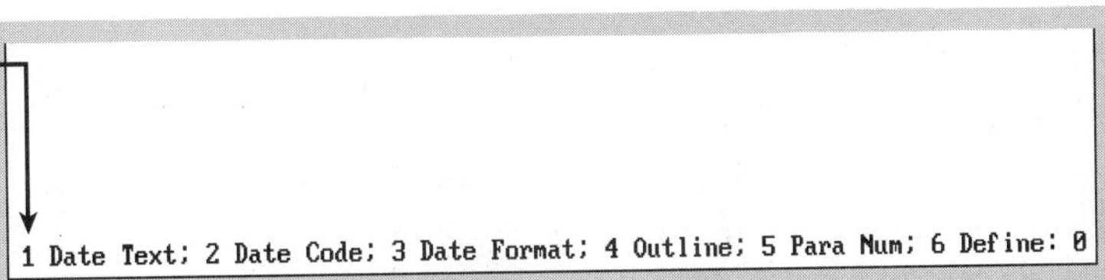

Figure 1-10
The Date/Outline
menu

```
1 Date Text; 2 Date Code; 3 Date Format; 4 Outline; 5 Para Num; 6 Define: 0
```

Remember that [Shift][F5] means that you press and hold down the [Shift] key, press the [F5] key, and then release both keys. This WordPerfect key is called Date/Outline because it displays a menu of items that include date features and outline features. You'll learn more about the outline features in Tutorial 5.

❷ Select **1** (Date **T**ext).

You can select this option by pressing 1, which is the option number, or by pressing T, which is the option mnemonic. WordPerfect inserts today's date into the document. At this point, if you have followed all the previous examples, including those with mouse commands, the current date appears four times on your screen.

❸ Press **[Enter]** to move the cursor to the next line.

In most cases, when you press a function key with one of the modifier keys, WordPerfect displays a menu, such as the one shown in Figure 1-10. You can then select an option from the menu by pressing the number that corresponds to the menu item you want or by pressing the mnemonic letter (the highlighted letter in the menu item).

Pull-Down Menus vs. Function Keys

You've seen various ways of executing WordPerfect commands using pull-down menus, both with the keyboard and with the mouse. You've also seen how to execute the same WordPerfect commands using the function keys and the function-key template. But which method is better, pull-down menus or function keys?

The answer depends on your level of experience and your personal preference. Most commands require fewer keystrokes if you use the function keys rather than the pull-down menus with the keyboard, but the pull-down menus are usually easier to learn. Using pull-down menus with the mouse is sometimes easier than using the function keys. Even when it is more time consuming, some people simply prefer using the pull-down menus to using the function keys. In these WordPerfect tutorials, we give you a choice of how to execute a command. You can follow whichever method you prefer or whichever method your instructor requires.

When we ask you to execute a command, we first instruct you how to issue the command from a pull-down menu, which you can select using the keyboard or the mouse. We then tell you how to issue the same command using a function key. For example, an instruction to execute the Date Text command would be "Select Date Text from the Tools menu or press [Shift][F5] (Date/Outline) and select 1 (Date Text)." To execute this command using pull-down menus, you would press [Alt][=] or press the right mouse button to display the menu bar, pull down the Tools menu, and then select Date Text. To execute this command using the function keys, you would press [Shift][F5] (Date/Outline) and then either press 1 (or T) or click the mouse pointer on Date Text. In those operations where you can use only the keyboard but not the mouse, we will just tell you what keys to press.

Getting Help

How do you know which menu item to select or which function key to press, for example, to change the margins, to number pages, or to perform any other WordPerfect command? The best way is through training and continued experience in using WordPerfect. These WordPerfect tutorials will give you the training and the experience you need to perform the most important WordPerfect operations.

But WordPerfect provides another way for you to learn what commands are available and how to execute them: the WordPerfect Help feature. Both the main menu bar and the template list the Help feature. When you select Help from the menu bar or press [F3] (Help), WordPerfect displays a help screen and waits for you to do one of the following:

- Press a letter to get an alphabetical list of features whose names start with that letter
- Press [F3] (Help) again to display an illustration of the function key template
- Press any other function key or any cursor-movement or deletion key to get a description of that key
- Click the right mouse button or press [Enter] to exit Help and return to the document screen

Let's use each of these commands to get help with WordPerfect features.

Getting Help with a List of Features

Suppose you forget how to execute the WordPerfect command for inserting the date into a document. You can use the Help feature to get information on "Date" by using the alphabetical list of features. Let's do that now.

To get an alphabetical list of features that start with the letter D:

❶ Select Help from the menu bar or press **[F3]** (Help). WordPerfect displays the Help screen. See Figure 1-11.

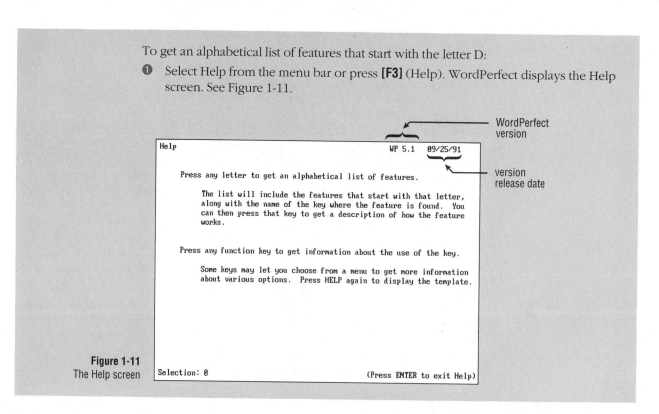

Figure 1-11
The Help screen

❷ Press **D**.

WordPerfect displays a list of the features that start with the letter D, including "Date Format," "Date/Time," "Default Codes," "Delete," and "Document Format." See Figure 1-12. The list gives the name of the feature, the name of the WordPerfect key on the function-key template, and the keystrokes you would press to execute the command.

features that
start with D

names of WordPerfect
keys on template

function-key commands
and other keystrokes

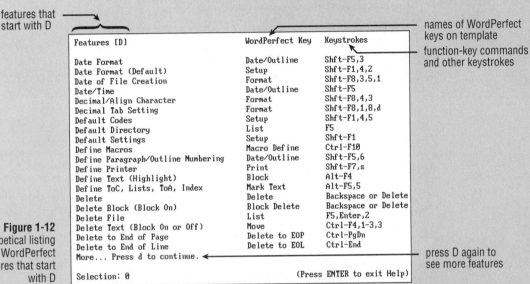

```
Features [D]                        WordPerfect Key   Keystrokes

Date Format                         Date/Outline      Shft-F5,3
Date Format (Default)               Setup             Shft-F1,4,2
Date of File Creation               Format            Shft-F8,3,5,1
Date/Time                           Date/Outline      Shft-F5
Decimal/Align Character             Format            Shft-F8,4,3
Decimal Tab Setting                 Format            Shft-F8,1,8,d
Default Codes                       Setup             Shft-F1,4,5
Default Directory                   List              F5
Default Settings                    Setup             Shft-F1
Define Macros                       Macro Define      Ctrl-F10
Define Paragraph/Outline Numbering  Date/Outline      Shft-F5,6
Define Printer                      Print             Shft-F7,s
Define Text (Highlight)             Block             Alt-F4
Define ToC, Lists, ToA, Index       Mark Text         Alt-F5,5
Delete                              Delete            Backspace or Delete
Delete Block (Block On)             Block Delete      Backspace or Delete
Delete File                         List              F5,Enter,2
Delete Text (Block On or Off)       Move              Ctrl-F4,1-3,3
Delete to End of Page               Delete to EOP     Ctrl-PgDn
Delete to End of Line               Delete to EOL     Ctrl-End
More... Press d to continue.

Selection: 0                                 (Press ENTER to exit Help)
```

Figure 1-12
An alphabetical listing
of WordPerfect
features that start
with D

press D again to
see more features

❸ Press **[Shift][F5]** (Date/Outline). WordPerfect displays information about Date/Outline, including a menu of the features you can select after you issue the Date/Outline command. See Figure 1-13. To get an explanation of any feature in this menu, select that item. In this case, you want an explanation of WordPerfect's Date Text option, so you will select Option 1 (Date Text).

```
Date/Outline

     Includes options which assist you in inserting the current date into your
     document.  You may also create outlines and numbered paragraphs.

     1 - Date Text

     2 - Date Code

     3 - Date Format

     4 - Outline

     5 - Paragraph Numbering

     6 - Define



Selection: 0                               (Press ENTER to exit Help)
```

Figure 1-13
The Date/Outline
Help screen

❹   Select **1** (Date **T**ext) from the menu. WordPerfect displays a detailed explanation of the feature you selected, namely, Date Text. See Figure 1-14.

```
Date Text/Code

    Inserts the date and time into your text at the current cursor location.
    The date and time used is the "system" date and time.  You specify how the
    date and time should be displayed with Date Format (Shift-F5,3).

    Date Text - Inserts the current date and time as text.

    Date Code - Inserts the current date and time as a WordPerfect code.  The
        code will always print the current date and time.
```

Figure 1-14
The Date Text/Code
Help screen

❺   Press **[Enter]** when you are ready to exit Help and return to the document screen.

Getting Help with the Function-Key Templates

If you don't have a WordPerfect function-key template on your computer keyboard, you can use Help to see the template. In the following steps, you'll view the enhanced and the standard keyboard templates.

To use Help to display the function-key templates:

❶   Select Help from the Help menu or press **[F3]** (Help) to display the Help screen.

❷   Press **[F3]** (Help) again to display the function-key template for a 101-key enhanced keyboard. See Figure 1-15.

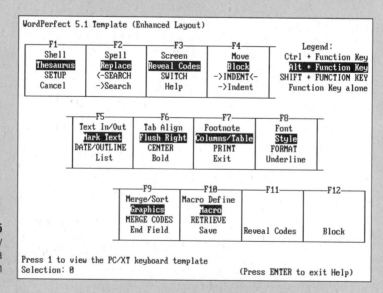

Figure 1-15
The 101-key
template shown on a
Help screen

This screen template lists the function keys (with and without modifier keys) that you would press to execute WordPerfect commands.

❸ Press **1** to display the function-key template for an IBM PC/XT-style keyboard. See Figure 1-16.

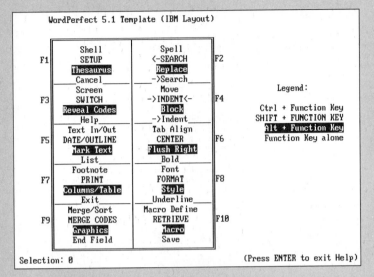

Figure 1-16
The 83-key template shown on a Help screen

❹ Press **[Enter]** when you are ready to exit Help and return to the document screen.

Getting Help with Special Keys

Suppose you wanted information on using the right arrow key [→]. You could again use the Help feature for assistance.

To get help on a cursor-movement key or any other special key (such as [Backspace], [Del] or [Tab]):

❶ Select Help from the Help menu or press **[F3]** (Help).

❷ Press the key you want an explanation of, in this case, **[→]**. WordPerfect explains how to use the left arrow [←] and the right arrow [→] keys alone and with the [Home], [Esc], and [GoTo] keys. See Figure 1-17 on the next page. Your screen might look slightly different depending on your version of WordPerfect.

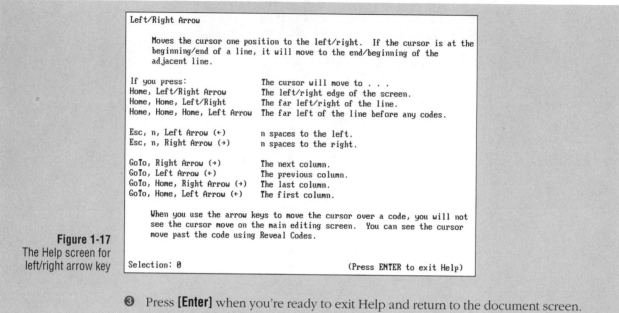

```
Left/Right Arrow

     Moves the cursor one position to the left/right.  If the cursor is at the
     beginning/end of a line, it will move to the end/beginning of the
     adjacent line.

If you press:                      The cursor will move to . . .
Home, Left/Right Arrow             The left/right edge of the screen.
Home, Home, Left/Right             The far left/right of the line.
Home, Home, Home, Left Arrow       The far left of the line before any codes.

Esc, n, Left Arrow (←)             n spaces to the left.
Esc, n, Right Arrow (→)            n spaces to the right.

GoTo, Right Arrow (→)              The next column.
GoTo, Left Arrow (←)               The previous column.
GoTo, Home, Right Arrow (→)        The last column.
GoTo, Home, Left Arrow (←)         The first column.

     When you use the arrow keys to move the cursor over a code, you will not
     see the cursor move on the main editing screen.  You can see the cursor
     move past the code using Reveal Codes.


Selection: 0                                      (Press ENTER to exit Help)
```

Figure 1-17
The Help screen for
left/right arrow key

❸   Press **[Enter]** when you're ready to exit Help and return to the document screen.

Correcting Errors

Beginners and experienced WordPerfect users alike make mistakes. One of the advantages of using a word processor is that when you make a mistake, you can correct it quickly and cleanly. The following steps show you several ways to correct errors when you're entering text or executing a command. First, you'll learn how to use the Backspace key to correct typing errors.

To use [Backspace] to correct typing errors:

❶   Make sure the cursor is on the blank line below the last date text you entered in the previous sections.

❷   Type **Andria**. See Figure 1-18. This is a misspelled version of Andrea Simone's first name.

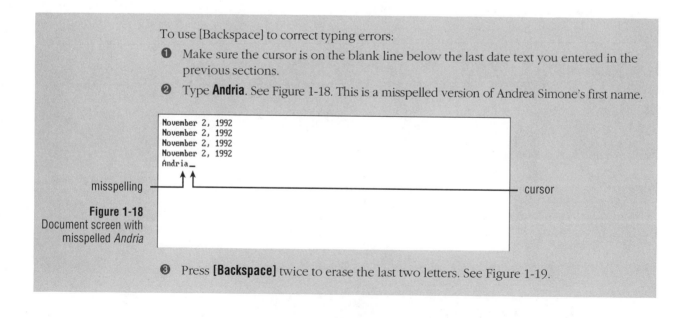

```
November 2, 1992
November 2, 1992
November 2, 1992
November 2, 1992
Andria_
```

misspelling ———   ——— cursor

Figure 1-18
Document screen with
misspelled *Andria*

❸   Press **[Backspace]** twice to erase the last two letters. See Figure 1-19.

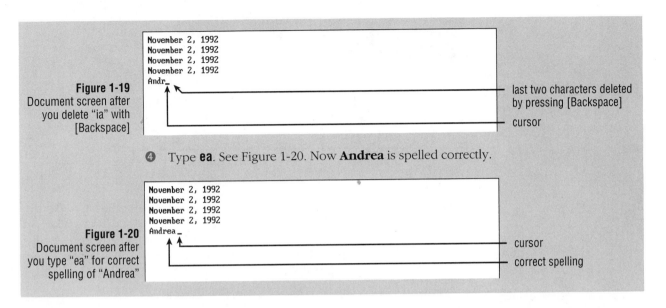

Figure 1-19
Document screen after
you delete "ia" with
[Backspace]

```
November 2, 1992
November 2, 1992
November 2, 1992
November 2, 1992
Andr_
```

last two characters deleted
by pressing [Backspace]

cursor

❹ Type **ea**. See Figure 1-20. Now **Andrea** is spelled correctly.

Figure 1-20
Document screen after
you type "ea" for correct
spelling of "Andrea"

```
November 2, 1992
November 2, 1992
November 2, 1992
November 2, 1992
Andrea _
```

cursor

correct spelling

These steps demonstrate that if you discover a typing error soon after you have made it, you can press [Backspace] to erase the characters to the left of the cursor, back to and including the error, and then type the correct characters. You can also eliminate unwanted space. For example, if you accidentally press [Enter] or [Space], you can use [Backspace] to return the cursor to where you want it. If you make an error and discover it some time later, you can use the arrow keys ([←], [→], [↑], and [↓]) to move the cursor to the error, delete the error, and type the correct characters.

To use the left arrow key to correct a typing error:

❶ Press **[Space]** and type **Semone**. This is a misspelled version of Andrea Simone's last name.

❷ Press [←] until the cursor is at the first "e" in "Semone." See Figure 1-21.

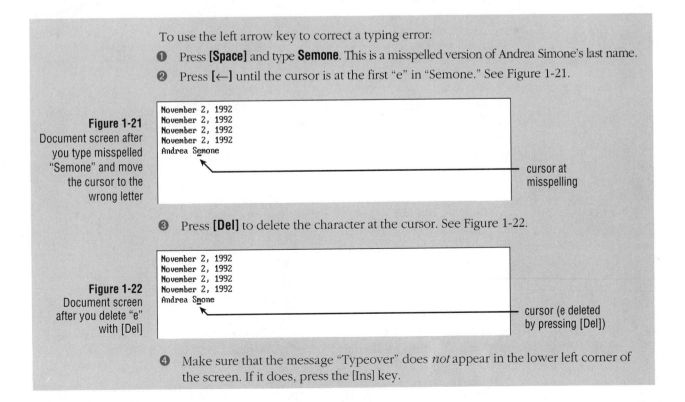

Figure 1-21
Document screen after
you type misspelled
"Semone" and move
the cursor to the
wrong letter

```
November 2, 1992
November 2, 1992
November 2, 1992
November 2, 1992
Andrea Semone
```

cursor at
misspelling

❸ Press **[Del]** to delete the character at the cursor. See Figure 1-22.

Figure 1-22
Document screen
after you delete "e"
with [Del]

```
November 2, 1992
November 2, 1992
November 2, 1992
November 2, 1992
Andrea Smone
```

cursor (e deleted
by pressing [Del])

❹ Make sure that the message "Typeover" does *not* appear in the lower left corner of the screen. If it does, press the [Ins] key.

⑤ Type **i** to insert the correct letter. See Figure 1-23.

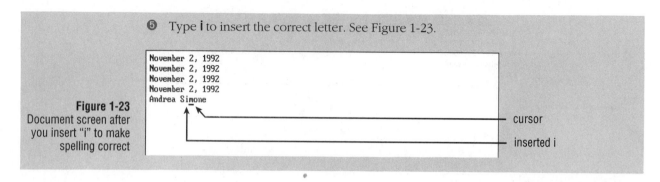

Figure 1-23
Document screen after
you insert "i" to make
spelling correct

You'll learn other methods of correcting typing errors later in this tutorial and in future tutorials. Another mistake that all WordPerfect users make is pressing the wrong function key. In the following steps, you'll learn two ways to correct this kind of mistake: by pressing [F1] (Cancel) and by using a menu option to close a menu and return to the document screen.

To use the [F1] (Cancel) key to close a menu and return to the document screen:

❶ Press **[Shift][F5]** (Date/Outline).

WordPerfect displays a one-line menu on the status line at the bottom of the screen. Let's assume now that you really didn't want to press [Shift][F5] (Date/Outline), but you meant to press something else.

❷ Press **[F1]** (Cancel) to close the menu and return to the document screen.

Sometimes you may have to press [F1] (Cancel) more than once to get back to the document screen.

Now let's try the second way to correct pressing the wrong function key.

To use an option to close a menu and return to the document screen:

❶ Press **[Shift][F5]** (Date/Outline). A zero (0) appears on the far right side of the one-line menu on the status line. See Figure 1-24.

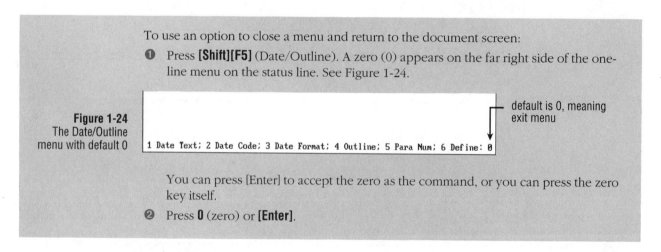

Figure 1-24
The Date/Outline
menu with default 0

You can press [Enter] to accept the zero as the command, or you can press the zero key itself.

❷ Press **0** (zero) or **[Enter]**.

Most WordPerfect menus display a zero as an option. You can press the zero key or [Enter] to close the menu and return to the document screen.

Clearing the Document Screen

You are now ready to begin typing Andrea's letter to Learning Videos. But before you can type the letter, you must be sure that the WordPerfect document screen is clear. If you don't clear the screen before starting the letter, all the text that now appears on the document screen will be part of the document when you print it. Let's clear the screen now.

To clear the document screen:

❶ Select Exit from the File menu or press **[F7]** (Exit).

WordPerfect displays the prompt "Save document?" at the bottom of the screen and pauses for you to answer "yes" or "no." See Figure 1-25.

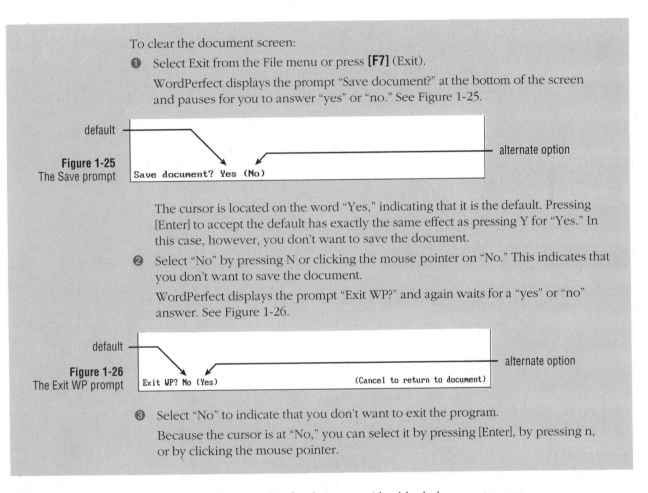

Figure 1-25
The Save prompt

The cursor is located on the word "Yes," indicating that it is the default. Pressing [Enter] to accept the default has exactly the same effect as pressing Y for "Yes." In this case, however, you don't want to save the document.

❷ Select "No" by pressing N or clicking the mouse pointer on "No." This indicates that you don't want to save the document.

WordPerfect displays the prompt "Exit WP?" and again waits for a "yes" or "no" answer. See Figure 1-26.

Figure 1-26
The Exit WP prompt

❸ Select "No" to indicate that you don't want to exit the program.

Because the cursor is at "No," you can select it by pressing [Enter], by pressing n, or by clicking the mouse pointer.

You are still in WordPerfect but now with a blank document screen.

Entering Text

With a blank document screen on your computer monitor and the cursor at Ln 1" Pos 1", you're ready to type Andrea's letter (Figure 1-3). Let's begin by typing the date, the inside address, and the salutation of the letter.

To type the date, the inside address, and the salutation:

❶ Press **[Enter]** six times.

This moves the cursor down one inch from the top margin, giving a total of about two inches of space at the top of the page and allowing room for the Clearwater Valve Company letterhead. The line number on the status line should read Ln 2″ (or some number close to 2), indicating that the cursor is two inches from the top of the page. See Figure 1-27. If you pressed [Enter] too many times, just press [Back-space] to delete the extra blank lines. If the line number on your screen has a slightly different value, like Ln 1.95 or Ln 2.12, don't worry. Different printers produce slightly different measurements when you press [Enter].

Andrea is now ready to insert the date.

cursor

Figure 1-27
Document screen after
you clear screen and
press [Enter] six times

vertical position is two
inches from top of page

Doc 1 Pg 1 Ln 2″ Pos 1″

❷ Select Date Text from the Tools menu or press **[Shift][F5]** (Date/Outline) and select **1** (Date **T**ext). (The date that appears in your document most likely will differ from the date in Figure 1-3.)

❸ Press **[Enter]** twice to insert a double space between the date and the inside address.

Next Andrea enters the inside address, which she got from Steve's note.

❹ Type **Mr. Peter Argyle** and press **[Enter]**. Type **Learning Videos Inc.** and press **[Enter]**. Type **862 Pinewood Road, Suite #210** and press **[Enter]**. Finally, type **Pecos, TX 79772** and press **[Enter]** twice, once to end the line and once to add an extra blank line. See Figure 1-28.

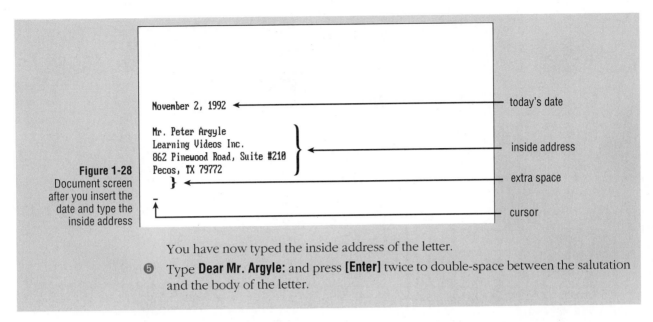

Figure 1-28
Document screen
after you insert the
date and type the
inside address

You have now typed the inside address of the letter.

⑤ Type **Dear Mr. Argyle:** and press **[Enter]** twice to double-space between the salutation and the body of the letter.

Andrea has now completed the date, the inside address, and the salutation of her letter, using a standard format for business letters. See Figure 1-29.

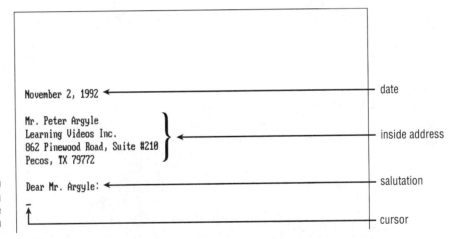

Figure 1-29
Document screen
after you type the
salutation

Saving a Document

The letter that you're typing is currently stored in your computer's memory but not on a disk. If you were to exit WordPerfect without saving your letter, turn off your computer, or experience an accidental power failure right now, the information you have typed would be lost. You should get in the habit of frequently saving your document to a disk. Unless a document is very short, don't wait until you've typed the whole document before saving it. As a rule of thumb, save your work about every 15 minutes.

Although Andrea hasn't been working on this letter for 15 minutes yet, she decides, just to be safe, to save the document now.

To save a document:

❶ Insert the WordPerfect data diskette into drive A and close the drive door.

This tutorial assumes that you have a hard disk — drive C — and at least one diskette drive.

❷ Select Save from the File menu. See Figure 1-30. Alternatively you can press [F10] (Save).

Save option highlighted →

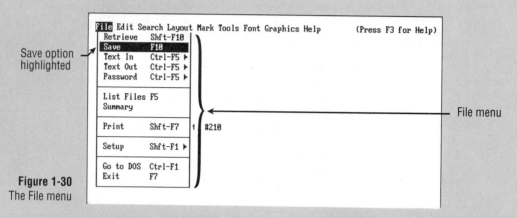

File menu

Figure 1-30
The File menu

WordPerfect displays the prompt "Document to be saved:" on the status line and waits for you to type a name for the document.

❸ Type **a:\s1file1.dft**. See Figure 1-31. Press **[Enter]**.

save prompt →

Figure 1-31
The Save prompt
with the filename

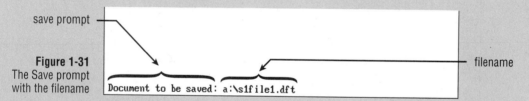

filename

WordPerfect saves the document file to the diskette in drive A. If the error message "Drive not ready reading drive A. 1 Retry; 2 Cancel" appears, make sure the diskette in drive A is positioned properly and the drive door is completely closed. Then select 1 (Retry). If the error message "General failure reading drive A. 1 (Retry); 2 (Cancel)" appears, your diskette is probably not formatted. Remove it from the drive, insert a formatted diskette, close the drive door, and select 1 (Retry).

Figure 1-32 shows the process that occurs when you save a document. WordPerfect copies the file in the computer's memory to your computer's disk storage. Now identical copies of the file exist both in computer memory and on the diskette.

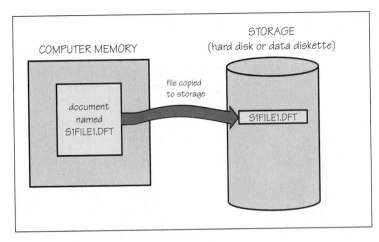

Figure 1-32
Saving a document

After you save the document to the diskette, the path and filename of the document, "A:\S1FILE1.DFT," appear on the screen (Figure 1-33).

document name

path

Figure 1-33
Status line showing
the path and the
document name

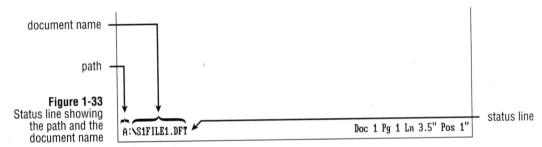

A:\S1FILE1.DFT   Doc 1 Pg 1 Ln 3.5" Pos 1"   status line

Document Filenames

Besides saving your documents frequently, another good habit to follow is to use descriptive filenames that help identify the contents of your files. Document filenames can be any legal DOS filename and may contain the path (such as "a:\" or "c:\wpfiles\"). The filename may contain from one to eight characters and may include a filename extension of one to three characters. In S1FILE1.DFT the filename extension DFT stands for "draft," indicating that this is Andrea's first draft of the letter.

Eight characters in the filename and three in the filename extension often don't allow you to use complete names, but you can at least create meaningful abbreviations. For example, since Andrea is writing a letter to Learning Videos Inc., she could save the final version of her letter with the filename LVI.LET, where LVI is an abbreviation of the name of the company, and LET reminds her that the document is a letter. If she were to write a memo to Clearwater employees about the 1992 budget, she might name the memo 92BUDGET.MEM, where the filename extension MEM stands for memo.

In this book, the six tutorials on WordPerfect involve many files. Therefore, we use filenames that will help you and your instructor recognize the origin and the content of the various documents. To name these files so you can recognize their contents, we have categorized them as follows:

File Category	Description
Tutorial Cases	The files you use to work through each tutorial
Tutorial Assignments	The files that contain the documents you need to complete the Tutorial Assignments at the end of each tutorial
Case Problems	The files that contain the documents you need to complete the Case Problems at the end of each tutorial
Saved Document	Any document you have saved

Let's take the filename S1FILE1.DFT, for example. At first glance this filename might appear to have no meaning, but it does contain meaningful abbreviations. The first character of the filename identifies the file as one of the four categories given above, as shown next:

If the first character is:	The file category is:
C	Tutorial **C**ase
T	**T**utorial Assignment
P	Case **P**roblem
S	**S**aved Document

Thus, S1FILE1.DFT is a document that you have saved.

The second character of the document filename identifies the tutorial from which the file comes. Thus, S1FILE1.DFT is a file you saved from Tutorial 1. The remaining six characters of the filename identify the specific file. All documents in the tutorials are named FILE, followed by a number. Each time you save a file, you will increase the number after FILE by 1. The filename extensions also help identify the file. A letter has the filename extension LET, a memo MEM, a report REP, and a draft of a document DFT. Thus, the filename S1FILE1.DFT tells you that this is the first draft that you saved in Tutorial 1.

The file T1FILE1.LET is the first document (a letter) found in the Tutorial Assignments from WordPerfect Tutorial 1, and C4FILE1.REP is the report you will use in a Tutorial Case for WordPerfect Tutorial 4. Files that you retrieve or save in the Tutorial Assignments and the Case Problems have a word or an abbreviation (other than FILE) to help identify the document. For example, P1IBM.LET is the filename of the Case Problem "Letter to IBM" from WordPerfect Tutorial 1.

Word Wrap

Having saved the first part of your document, you are now ready to complete the letter. As you type the body of the letter, do not press [Enter] at the end of each line. Instead allow WordPerfect to determine where one line ends and the next one begins. When you type a word that extends into the right margin, WordPerfect automatically moves the cursor and the word to the next line. This automatic movement of the cursor and a word to the next line is called **word wrap**. Word wrap ensures that each line of text is the proper length to fit between the left and right margins and eliminates the need for you to press [Enter] at the end of each line, as you would on a typewriter. If you happen to press [Enter] before word wrap occurs, press [Backspace] until the cursor moves back to the previous line, then continue typing. Let's see how word wrap works as you type the body of the letter.

To observe word wrap while you are typing a paragraph:

❶ Be sure the cursor is at the left edge of the screen and two lines below the salutation of the letter.

❷ Type **I have read the catalog description of your training video number**, press **[Space]**, and then slowly continue to type **LV18427**. As you type, notice that the cursor and LV18427 automatically jump to the next line. See Figure 1-34.

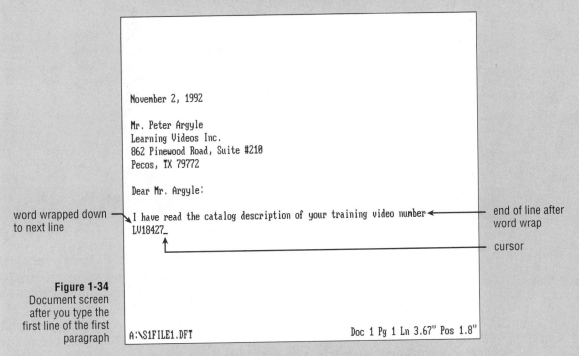

word wrapped down to next line

end of line after word wrap

cursor

Figure 1-34
Document screen after you type the first line of the first paragraph

Because different printers have different sized letters and numbers, the word at which word wrap occurs in your document may be different.

❸ Type the rest of the first paragraph of the body of the letter. See Figure 1-35.

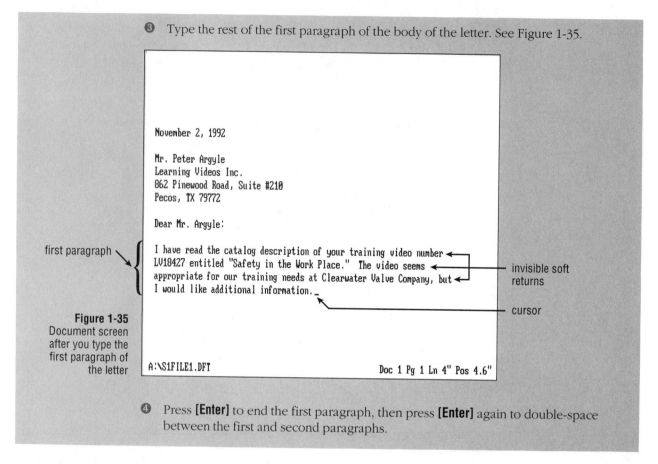

first paragraph

invisible soft returns

cursor

Figure 1-35
Document screen
after you type the
first paragraph of
the letter

❹ Press **[Enter]** to end the first paragraph, then press **[Enter]** again to double-space between the first and second paragraphs.

When you press [Enter], WordPerfect inserts an invisible code called a **hard return** into the document to mark the end of a line or the end of a paragraph. The word or punctuation immediately preceding a hard return always ends a line, regardless of how long or short the line is.

When a line ends with a word wrap, WordPerfect inserts an invisible code called a **soft return** into the document to mark the end of the line (Figure 1-35). The words before and after a soft return are not necessarily permanent — if you later add text to or delete text from the line, the word at which word wrap occurs may change.

Remember the following rule: As you type, press [Enter] only at the end of a paragraph or where you want a line to definitely end. This allows WordPerfect to automatically insert soft returns so that each line of a paragraph fits between the left and right margins.

Let's continue entering the text of the letter.

To enter the second paragraph of the letter:

❶ Type the first line of the second paragraph. See Figure 1-36.

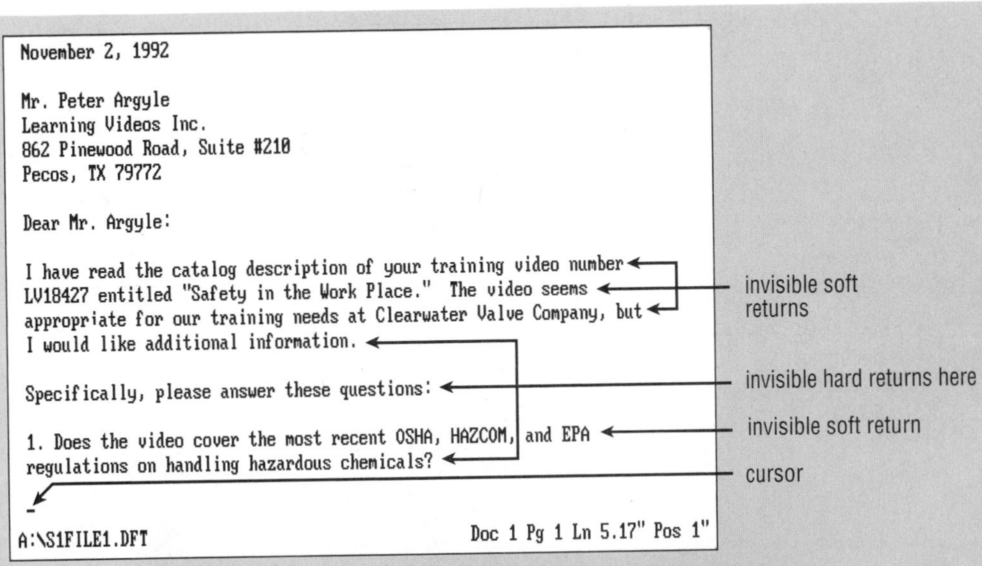
November 2, 1992

Mr. Peter Argyle
Learning Videos Inc.
862 Pinewood Road, Suite #210
Pecos, TX 79772

Dear Mr. Argyle:

I have read the catalog description of your training video number LV18427 entitled "Safety in the Work Place." The video seems appropriate for our training needs at Clearwater Valve Company, but I would like additional information.

Specifically, please answer these questions:

1. Does the video cover the most recent OSHA, HAZCOM, and EPA regulations on handling hazardous chemicals?

A:\S1FILE1.DFT Doc 1 Pg 1 Ln 5.17" Pos 1"
invisible soft returns
invisible hard returns here
invisible soft return
cursor

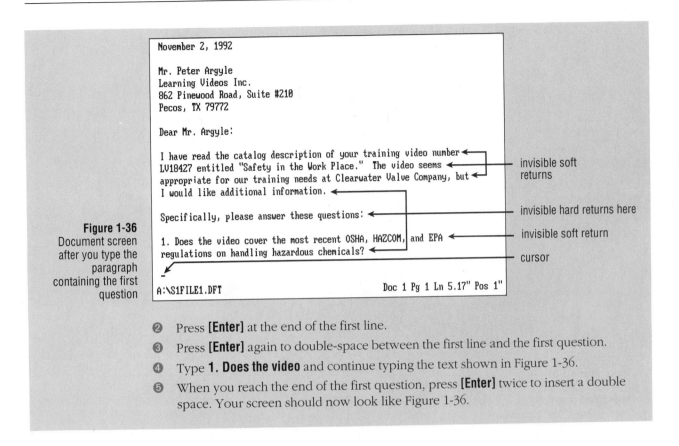

Figure 1-36 Document screen after you type the paragraph containing the first question

❷ Press **[Enter]** at the end of the first line.

❸ Press **[Enter]** again to double-space between the first line and the first question.

❹ Type **1. Does the video** and continue typing the text shown in Figure 1-36.

❺ When you reach the end of the first question, press **[Enter]** twice to insert a double space. Your screen should now look like Figure 1-36.

Scrolling

As you can see in Figure 1-36, the cursor is at the bottom of the screen and the screen is essentially filled with text. In the steps that follow, you will see that as you continue typing the letter, the text on the screen will shift up, so that the beginning lines of the letter disappear off the top of the screen. This shifting up or down of text, called **scrolling**, allows you to see one screenful at a time of a long document. The entire document is still in the computer's memory and available for editing; you just can't see it all at once (Figure 1-37 on the next page). Let's see the effect of scrolling as you insert the next several lines of text into Andrea's letter.

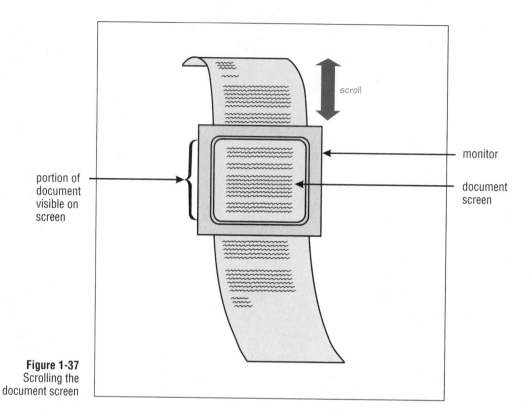

Figure 1-37
Scrolling the
document screen

Labels on figure:
- scroll
- portion of document visible on screen
- monitor
- document screen

To observe scrolling while you are entering text:

❶ Make sure the cursor is at the bottom of the screen, two lines below the end of the first question.

❷ Type the second question, shown in Figure 1-38, but stop before you press [Enter].

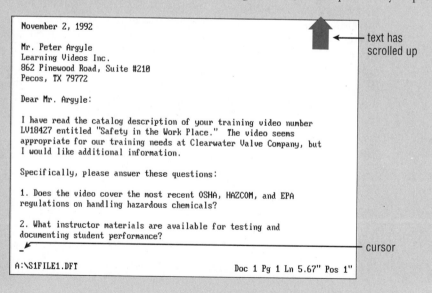

```
November 2, 1992

Mr. Peter Argyle
Learning Videos Inc.
862 Pinewood Road, Suite #210
Pecos, TX 79772

Dear Mr. Argyle:

I have read the catalog description of your training video number
LV18427 entitled "Safety in the Work Place."  The video seems
appropriate for our training needs at Clearwater Valve Company, but
I would like additional information.

Specifically, please answer these questions:

1. Does the video cover the most recent OSHA, HAZCOM, and EPA
regulations on handling hazardous chemicals?

2. What instructor materials are available for testing and
documenting student performance?
```

A:\S1FILE1.DFT   Doc 1 Pg 1 Ln 5.67" Pos 1"

Labels on figure:
- text has scrolled up
- cursor

Figure 1-38
Document screen
after you type the
second question

❸ With the cursor just to the right of the question mark in question 2, press **[Enter]** twice and watch what happens to the date at the top of the screen. See Figure 1-38. Your screen might not scroll at this point but will later.

❹ Type **Your attention to this matter** and continue typing to the end of the paragraph, then press **[Enter]** twice. See Figure 1-39.

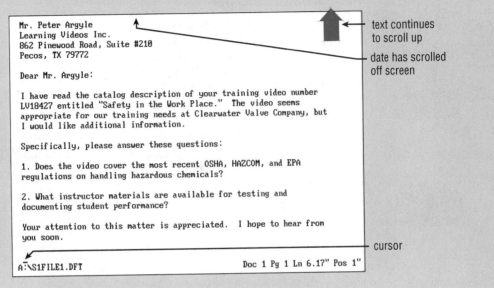

Figure 1-39
Document screen after the date has scrolled off the top of the screen

As you can see in Figure 1-39, the date no longer appears on the document screen. When you pressed [Enter] at the bottom of the screen, the text above the cursor scrolled up so that the date is no longer in view.

You are now ready to type the complimentary close of Andrea's letter, as well as her signature block.

To finish typing the letter:

❶ Make sure the cursor is two lines below the last paragraph, which ends with "hear from you soon." See Figure 1-39.

❷ Type **Sincerely yours,** (including the comma).

❸ Press **[Enter]** four times to allow space for the signature.

❹   Type **Andrea Simone**, press **[Enter]**, and type **Executive Assistant**. See Figure 1-40.

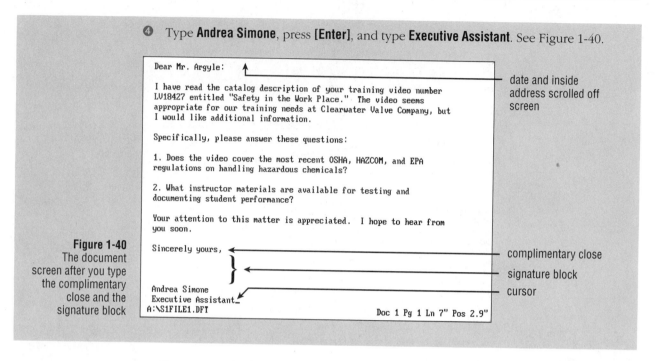

Figure 1-40
The document
screen after you type
the complimentary
close and the
signature block

As you type the last paragraph, the complimentary close and the signature block of the letter, the beginning lines of the letter scroll off the top of the screen so you can't see them any longer.

To see the beginning of the letter, you can use the arrow keys to scroll the text back into view.

To scroll the text using arrow keys:

❶   Press and hold down **[↑]** until the cursor is at the beginning of the letter and the line number reads Ln 1".

Notice that as you press **[↑]** when the cursor is at the top of the screen, the text of the letter scrolls down, so that the lines at the end of the letter disappear from the screen and the lines at the beginning reappear. When the cursor gets to the beginning of the document, scrolling stops because the cursor can't go any higher.

❷   Press and hold down **[↓]** until the cursor is at the end of the letter, on or below the line "Executive Assistant."

As you can see, the arrow keys allow you to scroll the document so you can move the cursor to part of the document that doesn't currently appear on the screen.

Take a few minutes to read over the letter you've just typed and compare it with Figure 1-3. Your letter should have the same text, but yours won't include the Clearwater letterhead, probably won't have the same date, and may have a different number of words on each line. Use the arrow keys ([↑], [↓], [→], and [←]) to move the cursor to various locations within the letter. If you find any errors, make the necessary corrections now.

Saving the Completed Letter

Having completed her letter, Andrea now wants to save the document to a diskette. Although she saved the letter earlier, the version currently on her diskette is incomplete. You must remember to save a document after you complete it, even though you've saved the document one or more times while you were creating it. Let's save the completed letter now.

To save the completed letter:

❶ Make sure the diskette you used earlier to save the partial letter is still in drive A.

It doesn't matter where the cursor is on the document screen when you save a document.

❷ Select Save from the File menu or press **[F10]** (Save).

WordPerfect displays the prompt "Document to be saved: A:\S1FILE1.DFT." Since you've already saved the file previously, WordPerfect displays the complete path and filename of the document.

❸ Press **[Enter]** to accept the given path and filename.

WordPerfect asks you if you want to replace the old version on the diskette with the new version on the screen. This is a helpful reminder that the filename you're using to save the document already exists on the diskette. If you didn't want to replace the current file on the diskette with the document file in memory, you would select "No" and then save the document using a new filename. In this case, however, you want to replace the old version with the new version.

❹ Select "Yes" to replace the old version with the new version.

The complete letter now exists as a document file on your diskette.

Previewing a Document

Andrea has completed her letter and is pleased with its content, organization, and style, but she really can't see the overall format of the letter. The document screen displays the text, but it doesn't show the margins or how the letter will fit onto the printed page.

Before Andrea prints the letter, she wants to make sure it has the proper format. WordPerfect provides a method for her to preview the letter before she prints it. Let's preview the letter you've just typed.

To preview a document:

❶ Select Print from the File menu or press **[Shift][F7]** (Print). WordPerfect displays the Print/Options menu. See Figure 1-41.

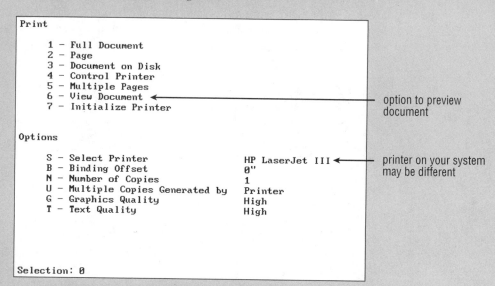

```
Print

    1 - Full Document
    2 - Page
    3 - Document on Disk
    4 - Control Printer
    5 - Multiple Pages
    6 - View Document          ◄──────────────   option to preview
    7 - Initialize Printer                        document


Options

    S - Select Printer                HP LaserJet III  ◄──   printer on your system
    B - Binding Offset                0"                      may be different
    N - Number of Copies              1
    U - Multiple Copies Generated by  Printer
    G - Graphics Quality              High
    T - Text Quality                  High




Selection: 0
```

Figure 1-41
The Print/Options
menu

The Print command is found in the File menu because printing is an operation that deals with the entire document file.

❷ Select **6** (**V**iew Document).

A picture of the document appears on the screen with a one-line menu at the bottom of the screen. See Figure 1-42. If your monitor doesn't support graphics mode, WordPerfect displays an error message, since the View Document command works only with graphics monitors.

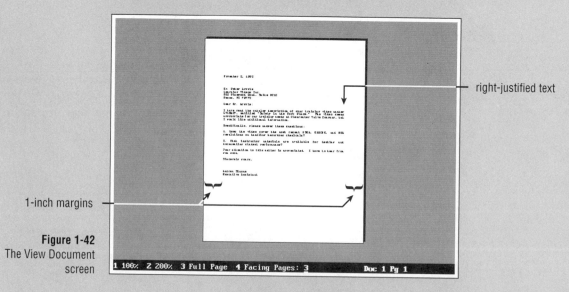

right-justified text

1-inch margins

Figure 1-42
The View Document
screen

❸ If you can't see the entire page of the letter, as shown in Figure 1-42, select **3** (Full Page).

Now you can see the one-inch margins on the left and right edges of the page. You can also see that the body of the letter will be printed with justified text, that is, the right edge of the text lines are aligned along the right margin.

The Full Page view lets you see how the entire page will look, but you can't actually read the text. To get a closer view of the document, you can select 1 (100%) to see the document in its actual size or 2 (200%) to see the document in twice its actual size.

❹ Select **1** (100%) to see the document in approximately its actual size.

Even in actual size the document is still hard to read on a graphics screen. For example, some of the commas may look like periods. Don't worry about this. When you print the document, it will be very readable.

❺ Press [↓] several times and [↑] several times to see how the page scrolls on the screen.

❻ Press **[F7]** (Exit) when you are ready to exit the *View Document* option and return to the normal document screen.

Andrea is satisfied with the format of the letter.

Printing a Document

Having typed, saved, and previewed the document, Andrea is now ready to print it. Let's print the letter now.

To print a document currently on the document screen:

❶ Make sure your printer is turned on and the paper is properly adjusted in the printer. If you have questions about setting up your printer for use with WordPerfect, see your technical support person.

❷ Select Print from the File menu or press **[Shift][F7]** (Print).

❸ Select **1** (**F**ull Document) to print the entire document.

WordPerfect prints the entire letter. Your printed letter should look similar to Figure 1-3, but without the letterhead.

Exiting WordPerfect

Andrea has now finished typing and printing her letter to Learning Videos Inc., so she is ready to exit WordPerfect. She knows that she should never just turn off the computer without first properly exiting WordPerfect. Let's see how to exit WordPerfect properly.

To exit WordPerfect:

❶ Select Exit from the File menu or press **[F7]** (Exit).

WordPerfect displays the prompt "Save document?" and waits for you to select "Yes" or "No." Since you have saved the document since the last modification, the message "(Text was not modified)" appears on the right side of the status line.

❷ Since you've already saved the completed document to the disk, select "No." (If you hadn't saved your document yet, you would select "Yes," type the document name, and press [Enter].) WordPerfect displays the prompt "Exit WP?" and again waits for you to select "Yes" or "No."

❸ Select "Yes" to exit WordPerfect. If you select "No" by accident, WordPerfect clears the document screen but leaves you in WordPerfect. In that case, repeat Steps 1 through 3.

You have now exited WordPerfect. The cursor returns to the DOS prompt if you entered WordPerfect from DOS or to a menu program if you entered WordPerfect through a menu.

Retrieving a Document

After Andrea types, saves, and prints the draft version of the letter to Learning Videos Inc., she gives the printed copy of the letter to her supervisor, Steve Morgan. Steve reads the letter and makes a note to Andrea to include a question about volume discounts (Figure 1-43). After she adds this question, Andrea will print the letter and mail it.

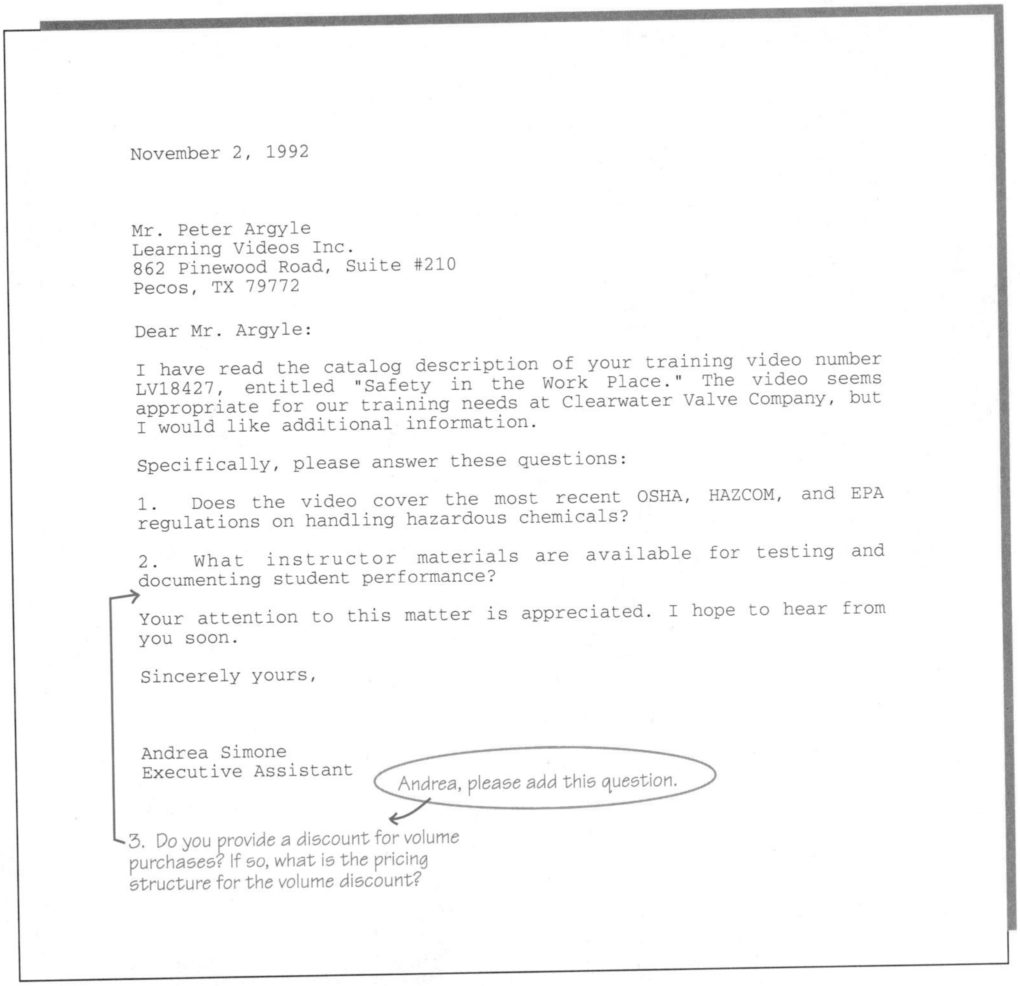

Figure 1-43
Andrea's draft with
Steve's addition

Andrea now needs to start WordPerfect again, retrieve the document file from the diskette into computer memory, add a third question to the letter, save the revised letter, and print the final version of the letter.

To retrieve a document file onto the document screen:

❶ Start WordPerfect as you did earlier, in the section "Starting WordPerfect."

❷ Make sure the document screen is blank.

   If necessary, clear the screen as explained in the section "Clearing the Document Screen."

❸ With a blank document screen, select Retrieve from the File menu or press **[Shift][F10]** (Retrieve).

   WordPerfect displays the prompt "Document to be retrieved:" and waits for you to type the document name.

❹ Make sure the diskette on which you saved the letter is in drive A.

❺ Type **a:\s1file1.dft** and press **[Enter]**.

WordPerfect retrieves the document from the diskette onto the document screen. See Figure 1-44.

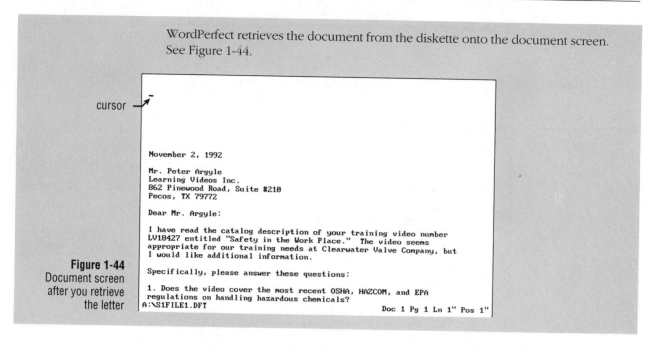

cursor

November 2, 1992

Mr. Peter Argyle
Learning Videos Inc.
862 Pinewood Road, Suite #210
Pecos, TX 79772

Dear Mr. Argyle:

I have read the catalog description of your training video number
LV18427 entitled "Safety in the Work Place." The video seems
appropriate for our training needs at Clearwater Valve Company, but
I would like additional information.

Specifically, please answer these questions:

1. Does the video cover the most recent OSHA, HAZCOM, and EPA
regulations on handling hazardous chemicals?

A:\S1FILE1.DFT   Doc 1 Pg 1 Ln 1" Pos 1"

Figure 1-44
Document screen
after you retrieve
the letter

When you retrieve a document from the diskette, WordPerfect copies the document file into the computer's memory (Figure 1-45). A copy of the document file remains on the diskette.

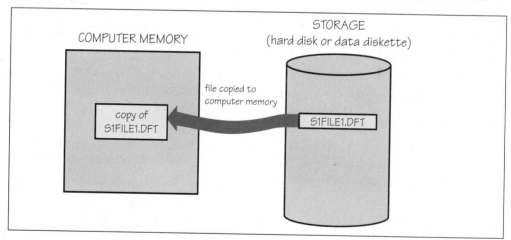

COMPUTER MEMORY

STORAGE
(hard disk or data diskette)

file copied to
computer memory

copy of
S1FILE1.DFT

S1FILE1.DFT

Figure 1-45
The process of
retrieving a file

Now that she has retrieved the file, Andrea is ready to make the addition to the letter as Steve requested. Let's modify the letter now.

To modify the letter:

❶ Press [↓] and [→] to move the cursor to the end of question 2, immediately after the phrase ". . . documenting student performance?"

❷ Make sure "Typeover" doesn't appear in the lower left corner of the screen. If it does, press [Ins].

❸ Press **[Enter]** twice to insert a double space after question 2.

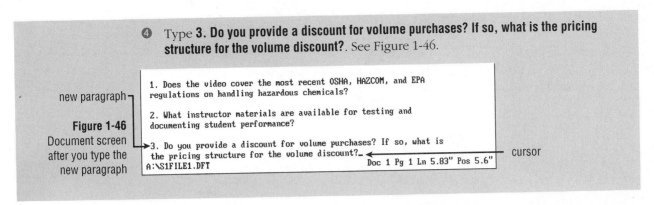

❹ Type **3. Do you provide a discount for volume purchases? If so, what is the pricing structure for the volume discount?**. See Figure 1-46.

new paragraph ⌐

Figure 1-46
Document screen
after you type the
new paragraph

```
1. Does the video cover the most recent OSHA, HAZCOM, and EPA
regulations on handling hazardous chemicals?

2. What instructor materials are available for testing and
documenting student performance?

3. Do you provide a discount for volume purchases? If so, what is
the pricing structure for the volume discount?_
A:\S1FILE1.DFT                          Doc 1 Pg 1 Ln 5.83" Pos 5.6"
```

cursor

The letter is now modified the way Steve wants it. Andrea looks over the letter one last time for any errors. She is ready to print the final version. But before she prints the letter, she realizes that she has to save this new, final version since the letter on the screen is different from the one on the diskette. Let's save the final version now.

To save the final version of the letter with a new filename:

❶ Select Save from the File menu or press **[F10]** (Save).

WordPerfect displays the prompt "Document to be saved: A:\S1FILE1.DFT." Remember, the name of the file of the document on the screen automatically appears in the prompt. But because this is the second time you're saving the letter and because you want to keep the previous version of the letter, now saved in S1FILE1.DFT, you'll use a new filename.

❷ Type **a:\s1file2.let** and press **[Enter]**.

Now a copy of the final letter on the screen is saved on the diskette as S1FILE2.LET. See Figure 1-47.

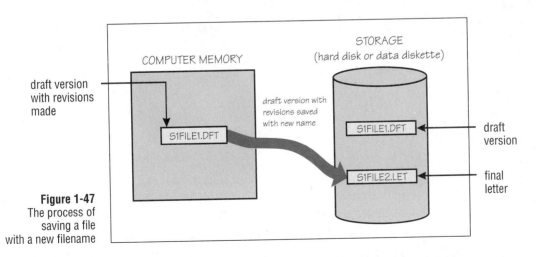

draft version
with revisions
made

Figure 1-47
The process of
saving a file
with a new filename

This completes Andrea Simone's letter to Learning Videos Inc. She can now print the final copy of the letter.

❸ Print the document. See Figure 1-48.

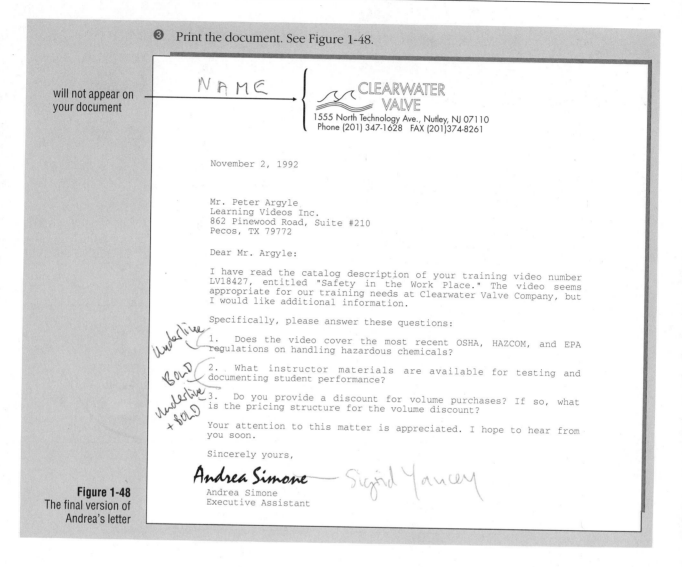

will not appear on
your document

Figure 1-48
The final version of
Andrea's letter

Exercises

1. If the cursor is at the DOS prompt and in the directory where the WordPerfect program is located, what do you type to start WordPerfect?

2. What does the status line message Ln 2" mean?

3. What does the status line message Pos 3.5" mean?

4. List two ways you can automatically insert today's date into a WordPerfect document.

5. How would you find out information on using [Del] (delete key) in WordPerfect?

6. What are the default margin settings in WordPerfect?

7. With the cursor in the document screen, what key(s) would you press to do the following?
   a. Display the menu bar
   b. Clear the WordPerfect document screen
   c. Double-space between paragraphs
   d. Move the cursor one character to the left
   e. Print the document that is on the document screen
   f. Exit WordPerfect

8. Define the following WordPerfect terms:
   a. Word wrap
   b. Retrieve
   c. Default format settings
   d. Function-key template
   e. Document screen
   f. Pull-down menu
   g. Scrolling
   h. Mnemonic letter
   i. Hard return
   j. Soft return

9. Name and describe four steps in planning a document.

10. Why should you usually save a document to your disk several times even before you finish typing it?

Tutorial Assignments

Be sure your WordPerfect data diskette is in drive A and clear the document screen. Then retrieve the file T1FILE1.DFT and do the following:

1. Delete the current date at the beginning of the letter, then use WordPerfect's Date Text command to insert today's date into the document.

2. Save the letter as S1FILE1.LET.

3. Preview the document to see what it will look like before you print it.

4. Print the document.

Clear the document screen, retrieve the letter T1FILE2.DFT from your data diskette and do the following:

5. In the body of the memo delete the space between "Clear" and "Water," and then delete the "W" and insert "w" so the word reads "Clearwater" instead of "Clear Water."

6. Save the document as S1FILE2.MEM.

7. Print the document.

Use Figure 1-49 to complete Assignments 8 through 12.

Date: November 13, 1992

To: Andrea Simone, Executive Assistant, Operations

From: Roberta Caldwell, Human Resources Manager

Re: Safety Training

Thanks for your help in setting up the safety training for our employees. Your care and attention to detail in selecting training videos, scheduling, instructors, and keeping training records has been extremely beneficial to Clearwater Valve Company.

cc: Steve Morgan

Figure 1-49

8. Type the memo, pressing [Space] twice after "Date:," "To:," "From:," and "Re:." For now use the date shown in the memo.

9. Delete the date in the memo and use WordPerfect's Date Text feature to insert today's date.

10. Save the memo as S1FILE3.MEM.

11. Preview the memo before printing it.

12. Print the memo.

Case Problems

1. Letter to IBM

Joseph Cardon is the manager of information systems for the public accounting firm of Armstrong, Black & Calzone. One of his responsibilities is to recommend which brand of personal computers employees should use. After reading an advertisement in which IBM Corporation offers a free copy of the book *How To Buy a Personal Computer for Your Small Business*, Joseph decides to write a letter requesting the book. He has already written the body of the letter and now needs only to insert the date, the inside address, the salutation, the complimentary close, and his name and title.

Retrieve the document P1IBM.LET from your data diskette and do the following:

1. Move the cursor to the beginning of the document and press [Enter] six times to insert sufficient space for a letterhead.

2. Use WordPerfect's Date Text feature to insert today's date.

3. Insert four blank lines after the date and, using the proper business-letter format, type the inside address: **IBM Corporation, P.O. Box 92835, Rochester, NY 14692**.

4. Insert a blank line after the inside address, then type the salutation **Dear Company Officers:**. Then insert another blank line.

5. Move the cursor to the end of the document and type the complimentary close and your name and title.

6. Save the letter as S1IBM.LET.

7. Preview the letter.

8. Print the letter.

2. Memo to Congratulate a Colleague

One of your colleagues at Clearwater Valve Company, Debora Stern, was recently given a company award as sales representative of the year.

1. Write a memo to Debora Stern congratulating her on receiving the award. Remember to use the four-part planning process. You should plan the content, organization, and style of the memo, and use the standard memo format shown in Figure 1-50.

Figure 1-50

Date:	*(today's date)*
To:	*(the name of the person to whom you are writing this memo)*
From:	*(your name)*
Re:	*(a brief description of the subject of the memo)*

2. Save the document as S1STERN.MEM.

3. Preview the memo.

4. Print the memo.

3. Letter of Introduction to a Prospective Client

Suppose you're a sales representative for Clearwater Valve Company. You have a list of prospective clients, one of whom is Mr. Ken Kikuchi of CryoTech Pharmaceuticals, 891 Avocado Avenue, Escondido, CA 92925.

1. Write a letter introducing yourself to Mr. Kikuchi and request the opportunity to visit him and others at CryoTech Pharmaceuticals.

2. Save the letter as S1CRYO.LET.

3. Preview the letter.

4. Print the letter.

Tutorial 2

Formatting and Editing a Document

Writing a Product Information Memo for an Ad Launch

Case: Decision Development Corporation

David Truong is an assistant product manager at Decision Development Corporation (DDC), a company that specializes in business software tools. David reports to Liz Escobar, the product manager. One of David's responsibilities is to write product description memos to the DDC advertising group explaining the key features and benefits of new products. The advertising group uses these memos to help them prepare for the launch meetings, at which the advertising campaigns for new products are planned.

Liz has just stopped by David's office and asked him to write a product description memo to the ad group about DDC's newest product, InTrack, an investment tracking program. Liz reminds David that, as usual, she wants him to submit his first draft to her for comments and corrections. After she returns the draft to him, he should make the necessary changes and print three copies of the memo — one for the advertising group, one for her, and one for the InTrack product file.

In this tutorial you'll plan, write, and edit David's memo for the ad launch.

OBJECTIVES

In this tutorial you will learn to:

■ Make large-scale cursor moves

■ Change margins

■ Justify text

■ Boldface and underline text

■ Reveal hidden format codes

■ Indent a paragraph

■ Delete words and lines of text and undo deletions

■ Use the insert and typeover modes

■ Insert a hard page break

■ Use the speller and the thesaurus

■ Print multiple copies of a document

Planning the Document

First David plans the four components of the document. He considers content, organization, style, and format.

Content

David has kept notes on the key features of InTrack and has a copy of the program specifications produced by the company software design team. His notes contain information he can use for the content of his product description memo. As he reads these notes, David realizes that they contain much more information than he needs to put in the memo. He decides to distill this information so the advertising group will understand the product and still have the necessary details to write the text of the advertisements, commonly called ad copy. He assumes that the ad group is familiar with computer software, so he feels free to use computer jargon.

Organization

Because the product description is a memo, David knows that his document will begin with the standard memo heading. He decides that the body of the memo will be a numbered list of the key features of InTrack.

Style

David assumes that the ad group will adapt and edit his information to a style that suits the needs of the ad campaign. His style, therefore, will be clear and straightforward, the best way to convey product information.

Format

David decides that in his first draft he will use WordPerfect's default format settings, which include one-inch margins and text aligned along the right margin. He knows that Liz might suggest format changes, but for now he'll use the defaults.

■   ■   ■

Having planned the document, David creates the rough draft of the memo. He submits it to Liz, who later returns the draft with her editing marks and notes (Figure 2-1). David looks over her comments and is ready to create the final draft of the InTrack product description memo.

Indent to 1.5" for 3-ring binder holes

DATE: January 15, 1993

TO: Advertising Group

FROM: David Truong, Assistant Product Manager
RE: *Product Description of InTrack*

turn off justification to make more informal

Liz has asked me to provide you the following list of key features of **InTrack** to help you plan the advertising campaign:

indent all paragraphs

run speller!

1. **InTrack** is a sophisticated yet easy-to-use investemnt management system. Customers will use the software to post all of their investment transactions; track commissions, dividends, and interest; create value projections; create tax information; and print reports on investment performance, portfolio values, capitol gains, investment income, and so forth. The mouse-supported menu-driven user interface is powerful and easy to learn.

repetitious; use better words

2. **InTrack** helps customers ~~keep~~ track ~~of~~ mutual funds, bonds, stocks, money market funds, certificates of deposit (CDs), real estate, annuities, trusts, and almost any other type of investment. ~~Customers can use the program to keep track of any kind of investment they want.~~

3. **InTrack** can be customized for any type of investment. Customers can print reports using built-in forms or can design their own reports.

4. **InTrack** is ideal for managing IRAs and Keog Plans. The the program will forecast the potential monthly and annual retirement income derived from IRAs and Keogh Plans.

5. **InTrack** provides internal telecommunications support. CUstomers can use the program to get on-line financial information from most of the electronic information services. Customers can also carry out transactions with their broker directly from within **InTrack**. *Dave, doesn't broker have to own InTrack?*

6. **InTrack** pays easily for itself within the first year of use, because (a) the program costs less than other products of this type on the market, (b) the cost of the program is tax deductible, (c) the program simplifies tax preparation, and (d) the program provides the necessary information to make smart investment decisions and allows customers to get the most return on their investment dollar.

3.0 (or higher)

7. **InTrack** runs on any IBM-compatible personal computer under DOS 3.2 (or higher) or under Windows. The program does not require a hard disk drive, but one is highly recommended. The fully installed program, with all features and auxiliary files, requires about 3.4 megabytes of disk space. *wasn't this lower?*   *Dave, what about other hardware options?*

Figure 2-1
The ad launch memo with Liz's edits and notes

In the instructions on editing the memo, you'll be given a choice of whether to use pull-down menus (with the keyboard or with the mouse) or to use the function-key template and the function keys to execute WordPerfect commands. You'll remember from Tutorial 1 that to use the pull-down menus you press [Alt][=] or the right mouse button to display the menu bar at the top of the document screen. Then you select a menu item by pressing the highlighted mnemonic key, by using an arrow key to highlight the menu item and pressing [Enter], or by clicking on the menu item. To use the template and a function key to execute a command, you press a modifier key ([Shift], [Alt], or [Ctrl]), if any, and a function key. We'll tell you the function-key combination to press and the name of the WordPerfect command listed on the function-key template. When a pull-down menu option or function-key command causes WordPerfect to display a menu, you select the appropriate option from that menu by pressing the number or mnemonic letter corresponding to the desired option or by clicking the mouse on that option.

Retrieving the Document

David begins by retrieving the first draft of his memo, which has the filename C2FILE1.DFT. The filename extension .DFT stands for "draft." Let's retrieve the memo now.

To retrieve the document:

❶ Start WordPerfect (if you haven't done so already) and make sure the document screen is clear. If necessary, refer to Tutorial 1 to see how to clear the document screen.

❷ Insert your WordPerfect data diskette into drive A and close the disk drive door.

❸ Select Retrieve from the File menu or press **[Shift][F10]** (Retrieve). The prompt "Document to be retrieved:" appears on the status line at the bottom of the screen.

❹ Type **a:\c2file1.dft** and press **[Enter]**. The rough draft of David Truong's memo appears on the screen. See Figure 2-2.

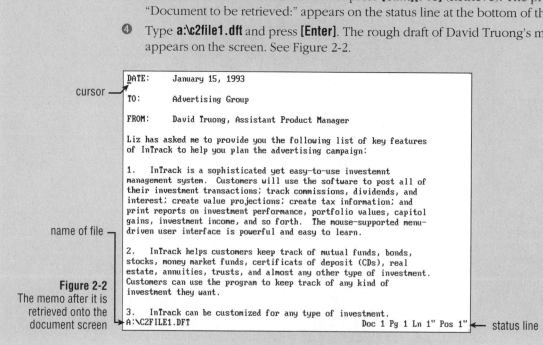

cursor —

name of file —

Figure 2-2
The memo after it is retrieved onto the document screen

status line

Making Large-Scale Cursor Moves

You're already familiar with the arrow keys ([→], [←], [↑], and [↓]) to move the cursor one character to the right or left or one line up or down. Now you'll see how to move the cursor more than one character or one line at a time. You should make an effort now to learn and remember these large-scale cursor moves because they will save you considerable time and energy when you have to move the cursor around to different parts of your documents.

In the following steps, you'll see how to move the cursor quickly from one place to another within the document.

Also, as you work through the following steps, you may notice several typographical and spelling errors. Don't correct the errors at this time. They appear in the document to help you learn various ways of editing the text and correcting the spelling.

To make large-scale cursor moves:

❶ Press **[Home]**, **[Home]**, and **[↓]**.

This sequence of keystrokes is separated by commas, meaning that you should press each key separately but don't type the commas. Notice that pressing these keys moves the cursor to the end of the document.

❷ Press **[Home]**, **[Home]**, and **[↑]** to move the cursor to the beginning of the document.

❸ Press **[↓]** enough times to move the cursor to the "1" in the first numbered paragraph of the memo. See Figure 2-3.

```
DATE:     January 15, 1993

TO:       Advertising Group

FROM:     David Truong, Assistant Product Manager

Liz has asked me to provide you the following list of key features
of InTrack to help you plan the advertising campaign:

1.   InTrack is a sophisticated yet easy-to-use investemnt
management system.  Customers will use the software to post all of
their investment transactions; track commissions, dividends, and
interest; create value projections; create tax information; and
print reports on investment performance, portfolio values, capitol
gains, investment income, and so forth.  The mouse-supported menu-
driven user interface is powerful and easy to learn.

2.   InTrack helps customers keep track of mutual funds, bonds,
stocks, money market funds, certificats of deposit (CDs), real
estate, annuities, trusts, and almost any other type of investment.
Customers can use the program to keep track of any kind of
investment they want.

3.   InTrack can be customized for any type of investment.
A:\C2FILE1.DFT                              Doc 1 Pg 1 Ln 2.5" Pos 1"
```

cursor →

Figure 2-3
The cursor position at
paragraph 1

❹ Press **[End]** to move the cursor to the end of the current line. This method is much faster in moving the cursor to the end of the line than if you repeatedly press [→] until the cursor gets to the end of the line.

❺ Press **[Home]** and **[←]** to move the cursor to the beginning of the current line.

❻ Press **[Ctrl][→]** (Word Right) three times to move your cursor to the word "a," then press **[Ctrl][←]** (Word Left) three times to move the cursor back to the "1."

As you can see, [Ctrl][→] moves the cursor one word to the right, and [Ctrl][←] moves the cursor one word to the left.

❼ With Num Lock off, press **[+]** (Screen Down) on the numeric keypad once to move the cursor to the bottom of the screen. Press it again to move the cursor down another screen. See Figure 2-4. Your screen may look different due to differences in font size.

cursor ⟶

```
the program simplifies tax preparation, and (d) the program
provides the necessary information to make smart investment
decisions and allows customers to get the most return on their
investment dollar.

7.   InTrack runs on any IBM-compatible personal computer under DOS
3.2 (or higher) or under Windows.  The program does not require a
hard disk drive, but one is highly recommended.  The fully
A:\C2FILE1.DFT                              Doc 1 Pg 1 Ln 8.83" Pos 1"
```

Figure 2-4
The cursor after you use the Screen Down command

Pressing [+] on the keypad with Num Lock off moves the cursor to the bottom of the current screen. When you press it again, the cursor moves to the bottom of the next screenful of text. You must remember to use the plus-sign key [+] *on the keypad* and to have Num Lock off. If you press the plus key on the typewriter section of the keyboard or on the keypad with Num Lock on, a plus character will be inserted into the document.

❽ Press **[−]** (Screen Up) on the numeric keypad twice.

Pressing [−] on the keypad once moves the cursor to the top of the current screen. Pressing it again moves the cursor up another screenful. See Figure 2-5. Your cursor might be in a slightly different position because of differences in font size.

cursor at beginning of document ⟶

```
DATE:     January 15, 1993

TO:       Advertising Group

FROM:     David Truong, Assistant Product Manager

Liz has asked me to provide you the following list of key features
of InTrack to help you plan the advertising campaign:

1.   InTrack is a sophisticated yet easy-to-use investemnt
management system.  Customers will use the software to post all of
their investment transactions; track commissions, dividends, and
interest; create value projections; create tax information; and
print reports on investment performance, portfolio values, capitol
gains, investment income, and so forth.  The mouse-supported menu-
```

Figure 2-5
The cursor after you use the Screen Up command

The cursor-movement keys demonstrated in the preceding steps are only a few of the many ways you can move the cursor in WordPerfect. Figure 2-6 lists most of the WordPerfect cursor-movement commands. You'll use some of the other cursor-movement keys in later tutorials.

Cursor Key	Movement
[←]	Left one character
[→]	Right one character
[↑]	Up one line
[↓]	Down one line
[Ctrl][←]	Left one word
[Ctrl][→]	Right one word
[Home], [←]	Far left side of screen
[Home], [→]	Far right side of screen
[Home], [Home], [←]	Beginning of line (even when the line extends beyond the left edge of the screen)
[Home], [Home], [→] or [End]	End of line (even when the line extends beyond the right edge of the screen)
[Home], [↑] or keypad [-]	Top of screen, then up one screen at a time
[Home], [↓] or keypad [+] ·	Bottom of screen, then down one screen at a time
[PgUp]	First line of previous page
[PgDn]	First line of next page
[Home], [Home], [↑]	Beginning of document (after any formatting codes)
[Home], [Home], [↓]	End of document (after any formatting codes)

Figure 2-6
WordPerfect
cursor-movement
keys

As you move the cursor through a document, you'll discover that the cursor won't move to a region of the screen not occupied by text. If the cursor were at the end of a document, for example, and you pressed [+] (Screen Down), the cursor wouldn't move, since it couldn't go down lower than the end of the document. Similarly if the cursor were at the end of a short line of text and you pressed [→], the cursor wouldn't go any farther to the right, but would move to the first character of the next line.

Sometimes as you move the cursor through a document, you'll see WordPerfect reformat the screen by shifting text left or right, wrapping words from one line to another, and so forth. This happens because some format changes don't actually appear on the screen until you move the cursor through the affected text.

Changing Margins

David's first task in editing the memo is to increase the left margin to 1.5 inches. Because the left margin affects the length of text lines, David will use the Line menu to change the margin. Let's change the margin now.

To change the left margin:

❶ Press **[Home]**, **[Home]**, **[↑]** to make sure the cursor is at the beginning of the document.

If you want to change a margin for an entire document, you must move the cursor to the beginning of the document before you set the new margin value. If you were to change a margin or other format value when the cursor was in the middle of the document, the change would be in effect only from the location of the cursor to the end of the document.

❷ Select Line from the Layout menu (Figure 2-7).

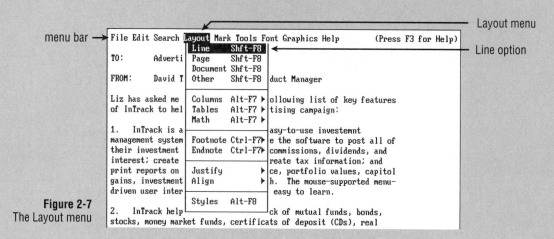

menu bar →

Layout menu

Line option

Figure 2-7
The Layout menu

Alternatively, press **[Shift][F8]** (Format) to display the menu shown in Figure 2-8, and select **1** (**L**ine).

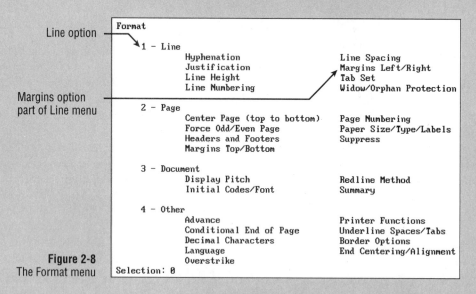

Line option

Margins option
part of Line menu

Figure 2-8
The Format menu

The Format: Line menu now appears on the screen. See Figure 2-9. You'll learn the meaning of the many Line commands as you go through these tutorials. For now you are interested only in option 7 (Margins). To the right of this option WordPerfect displays the current margins: Left 1" and Right 1". You want to change the value for the left margin.

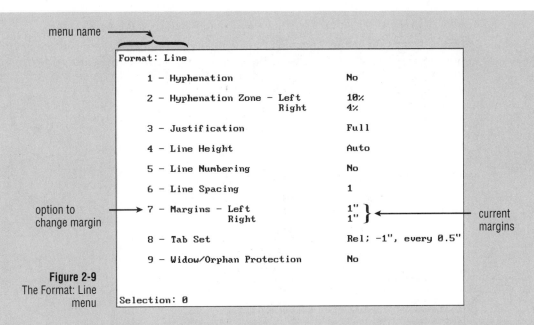

menu name

```
Format: Line
        1 - Hyphenation                  No
        2 - Hyphenation Zone - Left      10%
                             Right        4%
        3 - Justification               Full
        4 - Line Height                 Auto
        5 - Line Numbering              No
        6 - Line Spacing                1
        7 - Margins - Left              1" ⎫
                      Right             1" ⎭
        8 - Tab Set                     Rel; -1", every 0.5"
        9 - Widow/Orphan Protection     No

Selection: 0
```

option to
change margin

current
margins

Figure 2-9
The Format: Line
menu

❸ Select **7** (**M**argins).

To select this option you can press 7, press M, or click the mouse pointer on
"7 - Margins." The cursor moves to the right of the Margin option. You can now
type the new value for the left margin.

As Figure 2-1 shows, Liz asked David to make the left margin 1½ inches.

❹ Type **1.5** and press **[Enter]**.

The cursor moves to the value for the right margin. If you wanted to change that
value, you would type a new number. But in this case, you want to leave the right
margin at 1 inch, because Liz didn't ask David to change the right margin.

❺ Press **[Enter]** to accept the current value.

As a general rule in WordPerfect, you just press [Enter] to accept a current setting,
value, or name.

❻   Press **[F7]** (Exit) to exit the Format: Line menu and return to the main document.

The text along the left margin moves to the right. See Figure 2-10. Your screen may not show the full effect of changing the margin until you move the cursor down through the text or you tell WordPerfect to "rewrite" the screen, that is, to show you what the entire screen looks like with any changes.

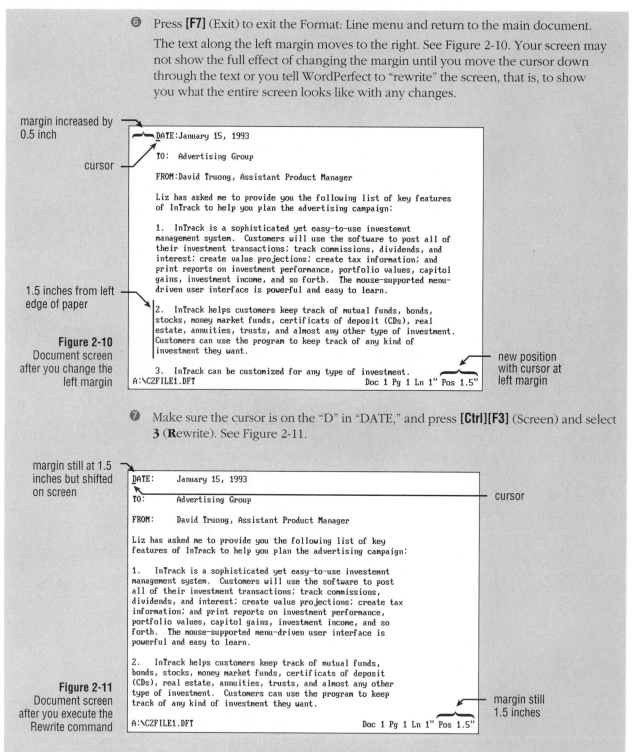

margin increased by 0.5 inch

cursor

1.5 inches from left edge of paper

Figure 2-10
Document screen after you change the left margin

new position with cursor at left margin

❼   Make sure the cursor is on the "D" in "DATE," and press **[Ctrl][F3]** (Screen) and select **3** (**R**ewrite). See Figure 2-11.

margin still at 1.5 inches but shifted on screen

cursor

Figure 2-11
Document screen after you execute the Rewrite command

margin still 1.5 inches

This command causes WordPerfect to rewrite the screen to show the effect of changing the margin. In most cases you won't have to use the Rewrite command because WordPerfect automatically reformats the screen when you move the cursor into that region of the screen.

As you can see, when you want to change the margins or any other format setting, you first move the cursor to the position where you want the new format to begin and then set the new format feature. The new format setting takes effect from that point in the document to the end of the document, unless you change the format setting later. In our example, David and Liz wanted the left margin to be 1.5 inches for the entire document, so you moved the cursor to the beginning of the document before you changed the margin.

Justifying Text

Justification usually means adjusting the spacing between characters so that text is aligned along the right margin as well as along the left margin. Modern word processors and desktop publishing software, however, define justification to mean more than right-aligned margins. Specifically WordPerfect allows for four types of justified text: left, center, right, and full (Figure 2-12).

```
Full Justification
This paragraph is an example of full justification. The lines
of  text  are  aligned  along  the  left  and  the  right
margins.   This gives an ordered look to the document but is
generally more difficult to read than left-justified text.
Full justification is the default setting in WordPerfect.


Left Justification
This paragraph is an example of left justification.
The lines of text are aligned along the left margin but are
"ragged" along the right margin.   This gives a less
ordered look to the document but is generally easier to
read than fully justified text.


Right Justification
       This paragraph is an example of right justification. The
           lines of text are aligned along the right margin but
      ragged along the left margin.   You would never use right
        justification in the body of a normal document, but you
                              might use it for special effects.


Center Justification
                This paragraph is an example of center
            justification. The lines of text are centered
            between the left and the right margins.   You
            would never use center justification in the
             body of a normal document, but you would
              frequently use it in creating title pages.
```

Figure 2-12
Examples of justification

The WordPerfect default format setting is full justification, and that is how David formatted the first draft of his product description memo. But Liz has suggested that he change the format setting to left justification to make the memo appear less formal. David can do this by using the Format: Line menu, which you have already used. Let's change the justification of the memo that appears on your screen.

To change text justification using the pull-down menus:

❶ Press **[Home]**, **[Home]**, **[↑]** to make sure the cursor is at the beginning of the document.

Remember that since you want to change justification for the entire document, you must move the cursor to the beginning of the document before you change the format setting. Otherwise, justification will be in effect only from the current location of the cursor to the end of the document.

❷ Press **[Shift][F8]** (Format) and select **1** (**L**ine); then from the Format: Line menu, select **3** (**J**ustification). WordPerfect displays the one-line Justification menu at the bottom of the screen. See Figure 2-13.

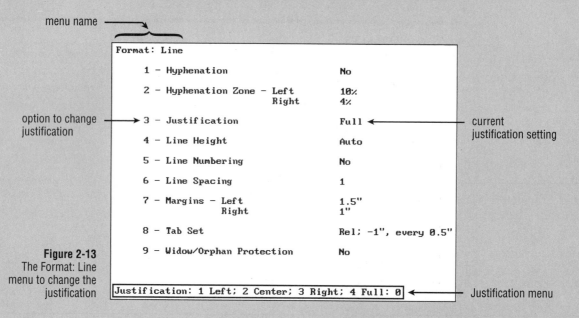

menu name

```
Format: Line

        1 - Hyphenation                     No

        2 - Hyphenation Zone - Left         10%
                             Right          4%

     →  3 - Justification                   Full  ←

        4 - Line Height                     Auto

        5 - Line Numbering                  No

        6 - Line Spacing                    1

        7 - Margins - Left                  1.5"
                      Right                 1"

        8 - Tab Set                         Rel; -1", every 0.5"

        9 - Widow/Orphan Protection         No


 Justification: 1 Left; 2 Center; 3 Right; 4 Full: 0  ←
```

option to change justification →

current justification setting ←

Figure 2-13
The Format: Line menu to change the justification

Justification menu ←

❸ Select **1** (**L**eft) to set the document to left justification.

❹ Press **[F7]** (Exit) to exit the menu and return to the document screen.

To use the pull-down menus to set left justification, you would select Justify from the Layout menu and then select Left from the Justify menu. See Figure 2-14.

menu name

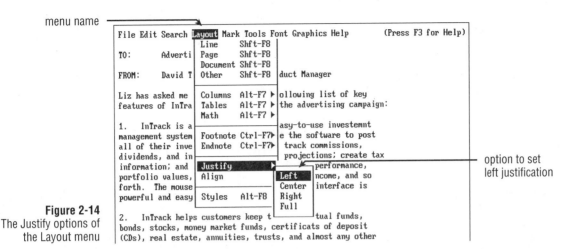

option to set
left justification

Figure 2-14
The Justify options of
the Layout menu

From the cursor's current location — the beginning of the memo in this instance — to the end of the document, the text is now left-justified. Since the document screen looks the same for full and for left justification, you will not see any changes until you use View Document to preview the document or until you print it. Let's preview the document to see what the left justification looks like.

To preview the document:

❶ Select Print from the File menu or press **[Shift][F7]** (Print) to display the Print/Options menu.

❷ Select **6** (**V**iew Document) to see what the document will look like when you print it. See Figure 2-15.

left-justified

ragged right margin

Figure 2-15
The View Document
screen showing
left-justified text

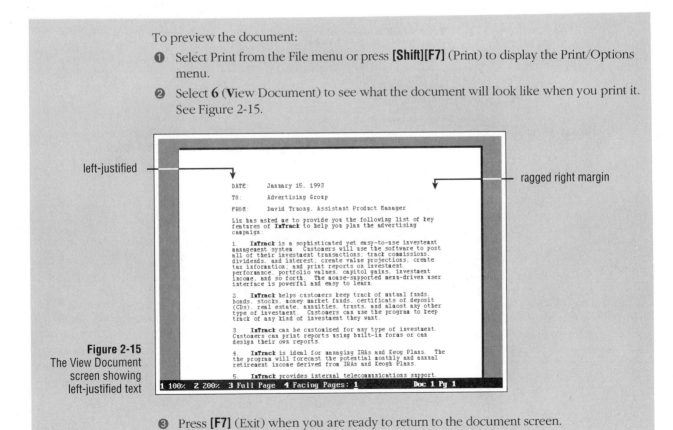

❸ Press **[F7]** (Exit) when you are ready to return to the document screen.

The document is left-justified, that is, aligned along the left margin but ragged along the right margin.

Using Tabs

As Figure 2-1 shows, David's next task in revising the memo is to insert the "RE," or reference, line below the "FROM" line. In the following steps you'll use [Enter] to insert new lines and then use the [Tab] key to insert space between the word "RE:" and the word "Product," as was already done between "TO:" and "Advertising" (Figure 2-16).

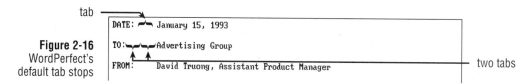

Figure 2-16
WordPerfect's
default tab stops

The [Tab] key indents text by inserting space from the current cursor location to the next tab stop. **Tab stops** are precise locations on the text lines; WordPerfect's default settings of the tab stops are every one-half inch from the left margin. Tabs are useful in aligning text vertically in your document. In the case of David's memo, the tab stops after "DATE:," "TO:," and "FROM:" keep the text precisely aligned (Figure 2-17). You should not use [Space] to align text; the text might appear aligned on the document screen, but when you print the document, the text might not be aligned. Let's use [Tab] to insert space between "RE:" and the word "Product."

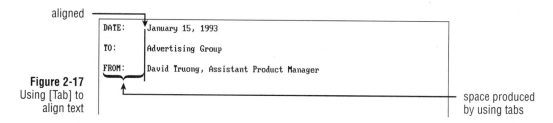

Figure 2-17
Using [Tab] to
align text

To use [Tab] to insert space:

❶ Move the cursor to the "F" in "FROM" on the third line of text in the memo.

❷ Press **[End]** to move the cursor to the end of the line, after the word "Manager."

❸ Press **[Enter]** twice to double space after the "FROM" line.

❹ Type **RE:** and press **[Tab]** twice.

Pressing [Tab] twice inserts space between "RE:" and the tab stop at Pos 2.5". The cursor is now directly beneath the word "David."

❺ Type **Product Description of** and press **[Space]**.

You're now ready to type the word "InTrack" in boldface.

Boldfacing Text

One way to highlight a word in your document is to use boldfacing. **Boldfaced text** is text with thicker characters than normal text. Let's now type the word "InTrack" in boldfaced text in David's memo.

To boldface text:

1. Make sure the cursor is to the right of the space after the phrase "Product Description of" that you typed in the previous section.

2. Press **[F6]** (Bold).

   After you press **[F6]** (Bold), the position number after "Pos," on the far right side of the status line, appears in bold. With bold turned on, whatever text you type will appear as bold on the screen and in your printed document.

3. Type **InTrack** and press **[F6]** (Bold) again to turn off bold. See Figure 2-18.

Figure 2-18
Document screen
after you type
boldfaced "InTrack"

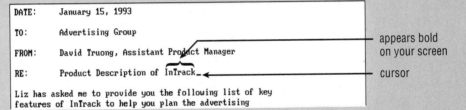

```
DATE:      January 15, 1993

TO:        Advertising Group

FROM:      David Truong, Assistant Product Manager          ——— appears bold
                                                                on your screen
RE:        Product Description of InTrack.  ←——————————————— cursor

Liz has asked me to provide you the following list of key
features of InTrack to help you plan the advertising
```

When you press [F6] (Bold) the second time, bold is turned off. The "Pos" number on the status line returns to normal text.

As you can see from these steps, [F6] (Bold) is a toggle key. A **toggle key** is any key that turns on a feature the first time you press the key and turns off the feature the next time you press the key. Thus, pressing [F6] once turns bold on, and pressing [F6] again turns bold off.

You can also turn on or turn off bold by selecting Appearance from the Font menu and then selecting Bold from the Appearance menu (Figure 2-19 on the next page). This method, however, would require five keystrokes — [Alt][=], O, A, and B — instead of just one, [F6].

menu name

option to change
appearance

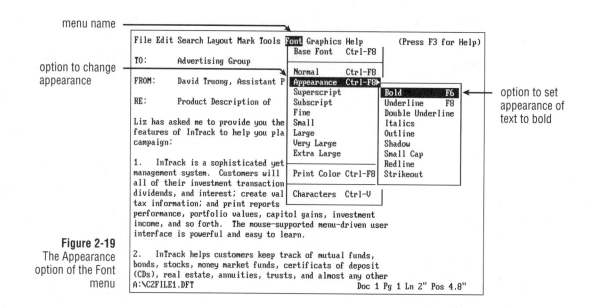

option to set
appearance of
text to bold

Figure 2-19
The Appearance
option of the Font
menu

Underlining Text

David next wants to address Liz's question at the end of paragraph 5 in the memo. David decides to insert a note explaining that brokers must also have InTrack to use this option. He wants the note to be in parentheses, with the word "Note" underlined.

To underline text:

❶ Move the cursor to the end of paragraph numbered 5, after the phrase ". . . directly from within InTrack."

❷ Press **[Space]** twice to insert two spaces at the end of the sentence and type **(** (left parenthesis).

❸ Press **[F8]** (Underline).

The position number on the status line indicates underline mode. See Figure 2-20. On a color monitor the position number changes colors or appears in reverse video. On most monochrome monitors the position number is underlined. With underline turned on, whatever text you type will be underlined, color-coded, or in reverse video on the screen and underlined in your printed document. [F8] (Underline) is a toggle key.

Figure 2-20
Document screen just
before you type with
underlining on

```
5.   InTrack provides internal telecommunications support.
CUstomers can use the program to get on-line financial
information from most of the electronic information
services.  Customers can also carry out transactions with
their broker directly from within InTrack.  (
A:\C2FILE1.DFT                          Doc 1 Pg 1 Ln 7.5" Pos 6"
```

cursor

underline on

❹ Type **Note** and then press **[F8]** (Underline) to toggle off underlining.

Notice that the position number no longer indicates underlining and that the word "Note" is underlined, color-coded, or in reverse video, depending on your type of monitor. See Figure 2-21.

Figure 2-21
Document screen
after you type
underlined "Note"

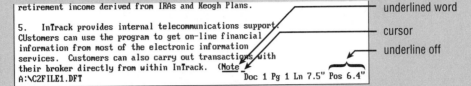

Type a colon (:), press **[Space]** twice, then type **Their broker must also have** and press **[Space]**.

⑥ Press **[F6]** (Bold) to turn on boldfacing for the word "InTrack."

⑦ Type **InTrack** and press **[F6]** (Bold) to toggle off boldfacing.

⑧ Press **[Space]** and type **to use this option.)**. See Figure 2-22.

Figure 2-22
Document screen
after you type the
note

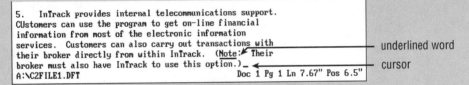

You can also turn on or turn off underlining by selecting Appearance from the Font menu and then selecting Underline from the Appearance menu. This method, however, would require five keystrokes — [Alt][=], O, A, and U — instead of just one, [F8].

Saving an Intermediate Version of the Document

David has now worked on the document for over 15 minutes and feels that it's time to save his changes. Let's save the document now.

To save the document:
❶ Make sure your WordPerfect data diskette is still in drive A.
❷ Select Save from the File menu or press **[F10]** (Save).

WordPerfect displays the prompt "Document to be saved: A:\C2FILE1.DFT" on the status line.

If you wanted to save the document using the old name, you would press [Enter] to accept the default filename, C2FILE1.DFT. In this case, however, you want to keep the original version on your diskette and save the file to a new filename.

❸ Type the new filename **a:\s2file2.dft** and press **[Enter]**.

WordPerfect saves the edited memo to your data diskette using the filename S2FILE2.DFT.

Revealing Format Codes

Whenever you execute a WordPerfect format command (for example, to left-justify text) or change the text appearance (for example, to boldface or underline text), WordPerfect inserts an invisible format code into your document. These codes tell WordPerfect how to format the document on the screen and how the document will appear when you print it.

When you are typing a document, you usually don't need to see these format codes. But every once in a while — such as when you've pressed the wrong key or you want to change one of the format codes — you need to reveal these codes. In the following steps, you'll move the cursor to the beginning of the document and reveal the format codes.

To reveal the format codes:

❶ Move the cursor to the beginning of the document by pressing **[Home]**, **[Home]**, **[↑]**.

❷ Select Reveal Codes from the Edit menu (Figure 2-23) or press **[Alt][F3]** or **[F11]** (Reveal Codes). (The [F11] key is found only on an enhanced 101-key keyboard, not on a standard 83-key keyboard.)

menu name ⟶

Figure 2-23
The Reveal Codes
option of the Edit
menu

```
File  Edit Search Layout Mark Tools Font Graphics Help       (Press F3 for Help)
      [Move (Cut)    Ctrl-Del ]
TO:   [Copy          Ctrl-Ins ]
      Paste
FROM: [Append                 ] Product Manager

RE:   Delete         Del        nTrack
      Undelete       F1
Liz h                            e following list of key
featu Block          Alt-F4      an the advertising
campa Select               ▶
      Comment        Ctrl-F5 ▶
1.    [Convert Case   Shft-F3 ]  t easy-to-use investemnt
manag [Protect Block  Shft-F8 ]   use the software to post
all o                            ns; track commissions,
divid Switch Document Shft-F3    lue projections; create
tax i Window         Ctrl-F3     on investment
perfo                            itol gains, investment
incom  Reveal Codes   Alt-F3     upported menu-driven user
inter                            learn.
```

option to display
format codes

The screen is now divided in half. The top half is the document window and the bottom half is the Reveal Codes window. See Figure 2-24.

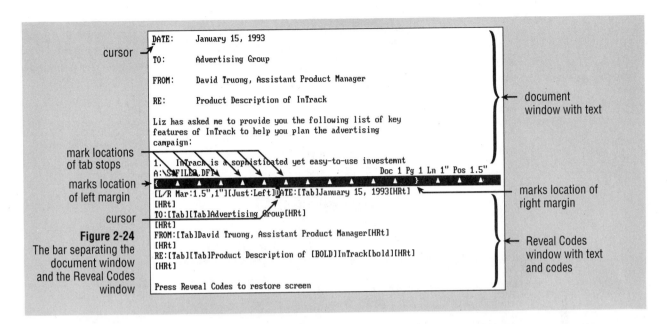

cursor

document
window with text

mark locations
of tab stops

marks location
of left margin

marks location of
right margin

cursor

Figure 2-24
The bar separating the
document window
and the Reveal Codes
window

Reveal Codes
window with text
and codes

The bar separating the document window and the Reveal Codes window contains a left brace (⎸) to mark the left margin, a right brace (⎹) to mark the right margin, and triangles (▲) to mark the tab stops.

You can tell the location of the cursor in the Reveal Codes window because the code or character at the cursor is highlighted. For example, in Figure 2-24 the cursor is on the "D" in "DATE", so the "D" is highlighted in the Reveal Codes window. Since both the document window and the Reveal Codes window have a cursor, the screen actually shows two cursors. Let's move the cursor to demonstrate how the two cursors move together.

To move the cursor with Reveal Codes on:

❶ Move the cursor down to the 3 at the beginning of paragraph 3.

As you press [↓], the text in the document window and the information in the Reveal Codes windows scroll up.

❷ Press and hold down [→] for two or three seconds to watch how the two cursors move across the screen.

As you can see, the two cursors always move together through the document.

❸ Press **[Home]**, **[Home]**, **[↑]** to return to the top of the document.

In the Reveal Codes window, the highlighted words in square brackets are the format codes (Figure 2-25). Notice that the first code is [L/R Mar:1.5",1"]. This code was inserted into the document when you changed the margin settings earlier in this tutorial. The next code is [Just:Left], to indicate that you have specified left justification.

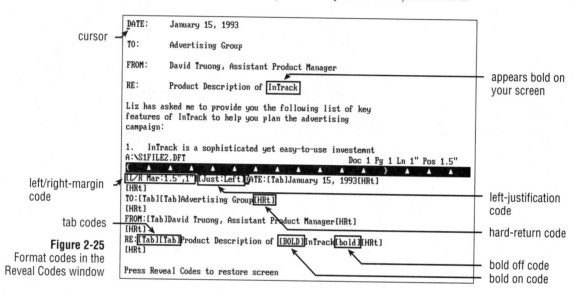

cursor

appears bold on your screen

left/right-margin code

tab codes

Figure 2-25
Format codes in the
Reveal Codes window

left-justification code

hard-return code

bold off code
bold on code

Other format codes include [Tab] to mark where you pressed [Tab] to move the text to the next tab stop on the RE line of the heading, [HRt] for the hard returns, and the paired codes [BOLD] to mark the beginning of boldfaced text and [bold] to mark the end of boldfaced text.

Figure 2-26 is a list of common WordPerfect format codes. Some of these codes won't make sense to you now, but their meanings will become clear as you work through this and later tutorials.

Codes	Meaning
[ ]	Hard space
[-]	Hyphen
-	Soft hyphen
/	Cancel hyphenation
[Dec Tab]	Decimal align in Tab
[BOLD][bold]	Bold begin and end
[Block]	Block begin
[Center]	Center
[Flsh Rgt]	Flush right
[HPg]	Hard page break
[HRt]	Hard return
[Hyph On/Off]	Hyphenation on or off
[→Indent]	Indent
[→Indent←]	Left/Right indent
[Just:Left]	Left justification
[L/R Mar:n,n]	Left and right margin values
[Ln Spacing:n]	Line spacing
[SPg]	Soft page break
[SRt]	Soft return
[SUBSCPT][subscpt]	Subscript begin and end
[SUPRSCPT][suprscpt]	Superscript begin and end
[Tab]	Tab (move to next tab stop)
[T/B Mar:n,n]	Top and bottom margin values
[UND][und]	Underline begin and end
[W/O On/Off]	Widow/orphan protection on or off

Figure 2-26
Common
WordPerfect
format codes — *n*
represents the
number you type

Keep Reveal Codes on, because in the next section you'll use the Reveal Codes window to help you edit the document.

Indenting a Paragraph

The Reveal Codes window will help David perform his next task. One of Liz's suggestions for the product description memo is to indent the numbered paragraphs. David realizes that he can't use tabs to do this because a tab inserts space only on the line where [Tab] was pressed. Instead, he must use the [F4] (Indent) command, which indents not just the first line of the paragraph but all subsequent lines until the end of the paragraph, which is marked by a hard return. David's task, therefore, is to change the [Tab] format code to the [→Indent] format code at the beginning of each numbered paragraph.

To change [Tab] codes to [→Indent] codes:

❶ Make sure the Reveal Codes window appears on the screen.

If necessary, select Reveal Codes from the Edit menu or press [Alt][F3] or [F11] (Reveal Codes).

❷ Move the cursor to the "1" of the first numbered paragraph. You can now see a **[Tab]** code to the right of the 1.

❸ Press [→] twice to put the cursor on the [Tab] code. See Figure 2-27.

cursor

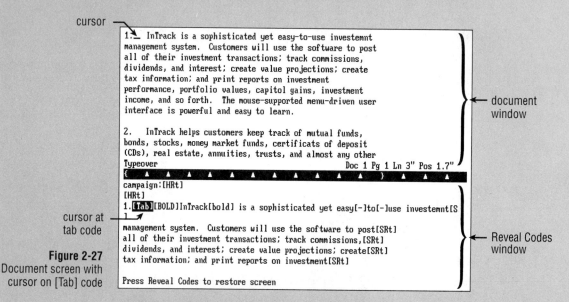

cursor at tab code

Figure 2-27
Document screen with cursor on [Tab] code

document window

Reveal Codes window

❹ Press **[Del]** to delete the [Tab] code. (Remember that if you use the [Del] key on the numeric keypad, Num Lock must be off.)

The [Tab] code disappears and the text beginning with "InTrack is a . . ." moves next to the 1.

❺ Press **[F4]** (Indent). The [→Indent] code is inserted into the document. See Figure 2-28.

As you can see, the [→Indent] code appears in the Reveal Codes window, and the paragraph is fully indented. If you don't see the entire paragraph indented, press [Ctrl][F3] (Screen) and select 3 (Rewrite) to tell WordPerfect to reformat the screen.

entire paragraph
indented

cursor

indent code

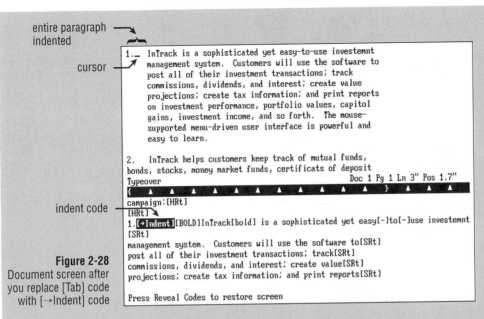

Figure 2-28
Document screen after
you replace [Tab] code
with [→Indent] code

The amount of space that the text is indented depends on the location of the tab stops. Since WordPerfect's default format settings have a tab stop at every 0.5 inch, the paragraph is indented 0.5 inch from the left margin, or 2 inches from the left edge of the page.

⑥ Move the cursor to the [Tab] code at the beginning of the next numbered paragraph, delete the code, and press **[F4]** (Indent) to insert the [→Indent] code at that location. Repeat this step until you have indented all seven paragraphs.

⑦ Select Reveal Codes from the Edit menu or press **[Alt][F3]** or **[F11]** (Reveal Codes) to close the Reveal Codes window and display a full document screen.

The document screen should now look similar to Figure 2-29. As you can see, Reveal Codes is a toggle key: selecting it a first time opens the Reveal Codes window and selecting it a second time closes the Reveal Codes window.

indented paragraphs

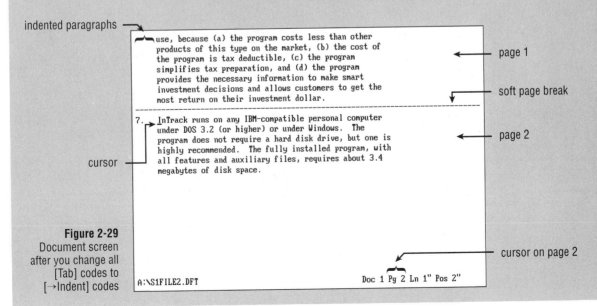

Figure 2-29
Document screen
after you change all
[Tab] codes to
[→Indent] codes

page 1

soft page break

page 2

cursor

cursor on page 2

As you made these changes, WordPerfect automatically inserted a **soft page break** — a code that indicates where one page ends and another page begins. The location of a soft page break is shown as a broken line across the screen (Figure 2-29). It is called a *soft* page break because if you add or delete text before the break, the page break location may change.

In this section, you've learned how to reveal format codes, delete the codes, and insert other codes. You've also seen how to indent a paragraph using the [F4] (Indent) key. You can use these methods to change any format code. For example, if you decide that you want to change some boldfaced text back to normal appearance, you could turn on Reveal Codes, move the cursor to the code that marks the beginning or the end of the boldfaced text, and delete the code. When you delete either code, WordPerfect automatically deletes the other.

Deleting Words and Lines of Text

David is already familiar with using [Backspace] to delete a character or a code to the left of the cursor and with using [Del] to delete a character or a code at the cursor. But WordPerfect also provides ways for you to delete larger chunks of text.

For example, on the first line of paragraph 2 in the product description memo, Liz suggested that the phrase "keep track of" be simplified to "track." David will use WordPerfect's [Ctrl][Backspace] (Delete Word) to delete the words "keep" and "of." Let's make the change in your document.

To delete a word from the text:

❶ Move the cursor to the first letter of the word "keep" in the first line of paragraph 2 in the product description memo.

To use the [Ctrl][Backspace] (Delete Word) command, you can move the cursor anywhere within the word or to the space just to the right of the word that you want to delete.

❷ Press **[Ctrl][Backspace]** (Delete Word). The word and the space after it disappear from the document.

❸ Press **[Ctrl][→]** (Word Right) to move the cursor past "track" and to the word "of."

❹ Press **[Ctrl][Backspace]** (Delete Word). The word and the space after it disappear from the document. See Figure 2-30.

Figure 2-30
Document screen
after you use
[Ctrl] [Backspace]
(Delete Word)

```
on investment performance, portfolio values, capitol
gains, investment income, and so forth.  The mouse-
supported menu-driven user interface is powerful and
easy to learn.

2.   InTrack helps customers track mutual funds, bonds,
     stocks, money market funds, certificats of deposit
A:\S1FILE2.DFT                          Doc 1 Pg 1 Ln 4.67" Pos 5"
```
— words deleted

Another valuable deletion command is [Ctrl][End] (Del to EOL), which instructs WordPerfect to "delete from the cursor to the end of the current line." You can use this command to delete a complete or partial line of text. In the product description memo, Liz wants David to delete the last sentence of paragraph 2, since the sentence is redundant. Let's use [Ctrl][End] (Del to EOL) to delete this sentence.

To delete from the cursor to the end of a line:

❶ Move the cursor to the end of the first sentence in paragraph 2. See Figure 2-31.

Figure 2-31
Document screen
before you use
[Ctrl][End]
(Del to EOL)

```
2.   InTrack helps customers track mutual funds, bonds,
     stocks, money market funds, certificats of deposit
     (CDs), real estate, annuities, trusts, and almost any
     other type of investment.  Customers can use the
A:\S1FILE2.DFT                           Doc 1 Pg 1 Ln 5.17" Pos 4.5"
```
— cursor

❷ Press **[Ctrl][End]** (Del to EOL).

The text from the cursor to the end of the line is deleted, and the remaining text in the sentence moves into the place of the deleted text. See Figure 2-32.

Figure 2-32
Document screen
after you press
[Ctrl][End]
(Del to EOL)

after deletion, text from lower line moves up to this line

```
2.   InTrack helps customers track mutual funds, bonds,
     stocks, money market funds, certificats of deposit
     (CDs), real estate, annuities, trusts, and almost any
     other type of investment. program to keep track of any
A:\S1FILE2.DFT                           Doc 1 Pg 1 Ln 5.17" Pos 4.5"
```
— cursor

❸ Press **[Ctrl][End]** (Del to EOL) until you finish deleting the sentence.

In addition to [Ctrl][Backspace] (Delete Word) and [Ctrl][End] (Del to EOL), you can use the keystrokes shown in Figure 2-33 to delete text. As you become more familiar with WordPerfect, you'll be able to use these other delete commands in your own documents.

Figure 2-33
WordPerfect
deletion keystrokes

Key(s)	Deletion
[Del]	Character at the cursor
[Backspace]	Character to the left of the cursor
[Ctrl][Backspace]	Word at the cursor
[Ctrl][End]	From the cursor to the end of the line
[Ctrl][PgDn]	From the cursor to the end of the page
[Home], [Backspace]	From the cursor to the beginning of the word
[Home], [Del]	From the cursor to the end of the word

Undeleting Text

Whenever you delete text from a document, WordPerfect temporarily saves the deleted text, just in case you want to **undelete**, or restore, it later. WordPerfect doesn't store all your deletions, *only the last three.* Let's use WordPerfect's Undelete capability to delete and then restore the word "investment."

To undelete text:

❶ Make sure the cursor is still at the end of paragraph 2 in the product description memo.

❷ Press **[Ctrl][←]** (Word Left) to move the cursor to the beginning of the word "investment."

❸ Press **[Ctrl][Backspace]** (Delete Word) to delete the word "investment" and the period.

Let's suppose that now you want the word and the period back in your document.

❹ Select Undelete from the Edit menu or press **[F1]** (Cancel).

WordPerfect immediately restores the most recent deletion to the screen, keeps the undeleted text highlighted, and displays the Undelete menu on the status line. See Figure 2-34. To see the next-to-the-last deletion, you would select 2 (Previous Deletion); to see the deletion before that, you would select 2 (Previous Deletion) again.

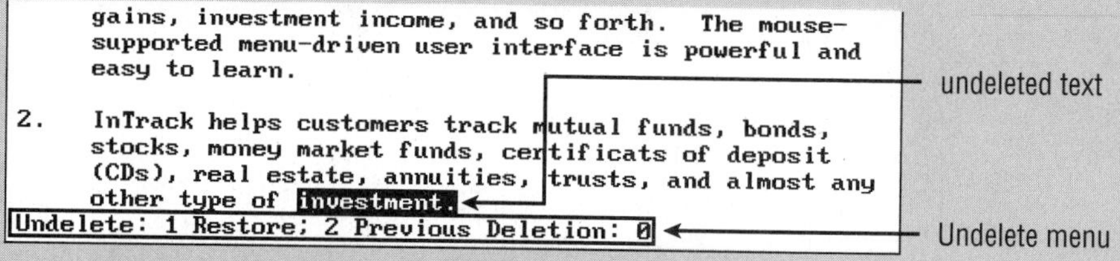

Figure 2-34
The Undelete menu

```
gains, investment income, and so forth.  The mouse-
supported menu-driven user interface is powerful and
easy to learn.

2.   InTrack helps customers track mutual funds, bonds,
     stocks, money market funds, certificats of deposit
     (CDs), real estate, annuities, trusts, and almost any
     other type of investment.
Undelete: 1 Restore; 2 Previous Deletion: 0
```

— undeleted text

— Undelete menu

❺ Select **1** (**R**estore). The deleted word "investment" and the accompanying period are restored to the document as if they had never been deleted.

After deleting text, you can type new text, move the cursor, or execute other commands before you undelete the deleted text. For example, if you pressed [F1] (Cancel) and selected 1 (Restore), WordPerfect would restore the deleted text at the current location of the cursor, not where the deleted text originally appeared. David can, therefore, use Undelete to move a word or a phrase from one location to another. Let's try this by deleting the word "pays" in paragraph 6 and restoring it after the word "easily" to switch the order of the words, as Liz suggested.

To use Undelete to move a word:

❶ Move the cursor to the word "pays" on the first line in paragraph 6.

❷ Press **[Ctrl][Backspace]** (Delete Word) to delete the word.

❸ Press **[Ctrl][→]** (Word Right) to move the cursor past "easily" to the "f" in the word "for."

❹ Select Undelete from the Edit menu or press **[F1]** (Cancel) and select **1** (**R**estore). See Figure 2-35.

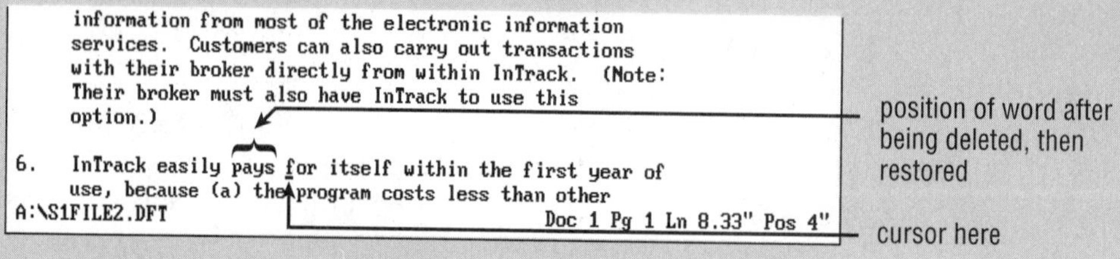

Figure 2-35
Document screen after you delete, then restore a word

```
information from most of the electronic information
services.  Customers can also carry out transactions
with their broker directly from within InTrack.  (Note:
Their broker must also have InTrack to use this
option.)

6.   InTrack easily pays for itself within the first year of
     use, because (a) the program costs less than other
A:\S1FILE2.DFT                              Doc 1 Pg 1 Ln 8.33" Pos 4"
```

— position of word after being deleted, then restored

— cursor here

Now the phrase reads "InTrack easily pays for itself," as Liz suggested.

Using Typeover Mode

When you start WordPerfect, the document screen starts out in **insert mode**, which means that the characters you type are inserted into the document at the cursor and existing characters move to the right.

If you press [Ins] (Insert), the document screen changes from insert mode to **typeover mode**, which means that the characters you type replace existing text at the cursor. When typeover mode is on, the word "Typeover" appears on the left side of the status line at the bottom of the screen. The filename of the document no longer appears on the status line.

As shown in Figure 2-1, Liz wants David to add "3.0 or higher" to the second line of paragraph 7. Let's use insert mode to insert "3.0 or higher" and then use typeover mode to change "3.4" to "2.5" in the last line of the same paragraph.

To use insert mode:

❶ Move the cursor to the period (.) after the word "Windows" at the end of the first sentence in paragraph 7.

❷ Make sure "Typeover" does *not* appear on the status line. If it does, press **[Ins]** to return to insert mode.

❸ Press **[Space]** and type **3.0 (or higher)**.

When you type this short phrase, watch as the sentence "The program does not require . . ." is pushed to the right and then wrapped to the next line.

Next let's use typeover mode to change "3.4" to "2.5".

To use typeover mode:

❶ Move the cursor to the "3" in "about 3.4 megabytes" in the last line of paragraph 7.

❷ Press **[Ins]**. The word "Typeover" appears on the left side of the status line at the bottom of the screen, replacing the document name.

❸ Type **2.5**. With typeover mode on, the new characters replace, or type over, the original characters at the cursor. In this case "2.5" replaces "3.4." See Figure 2-36.

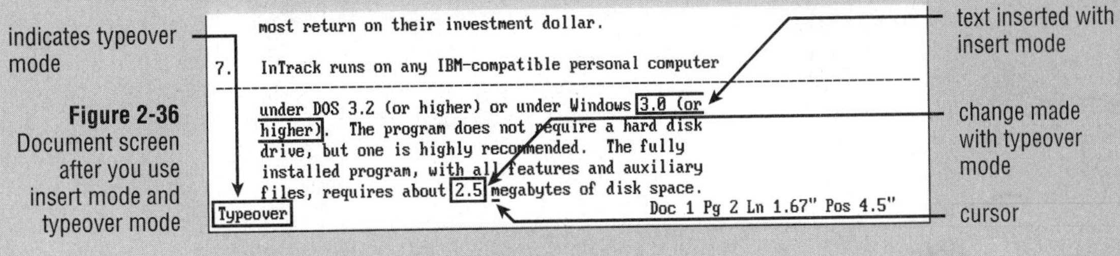

Figure 2-36
Document screen after you use insert mode and typeover mode

❹ Press **[Ins]** to turn off typeover mode and return to insert mode.

As you can see, [Ins] is a toggle key: pressing it once changes the document screen from insert mode to typeover mode; pressing it a second time changes the document screen from typeover mode back to insert mode.

Inserting a Hard Page Break

Look at Liz's question at the bottom of Figure 2-1: "Dave, what about other hardware options?" In response to this question, David decides to add a paragraph at the end of the product description.

To add a paragraph to the memo:

❶ Press **[Home]**, **[Home]**, **[↓]** to move the cursor to the end of the document.

❷ Press **[Enter]** twice to double-space between paragraph 7 and the new paragraph you're about to type.

❸ Type **8.** (the number 8 and a period) and press **[F4]** (Indent) to indent the new paragraph.

❹ Press **[F6]** (Bold) to turn on bold, type **InTrack**, press **[F6]** (Bold) again to turn off bold, and press **[Space]**.

❺ Type the remainder of the paragraph: **supports, but does not require, the following hardware items: VGA color graphics, Microsoft-compatible mouse, and Hayes-compatible modem.** See Figure 2-37.

Figure 2-37
Document screen
after you type
paragraph 8

```
under DOS 3.2 (or higher) or under Windows 3.0 (or
higher).  The program does not require a hard disk
drive, but one is highly recommended.  The fully
installed program, with all features and auxiliary
files, requires about 2.5 megabytes of disk space.

8.   InTrack supports, but does not require, the following
     hardware items: VGA color graphics, Microsoft-
     compatible mouse, and Hayes-compatible modem._
A:\S1FILE2.DFT                          Doc 1 Pg 2 Ln 2.33" Pos 6.5"
```

new text

cursor

This last paragraph completes the text of the memo. But notice that paragraph 7 is split between page 1 and page 2. On your screen paragraph 7 might not be split between two pages. Even if it is not split, continue reading and follow the next set of steps. David doesn't want a page break within a numbered paragraph, so he decides to use what is called a hard page break just before paragraph 7. A **hard page break** is a format code that forces all text after it onto the next page. Regardless of how much text you might add or delete before a hard page break, the text on the page will end at that point, and the text that follows will go onto the next page. WordPerfect marks the location of a hard page break with a horizontal line of double dashes that extend across the width of the screen.

Let's insert a hard page break to force paragraph 7 and the text that follows it onto the next page.

To insert a hard page break:

❶ Move the cursor to the "7" at the beginning of paragraph 7.

❷ Press **[Ctrl][Enter]** (Hard Page) to force paragraph 7 onto the next page. The hard page break appears on the screen. See Figure 2-38.

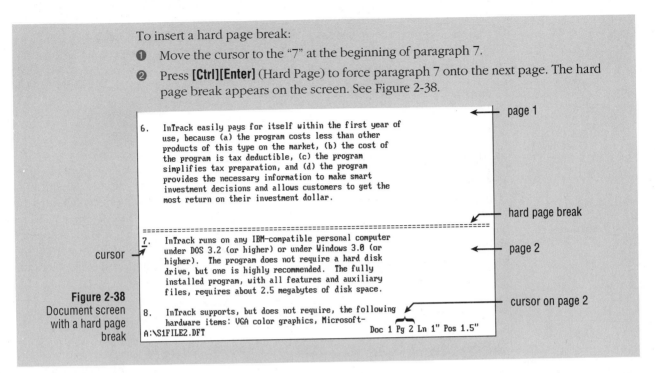

Figure 2-38
Document screen with a hard page break

The format code for a hard page break is [HPg]. You can use this code as you have the other codes you've already learned about. For example, to delete a hard page break, you would move the cursor to the location of the page break, turn on Reveal Codes, move the cursor to the [HPg] code, and press [Del] to delete it.

Checking the Spelling in a Document

David's product description memo still contains misspelled words and other typographical errors, commonly called "typos." You can catch most misspellings and typos by running the **speller** — a WordPerfect feature that checks the spelling within a document — as Liz suggested to David in the first paragraph of the memo. When you run the speller, WordPerfect checks each word in your document against the WordPerfect **dictionary**, a file on the disk that contains a list of correctly spelled words.

Let's correct the spelling errors in David's memo by using the speller.

Running the Speller

To run the speller:

❶ Select Spell from the Tools menu or press **[Ctrl][F2]** (Spell). WordPerfect displays the one-line speller menu on the status line. See Figure 2-39.

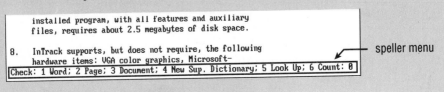

Figure 2-39
The speller menu

❷ Select **3** (**D**ocument) to check the spelling of the entire document. WordPerfect automatically starts checking from the beginning of the document, no matter where the cursor is.

Skipping a Word Not Found in the Dictionary

The first "misspelled" word detected by WordPerfect is "Truong" (Figure 2-40). Although "Truong" is spelled correctly, it's not in WordPerfect's dictionary. WordPerfect highlights the word to flag it as a potential error and divides the screen in two, with the document window on top and the dictionary window on bottom. A list of suggested "correct spellings" appears in the dictionary window, and the one-line Not Found menu appears at the bottom of the screen. Since we don't want to change "Truong" to any of the suggested spellings, let's tell WordPerfect to skip this word from now on.

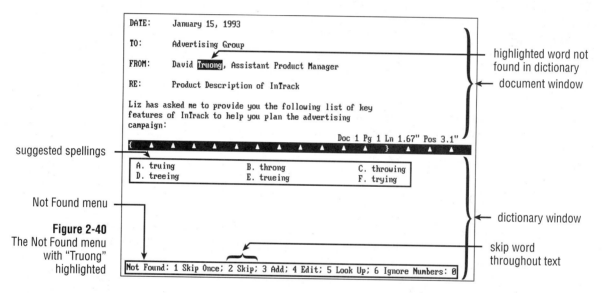

suggested spellings

Not Found menu

Figure 2-40
The Not Found menu
with "Truong"
highlighted

highlighted word not
found in dictionary

document window

dictionary window

skip word
throughout text

To skip a word not found in WordPerfect's dictionary:

❶ Select **2** (Skip). This option tells WordPerfect to skip all occurrences of the word "Truong" here and in the remainder of the document.

WordPerfect next stops at "InTrack." This is another example of a correctly spelled word that isn't in WordPerfect's dictionary.

❷ Select **2** (Skip) to skip this and all future occurrences of "InTrack."

WordPerfect continues checking words in the document against words in the dictionary until it comes to the next word not found in the dictionary.

Selecting a Suggested Spelling

The first word that David actually misspelled is "investemnt." WordPerfect highlights the word, gives a suggested spelling ("investment"), and displays the Not Found menu at the bottom of the screen (Figure 2-41).

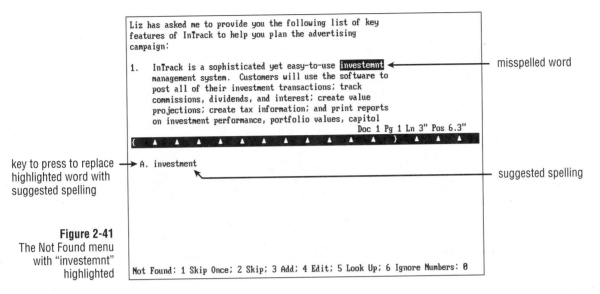

misspelled word

key to press to replace highlighted word with suggested spelling

suggested spelling

Figure 2-41
The Not Found menu with "investemnt" highlighted

In the following steps, you'll select a replacement word from the dictionary window. WordPerfect will then replace the misspelled word in the document with the selected word from the dictionary window.

To select a suggested spelling from the dictionary window:

❶ Press the letter next to the correct word in the dictionary window. In this example, press **A** or **a**. WordPerfect immediately replaces the misspelled word with "investment" and continues the spell checking.

The next misspelled word is "certificats." WordPerfect displays two suggested words in the dictionary window. See Figure 2-42.

```
      gains, investment income, and so forth.  The mouse-
      supported menu-driven user interface is powerful and
      easy to learn.

2.    InTrack helps customers track mutual funds, bonds,
      stocks, money market funds, certificats of deposit
      (CDs), real estate, annuities, trusts, and almost any
      other type of investment.

3.    InTrack can be customized for any type of investment.
      Customers can print reports using built-in forms or can
                              Doc 1 Pg 1 Ln 4.83" Pos 4.8"

A. certificate          B. certificates
```

misspelled word

key to press

Figure 2-42
The Not Found menu with "certificats" highlighted

❷   Press **B** (or **b**) to select "certificates" from the dictionary window.

Skipping a Word Once

WordPerfect next stops at the word "CDs," an abbreviation for "certificates of deposit," and presents a long list of possible words in the dictionary window (Figure 2-43). Since none of these words is correct, let's tell WordPerfect to skip this word once but to flag any later occurrence of "CDs" or "cds" in the document.

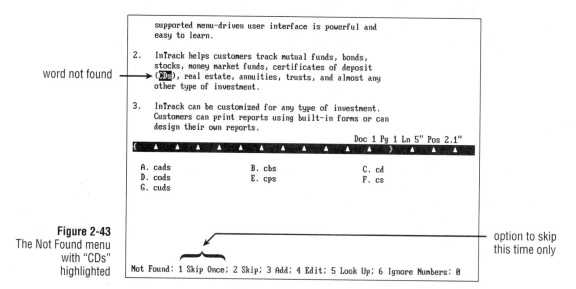

word not found

Figure 2-43
The Not Found menu
with "CDs"
highlighted

option to skip
this time only

To skip a word once:

❶   Select **1** (Skip Once). This option tells WordPerfect that you want to skip the word this time only.

The next "misspelled" word is "IRAs."

❷   Select **2** (Skip) to skip this and all future occurrences of "IRAs" in the document.

As a general rule, select 1 (Skip Once) if there's a chance that the flagged word may actually be a misspelling later in the document. Select 2 (Skip) if you know that the word will appear again later in the document but you don't want the speller to flag it.

Editing a Misspelled Word

WordPerfect next stops at the word "Keog" and displays several suggested words in the dictionary window (Figure 2-44). The correct word is "Keogh," which is the name of a retirement investment plan. In this case, "Keog" is not a correct spelling, but the correct spelling is not found in the WordPerfect dictionary either. Thus, you need to edit the word, that is, change the word so that it is spelled correctly.

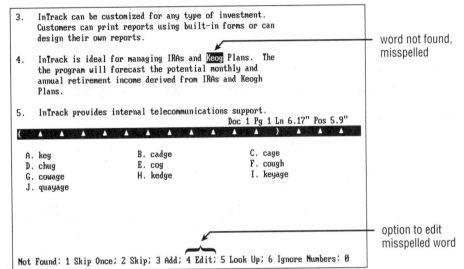

word not found, misspelled

option to edit misspelled word

Figure 2-44
The Not Found menu with "Keog" highlighted

To edit a misspelled word:

❶ Select **4** (Edit). The cursor moves into the document window at the beginning of the misspelled word, and the dictionary window disappears.

❷ Move the cursor to the space after "Keog," type **h** to make the word "Keogh," and press **[F7]** (Exit) to exit the document window and return to the speller.

The word is now spelled the way you want it. However, it's still not in the WordPerfect dictionary, so it remains highlighted.

❸ Select **2** (Skip) to skip this and all future occurrences of the word "Keogh" in the document.

Correcting Double Words

WordPerfect next stops at the double words "The the" and displays the Double Word menu on the status line (Figure 2-45).

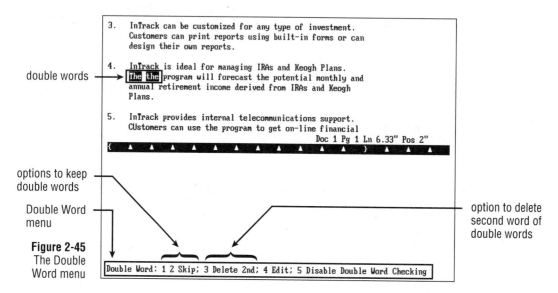

double words

options to keep double words

Double Word menu

option to delete second word of double words

Figure 2-45
The Double Word menu

To correct double words:

❶ Press **3** (Delete 2nd) to delete the second occurrence of the word "the."

You would select option 1 or 2 if you wanted to skip the double words and leave both words in your document.

Your document now has only "The" instead of "The the" at that location in the document.

Correcting Irregular Case

The next typo that WordPerfect encounters is an irregular case error. An "irregular case" error is a word that has some lowercase letters and one or more uppercase letters after the initial letter. When David typed the rough draft of the memo, he accidentally held the [Shift] key down too long and typed "CUstomer" instead of "Customer." When such an error occurs, WordPerfect highlights the erroneous word and displays the Irregular Case menu (Figure 2-46).

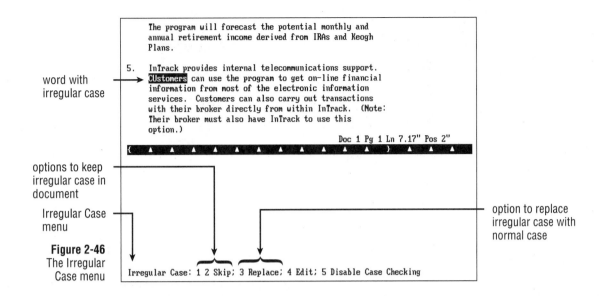

word with
irregular case

options to keep
irregular case in
document

Irregular Case
menu

Figure 2-46
The Irregular
Case menu

option to replace
irregular case with
normal case

To correct irregular case:

❶ Select **3** (Replace) to replace the irregular case word "CUstomer" with correct word "Customer."

❷ When the speller stops at any other word not found in the dictionary (such as "VGA" or "Microsoft"), select 1 (Skip Once) or 2 (Skip). Repeat this step until the speller reaches the end of the document and displays the word count.

You have now completed the spell checking of the document. WordPerfect displays the number of words (355) in the document. You are ready to exit the speller.

To exit the speller:

❶ Press any key to exit the speller and return to the normal document screen.

Checking for Misused Words

Keep in mind that the WordPerfect speller checks only spelling, not meaning or usage. For example, in paragraph 1 of the product description memo, David used the word "capitol," which means a building in which a legislature convenes, instead of "capital," which means assets or wealth. WordPerfect doesn't have a program to help you catch this type of error, so you must carefully proofread your document for correct usage. Let's correct the error now.

To correct a misused word:

❶ Move the cursor to the "o" in "capitol" in paragraph 1 of the memo.

❷ Press **[Ins]** to turn on typeover mode.

❸ Type **a** to change "capitol" to "capital."

❹ Press **[Ins]** to turn off typeover mode and return to insert mode.

Using the Thesaurus

David is now ready to address Liz's last suggestion. In paragraph 1, David used the verb "create" twice in the same series of items. Liz thinks this is repetitious and suggests he choose better words. He agrees but isn't sure what words to use in their place. He realizes that WordPerfect's thesaurus can help him with his problem. The **thesaurus** is a WordPerfect file that contains a list of words and their synonyms and antonyms. In the following steps, you'll see how to use the thesaurus.

To use the thesaurus:

❶ Move the cursor to the first occurrence of "create" on the fourth line of the first numbered paragraph.

The cursor can be anywhere in the word or at the space just after the word.

❷ Select Thesaurus from the Tools menu or press **[Alt][F1]** (Thesaurus). WordPerfect displays a list of the synonyms and antonyms of "create" in the thesaurus window. See Figure 2-47.

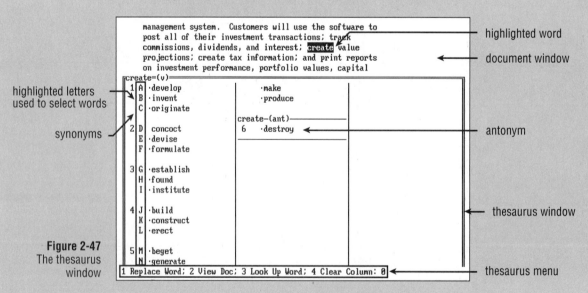

Figure 2-47
The thesaurus window

David looks over the words and decides that the word "make" is the best choice. Notice that "make" is in the second column of synonyms, but the uppercase highlighted letters you use to select a word are in the first column. Let's move the highlighted letters to the second column so we can choose a word from that column.

❸ Press [→] to move the highlighted letters to the second column. See Figure 2-48.

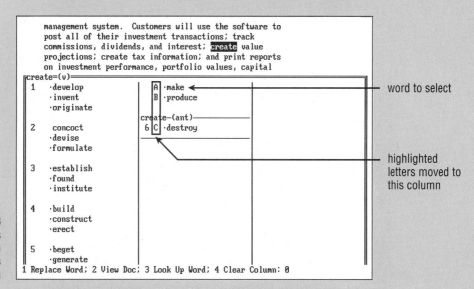

Figure 2-48
The thesaurus window after you move selection letters to second column

```
    management system.  Customers will use the software to
    post all of their investment transactions; track
    commissions, dividends, and interest; create value
    projections; create tax information; and print reports
    on investment performance, portfolio values, capital
┌create=(v)
│1   ·develop          A ·make                         word to select
│    ·invent           B ·produce
│    ·originate
│              create-(ant)
│2    concoct        6 C ·destroy
│    ·devise
│    ·formulate
│                                                       highlighted
│3   ·establish                                         letters moved to
│    ·found                                             this column
│    ·institute
│
│4   ·build
│    ·construct
│    ·erect
│
│5   ·beget
│    ·generate
│1 Replace Word; 2 View Doc; 3 Look Up Word; 4 Clear Column; 0
```

❹ Select **1** (Replace Word) and press **A** or **a** to replace "create" with "make." WordPerfect makes the replacement and closes the thesaurus window.

David wants to replace the second occurrence of "create" with the word "generate." Because WordPerfect closes the thesaurus window after an option is selected from the thesaurus menu, David has to reissue the Thesaurus command.

❺ Move the cursor to the second occurrence of "create" and execute the Thesaurus command.

❻ Select **1** (Replace Word) and press **N** to replace "create" with "generate."

As you can see, the thesaurus is a powerful tool for helping you choose synonyms and antonyms for words in your document.

Saving the Final Version of the Document

David has now completed all the changes in the document that Liz suggested. Your document should now look like Figure 2-49 on the following pages.

DATE: January 15, 1993

TO: Advertising Group

FROM: David Truong, Assistant Product Manager

RE: Product Description of **InTrack**

Liz has asked me to provide you the following list of key features of **InTrack** to help you plan the advertising campaign:

1. InTrack is a sophisticated yet easy-to-use investment management system. Customers will use the software to post all of their investment transactions; track commissions, dividends, and interest; make value projections; generate tax information; and print reports on investment performance, portfolio values, capital gains, investment income, and so forth. The mouse-supported menu-driven user interface is powerful and easy to learn.

2. **InTrack** helps customers track mutual funds, bonds, stocks, money market funds, certificates of deposit (CDs), real estate, annuities, trusts, and almost any other type of investment.

3. **InTrack** can be customized for any type of investment. Customers can print reports using built-in forms or can design their own reports.

4. **InTrack** is ideal for managing IRAs and Keogh Plans. The program will forecast the potential monthly and annual retirement income derived from IRAs and Keogh Plans.

5. **InTrack** provides internal telecommunications support. Customers can use the program to get on-line financial information from most of the electronic information services. Customers can also carry out transactions with their broker directly from within **InTrack.** (<u>Note</u>: Their broker must also have **InTrack** to use this option.)

6. **InTrack** easily pays for itself within the first year of use, because (a) the program costs less than other products of this type on the market, (b) the cost of the program is tax deductible, (c) the program simplifies tax preparation, and (d) the program provides the necessary information to make smart investment decisions and allows customers to get the most return on their investment dollar.

Figure 2-49
Page one of the
final version of the
document
(continued on next
page)

```
      7.    InTrack runs on any IBM-compatible personal computer
            under DOS 3.2 (or higher) or under Windows 3.0 (or
            higher). The program does not require a hard disk
            drive, but one is highly recommended. The fully
            installed program, with all features and auxiliary
            files, requires about 2.5 megabytes of disk space.

      8.    InTrack supports, but does not require, the following
            hardware items: VGA color graphics, Microsoft-
            compatible mouse, and Hayes-compatible modem.
```

Figure 2-49
Page two of the
final version of the
document
(continued from
previous page)

After editing any document, you should save it to the diskette; otherwise, the diskette copy of the document will still be the previous version without any of the corrections you made since your last save. In this case, let's assume David wants to keep a record of his original rough draft (C2FILE1.DFT) and the most recently saved version (S2FILE2.DFT). He saves the final version of the memo as S2FILE3.MEM.

To save the final version of the document:

❶ Make sure your WordPerfect data diskette is still in drive A.

❷ Select Save from the File menu or press **[F10]** (Save). WordPerfect displays the prompt "Document to be saved: A:\S2FILE2.DFT" on the status line.

❸ Type the new filename **a:\s2file3.mem** and press **[Enter]**.

WordPerfect saves the final version of the memo to your diskette using the filename S2FILE3.MEM. See Figure 2-50.

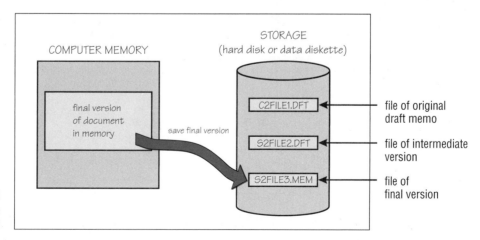

Figure 2-50
Saving the
final version

Printing Multiple Copies of a Document

David's last task is to print three copies of the memo. He could simply execute the print command three times, but there is an easier way. Let's use WordPerfect's Number of Copies feature to print three copies of the memo.

To print multiple copies of a document:

❶ Select Print from the File menu or press **[Shift][F7]** (Print) to display the Print/Options menu. See Figure 2-51.

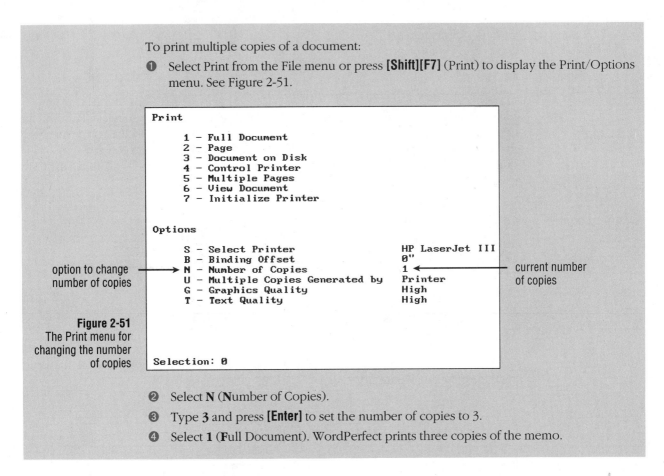

option to change
number of copies

current number
of copies

Figure 2-51
The Print menu for
changing the number
of copies

❷ Select **N** (**N**umber of Copies).

❸ Type **3** and press **[Enter]** to set the number of copies to 3.

❹ Select **1** (**F**ull Document). WordPerfect prints three copies of the memo.

This completes Tutorial 2. If you want to exit WordPerfect, press [F7] (Exit), then N (No), and then Y (Yes).

■   ■   ■

Exercises

1. Which key(s) do you press to move the cursor in the following directions?
   a. To the left side of the screen
   b. To the right side of the screen
   c. To the beginning of the document
   d. To the end of the document
   e. One word to the left

2. Describe what you would do to change the right margin of a document to 1.5 inches.

3. What key(s) would you press to do the following?
    a. Turn on boldfacing
    b. Turn off boldfacing
    c. Turn on underlining
    d. Turn off underlining

4. What would you do to see the format code that marks the location where you changed the margins within a document?

5. What is the WordPerfect code for each of the following?
    a. Soft return
    b. Hard return
    c. Soft page break
    d. Hard page break
    e. Tab

6. What is the difference between a soft return and a hard return?

7. Explain the meaning of each of the following WordPerfect terms:
    a. Full justification
    b. Left justification
    c. Right justification
    d. Center justification

8. Explain the difference between [Tab] and [F4] (Indent).

9. Explain the difference between insert mode and typeover mode. What key do you press to change from one mode to the other?

10. What key(s) do you press to force a page break? Why would you want to force a page break?

11. What key(s) do you press to delete the following portions of a document? *Hint:* See Figure 2-33.
    a. The word at the cursor
    b. From the cursor to the end of the line
    c. From the cursor to the beginning of a word
    d. From the cursor to the end of a word

12. After you've deleted a word or a phrase, how do you undelete, or restore, the word or phrase?

13. How many groups of deleted text does WordPerfect save for future undelete operations?

14. Name at least three types of errors that the WordPerfect speller can find.

15. If you type the sentence "That is just to bad!" and then run the speller, why won't the speller detect the incorrect usage of the word "to"?

16. Besides synonyms what does the WordPerfect thesaurus list?

17. What procedure would you follow to print five copies of a memo?

18. Define the word "toggle" as it is used in WordPerfect.

Tutorial Assignments

> In the following Tutorial Assignments, make sure you clear the document screen before retrieving each file.

Retrieve the file T2FILE1.DFT and do the following:

1. Change the justification from full to left for the entire document.

2. In the numbered paragraphs change the tabs to indents.

3. Use the WordPerfect speller to correct misspelled words, double words, and irregular case words.

4. Carefully read the document and make a list of the words that are "misspelled" or incorrectly used but that the speller failed to flag. Edit the document to correct these words.

5. Save the document as S2FILE1.MEM.

6. Print the document.

Retrieve the file T2FILE2.DFT and do the following:

7. Use the thesaurus to substitute the word "plethora" for a simpler word that has the same meaning.

8. Use the thesaurus to list the antonym(s) of the word "abstruse," then reword the entire sentence using an antonym.

9. Save the document as S2FILE2.MEM.

10. Print three copies of the document by changing the Number of Copies option on the Print and Options menu.

Retrieve the file T2FILE3.DOC and do the following:

11. Insert a hard page break after the company telephone number, so the first six lines become a title page and the rest of the document is on a separate page.

12. At the beginning of the second page, just after the page break, change the justification to left.

13. Save the document as S2FILE2.DOC.

14. Print one copy of the document.

Retrieve the file T2FILE4.DFT and do the following:

15. After the first paragraph to the right of the colon, type "InTrack can really help improve the return on your investments." Put "InTrack" in boldfaced type.

16. Use typeover mode to change the number "4,827.29" to "5,216.41."

17. Run the speller to correct the typos in the document.

18. Save the document as S2FILE4.MEM.

19. Print one copy of the document.

Retrieve the file T2FILE5.DOC and do the following *in the order given*:

20. Turn on Reveal Codes and make a handwritten list of all the format codes you can see in the document.

21. Clear the document screen, then type the list of format codes you found. Type only one code per line.

22. Number each code in the list and indent ([F4]) after each number.

23. After each format code, type a colon (:), then type the meaning of the code.

24. Save the document as S2CODES.DOC.

25. Print the document.

Case Problems

1. CompuLearn Inc.

Sharon Pincus is a computer consultant working for CompuLearn Inc. of Biloxi, Mississippi. One of CompuLearn's potential clients is Mr. Michael Jensen, the office manager of Boyer and Stephenson Law Offices, 841 Magnolia Avenue, Jackson, MI 93204. Mr. Jensen has requested information from CompuLearn about the experience and the qualifications of the computer trainer who would be assigned to his office. Sharon has been assigned to this account, so she has to write Mr. Jensen to tell him about her experience and qualifications.

Retrieve the file P2JENSEN.DFT and do the following:

1. Set the entire document to left justification.

2. Change the margins to 1.5 inches on the left and the right.

3. Insert today's date, the inside address, and the salutation at the beginning of the document.

4. Number the three paragraphs that explain Sharon's qualifications. Indent all the lines of the paragraph *after* the paragraph number.

5. At the end of the third numbered paragraph, add: **I also know all aspects of <u>WordPerfect</u>, including basic document editing, graphics, styles, macros, and desktop publishing**.

6. Run the speller to correct any typos and spelling errors. Proofread the document for errors that the speller may have missed.

7. Since the use of the word "aspect" twice in the third numbered paragraph is repetitive, use the thesaurus to replace the second occurrence of "aspects" with a synonym. After you make the replacement, be sure to make the synonym plural.

8. Save the document as S2JENSEN.LET.

9. Print two copies of the letter.

2. Z & Z Electronics Product Description

Carlos Gallegos is the product manager of Z & Z Electronics. Carlos has to prepare a brief description of a new computer cabinet manufactured by Z & Z. The product description must include a cover sheet (Figure 2-52a on the next page) and, on a separate sheet, the body of the document (Figure 2-52b on the following page).

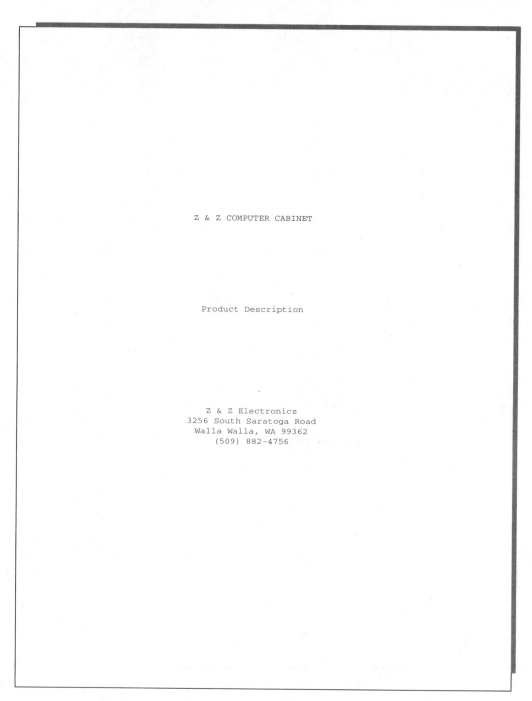

Z & Z COMPUTER CABINET

Product Description

Z & Z Electronics
3256 South Saratoga Road
Walla Walla, WA 99362
(509) 882-4756

Figure 2-52a

The Z & Z Computer Cabinet

Dimensions: 6 ft. wide, 5 ft. 6 in. tall, 2 ft. 8
in. deep

Material: Composition board with walnut or maple
veneer

Features: Retractable keyboard drawer, 4-inch high
monitor stand, printer shelf (large
enough to accommodate any laser
printer), four book shelves, three
drawers for office supplies and for
computer paper, built-in power strip and
separate on/off switch for the computer
and each peripheral.

Price: $285.00 (suggested retail)

Figure 2-52b

Do the following:

1. Type the cover sheet of the document with center-justified text.

2. Insert a hard page break after the cover sheet.

3. For the body of the product description, set the margins to 2.0 inches on the left and 1.0 inch on the right.

4. Make the document left-justified.

5. Type the body of the product description as shown in Figure 2-52. Notice that the descriptive text on the right is indented and that some of the words and phrases are boldfaced or underlined.

6. Save the document as S2COMCAB.DOC, where COMCAB stands for computer cabinet.

7. Print a copy of the document.

3. Celebrity Management Corporation Statement of Goals

Cecilia Jordon is president of Celebrity Management Corporation, a small Los Angeles company that manages the personal appearances, endorsements, and investments of actors, radio personalities, and sports figures. Cecilia is preparing a memo listing proposed goals for the company. She first writes a rough draft of the memo (Figure 2-53).

```
                                    November 9, 1992
        MEMORANDUM TO:   Members, Executive Committee
                         Celebrity Management Corporation

                         Jim Aguilar
                         Samantha Clark
                         Ellen Inouye
                         George Koerner

        FROM:            Cecilia Jordon, President

        SUBJECT:         Company Goals

        In advance of our executive meeting on November 16,
        1992, please consider the following list of tentative
        annual company goals. Keep in mind that our goals
        should be aggressive, measurable, and attainable.

            1.   Increase the number of clients by 20%.
            2.   Increase the average income/dividend per
                 client by 5%.
            3.   Develop a company culture.
            4.   Expand our current office space by 14,000
                 square feet.
            5.   Hire four new agents.

        If you have comments or questions prior to the planning
        meeting, please contact me.
```

Figure 2-53

Do the following:

1. With a clear document screen, set the margins to 1.5 inches on the left and the right.

2. Set the document to left justification.

3. Type the rough draft of the document as shown in Figure 2-53.

4. Save the document as S2CMC1.DFT.

5. Print the document.

   Cecilia has her assistant proofread and edit the document. Cecilia then approves the changes (Figure 2-54) and has her assistant make them.

```
                                              November 9, 1992

          MEMORANDUM TO:   Members, Executive Committee
                           Celebrity Management Corporation

                           Jim Aguilar
                           Samantha Clark
                           Ellen Inouye
                           George Koerner

          FROM:            Cecilia Jordon, President

          SUBJECT:         Company Goals
                                      planning
          In advance of our executive meeting on November 16,
          1992, please consider the following list of tentative  for 1993
          annual company goals. Keep in mind that our goals
          should be aggressive, measurable, and attainable.

             1.   Increase the number of clients by 20%.
             2.   Increase the average income/dividend per
                  client by 5%.             not measurable
             3.   Develop a company culture.
            3 4.  Expand our current office space by 14,000
                  square feet.
            4 5.  Hire four new agents.

          If you have comments or questions prior to the planning
          meeting, please contact me.
```

Figure 2-54

6. Revise the document according to the editing marks shown in Figure 2-54.

7. Save the new version of the memo as S2CMC2.MEM.

8. Print three copies of the memo.

Tutorial 3

Using Additional Editing Features

Writing an Inventory Observation Memo

Case: Sorority Designs Inc.

Melissa Walborsky graduated last June with a degree in accounting and has earned her C.P.A. certificate. She recently began work on the audit staff at McDermott & Eston, an accounting firm in Syracuse, New York. One of Melissa's first assignments is an audit of Sorority Designs Inc. (SDI), a clothing company that markets stylish apparel designed for college-age women. As a member of the audit team, she observed the inventory at SDI's warehouse in Syracuse. Susan Guttmann, Melissa's manager, has asked her to write the inventory observation memo for the audit working papers (documents that verify the nature of an audit and the results). Melissa will write a first draft of the memo. Then based on her own analysis and proofreading, she will revise it. Finally she will submit her draft to Susan for approval, in accordance with the established policy for all McDermott & Eston documents.

OBJECTIVES

In this tutorial you will learn to:

- Align text flush right

- Center a line of text

- Search and replace text

- Use block operations to move, delete, and copy text

- Use block operations to change the appearance of existing text

- Use block operations to convert existing text to all uppercase

Planning the Document

Before writing the memo, Melissa looks at her own notes, the audit working papers, and several other inventory observation memos to help her determine the content, organization, style, and format of her document.

Content

Melissa decides to base the content of her memo primarily on her notes (Figure 3-1) and her personal recollection of the inventory.

Inventory Observation, Syracuse warehouse, June 30, 1993

– Arrived 7:20 a.m.
– No merchandise shipped that day.
– Slow moving and damaged merchandise: shipped to Ithaca outlet.
– Periodic test counts on 31% of inventory.
– Cutoff controls: noted apparel received on June 28 and noted no merchandise shipped on June 29.

Figure 3-1
Notes Melissa took during inventory observations

Organization

Melissa's document will follow the standard organization for an inventory observation memo, with the headings "Observation of Inventory Taking," "Slow Moving and Damaged Merchandise," "Test Counts," "Cutoff Controls," and "Conclusions." She determines that the memo needs only one or two paragraphs under each heading.

Style

Melissa decides to use a straightforward writing style but also to include the usual auditing jargon, since she knows that her audience will be other accountants at McDermott & Eston.

Format

Melissa decides not to change any of WordPerfect's default format settings. She leaves the margins at one inch on the left, right, top, and bottom and keeps the default of full justification. Melissa will modify the format of the heading, however, so that the document follows the standard McDermott & Eston format for inventory observation memos.

Retrieving the Document Using List Files

Let's begin by retrieving Melissa's rough draft of her inventory observation memo. But instead of using the Retrieve feature, let's use WordPerfect's List Files feature. List Files allows you to list the files on a disk or in a directory and to retrieve, delete, rename, or print the document files. The advantage of List Files in retrieving a document is that you don't have to remember the exact name of a document file — you can look over the list of filenames and select the one you want.

To retrieve the document using List Files:

❶ Insert your WordPerfect data diskette into drive A and make sure the document screen is clear.

❷ Select List Files from the File menu. See Figure 3-2. Alternatively press **[F5]** (List). WordPerfect displays the word "Dir" followed by the name of the default directory on the status line.

You can now type a root directory or a directory path to get a directory listing.

menu name ⟶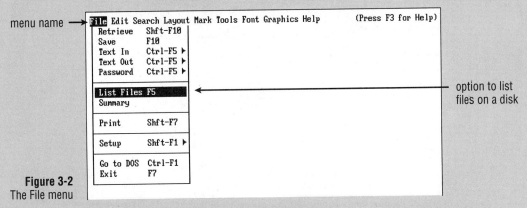

Figure 3-2
The File menu

❸ Type **a:** and press **[Enter]**. WordPerfect displays a List Files menu, similar to the one in Figure 3-3.

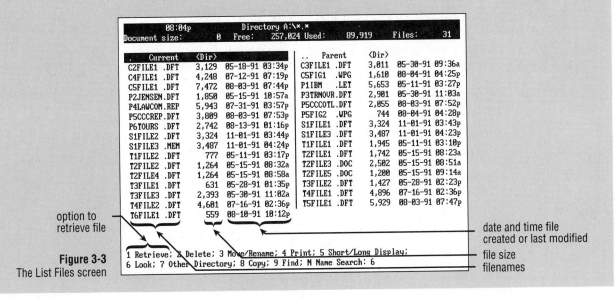

Figure 3-3
The List Files screen

❹ Move the cursor so the filename C3FILE1.DFT is highlighted.

You can use the mouse pointer to click on the filename C3FILE1.DFT or use the keyboard cursor-movement keys to move the cursor to C3FILE1.DFT.

❺ Select **1** (**R**etrieve). If WordPerfect displays the prompt "Retrieve into current document?", your document screen already contains a document. You should select "No," press **[F7]** (Exit) to return to the document screen, clear the screen, and return to Step 1.

The rough draft of the inventory observation memo appears on the WordPerfect document screen. Your screen will look similar to Figure 3-4.

cursor →

```
Prepared by:  Melissa Walborsky Date: 7/5/93
Reviewed by:  Susan Guttmann


Sorority Designs Inc.
Inventory Observation Memorandum - Syracuse Warehouse
6/30/93



OBSERVATION OF INVENTORY TAKING
      The audit staff who participated in this observation were Mike
Newman, Harvey Strauss, Edith Kaplan, and I.  We arrived at the
Syracuse warehouse at 7:20 a.m. on June 30, 1993.
      We all observed and noted the care with which the warehouse
personnel counted the inventory and used the inventory count
sheets.  They appeared to follow the required procedures.  Standard
inventory protocols were observed.

SLOW MOVING AND DAMAGED MERCHANDISE
      We questioned the SDI warehouse personnel about slow moving
and damaged merchandise.  We were told that SDI monitors this
merchandise and periodically transfers it to the SDI clothing
A:\C3FILE1.DFT                           Doc 1 Pg 1 Ln 1" Pos 1"
```

Figure 3-4
The rough draft as it appears on the document screen

filename of rough draft

Remember that this is Melissa's *rough draft*, which she has not yet revised. It contains formatting, spelling, and other errors. In the following section Melissa will revise the memo before she submits it to Susan. Take time now to read through the entire document to familiarize yourself with its content and some of its problems (Figure 3-5).

Prepared by: Melissa Walborksy Date: 7/5/93
Reviewed by: Susan Guttmann

Sorority Designs Inc.
Inventory Observation Memorandum - Syracuse Warehouse
6/30/93

OBSERVATION OF INVENTORY TAKING
    The audit staff who participated in this observation were Mike Newman, Harvey Strauss, Edith Kaplan, and I. We arrived at the Syracuse warehouse at 7:20 a.m. on June 30, 1993.
    We all observed and noted the care with which the warehouse personnel counted the inventory and used the inventory count sheets. They appeared to follow the required procedures. Standard inventory protocols were observed.

SLOW MOVING AND DAMAGED MERCHANDISE
    We questioned the SDI warehouse personnel about slow moving and damaged merchandise. We were told that SDI monitors this merchandise and periodically transfers it to the SDI clothing outlet store in Ithica. We observed a holding area wherein such merchandise is stored until the next shipment to Ithica. Thus, we did not include the slow moving and damaged merchandise in the count.

TEST COUNTS
    We made test counts on approximately 31% the inventory. We recorded our findings in our work papers and noted that these counts substantiated SDI's counts.

CUTOFF CONTROLS
    We took time to gain access to and examine the Receipt Log and the Shipping Log for this warehouse. We noted the merchandise received on June 28, 1993; we also noted that no merchandise was shipped on June 29, 1993. We used the June 28 numbers for our subsequent purchases and sales cutoff tests.

Conclusions
    I believe we made an accurate count of all saleable merchandise in the Syracuse warehouse on June 30, 1993, because the SDI personnel followed all required procedures and because the merchandise held for delivery to the Ithica outlet store was not counted.

Figure 3-5
Melissa's rough draft

Using Flush Right

Melissa begins by observing that in most of the other company memos the date on the top line of the document appears flush against the right margin. She decides, therefore, to use WordPerfect's Flush Right feature to move the date to the right margin. Let's use Flush Right to position the date on the right margin.

To move existing text flush right:

❶ Move the cursor to the "D" in "Date" on the first line of the document.

Whenever you use this feature, move the cursor to the first letter of the group of words that you want flush right.

❷ Select Flush Right from the Align option of the Layout menu. See Figure 3-6. Alternatively press **[Alt][F6]** (Flush Right).

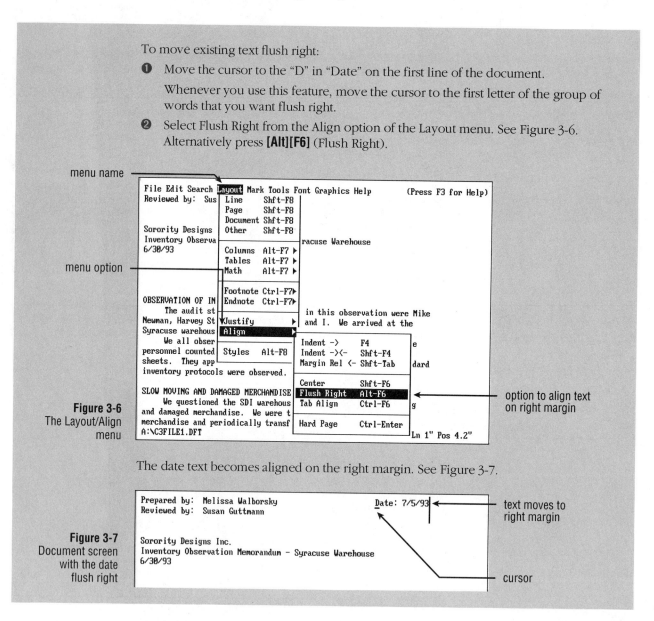

Figure 3-6
The Layout/Align menu

The date text becomes aligned on the right margin. See Figure 3-7.

Figure 3-7
Document screen with the date flush right

Melissa then decides to add the date that she thinks Susan Guttmann will review the memo, knowing that the date may change.

To type flush-right text:

❶ Move the cursor to the end of the second line, after "Susan Guttmann."

❷ Select Flush Right from the Align option of the Layout menu or press **[Alt][F6]** (Flush Right). The cursor is now at the far right margin of the document.

❸ Type **Date: 7/9/93**.

Notice that as you type the cursor stays in the same place, rather than moving from left to right. Instead the characters move from right to left, away from the right margin. See Figure 3-8.

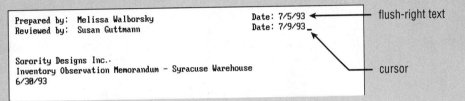

```
Prepared by:  Melissa Walborsky            Date: 7/5/93  ◄──────── flush-right text
Reviewed by:  Susan Guttmann               Date: 7/9/93 _

Sorority Designs Inc..
Inventory Observation Memorandum - Syracuse Warehouse    ──────── cursor
6/30/93
```

Figure 3-8
Document screen with second date flush right

Centering Text

Melissa realizes that the three title lines in the inventory observation memo — starting with "Sorority Designs" and ending with the date of the audit, "6/30/93" — should be centered between the left and the right margins. Let's use WordPerfect's Center command to format these three lines of text.

To center text:

❶ Move the cursor to the "S" in "Sorority," at the beginning of the third line of the document.

To center any line of text, you first place the cursor at the beginning of that line.

❷ Select Center from the Align option of the Layout menu or press **[Shift][F6]** (Center). As soon as you select the Center command, WordPerfect centers the line of text between the margins. See Figure 3-9.

```
Prepared by:  Melissa Walborsky            Date: 7/5/93
Reviewed by:  Susan Guttmann               Date: 7/9/93


                    Sorority Designs Inc. ◄──────── first line of
Inventory Observation Memorandum - Syracuse Warehouse    title centered
6/30/93
```

Figure 3-9
Document screen with first title line centered

❸ Move the cursor to the beginning of the next line.

❹ Select Center from the Align option of the Layout menu or press **[Shift][F6]** (Center).

⑤   Use the same procedure to center the next line of text. See Figure 3-10.

Figure 3-10
Document screen
with all three title
lines centered

all three lines
centered

⑥   Turn on Reveal Codes to see the [Flsh Rgt] and the [Center] format codes that
WordPerfect inserted into the document in this and the previous set of steps. (You
will have to move the cursor up near the beginning of the document to see the
[Flsh Rgt] codes.) After you have viewed the codes, turn off Reveal Codes.

As a general rule, when you want to center many lines of text, such as all the lines on a
title page of a report, use the Center Justification command, which you learned in
WordPerfect Tutorial 2. When you want to center only a few lines of text, use the Center
command.

Searching for Text

When you're working with a short document — a half page in length, for example — you
can find a specific word or phrase or move the cursor to a specific location just by using the
cursor-movement keys. But when you're working with a longer document, the best way to
find a specific word or phrase or to move to a specific location may be with the Search
command. A **search** is an operation you use to position the cursor at a specified sequence
of characters or codes, called the **search string**. The search string may include a single
character, such as "T" or "4"; a format code, such as [→Indent] or [HRt]; a word or group of
words, such as "inventory" or "shipping log"; or any combination of characters, codes, or
words.

Let's look at an example of how you would use the Search command. Melissa notices
that in her inventory observation memo she left out the word "of" after "31%" in the first line
under "TEST COUNTS." She decides to use WordPerfect's Search command to move the
cursor quickly to that location in the memo.

To search for text:

❶   Move the cursor to the beginning of the document.

Since you will tell WordPerfect to search forward from the cursor toward the end
of the document, you want to move the cursor to the beginning of the document
to make sure that you find the specified search string.

❷   Select Forward from the Search menu. See Figure 3-11. Alternatively press **[F2]**
(Search).

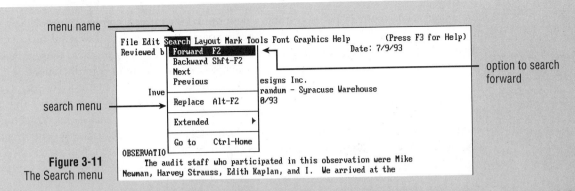

menu name

option to search forward

search menu

Figure 3-11
The Search menu

WordPerfect displays the prompt "-> Srch:" and waits for you to type the search string. The "->" in the prompt represents a forward arrow, meaning that WordPerfect will search from the cursor toward the end of the document.

❸   Type **31%** and press **[F2]** (Search).

Do *not* press [Enter], because that would insert a hard-return code [HRt] into the search string, and WordPerfect would search for the string "31%[HRt]" instead of just "31%." If you accidentally pressed [Enter] and have not yet pressed [F2], just press [Backspace] to erase the [HRt] code. Similarly be careful not to type a space or a period as part of the search string. In other words, type *only* the characters that you want WordPerfect to search for. WordPerfect searches through the document until it finds the next occurrence of the search string — "31%" — and then positions the cursor immediately after the string. In Melissa's inventory observation memo the string "31%" occurs only once, so the cursor moves to just after "31%."

❹   Press **[Space]** and type **of** to add the missing word. See Figure 3-12.

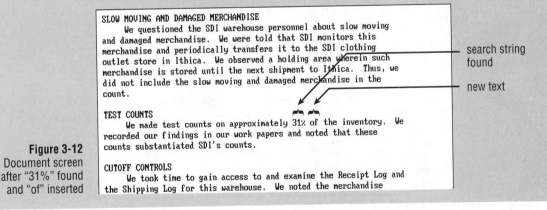

search string found

new text

Figure 3-12
Document screen after "31%" found and "of" inserted

After you have had some practice, you'll find that using the Search command to move the cursor to specific locations within your document is usually much faster than using only the cursor-movement keys.

Searching and Replacing

Search and replace, sometimes simply called **replace**, is an operation that searches through a document for a search string and then replaces one or more occurrences of that search string with another specified string, called the **replacement string**. The replacement string, like the search string, can be any combination of characters, codes, or words. You can use search and replace to change one word to another word, one phrase to another phrase, one set of format codes to another set of format codes, and so forth, throughout your document.

Let's use search and replace to change an incorrect word in the inventory observation memo to the correct word. For example, Melissa notices that she misspelled "Ithaca" throughout the document. She can't use WordPerfect's speller to make the correction, because "Ithaca" is not in the speller dictionary. She decides, therefore, to use WordPerfect's Replace feature to search for all occurrences of "Ithica" and replace them with "Ithaca."

To search and replace a string of text:

❶ Move the cursor to the beginning of the document.

The Replace feature works from the position of the cursor to the end of the document. Thus, to perform the operation for an entire document, you need to move the cursor to the beginning of the document.

❷ Select Replace from the Search menu or press **[Alt][F2]** (Replace). WordPerfect displays the "w/Confirm?" prompt. See Figure 3-13.

Figure 3-13
The "w/Confirm" prompt

prompt to select search and replace with or without confirmations

Selecting "Yes" instructs WordPerfect to pause at every occurrence of the search string and wait for you to decide whether you want that occurrence of the search string replaced.

❸ Select "No" by pressing **N** or by pressing **[Enter]** (since "No" is the default), or by clicking the mouse pointer on "No."

Selecting "No" tells WordPerfect that you don't want to confirm the replacements. That is, WordPerfect will automatically replace every occurrence of the search string, "Ithica", with the replacement string, "Ithaca", throughout your document, without pausing to ask for confirmation.

The "-> Srch:" prompt appears on the status line followed by the previous search string. See Figure 3-14.

Figure 3-14
The "-> Search" prompt with previous search string

prompt for search string

previous search string

❹ Ignore the previous search string and type **Ithica**, then press **[F2]** (Search). "Ithica" becomes the new search string. The prompt "Replace with:" appears on the status line.

❺ Type **Ithaca** and press **[F2]** (Search). "Ithaca", the correct spelling of the city, becomes the replacement string.

WordPerfect carries out the search and replace, changing all occurrences of "Ithica" to "Ithaca." If you scroll the screen up to the first occurence of "Ithaca", your screen will look like Figure 3-15.

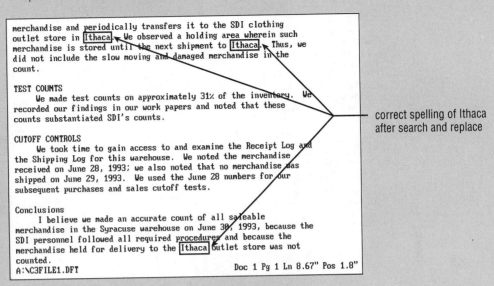

```
merchandise and periodically transfers it to the SDI clothing
outlet store in  Ithaca .  We observed a holding area wherein such
merchandise is stored until the next shipment to  Ithaca .  Thus, we
did not include the slow moving and damaged merchandise in the
count.

TEST COUNTS
     We made test counts on approximately 31% of the inventory.  We
recorded our findings in our work papers and noted that these
counts substantiated SDI's counts.

CUTOFF CONTROLS
     We took time to gain access to and examine the Receipt Log and
the Shipping Log for this warehouse.  We noted the merchandise
received on June 28, 1993; we also noted that no merchandise was
shipped on June 29, 1993.  We used the June 28 numbers for our
subsequent purchases and sales cutoff tests.

Conclusions
     I believe we made an accurate count of all saleable
merchandise in the Syracuse warehouse on June 30, 1993, because the
SDI personnel followed all required procedures and because the
merchandise held for delivery to the  Ithaca  outlet store was not
counted.
A:\C3FILE1.DFT                          Doc 1 Pg 1 Ln 8.67" Pos 1.8"
```

correct spelling of Ithaca after search and replace

Figure 3-15
Document screen after the Replace operation

As Melissa reads through her draft of the memo, she realizes that she has used the word "merchandise" excessively. She decides that in some places she could use the word "apparel" instead, since apparel is the only type of merchandise that SDI sells. To avoid the repetitive use of "merchandise," she performs a search and replace *with confirmation*. This means that at each occurrence of "merchandise" in the document, WordPerfect will stop and ask her if she wants to replace "merchandise" with "apparel."

In this example, we'll use the search string "merchandise" in all lowercase letters. This instructs WordPerfect to stop at *all* occurrences of "merchandise" with either uppercase or lowercase letters, such as "Merchandise" or "MERCHANDISE." When you use uppercase letters in a search string, WordPerfect searches only for a string with those uppercase letters. For example, if "Ithica" were the search string, WordPerfect would stop at "Ithica" and "ITHICA" but not at "ithica."

Let's use search and replace with confirmation to change some of the occurrences of "merchandise" to "apparel." In the following steps, the choice of when to change a word and when to leave it unchanged is based on whatever seems better to Melissa, not on any rules.

To search and replace with confirmation:

❶ Move the cursor to the beginning of the document and select Replace from the Search menu or press **[Alt][F2]** (Replace).

❷ At the prompt "w/Confirm?" select "Yes."

Selecting "Yes" instructs WordPerfect to stop at all occurrences of the search string and to prompt for confirmation before replacing the text.

❸ Type **merchandise** and press **[F2]** (Search). The word "merchandise" becomes the search string.

❹ Type **apparel** and press **[F2]** (Search).

The word "apparel" becomes the replacement string. The cursor now stops at the first occurrence of "merchandise," located in the second heading, and WordPerfect waits for you to accept or decline the replacement. See Figure 3-16.

```
SLOW MOVING AND DAMAGED MERCHANDISE                                    ─── cursor
     We questioned the SDI warehouse personnel about slow moving
and damaged merchandise.  We were told that SDI monitors this
merchandise and periodically transfers it to the SDI clothing
outlet store in Ithaca.  We observed a holding area wherein such
merchandise is stored until the next shipment to Ithaca.  Thus, we
did not include the slow moving and damaged merchandise in the
count.

TEST COUNTS
     We made test counts on approximately 31% of the inventory.  We
recorded our findings in our work papers and noted that these
counts substantiated SDI's counts.
Confirm? No (Yes)                            Doc 1 Pg 1 Ln 4.33" Pos 3.5"  ─── confirmation prompt
```

Figure 3-16
The confirmation prompt with the cursor on "MERCHANDISE"

❺ Select "Yes" to replace "merchandise" with "apparel" in the second heading. The cursor then continues to move to each occurrence of "merchandise," stopping each time for you to accept or decline the replacement.

❻ The word "merchandise" occurs four times in the paragraph following the second heading. Select "Yes" to accept the replacement in the first sentence of the paragraph, select "No" to decline the replacement in the second sentence, select "No" again to decline replacement in the third sentence, and select "Yes" to accept the replacement in the last sentence.

❼ Select "No" twice to decline replacement of both occurrences of "merchandise" in the paragraph under "CUTOFF CONTROLS."

❽ Select "Yes" to accept replacement of the first occurrence of "merchandise" in the final paragraph, then select "No" to decline replacement of the last occurrence of "merchandise" in the document.

The search and replace operation is now complete. Your printed document will look similar to Figure 3-17. The word "Apparel" in the second heading isn't in all uppercase letters, as it should be, but you'll fix that problem later. The first letter of "Apparel" is uppercase because, in a search and replace, WordPerfect automatically capitalizes the first letter of the *replacement* word when the first letter of the *replaced* word is uppercase.

Prepared by: Melissa Walborksy   Date: 7/5/93
Reviewed by: Susan Guttmann   Date: 7/9/93

Sorority Designs Inc.
Inventory Observation Memorandum - Syracuse Warehouse
6/30/93

OBSERVATION OF INVENTORY TAKING

The audit staff who participated in this observation were Mike Newman, Harvey Strauss, Edith Kaplan, and I. We arrived at the Syracuse warehouse at 7:20 a.m. on June 30, 1993.

We all observed and noted the care with which the warehouse personnel counted the inventory and used the inventory count sheets. They appeared to follow the required procedures. Standard inventory protocols were observed.

SLOW MOVING AND DAMAGED Apparel

We questioned the SDI warehouse personnel about slow moving and damaged apparel. We were told that SDI monitors this merchandise and periodically transfers it to the SDI clothing outlet store in Ithaca. We observed a holding area wherein such merchandise is stored until the next shipment to Ithaca. Thus, we did not include the slow moving and damaged apparel in the count.

TEST COUNTS

We made test counts on approximately 31% of the inventory. We recorded our findings in our work papers and noted that these counts substantiated SDI's counts.

CUTOFF CONTROLS

We took time to gain access to and examine the Receipt Log and the Shipping Log for this warehouse. We noted the merchandise received on June 28, 1993; we also noted that no merchandise was shipped on June 29, 1993. We used the June 28 numbers for our subsequent purchases and sales cutoff tests.

Conclusions

I believe we made an accurate count of all saleable apparel in the Syracuse warehouse on June 30, 1993, because the SDI personnel followed all required procedures and because the merchandise held for delivery to the Ithaca outlet store was not counted.

Figure 3-17
Melissa's revised draft of the memo

Saving and Printing the Document

Melissa now feels that the inventory observation memo is ready to save to the disk and to print for review by her manager, Susan.

To save and print the document:

❶ Make sure your data diskette is in drive A.

❷ Save the document using the path and filename A:\S3FILE2.DFT.

Melissa uses the filename extension .DFT to signify that this is still a draft of the memo. Before saving and printing the final version, she wants Susan to read it.

❸ Make sure your printer is turned on and ready to print, then print the document.

After she prints the document, Melissa gives it to Susan, who notes errors and makes other changes. Susan returns the edited document to Melissa and asks her to make the changes before printing a copy for the file (Figure 3-18). Because Susan did, in fact, review the memo on 7/9/93, she doesn't tell Melissa to change that date.

Block Operations

One of the most powerful editing features in WordPerfect is the Block command, which executes block operations. A **block operation** is a set of commands that allows you to modify or otherwise act on an existing unit of text. The unit of text may be any portion of your document — a single character, a phrase, a sentence, a paragraph, a page, or a group of pages.

Block operations are powerful because they allow you to change a block of text all at one time instead of changing each word individually. For example, you could change all the text in a paragraph from normal to boldfaced, from left-justified to centered, or from uppercase and lowercase to all uppercase. You can also use block operations to delete a block of text, save a block of text to a disk, or move a block of text from one location to another within your document.

```
Prepared by:  Melissa Walborksy          Date:  7/5/93
Reviewed by:  Susan Guttmann              Date:  7/9/93
```

Sorority Designs Inc. (bf)   (underline)
Inventory Observation Memorandum - Syracuse Warehouse
6/30/93

OBSERVATION OF INVENTORY TAKING
     The audit staff who participated in this observation were Mike
Newman, Harvey Strauss, Edith Kaplan, and I. We arrived at the
Syracuse warehouse at 7:20 a.m. on June 30, 1993.
     We all observed and noted the care with which the warehouse
personnel counted the inventory and used the inventory count
sheets. They appeared to follow the required procedures. ~~Standard
inventory protocols were observed.~~

SLOW MOVING AND DAMAGED Apparel   ← (uppercase)
     We questioned the SDI warehouse personnel about slow moving
and damaged apparel. We were told that SDI monitors this
merchandise and periodically transfers it to the SDI clothing
outlet store in Ithaca. We observed a holding area wherein such
merchandise is stored until the next shipment to Ithaca. Thus, we
did not include the slow moving and damaged apparel in the count.

TEST COUNTS
     We made test counts on approximately 31% of the inventory. We
recorded our findings in our work papers and noted that these
counts substantiated SDI's counts.

CUTOFF CONTROLS
                                              d
     We ~~took time to gain access to and~~ examine the Receipt Log and
the Shipping Log for this warehouse. We noted the merchandise
received on June 28, 1993; we also noted that no merchandise was
shipped on June 29, 1993. We used the June 28 numbers for our
subsequent purchases and sales cutoff tests.

Conclusions ← (capitalize entire word)
     I believe we made an accurate count of all saleable apparel in
the Syracuse warehouse on June 30, 1993, because the SDI personnel
followed all required procedures and because the merchandise held
for delivery to the Ithaca outlet store was not counted.

Figure 3-18
Melissa's revised draft with Susan's edits

Figure 3-19 shows the many block features that are available in WordPerfect. Some of these features are familiar to you (such as Bold, Delete, and Flush Right), but many of them may be unfamiliar (such as Append, Comment, and Convert Case). You'll learn many of these features as you complete this and future tutorials.

Features	Description
Append	Add block to the end of an existing file
Bold	Boldface blocked text
Comment	Convert block to a document comment
Convert Case (Switch)	Switch all characters in block to uppercase or lowercase
Center	Center block horizontally
Copy	Make copy of block at another location in the document
Cut	Remove block and paste it into another location in document
Delete	Erase block
Flush Right	Align block against the right margin
Font	Change the size or appearance of blocked text
Macro	Macro acts upon block
Mark Text	Mark block for lists, index, table of contents
Move	Move block to another location in document
Print	Send block of text to the printer
Protect	Keep block of text together on same page to protect against page break
Replace	Search and replace words, phrase, or codes within block
Save	Save block of text to disk
Search	Search for text or codes within block
Shell	Append or save block of text to clipboard
Sort	Sort lines or records within block
Spell	Check spelling within block
Style	Insert style-formatting codes within block
Table	Convert block of text to table
Text In/Out	Save block as text file
Underline	Underline block

Figure 3-19
WordPerfect's
block features

Block operations involve first selecting, or highlighting, the block of text that you want to modify and then executing the appropriate WordPerfect command to act on the block of text. Let's illustrate this procedure by boldfacing an existing phrase in Melissa's inventory observation memo.

Boldfacing Existing Text

Look at Figure 3-18 and notice that Susan's first suggested change is to boldface the client's name in the document title. This is a common practice at McDermott & Eston.

Melissa already knows how to use [F6] (Bold) to boldface *new* text that she hasn't typed yet, but to boldface *existing* text, she has to use the Block feature. Let's use WordPerfect's Block command to boldface the client's name.

To boldface a block of existing text:

❶ Move the cursor to the "S" in "Sorority" in the document title.

In most block operations you first move the cursor to the beginning of the block of text that you want to modify.

You are now ready to turn on Block, that is, begin marking a block of text.

❷ Select Block from the Edit menu. See Figure 3-20. Alternatively press **[Alt][F4]** or **[F12]** (Block).

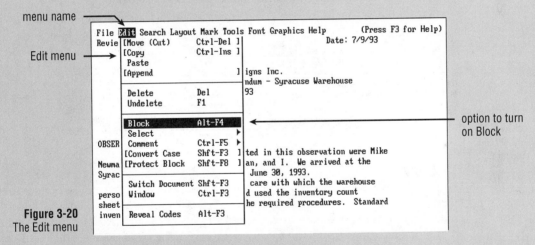

Figure 3-20
The Edit menu

WordPerfect displays the blinking message "Block on" at the bottom of the screen on the left side of the status line, to indicate that Block is on, and highlights the position number on the right side of the status line. See Figure 3-21 on the next page.

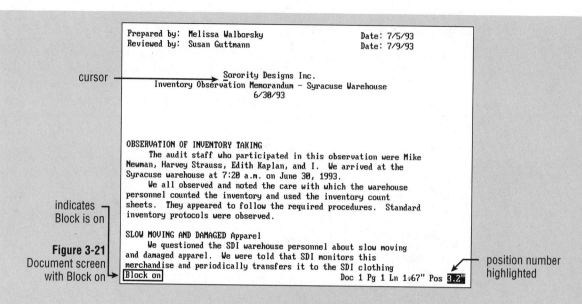

cursor

indicates Block is on

Figure 3-21
Document screen
with Block on

position number
highlighted

❸ Move the cursor to the end of the phrase "Sorority Designs Inc."

In most block operations you select the block by moving the cursor to the end of the block of text that you want to modify. WordPerfect then highlights the selected block of text. See Figure 3-22.

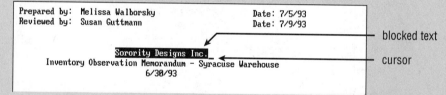

blocked text

cursor

Figure 3-22
Document screen
with blocked text

You can also use the mouse to highlight a block of text. Move the mouse pointer to the beginning of the block of text that you want to modify, press and hold down the left mouse button, drag the mouse pointer — that is, move the mouse pointer while you are still holding down the left button — to the end of the block of text, and release the mouse button. You can now use the mouse or the keyboard to execute other commands.

❹ Select Bold from the Appearance menu of the Font menu. See Figure 3-23. Alternatively press **[F6]** (Bold). The block of text becomes boldfaced, and Block is automatically turned off.

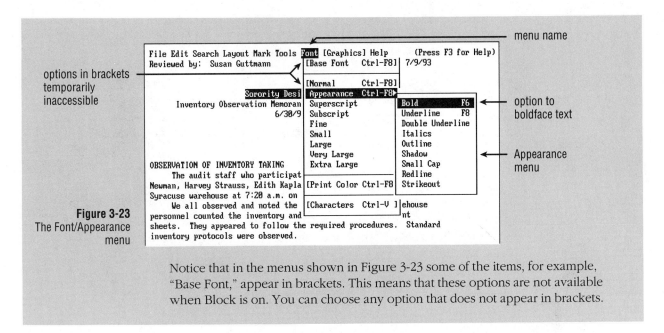

Figure 3-23
The Font/Appearance
menu

Notice that in the menus shown in Figure 3-23 some of the items, for example, "Base Font," appear in brackets. This means that these options are not available when Block is on. You can choose any option that does not appear in brackets.

As you have seen, WordPerfect's Block feature allows you to change the appearance of a blocked section of text to boldfaced, underlined, double underlined, and so forth.

If you accidentally boldface a block of text that you want in normal appearance, turn on Reveal Codes, move the cursor to the [BOLD] or [bold] code, and delete the code. When you delete either [BOLD] or [bold], WordPerfect automatically removes both codes from the document.

Underlining a Block of Text

Again look at Figure 3-18. Susan's next suggested change is to underline "Syracuse Warehouse" in the second line of the memo title. Let's use a block operation to underline this existing text.

To underline a block of existing text:

❶ Move the cursor to the "S" in "Syracuse," which is the beginning of the block of text that you want to highlight.

❷ Select Block from the Edit menu, press **[Alt][F4]**, or press **[F12]** (Block).

WordPerfect displays the blinking message "Block on" and highlights the position number on the status line.

❸   Move the cursor to the end of "Syracuse Warehouse." The selected block of text becomes highlighted. See Figure 3-24.

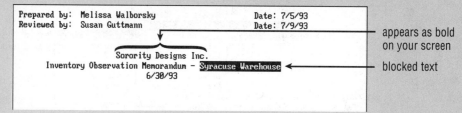

Figure 3-24
Document screen
with blocked text

appears as bold
on your screen

blocked text

Instead of using the keyboard to execute Steps 1 through 3, you could drag the mouse pointer over the text that you want to modify.

❹   Select Underline from the Appearance menu of the Font menu or press **[F8]** (Underline).

The block of text becomes underlined, and Block is automatically turned off.

Deleting a Block of Text

Another time-saving block feature is deleting a block of text. If you want to delete more than two or three words, you can save time by using Block. For example, in Figure 3-18 in the paragraph headed "CUTOFF CONTROLS," Susan suggests that Melissa delete the unnecessary and wordy phrase "took time to gain access to and". Let's use a block operation to delete this phrase.

To delete a block of text:

❶   Highlight the phrase "took time to gain access to and" by moving the cursor to the "t" in "took," just below the heading "CUTOFF CONTROLS," turning on Block, then moving the cursor to the "d" in "and". Alternatively you can highlight the phrase by dragging the mouse pointer over it.

❷   Press **[Backspace]** or **[Del]**. WordPerfect displays the prompt "Delete Block?" See Figure 3-25.

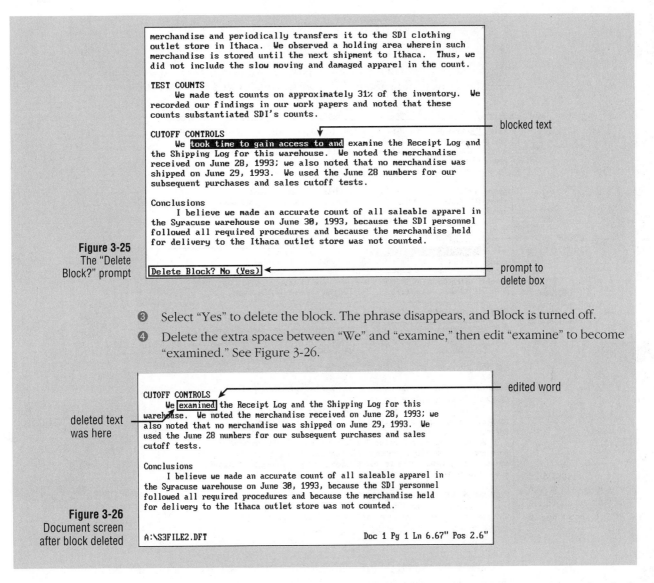

Figure 3-25
The "Delete
Block?" prompt

blocked text

prompt to
delete box

Figure 3-26
Document screen
after block deleted

deleted text
was here

edited word

❸ Select "Yes" to delete the block. The phrase disappears, and Block is turned off.

❹ Delete the extra space between "We" and "examine," then edit "examine" to become
"examined." See Figure 3-26.

The more text you have to delete, the more keystrokes you will save by using the Block
feature.

If you accidentally delete the wrong block of text, you can restore it by selecting Undelete
from the Edit menu or by pressing [F1] (Cancel) and then selecting 1 (Restore).

Converting a Block of Text to All Uppercase

In Figure 3-18 Susan's next editing mark is in the second heading. When Melissa used search
and replace to change "merchandise" to "apparel," she forgot to change "Apparel" to all
uppercase in the heading. Melissa knows that she can use a block feature to convert case.

To convert the case of a block of text:

❶ Highlight the word "Apparel" in the first heading using the keyboard or the mouse.

❷ Select To Upper in the Convert Case menu of the Edit menu. See Figure 3-27. Alternatively press **[Shift][F3]** (Switch) and select **1** (**U**ppercase).

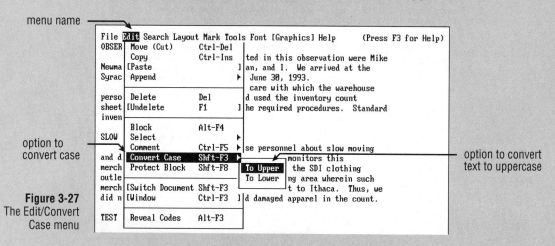

menu name →

option to convert case →

option to convert text to uppercase →

Figure 3-27
The Edit/Convert
Case menu

The word "Apparel" is converted to the all uppercase "APPAREL," and Block is turned off. See Figure 3-28.

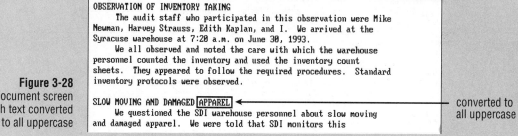

Figure 3-28
Document screen
with text converted
to all uppercase

converted to
all uppercase →

Susan also noted that the last heading, "Conclusions," should also be in all uppercase letters. Let's correct this error as well using a block operation.

❶ Highlight the word "Conclusions" just above the last paragraph of the memo.

❷ Select To Upper in the Convert Case menu of the Edit menu or press **[Shift][F3]** (Switch) and select **1** (**U**ppercase).

The word "Conclusions" becomes "CONCLUSIONS." Your document screen should now appear similar to Figure 3-29.

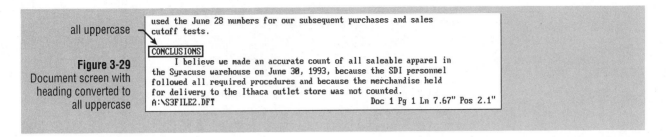

all uppercase

```
used the June 28 numbers for our subsequent purchases and sales
cutoff tests.
┌─────────┐
│CONCLUSIONS│
└─────────┘
     I believe we made an accurate count of all saleable apparel in
the Syracuse warehouse on June 30, 1993, because the SDI personnel
followed all required procedures and because the merchandise held
for delivery to the Ithaca outlet store was not counted.
A:\S3FILE2.DFT                              Doc 1 Pg 1 Ln 7.67" Pos 2.1"
```

Figure 3-29
Document screen with heading converted to all uppercase

You can also use the Convert Case feature to convert a block of text to all lowercase characters.

Moving a Block of Text

One of the most important uses of Block is to move text. Suppose, for example, you have typed a paragraph into a document but then realize the paragraph is in the wrong place. You could solve the problem by deleting the paragraph and then retyping it at the new location. But a much more efficient approach would be to use a block operation to move the paragraph. This is sometimes called "cut and paste," because after highlighting the block of text that you want to move, you cut (delete) it from the text and then paste (restore) it back again (Figure 3-30).

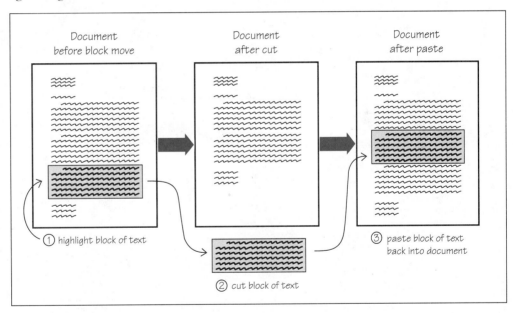

Figure 3-30
The cut and paste operation

In Figure 3-18 Susan suggests that Melissa move the "TEST COUNTS" section so that it is the second section in the memo instead of the third. Melissa knows that instead of deleting and retyping the paragraph she can use the Block and Move commands to move the entire section. Let's do this now. You can move the text using either the keyboard or a mouse.

To move a block of text using the keyboard:

➊ Move the cursor to the first "T" in "TEST COUNTS," turn on Block, then move the cursor to the "C" in "CUTOFF" to highlight the entire block that you want to move.

Because you want to move the entire section of text, you block from the beginning of one heading to the beginning of the next heading to include the blank line after the paragraph. The blank line is not highlighted, because Block highlights only existing text. See Figure 3-31.

blocked text →

```
     We questioned the SDI warehouse personnel about slow moving
and damaged apparel.  We were told that SDI monitors this
merchandise and periodically transfers it to the SDI clothing
outlet store in Ithaca.  We observed a holding area wherein such
merchandise is stored until the next shipment to Ithaca.  Thus, we
did not include the slow moving and damaged apparel in the count.

TEST COUNTS
     We made test counts on approximately 31% of the inventory.  We
recorded our findings in our work papers and noted that these
counts substantiated SDI's counts.

CUTOFF CONTROLS
     We examined the Receipt Log and the Shipping Log for this
warehouse.  We noted the merchandise received on June 28, 1993; we
also noted that no merchandise was shipped on June 29, 1993.  We
```
→ cursor

Figure 3-31
Document screen with blocked text for moving

➋ Select Move (Cut) from the Edit menu. See Figure 3-32.

menu name →

option to move block →

```
File Edit Search Layout Mark Tools Font [Graphics] Help        (Press F3 for Help)
and d ┌─────────────────────────────┐ that SDI monitors this
merch │ Move (Cut)      Ctrl-Del    │ fers it to the SDI clothing
outle │ Copy            Ctrl-Ins    │ ed a holding area wherein such
merch │ [Paste                    ] │ xt shipment to Ithaca.  Thus, we
did n │ Append                    ▶ │ d damaged apparel in the count.
      │                             │
      │ Delete          Del         │
TEST  │ [Undelete        F1       ] │ imately 31% of the inventory.  We
      │                             │ papers and noted that these
recor │ Block           Alt-F4      │
count │ Select                    ▶ │
      │ Comment         Ctrl-F5   ▶ │
CUTOF │ Convert Case    Shft-F3   ▶ │
      │ Protect Block   Shft-F8     │ nd the Shipping Log for this
wareh │                             │ se received on June 28, 1993; we
also  │ [Switch Document Shft-F3  ] │ shipped on June 29, 1993.  We
used  │ [Window         Ctrl-F3   ] │ ubsequent purchases and sales
cutof │                             │
      │ Reveal Codes    Alt-F3      │
      └─────────────────────────────┘
```

Figure 3-32
The Edit menu with Move highlighted

Alternatively press **[Ctrl][F4]** (Move) to display the Move menu and select **1** (**B**lock), then **1** (**M**ove). See Figure 3-33.

```
     I believe we made an accurate count of all saleable apparel in
the Syracuse warehouse on June 30, 1993, because the SDI personnel
followed all required procedures and because the merchandise held
for delivery to the Ithaca outlet store was not counted.
┌──────────────────────────────────────────────────┐
│ Move: 1 Block; 2 Tabular Column; 3 Rectangle: 0   │ ← move menu
└──────────────────────────────────────────────────┘
```

Figure 3-33
The Move menu

This cuts, or deletes, the selected block of text from the document. The prompt "Move cursor; press Enter to retrieve" appears on the status line. See Figure 3-34. This prompt tells you to move the cursor (using the cursor-movement keys or a search operation) to the position where you want to move the deleted text and then to press [Enter] to restore the text into the memo.

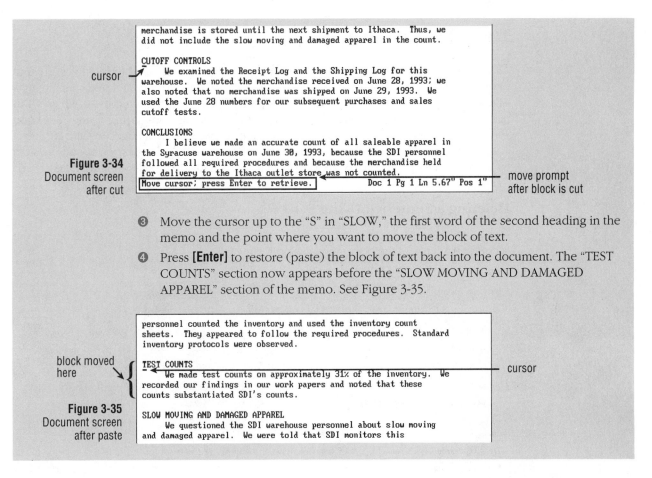

Figure 3-34
Document screen
after cut

cursor

move prompt
after block is cut

❸ Move the cursor up to the "S" in "SLOW," the first word of the second heading in the memo and the point where you want to move the block of text.

❹ Press **[Enter]** to restore (paste) the block of text back into the document. The "TEST COUNTS" section now appears before the "SLOW MOVING AND DAMAGED APPAREL" section of the memo. See Figure 3-35.

block moved
here

cursor

Figure 3-35
Document screen
after paste

If you are using a mouse follow these steps.

To move a block of text using the mouse:

❶ Move the mouse pointer to the "T" in "TEST COUNTS," press and hold down the left mouse button, move the mouse pointer to the "C" in "CUTOFF," and release the mouse button. This highlights the entire block that you want to move.

Because you want to move the entire section of text, you block from the beginning of one heading to the beginning of the next heading to include the blank line after the paragraph.

❷ Select Move (Cut) from the Edit menu.

This cuts, or deletes, the selected block of text from the document. The prompt "Move cursor; press Enter to retrieve" appears on the status line.

❸ Move the mouse pointer to the "S" in "SLOW," the first word of the second heading in the memo and the point where you want to move the block of text, then click the left mouse button.

❹ Select Paste from the Edit menu. The "TEST COUNTS" section now appears before the "SLOW MOVING AND DAMAGED APPAREL" section of the memo. See Figure 3-35.

The Select Command

As you saw in the previous section, you can use the Block command to highlight any unit of text. WordPerfect provides another method, called Select, for highlighting specific units of text. Select, however, allows you to highlight only sentences, paragraphs, and pages, but not other groups of text such as partial sentences or multiple paragraphs. Using Select you can move the cursor to any location within a sentence, paragraph, or page, execute the Select command to highlight the desired unit of text, and then perform the desired operation, such as Move or Delete. This procedure is usually faster than using Block to highlight text.

Deleting a Sentence Using Select

Melissa will use the Select command to delete the unnecessary sentence at the end of the second paragraph in the document, as Susan suggests.

To delete a sentence using the Select command:

❶ Move the cursor anywhere within the sentence "Standard inventory protocols . . ."

With the Select command, you can move the cursor to anywhere in the sentence or to the punctuation mark at the end of the sentence.

❷ Select Sentence from the Select menu of the Edit menu. See Figure 3-36. Alternatively you can press **[Ctrl][F4]** (Move) and select **1** (**S**entence).

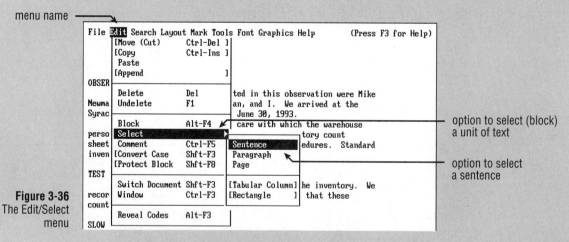

menu name

option to select (block) a unit of text

option to select a sentence

Figure 3-36
The Edit/Select menu

The entire sentence is highlighted, just as if you had used the Block command, and a one-line menu appears at the bottom of the screen. See Figure 3-37.

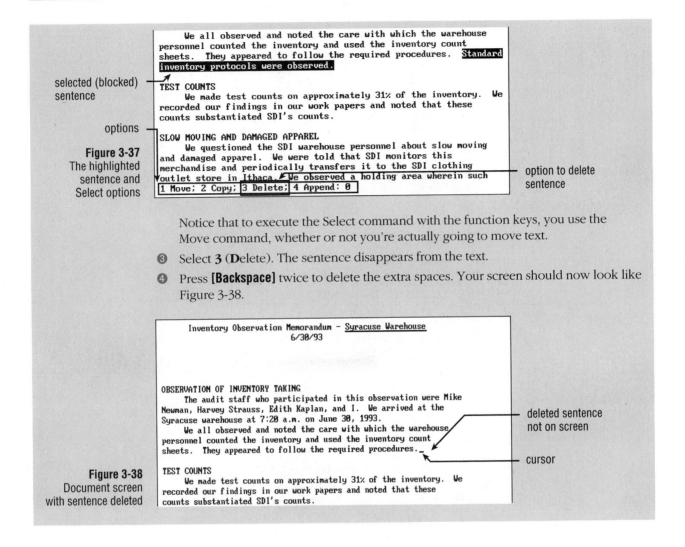

selected (blocked)
sentence

options

Figure 3-37
The highlighted
sentence and
Select options

option to delete
sentence

Notice that to execute the Select command with the function keys, you use the
Move command, whether or not you're actually going to move text.

❸ Select **3** (**D**elete). The sentence disappears from the text.

❹ Press **[Backspace]** twice to delete the extra spaces. Your screen should now look like
Figure 3-38.

deleted sentence
not on screen

cursor

Figure 3-38
Document screen
with sentence deleted

Copying a Paragraph Using Select

You can also use the Move command to copy a sentence, a paragraph, or a page. Although
Melissa has no reason to copy text in her memo, let's copy the second paragraph to the end
of the memo, for illustration purposes only, and then use Select to delete the copy.

To copy a paragraph:

❶ Leave the cursor to the right of the period following "required procedures," or move the cursor anywhere within the second paragraph of the memo.

❷ Select Paragraph from the Select menu of the Edit menu or press **[Ctrl][F4]** (Move) and select **2** (**P**aragraph). The entire paragraph that you want to copy is highlighted. See Figure 3-39.

selected (blocked) paragraph

options

Figure 3-39
The selected paragraph to copy

option to copy paragraph

```
Newman, Harvey Strauss, Edith Kaplan, and I.  We arrived at the
Syracuse warehouse at 7:20 a.m. on June 30, 1993.
     We all observed and noted the care with which the warehouse
personnel counted the inventory and used the inventory count
sheets.  They appeared to follow the required procedures.

TEST COUNTS
     We made test counts on approximately 31% of the inventory.  We
recorded our findings in our work papers and noted that these
counts substantiated SDI's counts.

SLOW MOVING AND DAMAGED APPAREL
     We questioned the SDI warehouse personnel about slow moving
and damaged apparel.  We were told that SDI monitors this
merchandise and periodically transfers it to the SDI clothing
outlet store in Ithaca.  We observed a holding area wherein such
1 Move; 2 Copy; 3 Delete; 4 Append: 0
```

❸ Select **2** (**C**opy). WordPerfect leaves the selected paragraph intact, turns off the highlight, and displays the prompt "Move cursor; press Enter to retrieve" on the status line.

Now you need to move the cursor to the location where you want the second copy of the paragraph.

❹ Move the cursor to the end of the document.

❺ Select Paste from the Edit menu or press **[Enter]** to insert the copy of the paragraph into the text. Press **[Enter]** twice to insert hard returns so that the new copy of the paragraph appears two lines below the preceding paragraph. A copy of the original paragraph appears at this new location in the text. See Figure 3-40.

Figure 3-40
Document screen after paragraph copied

copied paragraph

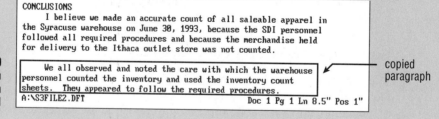

```
CONCLUSIONS
     I believe we made an accurate count of all saleable apparel in
the Syracuse warehouse on June 30, 1993, because the SDI personnel
followed all required procedures and because the merchandise held
for delivery to the Ithaca outlet store was not counted.

     We all observed and noted the care with which the warehouse
personnel counted the inventory and used the inventory count
sheets.  They appeared to follow the required procedures.
A:\S3FILE2.DFT                              Doc 1 Pg 1 Ln 8.5" Pos 1"
```

Deleting a Paragraph with Select

Just as you can delete a sentence using Select, you can also delete a paragraph using Select. To demonstrate this feature, let's delete the paragraph that we just copied to the end of the memo.

To delete a paragraph with Select:

① Make sure the cursor is somewhere in the paragraph beginning "We all observed and noted" at end of the document.

② Select Paragraph from the Select menu of the Edit menu or press **[Ctrl][F4]** (Move) and select **2** (**P**aragraph). The entire paragraph that you want to delete is highlighted. See Figure 3-41.

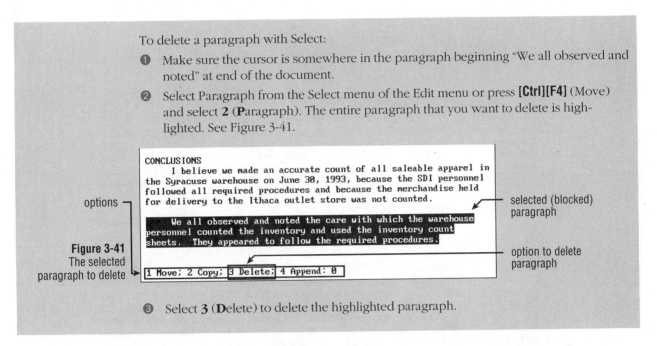

options ⌐

Figure 3-41
The selected
paragraph to delete ➤

selected (blocked)
paragraph

option to delete
paragraph

③ Select **3** (**D**elete) to delete the highlighted paragraph.

The final version of your document should now look similar to Figure 3-42 on the next page.

```
Prepared by:  Melissa Walborksy          Date:  7/5/93
Reviewed by:  Susan Guttmann              Date:  7/9/93
```

Sorority Designs Inc.
Inventory Observation Memorandum – <u>Syracuse Warehouse</u>
6/30/93

OBSERVATION OF INVENTORY TAKING
    The audit staff who participated in this observation were Mike Newman, Harvey Strauss, Edith Kaplan, and I. We arrived at the Syracuse warehouse at 7:20 a.m. on June 30, 1993.
    We all observed and noted the care with which the warehouse personnel counted the inventory and used the inventory count sheets. They appeared to follow the required procedures.

TEST COUNTS
    We made test counts on approximately 31% of the inventory. We recorded our findings in our work papers and noted that these counts substantiated SDI's counts.

SLOW MOVING AND DAMAGED APPAREL
    We questioned the SDI warehouse personnel about slow moving and damaged apparel. We were told that SDI monitors this merchandise and periodically transfers it to the SDI clothing outlet store in Ithaca. We observed a holding area wherein such merchandise is stored until the next shipment to Ithaca. Thus, we did not include the slow moving and damaged apparel in the count.

CUTOFF CONTROLS
    We examined the Receipt Log and the Shipping Log for this warehouse. We noted the merchandise received on June 28, 1993; we also noted that no merchandise was shipped on June 29, 1993. We used the June 28 numbers for our subsequent purchases and sales cutoff tests.

CONCLUSIONS
    I believe we made an accurate count of all saleable apparel in the Syracuse warehouse on June 30, 1993, because the SDI personnel followed all required procedures and because the merchandise held for delivery to the Ithaca outlet store was not counted.

Figure 3-42
The final version of the memo

Select vs. Block

You might not know whether it's better to use Select or Block when you want to modify some existing text. Keep in mind the following information. You can use Select or Block to move, copy, or delete text, but you can use only Block, not Select, to perform other operations such as changing the case, converting from normal text to boldfaced text, or centering the text. Furthermore, Select works only with a clearly defined unit of text — namely, a sentence, a paragraph, or a page — while Block can work with any section of text, such as a word, a phrase, or a group of adjacent paragraphs. Therefore, to move, copy, or delete a sentence, a paragraph, or a page, it would probably be better to use Select. If, on the other hand, you want to do anything else — such as change the case of a phrase or a sentence, delete two adjacent sentences, boldface a paragraph, or copy two adjacent paragraphs — you should use the Block command.

Saving and Printing the Memo

Melissa has completed all the corrections that Susan suggested and can now save and print the finished memo. Melissa should also run the speller before she prints the final copy of her memo. She might also want to use View Document to see how the memo will look on the printed page before she prints it. We'll assume that she's already done these things, and so we won't do them here.

To save and print the memo:

❶ Make sure your data diskette is still in drive A.

❷ Save the document as A:\S3FILE3.MEM.

The .MEM filename extension signifies that this is the final version of the memo. WordPerfect saves the final version of the memo to the diskette.

❸ Make sure your printer is on and ready to print, then print the document.

Exercises

1. What keys(s) would you press to do the following?
   a. Move a phrase flush against the right margin of the page
   b. Center a line of text between the left and the right margins
   c. Search for the first occurrence of the word "payment" in a document
   d. Search for a previous occurrence (that is, earlier in the document than where the cursor is currently located) of the word "audit" in a document

2. Describe an example of when you would use each of the following function-key commands.
    a. [Alt][F4] or [F12] (Block)   c. [Shift][F2] (Search Left)
    b. [Ctrl][F4] (Move)   d. [Alt][F2] (Replace)

3. List five common commands that you can execute with Block on.

4. Describe how you would boldface text as you type it and then describe how you would boldface text that already exists in a document.

5. What happens when you press the following key(s) with Block on? *Hint:* Look at Figure 3-19.
    a. [Ctrl][F2] (Spell)   c. [Del]
    b. [Shift][F3] (Switch), 2 (Lowercase)   d. [F10] (Save)

6. How would you copy a sentence in your document?

7. For which of the following operations would you use the Block command? For which would you use the Select command?
    a. Deleting three adjacent paragraphs of text
    b. Deleting an entire page of text
    c. Deleting a sentence
    d. Copying a paragraph
    e. Copying a page
    f. Copying a phrase

8. Under what conditions could you safely carry out a search and replace operation without confirmation? Under what conditions would you need to carry out search and replace with confirmation?

Tutorial Assignments

For the following Tutorial Assignments, make sure the document screen is clear before you retrieve a document.

Retrieve the file T3FILE1.DFT and do the following:

1. Center the first three lines of text. Do not use the center-justification feature.

2. Without retyping the title, change it to all uppercase letters.

3. Boldface the title.

4. Do a search and replace operation to change all occurrences of "SDI" to "Sorority Designs."

5. Save the document as S3MISSON.DOC.

6. Print the document.

Retrieve the file T3FILE2.DFT and do the following:

7. Use Flush Right to right-justify the date in the top line of the memo.

8. Center the title lines, the two lines under Melissa Walborsky's name.

9. Make the title "Solving the Inventory Reduction Problems" uppercase and bold.

10. Move paragraph number 3 above paragraph number 2, then renumber the paragraphs.

11. Without retyping them, underline the words "surprise" in paragraph 3 and "ink" in paragraph 4.

12. Copy the current paragraph 3 to the end of the document and change its paragraph number to 5.

13. In the new paragraph 5, change "audits of their inventories" to "observations of trash cans and dressing rooms." In the second sentence of paragraph 5, change "audits" to "observations."

14. In paragraph 1, move the second sentence, which begins "These beginning figures," to the end of the paragraph.

15. Save the document as S3INVCON.MEM.

16. Print the document.

Retrieve the file T3FILE3.DFT and do the following:

17. Use [Alt][F2] (Replace) to replace all occurrences of the invisible [Tab] code with the code [→Indent]. *Hint:* In the search and replace operation, press **[Tab]** to create the search string and **[F4]** (Indent) to create the replacement string. You may want to turn on Reveal Codes here, but you can execute the command with Reveals Codes off.

18. Use search and replace with confirmation to change all occurrences of "Ithaca Clothing Outlet Store" to "ICOS" in the body of the report but not in the title.

19. Save the document as S3ICOS.MEM.

20. Print the document.

Case Problems

1. Employee Turnover Memo

Aisha Kadar, the director of human resources for the public accounting firm of Armstrong, Black & Calzone (ABC), sends a report each month to the senior partners to summarize employee turnover. The data on turnover rates, including comparisons with previous periods and with industry averages, appear in a Lotus 1-2-3 spreadsheet that accompanies the memo. The main purpose of this quarter's memo is to summarize and explain a higher than normal employee turnover rate.

Do the following:

1. Retrieve the file P3TRNOVR.DFT.

2. In the first line make the date (including the word "Date") flush against the right margin.

3. Center the two title lines of the memo.

4. Boldface the title line "Employee Turnover Memorandum."

5. Change the three headings (which start "Turnover during," "Reasons for," and "Items to") to all uppercase characters.

6. Use a block move operation to switch around reasons number 2 and 3. Revise the paragraph numbers so they are consecutive.

7. Move the first sentence of the last paragraph to the end of the paragraph.

8. Where such changes wouldn't cause an error in the meaning of the text, carry out a search and replace operation to change all occurrences of "the firm" to "ABC."

9. Carry out a search and replace with confirmation to change the tabs ([Tab] codes) after the numbers in the numbered paragraphs to indents ([→Indent] codes).

10. Save the document as S3TRNOVR.MEM.

11. Print the memo.

2.   Restaurant Review for *Restaurant Happenings*

Gene Marchand is a freelance writer for *Restaurant Happenings*, a weekly magazine published nationally whose audience is restaurant owners and managers. His editor has asked him to write an article on Pizza Now!, a new chain of drive-in pizza franchises. Figure 3-43 shows the first five paragraphs of Gene's rough draft of the article.

Do the following:

1. Clear the document screen and type the header lines, as shown in Figure 3-43, at the beginning of the document. This header is a standard format used by freelance writers.
   a.   On the left type the author's name, address, and phone number.
   b.   Flush right on the first line, type the word count for the article.
   c.   Flush right on the second line, type the rights that the author is offering: "First North American Serial Rights."

2. Type the title in boldface type and centered between the left and the right margins.

3. Type the author's byline centered between the left and right margins.

4. Type the rest of the article as shown in Figure 3-43.

5. Save the article as S3PIZZA.DOC.

6. Print the document.

```
Gene Marchand                          Word Count (approx):  1800
315 Eastern Parkway #921         First North American Serial Rights
Brooklyn, NY 11201
(718) 812-4875



                    Can Food Be Fast and Good?
                      Pizza Now! Says Yes


                         by Gene Marchand




         Phillip Goldman is the founder and CEO of Pizza Now! Inc., a
    franchiser of drive-through fast-food pizza restaurants. He knows
    he has a tough job convincing the public that fast-food pizza can
    taste good, but he's convinced me.
         I'll take that back. He didn't convince me. His pizza did.
         When I drove through one of his Pizza Now! restaurants in
    Pheonix, Arizona, I was in for a pleasant surprise. Not only did I
    get my two slices of pizza and a small tossed salad in less time
    that it takes to get a Big Mac at McDonald's, but I also found the
    pizza to be good tasting. Very good tasting.
         If you like Pizza Hut's, Domino's, or Little Caesar's pizza,
    you'll love Pizza Now!'s pizza.
         So what is Goldman's secret to high quality pizza in record
    time? I recently talked with him at his company headquarters in
    Mesa, just outside of Phoenix. He had some interesting views about
    his franchise business and about his pizza.
```

Figure 3-43

3. Life Success Inc.

Michael Thompson is director of Life Success Inc. This nonprofit organization gives one-day training seminars in major cities across the United States to help high school students improve their self-esteem and to realize their full potential as responsible family members, employees, and citizens. Michael is planning the program for the Life Success seminar to be held March 27, 1993, at the Balboa Park Auditorium in San Diego, California. A copy of his tentative program is shown in Figure 3-44 on the next page.

```
                          Life Success Seminar
                     Balboa Park, San Diego, California
                             March 27, 1993


Welcome . . . . . . . . . . . . . . . . . Michael Thompson
                                     Director, Life Success Inc.

Musical Number . . . . . . . . . . . . . La Jolla Youth Chorus
       "The Wind Beneath My Wings" by Larry Henley and Jeff Silbar
                        Directed by Patricia Wilson

Speaker . . . . . . . . . . . . . . . . Alisha Whiting Robinson
                                   Professor of Sociology, UCSD
                    "Finding Role Models"

Musical Number . . . . . . . . . . . . . La Jolla Youth Chorus
              "From a Distance" by Julie Gold
                     Directed by Patricia Wilson

Introduction of Guest Speaker . . . . . . . . Michael Thompson

Guest Speaker . . . . . . . . . . . . . . . . . . . Bruce Hurst
                             Star Pitcher, San Diego Padres
                   "Living Up to Your Potential"
```

Figure 3-44

Do the following:

1. Clear the document screen and type the three title lines of the program.

2. Center and boldface all of the title lines.

3. Type the first three items in the program. Press **[Alt][F6]** (Flush Right) *twice* after the first item on each line to produce text that is flush right, with dot leaders.

4. To create the fourth item in the program (the second musical number), use a block operation to copy the second item (the first musical number), then edit the song title rather than retype the entire text.

5. Save the document as S3LIFE.DOC.

6. Print the document.

Tutorial 4

Formatting Multiple-Page Documents

Writing a Sales Report

Case: Camino Office Equipment Corporation

Steven Tanaka is a sales representative for the Camino Office Equipment Corporation (COEC), which sells photocopy machines, fax machines, dictaphones, telephone answering equipment, and other high-technology office equipment. At the end of every year, Steven writes a report that summarizes his sales results, compares these results with previous years' sales, and discusses strategies for future sales. Steven is currently working on his 1992 annual sales report.

Planning the Document

Steven wrote his first annual sales report in 1989. At that time he was trained by company personnel on how to write reports, and he read several reports by successful COEC sales representatives. He now plans his annual report throughout the year by filing notes and data on his sales activities and results. At the end of the year, he organizes and analyzes this information and uses the company guidelines for the content, organization, style, and format of his report.

Content

The main contents of Steven's annual report, besides his own notes and observations, are the quarterly sales figures for the current year and the previous two years. He obtains prior-year sales figures from previous annual reports and total annual sales figures from COEC's main office.

OBJECTIVES

In this tutorial you will learn to:

- Change line spacing

- Center a page from top to bottom

- Change tab settings

- Number pages

- Create headers and footers

- Suppress headers, footers, and page numbers

- Create and use styles

- Create tables

- Set Conditional End of Page

- Set Widow/Orphan Protection

Just as important as the data are his interpretations of the data. Steven knows that a good sales report includes analysis and recommendations.

Organization

Steven organizes his report according to company policy, with a title page, an introduction, a presentation and interpretation of the gross sales for the current and the previous two years, an analysis and summary of the year's sales effort, and recommendations for improved sales in the future.

Style

The report follows established standards of style, emphasizing clarity, simplicity, and directness.

Format

In accordance with COEC policy, Steven's report will include a title page, with each line of text centered between the left and the right margins and the entire text centered between the top and the bottom margins. The lines of text in the body of the report will be double-spaced. Every page, except the title page, will include a header and a page number. Tabs at the beginning of each paragraph will be 0.3 inch. Some information will be presented in a table.

Changing the Line Spacing

Steven has already written and edited the body of his report, but he has yet to type the title page and format the report as COEC requires. He marks a copy of his document with the changes he needs to make (Figure 4-1). As he looks over his copy, Steven decides that first he should retrieve the document and double-space the text. Let's change the line spacing in Steven's report.

To change the line spacing:

1. Retrieve the document C4FILE1.DFT from your data diskette in drive A.
2. Make sure the cursor is at the beginning of the document.

Remember that WordPerfect's formatting features take effect from the point in the document where you make the change to the end of the document. If you want to set new line spacing for the entire document, you must move the cursor to the beginning of the document before you change the line spacing.

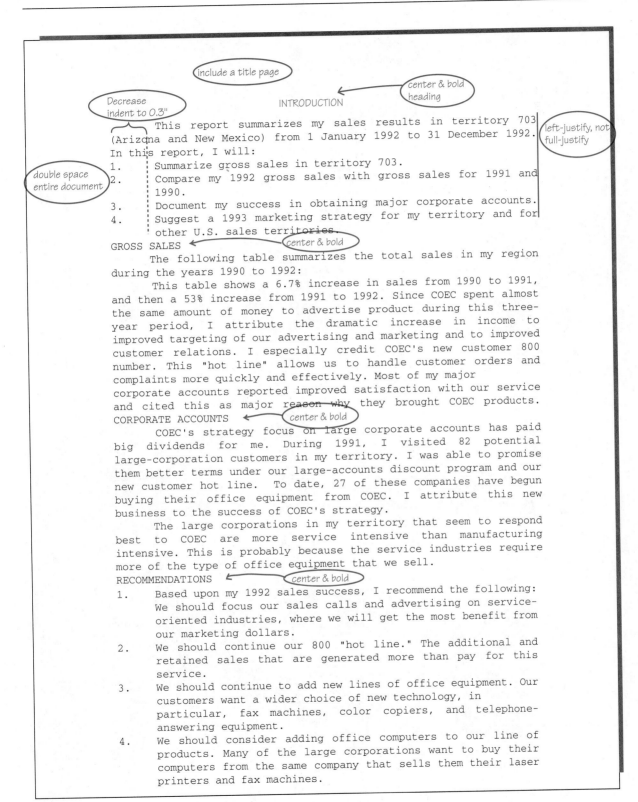

include a title page

center & bold heading

Decrease indent to 0.3"

INTRODUCTION

left-justify, not full-justify

This report summarizes my sales results in territory 703 (Arizona and New Mexico) from 1 January 1992 to 31 December 1992. In this report, I will:

double space entire document

1. Summarize gross sales in territory 703.
2. Compare my 1992 gross sales with gross sales for 1991 and 1990.
3. Document my success in obtaining major corporate accounts.
4. Suggest a 1993 marketing strategy for my territory and for other U.S. sales territories.

GROSS SALES   *center & bold*

The following table summarizes the total sales in my region during the years 1990 to 1992:

This table shows a 6.7% increase in sales from 1990 to 1991, and then a 53% increase from 1991 to 1992. Since COEC spent almost the same amount of money to advertise product during this three-year period, I attribute the dramatic increase in income to improved targeting of our advertising and marketing and to improved customer relations. I especially credit COEC's new customer 800 number. This "hot line" allows us to handle customer orders and complaints more quickly and effectively. Most of my major corporate accounts reported improved satisfaction with our service and cited this as major reason why they brought COEC products.

CORPORATE ACCOUNTS   *center & bold*

COEC's strategy focus on large corporate accounts has paid big dividends for me. During 1991, I visited 82 potential large-corporation customers in my territory. I was able to promise them better terms under our large-accounts discount program and our new customer hot line. To date, 27 of these companies have begun buying their office equipment from COEC. I attribute this new business to the success of COEC's strategy.

The large corporations in my territory that seem to respond best to COEC are more service intensive than manufacturing intensive. This is probably because the service industries require more of the type of office equipment that we sell.

RECOMMENDATIONS   *center & bold*

1. Based upon my 1992 sales success, I recommend the following: We should focus our sales calls and advertising on service-oriented industries, where we will get the most benefit from our marketing dollars.
2. We should continue our 800 "hot line." The additional and retained sales that are generated more than pay for this service.
3. We should continue to add new lines of office equipment. Our customers want a wider choice of new technology, in particular, fax machines, color copiers, and telephone-answering equipment.
4. We should consider adding office computers to our line of products. Many of the large corporations want to buy their computers from the same company that sells them their laser printers and fax machines.

Figure 4-1
The rough draft of Steven's report with his editing marks

③ Select Line from the Layout menu. See Figure 4-2. Alternatively, press **[Shift][F8]** (Format) and select **1** (**Line**).

menu name

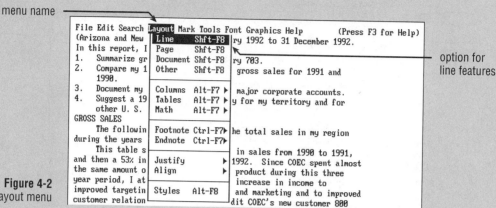

option for
line features

Figure 4-2
The Layout menu

WordPerfect displays the full-screen menu shown in Figure 4-3.

option to change
line spacing

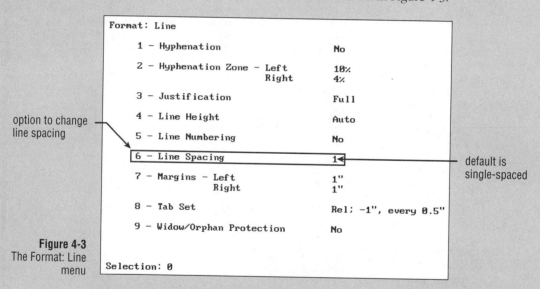

default is
single-spaced

Figure 4-3
The Format: Line
menu

Notice that option 6 is Line Spacing and that to the right of the option is the current line spacing. If you want to make the document double-spaced, you have to change this value from 1 (single spacing) to 2 (double spacing).

④ Select **6** (Line **S**pacing). The cursor moves to the current value of the line spacing.

⑤ Type **2** and press **[Enter]** to set the spacing to 2.

⑥ Press **[F7]** (Exit) to return to the document screen. The text of the report is double-spaced. See Figure 4-4.

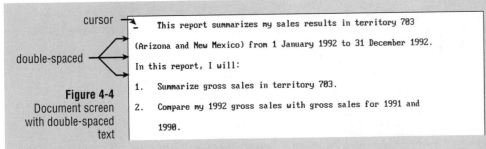

Figure 4-4
Document screen
with double-spaced
text

❼ Turn on Reveal Codes to view WordPerfect's format code for double spacing and then turn off Reveal Codes.

The code for double spacing is [Ln Spacing:2]. This code is a signal to WordPerfect to double-space the text from that point until the end of the document or until the next [Ln Spacing] code.

You can set the line spacing to any value you want, from 0.01 to 255.99 inches. The most common line spacings, however, are 1 for single spacing, 1.5 for one and one-half spacing, 2 for double spacing, and 3 for triple spacing.

Centering a Page Top to Bottom

Steven next decides to create the title page. He will first insert a hard page break at the beginning of the document, instruct WordPerfect to center the lines between the left and the right margins, and then type the title page.

To create the title page:

❶ Make sure the cursor is at the beginning of the document, just to the right of the [Ln Spacing:2] code.

If necessary turn on Reveal Codes to make sure the cursor is in the right place, and then turn off Reveal Codes.

❷ Press **[Ctrl][Enter]** (Hard Page) to force a hard page break.

The hard page break mark appears on the screen, and the status line indicates that the cursor is now on page 2. See Figure 4-5. You have now created a separate page where you'll type the title of the report.

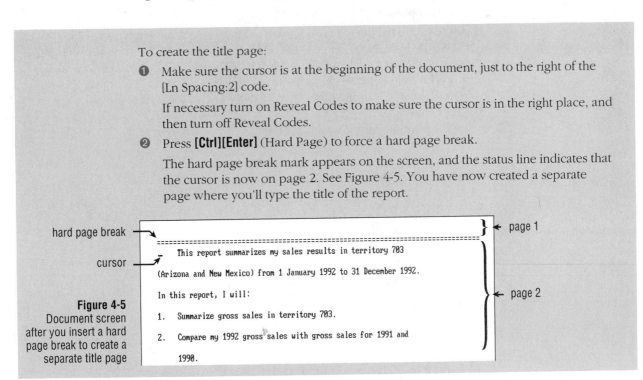

Figure 4-5
Document screen
after you insert a hard
page break to create a
separate title page

❸ Set the document to left justification by selecting Left from the Layout/Justify menu. See Figure 4-6. Alternatively press **[Shift][F8]** (Format); select **1** (**L**ine), **3** (**J**ustification), and **1** (**L**eft); and press **[F7]** (Exit).

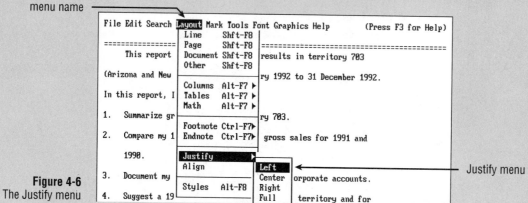

Figure 4-6
The Justify menu

Setting left justification accomplishes two things. First, it sets the body of the report to left justification, which Steven wants. Second, it prevents a problem later on when you set the beginning of the title page to center-justify the title. The problem is that when you set center justification, WordPerfect automatically strips all [Tab] codes from the center-justified text. By setting left justification here, WordPerfect won't center-justify the body of the text when you center-justify the title page.

❹ Move the cursor back to the first page.

❺ Execute the Center Justification command, using the menus or keystrokes similar to those for setting left justification. This causes all the text on the title page (page 1) to be center-justified.

❻ Type the text of the title page, as shown in Figure 4-7. After you type the title ("1992 ANNUAL SALES REPORT") in boldfaced characters, turn off bold and press **[Enter]** four times to insert four blank lines. Then type the next block of text (name, title, territory) and press **[Enter]** five times to insert five more blank lines. Finally insert today's date using WordPerfect's Date Text command. Your screen should look similar to Figure 4-7.

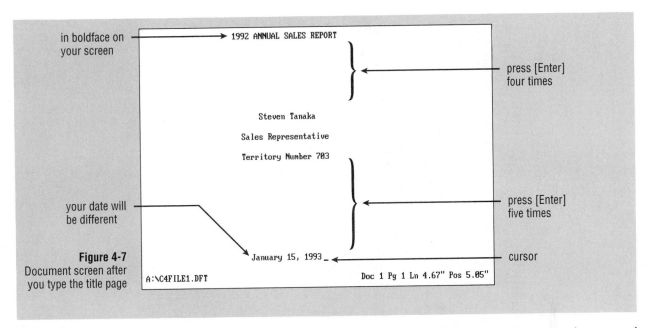

in boldface on your screen

press [Enter] four times

your date will be different

press [Enter] five times

Figure 4-7
Document screen after you type the title page

cursor

1992 ANNUAL SALES REPORT

Steven Tanaka

Sales Representative

Territory Number 703

January 15, 1993

A:\C4FILE1.DFT

Doc 1 Pg 1 Ln 4.67" Pos 5.05"

These steps create the title page, but COEC requires that the text of the page be centered between the top and bottom margins on the page. As you can see from the View Document screen (Figure 4-8), the text of the title page is too high up on the page. You could insert hard returns at the beginning of the page until the text is centered. But WordPerfect provides an easier, more accurate method to center text on a page — a feature called Center Page Top to Bottom. Once Steven sets this feature at the beginning of a page, the text will stay centered between the top and the bottom margins, regardless of how much or how little text is on the page.

Let's center the title page now.

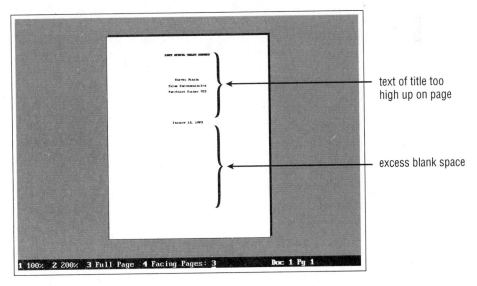

text of title too high up on page

excess blank space

Figure 4-8
View Document screen of title page

1 100%   2 200%   3 Full Page   4 Facing Pages: 3   Doc 1 Pg 1

To center the page top to bottom:

❶ Press **[Home]**, **[Home]**, **[Home]**, **[↑]** to move the cursor to the very beginning of the document, prior to any format codes.

For the Center Page Top to Bottom feature to work, the cursor must be located before any text on the page and before any format code that affects the appearance of the first line of text on the page, such as [HRt], [Tab], or [BOLD]. Pressing [Home] three times prior to pressing [↑] moves the cursor before all text and all codes in the document.

❷ Select Page from the Layout menu or press **[Shift][F8]** (Format) and select **2** (**P**age). The Format: Page menu appears on the screen. See Figure 4-9.

menu name ⟶

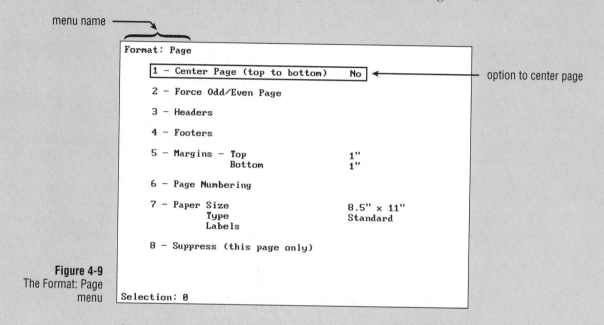

```
Format: Page

        1 - Center Page (top to bottom)     No  ◄──────── option to center page

        2 - Force Odd/Even Page

        3 - Headers

        4 - Footers

        5 - Margins - Top                 1"
                      Bottom              1"

        6 - Page Numbering

        7 - Paper Size                    8.5" x 11"
                      Type                Standard
                      Labels

        8 - Suppress (this page only)


Selection: 0
```

Figure 4-9
The Format: Page
menu

❸ Select **1** (**C**enter Page top to bottom), select "Yes" to verify that you do want to center the page, and press **[F7]** (Exit) to return to the document screen. WordPerfect inserts the [Center Pg] code into your document at the location of the cursor, as you can see if you turn on Reveal Codes. Turn off Reveal Codes before going to Step 4.

❹ Select View Document from the Print/Options menu to see how the page is centered. See Figure 4-10. After you have viewed the document, press **[F7]** (Exit) to return to the document screen.

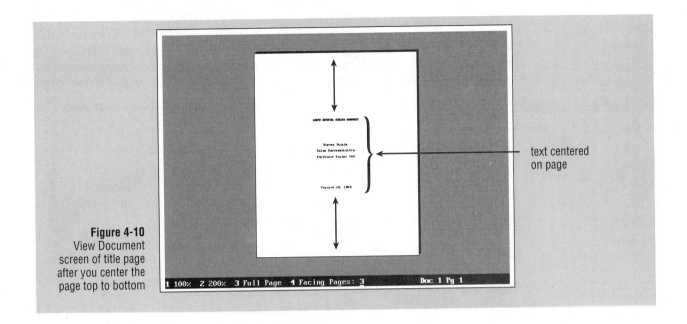

Figure 4-10
View Document
screen of title page
after you center the
page top to bottom

text centered
on page

Changing the Tab Stops

Steven looks over his edited report (Figure 4-1) and decides to next change the amount of indented space at the beginning of each paragraph from 0.5 inch to 0.3 inch, according to COEC requirements.

When Steven wrote the draft of his report, he pressed [Tab] at the beginning of each paragraph. This created a 0.5-inch space at the beginning of each paragraph, because the first tab stop to the right of the left margin was at 0.5 inch. A **tab stop** is a location (usually specified in inches) along each text line to which the cursor will move when you press [Tab] or [Indent] (Figure 4-11). In WordPerfect the default setting of the tab stops is every 0.5 inch from the left margin. With a 1-inch left margin and the cursor located at the left margin (Pos 1", as indicated on the status line), pressing [Tab] will move the cursor and all text to the right of the cursor to the tab stop at Pos 1.5".

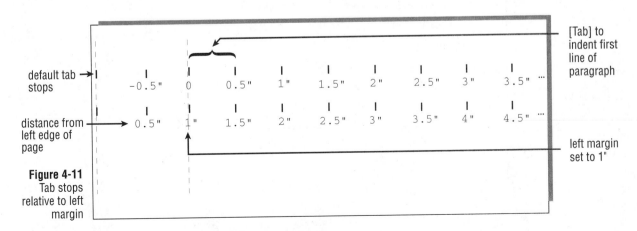

[Tab] to
indent first
line of
paragraph

default tab
stops

distance from
left edge of
page

left margin
set to 1"

Figure 4-11
Tab stops
relative to left
margin

To create the numbered paragraphs, Steven typed a number and a period, which positioned the cursor at about Pos 1.2", and then he pressed [F4] (Indent). This caused the entire paragraph to be indented to the next tab stop at Pos 1.5" (Figure 4-12). The cursor will return to the left margin at Pos 1" after you press [Enter] at the end of the paragraph.

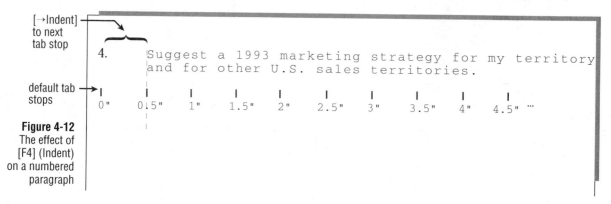

Figure 4-12
The effect of
[F4] (Indent)
on a numbered
paragraph

Because the COEC format calls for the first line of each paragraph to be indented 0.3 inch, Steven has to change the tab stops. Let's first instruct WordPerfect to display the Tab menu, which indicates the location of the current tab stops.

To display the Tab menu:

❶ Make sure the cursor is at the beginning of the document so that the change in location of tab stops will affect the entire document, from beginning to end.

❷ Select Line from the Layout menu or press **[Shift][F8]** (Format) and select **1** (**L**ine). WordPerfect displays the Format: Line menu, as shown in Figure 4-13.

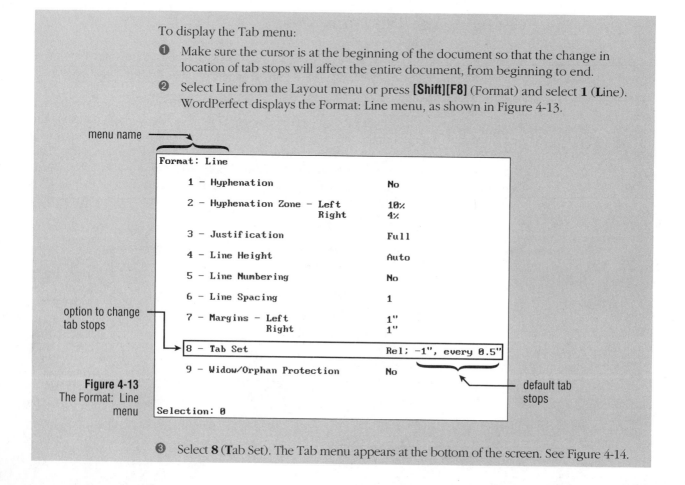

Figure 4-13
The Format: Line
menu

❸ Select **8** (**T**ab Set). The Tab menu appears at the bottom of the screen. See Figure 4-14.

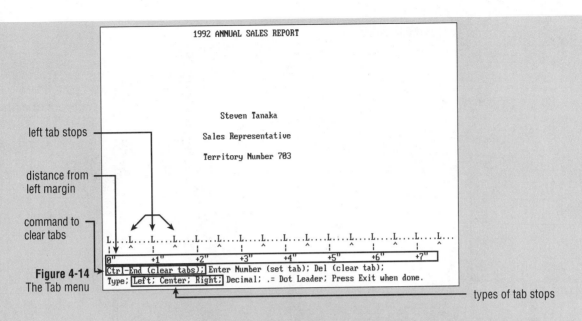

Figure 4-14
The Tab menu

The menu consists of a tab scale, usually labeled in inches, that indicates the location of each tab stop. Each tab stop is marked with the letter L, which stands for left tab stop. A left tab stop allows you to align words and phrases along their left edges, as shown in Figure 4-15, which also demonstrates center and right tabs.

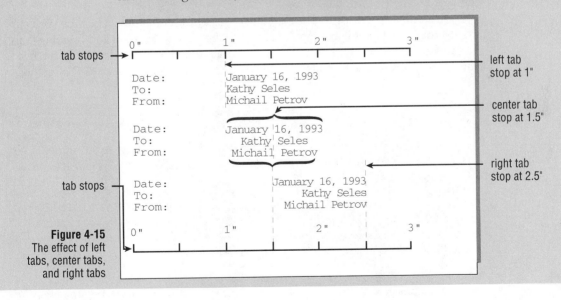

Figure 4-15
The effect of left tabs, center tabs, and right tabs

Next let's clear the current tab stops so we can set new ones.

To clear the tab stops:

❶ Make sure the cursor is located at 0" on the tab scale.

You can use [←] and [→] to move the cursor, or you can type the value (in this case, 0 or zero) and press **[Enter]**, to position the cursor on the tab scale. The 0" means that the cursor is zero inches from the left *margin* of the page, not from the left edge of the page.

❷ Press **[Ctrl][End]** (Del to EOL) to delete the tab stops from the cursor to the end of the line. See Figure 4-16.

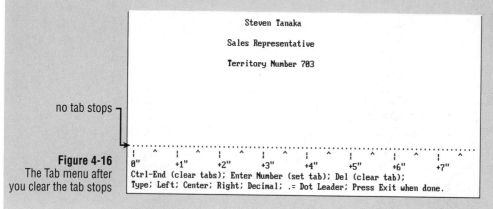

no tab stops

Figure 4-16
The Tab menu after
you clear the tab stops

```
                          Steven Tanaka

                     Sales Representative

                     Territory Number 703




 !    ^   !    ^   !    ^   !    ^   !    ^   !    ^   !    ^   !    ^
 0"    +1"    +2"    +3"    +4"    +5"    +6"    +7"
Ctrl-End (clear tabs); Enter Number (set tab); Del (clear tab);
Type; Left; Center; Right; Decimal; .= Dot Leader; Press Exit when done.
```

With all the old tab stops cleared, you are ready to set the new tab stops. You can set tab stops one at a time by moving the cursor to the desired location and pressing [Tab], or you can set several evenly spaced tabs in one operation. Let's begin by setting a tab stop at 0" and then set evenly spaced tabs, starting at 0.3" and continuing every 0.5" after that.

To set the tab stops:

❶ Press **[Tab]** to set the tab at the current cursor position. In this case the cursor is at 0", so an "L" (for left tab) appears on the tab scale at that location. You can also press L to set a left tab.

A tab stop at 0" is required in case you release the left margin (by pressing [Shift][Tab] (Left Margin Release) so the cursor moves into the left margin); you then can press [Tab] to get back to the left margin. You would need tab stops to the left of 0" if you planned to type text inside the left margin in your document.

Next let's set the evenly spaced tabs. In WordPerfect, to set evenly spaced tabs, you first type the distance from the left margin where you want the tabs to begin, type a comma, and then, without typing a space after the comma, type the spacing between the tabs.

❷ Type **0.3,0.5** and press **[Enter]**.

Be sure to include the 0 (zero) in front of the decimal when you type these numbers. The command **0.3,0.5** tells WordPerfect to set a tab stop at 0.3 inch from the left margin and subsequent tabs at every 0.5 inch from that location. The new tab settings appear on the tab scale. See Figure 4-17.

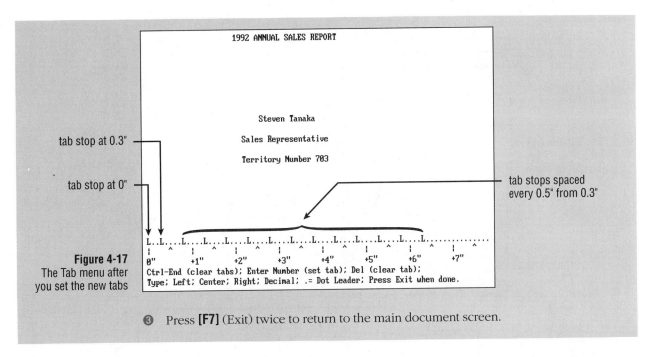

tab stop at 0.3"

tab stop at 0"

tab stops spaced
every 0.5" from 0.3"

❸ Press **[F7]** (Exit) twice to return to the main document screen.

Now scroll down through the body of the document. Notice that the first line of each paragraph is indented 0.3 inch from the left margin rather than 0.5 inch.

Numbering Pages

Since the report is longer than one page, Steven wants to number the pages. He can do this automatically with the Page Numbering feature. The COEC standard format requires that reports have page numbers centered at the bottom of each page.

To set page numbering:

❶ Make sure the cursor is at the beginning of the document before any text and before any code that affects the first line of text. This ensures that page numbering is turned on for the entire document. You may need to turn on Reveal Codes and move the cursor to the right of [Ln Spacing:2] and on [Just:Center].

❷ Select Page from the Layout menu or press **[Shift][F8]** (Format) and select **2** (**P**age). The Format: Page menu appears on the screen.

❸ Select **6** (Page **N**umbering). The Format: Page Numbering menu appears on the screen. See Figure 4-18 on the next page.

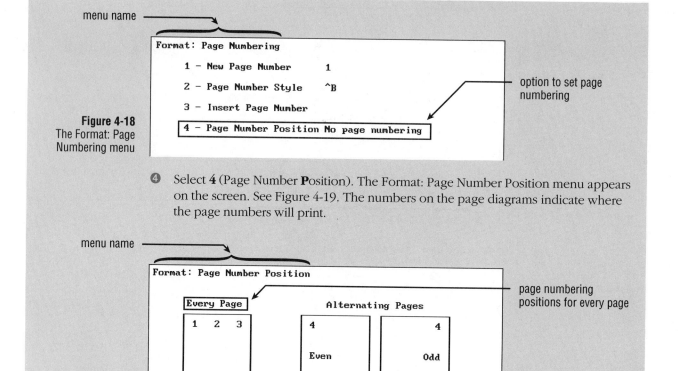

menu name ⟶

Format: Page Numbering

   1 — New Page Number   1

   2 — Page Number Style   ^B

   3 — Insert Page Number

   4 — Page Number Position No page numbering

option to set page numbering

Figure 4-18
The Format: Page Numbering menu

④ Select **4** (Page Number **P**osition). The Format: Page Number Position menu appears on the screen. See Figure 4-19. The numbers on the page diagrams indicate where the page numbers will print.

menu name ⟶

Format: Page Number Position

Every Page   Alternating Pages

1 2 3   4   4

              Even   Odd

5 6 7   8   8

9 — No Page Numbers

page numbering positions for every page

option to set page numbering centered at bottom of page

Figure 4-19
The Format: Page Number Position menu

Remember that Steven wants his page numbers centered at the bottom of each page, so you should select option 6.

⑤ Select **6** and then press **[F7]** (Exit) to return to the document screen.

This instructs WordPerfect to print a page number at the bottom center of every page, below the last line of text and just above the bottom margin. Page numbers do not appear on the document screen.

Creating Headers and Footers

Steven next wants to instruct WordPerfect to print the title of his report and his name at the top of every page. Text printed at the top of each page is called a **header**. Most books have headers on each page to guide the reader. Headers contain, for example, the page number and the name of the book or the chapter name or number. Similarly a **footer** is one or more lines of text printed at the bottom of each page that serve the same purpose as the header.

When you create a header, WordPerfect prints it just below the top margin and then inserts a blank line between the header and the first line of text on the page. Similarly

WordPerfect prints a footer just above the bottom margin and inserts a blank line between the footer and the last line of text on the page.

Let's create a header that includes the name of the report and Steven's full name.

To create a header:

1 Make sure the cursor is still at the beginning of the document before any text or code that affects the first line of text.

2 Invoke the Format: Page menu by selecting Page from the Layout menu or pressing **[Shift][F8]** (Format) and selecting **2** (**P**age).

3 Select **3** (**H**eaders).

WordPerfect lets you define up to two different headers at a time, Header A and Header B. In this report you'll use only one header. In other documents, you might want two headings — one heading, such as the title, on odd-numbered pages, and another heading, such as the author's name, on even-numbered pages.

4 Select **1** (Header **A**). The one-line menu shown in Figure 4-20 appears at the bottom of the screen. You'll use this menu to select the pages on which the report should have headers. This menu also allows you to discontinue any current header or to edit an existing header.

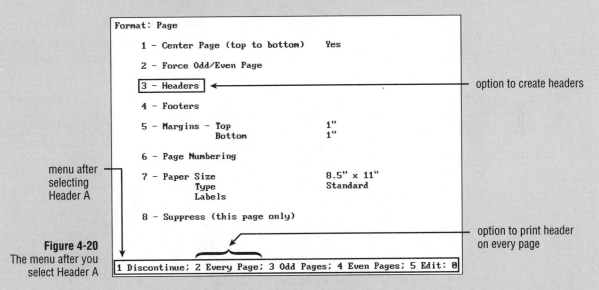

option to create headers

menu after selecting Header A

option to print header on every page

Figure 4-20
The menu after you select Header A

5 Select **2** (Every **P**age). WordPerfect displays the header edit screen.

6 Type **1992 ANNUAL SALES REPORT**, press **[Alt][F6]** (Flush Right), type **Steven Tanaka**, and press **[Enter]**. See Figure 4-21 on the next page. Because WordPerfect automatically inserts one blank line between the header and the body of the page text, pressing [Enter] here inserts an additional blank line after the header.

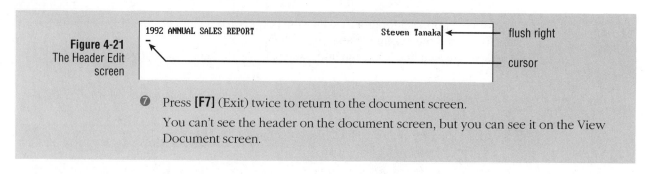

Figure 4-21
The Header Edit
screen

⑦ Press **[F7]** (Exit) twice to return to the document screen.

You can't see the header on the document screen, but you can see it on the View Document screen.

To create a footer, you use the same procedure except that in step 4, you select 4 (Footers) instead of 3 (Headers). To edit a header or a footer, select 5 (Edit) in Step 5.

If you want the page numbers to be part of headers or footers, do *not* set page numbering. Instead, include the page number in the definition of the headers or footers by pressing [Ctrl][B] to insert the ^B code into the text of the header or footer. Then when you print the document, the page numbers will appear where ^B appears in the definition of the header or footer. In his report Steven put page numbering at the bottom of the page, so it won't interfere with the headers.

Suppressing Page Numbering, Headers, and Footers

Steven has inserted the codes for page numbering and a header, but he doesn't want these page features to appear on the title page. To eliminate headers, footers, and page numbering on any particular page, you can use the Page Suppress feature. Let's use this feature now.

To suppress the page numbering and the header on the current page:

① Make sure the cursor is at the beginning of the title page, just after the format code for Header A. Use Reveal Codes to position the cursor properly.

② Invoke the Format: Page menu and select **8** (Su**pp**ress). WordPerfect displays the Format: Suppress (this page only) menu. See Figure 4-22.

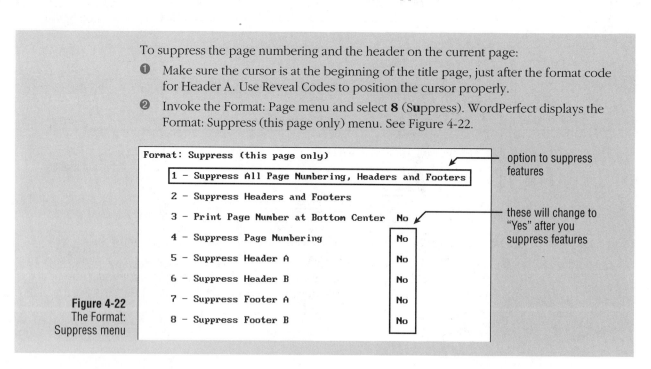

Figure 4-22
The Format:
Suppress menu

❸ Select **1** (**S**uppress All Page Numbering, Headers and Footers). As you do, notice how options 4 through 8 change to indicate "Yes," so that no page numbering, header, or footer will be printed on the current page.

❹ Press **[F7]** (Exit) to return to the document screen.

Now when Steven prints his annual report, no page number or header will appear on the title page.

Setting a New Page Number

Even though a page number won't appear on the title page when Steven prints the report, the title page is still page 1 of the document, and the body of the report begins on page 2. But Steven wants the body of the report to begin on page 1. This requires that he change the page numbering for the document beginning on the page after the title page. Let's use WordPerfect's Page Numbering feature to set a new page number.

To set a new page number:

❶ Move the cursor to the beginning of page 2, so that the cursor is just after the [HPg] code and on the [Just:Left] code. You may have to turn on Reveal Codes to position the cursor properly, and then turn off Reveal Codes.

❷ Invoke the Format: Page menu and select **6** (Page **N**umbering). As before, WordPerfect displays the Format: Page Numbering menu.

❸ Select **1** (**N**ew Page Number). The cursor moves to the right of the New Page Number option, and WordPerfect waits for you to type the new page number.

❹ Type **1** and press **[Enter]**.

❺ Press **[F7]** (Exit) to return to the document screen. WordPerfect inserts the [Pg Num:1] code into the document.

Now when Steven prints the document, the beginning of the body of the report will be page 1, the page after that will be page 2, and so forth.

Viewing and Saving the Document

There is no way of seeing headers, footers, or page numbers on the document screen, but you can see these features on the View Document screen. Let's see how Steven's document looks now.

To view the document:

❶ Make sure the cursor is still on the first page of the body of the report.

❷   Select Print from the File menu or press **[Shift][F7]** (Print) to display the Print/Options menu.

❸   Select **6** (**View** Document), then select **3** (Full Page) so you can see the entire page at once. See Figure 4-23.

header ——

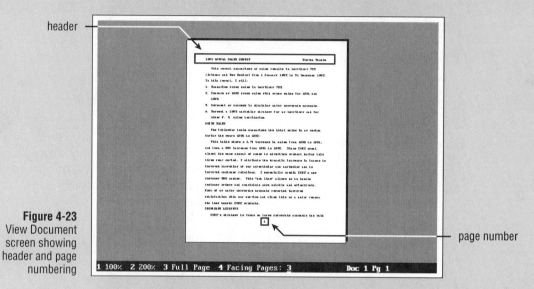

—— page number

Figure 4-23
View Document
screen showing
header and page
numbering

Even though the words are too small to read, you can see the position of the header at the top of the page and the page number at the bottom of the page.

❹   Select **1** (100%) so you can read the header at the top of the page. Then scroll the screen so you can read the page number at the bottom of the page.

❺   Press **[PgDn]** to view a subsequent page of the document or **[PgUp]** to view a previous page of the document.

❻   Press **[F7]** (Exit) when you are ready to return to the main document screen.

Having worked on this version of his report for about 15 minutes, Steven decides to save the document with the changes he's made so far. Let's save the document.

To save the document:

❶   Select Save from the File menu or press **[F10]** (Save).

❷   Type **a:s4file2.dft** and press **[Enter]** to save this draft of the report.

WordPerfect Styles

One of the most powerful features in WordPerfect is the Styles feature. A WordPerfect **style** is a set of format codes or other codes and text that you can apply to words, phrases, paragraphs, or even entire documents to change their appearance or format. Once you define the format codes of a particular style, WordPerfect saves the style as part of the document so you can use the style over and over again to specify a particular format without having to go through the formatting keystrokes each time. For example, Steven wants to use a style in his report to specify the format for section headings within his document. He can create a style that tells WordPerfect to insert an extra blank line just before each heading and to center and boldface the text in the heading.

The advantages of using styles to format titles, headings, and other elements of your document include the following:

- **Efficiency**. Once you specify the format codes within a style, you can use the style in every similar element of the document. For example, when Steven creates the style for the headings in his annual report, he has to set center and bold only once; he can then use that style with all the headings in his document.

- **Flexibility**. If you later decide to change the style, you have to change the style only once, and the format of all the headings throughout the document will automatically change. For example, if Steven decided that he wanted all headings to be underlined instead of boldfaced, he could go through the entire document and change each heading individually. With a style he would have to make the change only once, in the style itself.

- **Consistency**. Without styles you can sometimes forget exactly how you formatted a document element. With styles the same format codes apply to every instance. For example, Steven can be confident that his report will follow the required COEC style and that all headings will have the same format.

Once you understand how to create and use styles, you'll want to create styles for document titles, headings, numbered lists, and other features within your document that require special formatting.

Creating a Style

Steven notices that the headings in his report don't follow the required COEC format. He decides to create a style to format all the headings efficiently and consistently. Let's create the heading style now.

To create a style:

❶ With the cursor anywhere in the document screen, select Styles from the Layout menu or press **[Alt][F8]** (Style). WordPerfect displays the Styles menu. See Figure 4-24. Your Styles menu may already include one or more existing styles.

blank Styles menu

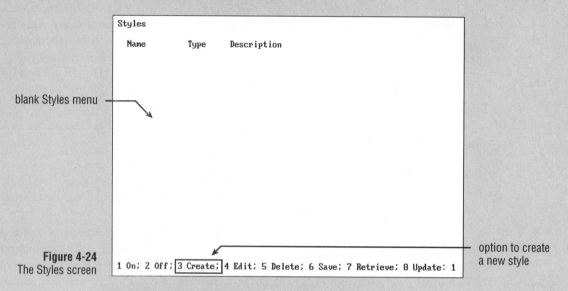

option to create
a new style

Figure 4-24
The Styles screen

Creating a style doesn't insert a code into the document, so the cursor can be anywhere in the document when you define the style.

❷ Select **3** (**C**reate). The Styles: Edit menu, where you create and edit styles, now appears on the screen. See Figure 4-25.

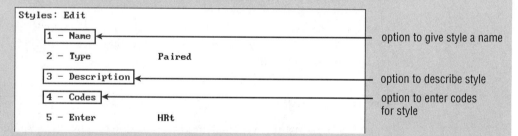

option to give style a name

option to describe style

option to enter codes
for style

Figure 4-25
The Styles: Edit
menu

Next you want to name the style that you're going to create. Let's call the style "Heading."

❸ Select **1** (**N**ame), type **Heading**, and press **[Enter]**.

Notice on the Styles: Edit menu that option 2 is Type. WordPerfect allows three types of styles: paired, open, and outline. "Paired" means that when you turn the style on, the new formatting features begin, and when you turn it off, these features end. "Open" means that when you turn the style on, the new formatting features begin and remain turned on until the end of the document or until the formatting features are changed. "Outline" means that the style is part of outlining or paragraph numbering. Steven wants to keep the Heading style paired, so you won't change the default setting for Type.

Next you'll give the style a description so you can remember the style's purpose.

④ Select **3** (**D**escription), type **Heading of a section of text**, and press **[Enter]**.

You'll next enter the format codes for the Heading style.

⑤ Select **4** (**C**odes) to display the Style Codes screen. See Figure 4-26.

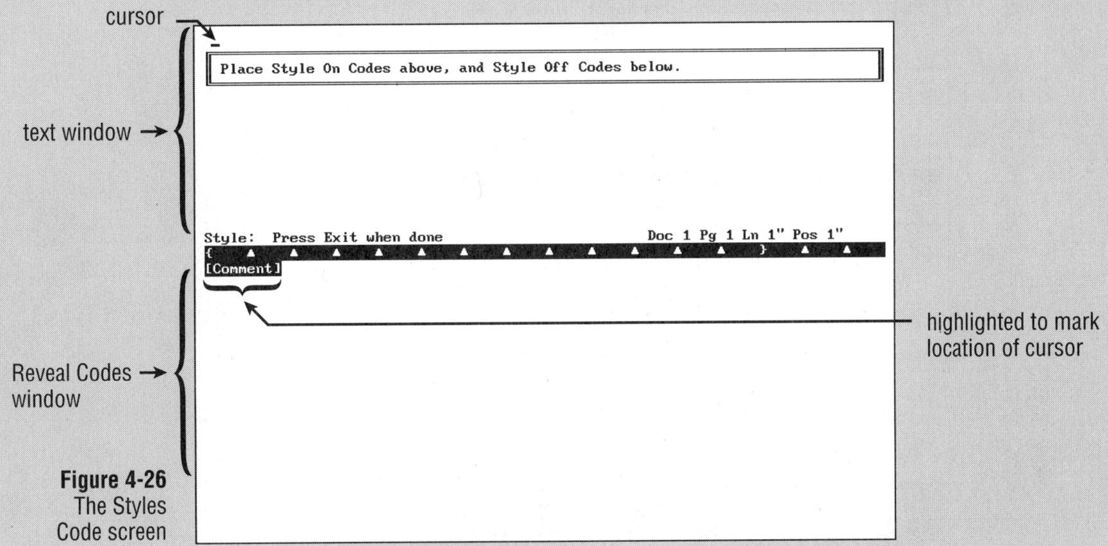

cursor

text window →

Place Style On Codes above, and Style Off Codes below.

Style: Press Exit when done   Doc 1 Pg 1 Ln 1" Pos 1"
[Comment]

Reveal Codes →
window

highlighted to mark
location of cursor

Figure 4-26
The Styles
Code screen

The top half of the Styles Code screen is a text window, where you see any text that you enter as part of the style. The bottom half of the screen is the Reveal Codes window, where you see any format codes that you enter as part of the style. The text window contains a comment box with the message "Place Style On Codes above, and Style Off Codes below." The [Comment] code indicates the location of the comment box in the Reveal Codes window. The purpose of the comment box is to mark the location of the text to which you will apply the style. For example, if you're going to apply the style to your major headings, imagine that the comment box is one of those headings. Any code that precedes the comment box will turn on the specified format or appearance for that heading. Any code that comes after the comment box will turn off the specified format or appearance.

You'll now add the format codes to the codes screen. In the next two steps you'll instruct WordPerfect to insert a blank line, to center the text, and to boldface the text to which the style is applied.

To add format codes to the Styles Code screen:

① Make sure the cursor is above the comment box in the text window. The [Comment] code in the Reveal Codes window should be highlighted.

Now let's instruct WordPerfect to insert a blank line and to center and boldface the text.

② Press **[Enter]**, **[Shift][F6]** (Center), and **[F6]** (Bold). These keystrokes insert the codes [HRt] (hard return), [Center], and [BOLD] before the comment in the Reveal Codes window.

❸ Move the cursor below the comment box in the text window, which is to the right of [Comment] in the Reveal Codes window, and press **[F6]** (Bold). This inserts the code [bold] to turn off bold after the heading. See Figure 4-27.

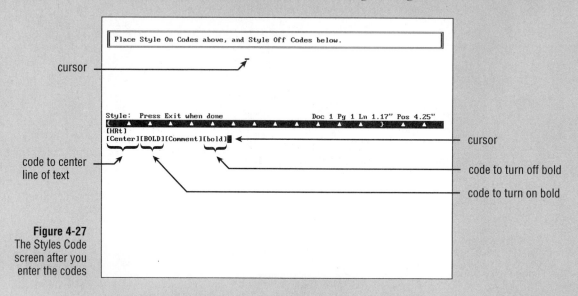

Figure 4-27
The Styles Code
screen after you
enter the codes

You have now inserted the desired codes into the style.

❹ Press **[F7]** (Exit) to exit the Styles Code screen and return to the Styles: Edit screen.

Normally, when you press [Enter] while using a style, WordPerfect inserts a hard return; but in this style, we want to instruct WordPerfect that pressing [Enter] should turn off the style.

❺ Select **5** (**Enter**) and select **2** (**Off**).

❻ Press **[F7]** (Exit) twice to return to the main document screen.

You have finished creating the style named "Heading," which contains the codes that Steven wants for the headings. In the next section you use the style to format the headings in the report.

Using a Style

Steven is now ready to use the Heading style to create a heading for a section of text.

To use the Heading style:

❶ Turn on Reveal Codes and move the cursor to the right of the [Just:Left] code at the beginning of the second page. The cursor should highlight the [Tab] code at the beginning of the first paragraph.

❷ Press **[Enter]** to create a blank line for the heading, then move the cursor back to the blank line. The cursor should be on the [HRt] code.

❸ Select Styles from the Layout menu or press **[Alt][F8]** (Style) to display the Styles menu. The Styles menu displays the name and the description of the Heading style that you just created. See Figure 4-28.

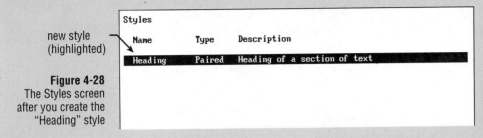

new style
(highlighted)

Figure 4-28
The Styles screen
after you create the
"Heading" style

❹ Make sure "Heading" is highlighted and select **1** (**On**). This turns on the style and returns you to the document screen. Any text that you type will be centered and boldfaced until you turn off the style by pressing [Enter].

❺ Type **INTRODUCTION** and press **[Enter]** to end the style.

You can see how this page of your document will appear by executing the View Document command (Figure 4-29). The first line below the top margin is the header, and four lines below that is the heading, centered and boldfaced. After you have viewed the page, return to the main document screen.

Figure 4-29
The INTRODUCTION
heading formatted
with the Heading style

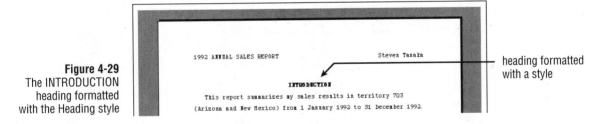

heading formatted
with a style

Using a Style with Existing Text

Steven has already typed the other headings of the report: "GROSS SALES," "CORPORATE ACCOUNTS," and "RECOMMENDATIONS." He can apply his Heading style to these headings without retyping them, just as you can apply WordPerfect's bold feature to a phrase without retyping it.

To use a style with existing text:

❶ Move the cursor to the beginning of the next heading, to the "G" in "GROSS SALES."

To apply a style, you first block the text you want in that style.

❷ Select Block from the Edit menu or press **[Alt][F4]** or **[F12]** (Block).

❸ Press **[End]** to move the cursor to the end of the heading. This blocks (highlights) the heading.

❹ Select Styles from the Layout menu or press **[Alt][F8]** (Style).

⑤ ` Make sure "Heading" is highlighted and select **1** (**On**). This turns on the style at the beginning of the blocked text and turns it off at the end of the blocked text. The heading immediately moves down one line and becomes centered and boldfaced.

⑥ Repeat these steps for the other two headings, "CORPORATE ACCOUNTS" and "RECOMMENDATIONS."

The headings within the report now all have the same format.

WordPerfect Tables

Steven decides to include in his report a table of data that summarizes the gross sales for the previous three years. Before modern word processors were available, typists faced a tedious process when they had to create tables. But with WordPerfect's Tables feature, creating a table is relatively simple. You can specify the number of columns and rows, insert or delete columns and rows, change the width of columns, draw or remove lines between columns and rows, change the format of text and numbers within the table, and perform other tasks to make the table attractive and readable, without having to retype the table's data.

Creating a Table

Steven will use the Tables feature to produce a table of his annual sales (Figure 4-30). Let's make this table now as part of the report.

TERRITORY 703 GROSS SALES (in dollars)					
Year	Qtr. 1	Qtr. 2	Qtr. 3	Qtr. 4	TOTAL
1990	542,197	591,287	588,841	498,276	2,220,601
1991	562,422	681,647	584,892	540,699	2,369,660
1992	891,322	904,498	896,217	934,228	3,626,265

Figure 4-30
Data table for
Steven's report

To create a table:

❶ Move the cursor to the end of the first line of the section "GROSS SALES," just after the colon at the end of the phrase "during the years 1990 to 1992." This moves the cursor to the location in the document where you want the table to appear.

❷ Press **[Enter]** to insert a line between the text and the table. See Figure 4-31.

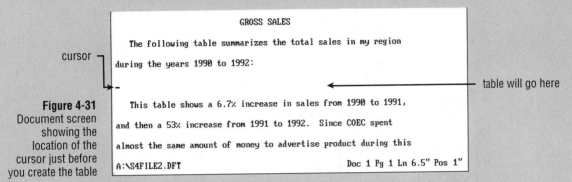

cursor

table will go here

Figure 4-31
Document screen
showing the
location of the
cursor just before
you create the table

❸ Select Create from the Tables menu of the Layout menu. See Figure 4-32. Alternatively press **[Alt][F7]** (Columns/Tables), select **2** (**T**ables), then **1** (**C**reate).

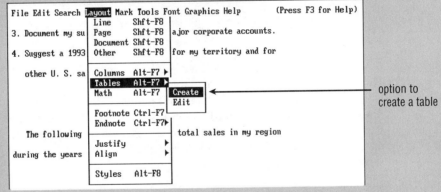

option to
create a table

Figure 4-32
The Tables menu

WordPerfect prompts you for the number of columns in the table. Steven's table has six columns.

❹ Type **6** and press **[Enter]**.

WordPerfect prompts you for the number of rows in the table. Steven's table has five rows.

⑤ Type **5** and press **[Enter]**. The Table Edit menu appears on the screen, with the table cursor in cell A1. See Figure 4-33. This menu allows you to create new tables and edit existing tables.

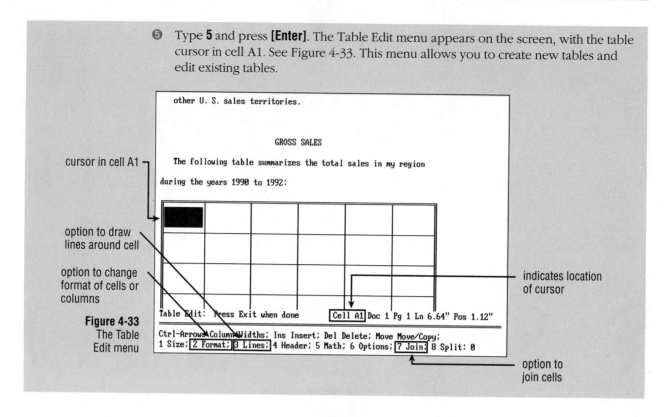

Figure 4-33
The Table
Edit menu

In a WordPerfect table, a **cell** is a single box into which you can type a number or text. To identify a specific cell within a table, WordPerfect assigns letters to the columns of the table, with the first column on the far left named column "A," the next column "B," and so on in alphabetical order. WordPerfect numbers the rows of a table from top to bottom, starting with row 1. Each cell, therefore, is designated by a letter and a number. The cell in the upper left corner is A1; the cell to its right is B1; the cell below A1 is A2; and so forth, as shown in Figure 4-34.

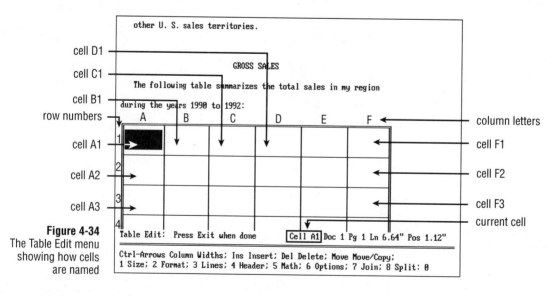

Figure 4-34
The Table Edit menu
showing how cells
are named

While the Table Edit menu is active, you can move the cursor from cell to cell by using the arrow keys ([→], [←], [↑], [↓]), [Tab] (to move right), or [Shift][Tab] (to move left). You can use [End] to move to the far right column and [Home], [←] to move to the far left column. Practice using these cursor-movement keys to move the cursor around the table.

Formatting a Table

Steven realizes that he'll have to modify the format of his table to make it attractive and readable. First he'll join the cells in the top row into one large cell so it can contain the title of the table, as shown in Figure 4-30.

To join cells in a table:

❶ Make sure the cursor is in cell A1, the first cell in the group of cells we want to join.

❷ Press **[Alt][F4]** or **[F12]** (Block) and **[End]** to highlight the top row of cells.

You can't use the pull-down menus to turn Block on while the Table Edit menu is active. If you accidentally press the right mouse button, WordPerfect will exit the Tables menu. To return to the Tables menu, make sure the cursor is in one of the table cells and press **[Alt][F7]** (Columns/Tables).

❸ Select **7** (**J**oin) to display the prompt "Join cells?" See Figure 4-35.

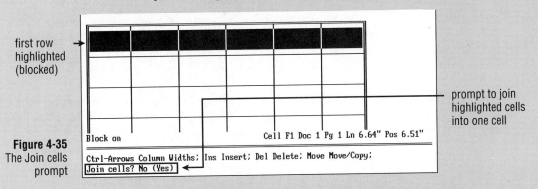

first row
highlighted
(blocked)

prompt to join
highlighted cells
into one cell

Block on   Cell F1 Doc 1 Pg 1 Ln 6.64" Pos 6.51"

Figure 4-35
The Join cells
prompt

Ctrl-Arrows Column Widths; Ins Insert; Del Delete; Move Move/Copy;
Join cells? No (Yes)

❹ Select "Yes" to join the top row of cells into one cell. The top row is now a single cell in which you can type the title of the table.

Next Steven decides to draw double lines under the top row to separate the title from the rest of the table.

To draw a double line under a cell:

❶ Make sure the cursor is still in cell A1.

❷ Select **3** (**L**ines), **4** (**B**ottom), and **3** (**D**ouble) to draw a double line at the bottom of the top cell.

Steven next wants to draw a double line below each cell of row 2. As shown in Figure 4-30, these double lines will separate the column labels from the data in the columns.

To draw a double line under a row of cells:

❶ Move the cursor to cell A2.

❷ Press **[Alt][F4]** or **[F12]** (Block) and **[End]** to highlight the second row, then use the same keystrokes given in the previous Steps to draw a double line across the bottom of this row.

Next Steven decides that the labels and the numbers in the columns should be right-justified, that is, aligned flush against the right side of the cells. Let's change the format of the columns to be right-justified.

To right-justify text in columns of cells:

❶ Move the cursor back to cell A2.

❷ Block the entire row of cells as you did before.

❸ Press **2** (Format), **2** (Column), **3** (Justify), and **3** (**R**ight) to set right justification for all the columns of the table. Any text that you type into the table will be flush right in the cells. Notice how the cursor now appears in the upper right corner of cell F2.

Having set all the columns to right justification, Steven realizes that he wants the title, in cell A1, to be centered between the left and the right edges of the table, as shown in Figure 4-30. Let's set center justification for cell A1.

To center-justify a cell:

❶ Move the cursor to cell A1.

❷ Press **2** (Format), **1** (**C**ell), **3** (Justify), and **2** (**C**enter) so any text typed in that cell will be centered.

By changing only this cell to center justification, the other cells stay set to right justification.

Steven now wants to decrease the width of column A, the Year column. The key combination to decrease the width of a column is [Ctrl][←]. Let's decrease the column width now.

To decrease the width of a column:

❶ Move the cursor to cell A2 to position the cursor in the column whose width you want to change.

❷ Press **[Ctrl][←]** twice to decrease the width of the column.

Steven now wants to increase the width of column F, the Totals column. This column has to be wider to accommodate the larger numbers of the totals. The key combination to increase the width of a column is [Ctrl][→]. Let's increase the column width now.

To increase the width of a column:

❶ Move the cursor to cell F2.

❷ Press **[Ctrl][→]** twice to increase the width of the column.

Now that he has completed the format changes of the table, Steven can exit the Table Edit menu, return to the document screen, and enter the text and data into the tables.

To exit the Table Edit menu:

❶ Press **[F7]** (Exit) to exit the Table Edit menu and to return to the document screen.

Your screen should now look similar to Figure 4-36. You can't change the format of the table when the cursor is in the document screen. You can only enter, edit, or delete information in the cells of the table.

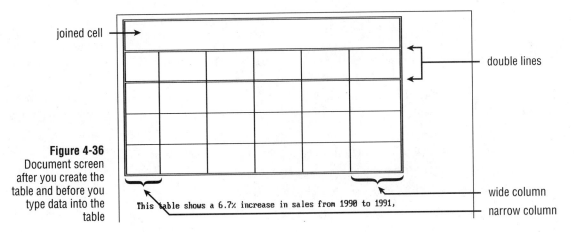

Figure 4-36
Document screen after you create the table and before you type data into the table

joined cell

double lines

wide column

narrow column

This table shows a 6.7% increase in sales from 1990 to 1991,

Entering Labels and Data into the Table

Having created and formatted the table, Steven is now ready to enter data into the table. Entering data is not difficult, since you can use most of the standard WordPerfect cursor-movement keys and deletion keys. Besides those keys, you can use [Tab] to move the cursor to the right one cell (without inserting a [Tab] code) and [Shift][Tab] moves the cursor to the left one cell. Let's enter the labels and the data into the table now.

To enter data into the table:

❶ Move the cursor to cell A1 and type the title of the table as shown in Figure 4-30.

❷ Type the data into the other cells of the table as shown in Figure 4-30.

Your screen should now look like Figure 4-37.

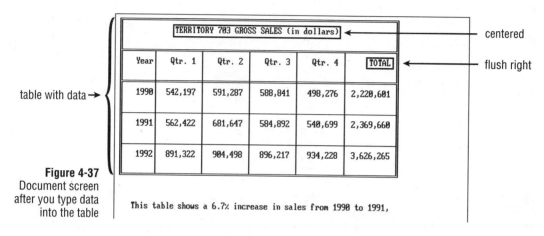

table with data →

centered

flush right

Figure 4-37
Document screen
after you type data
into the table

Editing the Table Format

After completing the table, Steven decides that the "TOTAL" label in column F should be centered in the column rather than right-justified. Thus, he needs to edit the table.

To edit the table:

❶ Move the cursor anywhere within the table. The current-cell designation (letter and number) appears on the status line.

❷ Press **[Alt][F7]** (Columns/Tables). The Table Edit menu appears on the screen. You can now select any of the options in the menu.

❸ Move the cursor to cell F2.

❹ Press **2** (Format), **1** (Cell), **3** (Justify), and **2** (Center).

The text ("TOTAL") becomes centered in the cell.

❺ Press **[F7]** (Exit) to return to the document screen.

You have now completed the table. Your screen should look like Figure 4-38.

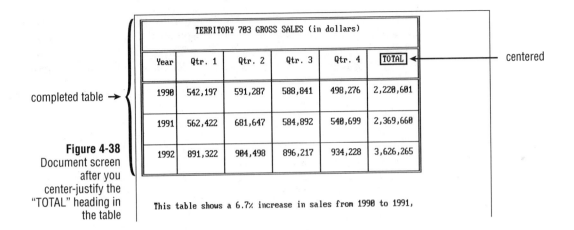

completed table →

Figure 4-38
Document screen
after you
center-justify the
"TOTAL" heading in
the table

centered

Setting a Conditional End of Page

After he has created the table, Steven looks over the document and notices a serious formatting problem: the heading "RECOMMENDATIONS" is isolated at the bottom of page 2 (Figure 4-39). (Because of differences in type size among printers, your document might not have the heading isolated at the bottom of the page. Do the steps in this section anyway.)

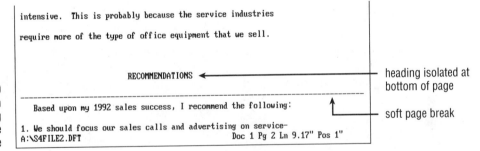

Figure 4-39
Document screen
with a heading
isolated at the
bottom of the page

heading isolated at
bottom of page

soft page break

One solution to the problem would be to press [Ctrl][Enter] (Hard Page) to insert a hard page break just before the heading. The drawback of this solution is that if Steven later adds or removes text anywhere before the hard page break, the location of the page break probably would be unacceptable. For example, if Steven adds three or four lines on page 2, one or two of the lines would spill over to page 3, the rest of page 3 would be blank, and "RECOMMENDATIONS" would start on page 4, as shown in Figure 4-40.

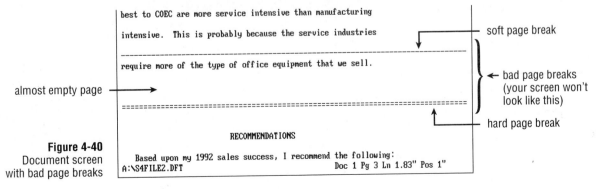

almost empty page →

Figure 4-40
Document screen
with bad page breaks

soft page break

bad page breaks
(your screen won't
look like this)

hard page break

A better solution would be to use WordPerfect's Conditional End of Page feature. Conditional End of Page is a command that allows you to specify the number of lines of text that should be kept together on one page. For example, if you specify that six lines of text should be kept together, WordPerfect inserts a soft page break if the six lines would otherwise be split between two pages (Figure 4-41).

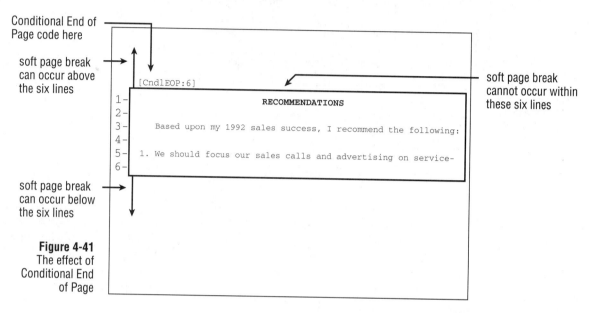

Conditional End of
Page code here

soft page break
can occur above
the six lines

soft page break
cannot occur within
these six lines

[CndlEOP:6]

RECOMMENDATIONS

Based upon my 1992 sales success, I recommend the following:

1. We should focus our sales calls and advertising on service-

soft page break
can occur below
the six lines

Figure 4-41
The effect of
Conditional End
of Page

Steven decides to use the Conditional End of Page code above the "RECOMMENDATIONS" heading. That way, regardless of any changes he makes to the document, the heading will never be isolated at the bottom of a page.

To set Conditional End of Page:

❶ Move the cursor on the blank line below the paragraph that ends "office equipment that we sell" and above the heading "RECOMMENDATIONS."

When you specify Conditional End of Page, move the cursor to the line *above* the text that you want kept together.

❷ Select Other from the Layout menu or press **[Shift][F8]** (Format) and select **4** (**Other**) to display the Format: Other menu. See Figure 4-42.

menu name

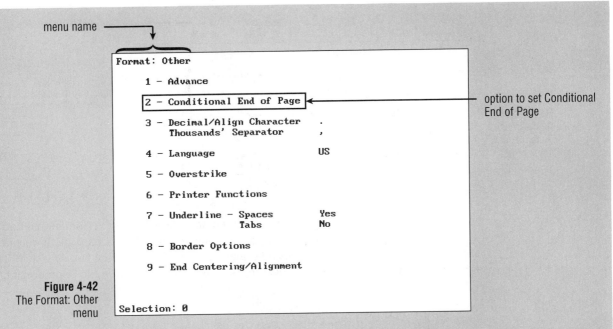

option to set Conditional End of Page

Figure 4-42
The Format: Other menu

❸ Select **2** (**C**onditional End of Page). A prompt asks you for the number of lines that you want kept together. See Figure 4-43.

Figure 4-43
The prompt after you select Conditional End of Page

prompt after selecting Conditional End of Page

The number of lines requested includes the blank lines in double-spaced text. So if you want the heading and the first two lines of text in the paragraph under the heading to be kept together, you should specify six (three lines of double-spaced text) as the number of lines to keep together.

❹ Type **6** and press **[Enter]**.

❺ Press **[F7]** (Exit) to exit the Format: Other menu and return to the document screen. WordPerfect has inserted the format code [Cndl EOP:6], which you can see by turning on Reveal Codes.

❻ Rewrite the screen by pressing **[Ctrl][F3]** (Screen) and selecting **3** (**R**ewrite). WordPerfect inserts a soft page break above the heading so that the heading is on page 3. See Figure 4-44 on the next page.

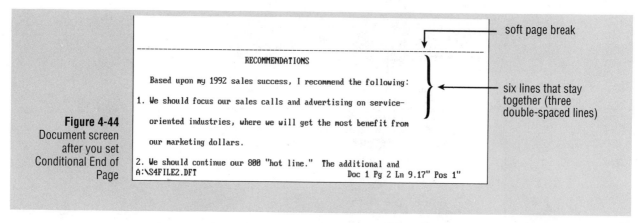

Figure 4-44
Document screen
after you set
Conditional End of
Page

soft page break

six lines that stay
together (three
double-spaced lines)

Steven realizes that every heading in the document should have the Conditional End of Page command, so that no heading ever gets isolated at the bottom of a page. It occurs to Steven that he really should put the Conditional End of Page code in the Heading style. The code would then take effect at every heading automatically. Let's insert the Conditional End of Page code into the Heading style.

To set Conditional End of Page in the style:

❶ Select Styles from the Layout menu or press **[Alt][F8]** (Style) to display the Styles screen.

❷ With "Heading" highlighted, select **4** (**E**dit) and **4** (**C**odes), so you can edit the "Heading" style in the codes screen.

❸ With the cursor at the beginning of the style codes, select Other from the Layout menu or press **[Shift][F8]** (Format) and select **4** (**O**ther) to display the Format: Other menu.

❹ Select **2** (**C**onditional End of Page), type **6**, and press **[Enter]**, and press **[F7]** (Exit). The code [Cndl EOP:6] appears in the style.

❺ Press **[F7]** (Exit) until you return to the main document screen.

With Conditional End of Page in the heading style, you don't need the code that you inserted above the "RECOMMENDATIONS" heading, although the extra code won't hurt anything. (If you like, you can turn on Reveal Codes and delete the [Cndl EOP:6] code above "RECOMMENDATIONS.") Because the code is in the Heading style, everywhere the style is applied, six lines of text after the start of the style will move as one inseparable block of text.

Setting Widow/Orphan Protection

Steven now notices another formatting problem: underneath the table at the bottom of page 1 is a single line of text isolated from the rest of its paragraph. Because of differences in type sizes, your document might not have this line under the table at the bottom of page 1. This is called an **orphan** — the first line of a paragraph appearing alone at the bottom of a page. Similarly a **widow** is the last line of a paragraph appearing alone at the top of a page. Widows and orphans detract from the appearance and readability of a document. Fortunately you can solve the problem of widows and orphans by using WordPerfect's Widow/Orphan Protection. Let's set widow/orphan protection in Steven's report.

To set widow/orphan protection:

❶ Move the cursor to the beginning of the document before any text.

❷ Select Line from the Layout menu or press **[Shift][F8]** (Format) and select **1** (**L**ine). The Format: Line menu appears on the screen.

❸ Select **9** (**W**idow/Orphan Protection). WordPerfect displays the prompt shown in Figure 4-45.

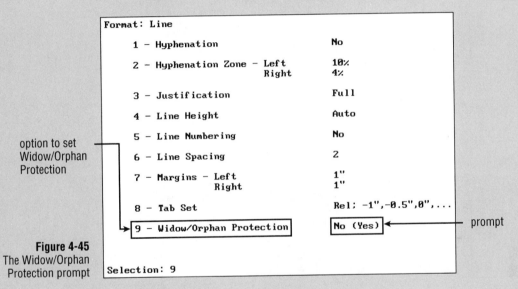

option to set Widow/Orphan Protection

Figure 4-45
The Widow/Orphan Protection prompt

prompt

```
Format: Line

     1 - Hyphenation                    No

     2 - Hyphenation Zone - Left        10%
                           Right        4%

     3 - Justification                  Full

     4 - Line Height                    Auto

     5 - Line Numbering                 No

     6 - Line Spacing                   2

     7 - Margins - Left                 1"
                   Right                1"

     8 - Tab Set                        Rel; -1",-0.5",0",...

     9 - Widow/Orphan Protection        No (Yes)

Selection: 9
```

❹ Select "Yes" to verify that you do want Widow/Orphan protection turned on.

❺ Press **[F7]** (Exit) to return to the document screen. WordPerfect inserts the code [W/O On] into the document.

Now move the cursor to the bottom of page 1 and then to the top of page 2. If there was an orphan before, the orphan is gone. The first line of the paragraph has moved below the soft page break, to page 2.

Saving and Printing the Report

Save Steven's report as S4FILE3.REP, view the document, and then print the report. Your final copy of the report should look like Figure 4-46 on the following pages.

1992 ANNUAL SALES REPORT

Steven Tanaka
Sales Representative
Territory Number 703

January 15, 1993

1992 ANNUAL SALES REPORT   Steven Tanaka

INTRODUCTION

This report summarizes my sales results in territory 703 (Arizona and New Mexico) from 1 January 1992 to 31 December 1992. In this report, I will:

1. Summarize gross sales in territory 703.
2. Compare my 1992 gross sales with gross sales for 1991 and 1990.
3. Document my success in obtaining major corporate accounts.
4. Suggest a 1993 marketing strategy for my territory and for other U. S. sales territories.

GROSS SALES

The following table summarizes the total sales in my region during the years 1990 to 1992:

TERRITORY 703 GROSS SALES (in dollars)					
Year	Qtr. 1	Qtr. 2	Qtr. 3	Qtr. 4	TOTAL
1990	542,197	591,287	588,841	498,276	2,220,601
1991	562,422	681,647	584,892	540,699	2,369,660
1992	891,322	904,498	896,217	934,228	3,626,265

1

Figure 4-46
The final version of
Steven's annual
sales report

1992 ANNUAL SALES REPORT   Steven Tanaka

This table shows a 6.7% increase in sales from 1990 to 1991, and then a 53% increase from 1991 to 1992. Since COEC spent almost the same amount of money to advertise product during this three year period, I attribute the dramatic increase in income to improved targeting of our advertising and marketing and to improved customer relations. I especially credit COEC's new customer 800 number. This "hot line" allows us to handle customer orders and complaints more quickly and effectively. Most of my major corporate accounts reported improved satisfaction with our service and cited this as a major reason why they bought COEC products.

CORPORATE ACCOUNTS

COEC's strategy to focus on large corporate accounts has paid big dividends for me. During 1991, I visited 82 potential large-corporation customers in my territory. I was able to promise them better terms under our large-accounts discount program and our new customer hot line. To date, twenty-seven of these companies have begun buying their office equipment from COEC. I attribute this new business to the success of COEC's strategy.

The large corporations in my territory that seem to respond best to COEC are more service intensive than manufacturing intensive. This is probably because the service industries require more of the type of office equipment that we sell.

2

1992 ANNUAL SALES REPORT   Steven Tanaka

RECOMMENDATIONS

Based upon my 1992 sales success, I recommend the following:

1. We should focus our sales calls and advertising on service-oriented industries, where we will get the most benefit from our marketing dollars.

2. We should continue our 800 "hot line." The additional and retained sales that are generated more than pay for this service.

3. We should continue to add new lines of office equipment. Our customers want a wider choice of new technology, in particular, fax machines, color copiers, and telephone-answering equipment.

4. We should consider adding office computers to our line of products. Many of the large corporations want to buy their computers from the same company that sells them their laser printers and fax machines.

3

Figure 4-46
(continued)

■   ■   ■

Exercises

1. Define or describe the following terms:
    a. line spacing   d. header
    b. style (for formatting) e. footer
    c. page numbering

2. How would you create a header that prints your name in the upper left corner of every page?

3. How would you create a footer that prints your name in the lower right corner of every page?

4. Why would you use each of the following features?
    a. Conditional End of Page   d. Tables
    b. Widow/Orphan Protection   e. Suppress (this page only)
    c. Line Spacing   f. Style

5. What are the advantages of using a WordPerfect style to format the headings in your documents?

6. How would you set tabs every one-fourth inch from the left margin of a document?

7. When you use WordPerfect's Tables feature to create or edit a table, how would you do each of the following?
    a. Draw double lines at the bottom of a cell
    b. Set the alignment (justification) to Center
    c. Create a single horizontal box that spans the entire width of the table

Tutorial Assignments

Retrieve the file T4FILE1.DFT from the data diskette and do the following:

1. Center the title page between the top and the bottom margins.

2. Change the line spacing to triple spacing.

3. Number all the pages of the document in the top right corner of each page.

4. Suppress page numbering on the title page.

5. Change the tabs from 0.5-inch intervals to 0.3-inch intervals (from the left margin).

6. Save the file as S4FILE1.DOC and print it.

Retrieve the file T4FILE2.DFT from the data diskette and do the following:

7. Create a header that prints your name in the upper left corner of each page and prints the page number in the upper right corner of the page. *Hint:* Within a header, press [Ctrl][B] to insert the code ^B for page numbers.

8. Create a style that centers a title page top to bottom, centers the lines of the title between the left and the right margins, and suppresses page numbering and your

header. Then use the style to create a title page with the title "Preparing for Sales Calls," your name, and the current date.

9. Create a style that formats the headings. Each heading should include a Conditional End of Page code (with six lines kept together) and a blank line. The text of the heading should be underlined and centered. Apply this style to the three headings in the document.

10. Save the file as S4FILE2.DOC and print it.

Clear the document screen and do the following:

11. Create an empty table that has four columns and six rows.

12. Make the top row of cells into one cell, change its justification to center, and type the heading **New Clients in Territory 703**.

13. In the second row of cells type the following headings (one heading per cell): **Company Name**, **Purchasing Agent**, **Phone Number**, and **City**. Adjust the widths of the cells so that each heading fits neatly on one line within the cell.

14. In the other four rows of the table type the data in Figure 4-47.

Figure 4-47

Kaibab Construction Co., Matt Bringhurst, (602) 834-1763, Tucson
Sandia Electronics Corp., Megan Tartakov, (602) 418-8930, Mesa
Santa Fe Travel, Inc., Bertha Lopez, (505) 128-4747, Santa Fe
White Sands Manufacturing Corp., Carl Wilson, (505) 311-4800, Las Cruces

15. Adjust the width of the columns so that the information fits neatly in each cell.

16. Save the file as S4FILE3.TAB and print it.

Case Problems

1. Report on Computer Use in a Law Firm

Laura Eisel is the office manager for Orehoski, Donaldson & McAllister, Attorneys at Law, a large law firm headquartered in Seattle. When Laura joined the firm 18 months ago, she began updating the office computer system with IBM-compatible machines networked together using Novell NetWare. Now after the office has used the updated system for a full year, she has been asked to write a report to the senior partners of the firm on how the computer system has affected the firm and to make recommendations on updating the computer system at the firm's Portland, Oregon, office.

Do the following:

1. Retrieve the body of Laura's report (P4LAWCOM.REP) from the data diskette.

2. Change the line spacing to double spacing.

3. Prepare a title page for the document as follows:
   a. The title is "PCs in the Law Office."
   b. The subtitle is "Report on the New Computer System at Orehoski, Donaldson & McAllister."
   c. The author is Laura Eisel.
   d. The date is the current date.
   e. Format this title page to improve its appearance.

4. Add page numbering to the document, so that WordPerfect prints the page number in the lower right corner of every page except the title page.

5. Include a header that prints on every page except the title page. On the left margin of the header, insert "REPORT ON COMPUTER USE" and insert the author's name flush right on the same line.

6. Make sure the report has no isolated headings, widows, or orphans.

7. Save the file as S4LAWCOM.REP and print it.

2. Financial Information on Professional Basketball Teams

Catarina Calderon is the assistant marketing manager for NBAHoops of Durham, North Carolina, a major publisher of basketball collection cards. She recently read a report on the worth of America's professional sports teams in *Financial World* magazine and has decided to write a memo to marketing and sales personnel in her company summarizing key information on the top National Basketball Association (NBA) teams.

Do the following:

1. Type a standard memo heading with the following information: **DATE: January 16, 1992; TO: Marketing and Sales Personnel; FROM: Catarina Calderon, Asst. Marketing Manager.**

2. For the body of the memo type the following sentence: **The following table summarizes financial data about the top ten NBA teams in order of estimated franchise value.**

3. Below the sentence create the following table. Your table should look as much like the one in Figure 4-48 as possible.

4. Save the file as S4NBATAB.MEM and print it.

TOP TEN NBA TEAMS IN FRANCHISE VALUE (All values in millions of dollars)			
Team Name	Annual Revenues	Player Salaries	Franchise Value (Est.)
Los Angeles Lakers	62.2	12.6	200
Boston Celtics	30.7	10.5	180
Detroit Pistons	47.3	10.9	150
Chicago Bulls	27.4	9.3	100
New York Knicks	25.6	13.3	100
Phoenix Suns	20.7	8.8	99
Philadelphia 76ers	20.4	9.8	75
Cleveland Cavaliers	22.6	9.0	61
Orlando Magic	22.5	13.3	61
Portland Trailblazers	21.4	11.2	60

Figure 4-48

3. Report on Advantages of Word Processing in Business

Write a three- to four-page report, including a title page, on the advantages of using a word processor in business. Compare writing letters, memos, and reports with a typewriter versus a computer. Include the major time-saving features of a word processor.

As part of the report, do the following:

1. Include a table showing the amount of time required to produce various types of document with a typewriter and with a word processor. The table should look like Figure 4-49.

Estimated Time (Minutes) to Type a Document		
Type of Document	Typewriter	WordPerfect
memo	8	6
letter	15	10
sales report	120	70
financial report	240	140

Figure 4-49

2. Double-space the report.

3. Include a header with the name of the report and your name.

4. Include page numbering in the bottom right corner of every page.

5. Create a WordPerfect style that you'll use to create headings within the report. Use the style to create three or more headings that divide the report into sections.

6. Save the file as S4WP.REP and print it.

Tutorial 5

Using Special Word Processing Features

Writing a Feasibility Report

Case: Connolly/Bayle Publishing Company

Since graduating last year with a degree in business management, Jonathan Lew has worked in outside sales for Connolly/Bayle (C/B) Publishing Company, which publishes computer magazines. Recently Jonathan took an in-house job as an assistant to Ann McMullen, the business manager for C/B Publishing. The company's cofounders, Stephen Connolly and John Bayle, have asked Ann to head a task force to investigate the feasibility of starting a new magazine aimed at graphic designers who use personal computers. The task force consists of Ann, Jonathan, two marketing managers, and two editors who manage other magazines at C/B Publishing.

The task force first met to map out strategies for the feasibility study. They decided to send out questionnaires, conduct interviews, and make financial projections with David Palermo, an accountant at C/B Publishing. After completing the study, the task force met again to analyze the information, draw conclusions, and make recommendations. Ann asked Jonathan to draft the outline for the final report and to distribute copies of the outline to the other task members for their approval. Once the outline has been approved, Ann will write the main body of the actual report and Jonathan will prepare the report for final distribution by adding footnotes, section headings, and other features.

OBJECTIVES

In this tutorial you will learn to:

- Use the Outline feature
- Switch between two documents
- Use split-screen windows
- Create and use macros
- Create footnotes
- Use hyphenation

Planning the Document

The responsibility for planning the document rests with all members of the task committee, even though Ann will write the actual body of the report.

Content

The content of the feasibility report will come from the results of the feasibility study, from the financial analysis, and from notes that Ann and Jonathan took in the task force meetings.

Organization

Jonathan will organize the feasibility report by creating an outline. He decides to have an introduction section, which states the purposes of the report and explains how the data for the report were gathered. He will then include sections on the target audience, expenses, and projected income for the magazine. The report will conclude with a summary and the recommendation of the task force.

Style

Jonathan wants the feasibility report to be like any other business document and follow a straightforward, clear style.

Format

C/B Publishing has no policy on how to format reports. Jonathan will use WordPerfect's default settings for margins, tabs, and justification and the standard format he learned in college for titles, headings, and page numbering.

■   ■   ■

The Outline Feature

Jonathan's task is to organize the data collected in the feasibility study and to outline the report. He decides to use WordPerfect's Outline feature. Each paragraph in an outline is preceded by a paragraph number. **Paragraph numbers** in a WordPerfect outline are Roman numerals (I, II, III, etc.), Arabic numerals (1, 2, 3, etc.), uppercase letters (A, B, C, etc.), and lowercase letters (a, b, c, etc.) that label the paragraphs and the subparagraphs of an outline to show the relationships between ideas and information. To show these relationships, the paragraph numbers represent **levels**: level-1 paragraphs (major ideas) are usually preceded by Roman numerals, level-2 paragraphs (supporting ideas) by uppercase letters, level-3 paragraphs by Arabic numerals, level-4 paragraphs by lowercase letters, and so forth (Figure 5-1). WordPerfect's Outline feature allows up to eight levels of paragraph numbers.

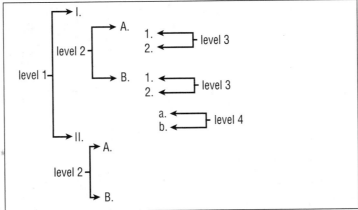

Figure 5-1
Outline levels

The advantage of WordPerfect's Outline feature is that paragraph numbering is automatic. When Outline is on and you press [Enter] to end one paragraph and start a new one, WordPerfect automatically inserts the next paragraph number of the outline. With a simple keystroke, you can change a paragraph number from a higher level to a lower level or from a lower level to a higher level. When you move a paragraph or a group of paragraphs in the outline, WordPerfect automatically renumbers the paragraphs.

Creating an Outline

The first draft of Jonathan's outline is shown in Figure 5-2. In the following steps you'll use WordPerfect's Outline feature to create this outline.

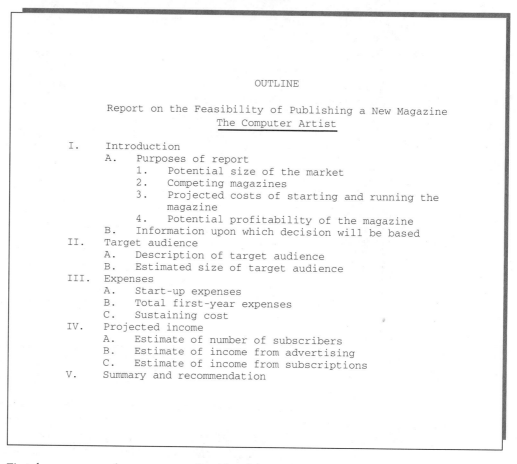

```
                              OUTLINE

         Report on the Feasibility of Publishing a New Magazine
                         The Computer Artist

     I.    Introduction
           A.   Purposes of report
                1.   Potential size of the market
                2.   Competing magazines
                3.   Projected costs of starting and running the
                     magazine
                4.   Potential profitability of the magazine
           B.   Information upon which decision will be based
     II.   Target audience
           A.   Description of target audience
           B.   Estimated size of target audience
     III.  Expenses
           A.   Start-up expenses
           B.   Total first-year expenses
           C.   Sustaining cost
     IV.   Projected income
           A.   Estimate of number of subscribers
           B.   Estimate of income from advertising
           C.   Estimate of income from subscriptions
     V.    Summary and recommendation
```

Figure 5-2
Jonathan's outline
of the report

First, however, you have to create the title of the outline.

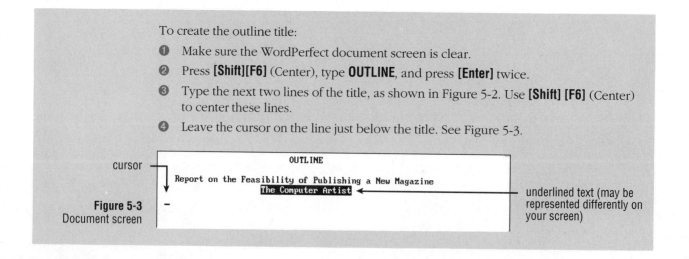

To create the outline title:

1 Make sure the WordPerfect document screen is clear.

2 Press **[Shift][F6]** (Center), type **OUTLINE**, and press **[Enter]** twice.

3 Type the next two lines of the title, as shown in Figure 5-2. Use **[Shift] [F6]** (Center) to center these lines.

4 Leave the cursor on the line just below the title. See Figure 5-3.

cursor ———

```
                          OUTLINE

     Report on the Feasibility of Publishing a New Magazine
                    The Computer Artist
```

underlined text (may be
represented differently on
your screen)

Figure 5-3
Document screen

Now you're ready to turn on WordPerfect's Outline feature and to create the outline. With Outline on, whenever you press [Enter], WordPerfect automatically inserts a new paragraph number into the document. You can then press [F4] (Indent) and type the text of the paragraph; change the paragraph number from a higher level to a lower level (for example, from II to A) by pressing [Tab] or from a lower level to a higher level (for example from A to II) by pressing [Shift][Tab] (Left Margin Release); or delete the paragraph number entirely by pressing [Backspace]. As you work through the following steps, you'll see how these commands work to help you create an outline quickly and efficiently.

To create an outline:

❶ With the cursor at the left margin on the first line after the title, select Outline from the Tools menu, then select On to turn on Outline. See Figure 5-4.

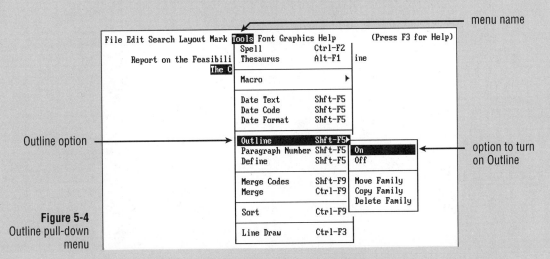

menu name

Outline option

option to turn on Outline

Figure 5-4
Outline pull-down menu

Alternatively press **[Shift][F5]** (Date/Outline) and select **4** (**O**utline) to display the Outline menu. See Figure 5-5. Select **1** (**O**n) from the Outline menu to turn on Outline. The message "Outline " appears on the left side of the status line at the bottom of the screen.

option to turn on Outline

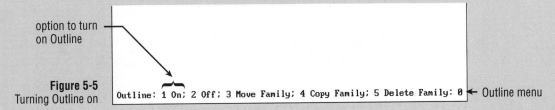

Outline: 1 On; 2 Off; 3 Move Family; 4 Copy Family; 5 Delete Family: 0 ◄ Outline menu

Figure 5-5
Turning Outline on

❷ Press **[Enter]**. WordPerfect inserts a paragraph number (in this case, a Roman numeral I) and a period at the beginning of this new line. With Outline on, every time you press [Enter], a new paragraph number appears on the screen.

❸ Press **[F4]** (Indent). This command indents after the paragraph number so you can type the text of the paragraph.

Pressing [F4] (Indent) keeps the same paragraph number. If you accidentally pressed [Tab], WordPerfect would indent and change the paragraph number from

"I" to "A." If this happens, press [Shift][Tab] (Left Margin Release) to "unindent" and to instruct WordPerfect to change from a lower level (A) back to the next higher level of paragraph number (I).

❹   Type **Introduction**. See Figure 5-6.

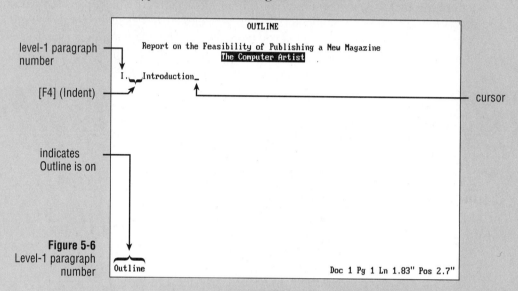

level-1 paragraph number

[F4] (Indent)

cursor

indicates Outline is on

Figure 5-6
Level-1 paragraph number

❺   Press **[Enter]** to move the cursor to the next line. WordPerfect automatically inserts the next level-1 paragraph number (II).

As you can see from Figure 5-2, you want the level-2 paragraph number A, not paragraph number II, on this line. To indent and change the paragraph number, you press [Tab].

❻   Press **[Tab]** to change from the level-1 paragraph number I to the level-2 paragraph number A and indent to the next tab stop.

❼   Press **[F4]** (Indent) to indent without changing the paragraph number, then type **Purposes of report**. See Figure 5-7.

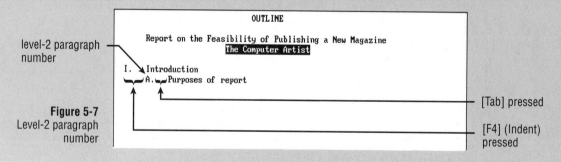

level-2 paragraph number

[Tab] pressed

Figure 5-7
Level-2 paragraph number

[F4] (Indent) pressed

Now let's continue creating the outline shown in Figure 5-2.

To continue the outline:

❶ Press **[Enter]** to move to the next line and to insert the next paragraph number (B) into the text.

❷ Press **[Tab]** to change from a level-2 to a level-3 paragraph number and to indent to the next tab stop. The paragraph number "B" changes to "1."

❸ Press **[F4]** (Indent) and type **Potential size of the market**.

❹ Press **[Enter]** to move to the next line and to insert the next paragraph number (the level-3 paragraph number 2), press **[F4]** (Indent), and type **Competing magazines**.

❺ Press **[Enter]** to insert the next paragraph number (3), press **[F4]** (Indent), and type **Projected costs of starting and running the magazine**.

❻ Press **[Enter]**, press **[F4]** (Indent), and type **Potential profitability of the magazine**.

You have now completed four items at level-3 paragraph numbering (Figure 5-8). In the next steps, you'll instruct WordPerfect to change a lower-level paragraph number to a higher-level paragraph number.

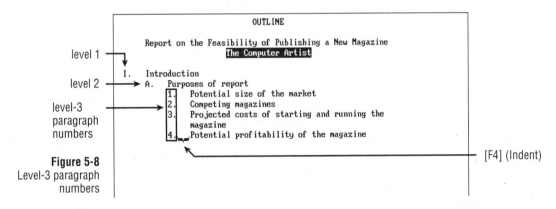

Figure 5-8
Level-3 paragraph numbers

To change from a lower-level to a higher-level paragraph number:

❶ Press **[Enter]**. WordPerfect inserts the level-3 paragraph number 5, which you don't want.

To change from a level-3 to a level-2 paragraph number, you press [Shift][Tab] (Left Margin Release).

❷ Press **[Shift][Tab]** (Left Margin Release) to return to the next higher level of paragraph numbering.

❸ Press **[F4]** (Indent) and type **Information upon which decision will be based**. Your screen should now look like Figure 5-9.

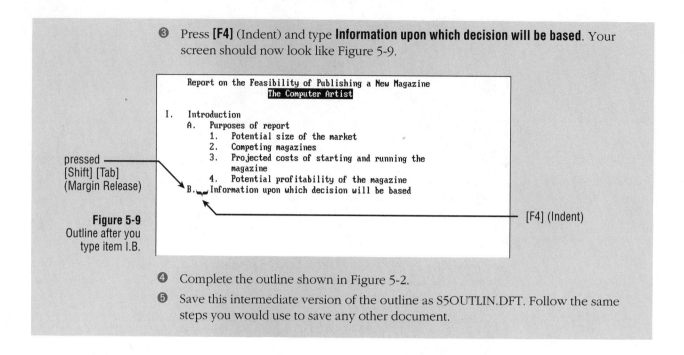

pressed — [Shift] [Tab] (Margin Release)

Figure 5-9 Outline after you type item I.B.

[F4] (Indent)

❹ Complete the outline shown in Figure 5-2.

❺ Save this intermediate version of the outline as S5OUTLIN.DFT. Follow the same steps you would use to save any other document.

Editing an Outline

Jonathan gives the task force members a copy of the outline at their next meeting. The task force decides to add a new section on competing magazines, as shown in Figure 5-10. They also suggest that current items III ("Expenses") and IV ("Projected income") be switched, so that projected income is discussed before expenses. Finally they suggest that items B and C under "Projected income" be switched, so that the estimate of income from subscriptions comes immediately after the estimate of the number of subscribers. Jonathan decides to use WordPerfect's powerful outline editing features to make these changes.

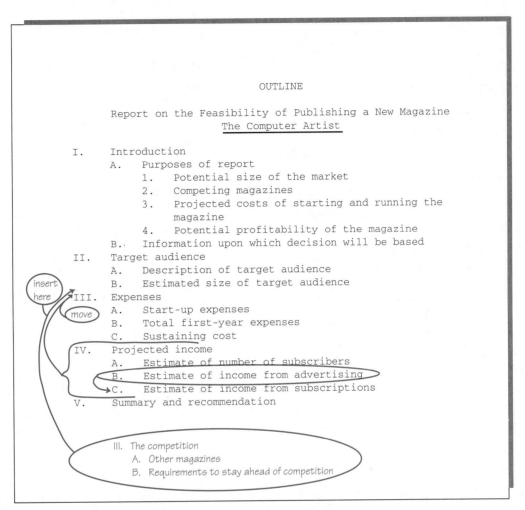

Figure 5-10
The task force's
suggested changes
to the outline

Moving the Cursor through an Outline

You can use all the standard WordPerfect cursor-movement commands in an outline, but WordPerfect also provides four special cursor-movement commands, shown in Figure 5-11. These special commands require an enhanced keyboard with separate cursor-movement keys. (If you don't have an enhanced keyboard, go to the next section.) Let's practice using the special cursor-movement commands.

Figure 5-11
Special outline
cursor-movement
keys

Keys	Description
[Alt] [→]	Move cursor to next paragraph number.
[Alt] [←]	Move cursor to previous paragraph number.
[Alt] [↓]	Move cursor to next paragraph number at same outline level or higher.
[Alt] [↑]	Move cursor to previous paragraph number at same outline level or higher.

To use the special cursor-movement commands to move the cursor through the outline:

❶ Make sure the intermediate version of the outline, S5OUTLIN.DFT, is on the WordPerfect document screen.

❷ Use the standard cursor-movement keys to move the cursor to the "I" in "Introduction," to the right of Roman numeral I.

❸ Press **[Alt][→]** several times and then **[Alt][←]** several times. Observe the behavior of the cursor.

As you can see, the cursor moves forward to the next paragraph number each time you press [Alt][→] and backward to the previous paragraph number each time you press [Alt][←].

❹ Press **[Alt][↓]** several times and **[Alt][↑]** several times. Observe the behavior of the cursor.

As you can see, pressing [Alt][↑] moves the cursor backward to the previous paragraph number of the same level or higher, and pressing [Alt][↓] moves the cursor forward to the next paragraph number of the same level or higher.

With these special cursor-movement commands, you can move the cursor quickly from one place to another within an outline.

Inserting New Paragraph Numbers into an Outline

After the task force meeting Jonathan returns to his office and edits a copy of the outline according to the committee's suggestions (Figure 5-10). Let's first insert the text on competing magazines, which begins with outline paragraph number III.

To insert new paragraph numbers into an outline:

❶ Move the cursor to the end of item II.B., "Estimated size of target audience," that is, to the end of the line above the paragraph number that you want to insert.

❷ Press **[Enter]**. WordPerfect inserts a hard return, moves the cursor down a line, and inserts the paragraph number "C" under the "B."

Because Jonathan wants a level-1 paragraph number (III) here, he must change the paragraph number "C" from a lower to a higher level.

❸ Press **[Shift][Tab]** (Left Margin Release) to change the paragraph number from a lower to a higher level.

The "C" disappears, the cursor moves one tab stop to the left, and "III" appears on the screen. WordPerfect automatically increments the subsequent level-1 paragraph numbers.

❹ Press **[F4]** (Indent) and type **The competition** to insert the level-1 paragraph.

Next you'll insert the two level-2 paragraphs of the revised outline.

❺ Press **[Enter]** to insert a hard return and insert a new paragraph number, press **[Tab]** to change to a lower level of paragraph number (A), press **[F4]** (Indent), and type **Other magazines**.

❻ Press **[Enter]**, press **[F4]** (Indent), and type **Requirements to stay ahead of competition**.

Your screen should now look like Figure 5-12. Jonathan has inserted the section on competing magazines, as suggested by the other members of the task force.

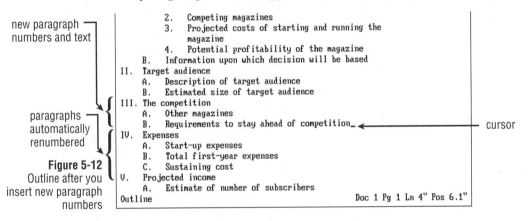

new paragraph numbers and text

paragraphs automatically renumbered

Figure 5-12
Outline after you insert new paragraph numbers

cursor

Moving an Outline Family

Jonathan's next task is to move an outline **family**, which is a group of paragraph numbers and accompanying text that includes the level where the cursor is located and all subordinate levels under that level (Figure 5-13) on the next page. In this case the outline family that you want to move is paragraph number V ("Projected income") and all subordinate paragraphs.

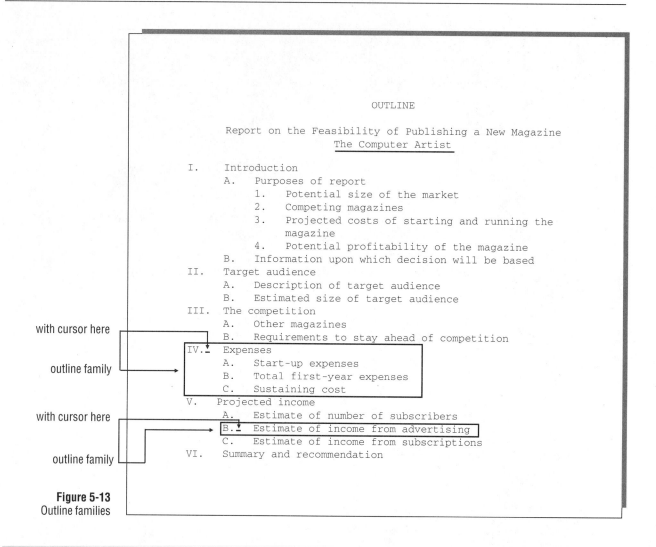

outline family

with cursor here

outline family

Figure 5-13
Outline families

To move an outline family:

❶ Move the cursor to the right of the paragraph number that heads the family you want to move. In this case move the cursor to the right of Roman numeral V, after the period and to the left of the "P" in "Projected income."

❷ Select Move Family from the Tools/Outline menu or press **[Shift][F5]** (Date/Outline), select **4** (**O**utline), and select **3** (**M**ove Family). The family you want to move becomes highlighted. See Figure 5-14.

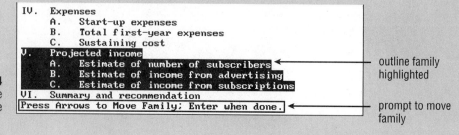

Figure 5-14
Highlighted outline
family before move

outline family
highlighted

prompt to move
family

❸ Press [↑] and then **[Enter]**. The highlighted family moves above the previous family, so the moved family begins with paragraph number IV instead of V. At the same time the old family that begins with "IV. Expenses" becomes the new family "V. Expenses."

You have now moved the "Projected income" family above the "Expenses" family. Your next task is to move the item "B. Estimate of income from advertising" underneath the item "C. Estimate of income from subscriptions." Let's use the Move Family command again to make the move.

❹ Move the cursor just to the right of "B." underneath "IV. Projected income."

❺ Select Move Family from the Tools/Outline menu or press **[Shift][F5]** (Date/Outline), select **4** (**O**utline), and select **3** (**M**ove Family). The line "B. Estimate of income from advertising" becomes highlighted.

❻ Press [↓] and then **[Enter]** to move the highlighted text down one line, as suggested by the task force committee.

You have now moved "Estimate of income from advertising" under "Estimate of income from subscriptions."

Turning Off Outline Mode

If your document doesn't contain any text after the outline, you do not have to turn off Outline mode. But if you want to insert additional text below the outline, you must turn off Outline mode.

To turn off Outline:

❶ Move the cursor to the end of the outline.

❷ Select Outline from the Tools menu, then select Off to turn off Outline. Alternatively press **[Shift][F5]** (Date/Outline) and select **4** (**O**utline) to display the Outline menu. Select **2** (**O**ff) from the Outline menu. The message "Outline" disappears from the status line.

❸ Save the outline as S5OUTLIN.DOC, print it, and clear the document screen.

The final version of your outline should now look like Figure 5-15 on the next page.

```
                              OUTLINE

           Report on the Feasibility of Publishing a New Magazine
                          The Computer Artist

     I.     Introduction
            A.    Purposes of report
                  1.    Potential size of the market
                  2.    Competing magazines
                  3.    Projected costs of starting and running the
                        magazine
                  4.    Potential profitability of the magazine
            B.    Information upon which decision will be based
     II.    Target audience
            A.    Description of target audience
            B.    Estimated size of target audience
     III.   The competition
            A.    Other magazines
            B.    Requirements to stay ahead of competition
     IV.    Projected income
            A.    Estimate of number of subscribers
            B.    Estimate of income from subscriptions
            C.    Estimate of income from advertising
     V.     Expenses
            A.    Start-up expenses
            B.    Total first-year expenses
            C.    Sustaining cost
     VI.    Summary and recommendation
```

Figure 5-15
Final version of
outline

Using the Two Document Screens

After approving Jonathan's revised outline, the task force agrees that Ann should begin writing the first draft of the report.

Retrieving a Document into the Second Document Screen

Ann wants to have the approved outline handy at all times without cluttering her desk; therefore, she decides to use WordPerfect's dual document feature. The **dual document feature** allows you to have two different documents in WordPerfect at once. You can then easily switch back and forth between the two documents. This is helpful if you want to read one document while creating another, copy text from one document to another, or edit two documents together. In this case Ann will write her report on document screen 1 (labeled "Doc 1" on the status line) and keep the outline on document screen 2 (labeled "Doc 2" on the status line). In that way she will always have access to the approved outline in WordPerfect. Let's use WordPerfect's dual document feature to begin writing the report.

To use document screen 2:

❶ Make sure you have saved the final version of the outline document as S5OUTLIN.DOC and cleared the document screen.

❷ Press **[Shift][F3]** (Switch) to switch from document screen 1 to document screen 2. The right side of the status line shows "Doc 2" instead of "Doc 1." See Figure 5-16.

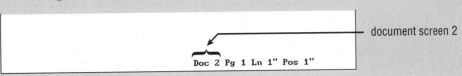

document screen 2

Doc 2 Pg 1 Ln 1" Pos 1"

❸ Retrieve S5OUTLIN.DOC. Now the outline is in Doc 2.

Copying Text between Doc 1 and Doc 2

Ann can now view the outline in Doc 2 whenever she wants and then return to Doc 1, where she will write the report. She uses [Shift][F3] (Switch) to switch between the two documents. So that she doesn't have to retype the title in creating her report, Ann will use dual documents to copy the title of the outline from Doc 2 to Doc 1. Let's copy the title from Doc 2 to Doc 1 using a block operation.

To copy text from Doc 2 to Doc 1:

❶ Make sure the current document screen is Doc 2, then move the cursor to the left margin of the line that begins "Report on the Feasibility." The cursor should be at Pos 1".

❷ Turn Block on by selecting Block from the Edit menu or by pressing **[Alt][F4]** or **[F12]** (Block).

❸ Move the cursor to the end of the line, after "The Computer Artist," to highlight the title.

❹ Select Copy from the Edit menu or press **[Ctrl][F4]** (Move) and select **1** (**B**lock) and **2** (**C**opy). The prompt "Move cursor; press Enter to retrieve" appears on the status line.

❺ Press **[Shift][F3]** (Switch) to switch to Doc 1, then press **[Enter]** to insert a copy of the title into the report. A copy of the title appears in Doc 1. See Figure 5-17.

Report on the Feasibility of Publishing a New Magazine
The Computer Artist

underlined

If "Outline" appears on the status line of Doc 1, you have accidentally copied the Outline code for Doc 2. You should then turn on Reveal Codes in Doc 1, delete [Outline], and turn off Reveal Codes.

These steps demonstrate that you can use the familiar copy and cut-and-paste operations to copy and move text not only within a document but also between documents.

Using Split-Screen Windows

Ann decides that she would really like to be able to see the outline while she is typing her report. Using [Shift][F3] (Switch) she can easily switch between the two documents, but she can't see them both on the screen at once. To see both documents on the screen at once, she will use the Window feature.

To use the Window feature to see both Doc 1 and Doc 2:

❶ Make sure that Doc 1 is still on your screen.

❷ Select Window from the Edit menu or press **[Ctrl][F3]** (Screen) and select **1** (**W**indow). The prompt "Number of lines in this window" appears on the status line. The default value, usually 24, appears with the prompt.

The total number of text lines on a document screen is normally 24. When you use split-screen windows, each document must have at least two lines; therefore, you can type any value from 2 to 22 as the number of lines in this window. In most cases, you'll want approximately the same number of lines in each window, that is, about 12 lines of text.

❸ Type **12** and press **[Enter]**. WordPerfect splits the screen into two windows, with Doc 1 on the top and Doc 2 on the bottom. See Figure 5-18.

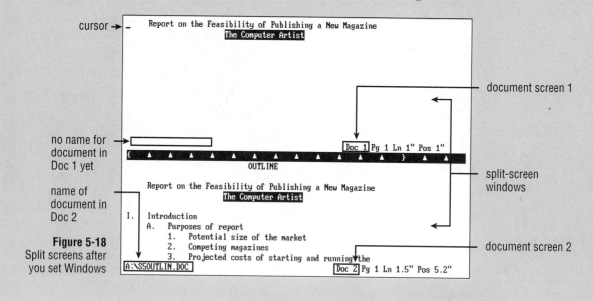

cursor →

document screen 1

no name for document in Doc 1 yet

name of document in Doc 2

Figure 5-18
Split screens after you set Windows

split-screen windows

document screen 2

Now Ann will be able to see both documents on the screen at once. She can edit only one document at a time, however, so the cursor will be in either one window or the other. She can move the cursor between the two windows by pressing [Shift][F3] (Switch).

Ann decides that her report should be double-spaced, so her next task is to set double spacing for the document in Doc 1. Let's insert the format code for double spacing.

To double-space the document in Doc 1:

1 Make sure the cursor is at the beginning of the document in Doc 1.

2 Select Line from the Layout menu or press **[Shift][F8]** (Format) and select **1** (**L**ine). The Format: Line menu appears on the screen.

3 Select **6** (Line **S**pacing), type **2** for double spacing, and press **[Enter]**.

4 Press **[F7]** (Exit) to return to the document screen.

Next Ann wants to type a heading for the first section of her report.

5 Move the cursor to the end of the document title, to the right of "The Computer Artist," after the Underline code, and press **[Enter]** to double-space after the title.

6 Press **[F6]** (Bold) to turn on boldfacing, type **Introduction**, press **[F6]** (Bold) again to turn off boldfacing, and press **[Enter]**.

With the outline in Doc 2, Ann continues to type the report in Doc 1. Except for copy and cut-and-paste operations, WordPerfect commands performed in one document don't affect the other document.

In the next steps, you'll retrieve the remainder of Ann's draft of the report and then turn off split-screen windows.

To retrieve the report and turn off split-screen windows:

1 With the cursor underneath the first heading ("Introduction") and with the WordPerfect data diskette in drive A, select Retrieve from the File menu or press **[Shift][F10]** (Retrieve), type **a:\c5file1.dft**, and press **[Enter]**.

2 Take a few minutes to read the report so you'll be familiar with its contents. Notice that the title of the magazine is missing from the first paragraph of the report. You'll fix that problem later.

3 Select Window from the Edit menu or press **[Ctrl][F3]** (Screen) and select **1** (**W**indows).

④ Type **24** and press **[Enter]** to tell WordPerfect that you want the current window to be 24 lines, or the entire screen. WordPerfect removes the split-screen windows so that Doc 1 and Doc 2 are on different screens. Your screen should look similar to Figure 5-19.

```
     Report on the Feasibility of Publishing a New Magazine
                        The Computer Artist

Introduction

cursor →  _   The purpose of this report is to examine the feasibility of

starting a new magazine tentatively entitled , which would be aimed

at graphic artists who use computers as their main tool for design

and production.  This report will describe the following:

1.   The potential size of the market audience.

2.   Competing magazines.

3.   Potential profitability of the magazine.

4.   Projected cost of starting and running the magazine.

     The conclusions reported here are the result of a study

                                        Doc 1 Pg 1 Ln 2" Pos 1"
```

Figure 5-19
Document screen
after you retrieve
report

Macros

Ann knows that while writing the feasibility study she will have to type the name of the proposed magazine, "The Computer Artist," several times. For any word-processing procedure that you have to repeat several times — a series of WordPerfect commands, a word, a phrase, or a combination of commands and text — you can create a macro to perform the procedure for you. A **macro**, in its simplest sense, is a "recording" of keystrokes that you can "play back" at any time by pressing just a few keystrokes.

Creating a macro to execute frequently pressed keystrokes has several advantages:

- Macros save time. By executing a macro, you can save many keystrokes, which means you can prepare your document faster.

- Macros are accurate. When you execute a macro, you don't have to worry about typos or other mistakes. If you created the macro correctly, every time you use it, the keystrokes are executed without error.

- Macros are consistent. Macros that insert text and formatting features create the same text and format each time.

Creating a Macro

Creating a macro requires five steps (Figure 5-20):

1. Turn on the "recording," that is, turn on macro definition.

2. Name the macro.

3. Describe the macro.

4. Record the keystrokes.

5. Turn off the "recording," that is, turn off macro definition.

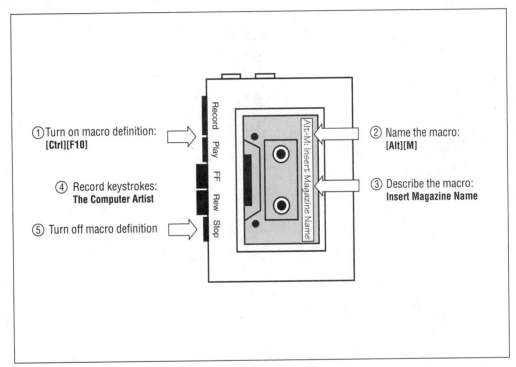

Figure 5-20
Five steps to create
a macro

When you create a macro, you can select one of three ways of naming the macro. An **Alt macro** is a macro you name by pressing [Alt] and a letter, for example, [Alt][M]. You can use any one of the 26 letters of the alphabet, but you can't use any other type of character, that is, no digits or symbols. To execute an Alt macro, that is, to "play back" the recorded keystrokes, you press [Alt] and the letter.

A **named macro** is a macro you name by typing a legal DOS filename. To execute a named macro, you issue the [Alt][F10] (Macro) command, type the filename of the named macro, and press [Enter].

An **Enter macro** is a macro without a name or a description. When WordPerfect asks you for the macro name to create or execute the macro, you just press [Enter]. In the steps that follow, you'll create and execute each of these three types of macros.

Before you create any macros, you should instruct WordPerfect about the disk and the directory where you want the macros saved. Since you will want WordPerfect to save your macros to your data diskette, let's specify drive A as the location of the macros.

To specify the location of macros:

❶ Insert your WordPerfect data diskette into drive A.

❷ Select Location of Files from the File/Setup menu. See Figure 5-21.

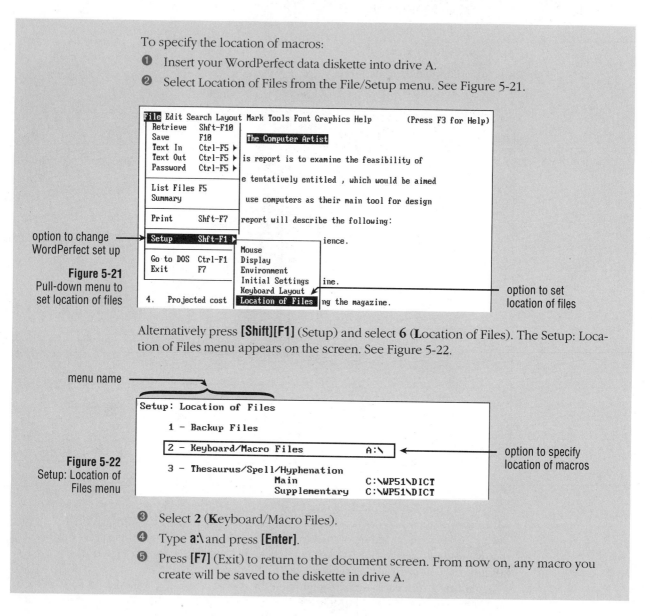

option to change WordPerfect set up

Figure 5-21
Pull-down menu to set location of files

option to set location of files

Alternatively press **[Shift][F1]** (Setup) and select **6** (**L**ocation of Files). The Setup: Location of Files menu appears on the screen. See Figure 5-22.

menu name

Figure 5-22
Setup: Location of Files menu

option to specify location of macros

❸ Select **2** (**K**eyboard/Macro Files).

❹ Type **a:** and press **[Enter]**.

❺ Press **[F7]** (Exit) to return to the document screen. From now on, any macro you create will be saved to the diskette in drive A.

In the following steps you'll define a macro that inserts the name of the proposed magazine.

To define a macro:

❶ Move the cursor to the comma after "tentatively entitled" in the second line of the first paragraph. When you create a macro, the keystrokes you record are executed in the document. If the macro will insert text, move the cursor to the position in the document where you want that text.

❷ Press **[Ctrl][F10]** (Macro Define) to turn on macro definition. The prompt "Define macro:" appears on the status line, and WordPerfect waits for you to give the macro a name.

For this macro, we'll create an Alt macro. And because this is a macro to insert the name of a magazine, we'll use "M" for "magazine."

❸ Press **[Alt][M]** to name the macro. This creates an Alt macro, which WordPerfect will save using the filename ALTM.WPM.

The prompt "Description:" appears on the status line. Let's type a description that will remind us of the macro's function.

❹ Type **Insert magazine name** and press **[Enter]**.

WordPerfect displays the message "Macro Def" in blinking bold characters on the left side of the status line. From this point on, until you turn off macro definition, WordPerfect will record every keystroke or mouse command that you execute. Now let's record the keystrokes for the Alt-M macro.

❺ Press **[F8]** (Underline), type **The Computer Artist**, and press **[F8]** (Underline). These keystrokes, which create the underlined title of the proposed magazine, are now recorded in the Alt-M macro.

Now that you have recorded the keystrokes for the Alt-M macro, you'll turn off macro definition.

❻ Press **[Ctrl][F10]** (Macro Define) to turn off macro definition. The message "Macro Def" disappears from the status line. WordPerfect saves the completed macro as ALTM.WPM.

You can use essentially the same procedure to record any sequence of keystrokes, such as your company name, your own name and address, or the keystrokes for setting double spacing.

Correcting an Error in a Macro

Take a moment to look at your document. Did you spell "The Computer Artist" correctly? Is it underlined? If you made a mistake, you can define the macro again. Let's assume you made an error and have to redefine the Alt-M macro.

To correct an error in a macro:

❶ Delete any text you typed while creating the macro and move the cursor to where you want to insert the text of the macro. In this case completely delete "The Computer Artist," including the underline code, that you inserted while creating the macro.

❷ Press **[Ctrl][F10]** (Macro Define) to turn on macro definition.

❸ Press **[Alt][M]** to name the macro. WordPerfect displays a prompt that a macro named ALTM.WPM already exists. See Figure 5-23.

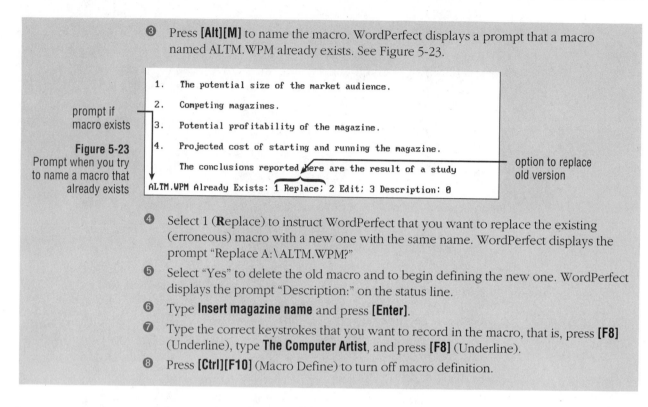

prompt if
macro exists

Figure 5-23
Prompt when you try
to name a macro that
already exists

1.   The potential size of the market audience.

2.   Competing magazines.

3.   Potential profitability of the magazine.

4.   Projected cost of starting and running the magazine.

     The conclusions reported here are the result of a study

ALTM.WPM Already Exists: 1 Replace; 2 Edit; 3 Description: 0

option to replace
old version

❹ Select 1 (**R**eplace) to instruct WordPerfect that you want to replace the existing (erroneous) macro with a new one with the same name. WordPerfect displays the prompt "Replace A:\ALTM.WPM?"

❺ Select "Yes" to delete the old macro and to begin defining the new one. WordPerfect displays the prompt "Description:" on the status line.

❻ Type **Insert magazine name** and press **[Enter]**.

❼ Type the correct keystrokes that you want to record in the macro, that is, press **[F8]** (Underline), type **The Computer Artist**, and press **[F8]** (Underline).

❽ Press **[Ctrl][F10]** (Macro Define) to turn off macro definition.

In general any time you make a mistake while you are creating a simple macro, just press [Ctrl][F10] (Macro Define) to turn off macro definition and then start over.

Executing an Alt Macro

Now that you've correctly created an Alt macro, you're ready to use the Alt-M macro to insert the magazine name into the document. To execute an Alt macro, you press [Alt] and, while holding it down, press the letter you used to create the macro.

To execute an Alt macro:

❶ Move the cursor to the location in your document where you want the macro executed. In this case move the cursor just to the right of the phrase "target audience" on the first line under the heading "The Target Audience."

❷ Press **[Space]**, type **of**, and press **[Space]**.

Now you're ready to insert the underlined name of the magazine. But instead of using the Underline command and typing the text, you'll execute the macro you just created.

❸ Press **[Alt][M]**. The underlined magazine title appears in the document.

❹ Now move the cursor after "The potential audience" at the beginning of the second sentence of the next paragraph.

❺ Insert the phrase "for <u>The Computer Artist</u>" using the Alt macro. Your screen should look similar to Figure 5-24.

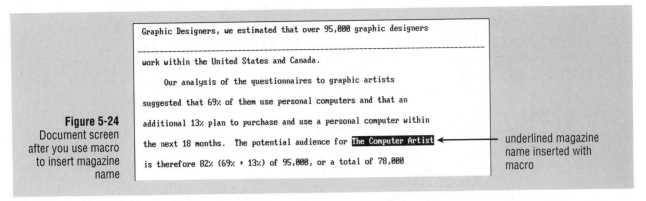

Figure 5-24
Document screen after you use macro to insert magazine name

underlined magazine name inserted with macro

Although Ann created and used the Alt-M macro while writing her feasibility report, the macro is not associated exclusively with the report but is saved to the disk as a separate file. She can use the Alt-M macro in this report and in any future documents she writes using the disk on which she saved the macro.

Creating a Named Macro

Ann knows that in this report and in other documents, she frequently will have to type the abbreviated name for Connolly/Bayle Publishing Company — C/B Publishing — so she decides to create a macro.

As you create the macro, you'll insert the name "C/B Publishing" into the document at the beginning of the title; later you'll use the macro to insert the name elsewhere in the document. First you'll have to prepare the report to insert a new title line.

To insert a new title line:

❶ Move the cursor to the beginning of the document so that the cursor is located after the initial formatting codes but before the title. You may have to turn on Reveal Codes to make sure that the cursor is on the first [Center] code. Turn off Reveal Codes after you position the cursor.

❷ Press **[Enter]** to insert a blank line at the beginning of the document, move the cursor back to the blank line, and press **[Shift][F6]** (Center).

You're now ready to create the macro to insert the abbreviated company name. Ann decides to define a named macro using the name "CB," which stands for "C/B Publishing." In a named macro you can use any legal DOS filename without a filename extension. WordPerfect automatically adds the .WPM extension. Let's create the named macro. Remember, if you make a mistake while recording keystrokes in the macro, turn off macro definition and start again.

To create a named macro:

❶ Press **[Ctrl][F10]** (Macro Define) to turn on macro definition. The prompt "Define macro:" appears on the status line, and WordPerfect waits for you to give the macro a name.

❷ Type **cb** and press **[Enter]** to name the macro. The prompt "Description:" appears on the status line.

❸ Type **Insert company name** and press **[Enter]** to describe the function of the macro. WordPerfect displays the message "Macro Def" in blinking bold characters on the left side of the status line.

❹ Type **C/B Publishing** but do *not* press [Enter]. If you did press [Enter], the macro would record the [Enter], and every time you executed the CB macro, a hard return would be inserted into the document. If you made a mistake, turn off macro definition and start over, replacing the original CB macro with the correct version.

❺ Press **[Ctrl][F10]** (Macro Define) to turn off macro definition. The message "Macro Def" disappears from the status line, and WordPerfect automatically saves the macro as CB.WPM.

Your screen should now look like Figure 5-25.

Figure 5-25
Document screen
after you type the
company name while
you are creating a
macro

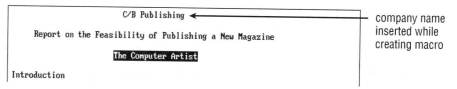

company name
inserted while
creating macro

Executing a Named Macro

To prepare for executing the CB macro or any other macro that inserts format codes or text, you have to move the cursor to the location in your document where you want the code or text.

To execute a named macro:

❶ Move the cursor to the right of the words "will help" just above the heading "The Target Audience" and press **[Space]**. This places the cursor where you want the name "C/B Publishing" inserted.

❷ Press **[Alt][F10]** (Macro). The prompt "Macro" appears on the status line for you to enter the name of the macro.

❸ Type **cb** and press **[Enter]**. The macro inserts the name of the company into the document at the location of the cursor.

Next let's use the CB macro to insert the company name elsewhere in the document.

❹ Move the cursor to the "b" at the beginning of "board of directors" in the middle of the paragraph under the heading "The Competition."

❺ Press **[Alt][F10]** (Macro), type **cb**, and press **[Enter]**. Press **[Space]** to leave a space after the company name.

Ann has now completed her work on this draft of the document and is ready to save the intermediate version to the disk.

❻   Save the document as S5FEAS1.DFT.

So far you have seen how to define two types of macros, Alt macros and named macros. The advantage of a named macro over an Alt macro is that the named macro is mnemonic, meaning that you can use easy-to-remember names for the macro. The advantage of the Alt macro is that it takes fewer keystrokes to execute than a named macro. For example, to execute the CB macro, you have to press [Alt][F10] (Macro), type "CB," and press [Enter] — a total of five keystrokes. To execute the Alt-M macro, you just press [Alt][M] — two keystrokes.

Creating an Enter Macro

Ann gives Jonathan a diskette that contains a copy of the file S5FEAS1.DFT and asks him to make any formatting changes that he feels would improve the appearance of the document. Jonathan decides that each heading should be preceded by three blank lines (not just the two lines currently in the double-spaced document) and that to simplify editing a Conditional End-of-Page command should be inserted just before each heading. Making these changes for the six headings would require many keystrokes, so Jonathan decides to create a macro to make the changes quickly and accurately.

Such a macro is applicable only to this report, because Jonathan doubts he would use it in future documents. He therefore decides to create an Enter macro instead of an Alt or a named macro. Unlike an Alt and a named macro, an Enter macro doesn't have a name or a description. To define or execute an Enter macro, you just press [Enter] when WordPerfect prompts you for the macro name.

Let's create an Enter macro to format the headings of Ann's report. As you create the macro, you'll record the keystrokes for formatting the first heading. Later you'll use the macro to format the other headings in the document.

As you create a macro, *the keystrokes are executed as you enter them*, thus modifying your document. If you press the wrong keys, your document could be altered *beyond repair*. Therefore, always save your document before you create or execute a complex macro. Make sure you have saved this document as S5FEAS1.DFT.

To create an Enter macro:

❶   Move the cursor to the beginning of the document. Because this Enter macro will search for the first occurrence of a heading, we'll start the macro at the beginning of the document.

❷   Press **[Ctrl][F10]** (Macro Define) to initiate the definition of the macro.

❸   Press **[Enter]**. This creates an Enter macro, with no name and no description. The blinking message "Macro Def" appears on the status line.

You're now ready to record the keystrokes of the macro. Because the headings contain the only boldfaced characters in the report, you'll begin the macro by searching for the [BOLD] code.

❹   Press **[F2]** (Search), then **[F6]** (Bold), then **[F2]** (Search).

The cursor moves to the first occurrence of boldfaced text, which is the heading "Introduction," just after the invisible [BOLD] code. The Pos value on the status line indicates that bold is on. To format the heading, you want the cursor before the [BOLD] code. In the keystrokes that follow, you'll move the cursor to the left of the [BOLD] code, then set conditional end of page.

⑤ Press [←] to move the cursor to the left of the [BOLD] code, press **[Shift][F8]** (Format), select **4** (**O**ther), select **2** (**C**onditional End of Page), type **6** (the number of lines that you want kept together), and press **[Enter]**. Keep the cursor on the Format: Other menu.

Next you want to add the codes necessary to insert one blank line just above the heading. You can't just press [Enter], because with the line spacing set to double, the [Enter] would insert two blank lines. Therefore, you must first set the spacing to single, press [Enter], then reset the spacing back to double.

⑥ Press **[Enter]** to return to the Format menu, select **1** (**L**ine), select **6** (Line **S**pacing), type **1** (for single spacing), and press **[Enter]**. Press **[F7]** (Exit) to return to the document screen. Press **[Enter]** to insert one blank line.

Now you have to set the spacing back to double.

⑦ Press **[Shift][F8]** (Format), select **1** (**L**ine), select **6** (Line **S**pacing), type **2** for double spacing, and press **[Enter]**. Press **[F7]** (Exit) to return to the document screen.

Now you have to move the cursor below the heading so that when you execute the macro, the cursor will be past the heading you've just edited and will find the next occurrence of a heading.

⑧ Press [↓] to move the cursor below the heading.

This sequence of keystrokes is long and tedious, which is why you want to do it only once, not at every heading.

⑨ Press **[Ctrl][F10]** (Macro Define) to turn off macro definition.

Executing an Enter Macro

Having formatted the first heading while he was creating the Enter macro, Jonathan is now ready to use the macro to format the other five headings. Since the only boldfacing in this document is in the headings, the macro will find and modify only headings. Don't use this macro in documents that may have boldfacing other than in headings.

To execute an Enter macro:

❶ Press **[Alt][F10]** (Macro). WordPerfect displays the "Macro" prompt.

❷ Press **[Enter]**.

The macro finds the next [BOLD] code, which occurs only in headings in this document, and inserts the desired formatting codes.

❸   Repeat Steps 1 and 2 to format the other four headings in the report.

Your screen should now look like Figure 5-26.

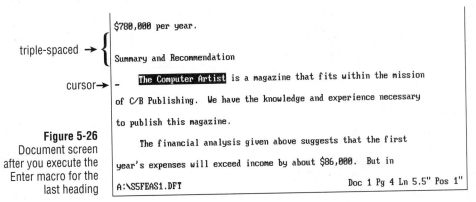

triple-spaced →

cursor→

Figure 5-26
Document screen
after you execute the
Enter macro for the
last heading

```
$780,000 per year.

Summary and Recommendation
     The Computer Artist is a magazine that fits within the mission
of C/B Publishing.  We have the knowledge and experience necessary
to publish this magazine.
     The financial analysis given above suggests that the first
year's expenses will exceed income by about $86,000.  But in
A:\S5FEAS1.DFT                              Doc 1 Pg 4 Ln 5.5" Pos 1"
```

Footnotes

Jonathan printed and distributed a copy of the feasibility report to the members of the task force, who then suggested some minor revisions. They felt that the report should include three footnotes: the first giving the source of the data published by the American Society of Graphic Designers, the second explaining how the task force arrived at the proposed subscription rate of $55, and the third giving the source of the expenses required to start up the proposed magazine.

Creating a Footnote

The three footnotes suggested by the task force are shown in Figure 5-27. Let's create them now.

Figure 5-27
The task force's
footnotes for the
report

> Jonathan, please add these footnotes to the text:
>
> After "American Society of Graphic Designers" add the footnote:
>   Report of the American Society of Graphic Designers,
>   Arbol Press, March 1990, p. 84.
>
> After "$55 per year" add the footnote:
>   Our questionnaire indicated that specialty magazines of
>   this type have subscription rates typically in the range
>   of $35 to $95 per year.
>
> After "721,000" add the footnote:
>   For a detailed breakdown of these expenses, contact
>   David Palermo in the Financial Office.

To create a footnote:

❶ Move the cursor to the location where you want the footnote number to appear in the text. In this case move the cursor to the right of the comma that follows the phrase "American Society of Graphic Designers" in the paragraph under "The Target Audience."

❷ Select Create from the Layout/Footnote menu. See Figure 5-28.

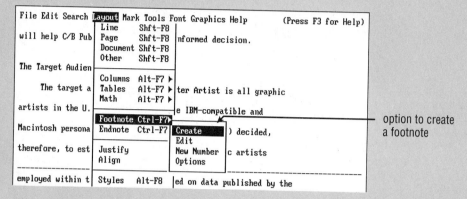

Figure 5-28
Pull-down menu to create a footnote

option to create a footnote

Alternatively press **[Ctrl][F7]** (Footnote) to display the one-line menu shown in Figure 5-29, then select **1** (**F**ootnote) to display the menu shown in Figure 5-30, and select **1** (**C**reate).

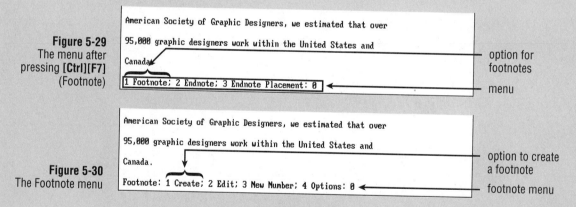

Figure 5-29
The menu after pressing **[Ctrl][F7]** (Footnote)

option for footnotes

menu

Figure 5-30
The Footnote menu

option to create a footnote

footnote menu

The blank Footnote Edit screen appears. See Figure 5-31. The screen contains an automatic tab and a superscript footnote number.

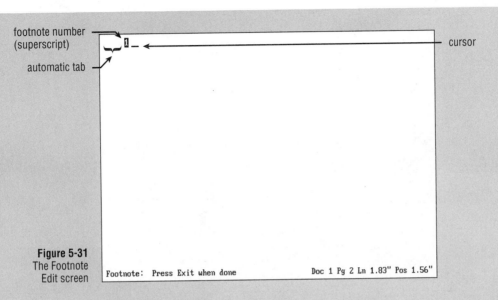

footnote number
(superscript)

cursor

automatic tab

Figure 5-31
The Footnote
Edit screen

Footnote: Press Exit when done   Doc 1 Pg 2 Ln 1.83" Pos 1.56"

❸   Without pressing [Space] or [Tab], type the text of the first footnote as shown in
    Figure 5-27.

❹   Press **[F7]** (Exit) to return to the document screen.

WordPerfect automatically inserts the correct footnote number into the body of the
report and formats the text of the footnote at the bottom of the page.

❺   Select View Document from the Print/Option menu, set the view to 100%, and scroll
    the screen so you can see the bottom of the page. See Figure 5-32.

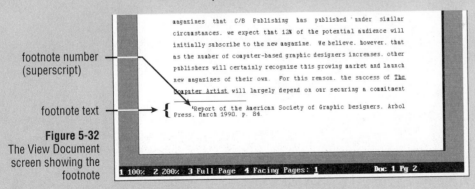

footnote number
(superscript)

footnote text

Figure 5-32
The View Document
screen showing the
footnote

magazines that C/B Publishing has published under similar
circumstances. we expect that 12% of the potential audience will
initially subscribe to the new magazine. We believe. however. that
as the number of computer-based graphic designers increases. other
publishers will certainly recognize this growing market and launch
new magazines of their own. For this reason. the success of The
Computer Artist will largely depend on our securing a commitment

¹Report of the American Society of Graphic Designers. Arbol
Press. March 1990. p. 84.

1 100%   2 200%   3 Full Page   4 Facing Pages: 1   Doc 1 Pg 2

The text of the footnote appears at the bottom of the page with a horizontal line separating the footnote from the body of the text.

❻   Exit the View Document screen and return to the document screen.

Editing a Footnote

After typing the first footnote, Jonathan remembers that the report cited in the footnote was published in 1991, not in 1990. The footnote from the task force was incorrect. Thus, he needs to edit the footnote to make this correction.

To edit a footnote:

❶ Select Edit from the Layout/Footnote menu or press **[Ctrl][F7]** (Footnote), select **1** (**F**ootnote), and select **2** (**E**dit). WordPerfect displays the prompt "Footnote Number?" with a default footnote number, either 1 or 2, depending on where your cursor is in the document.

❷ If the default number is 1, you can press **[Enter]** to accept the default. Otherwise, type the number of the footnote (in this case **1**) and press **[Enter]**. The footnote edit screen appears with the footnote text that you previously typed.

❸ Using the normal WordPerfect cursor-movement and edit keys, change "1990" to "1991."

❹ Press **[F7]** (Exit) to return to the document screen.

The text of footnote 1 is now correct.

Adding a New Footnote

Jonathan now wants to add the second and third footnotes.

To add a footnote:

❶ Move the cursor to the space after the final "r" in the phrase "$55 per year" in the second paragraph under "Projected income."

❷ Select Create from the Layout/Footnote menu or press **[Ctrl][F7]** (Footnote), select **1** (**F**ootnote), and select **1** (**C**reate). The cursor is now in a blank Footnote Edit screen, with footnote number 2 in the upper left corner of the screen.

❸ Type the text of the second footnote, as shown in Figure 5-27. Your screen should now look like Figure 5-33. Then press **[F7]** (Exit) to return to the document screen.

footnote number ———→

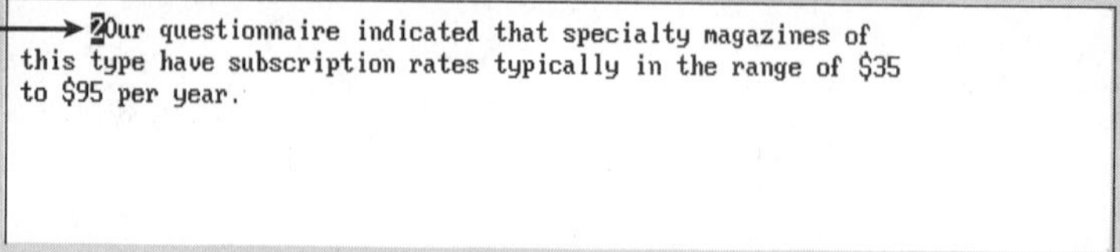

Figure 5-33
The Footnote Edit screen with footnote 2

```
2Our questionnaire indicated that specialty magazines of
this type have subscription rates typically in the range of $35
to $95 per year.
```

④ Use Steps 1 through 3 to help you create the third footnote shown in Figure 5-27. Put this footnote after the period following the number "$721,000" in the paragraph headed "Expenses."

Benefits of the Footnotes Feature

As you have seen, the Footnotes feature provides three benefits:

- WordPerfect automatically numbers the footnotes. If you add a footnote anywhere in the document, delete a footnote, or move a footnote, WordPerfect automatically renumbers all the footnotes so they appear consecutively.
- WordPerfect automatically formats the footnote text at the bottom of the page.
- WordPerfect allows you to edit the footnote.

What is true of footnotes is also true of **endnotes**, which are notes printed at the end of the document rather than at the bottom of each page. You can create and edit endnotes the same way you created and edited footnotes, except that you would select Endnotes rather than Footnotes from the Layout menu or from the menu that appears after you press [Ctrl][F7] (Footnote).

To delete a footnote, you move the cursor to the footnote and use the normal deletion keys to delete the footnote code. When you delete a footnote, WordPerfect automatically renumbers the footnotes to keep them in order.

To move a footnote, you move the cursor to the footnote, turn on Reveal Codes, block the footnote code, and use a normal cut-and-paste block operation to move the footnote to another point in your document.

Using Hyphenation

When text is fully justified, WordPerfect inserts small spaces between words and characters to keep the lines of text aligned along the right margin. Sometimes this causes unsightly "rivers," or blank regions, through the text. When text is only left-justified, an extremely ragged right edge may occur (Figure 5-34 on the next page). To solve these problems, you can use WordPerfect's automatic hyphenation feature. With hyphenation on, long words that would otherwise wrap to the next line are divided in two, so that part of the word stays on the original line. Thus, the number of "rivers" or the amount of raggedness along the right margin in decreased.

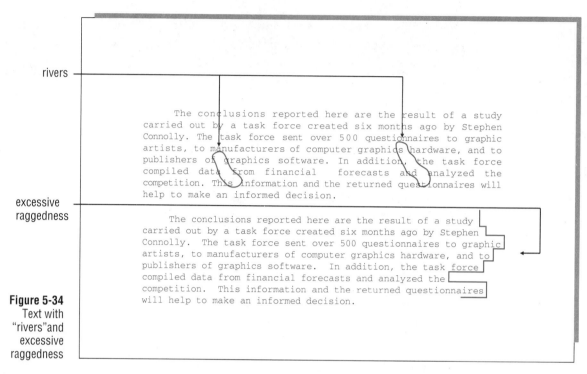

Figure 5-34
Text with "rivers"and excessive raggedness

rivers

excessive raggedness

When you turn on hyphenation and then move the cursor through your document, WordPerfect analyzes each word that falls at or near the end of a line and checks to see if it should be wrapped to the next line, kept on the same line without hyphenation, or hyphenated. If WordPerfect needs help in deciding how to hyphenate a word, a prompt appears on the status line to ask you where or if you want the word hyphenated.

As the final step in formatting his document, Jonathan decides to turn on hyphenation. You should turn on hyphenation as the *last step* in the final version of a document; otherwise, WordPerfect will constantly interrupt you with hyphenation prompts as you type and modify the text of your document.

To turn on hyphenation:

❶ Move the cursor to the beginning of the document.

Hyphenation occurs only from the point in the document where you turn on hyphenation to the end of the document. Since you want to hyphenate the entire document, you should move the cursor to the beginning of the document.

❷ Select Line from the Layout menu or press **[Shift][F8]** (Format) and select **1** (**L**ine). The Format: Line menu appears on the screen.

❸ Select **1** (**Hy**phenation), select "Yes" to verify that you want to turn on hyphenation, and press **[F7]** (Exit) to return to the document screen.

❹ Press **[Home]**, **[Home]**, **[↓]** to move the cursor to the end of the document, forcing WordPerfect to format the entire document.

As the cursor moves through the document, WordPerfect automatically hyphenates some words. If WordPerfect doesn't know how to hyphenate a word that needs hyphenation, it will stop and ask you for help in positioning the hyphen. You can then instruct WordPerfect where to hyphenate or not to hyphenate the word at all. For example, WordPerfect may stop at the word "approximately" and display the prompt shown in Figure 5-35. Depending on the size of type used by your printer, WordPerfect may stop at other words.

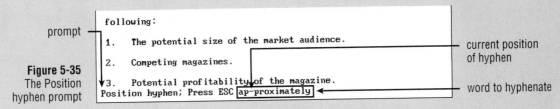

Figure 5-35
The Position
hyphen prompt

prompt

current position
of hyphen

word to hyphenate

⑤ Press [→] or [←] to change the location of the hyphen in the prompt and then press **[Esc]**.

For example, if WordPerfect stopped at "approximately," you would press [→] to move the hyphen so the word in the prompt is "approx-imately" and then press [Esc]. WordPerfect would accept this suggested position for the hyphen only if "approx-" could fit on the current line. If WordPerfect can't hyphenate a word in the suggested position, the hyphen automatically jumps back to the original position, and the "Position hyphen" prompt is displayed again.

⑥ If WordPerfect displays a "Position hyphen" prompt and you want to accept WordPerfect's suggested position of the hyphen, press **[Esc]**. If you don't want to hyphenate the word, press **[F1]** (Cancel).

⑦ If WordPerfect stops at any other words in the document, use your best judgment to position the cursor with [→] and [←], then press **[Esc]** when you're satisfied with the position of the hyphen. Press **[F1]** (Cancel) to instruct WordPerfect not to hyphenate the word.

The words that WordPerfect selects for hyphenation depend on the size of the font (typeface). If you make a mistake in hyphenating a word, move the cursor to the word and delete the hyphen.

This completes the feasibility report, as shown in Figure 5-36 on the following pages. Your document may look slightly different because of differences in font size and positions of the hyphens. You can now save and print the document and exit WordPerfect. Exiting WordPerfect with documents on both document screens (Doc 1 and Doc 2) requires some additional steps.

To save and print the document and exit WordPerfect:

❶ Save the document as S5FEASIB.REP and print it.

❷ Exit WordPerfect by pressing **[F7]** (Exit). The prompt "Save document?" appears on the screen.

❸ Select "No." WordPerfect displays the prompt "Exit doc 1?"

❹ Select "Yes." The cursor is now in Doc 2.

❺ Press **[F7]** (Exit) again, select "Yes" or "No" (depending on whether you want to save the document in Doc 2. WordPerfect displays the "Exit WordPerfect" prompt.

❻ Select "Yes" to exit WordPerfect.

C/B Publishing
Report on the Feasibility of Publishing a New Magazine
The Computer Artist

Introduction

The purpose of this report is to examine the feasibility of starting a new magazine tentatively entitled The Computer Artist, which would be aimed at graphic artists who use computers as their main tool for design and production. This report will describe the following:

1. The potential size of the market audience.
2. Competing magazines.
3. Potential profitability of the magazine.
4. Projected cost of starting and running the magazine.

The conclusions reported here are the result of a study carried out by a task force created six months ago by Stephen Connolly and John Bayle. The task force sent over 500 questionnaires to graphic artists, to manufacturers of computer graphics hardware, and to publishers of graphics software. In addition, the task force compiled data from financial forecasts and analyzed the competition. This information and the returned questionnaires will help C/B Publishing to make an informed decision.

The Target Audience

The target audience of The Computer Artist is all graphic artists in the U.S. and Canada who use IBM-compatible and Macintosh personal computers. We (the task force) decided, therefore, to estimate the total number of graphic artists employed within the

---

target area. Based on data published by the American Society of Graphic Designers,[1] we estimated that over 95,000 graphic designers work within the United States and Canada.

Our analysis of the questionnaires to graphic artists suggested that 69% of them use personal computers and that an additional 13% plan to purchase and use a personal computer within the next 18 months. The potential audience for The Computer Artist is therefore 82% (69% + 13%) of 95,000, or a total of 78,000 artists. We expect that this number will increase in the coming years because nearly 100% of the new graphic artists coming into the field will use computers on the job, while those retiring tend to be the artists who don't use computers. In the next five years, the target audience could number over 100,000.

The Competition

About eight trade magazines regularly cover the subjects of graphics software, desktop publishing, and graphic design, but no magazine published today focuses specifically on graphic design using personal computers. From experience with other professional magazines that C/B Publishing has published under similar circumstances, we expect that 12% of the potential audience will initially subscribe to the new magazine. We believe, however, that as the number of computer-based graphic designers increases, other publishers will certainly recognize this growing market and launch new magazines of their own. For this reason, the success of The Computer Artist will largely depend on our securing a commitment

---

[1] Report of the American Society of Graphic Designers, Arbol Press, March 1991, p. 84.

Figure 5-36
Pages one and two
of the final version
of the report

from the C/B Publishing board of directors to aggressive marketing and adherence to high publication standards. We must secure this commitment if we hope to increase or even maintain our subscription level two or three years into circulation. Being the first magazine to tap this market will help us, but we must be ever vigilant of the competition.

Projected Income

Our income from The Computer Artist has two sources, subscriptions and advertising.

From the estimated size of the potential audience (78,000 graphic designers in the U.S. and Canada) and the expected percentage of subscribers (12%), we project that we will have 9400 subscribers within the first year of publication. Assuming a subscription rate of $55 per year[2] and 9400 subscribers, the potential income from subscriptions will be $517,000.

Results of the questionnaires sent to manufacturers of computer graphics hardware and to publishers of graphics software were very encouraging. We have verbal commitments for full-page, half-page, and quarter-page advertisements from several large hardware and software companies who market graphics programs, laser printers, plotters, soft fonts, printer cartridges, and optical character recognition software. The marketing members of the task force are confident that with effort and focus, they can sell all of our advertisement space in The Computer Artist.

---

[2] Our questionnaire indicated that specialty magazines of this type have subscription rates typically in the range of $35 to $95 per year.

We have budgeted 16 of the 64-page issues for ad space. If we fill all 16 pages in 12 issues per year, and if we assume an average gross income per page of $4000, the total revenues from page advertisements will be approximately $768,000 per year.

The total projected income from publication of the magazine will, therefore, be approximately $1,285,000 per year.

Expenses

The cost of starting the magazine (including hiring six new staff members, renovating office space, meeting additional office expenses and other overhead costs, marketing expenses for the first two issues, and producing the first two issues) will be approximately $721,000.[3] Continued marketing expenses will be approximately $21,000 per month. Editorial and production expenses (based on our experience with our other magazines of similar size and format) will be approximately $44,000 per month. The total expense the first year will, therefore, be about $1,371,000, and the repeating expense after the initial investment will be about $780,000 per year.

Summary and Recommendation

The Computer Artist is a magazine that fits within the mission of C/B Publishing. We have the knowledge and experience necessary to publish this magazine.

The financial analysis given above suggests that the first year's expenses will exceed income by about $86,000. But in subsequent years, the income will exceed expenditures by about

---

[3] For a detailed breakdown of these expenses, contact David Palermo in the Financial Office.
$505,000.

Figure 5-36
Pages three and four of the final version of the report

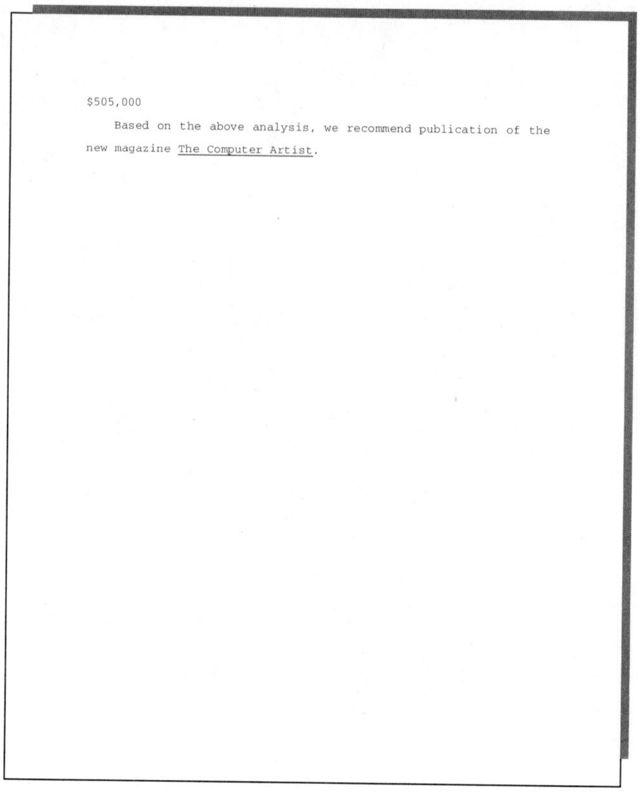

```
$505,000
    Based on the above analysis, we recommend publication of the
new magazine The Computer Artist.
```

Figure 5-36
Page five of the
final version of the
report

Exercises

1. Define or describe each of the following terms:
   a. paragraph number in an outline
   b. outline level
   c. outline family

2. How would you begin an outline?

3. How would you create a footnote?

4. How would you turn on hyphenation?

5. List the five steps in creating a macro.

6. Describe how to execute each of the following types of macros:
   a. Alt macro
   b. Named macro
   c. Enter macro

7. What is an advantage and a disadvantage of each of the three types of macros?

8. What would you do to be able to view two different documents on the screen simultaneously?

9. Suppose you needed to copy several nonconsecutive sentences and paragraphs from one document to another. How would you perform that task?

10. If WordPerfect needs help in positioning the hyphen when hyphenation is on, the "Position hyphen" prompt appears on the screen with a suggested position for the hyphen. What would you do to change the position of the hyphen and instruct WordPerfect to continue checking through the document?

Tutorial Assignments

Retrieve the file T5FILE1.DFT from your WordPerfect data diskette and do the following:

1. With T5FILE1.DFT in Doc 1, write an outline of the report in Doc 2, switching between your outline and the report as needed and using WordPerfect's outline feature. Use the headings and subheadings of the report to help in preparing the outline.

2. Save the outline as S5PUBLSH.OTL.

3. Print the outline.

4. In the report in Doc 1, turn on automatic hyphenation. Move the cursor to the end of the document to reformat the document, and respond to any hyphenation prompts that WordPerfect might display.

5. Create a macro named TITLE.WPM that boldfaces a heading and switches it to all upper-case letters (for example, "Introduction" to "**INTRODUCTION**"). *Hint:* To boldface or capitalize existing text, you have to use a block operation.

6. Use the macro you just created to boldface and capitalize the other three major headings in the report.

7. Save the report as S5PUBLSH.DFT.

8. Print the report.

9. Move the cursor to the right of the comma after the word Publish! in the first paragraph of the report. Insert the following footnote:

    Publish! is published monthly by PCW Communications, Inc., 501 Second St., San Francisco, CA 94107.

10. Move the cursor to the right of the article title "The Big Scan" (after the quotation mark) and insert the following footnote:

    Erik Holsinger and Bob Weibel, "The Big Scan," Publish!, March 1990, pp. 56–64.

11. Move the cursor to the right of the article title "Keep It In Color" (after the quotation mark) and insert the following footnote:

    Peter Vanags and Keith Baumann, "Keep It In Color," Publish!, March 1990, pp. 69–78.

12. Save the document as S5FILE1.REP.

13. Print the final version of the document.

Case Problems

1. Hartwell Pharmaceuticals' Corporate Fitness Program

Kawika Hemuli is an assistant business manager for Hartwell Pharmaceuticals Corporation, a 6,500-employee research and development company in Dubuque, Iowa. He wants to write a justification report, in memorandum format, to propose that the company create a corporate fitness program. His short report is shown in Figure 5-37.

Do the following:

1. Write a short outline of the contents of the report.

2. Save the outline as S5FITNES.OTL.

3. Print the outline.

4. Type the report until you get to the first occurrence of the phrase "corporate fitness program" in the SUBJECT of the memo.

Hartwell Pharmaceuticals Corporation

March 19, 1993
MEMO TO:Pablo Iquique
FROM:Kawika Hemuli
SUBJECT:Proposal to create a corporate fitness program

Purpose. To save money by improving employee morale and retention and lowering employee absenteeism.

Description of the Program. A corporate fitness program would allow employees (for a nominal fee of, for example, $25 per year) to enjoy the benefits of a fitness center--including exercycles, weight-lifting equipment, etc.--and fitness counseling--including exercise prescriptions and weight-loss programs. We would hire a fitness counselor (who has a degree in commercial fitness[1]) to set up and manage the program. We would renovate part of our current activity center to include the additional exercise equipment, and we would create five miles of paths for jogging, walking, or biking in the woods on the north and east ends of the company land.

Cost and Savings. The initial cost of setting up an employee fitness program would be approximately $280,000[2]--which includes consulting services, renovation of the activity center, creation of the jogging paths, printing of notices and program materials, and hiring a fitness counselor. The annual cost to the company would be approximately $35,000 in the beginning (a gross cost of $110,000 less about $75,000 in annual membership fees from employees). The company is currently losing an estimated $185,000 per year because of absenteeism and employee turnover. Other companies have experienced up to a 25% drop in absenteeism and turnover upon establishing a similar fitness program. Assuming that our program does the same, we would save $46,250. The net savings to the company would therefore be about $11,000 per year. The savings to the company would rise as more employees joined the program.

Proposal. I propose that Hartwell do the following:

1.   Retain a consulting firm to make recommendations regarding a fitness program and to design the fitness center and jogging trails.
2.   Hire a fitness counselor soon after the consulting firm provides its initial report. The fitness counselor could then help in the planning of facilities and programs.

_____

[1]Bachelor's degrees in commercial fitness are given by many large universities. The training usually includes exercise physiology, nutrition, and business management.

[2]This and all figures in this proposal are rough approximations only. The consulting firms who will help us plan the fitness program will be able to provide us with more realistic numbers.

Figure 5-37

```
    3.    Charge the fitness counselor with the task of signing up as
          many employees as possible, with the goal of eventually making
          the program self-sustaining.
    4.    Begin the renovation and construction of facilities.
    5.    Print information about the fitness program, and send it to
          all employees.
    6.    Recruit employees to participate in the fitness program.

    Conclusion.  A corporate fitness program would not only improve
    physical health and morale of our employees but, in the long run,
    would save the company money.  In addition, such a program would
    help in recruiting top personnel to our company.
```

Figure 5-37
(continued)

5. Create an Enter macro that inserts the phrase "corporate fitness program" into the document. Use the macro each time you need to type that phrase in the report.

6. Create a macro, named Alt-H, that formats the first heading ("Purpose") as shown in Figure 5-37. Use the macro to help you create subsequent headings in the report.

7. Finish typing the report, including footnotes, as shown in Figure 5-37.

8. Save the report as S5FITNES.REP.

9. Print the report.

2. Computer Consultants Corporation: Improving Office Efficiency

Robert Smith, who graduated with a bachelor's degree in business finance five years ago, works as a junior consultant for Computer Consultants Corp. (CCC), headquartered in New York City. He has just finished a study of the office automation needs of Central Park Medical Offices, a consortium of 12 physicians.

1. Retrieve into Doc 2 the outline of Robert's report, P5CCCOTL.DFT, from your WordPerfect data diskette.

2. Create a macro named Alt-U (for "up") that moves an outline family up one family (for example, from "4" to "3" or from "b" to "a").

3. Use the Alt-U macro to move the outline family that begins "2. CCC classes" up one family so that it is "1" instead of "2."

4. Use the Alt-U macro to move the item "D. Computerized accounting system" up one family so that it is "C" instead of "D."

5. Save the outline to the disk using the filename S5CCC.OTL.

6. Print the outline.

7. Retrieve Robert's report, P5CCCREP.DFT, into Doc 1.

8. Turn on hyphenation.

9. Add the following footnote at the end of recommendation number 1: To obtain a catalog of WordPerfect training tapes, write or phone LearnKey, Inc., 93 S. Mountain Way Dr., Orem, UT 84058, (800) 937-3279, which produces a wide selection of effective but inexpensive tapes.

10. Add the following footnote after the phrase "transcription costs" in recommendation number 2: "Prescription for Transcription," WordPerfect Magazine, July 1990, pp. 15–17.

11. Save the report to the file S5CCC.REP.

12. Print the report.

3. Report on Computers in Business

Write a double-spaced, three- to four-page report (700–1,000 words) on some facet of computers in business. Make the topic as narrow as possible to adequately cover the subject in three to four pages. Possible titles include:

- "Challenges in Learning to Use a Computer in Business"
- "How Computers Have Changed Small Businesses"
- "Using Computers in a Home Business"
- "The Advantages of a Local-Area Network in a Business Office"
- "Using a Word Processor to Make Money in Your Spare Time"
- "The Future of Computers in the Office"
- "How Computers Waste Time and Money"
- "How Computers Save Time and Money"

Possible sources of information include your own experience, interviews with business managers and owners, magazine articles, newspaper articles, and books.

If you have difficulty deciding on a topic or gathering information for your paper, consult a librarian at your university or municipal library or see your instructor.

Do the following:

1. Write an outline before you write the report, then revise the outline after you have completed your report. Submit both versions of the outline with this case problem.

2. Double-space the report.

3. Create a title page that contains the title of your article, your name, the title of your course, the date, and any other information your instructor wants you to include.

4. Turn on hyphenation for your report.

5. Include a header and page numbering.

6. Include at least two footnotes giving the sources of information for your report.

7. Create at least two macros to help you write the report. Make sure copies of the macro files are on the diskette that you submit to your instructor.

Tutorial 6

Merging Documents

Writing a Sales Form Letter

Case: Sanders Imports, Inc.

Immediately after graduating from high school, Whitney Sanders began working as a clerk in an import store owned by International Products, Ltd. (IPL), a large corporation with franchises throughout the United States. During the next six years, Whitney worked her way up to international buyer within IPL. Her job entailed traveling to foreign countries, especially Central and South America, to purchase specialty items such as rugs, wood carvings, picture frames, ceramics, and cast-iron furniture.

Although she enjoyed her job and was successful at it, Whitney wanted to go back to school and earn a degree in business administration. She felt such a degree would improve her professional opportunities. So after seven years with IPL, Whitney resigned and went back to school full time. Four years later she received a B.S. with a major in business administration and a minor in international relations from Howard University in Washington, D.C.

With degree in hand Whitney started her own import business called Sanders Imports, Inc. (SII), headquartered in Gaithersburg, Maryland, just outside Washington, D.C. Within 18 months her business was healthy and growing. Among her successes are several large contracts with three major discount department stores and over 20 specialty shops throughout the United States. Whitney markets to these clients by publishing a quarterly catalog that contains color photographs and descriptions of the items she imports.

Last week Whitney added two major items, Mexican iced-tea glass tumblers and Ecuadorian hand-carved chess sets, to her catalog. She is not scheduled to publish another catalog for two months, but she wants to advise her customers immediately about these highly marketable products. She decides to write a letter to her clients (Figure 6-1).

OBJECTIVES

In this tutorial you will learn to:

- Create primary and secondary merge files

- Merge files

- Sort a secondary file

- Create address labels

Sanders Imports, Inc.
429 Firstfield Road, Gaithersburg, MD 20878
Phone (301) 590-1000 Fax (301) 590-1825
Orders 1-800-IMPORTS

<u>   Date   </u>

First Name   Last Name
<u>   Company   </u>
<u>   Street Address   </u>
 City,   State   Zip

Dear   <u> NickName</u>:

    I am writing to let you know about two exciting new SII products that I'm certain will appeal to your customers.

    ICED TEA GLASS TUMBLERS, 16oz., finely painted patterns, imported from Mexico, suggested retail price $4.95 per set of four tumblers, your price $2.18 per set. These drinking glasses have heavy glass bottoms and clear glass sides and come in six different patterns. Sold in attractive cardboard carrying box. Because they are attractive yet inexpensive, these tumblers will sell well.

    HAND-CARVED CHESS SETS, Staunton pattern, weighted and felted bases, detailed knights, natural grain, U.S. Chess Federation approved, imported from Quito, Ecuador, suggested retail price $38.95, your price $16.68 per set. These sets are almost identical in appearance to the sets imported from India that sell for twice this amount.

    I have enclosed photographs of these products.

    <u>   NickName   </u>, please call me for more information or to receive samples of either of these items. As always, it is a pleasure doing business with <u>   Company   </u>.

                              Sincerely yours,

                              Whitney Sanders

                              Whitney Sanders
                              President, SII

Enclosures

Figure 6-1
Whitney's form
letter

The Merge Feature

Whitney wants to write a **form letter**, which is a letter that contains information pertinent to a large number of people (in this case, Whitney's clients) but that also contains information specific to the addressee. The specific information in Whitney's form letter is an inside address and salutation for each client and in the body of the letter the client's first name and the company's name.

To achieve these objectives efficiently, Whitney will use WordPerfect's Merge features. In general a **merge** is an operation that combines information from two documents to create several slightly different final documents.

Merge Documents

The merge operation employs two documents: a primary file and a secondary file. A **primary file** is a document — such as a letter or a contract — that, in addition to text, contains merge commands to mark where data — such as a name or an address — will be inserted. In Whitney's case, the primary file will be like Figure 6-1, except that instead of blanks the document will contain merge commands to mark the location for individualized names, addresses, and other data.

A **secondary file** is a document that contains specific information — such as names, street addresses, cities, states, and zip codes — that will be merged into the primary file. In Whitney's case, the secondary file will be an address list, similar to Figure 6-2, except that the file will have a slightly different format and will also contain merge commands to help WordPerfect merge the information into a primary file.

Figure 6-2
Client data for Whitney's secondary file

```
Malone, Rebecca C. (Becky)
415-825-1585
Compton Novelty Shop
8415 El Arbol Street
Compton, CA 90220

McArdy, Gregory P. (Paul)
719-448-0025
Paul's Imports
854 North Pike's Peak Road
Colorado Springs, CO 80902

Sorenson, Mary Beth (Mary)
218-968-1593
North Star Emporium
51 West Center Street
Bemidji, MN 56601

Pilar, F. Emilio (Emilio)
602-433-8878
Grand Canyon Imports
4851 Caibab Highway Suite 210
Flagstaff, AZ 86001

Gutanov, Mikhail Ivonov (Mike)
404-921-3722
Peachtree Emporium
88 Peachtree Plaza
Atlanta, GA 30304
```

The final document(s) produced by merging information from the secondary file into the primary file is called the **merged document** (Figure 6-3).

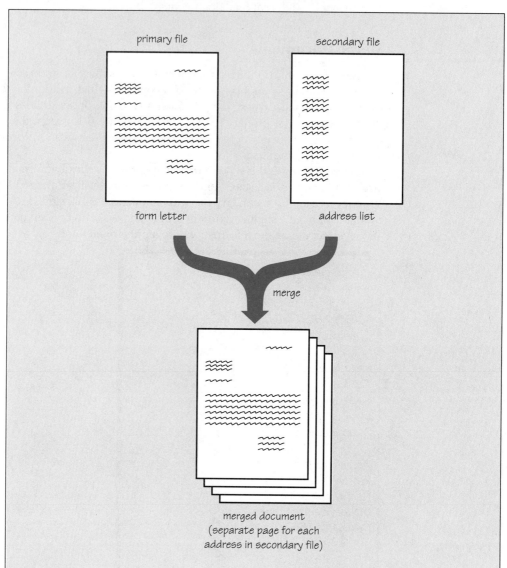

Merge Operations

During a merge operation, the merge commands in the primary file instruct WordPerfect to fetch specific information from the secondary file. For example, one merge command in the primary file might fetch a name, while another merge command might fetch a street address. For each name and street address in the secondary file, WordPerfect usually creates a separate page in the merged document. Thus, if Whitney's secondary file has, for example, five names and addresses of clients, the merge will produce five different letters, each with a different name and address and each on a separate page in the merged document (Figure 6-4).

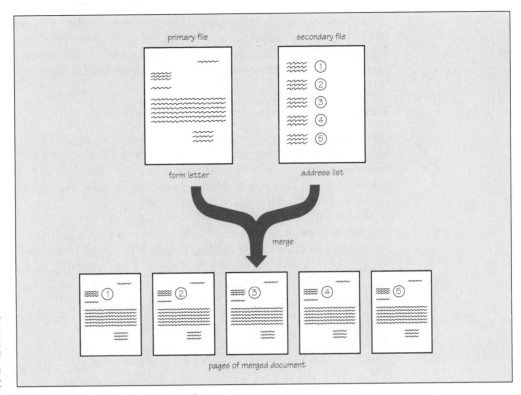

Figure 6-4
Pages of merged
document equal
number of
addresses in
address list

Records and Fields

The set of data on one individual in the secondary file is called a **record**. In Whitney's
secondary file each record contains information about one client (Figure 6-5). Each item
within a record is called a **field**. One field might be the client's name; another field, the client's
street address; another field, the client's city; and so forth. For a merge operation to work
properly, every record must have the same set of fields.

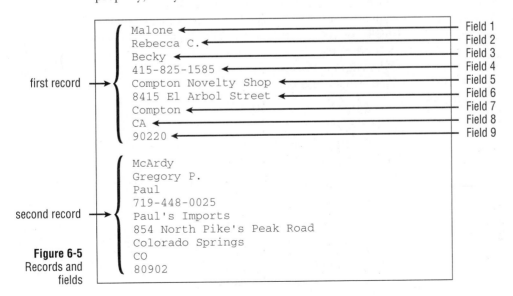

Figure 6-5
Records and
fields

Secondary files are not limited to records about clients. You could create a secondary file with employee records, another with records of suppliers, another with records of equipment, and so forth. Once you understand how to manage and manipulate the records in secondary merge files, you'll be able to use them for many different types of applications.

Merge Commands

Primary files usually contain merge commands that instruct WordPerfect which fields of each record to fetch and where to place those fields in the merged document. Primary files may also contain merge commands that insert the current date, get input from the keyboard, and perform other functions. Secondary files contain merge commands that mark the end of each record and that label the fields in each record.

Figure 6-6 is a table of the most common merge commands. Each merge command consists of a **merge code**, which appears in the primary document as an uppercase word enclosed in braces (curly brackets), such as {FIELD} or {DATE}. You don't actually type the characters in a merge code but rather use WordPerfect's Merge Codes command to insert the codes.

Merge Command	Action
{DATE}	Insert current date
{FIELD}FieldName~	Fetch data from field named *FieldName* in secondary file
{FIELD NAMES}*FieldName1~* *FieldName2~* *FieldName3~~*	List names of fields in secondary file
{END FIELD}	Mark end of the field
{END RECORD}	Mark end of the record

Figure 6-6
Common merge commands

Some merge commands also require a parameter. For example, the {FIELD} command requires a parameter that names a particular field within a record. The end of a parameter is marked with a tilde (~). Hence, a primary document that contained the merge command {FIELD}FirstName~ would instruct WordPerfect to fetch the field named "FirstName" from a record in the secondary file (Figure 6-7). In the {FIELDNAME} command a tilde marks the end of each field name and another tilde marks the end of the entire list of field names. The {DATE} command, which inserts the current date into the document, doesn't require a parameter.

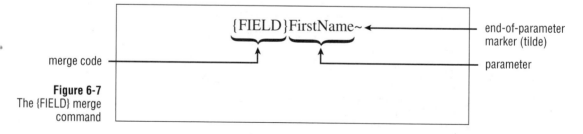

merge code

Figure 6-7
The {FIELD} merge command

Whitney's primary file, including the merge codes, is shown in Figure 6-8. Your task in the following section will be to create this primary file.

merge command
(no parameter)

merge commands
(codes and
parameters)

merge commands

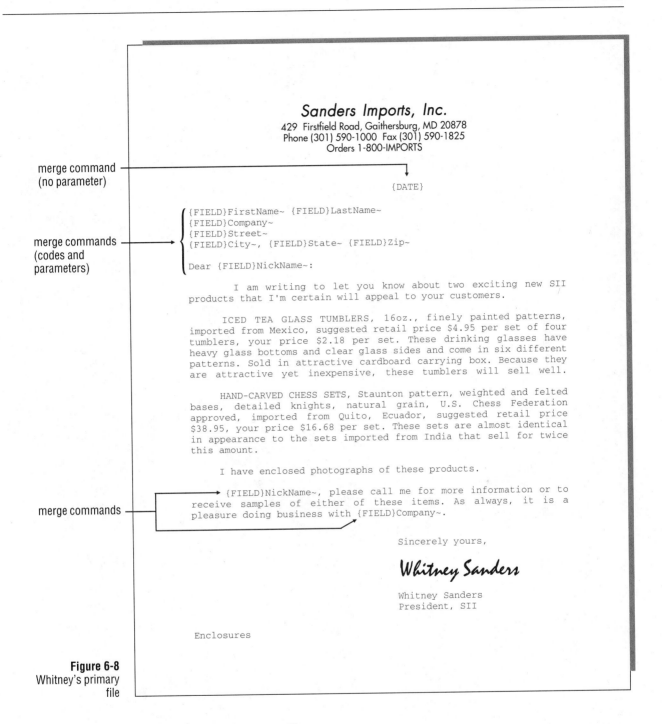

Figure 6-8
Whitney's primary
file

Creating a Primary File

A primary file contains text and merge commands. Creating a primary file is similar to creating any other type of WordPerfect document, except that you use [Shift][F9] (Merge Codes) to insert the merge commands into the primary file. You'll begin by inserting the {DATE} command.

To insert {DATE} into the primary file:

❶ Make sure the document screen is clear and press **[Enter]** until the cursor is at Ln 2.5" or lower.

This leaves room for the company letterhead at the top of the page. If your paper doesn't have a letterhead, the blank space will keep the text of the letter from being too high up on the page.

❷ Press **[Tab]** until the cursor is at Pos 4.5", where Whitney wants to put the date in the letter.

Now you're ready to instruct WordPerfect to insert the {DATE} code.

❸ Select More from the Tools/Merge Codes menu. See Figure 6-9.

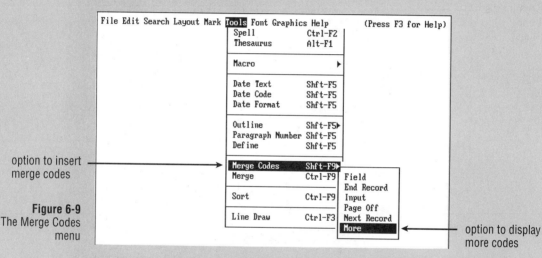

option to insert merge codes

option to display more codes

Figure 6-9
The Merge Codes menu

Alternatively press **[Shift][F9]** (Merge Codes) to display the one-line menu shown in Figure 6-10.

option to display more codes

Figure 6-10
Menu to select merge codes

Then select **6** (**M**ore). Because the merge code {DATE} doesn't appear on the pull-down menu or on the one-line menu, you must select More to get a listing of more merge codes. A window of merge codes appears in the upper right corner of the screen. See Figure 6-11. The window displays only a few of the many merge codes at any one time. You can use the arrow keys to scroll the contents of the window to display other codes.

Merge Codes window

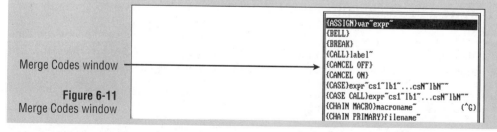

Figure 6-11
Merge Codes window

④ Use the cursor-movement keys or the mouse to move the cursor so that {DATE} is highlighted, then press **[Enter]**. You can also press **D** to tell WordPerfect to immediately move the cursor to the merge codes that begin with D, then you can use an arrow key to move the cursor to {DATE}. WordPerfect inserts the {DATE} code into the document, closes the Merge Codes window, and returns the cursor to the document screen.

Later, when Whitney executes the merge, WordPerfect will insert the current date at the location of the {DATE} code on each copy of the letter in the resulting merged document.

In the following steps, you'll insert the {FIELD} command into the primary file.

To insert the {FIELD} command into the primary file:

① Press **[Enter]** three times to triple space between the date and the inside address.

② Select Field from the Tools/Merge Codes menu or press **[Shift][F9]** (Merge Codes) and select **1** (**F**ield).

WordPerfect displays the prompt "Enter Field:" and waits for you to type the name of the field. The field name in the primary file must correspond to a field name in the secondary file. Since Whitney hasn't created the secondary file yet, she can use any field name she wants at this point. She'll have to remember these field names when she creates her secondary file.

③ Type **FirstName** and press **[Enter]**. WordPerfect inserts the {FIELD} command, the name of the field, and a tilde (~), which marks the end of the field name. See Figure 6-12.

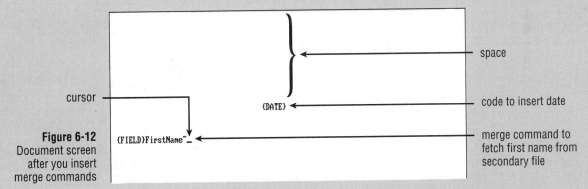

Figure 6-12
Document screen after you insert merge commands

space

cursor

code to insert date

{DATE}

{FIELD}FirstName~

merge command to fetch first name from secondary file

When Whitney executes the merge, WordPerfect will fetch the first name — which will include the first name and a middle name or a middle initial — from the secondary file and insert it into the document at that location.

④ Press **[Space]** to insert a space after the first name(s), then select Field from the Tools/Merge Codes menu or press **[Shift][F9]** (Merge Codes) and select **1** (**F**ield).

⑤ Type **LastName** and press **[Enter]**. See Figure 6-13.

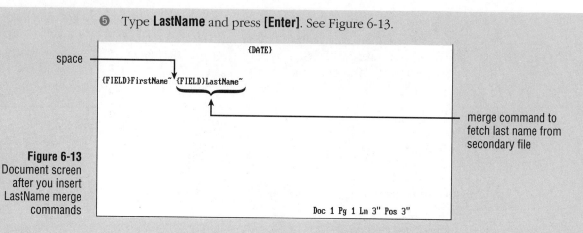

Figure 6-13
Document screen after you insert LastName merge commands

space

{DATE}

{FIELD}FirstName~ {FIELD}LastName~

merge command to fetch last name from secondary file

Doc 1 Pg 1 Ln 3" Pos 3"

⑥ Press **[Enter]** to move the cursor to the next line and insert the {FIELD} code with the field name "Company," as shown in Figure 6-8.

⑦ Continue typing the merge codes to insert the inside address and the salutation, until your screen looks like Figure 6-14. Remember, never *type* a merge code, such as "{FIELD}"; always use the Merge Codes command to insert the codes.

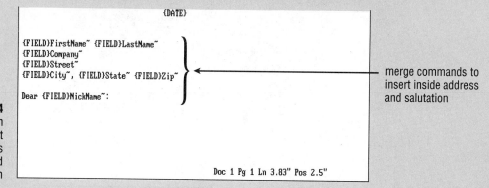

Figure 6-14
Document screen after you insert merge commands for address and salutation

{DATE}

{FIELD}FirstName~ {FIELD}LastName~
{FIELD}Company~
{FIELD}Street~
{FIELD}City~, {FIELD}State~ {FIELD}Zip~

Dear {FIELD}NickName~:

merge commands to insert inside address and salutation

Doc 1 Pg 1 Ln 3.83" Pos 2.5"

Carefully check over your document to make sure all the field names are spelled correctly.

⑧ Press **[Enter]** twice to double-space after the salutation.

The {FIELD}NickName~ command in the salutation tells WordPerfect to fetch a name that might be the same as the first name but is usually different. For example, the secondary file might list a client's first name as "Rebecca C." but her nickname as "Becky."

You'll now retrieve the rest of the form letter (the primary file) from the WordPerfect data diskette and insert two other merge commands.

To retrieve the file and insert merge commands:

❶ Insert the data diskette into drive A.

Because you will frequently use the diskette in drive A to save and retrieve files, you will now change the default directory to A:.

❷ Press **[F5]** (List), and then press **[=]** (equal sign). At the prompt "New directory = ," type **a:** and press **[Enter]**. Then press **[F1]** (Cancel) to cancel the directory listing.

❸ Retrieve the file C6FILE1.DFT from the data diskette in drive A.

WordPerfect may ask, "Retrieve into current file? No (Yes)." This is to help prevent you from accidentally combining an existing file with the file you presently have loaded. In this case, you *want* to combine them, so answer Yes.

❹ Move the cursor to the comma that begins the last paragraph of the letter.

❺ Insert the command {FIELD}NickName~.

❻ Move the cursor to the period at the end of the last paragraph.

❼ Insert the command {FIELD}Company~. See Figure 6-15. The merge commands in the last paragraph of the document will tell WordPerfect to insert the nickname and the company name of the client at these locations in the letter. By placing these merge commands in the body of the form letter, Whitney is able to personalize the letter.

Figure 6-15
Document screen after you insert merge commands in last paragraph

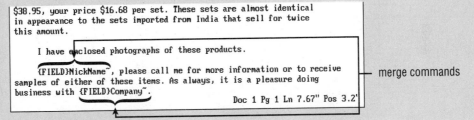

merge commands

```
$38.95, your price $16.68 per set. These sets are almost identical
in appearance to the sets imported from India that sell for twice
this amount.

    I have enclosed photographs of these products.

    {FIELD}NickName~, please call me for more information or to receive
samples of either of these items. As always, it is a pleasure doing
business with {FIELD}Company~.
                                    Doc 1 Pg 1 Ln 7.67" Pos 3.2'
```

❽ Save the file as S6SLSLET.PF.

The abbreviation "SLSLET" stands for "sales letter," and the filename extension "PF" stands for "primary file," to remind you that this is the primary file used in a WordPerfect merge operation.

Creating a Secondary File

As Whitney acquires new and potential clients, she types information about them into a WordPerfect secondary file. She can then merge the secondary file with a primary merge file to generate her sales letters.

Figure 6-16 on the next two pages shows the first five records of Whitney's secondary file. As you can see, the file contains merge codes that specify the names of the fields and that mark the ends of fields and records.

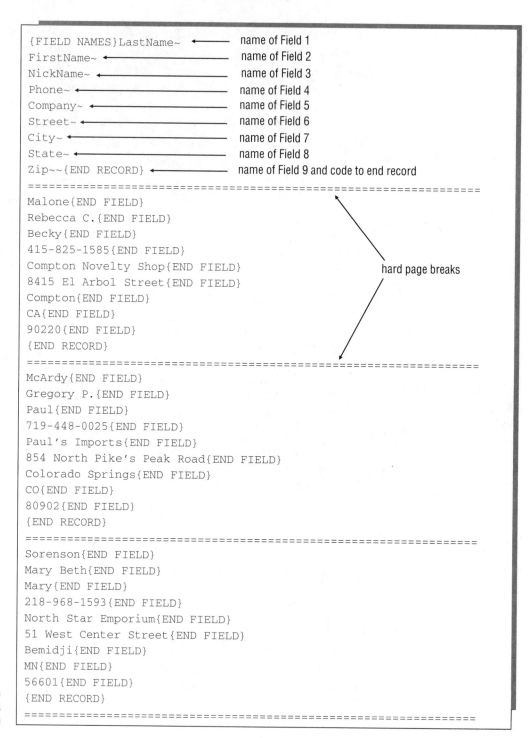

```
{FIELD NAMES}LastName~          ◄──────── name of Field 1
FirstName~        ◄────────────────────── name of Field 2
NickName~         ◄────────────────────── name of Field 3
Phone~  ◄──────────────────────────────── name of Field 4
Company~  ◄────────────────────────────── name of Field 5
Street~  ◄─────────────────────────────── name of Field 6
City~  ◄───────────────────────────────── name of Field 7
State~  ◄──────────────────────────────── name of Field 8
Zip~~{END RECORD}  ◄───────────────────── name of Field 9 and code to end record
=================================================================
Malone{END FIELD}
Rebecca C.{END FIELD}
Becky{END FIELD}
415-825-1585{END FIELD}
Compton Novelty Shop{END FIELD}               hard page breaks
8415 El Arbol Street{END FIELD}
Compton{END FIELD}
CA{END FIELD}
90220{END FIELD}
{END RECORD}
=================================================================
McArdy{END FIELD}
Gregory P.{END FIELD}
Paul{END FIELD}
719-448-0025{END FIELD}
Paul's Imports{END FIELD}
854 North Pike's Peak Road{END FIELD}
Colorado Springs{END FIELD}
CO{END FIELD}
80902{END FIELD}
{END RECORD}
=================================================================
Sorenson{END FIELD}
Mary Beth{END FIELD}
Mary{END FIELD}
218-968-1593{END FIELD}
North Star Emporium{END FIELD}
51 West Center Street{END FIELD}
Bemidji{END FIELD}
MN{END FIELD}
56601{END FIELD}
{END RECORD}
=================================================================
```

Figure 6-16
Whitney's
secondary file

```
Pilar{END FIELD}
F. Emilio{END FIELD}
Emilio{END FIELD}
602-433-8878{END FIELD}
Grand Canyon Imports{END FIELD}
4851 Caibab Highway Suite 210{END FIELD}
Flagstaff{END FIELD}
AZ{END FIELD}
86001{END FIELD}
{END RECORD}
================================================================
Gutanov{END FIELD}
Mikhail Ivonov{END FIELD}
Mike{END FIELD}
404-921-3722{END FIELD}
Peachtree Emporium{END FIELD}
88 Peachtree Plaza{END FIELD}
Atlanta{END FIELD}
GA{END FIELD}
30304{END FIELD}
{END RECORD}
================================================================
```

Figure 6-16
(continued)

To create a secondary file, you must follow certain procedures:

1. **Name the fields.** WordPerfect internally numbers each field within a record, but to make merge commands easier, you can tell WordPerfect the name of each field. In Figure 6-16, for example, the name of Field 1, the first field in each record, is "LastName." Wherever the primary file contains the merge command {FIELD}LastName~, WordPerfect will insert the information from the first field of the secondary file.

2. **Mark the end of the field names.** After you name all the fields, WordPerfect automatically inserts the {END RECORD} code to indicate that there are no more field names and inserts a hard page break.

3. **Insert data into the secondary file.** You type the text of a field and then insert the code {END FIELD} to mark the end of the field. You must follow exactly the format you used when you named the fields. For example, the first field of every record must be the last name; the second field of every record must be the first name; and so forth. If you change the order of entering information into the secondary file, Word-Perfect will insert the wrong information into the merge document during the merge operation. If the information for a particular field isn't available — for example, if you don't have a telephone number — you must still insert the Phone field by marking the end of the field with the {END FIELD} code. At the end of each record, you must insert the {END RECORD} code.

Let's create the secondary file of information about Whitney's clients. First we'll insert the merge command {FIELD NAMES}, which names the fields.

To insert the {FIELD NAMES} command:

❶   Clear the document screen.

❷   Select More from the Tools/Merge Codes menu or press **[Shift][F9]** (Merge Codes) and select **6** (**M**ore).

❸   Move the cursor to {FIELD NAMES} in the Merge Codes window and press **[Enter]**. WordPerfect displays the prompt "Enter Field 1:," as shown in Figure 6-17.

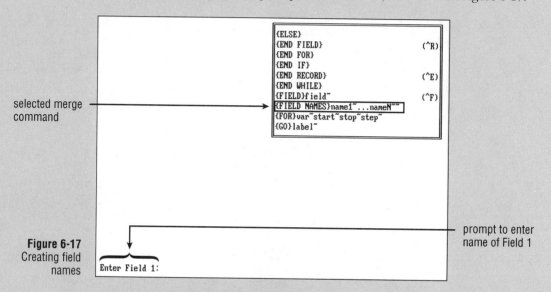

selected merge command

prompt to enter name of Field 1

Figure 6-17
Creating field names

❹   Type **LastName** and press **[Enter]** to specify that the first field in each record will contain the last name of the client.

Now WordPerfect prompts for the field name of Field 2, that is, the name of the second field of each record.

❺   Type **FirstName** and press **[Enter]**. WordPerfect displays the prompt for the name of Field 3.

❻   Type **NickName** and press **[Enter]**. This tells WordPerfect that the third field in each record will contain the client's nickname.

❼   Continue to type field names at the prompts, referring to Figure 6-16. The names of Fields 4 through 9 are "Phone," "Company," "Street," "City," "State," and "Zip."

WordPerfect automatically prompts you for the next field name until you tell WordPerfect to end the field names.

❽   After you have typed the last field name (Field 9, "Zip") and the prompt "Enter Field 10:" appears on the screen, press **[Enter]** without typing a name.

This signals WordPerfect that you have completed all the field names. The field names now appear across the top of the screen. See Figure 6-18. The {END RECORD} code and a hard page break appear after the last field name.

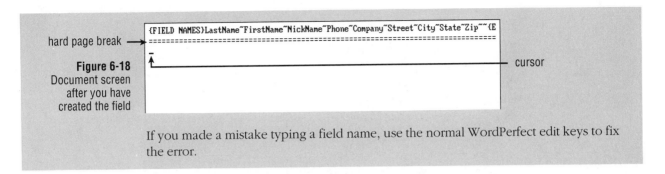

```
{FIELD NAMES}LastName~FirstName~NickName~Phone~Company~Street~City~State~Zip~~{E
================================================================================
```

hard page break →

Figure 6-18
Document screen
after you have
created the field

cursor

If you made a mistake typing a field name, use the normal WordPerfect edit keys to fix the error.

You can't see all the field names at once because the line is wider than one screen line. Let's insert a hard return at the end of each field name so each name appears on a separate second line.

To place the field names on separate lines:

❶ Move the cursor to the right of the first tilde (~), just after "LastName," and press **[Enter]**. The subsequent field names move to the next line.

❷ Move the cursor to the right of the tilde after each of the other field names and press **[Enter]**; then move the cursor below the page break. See Figure 6-19.

```
{FIELD NAMES}LastName~
FirstName~
NickName~
Phone~
Company~
Street~
City~
State~
Zip~~{END RECORD}
================================================================================


Field: LastName                              Doc 1 Pg 2 Ln 1" Pos 1"
```

hard returns
inserted after tildes
to put field names
on separate lines

cursor

Figure 6-19
Document screen
after you have
reformatted field
names

message to enter
data for Field 1
of first record

❸ Save the intermediate version of the secondary file as S6ADDR.INT. "ADDR" indicates that the file contains addresses, and the filename extension "INT" stands for "intermediate version" of the file.

The secondary file you have just created contains no records yet. You'll now enter the data for each record.

Entering Data into a Secondary File

After you create the {FIELD NAMES} command at the beginning of a secondary file, WordPerfect automatically inserts a hard page break after the {END RECORD} code, moves the cursor below the page break, and displays the current field on the left side of the status line at the bottom of the screen (Figure 6-19). Whitney is now ready to enter client information into the file, as shown in Figure 6-16. Let's begin by entering data into the first record.

To enter a record into a secondary file:

❶ With the cursor positioned just below the page break, type **Malone** and press **[F9]** (End Field). (If you pressed [Enter] instead of [F9] (End Field), press [Backspace] to delete the invisible [HRt] code.)

WordPerfect allows more than one line of text in a field. For example, you may want to include a department name and the company name on two separate lines in the Company field. In this particular file we will include only one line per field. WordPerfect inserts the merge code {END FIELD} to the right of "Malone" and automatically inserts a hard return to move the cursor to the next line. The message "Field: FirstName" appears on the status line. See Figure 6-20.

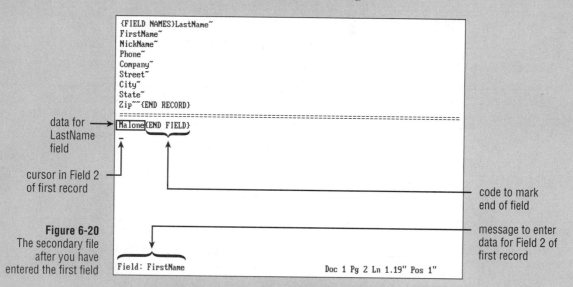

data for → LastName field

cursor in Field 2 of first record

code to mark end of field

message to enter data for Field 2 of first record

Figure 6-20
The secondary file
after you have
entered the first field

```
{FIELD NAMES}LastName~
FirstName~
NickName~
Phone~
Company~
Street~
City~
State~
Zip~~{END RECORD}
=====================================================================
Malone{END FIELD}
_
```

Field: FirstName   Doc 1 Pg 2 Ln 1.19" Pos 1"

❷ Type **Rebecca C.** and press **[F9]** (End Field) to insert the client's first name. Notice that this field also contains any middle name or middle initial of the client. WordPerfect inserts the {END FIELD} code and a hard return. The message "Field: NickName" appears on the status line.

❸ Type **Becky** and press **[F9]** (End Field) to insert the client's nickname. The NickName field contains only one name, the name that the client goes by. The nickname will often be the same as the client's first name.

WordPerfect displays the message "Field: Phone" on the status line. See Figure 6-21.

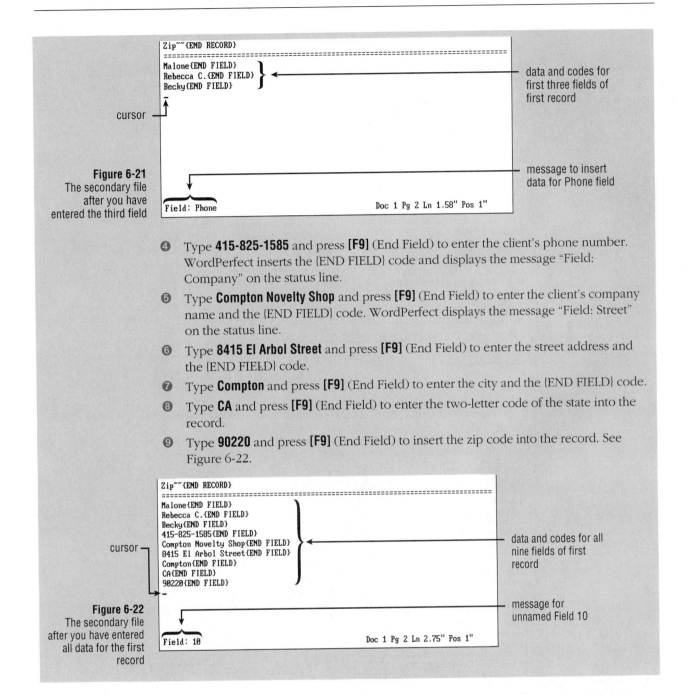

```
Zip~~{END RECORD}
========================================================================
Malone{END FIELD}
Rebecca C.{END FIELD}
Becky{END FIELD}
‾
▲
```

cursor

} data and codes for first three fields of first record

message to insert data for Phone field

```
Field: Phone                              Doc 1 Pg 2 Ln 1.58" Pos 1"
```

Figure 6-21
The secondary file after you have entered the third field

④ Type **415-825-1585** and press **[F9]** (End Field) to enter the client's phone number. WordPerfect inserts the {END FIELD} code and displays the message "Field: Company" on the status line.

⑤ Type **Compton Novelty Shop** and press **[F9]** (End Field) to enter the client's company name and the {END FIELD} code. WordPerfect displays the message "Field: Street" on the status line.

⑥ Type **8415 El Arbol Street** and press **[F9]** (End Field) to enter the street address and the {END FIELD} code.

⑦ Type **Compton** and press **[F9]** (End Field) to enter the city and the {END FIELD} code.

⑧ Type **CA** and press **[F9]** (End Field) to enter the two-letter code of the state into the record.

⑨ Type **90220** and press **[F9]** (End Field) to insert the zip code into the record. See Figure 6-22.

```
Zip~~{END RECORD}
========================================================================
Malone{END FIELD}
Rebecca C.{END FIELD}
Becky{END FIELD}
415-825-1585{END FIELD}
Compton Novelty Shop{END FIELD}
8415 El Arbol Street{END FIELD}
Compton{END FIELD}
CA{END FIELD}
90220{END FIELD}
‾
```

cursor

} data and codes for all nine fields of first record

message for unnamed Field 10

```
Field: 10                                 Doc 1 Pg 2 Ln 2.75" Pos 1"
```

Figure 6-22
The secondary file after you have entered all data for the first record

You have now entered all the data for the first record. The status line displays the message "Field: 10" instead of a field name, because the secondary file has only nine named fields. You now must mark the end of this record.

To mark the end of a record:

❶ Select End Record from the Tools/Merge Codes menu or press **[Shift][F9]** (Merge Codes) and select **2** (**E**nd Record). WordPerfect inserts the {END RECORD} command and a hard page break. See Figure 6-23.

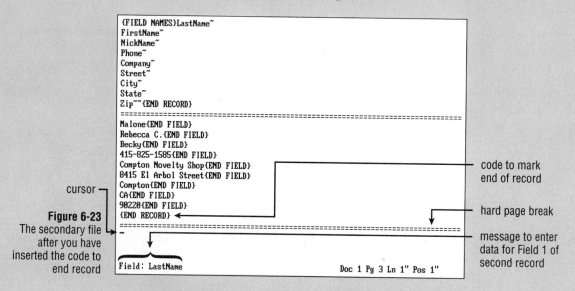

Figure 6-23
The secondary file after you have inserted the code to end record

Having created the first record in the secondary file, you can now enter the next four records of Whitney's client list, as shown in Figure 6-16.

❷ Finish entering the other four records into the secondary file. Your screen will look like Figure 6-24.

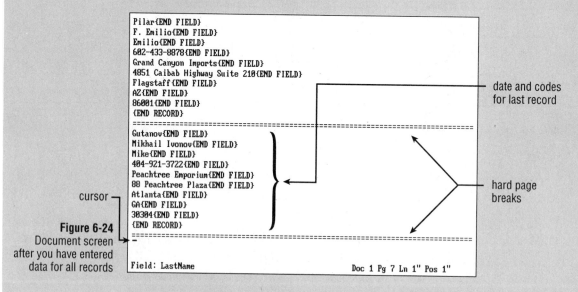

Figure 6-24
Document screen after you have entered data for all records

It's easy to make mistakes as you enter information for each record. Make sure you enter each item (last name, first name, nickname, phone number, company name, street, city, state, and zip code) into a separate field. Remember to press [F9] (End

Field) after you enter an item into a field and to select End Record at the end of each record.

After you have entered the final record, WordPerfect prompts you for the last name of another record (Figure 6-24). Ignore this prompt.

❸ After you have entered the data and double-checked it for accuracy, save the document as S6ADDR.SF. The filename extension "SF" stands for "secondary file."

Although Whitney's secondary file will eventually contain numerous records (one for each of her many clients), S6ADDR.SF contains only five records, a sufficient number to demonstrate WordPerfect's merge features.

Merging Primary and Secondary Files

Now that she has created her form letter (primary file) and her address list (secondary file), Whitney is ready to merge the two files to create individual letters to send to her clients. Let's merge S6SLSLET.PF (the primary file) with S6ADDR.SF (the secondary file).

To merge a primary file and a secondary file:

❶ Clear the document screen.

Because the results of the merge will appear in the document screen, you must clear the screen before you execute the merge.

❷ Select Merge from the Tools menu or press **[Ctrl][F9]** (Merge/Sort) and select **1** (**M**erge). The prompt "Primary file:" appears on the status line.

❸ Type **s6slslet.pf** and press **[Enter]**. This is Whitney's primary file, which contains her form letter. The prompt "Secondary file:" appears on the status line.

❹ Type **s6addr.sf** and press **[Enter]**. This is Whitney's secondary file, which contains her address list. WordPerfect merges the primary and secondary files to create the merged document.

The end of the merged document now appears on the document screen (Figure 6-25).

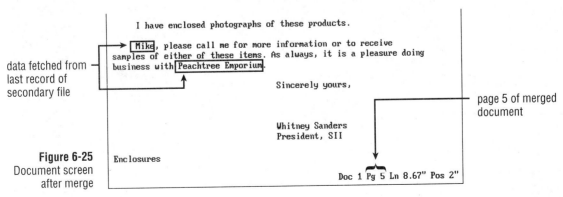

data fetched from last record of secondary file

page 5 of merged document

Figure 6-25
Document screen after merge

During the merge operation, WordPerfect extracted information from one record in the secondary file and inserted it into the primary file according to the merge commands in the primary file to create a letter. After each letter, WordPerfect inserted a hard page break so that each letter will print on a separate page. You can use the cursor-movement keys to move through the resulting merged document. As you can see, it contains five pages, one page for each of the five records in the primary file. The first page of the merged document, the letter to Rebecca Malone, appears in Figure 6-26.

this will not be on
your document

Sanders Imports, Inc.
429 Firstfield Road, Gaithersburg, MD 20878
Phone (301) 590-1000 Fax (301) 590-1825
Orders 1-800-IMPORTS

May 11, 1993

Rebecca C. Malone
Compton Novelty Shop
8415 El Arbol Street
Compton, CA 90220

Dear Becky:

I am writing to let you know about two exciting new SII products that I'm certain will appeal to your customers.

ICED TEA GLASS TUMBLERS, 16oz., finely painted patterns, imported from Mexico, suggested retail price $4.95 per set of four tumblers, your price $2.18 per set. These drinking glasses have heavy glass bottoms and clear glass sides and come in six different patterns. Sold in attractive cardboard carrying box. Because they are attractive yet inexpensive, these tumblers will sell well.

HAND-CARVED CHESS SETS, Staunton pattern, weighted and felted bases, detailed knights, natural grain, U.S. Chess Federation approved, imported from Quito, Ecuador, suggested retail price $38.95, your price $16.68 per set. These sets are almost identical in appearance to the sets imported from India that sell for twice this amount.

I have enclosed photographs of these products.

Becky, please call me for more information or to receive samples of either of these items. As always, it is a pleasure doing business with Compton Novelty Shop.

Sincerely yours,

Whitney Sanders

Whitney Sanders
President, SII

Enclosures

Figure 6-26
First page of
merged document

Sorting a Secondary File

As Whitney looks through the merged document with the letters to her clients, she observes one problem. She is going to use bulk mailing rates to send her letters, but the U.S. Postal Service requires bulk mailings to be divided into groups according to zip code. Currently the letters are in the order in which she added the client information to her secondary file. She must, therefore, sort the secondary file.

In WordPerfect, to **sort** means to arrange a list or a document in some specified order. WordPerfect allows you perform three types of sort: merge, line, and paragraph. A **merge sort** allows you to sort the records in a secondary file, as you'll see shortly. A **line sort** allows you to sort lines within a document (Figure 6-27). A **paragraph sort** allows you to sort the paragraphs within a document. You have to tell WordPerfect which type of sort you want to carry out.

Figure 6-27
Sorting lines in
a document

lines in document
before line sort

lines in document
after alphabetic
line sort

You also need to tell WordPerfect whether the sort involves only numbers, called a **numeric sort**, or numbers and letters, called an **alphanumeric sort**. For a merge sort, you need to instruct WordPerfect to sort by last name, by company name, by zip code, or by one of the other fields in the records. You also need to tell WordPerfect which word in the field to sort by. For example, if Whitney wanted to sort her secondary file by FirstName, which includes not only the first name but also any middle name or middle initial, she must tell WordPerfect to sort using the first word in the FirstName field.

Whitney decides that before printing the letters, she will sort the secondary file by zip code and then execute the merge again so that the letters are in order of zip code number. Let's do that now.

To sort the secondary file:

❶ Clear the merged document from the document screen and retrieve S6ADDR.SF, the secondary file with client information.

❷ Select Sort from the Tools menu or press **[Ctrl][F9]** (Merge/Sort) and select **2** (**S**ort). WordPerfect asks for the input file to sort. The input file is the file that you want to sort. The screen file is listed as the default. See Figure 6-28.

Figure 6-28
Prompt for input
file to sort

```
90220{END FIELD}
{END RECORD}
==================================================================
McArdy{END FIELD}
Gregory P.{END FIELD}
Paul{END FIELD}
Input file to sort: (Screen)
```

default input file

prompt to enter
input file

3 Press **[Enter]** to select the default input file (the screen). In other words, you want to sort the file currently on the document screen. If you wanted to sort a file on the disk, you would type the filename as the input file. WordPerfect now asks for the output file, that is, the file where the results of the sort will be saved. The input file and the output file may be the same file or different files. The screen is the default location for the output file.

4 Press **[Enter]** to select the default output file (the screen). WordPerfect displays the Sort menu in the window on the bottom half of the screen. See Figure 6-29. You will use this menu to specify the details of how you want WordPerfect to sort the file on the document on the screen.

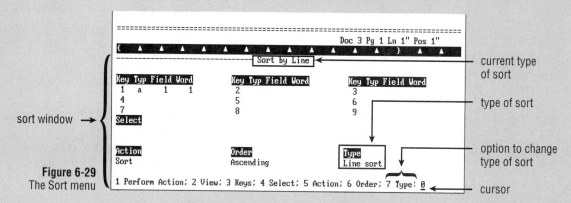

Figure 6-29
The Sort menu

First, let's instruct WordPerfect that you want to carry out a merge sort, not a line sort or a paragraph sort.

5 Select **7** (**T**ype) and **1** (**M**erge) to change the type of sort to merge. Now the title of the Sort menu is "Sort Secondary Merge File." See Figure 6-30.

Next you'll tell WordPerfect whether the sort is alphanumeric or numeric and specify the field and word by which you want to sort. You will enter this information into the **sort keys**, regions of the sort menu that instruct WordPerfect how to carry out the sort. Let's use the sort keys (Figure 6-30) to tell WordPerfect that we want to sort by Field 9 ("Zip").

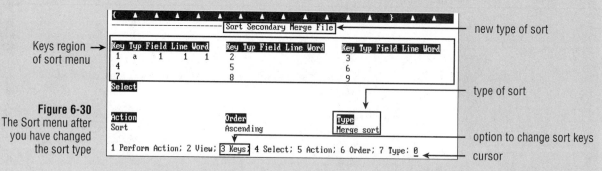

Figure 6-30
The Sort menu after you have changed the sort type

6 Select **3** (**K**eys) to move the cursor to the "a" in the Keys region of the Sort menu, under the "Typ" heading. See Figure 6-31.

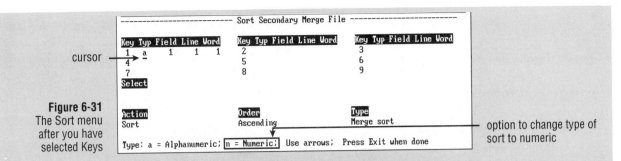

Figure 6-31
The Sort menu after you have selected Keys

option to change type of sort to numeric

Because you want to sort according to a number — the zip code — you'll tell WordPerfect to carry out a numeric sort rather than an alphanumeric sort.

❼ Press **n** to change the sort type from alphanumeric to numeric. The cursor automatically moves to the right of "1" under the "Field" heading.

❽ Type **9** to select Field 9 ("Zip"). See Figure 6-32.

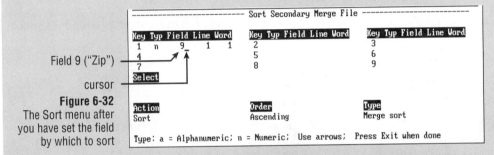

Field 9 ("Zip")

cursor

Figure 6-32
The Sort menu after you have set the field by which to sort

Since the Zip field is a number, you don't need to specify a word within the field. The Keys region of the Sort menu allows you to specify up to nine sort keys. You would use these other keys if, for example, your secondary file had many clients with the same zip code and you wanted WordPerfect to sort all records having the same zip code by the client's last name. You'd then move the cursor to the next key and specify the appropriate information to sort alphabetically on Field 1. In Whitney's secondary file, however, the order of the records having the same zip code doesn't matter, so she doesn't set any other sort keys.

❾ Press **[F7]** (Exit) to leave the Keys region of the Sort menu.

You have now specified all the information that WordPerfect needs to sort the secondary file by zip code. The Sort menu should look like Figure 6-33. Notice that the Order setting is "Ascending," which means that the sort will be from lowest to highest zip code number. If you wanted the sort to be "Descending," that is, to go from highest to lowest zip code number, you would select 6 (Order) and then 2 (Descending).

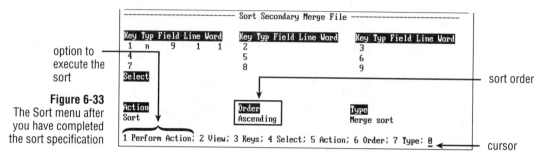

Figure 6-33
The Sort menu after you have completed the sort specification

You're now ready to perform the sort operation. You'll then save the secondary file, merge the primary and secondary files, and save and print the resulting merged document.

To perform the sort:

❶ Select **1** (**P**erform Action) to execute the sort.

WordPerfect sorts the secondary file, outputs the results to the document screen, exits the Sort menu, and returns the cursor to the document screen. The screen contains the secondary file with its records sorted according to zip code. See Figure 6-34. Use your cursor keys to move through the document to see that the first record is Mikhail Gutanov, with a zip code of 30304 (Georgia), and that the last record is Rebecca Malone, with a zip code of 90220 (California). You should now save the sorted secondary file.

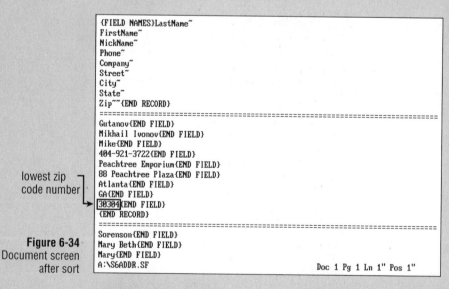

Figure 6-34
Document screen after sort

❷ Save the secondary file as S6ADDR2.SF.

❸ Clear the document screen and merge S6SLSLET.PF and S6ADDR2.SF.

❹ Save the merged document as S6MERGED.DOC.

❺ Print all five pages of the merged document.

As you can see, the letters print in order of zip code number, starting with the letter to Mike Gutanov, whose zip code is 30304, and ending with Becky Malone, whose zip code is 90220.

Printing Address Labels

Whitney wants to mail the form letters and accompanying photographs in 9-by-12-inch manila envelopes. Rather than typing the address on each envelope, she will use WordPerfect's labels and merge features to create mailing labels.

Creating the Labels Primary File

Whitney's first task is to create a primary file that specifies the format of the mailing label. The contents of the labels primary file is shown in Figure 6-35. As you can see, this primary file contains {FIELD} commands similar to those in Whitney's form letter. Let's create the labels primary file.

Figure 6-35
The primary file
to create labels

```
{FIELD}FirstName~ {FIELD}LastName~
{FIELD}Company~
{FIELD}Street~
{FIELD}City~, {FIELD}State~ {FIELD}Zip~
```

To create a primary file for labels:

❶ Clear the document screen.

❷ Create a document exactly like Figure 6-35. Use the Merge Codes command to enter the {FIELD} codes and then type the appropriate field names as shown.

❸ Save the file using the filename S6LABELS.PF.

Because the mailing labels contain only the names and addresses of the clients, this labels primary file includes no other text.

Merging the Labels Primary File with the Address List

Whitney's next task is to merge the labels primary file she has just created with the secondary file (the address list) she created earlier.

To merge the files:

❶ Clear the document screen.

❷ Select Merge from the Tools menu or press **[Ctrl][F9]** (Merge/Sort) and select **1** (**M**erge).

❸ Type **s6labels.pf** and press **[Enter]** to specify the name of the primary file.

❹ Type **s6addr2.sf** and press **[Enter]** to specify the name of the secondary file. WordPerfect carries out the merge to yield the merged document with one page for each record in the secondary file. See Figure 6-36.

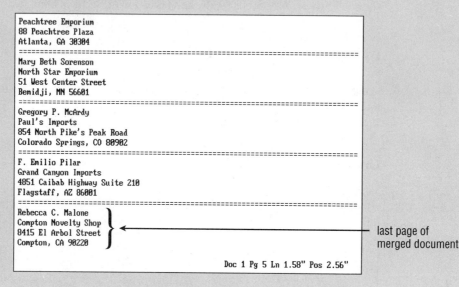

Figure 6-36
Document screen
of labels merged
document

last page of
merged document

Creating the Labels Document

If Whitney were to print the merged document as it appears now, she would get one address in the upper left corner of each printed page. She really wants the addresses to be printed on a standard sheet of gummed labels. Fortunately WordPerfect provides a method for creating a document that prints on gummed labels.

To format the merged document for labels, you need to change the page definition. WordPerfect's **page definition** is a set of instructions that specifies the page type and page size. By telling WordPerfect that the page definition is for labels and by specifying certain measurements about the labels, you can create a page definition for printing the clients' names and addresses on gummed labels.

Whitney has purchased Avery Laser Printer Labels number 5161/5162 from a local office supply store. She measures one of the labels and decides how she wants the addresses formatted on the labels (Figure 6-37). She also measures the distance between labels and the margins around the labels (Figure 6-38). If you use a different type of gummed label, set up your own page definition by measuring the size of the labels, the margins that you want within each label, the distances between labels, and the space between the labels and the edges of the labels page, as shown in Figures 6-37 and 6-38. You are now ready to define a labels page so that WordPerfect will format the merged document for the sheets of gummed labels.

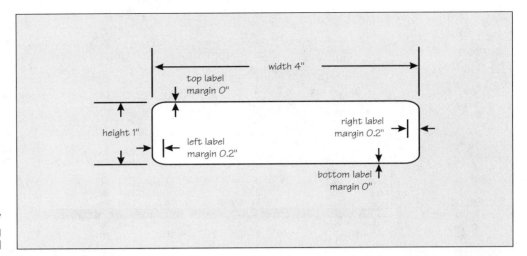

Figure 6-37
Data for defining
a label

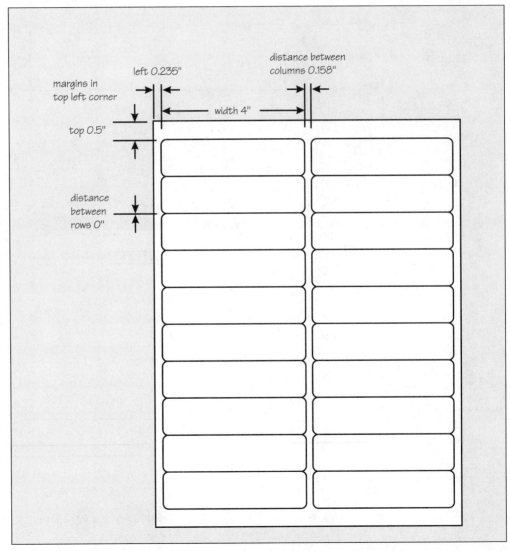

Figure 6-38
Data for defining
the labels page

To create a labels page definition:

❶ Move the cursor to the beginning of the merged document and select Page from the Layout menu or press **[Shift][F8]** (Format) and select **2** (**P**age). The Format: Page menu appears on the screen.

❷ Select **7** (Paper **S**ize). The Format: Paper Size/Type menu appears on the screen. See Figure 6-39.

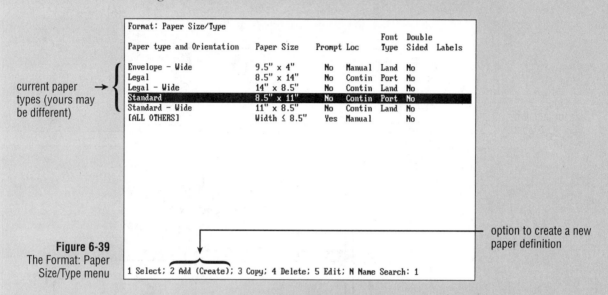

current paper types (yours may be different) →

option to create a new paper definition

Figure 6-39
The Format: Paper Size/Type menu

❸ Select **2** (**A**dd) to display the Format: Paper Type menu. This menu allows you to select a page type.

❹ Select **4** (**L**abels) to display the Format: Edit Paper Definition menu. See Figure 6-40.

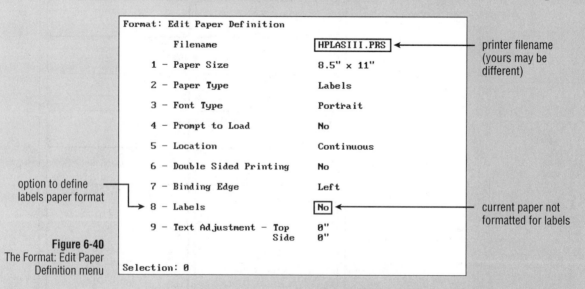

printer filename (yours may be different)

option to define labels paper format →

current paper not formatted for labels

Figure 6-40
The Format: Edit Paper Definition menu

❺ Select **8** (**L**abels) and select "Yes." The Format: Labels menu appears on the screen. See Figure 6-41.

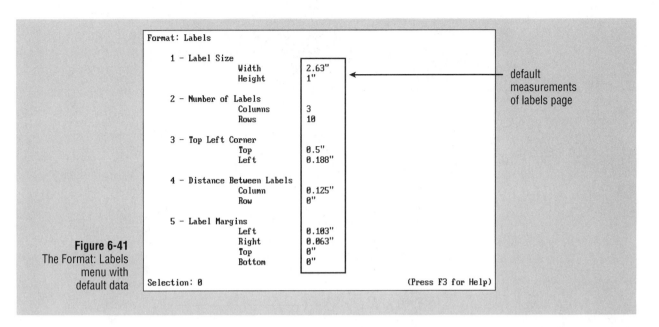

```
Format: Labels

    1 - Label Size
                  Width          2.63"
                  Height         1"

    2 - Number of Labels
                  Columns        3
                  Rows           10

    3 - Top Left Corner
                  Top            0.5"
                  Left           0.188"

    4 - Distance Between Labels
                  Column         0.125"
                  Row            0"

    5 - Label Margins
                  Left           0.103"
                  Right          0.063"
                  Top            0"
                  Bottom         0"

Selection: 0                              (Press F3 for Help)
```

default measurements of labels page

Figure 6-41
The Format: Labels menu with default data

The menu shown in Figure 6-41 allows you to specify the measurements of the labels shown in Figures 6-37 and 6-38. In the following steps you will enter the measurements for Whitney's labels (if you are using a different type of gummed label, enter your own measurements).

To specify the dimensions of the labels:

❶ Select **1** (Label **S**ize), type **4**, and press **[Enter]** to set the width to 4". Type **1** and press **[Enter]** to set the height to 1".

❷ Select **2** (**N**umber of Labels), type **2**, and press **[Enter]** to set the number of columns to 2, since the labels page has two columns of labels. Type **10** and press **[Enter]** to set the number of rows to 10, since the labels page has 10 rows of labels.

❸ Select **3** (**T**op Left Corner) and enter the data shown in Figure 6-38: Top 0.5" and Left 0.235".

❹ Select **4** (**D**istance Between Labels) and enter the data shown in Figure 6-38: Column 0.158" and Row 0".

❺ Select **5** (**L**abel Margins) and enter the data shown in Figure 6-37: Left 0.2", Right 0.2", Top 0", and Bottom 0".

Your screen should now look like Figure 6-42. Check all the data to make sure they are correct. If you find a mistake, select the appropriate menu item and retype the information. Once all the data are correct, you are ready to exit the Format: Labels menu.

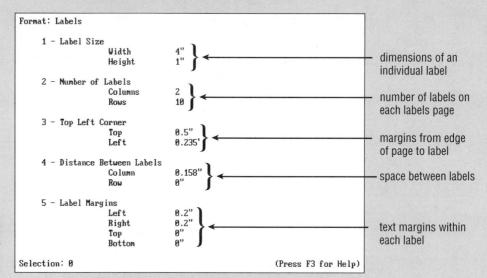

Figure 6-42
The Format: Labels menu after you have entered data

⑥ Press **[F7]** (Exit) twice to exit the Format: Labels menu and return to the Format: Paper Size/Type menu.

⑦ With Labels highlighted, press **1** (**S**elect). This selects the Labels page definition that you just created.

⑧ Press **[F7]** (Exit) to return to the document screen. The document is now ready for printing onto a sheet of gummed labels.

Defining the Labels page is a tedious process, but once you've done it, WordPerfect saves the definition for later use. Whitney will be able to use the Labels page definition whenever she prints mailing labels.

Printing the Labels

You can now view the document to see how it will look before you print it. Then you should save the document and print it.

To view, save, and print the labels document:

❶ Select Print from the File menu or press **[Shift][F7]** (Print).

❷ Select **6** (**V**iew Document). See Figure 6-43.

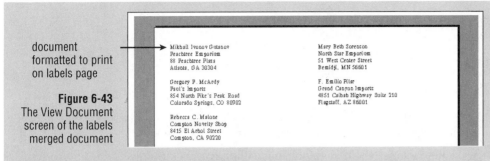

document formatted to print on labels page

Figure 6-43
The View Document screen of the labels merged document

❸   Press **[F7]** (Exit) to return to the document screen.

❹   Save the document as S6LABELS.DOC.

If you don't have a sheet of labels, you can print the screen document to an ordinary blank sheet of paper. If you're using an actual sheet of labels, consult your technical support person on how to feed the labels page into the printer.

❺   Print the labels document.

Whitney now has the letters and the labels necessary to send her sales letters. She attaches the gummed labels to the manila envelopes, inserts the sales letters and product photographs, and mails them.

■   ■   ■

Exercises

1.   Define or describe each of the following:
     a.   primary file   e.   record
     b.   secondary file   f.   field
     c.   merge code   g.   sort key
     d.   merged document

2.   Explain how you would insert the {DATE} merge command into a primary file.

3.   Suppose during a merge you wanted to insert a field named Company into a primary file. Explain how you would do this.

4.   How would you initiate a merge between a primary and a secondary file?

5.   When entering data into a secondary file, how do you mark the end of a field? the end of a record?

6.   What is the purpose of the {FIELD NAMES} merge code in a secondary file?

7.   How would you sort a secondary file using the last name as the sort key? Assume the last name is Field 1, named "Last," in the secondary file.

8.   Explain in general (without listing keystrokes) how you would use a secondary file to create mailing labels.

Tutorial Assignments

Retrieve the file T6FILE1.DFT and do the following:

1. To the right of "DATE:" in the memo, press **[Tab]** and insert the {DATE} merge code.

2. To the right of "MEMO TO:," press **[Tab]** and then insert {FIELD} merge commands for the fields First (for the first name) and Last (for the last name).

3. At the beginning of the body of the memo, before the word "please," insert the {FIELD} code for the field First, followed by a comma and a space.

4. Save the file as S6MEMO.PF.

Clear the document screen and do the following:

5. Insert the {FIELD NAMES} merge code to create the following field names: Last, First, and HomePhone.

6. Create a record for each of the following Sanders Imports employees. Enter the records in the order given:
   Sanders, Whitney, 285-2857
   Zayas, Gerry, 489-7765
   Creer, Paul, 288-8104
   Colón, Mario, 489-9147
   Ballentyne, Marsha, 384-0108
   Allen, Rachel, 285-9144
   Marchant, Philipe, 489-1215

7. Save the file as S6EMPL1.SF.

8. Sort the file by last name.

9. Save the sorted file as S6EMPL2.SF.

Clear the screen and do the following:

10. Merge the files S6MEMO.PF and S6EMPL2.SF.

11. Save the merged document as S6MEMO.MRG.

12. Print the file S6MEMO.MRG.

Case Problems

1. Ad Letter for White Water Tours

Peter Crow, a graduate in business management from the University of Arizona, is founder of White Water Tours. This small company allows Peter to combine his training in business with his love of travel and white-water rafting. He has obtained names of potential customers from many sources, such as sporting goods stores and outdoor clubs. Peter wants to send a form letter to these potential customers to announce his new Colorado River rafting tours. He will enclose with each letter a color brochure that explains the tours in more detail.

Do the following:

1. Retrieve P6TOURS.DFT, the body of Peter's ad letter from your data diskette.

2. Insert {FIELD} codes at the beginning of the document for the date, the inside address, and the salutation. You will create the secondary file later, so you may choose the names you give to each field. The secondary file will contain the following data: last name, first name, street address, city, state, and zip code.

3. At the beginning of the next to the last paragraph, insert the merge code to mark where you want WordPerfect to insert the first name.

4. Save the primary file as S6TOURS.PF.

5. Clear the screen and create a secondary file from the following information:
   Mikkelson, Aubry, 8551 Sun Valley Drive, Boise, ID 83708
   Wolfgramm, Stephen, 184 Atlantic Avenue, Stamford, CT 06904
   Sigimoto, Ken, 911 North Bradley Street, Greensboro, NC 27420
   Almaraz, Humberto, 591 West Black Hills Drive, Sioux Falls, SD 57101
   Cundick, Cole, 11821 Smokey Mountains Avenue, Kingsport, TN 37662
   Johnson, Tyrell, 841 South Pacific Drive, Redmond, WA 98052

6. Save the secondary file as S6CLIENT.SF.

7. Sort the secondary file by zip code and save the results using the same filename, S6CLIENT.SF.

8. Merge the files to create the final ad letters.

9. Save the merged document as S6TOURS.MRG.

10. Print the first three pages of S6TOURS.MRG.

2. Form Letter to Friends and Relatives

Do the following:

1. Write a one-page form letter — a primary merge file — to your friends and relatives. Include in the letter one or more of the following types of information:
   a. What you have learned about word processing from this class
   b. Your current class schedule, with a brief description of each class
   c. Your professional plans after graduation
   d. Your ideas for setting up your own business
   e. Merge codes to specify where names and addresses will be inserted into the merged document

2. Save the letter as S6PERLET.PF.

3. Create a secondary merge file containing the names and addresses of some of your friends and relatives. You may use fictitious names and addresses if you choose.

4. Sort the secondary file alphabetically by last name.

5. Save the sorted secondary file as S6FAMILY.SF.

6. Merge S6PERLET.PF and S6FAMILY.SF.

7. Save the merged document as S6FAMILY.MRG.

8. Print the first three pages of the merged document.

3. Managing a Collection

WordPerfect can help you manage lists of items such as client records, employee records, names and addresses of family members and friends, collections, and many other things. Your task is to create a secondary merge file for a collection. The collection can be compact discs, cassettes, wine, sports cards, coins, stamps, books in your personal library, or anything else you desire.

Do the following:

1. Create the secondary file with the following field names:
    a. "Item" for the name of item
    b. "Value" for the cost at the time of purchase or the current estimated cost
    c. "Source" for the name of the publisher or the location of the acquisition
    d. "Date" for the date of acquisition or the date of publication
    e. "Note" for a comment about the item

2. Include 10 records in the secondary file. If your collection doesn't have 10 items, include fictitious data.

3. Sort the file alphabetically, in ascending order, using Item as the sort key.

4. Save the file as S6COLLCT.SF.

5. Create a primary file that will generate a list of the 10 items in your collection.

6. Save the primary file as S6COLLCT.PF.

7. Merge the primary and secondary files.

8. Change the page breaks to hard returns in the merged document, so the list of all 10 items fits on one page.

9. Save the merged document as S6COLLCT.MRG.

10. Print S6COLLECT.MRG.

11. Sort the secondary file using Value as the sort key and going from highest value to lowest value. *Hint*: Set Order to Descending.

12. Save the resulting secondary file as S6COLLC2.SF.

13. Merge S6COLLC2.SF with S6COLLCT.PF.

14. Save the merged file as S6COLLC2.MRG.

15. Print S6COLLC2.MRG.

Additional Cases

Additional Case 1:
Resume and Letter of Application

Chelsie Randall will soon graduate from Southern Michigan State with a bachelor's degree in accounting. Having had experience in the automotive industry, she decides to apply for a job within that industry. One of the first jobs she applies for is a position as an accountant in the Detroit office of Lube-While-You-Shop Inc., which is headquartered in Providence, Rhode Island. Chelsie has written drafts of her resume and of a cover letter to accompany her application. She now wants to create final versions of these documents and send them to the director of personnel at Lube-While-You-Shop Inc.

Do the following:

1. Make sure your document screen is clear, then retrieve the draft of Chelsie's resume, PRESUME.DFT, from the WordPerfect data diskette.

2. Use block operations to center and boldface "CHELSIE RANDALL" at the beginning of the resume.

3. Center the next three lines of text, which include Chelsie's address and phone number.

4. Move the section titled "Education" above the section titled "Accounting Coursework."

5. Change the headings "Education" and "Accounting Coursework" from mixed uppercase and lowercase to all uppercase letters, to be consistent with the other headings in the resume.

In this case you will do the following:

- Enter text using insert and typeover modes

- Center, boldface, and underline text

- Position a phrase flush right

- Move (cut and paste) a block of text

- Switch existing text to all uppercase letters

- Change format codes

- Search and replace text

- Change the justification

- Use the Date Text features

- Use the Speller and Thesaurus

- Create, sort, and merge primary and secondary files

6. Underline "cum laude" in the third line under "EDUCATION."

7. In the section titled "EMPLOYMENT" underline the three job titles "Assistant Financial Manager," "Secretary/File Clerk," and "Staff Accountant."

8. In the last section of the resume, to the right of "REFERENCES," change the [Tab] code to [→Indent], so that both lines of the phrase are indented.

9. Search for and delete any period that appears at the end of a line in the resume.

10. Save the document as SRESUME.AUT. The filename extension AUT stands for "AUTOMOTIVE," to indicate that this is Chelsie's resume to the automotive industry.

11. Print the resume.

12. Clear the document screen and retrieve PAPPLIC.DFT, the draft of Chelsie's letter of application.

13. Change the justification so that the text along the right margin of the printed document is ragged instead of aligned.

14. Change the top margin to 2.5 inches so the letter isn't as high up on the page.

15. With the cursor six lines down from the beginning of the document, type Chelsie's street address, "64 Spartan Avenue," flush right on the first line of text and the rest of her address, "Dearborn, MI 48120" flush right on the second line of text.

16. Use WordPerfect's Date Text feature to insert today's date flush right on the third line of text.

17. Triple-space between the date and the inside address.

18. Underline the name of the newspaper *Ann Arbor Register* in the first paragraph.

19. Use a search-and-replace operation to change all occurrences of "car industry" to "automotive industry."

20. Run WordPerfect's Speller to check the spelling throughout the letter. Replace all misspelled words with the correctly spelled words.

21. Read the letter carefully to find and correct two words that are clearly typographical errors but that the Speller accepted as being correct.

22. Using typeover mode, correct Chelsie's phone number in the last paragraph from "313-463-3737" to "313-453-3637."

23. Insert the word "to" and a space after the telephone number in the last paragraph.

24. Save the letter as SAPPLIC.LET.

25. Print the letter.

Chelsie has found the names and addresses of several other automotive companies that want to hire accountants. She decides to create a secondary file with the company names and addresses and to modify her letter (SAPPLIC.LET) to make it a primary file.

Do the following:

26. Clear the document screen and create a secondary file with the following field names:

"Last," "First," "Title," "Department," "Company," "Street," "City," "State," and "Zip."

27. In the secondary file make three records with the following data. Each line in a record is a separate field.

Record 1:
Wardinsky
Patrice
Ms.
Personnel Department
Dearborn Design and Manufacturing Corp.
88 West Pontiac Drive
Dearborn
MI
48120

Record 2:
Almaraz
Manuel
Mr.
Accounting Department
Five-Star Automotive Supply Company
462 Harvest Drive
Detroit
MI
48104

Record 3:
Nemethy
Magan
Mrs.
Personnel Department
Johnson Motors, Inc.
8125 North University Avenue
Detroit
MI
48104

28. Save the secondary file as SAPPLIC.SF.

29. Print the secondary file.

30. Sort the secondary file alphabetically by the last name (field name "Last").

31. Save the sorted secondary file as SAPPLIC2.SF and print it.

32. Clear the document screen and retrieve SAPPLIC.LET.

33. Delete the current date from the the letter and insert the merge code to insert the date.

34. Delete the inside address and insert merge codes for fetching names and complete addresses from the secondary file.

35. Edit the salutation to include merge codes for the title and the last name.

36. Save the primary file as SAPPLIC.PF.

37. Merge the primary file SAPPLIC.PF and secondary file SAPPLIC2.SF.

38. Save the merged file as SAPPLIC.MRG.

39. Print all three pages of the merged document.

Additional Case 2: A Business Plan for Training in Management Excellence (T.I.M.E.)

Darren Czaja, a business management graduate, has worked as a part-time consultant to government and business managers in the Washington, D.C., area. He now wants to expand his consulting work and to open a consulting agency called T.I.M.E. (Training in Management Excellence). He has decided to apply to various banks for a loan to open his new office and to hire two full-time and one part-time employees. As part of his loan application, Darren must submit a business plan that describes his agency, provides evidence for potential success, and supplies other information needed by the banks.

Do the following:

1. Create the title page of the business plan as shown in Figure 1, according to the following instructions:
   a. Use Center Justification to center the lines between the left and right margins.
   b. Use Center Page Top to Bottom to center the title page between the top and bottom margins.
   c. Use Date Text to insert today's date, not the date shown in Figure 1.

2. Insert a hard page break after the date of the title page.

3. In preparation for typing the body of the report, change the justification to full at the beginning of page 2.

4. Instruct WordPerfect to protect against any widows and orphans that might occur in the text of the business plan.

5. At the beginning of page 2, change the page number to 1, so that the body of the report begins on page 1.

In this case you will do the following:

- Set text for center and full justification
- Insert a hard page break
- Protect a document against paragraph widows and orphans
- Use conditional end of page
- Create and use a style, a header, and a macro
- Position text flush right
- Insert page numbering
- Suppress headers, footers, and page numbering on a title page
- Change the tab settings
- Search and replace text
- Move (cut and paste) text
- Use automatic hyphenation
- Use the Outline feature

6. Create a Style according to the following instructions. (Remember that the cursor can be anywhere in the document.)
   a. Name the style "Heading."
   b. Create a paired Style.
   c. At the beginning of the Style, insert a code to tell WordPerfect to keep six lines together on a page.
   d. Insert a hard return to move the comment box down one line.
   e. Insert the necessary code so that headings will be boldfaced.
   f. Set the Enter feature of the Style so that when you press [Enter] with the Style on, the Style turns off.

7. Use the Style to create the heading "Introduction" at the beginning of the new page 1, just after the [Just:Full] code.

8. Insert blank lines to double-space after the "Introduction" heading.

```
                    BUSINESS PLAN AND LOAN REQUEST

                    Training In Management Excellence
                               (T.I.M.E.)




















                              Submitted by:

                            Darren M. Czaja
                          1667 Japonica Street
                         Springfield, VA  22150
                            (703) 846-1372










                            June 10, 1993
```

Figure 1

9. Retrieve PBUSPLN.DFT, the draft of the body of Darren's business plan.

10. Save the document as SBUSPLAN.DFT.

11. At the beginning of the document, before the [Just:Center] code on the title page, instruct WordPerfect to print a header on each page according to the following instructions:
    a. Create a Header A to be printed on every page.
    b. At the left margin of the header, type "BUSINESS PLAN, T.I.M.E."
    c. Flush right in the header, type "D. M. Czaja."

12. Instruct WordPerfect to print a page number at the bottom center of each page.

13. Instruct WordPerfect to suppress headers, footers, and page numbering on the title page.

14. Change the tab stops so that they begin at 0" (relative to the left margin) and occur every 0.4" along the tab ruler.

15. Use the "Heading" style that you just created to format the headings "My Experience and Background," "Business Description," "Marketing Plan," and "Financial Projection."

16. Move the cursor to the space after the phrase "allow me to expand" and before the word "Training" in the first paragraph. Then create an Alt macro with the name Alt-T to insert "T.I.M.E." into the document.

17. After "T.I.M.E." insert a space and then enclose the phrase "Training in Management Excellence" in parentheses.

18. Use the Search feature to find the phrase "The four goals" and, with the help of the macro that you just created, insert the phrase "of T.I.M.E." (The text should then read "The four goals of T.I.M.E are:".)

19. Use your macro to insert "T.I.M.E.'s" and a space into the heading "Marketing Plan," so that the heading reads "T.I.M.E.'s Marketing Plan."

20. In the numbered list after "The four goals of T.I.M.E. are:", change the tabs after the four numbers to indents, so that all the lines of the paragraphs after the numbers are indented.

21. Darren's initial calculations suggested that he needed a loan of $28,000, but after reconsideration, he realized that the loan request should be for $35,000. Use Search and Replace to change all occurrences of "$28,000" in the document to "$35,000."

22. After the quotation in the first sentence in the first paragraph under the heading "Business Description," insert a footnote with the following text (including the quotation marks around the name of the article): "Exhausted Executives: Time Management or Trivia?," The Time Management Journal, October 1988, p. 1348.

23. In the same paragraph underline the phrase "The Time Trap: How to Get More Done in Less Time," which is the name of a book.

24. Under the heading "T.I.M.E's Marketing Plan" there are three numbered subheadings, with a paragraph under each subheading. Move the subheading and the paragraph for "Market Growth" below the subheading and the paragraph for "Competition." Renumber the headings so they are in order.

25. Use Search to find the second occurrence in the document of the phrase "ability to obtain," then use the Thesaurus to replace the word "obtain" with an appropriate synonym.

26. Check the spelling of all the words in the document. Correct all errors in spelling, double words, and irregular case.

27. At the end of the document prepare the table with Darren's spending plan, as shown in Figure 2.

T.I.M.E. SPENDING PLAN		
Item	Expenses 1st month	Expenses 6 months
Furniture	$3,000	$3,000
Copy machine	2,000	2,000
Computer/Printer	4,000	4,000
Rent	1,500	9,000
Office Supplies	500	3,000
Salaries	7,500	45,000
TOTALS	$18,500	$66,000

Figure 2

28. Turn on hyphenation at the beginning of the document and move the cursor to the end of the document. Give WordPerfect any help it might need in deciding where to position a hyphen.

29. Save the final version of the business plan as SBUSPLN.FIN.

30. Print the document.

To ensure that his business plan is well organized, Darren decides to create an outline of the document.

31. With the business plan still on document screen 1, switch to document screen 2 and turn on Outline.

32. Referring to document screen 1, create an outline with each major heading in the business plan a level-1 outline paragraph and each subheading a level-2 outline paragraph.

33. Copy the title of the business plan from document screen 1 to the beginning of the document and above the outline on document screen 2.

34. Save the outline as SBUSPLN.OTL.

35. Print the outline.

Part Three

■ ■ ■

Lotus 1-2-3 Tutorials

■ **Tutorial 1 Creating a Worksheet**

■ **Tutorial 2 Modifying a Worksheet**

■ **Tutorial 3 Working with Larger Worksheets**

■ **Tutorial 4 Designing Professional Worksheets**

■ **Tutorial 5 Creating and Printing Graphs**

■ **Tutorial 6 Using a Database**

■ **Tutorial 7 Creating and Using Macros**

■ **Lotus 1-2-3 Additional Cases**

Tutorial 1

Creating a Worksheet

Preparing a Simple Payroll

Case: Krier Marine Services

Vince Diorio is an Information Systems major at the University of Rhode Island. To help pay for his tuition, he works part-time three days a week at a nearby marina, Krier Marine Services. Vince works in the Krier business office, and his responsibilities range from making coffee to keeping the company's books.

Recently, Jim and Marcia Krier, the owners of the marina, asked Vince if he could help them computerize the payroll for their four part-time employees. They explained to Vince that the employees work a different number of hours each week for different rates of pay. Marcia does the payroll manually and finds it time consuming. Moreover, whenever she makes errors, she is embarrassed and is annoyed at having to take additional time to correct them. Jim and Marcia hope that Vince can help them.

Vince immediately agrees to help. He tells the Kriers that he knows how to use Lotus 1-2-3 and that he can build a spreadsheet that will save Marcia time and reduce errors. But before we see how Vince solves this business problem, we must consider the key terms and concepts that are necessary to understand what a spreadsheet is and what it can do.

OBJECTIVES

In this tutorial you will learn to:

- Define worksheet terms

- Start Lotus 1-2-3

- Move the cell pointer

- Retrieve and save files

- Enter numbers, labels, and formulas

- Correct mistakes and erase entries

- Edit entries and use the Undo feature

- Define a range

- Print a worksheet

- Erase a worksheet

- Use on-line help

What Is a Spreadsheet?

If you have ever seen a budget, then you have seen a type of spreadsheet (Figure 1-1). This type of spreadsheet lists months across the top of a page and income and expense items vertically along the left side of a page. Historically a **spreadsheet** was a sheet of paper divided into rows and columns that accountants and bookkeepers used to perform calculations or produce reports. Until recently people had to use a calculator, pencil, and paper to perform calculations and enter results. Preparing a spreadsheet manually in this way took extensive amounts of time.

columns

	1 Jan	2 Feb	3 Mar	4 Apr	5 May	6 Jun
Income						
Sales Revenue	18000	20000	19000	18000	15000	20000
Expenses						
Insurance	2500	—	—	—	—	—
Utilities	400	400	400	400	400	400
Wages	3000	3000	3000	3000	3000	3000
Supplies	250	250	250	250	250	250
Advertising	300	300	300	500	350	500
Maintenance	100	100	100	100	100	100
Rent	3000	3000	3000	3000	3000	3000
Janitorial	450	450	450	450	450	450
Taxes	—	—	—	—	—	—
TOTAL COSTS	10000	7500	7500	7700	7550	7700

rows

a cell

Figure 1-1
Example of manual spreadsheet

With the advent of microcomputers came speedy electronic processing of spreadsheet applications such as sales projections, expense reports, income statements, and balance sheets. When you use spreadsheet software, a grid of columns and rows appears on your computer screen (Figure 1-2) that is similar to an accountant's paper spreadsheet. The spreadsheet software displays, manipulates, calculates, and prints rows and columns of numbers and text.

Electronic spreadsheets have become important business tools because of their simplicity, flexibility, and what-if capability. By *what-if* we mean you can ask a hypothetical question. For example, what if you wanted to see the impact on the budget if salaries, insurance, or advertising costs change? To consider alternatives you simply enter new data or change a formula. The computer immediately recalculates and changes all the related data for you.

The Worksheet

The **worksheet** is the basic structure for storing and organizing data when you are using spreadsheet software such as Lotus 1-2-3. In Lotus 1-2-3 the worksheet is a grid made up of columns and rows. The worksheet contains 8,192 rows and 256 columns.

```
B4: [W8] 15000                                                    READY

        A        B      C      D      E      F      G      H
1                Jan    Feb    Mar    Apr    May    Jun
2   Income
3   ----------
4   Sales Revenue 15000  20000  19000  10000  15000  20000
5
6   Expenses
7   ----------
8   Insurance    2500
9   Utilities    400    400    400    400    400    400
10  Wages        3000   3000   3000   3000   3000   3000
11  Supplies     250    250    250    250    250    250
12  Advertising  300    300    300    500    350    500
13  Maintenance  100    100    100    100    100    100
14  Rent         3000   3000   3000   3000   3000   3000
15  Janitorial   450    450    450    450    450    450
16  Taxes
17               ----------------------------------------
18  Total Costs  10000  7500   7500   7700   7550   7700
19
20                         UNDO
```

Figure 1-2

A **row number** in the left border of the worksheet identifies each row (Figure 1-3). Rows are numbered consecutively from 1 to 8192. A **column letter** in the top border of the worksheet identifies each column. Columns are lettered A-Z, then AA-AZ, then BA-BZ, and so on to column IV. A **cell** is a unit of the worksheet that stores data. It is formed by the intersection of a column and a row and is identified by its column letter and row number. For example, the intersection of column B and row 8 is cell B8. B8 is called the **cell address**; whenever you specify a cell address, be sure to name the column letter first and then the row number.

Notice the highlighted rectangle in cell B4 in Figure 1-3. This is called the **cell pointer**. The cell pointer appears in only one cell of the worksheet, but you can move the cell pointer to any cell of the worksheet. The **current cell** is the cell in which the cell pointer rests and in which you enter data.

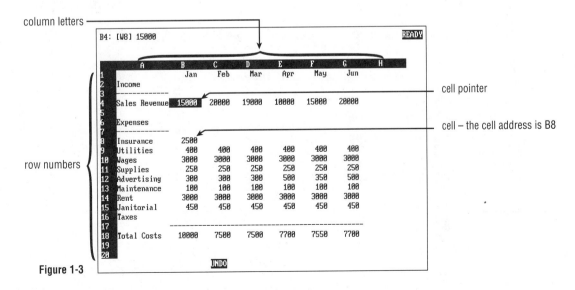

Figure 1-3

The 1-2-3 Screen

The 1-2-3 screen is made up of three areas: the **worksheet area**, the **control panel**, and the **status line** (Figure 1-4). The 1-2-3 screen cannot display all 8,192 rows and 256 columns of a worksheet at one time. Typically a 1-2-3 screen displays 20 rows and eight columns at a time (the number of columns might vary if the width of a column has changed). The rows and columns that appear on your screen are a window into your worksheet and represent the worksheet area.

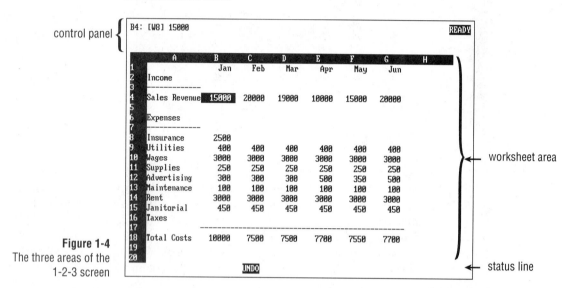

Figure 1-4
The three areas of the
1-2-3 screen

The top three lines of the 1-2-3 screen contain the control panel. The **control panel** displays information about what 1-2-3 is doing and about your work (Figure 1-5).

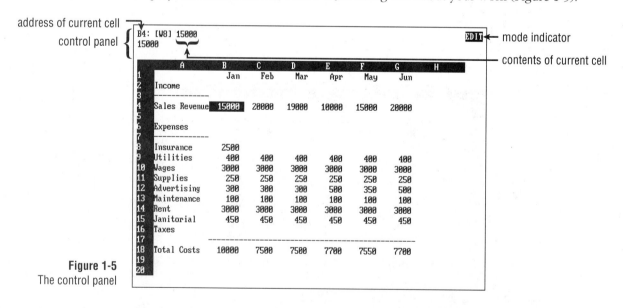

Figure 1-5
The control panel

The *first line* of the control panel displays information about the current cell and the mode, or state, of 1-2-3. At the far left of the first line, 1-2-3 displays the **address**, or location, of the current cell and its contents. 1-2-3 also displays the entry in the current cell, if the cell contains an entry.

At the far right of the first line of the control panel, 1-2-3 displays the **mode indicator**, which tells you what **mode**, or state, 1-2-3 is currently in. For example, when 1-2-3 is ready for you to type or select a command, 1-2-3 is in READY mode. When you are performing a task in 1-2-3, the mode indicator changes to show the current status of the task. Figure 1-6 lists some of the mode indicator messages.

Mode indicator	Meaning
EDIT	You pressed [EDIT] (F2) to edit an entry or entered a formula incorrectly.
ERROR	1-2-3 is displaying an error message. Press [HELP] (F1) to display a Help screen that describes the error; or press [Esc] or [Enter] to clear the error message.
FILES	1-2-3 is displaying a menu of filenames in the control panel. Press [NAME] (F3) to display a full-screen menu of filenames.
FIND	You selected /Data Query Find or pressed [Query] (F7) to repeat the last /Data Query Find you specified, and 1-2-3 is highlighting a database record that matches your criteria.
FRMT	You selected /Data Parse Format-Line Edit to edit a format line.
HELP	You pressed [HELP] (F1) and 1-2-3 is displaying a Help screen.
LABEL	You are entering a label.
MENU	You pressed / (Slash) or < (Less-than symbol), and 1-2-3 is displaying a menu of commands.
NAMES	1-2-3 is displaying a menu of range names, graph names, or attached add-in names.
POINT	1-2-3 is prompting you to specify a range or you are creating a formula by highlighting a range.
READY	1-2-3 is ready for you to enter data or select a command.
STAT	You selected /Worksheet Status or /Worksheet Global Default Status, and 1-2-3 is displaying the corresponding status screen.
VALUE	You are entering a value (a number or formula).
WAIT	1-2-3 is completing a command or process.

Figure 1-6
Mode indicator
messages

The *second line* of the control panel displays the current entry when you are creating or editing the entry. It can also display the **main menu**, which is a list of commands, and the submenus that appear after you make a selection from the main menu. The rectangular highlight that appears on a command in the menu is called the **menu pointer**.

The *third line* of the control panel displays information about the command highlighted by the menu pointer. 1-2-3 lists either the submenu commands for the highlighted command or a description of the highlighted command.

The **status line** (Figure 1-7) is the bottom line of the screen. It displays the date-and-time indicator, the status indicators, and error messages.

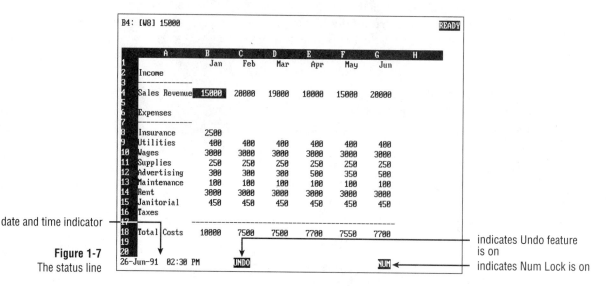

date and time indicator

Figure 1-7
The status line

indicates Undo feature is on

indicates Num Lock is on

The **date-and-time indicator** appears in the left corner of the status line. It usually displays the current date and time.

An **error message** appears in place of the date-and-time indicator when 1-2-3 detects a mistake or cannot perform a task. If an error message appears, press the function key F1 (HELP) for a description of the error message and why it occurred; or press [Esc] or [Enter] to clear the error and continue working.

A **status indicator** appears when you use certain 1-2-3 keys and when a particular program condition exists. For example, UNDO indicates you can press the function key F4 [UNDO] to undo your last action, and NUM indicates the [NUM LOCK] key is on.

Now that you have learned some basic worksheet terms and concepts, we are ready to see how Vince creates the worksheet for Mrs Krier. But before he begins, Vince recalls some advice from his college course: effective worksheets are well planned and carefully designed. So Vince does not start working with the 1-2-3 software immediately; he first sits down and follows a process he learned in his course.

Planning the Worksheet

Planning the worksheet first is a good habit to establish. If you plan first, your worksheet will be clear, accurate, and useful. Your plan will guide you as you try to solve business problems using 1-2-3.

You can divide your planning into four phases:

- Defining the problem
- Designing the worksheet
- Building the worksheet
- Testing the worksheet

Defining the Problem

Begin by outlining what you want to accomplish. Take a piece of paper and pencil and do the following:

1. List your goal(s).

2. Identify and list the results you want to see in the worksheet. This information is often called *output*.

3. Identify and write down the information you want to put into the worksheet. This information is often called *input*.

4. Determine and list the calculations that will produce the results you desire. These calculations become the *formulas* you will use in the worksheet.

When you finish, you will have completed the first phase of planning. You will have defined the problem and be ready to design the worksheet. Figure 1-8a shows how Vince defined the Krier payroll problem.

Figure 1-8a
Vince's planning
sheet

> My Goal(s):
>   Develop a worksheet that calculates the
>   Krier Marine Services payroll.
>
> What results do I want to see?
>   Weekly Payroll Report
>
> What information do I need?
>   Employee name
>   Number of hours each employee worked
>   during the week
>   Employee's rate of pay per hour
>
> What calculations will I perform?
>   Gross pay for each employee

Designing the Worksheet

Next, on a piece of paper, sketch what you think the worksheet should look like. Include titles, row and column headings, totals, and other items of the worksheet. Figure 1-8b on the next page shows Vince's sketch.

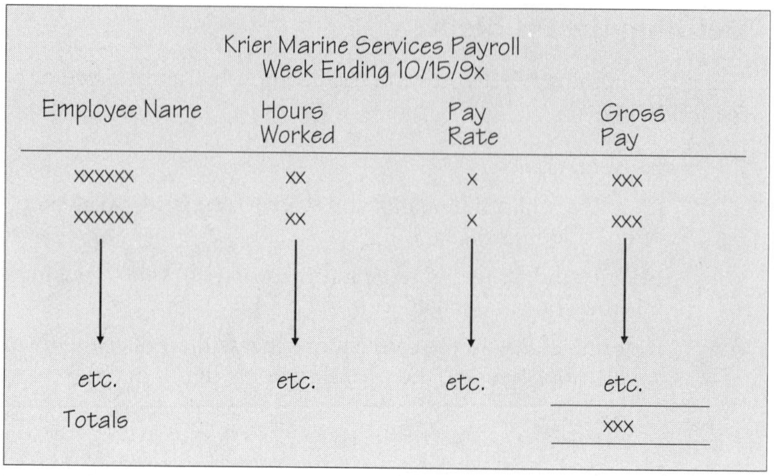

Figure 1-8b
Vince's sketch

Building the Worksheet

After defining the problem and sketching the worksheet, you are ready to type your worksheet design into 1-2-3. You enter titles, labels, formulas, input, and other items you listed and sketched when you defined your goal(s) and designed the worksheet.

Testing the Worksheet

After you have built a new worksheet, you should test it before you start to use it. If possible, develop some sample data, also known as test data, and manually calculate the results. Then put the same test data into your 1-2-3 worksheet. Are the results the same? If you discover any differences, you should find the reason(s) and correct any errors in the worksheet.

After completing this fourth phase, you are ready to begin using the worksheet.

■   ■   ■

In Tutorial 1, you will use Vince's problem definition and sketch (Figures 1-8a and 1-8b) as a guide when you build the worksheet for the Krier Marine Services payroll. You will create the worksheet that Vince developed for the Kriers. First you will retrieve a partially completed worksheet, which will serve as your starting point. Next you will enter the payroll data, employee names, hours worked, and rates of pay. Then you will enter formulas to calculate total gross pay for each employee. Finally you will calculate the gross pay for all employees. When the worksheet is complete, you will learn how to print and save it.

Starting 1-2-3

Start your computer. Be certain that the DOS prompt appears. If you are using 1-2-3 in a lab, you might need to ask your instructor or technical support person for instructions.

To start 1-2-3:

❶ Make sure you have the Lotus 1-2-3 data diskette ready. If you haven't already created the Lotus 1-2-3 data diskette, follow the instructions on page 79.

❷ If you have a *two-diskette system*, insert the Lotus 1-2-3 System Disk in drive A. Also insert your Lotus 1-2-3 data diskette in drive B. Then type **a:** and press **[Enter]**.

If you have a *hard-disk system*, insert the Lotus 1-2-3 data diskette in drive A. Then type **cd\123** and press **[Enter]**.

This makes the drive that contains the 1-2-3 program files the current directory.

❸ At the DOS prompt, type **123** and press **[Enter]**.

An introductory screen appears, followed by a blank 1-2-3 worksheet. See Figure 1-9. If the worksheet does not appear, your copy of 1-2-3 may not be installed correctly. Check you installation instructions or consult your technical support person.

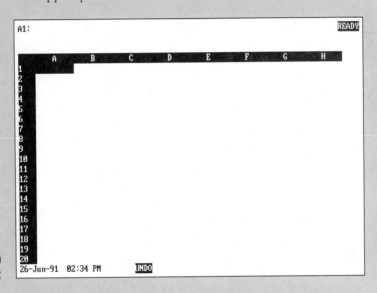

Figure 1-9
Blank worksheet

Moving the Cell Pointer

To be able to enter or view data in your worksheet, you will need to learn how to move the cell pointer. **Pointer-movement keys** enable you to move the cell pointer from cell to cell within your worksheet. You move the cell pointer up, down, left, and right with the pointer-movement keys on your keyboard. Let's try moving the cell pointer one cell at a time and several cells at a time. As you move it within the worksheet, notice how the location of the cell pointer changes in the status line of the control panel.

To move the cell pointer in the worksheet:

❶ Press **[Home]** once to move the cell pointer to cell A1, if it is not currently in cell A1.

❷ Press **[→]** once to move the cell pointer to cell B1.

❸ Press **[↓]** once to move the cell pointer to cell B2.

❹ Press **[PgDn]** once to move the cell pointer down one screen. See Figure 1-10.

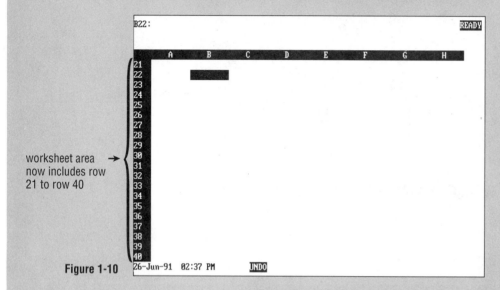

worksheet area → now includes row 21 to row 40

Figure 1-10

Then press **[PgUp]** to move the cell pointer back up one screen. When a pointer-movement keystroke moves the pointer into a cell not currently in the worksheet area, 1-2-3 shifts the worksheet area to display a different part of the worksheet.

❺ Press **[Tab]** once to move the cell pointer right one screen. Press **[Shift][Tab]** to move left one screen. Remember that to use the key combinations, such as [Shift][Tab], you press and hold the first key. Then while holding the first key, you press the second key. Then release both.

❻ Press **[End]** once and then press **[↓]** once to move to the last row of the worksheet. The cell pointer should be in cell A8192.

❼ Press **[End]** and then press **[→]** to move to the last column of the worksheet. The cell pointer should be in cell IV8192.

❽ Press **[Home]** to return to cell A1.

Figure 1-11 lists the most commonly used pointer-movement keys.

Key	Moves cell pointer
[→]	Right one cell
[←]	Left one cell
[↓]	Down one cell
[↑]	Up one cell
[Tab]	Right one screen
[Shift][Tab]	Left one screen
[Ctrl][→]	Right one screen
[Ctrl][←]	Left one screen
[Home]	To cell A1
[PgDn]	Down one screen
[PgUp]	Up one screen

Figure 1-11
Commonly used
pointer-movement
keys

Retrieving the Worksheet

Vince Diorio has started working on the spreadsheet for Krier Marine Services. His worksheet is stored as a file on the *Microcomputer Applications for Business* Sample Files Disk. Let's retrieve this file now. The file from which you work will be on either a diskette copy of the Sample Files Disk or a copy of the files that you copied onto your hard disk. If you want to start over for any reason, such as to recover from a mistake, retrieve C1FILE1.WK1 again and repeat the steps. You will learn how to correct mistakes as you work through this tutorial.

To retrieve a 1-2-3 worksheet file:

❶   Press **/** (Slash) to activate the 1-2-3 main menu, which shows a list of commands you may choose. See Figure 1-12.

main menu →

```
A1:                                                    MENU
Worksheet  Range  Copy  Move  File  Print  Graph  Data  System  Add-In  Quit
Global   Insert  Delete  Column  Erase  Titles  Window  Status  Page  Learn
         A        B        C        D        E        F        G        H
1
2
3
4
5
6
7
8
```

changed mode
indicator

Figure 1-12
The 1-2-3 main
menu

The mode indicator in the upper right corner has changed from READY to MENU and a command menu appears on the second and third lines of the control panel. The second line lists the main actions or commands from which you may select. The third line, or submenu, lists the commands available if you select the command currently highlighted in the second line.

There are two ways to select a command from the command line:

- You can highlight a menu choice by pressing [→] or [←] to move the highlight to the command you want and press [Enter].

- You can type the first character of the command you wish to select. For example, to select File you type F.

❷ Select File (**F**). The choices available from the File Menu now appear on the second line of the control panel. See Figure 1-13.

action of highlighted option from line 2 →

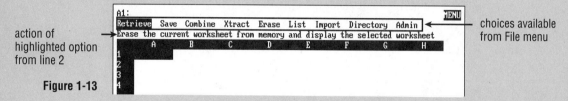

choices available from File menu

Figure 1-13

❸ Select Retrieve (**R**) to display the names of some of the worksheet files in the control panel. The top of your screen should look similar to Figure 1-14.

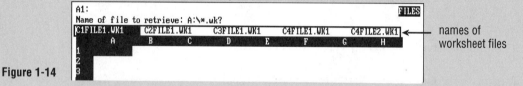

names of worksheet files

Figure 1-14

If the filenames do not appear press [Esc] to return to READY mode and see page 379 for assistance. Also if you accidentally press the wrong key and select the wrong command from the menu, you can return to the previous step by pressing the [Esc] key. If you continue to press [Esc], you back up a step at a time until you return to READY mode.

❹ Using the [→] or [←] key, highlight the worksheet file C1FILE1.WK1. Then press **[Enter]**. 1-2-3 retrieves the file you selected. See Figure 1-15.

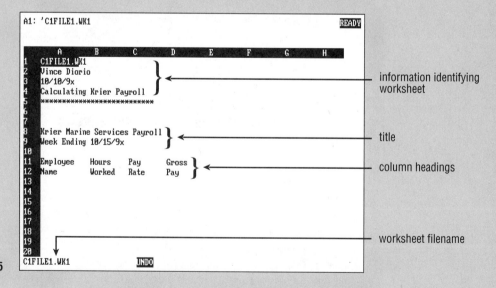

information identifying worksheet

title

column headings

worksheet filename

Figure 1-15

If the filename does not appear in the lower left corner of the screen, see page 379 for assistance.

The worksheet file you retrieved contains the beginning of the worksheet that Vince plans to use in developing the payroll worksheet. Currently, the worksheet consists of a title and descriptive column headings. These headings represent the data he will enter or calculate.

You no doubt have noticed that beginning in cell A1 there are four lines of identifying information:

- the name of the worksheet file
- the name of the person who developed the worksheet
- the date the worksheet was created or last modified
- a description of the worksheet

You should include such a section of identifying information in *every* worksheet you develop, to remind you about what the worksheet contains.

To help you understand what occurs when you retrieve a worksheet file, look at Figure 1-16. When you select File Retrieve and then select the worksheet file C1FILE1.WK1, 1-2-3 copies the worksheet file from the disk to the computer's memory. C1FILE1.WK1 is, therefore, in both the computer memory and disk storage.

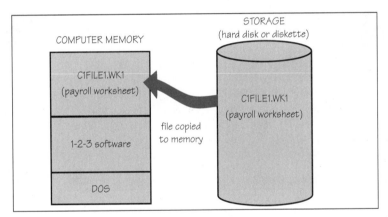

Figure 1-16
The process of retrieving a file

Entering Labels

Most of the data you enter into a worksheet will be descriptive text, numbers, or formulas. To enter data into a worksheet, you move the cell pointer to the cell where you want the data to appear. You then type the data and press the [Enter] key. 1-2-3 stores what you typed in the cell.

1-2-3 categorizes all entries you type in a cell as either labels or values. **Labels** are descriptive text such as column headings or textual data. If the first character you type is a letter, 1-2-3 assumes you are entering a label in that cell. Also, if you begin typing with one of the four special characters ' " ^ \, 1-2-3 will store any characters that follow as a label. As soon as you begin entering a letter or one of these special characters, you'll notice that the mode indicator, in the upper right corner of your screen, changes from READY to LABEL.

The next step in developing Vince's worksheet is to enter the names of the Krier part-time employees. These entries are labels.

To enter an employee name:

❶ Press [↓] to move the cell pointer to cell A14.

❷ Type **Bramble**. Before you press [Enter], look at the top left of the screen. See Figure 1-17.

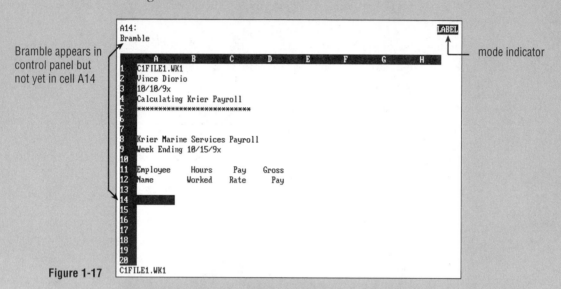

Bramble appears in control panel but not yet in cell A14

mode indicator

Figure 1-17

Notice that Bramble appears in the control panel but not in cell A14. Also notice that the mode indicator in the upper right corner of your screen has changed from READY to LABEL mode. This is because when you typed the letter B, 1-2-3 recognized that the entry was a label.

❸ Press **[Enter]**. Bramble now appears in cell A14. See Figure 1-18.

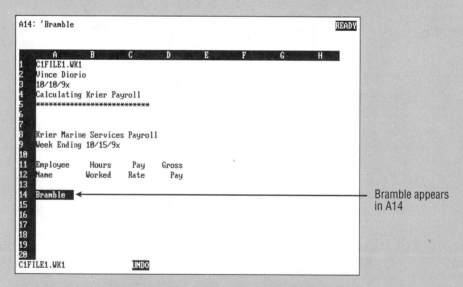

Bramble appears in A14

Figure 1-18

When you press the [Enter] key, the cell pointer remains in cell A14.

To enter the name of the second employee:

④ Press [↓] once to move the cell pointer to cell A15.

⑤ Type **Juarez** and then press **[Enter]**.

To enter the third employee:

⑥ Press [↓] once to move the cell pointer to cell A16.

⑦ Type **Smith** and then press **[Enter]**.

To enter the fourth employee:

⑧ Press [↓] once to move the cell pointer to cell A17.

⑨ Type **Diorio** and then press **[Enter]**.

The names of the four employees should now appear on your worksheet. See Figure 1-19.

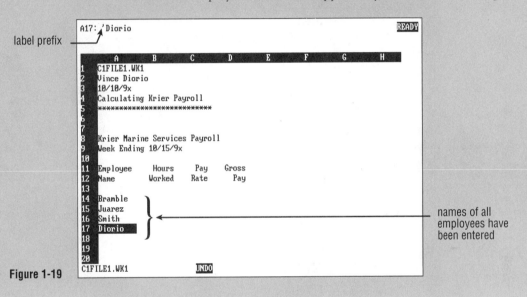

Figure 1-19

When the cell pointer is in a cell that contains a label, the control panel displays the cell address, followed by a colon, an apostrophe, and the label you entered. See Figure 1-19. The apostrophe before the label is called a **label prefix**. 1-2-3 automatically enters a label prefix whenever you enter labels in a worksheet.

Correcting Errors

The following steps show you two of the many ways to correct errors you make when you are entering text or numbers.

To correct errors as you are typing:

① Move the cell pointer to A16 and type **Smiht** but do not press [Enter]. Clearly this label is misspelled. Since you haven't pressed [Enter], you can use [Backspace] to correct the error. On most keyboards, this key is above the [Enter] key.

❷   Press **[Backspace]** twice to erase the last two characters you typed.

❸   Type the correct text — **th** — and press **[Enter]**.

If you notice an error any time *after* the text or value appears in the cell, you can correct the error by retyping the entry.

To correct errors in a cell:

❶   Be sure the cell pointer is in cell A16 and type **Smiht.** Press **[Enter]**. Smiht appears in cell A16. See Figure 1-20.

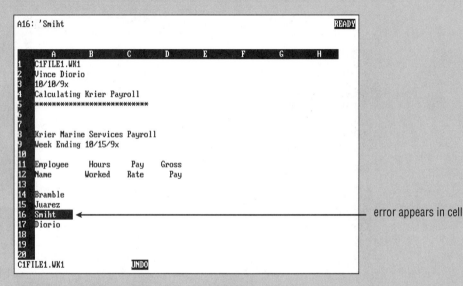

```
A16: 'Smiht                                                    READY

           A        B        C        D        E        F        G        H
  1   C1FILE1.WK1
  2   Vince Diorio
  3   10/10/9x
  4   Calculating Krier Payroll
  5   *****************************
  6
  7
  8   Krier Marine Services Payroll
  9   Week Ending 10/15/9x
 10
 11   Employee     Hours     Pay     Gross
 12   Name         Worked    Rate     Pay
 13
 14   Bramble
 15   Juarez
 16   Smiht    ◄─────────────────────────────────────  error appears in cell
 17   Diorio
 18
 19
 20
      C1FILE1.WK1                UNDO
```

Figure 1-20

❷   Type **Smith** in cell A16 and press **[Enter]**. As you can see, 1-2-3 enters the new text over the old. This is commonly called *typing over.*

Entering Values

A value in 1-2-3 can be a number or a formula. 1-2-3 interprets an entry in a cell as a **value** if the first character you type is a number (0 through 9) or one of the special characters + − @ . (# $. As soon as you begin entering a number or one of these special characters, you'll notice that the mode indicator changes from READY to VALUE.

Next, enter the hours worked by each employee at Krier Marine Services.

To enter the hours worked:

❶ Move the cell pointer to cell B14, the location of Bramble's hours worked.

Bramble worked 15 hours.

❷ Type **15** and press **[Enter]**. Do not include any symbols or punctuation, such as a dollar sign or a comma, when entering values.

❸ Press **[↓]** once to move the cell pointer to cell B15, the location of Juarez's hours worked. Juarez worked 28 hours.

❹ Type **28** and press **[Enter]**.

Smith worked 40 hours.

❺ Press **[↓]** once to move the cell pointer to cell B16, the location of Smith's hours worked.

❻ Type **40** and press **[Enter]**.

Diorio worked 22 hours.

❼ Press **[↓]** to move the cell pointer to cell B17, the location of Diorio's hours worked.

❽ Type **22** and press **[Enter]**. Your screen should look like Figure 1-21.

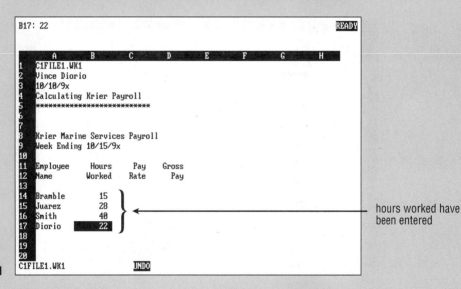

Figure 1-21

There is another, faster way to enter data. You can enter data in a cell and move the cell pointer to a cell on any side of that cell in one step by pressing a pointer-movement key instead of [Enter]. The **pointer-movement keys** are the directional keys, such as [→], [←], [↑], [↓], [PgDn], and [PgUp] which you press to move the pointer in the worksheet. To learn how to do this, let's enter the hourly pay rates for each employee.

To enter hourly pay rates using pointer-movement keys:

❶ Move the cell pointer to C14, the location of Bramble's pay rate.

Bramble earns $7 an hour.

❷ Type **7** and press [↓] instead of the [Enter] key. Notice that you entered the value in cell C14 and moved the cell pointer to cell C15, the cell immediately below C14. C15 is the location of Juarez's pay rate.

Juarez earns $5 an hour.

❸ With the cell pointer in C15, type **5** and press [↓].

Smith earns $7 an hour.

❹ In cell C16 type **7** and press [↓].

Diorio earns $5 an hour.

❺ In cell C17 type **5** and press **[Enter]**. You have now entered all the data. Your worksheet should be similar to Figure 1-22.

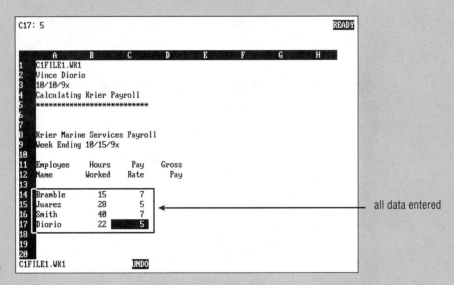

Figure 1-22

Saving a Worksheet

When you create or modify a worksheet, it is only temporarily stored in the computer's memory. To store your work permanently, you must save the worksheet to your hard disk or data diskette. It is always a good idea to save frequently as you work, rather than waiting until you've finished. Suppose the power goes out or you step away from your computer and someone starts working with another file. Unless you have been saving as you go along, all of your work could be lost.

Next we'll save all the entries you have made so far to a new file named S1FILE1.WK1. Before you save the file you should change cell A1 to S1FILE1.WK1 so the identifying information in the worksheet will be consistent with the new filename.

To change the filename in cell A1 and the save the file:

❶ Press **[Home]** to move the cell pointer to cell A1.

❷ Type **S1FILE1.WK1** and press **[Enter]**.

❸ Select /File Save (**/FS**). Notice that the mode indicator in the upper right corner changes to EDIT. See Figure 1-23.

1-2-3 prompts you for a filename in the control panel. It also shows the current filename and the drive from which you retrieved the file.

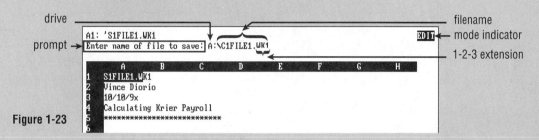

Figure 1-23

❹ Type **S1FILE1**. Notice that you do not have to erase the current filename.

In 1-2-3, all filenames must consist of not more than eight characters. You can use uppercase or lowercase letters, numbers, and the special characters $ & % ( ) { } – _ to create a filename. 1-2-3 converts any lowercase letters to uppercase letters once you press [Enter]. You cannot use spaces in a filename.

❺ Press **[Enter]** to save the file in the drive and directory you specified. 1-2-3 will automatically add the file extension .WK1 to the filename.

Figure 1-24 shows the process that occurs when you select File Save and type S1FILE1. 1-2-3 copies the worksheet file from the computer's memory to your disk storage.

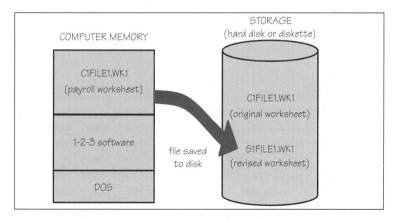

Figure 1-24
The process of saving a file

You have now saved your worksheet, including all the employee data you entered. If you previously saved this file with the name S1FILE1 and now see the prompt "Cancel Replace Backup," select Replace (R) to replace the previous version of this file.

Worksheet Filenames in This Book

Besides saving frequently, another good habit to follow is to use descriptive names that will help you identify the contents of your files. Worksheet filenames can contain up to eight characters. These characters can be letters, numbers, and all symbols except for spaces, commas, colons, and asterisks. Although eight characters do not often allow you to create complete names, you can create meaningful abbreviations. For example, your data diskette contains over 50 files. To name these files so that you can recognize their contents, we categorized them as follows:

File Category	Description
Tutorial Case	The files you use to work through each tutorial
Tutorial Assignment	The files that contain the worksheets you need to complete the Tutorial Assignments at the end of each tutorial
Case Problem	The files that contain the worksheets you need to complete the Case Problems at the end of each tutorial or the Additional Cases at the end of this part of the book
Saved Worksheet	Any worksheet that you have saved

We used these categories to help name the worksheet files on your data diskette. Let's take the filename C1FILE1, for example. This name may appear to have no meaning, but it does contain meaningful abbreviations. The first character of every worksheet filename on your data diskette identifies the file as one of the four file categories discussed above. Thus,

If the first character is:	The file category is:
C	Tutorial **C**ase
T	**T**utorial Assignment
P	Case **P**roblem
S	**S**aved Worksheet

Based on these categories, we know that the file C1FILE1 is a Tutorial Case file.

The second character of every worksheet file identifies the tutorial from which the file comes. Thus, C1FILE1 is a Tutorial Case from Tutorial 1. The remaining six characters of the filename identify the specific file. All worksheets in tutorials are named FILE, and the number that follows the name FILE indicates a version number. Thus, C1FILE1 is the first Tutorial Case worksheet from Tutorial 1. T1FILE1 is the first worksheet found in the Tutorial Assignments from Tutorial 1, while T1FILE2 is a second version of this worksheet. As another example, P1TOYS is the filename of the Case Problem "Sales in Toyland" from Tutorial 1. Remember also that when you save a file, 1-2-3 automatically adds a three-character extension to the filename. In these 1-2-3 tutorials the extension for your saved files will always be WK1.

Entering Formulas

Next you will calculate the gross pay for each employee. To calculate gross pay, you use a formula. A formula is an entry in a worksheet that performs a calculation. Formulas normally refer to data stored in other cells. To use the cell-referencing capability of 1-2-3, you include in the formula the addresses of the cells holding the values you want to calculate. For example, if you enter the formula +B14+B15 in cell B19, 1-2-3 adds the value in cell B14 to the value in cell B15 and places the result in cell B19.

Using formulas is one way to tap into the power of a spreadsheet like 1-2-3. Once you have entered a formula, you can make changes to your data and get the new results immediately.

Now let's calculate the gross pay for each employee. Gross pay is the number of hours worked multiplied by the rate of pay (hours worked × rate of pay). You do not need to do the multiplication yourself; you enter a formula, such as +B14*C14 that tells 1-2-3 which cells to multiply. The [*] (Asterisk) represents multiplication. 1-2-3 performs the calculations immediately and displays the results in the cell containing the formula. The following steps show you one way to enter a formula.

To enter a formula to compute Bramble's gross pay:

❶   Move the cell pointer to cell D14, the location of Bramble's gross pay.

❷   Type **+B14*C14**. The plus sign is one symbol you can use to indicate to 1-2-3 that you are entering a formula and not a label.

Notice that the formula appears in the control panel as you type and that 1-2-3 is now in VALUE mode. See Figure 1-25. Remember, if you make a mistake, you can use [Backspace] if you are still entering the formula, or you can retype the formula if you have pressed [Enter].

formula to calculate Bramble's gross pay

mode has changed

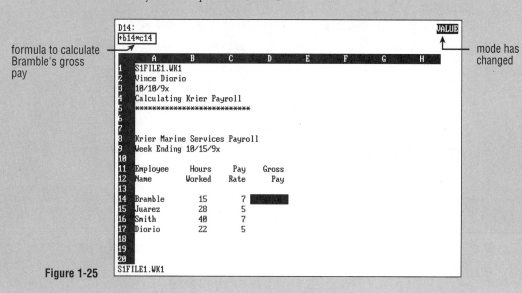

Figure 1-25

❸ Press **[Enter]**. 1-2-3 calculates the formula's value, 105, and the result appears in cell D14. If you get a different result, check the formula or the data values in B14 and C14. Retype if you find any errors. See Figure 1-26.

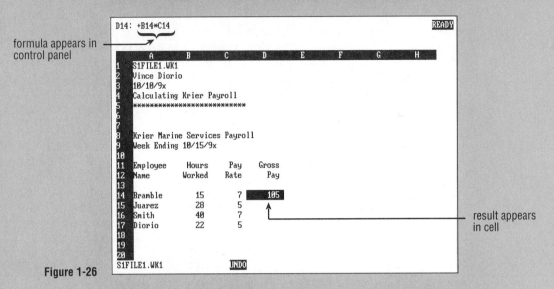

formula appears in control panel

result appears in cell

Figure 1-26

Now enter the formula in cell D15 to calculate Juarez's gross pay.

❹ Move the cell pointer to cell D15. Type **+B15*C15** and press **[Enter]**. The result, 140, appears in cell D15.

Now enter the formula in cell D16 to calculate Smith's gross pay.

❺ Move the cell pointer to cell D16, type **+B16*C16**, and press **[Enter]**. The gross pay for Smith is 280, which appears in cell D16.

Finally, enter the formula in cell D17 to calculate Diorio's gross pay.

❻ Move the cell pointer to cell D17, type **+B17*C17**, and press **[Enter]**. Diorio's pay is 110, which appears in cell D17.

Figure 1-27 shows the gross pay calculated for all the employees.

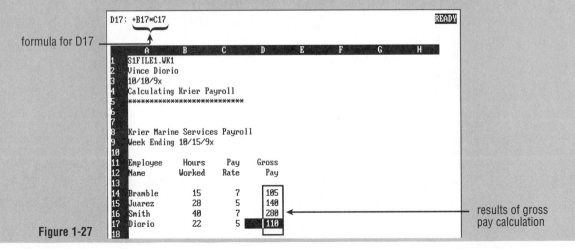

formula for D17

results of gross pay calculation

Figure 1-27

Calculating a Sum

Now let's calculate the total gross pay for all employees by adding the gross pay of Bramble, Juarez, Smith, and Diorio, that is, adding the values of cells D14, D15, D16, and D17.

To calculate a sum:

❶ Move the cell pointer to cell A19. Type the label **Totals** and press **[Enter]**.

❷ Move the cell pointer to D19. This is the cell in which we want to put the total gross pay.

The correct formula to calculate gross pay is +D14+D15+D16+D17. But for now, let's intentionally enter an incorrect formula.

❸ Type **+D14+D15+C17+D17** and press **[Enter]**. 1-2-3 calculates a total using this formula, and 360 appears in cell D19. See Figure 1-28.

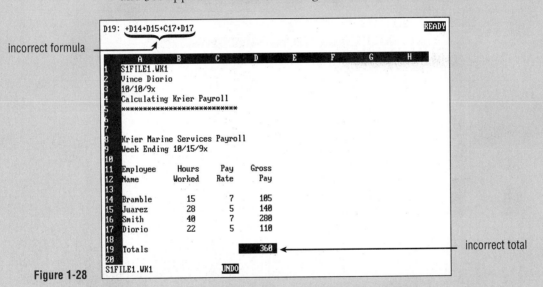

incorrect formula

incorrect total

Figure 1-28

Is the sum correct? If you add the gross pay of each employee (105 + 140 + 280 + 110), you get 635. Why does 360 appear in cell D19? Look at the formula in the control panel. The correct formula is +D14+D15+D16+D17, but your panel shows +D14+D15+C17+D17.

We made this error intentionally to demonstrate that you always run the risk of making errors when you create a worksheet. Be sure to check your entries and formulas. In this case, you would add the results manually and compare them to the value in the worksheet.

Editing Entries in a Cell

If you notice an error in your worksheet, you have already learned that you can move the pointer to the cell with the error and retype the entry that contains the error. You can also use EDIT mode to correct the problem. EDIT mode is sometimes faster and easier to use, because you change only the incorrect characters and leave the rest of the entry intact. In 1-2-3, you use [F2] (EDIT) to edit an entry. In the following steps, you'll edit cell D19, which contains the incorrect formula for total gross pay.

To edit the contents of a cell:

❶ Be sure the cell pointer is in cell D19.

❷ Press **[F2]** (EDIT). The formula +D14+D15+C17+D17 appears in the second line of the control panel. See Figure 1-29.

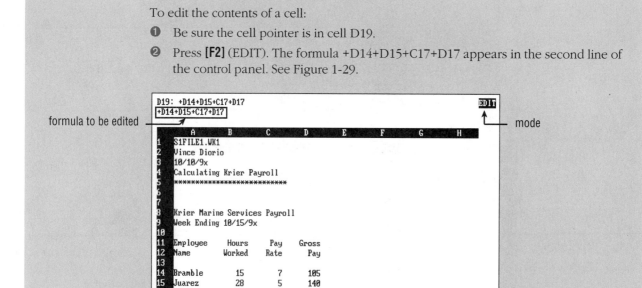

formula to be edited ——→   mode

Figure 1-29

❸ Press **[←]** to position the cursor under the letter C in the formula. Press **[Del]** three times to erase C17, the incorrect portion of the formula.

❹ Type **D16**. Press **[Enter]** and, as you do, notice that the value in D19 changes to 635, the correct total gross pay. Notice also that the correct formula, +D14+D15+D16+D17, appears in the control panel. See Figure 1-30.

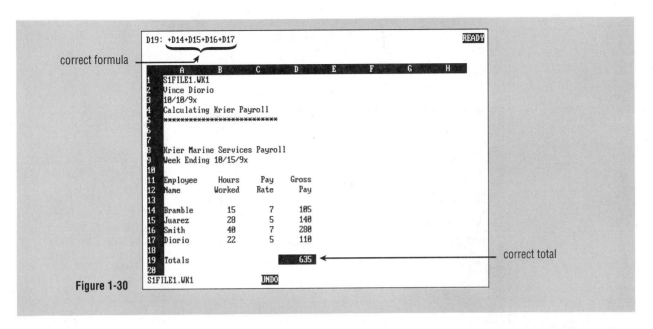

correct formula

D19: +D14+D15+D16+D17   READY

```
           A        B       C       D       E       F       G       H
 1  S1FILE1.WK1
 2  Vince Diorio
 3  10/10/9x
 4  Calculating Krier Payroll
 5  *******************************
 6
 7
 8  Krier Marine Services Payroll
 9  Week Ending 10/15/9x
10
11  Employee    Hours    Pay    Gross
12  Name        Worked   Rate    Pay
13
14  Bramble       15       7     105
15  Juarez        28       5     140
16  Smith         40       7     280
17  Diorio        22       5     110
18
19  Totals                       635
20
S1FILE1.WK1              UNDO
```

correct total

Figure 1-30

Be sure to take advantage of the [F2] (EDIT) key. It is often easier and more efficient to correct mistakes by typing only what needs to be changed.

Entering Lines

Worksheets often contain a row of lines below column headings and above and below subtotals to make the worksheet more readable. In addition, double lines are often used to indicate final totals. You could enter as many minus signs (–) or equal signs (=) as you need to create lines, but 1-2-3 provides a more convenient way. You first type \ (Backslash, not the slash symbol, /) and then type the character you want to use to draw the line. The backslash is a special label prefix that instructs 1-2-3 to repeat the character that follows it until the cell is filled.

To fill a cell with characters:

❶ Move the cell pointer to cell A13. This is a blank cell under a column heading.

❷ Type \ (Backslash) followed by a – (Minus Sign) to fill the cell with minus signs.

❸ Press **[Enter]**. See Figure 1-31. Notice how minus signs fill cell A13, producing a line in this cell.

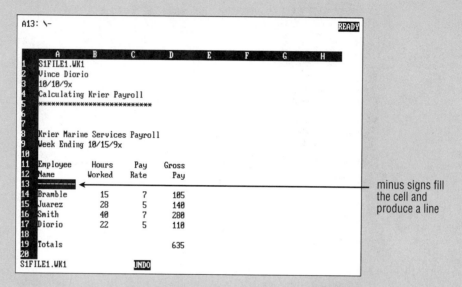

Figure 1-31

❹ Move the cell pointer to cell B13 and type **\–**, then press **[Enter]**.

❺ Move the cell pointer to cell C13, type **\–**, then press **[Enter]**.

❻ Move the cell pointer to cell D13, type **\–**, then press **[Enter]**. You have now entered a line across row 13.

❼ Move the cell pointer to cell D18, type **\–**, then press **[Enter]**. This enters a line in the gross pay column.

Your screen should be similar to Figure 1-32.

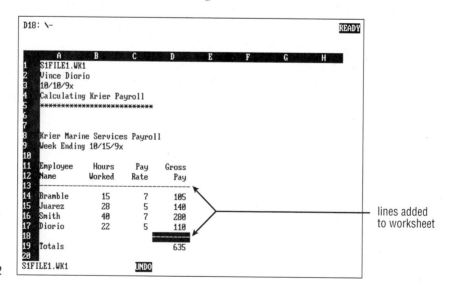

Figure 1-32

Using UNDO to Correct Mistakes

What would you do if you accidentally typed over or erased a complicated formula? It would probably be a lot of work to figure out the formula again and reenter it. UNDO can help. You can use it to cancel the *most recent* operation you performed on your worksheet.

To use UNDO, two indicators must appear on the screen. The word UNDO must appear in the status indicator at the bottom of your screen. Also, the word READY must appear in the mode indicator in the upper right corner of the screen. This means that your worksheet is in READY mode and can accept a keystroke.

Let's make an intentional mistake and use UNDO to correct it. Instead of typing the label ========= in cell D20, where it belongs, you will type it in cell D19, where it will erase the formula for total gross pay. Then you'll restore the original formula by using UNDO.

To intentionally make a mistake:

❶ Move the cell pointer to cell D19, the cell that contains the formula for total gross pay.

❷ Type \ = and press **[Enter]**. See Figure 1-33.

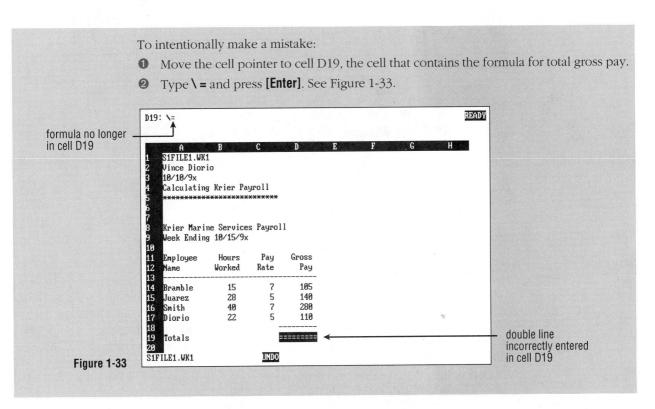

formula no longer in cell D19

double line incorrectly entered in cell D19

Figure 1-33

You have erased the entire formula and replaced it with =========, but don't worry. You can undo the mistake.

To use UNDO to cancel your *most recent* operation:

❶ Press the **[Alt]** key and, while holding it down, press the **[F4]** key ([Alt][F4]). Then release both keys. [Alt][F4] (UNDO) undoes your intentional mistake and restores the formula in D19. The value in D19 should again be 635.

❷   Now move the cell pointer to D20, the cell in which you should enter the double line. Type **\ =** and press **[Enter]**. See Figure 1-34.

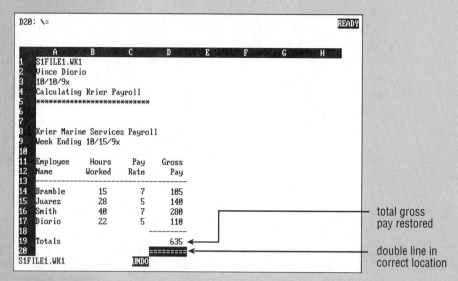

Figure 1-34

❸   Select /File Save (**/FS**) and press **[Enter]**. Select Replace (**R**) to save your work again as S1FILE1.

Understanding Ranges

Vince has completed the payroll worksheet for Krier Marine Services. Now he wants to print it. The Print command requires you to identify the range of cells that you want to print. Therefore, you need to understand the term *range* before using the Print command.

A **range** in 1-2-3 consists of one or more cells forming a rectangular shape. A range may be a single cell, a row of cells, a column of cells, or a rectangular block of cells. To define a range, you indicate the upper left corner cell of the rectangle and the lower right corner cell of the rectangle. Two periods [..] separate these entries and represent all the values between the beginning cell and ending cell, for example C14..C17.

Figure 1-35 illustrates several examples of ranges that you can define in a worksheet.

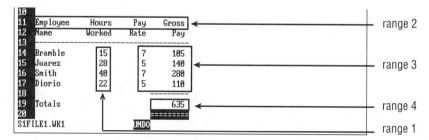

Figure 1-35

- The first example, labeled range 1, is identified as B14..B17. This forms a column of cells located in column B, beginning in row 14 and ending in row 17.
- The second example, range 2, represents a row of cells. The range is defined as A11..D11, which means the range of cells beginning at cell A11 and ending at D11.
- The third example, range 3, represents the rectangular block of cells C14..D17. A block of cells is identified in a worksheet by specifying a pair of diagonally opposite corner cells. C14, the upper left corner, and D17, the bottom right corner, define a block of eight cells.
- The fourth example, range 4, represents the single cell D19..D19. A single cell defined as a range has the same starting and ending cell.

Using the Print Command

You have entered the data, calculated gross pay and totals, saved your worksheet, and learned about ranges. You are now ready to print the Krier payroll worksheet and learn the basics of using the Print command. In 1-2-3, you print by first specifying a range to print and then printing the worksheet. You can print all or part of your worksheet by first defining a rectangular range of cells that you want to print. Vince wants to print the payroll report using the range A8 through D20.

To specify the print range A8..D20:

❶ Select /Print Printer (**/PP**). 1-2-3 displays a print settings sheet. See Figure 1-36.

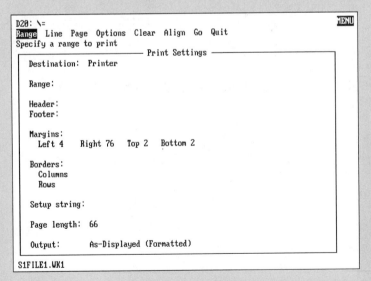

Figure 1-36
The print settings sheet

```
D20: \=                                                    MENU
Range  Line  Page  Options  Clear  Align  Go  Quit
Specify a range to print
                          ┌──── Print Settings ────
    Destination:  Printer

    Range:

    Header:
    Footer:

    Margins:
      Left 4     Right 76    Top 2    Bottom 2

    Borders:
      Columns
      Rows

    Setup string:

    Page length:  66

    Output:       As-Displayed (Formatted)

S1FILE1.WK1
```

Anytime you print, the printed output will be formatted according to the specifications on this sheet. If you want to see the worksheet instead of the print settings sheet, you can press the function key [F6]. Press [F6] again and the print settings sheet reappears.

❷ Select Range (**R**). The worksheet reappears.

To define the print range, you must specify two cell addresses that are diagonally across from one another. Usually, the upper left corner and the lower right corner cells define the range.

❸ Move the cell pointer to A8, the upper left corner cell in the print range. See Figure 1-37.

beginning of print range →

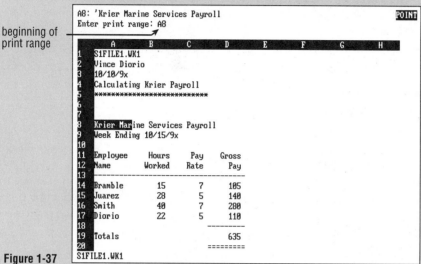

Figure 1-37

❹ Type **.** (Period). This fixes, or **anchors**, the cell. Whenever you want to specify a range, you should move the cell pointer to the top left corner cell of a range and anchor this position by pressing **.** (Period). See Figure 1-38 and compare it to Figure 1-37. Notice how 1-2-3 now indicates that cell A8 is anchored.

.. indicates range is now anchored →

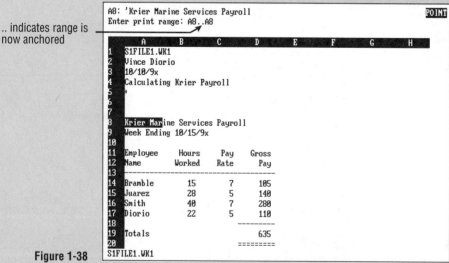

Figure 1-38

Once the range is anchored, you can expand it by using the cursor-movement keys. Pressing these keys highlights the range.

⑤ Press [↓] and [→], as needed, to highlight the range A8..D20. The highlighted range appears in the control panel. See Figure 1-39.

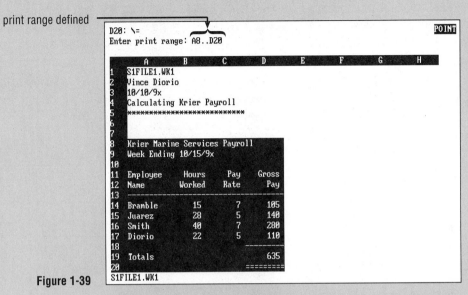

print range defined

Figure 1-39

⑥ Press **[Enter]**. This completes the definition of the range, which now appears in the print settings sheet. See Figure 1-40.

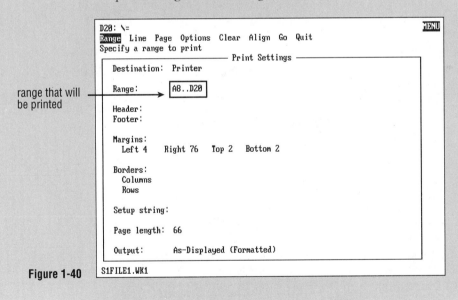

range that will be printed

Figure 1-40

Now that you've instructed 1-2-3 what cells you want to print, you are ready to print the worksheet.

To print a specified range:

➊ Make sure your paper is positioned properly in your printer and the printer is on-line.

➋ Select Align (**A**) to tell 1-2-3 that the paper is correctly positioned and ready for printing. You should always choose Align before beginning to print.

➌ Select Go (**G**) to print the specified range. If the range does not print, your copy of 1-2-3 may not be installed correctly.

➍ Select Page (**P**). You need not wait for the printing to finish before you select Page. The Page command tells 1-2-3 to advance the paper to the top of the next page when it is finished printing. See Figure 1-41.

```
Lotus 1-2-3 Student Business Series          Vince Diorio


Krier Marine Services Payroll
Week Ending 10/15/9x

Employee     Hours    Pay      Gross
Name         Worked   Rate     Pay
-----------------------------------------
Bramble       15        7       105
Juarez        28        5       140
Smith         40        7       280
Diorio        22        5       110
                               ---------
Totals                          635
                               =========
```

Figure 1-41
Printout of Krier
Marine Services
payroll worksheet

➎ Select Quit (**Q**) to leave the Print menu and return to READY mode with your worksheet displayed on your screen.

➏ Save your worksheet as S1FILE1 one last time (**/FS**). Press **[Enter]** and select Replace (**R**). This saves the print setting with the worksheet.

Erasing the Entire Worksheet

Once you have completed a worksheet, you may wish to start a new one. You can do this easily, but always remember to save your current worksheet. Then you can clear the worksheet from memory by using the Worksheet Erase command. You can also use this command if you begin a worksheet but decide you don't want it and have to start over. Let's erase the Krier payroll worksheet.

To erase a worksheet:

❶ Select /Worksheet Erase (**/WE**).

❷ Type **Y** (Yes) if you are sure you want to erase the worksheet. After you type Y, the worksheet disappears from the screen. See Figure 1-42. 1-2-3 *does not* erase the worksheet from your data diskette, only from the computer's memory.

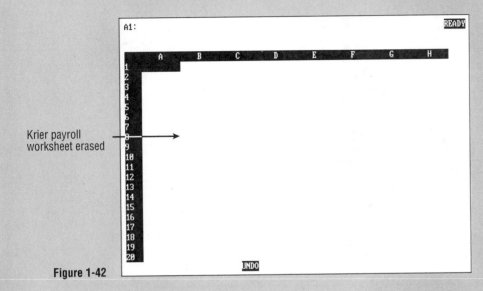

Krier payroll
worksheet erased

Figure 1-42

Using On-line Help

If you have difficulty using a 1-2-3 command, you can press [F1] (Help) at any time while you are using 1-2-3 to get helpful information on many topics. When a Help screen appears, the worksheet on which you are working temporarily disappears.

To use Help:

❶ If you are using a 5¼-inch *two-diskette system*, insert the Help Disk in drive A. If you are using a *hard-disk system*, go to Step 2.

❷ Press **[F1]** (Help).

1-2-3 displays the Help index. See Figure 1-43 on the next page.

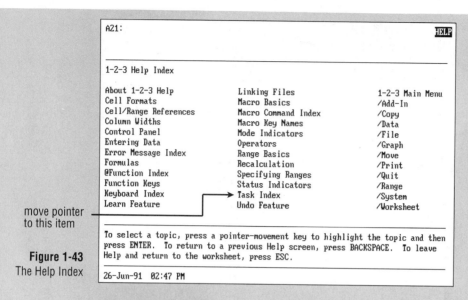

move pointer
to this item

Figure 1-43
The Help Index

❸ Use the pointer-movement keys to move the rectangular highlight to the item listed as "Task Index" and press **[Enter]**. See Figure 1-44.

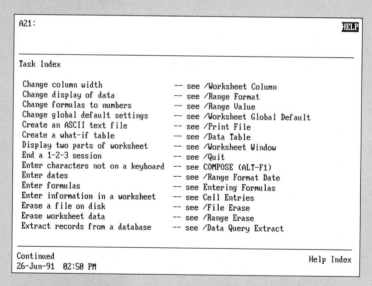

Figure 1-44
Help screen for
Task Index

1-2-3 displays a Help screen. On the left is a list of tasks you might want to do and on the right are the corresponding 1-2-3 commands. This Task Index is very useful when you are first learning 1-2-3.

❹ Move the highlight to one of the commands and press **[Enter]** to display additional help.

❺ When you are ready to return to the worksheet, press **[Esc]**.

1-2-3 Help is *context sensitive*. This means if you press [F1] (Help) while you are performing a particular task or if you have just made an error, you will get Help on that task or the error that has just occurred.

Quitting 1-2-3

When you are ready to quit 1-2-3, you choose the Quit command. You will be returned to the operating system prompt.

To quit a 1-2-3 session:
❶ Select /Quit Yes (**/QY**).

Exercises

1. Would you enter the following data items as labels or values?
   a. 227-3541   (phone number)
   b. 6.45   (pay rate)
   c. 02384   (zip code)
   d. 46 Main Street   (address)
   e. 25   (units on hand)

2. The contents of cell B5 is 20 and the contents of B6 is 15. What result appears in cell B7 if the following formula is entered in B7?
   a. +B5-B6   c. +B6*B5
   b. +B5*B6   d. +B6/B5

3. Which of the following ranges defines a row of cells? Which range defines a block of cells?
   a. B1..B7   c. B1..E1
   b. B1..D7   d. B1..B1

4. How can you display a series of plus signs, +++++++++, in a cell?

5. Which of the following filenames can be used to name a 1-2-3 worksheet?
   a. Q1.WK1   d. ACCT REC.WK1
   b. 1991.WK1   e. ACCT_REC.WK1
   c. ACCTREC.WK1   f. ACCT.REC.WK1

6. What key(s) would you press to accomplish the following tasks?
   a. Get to the Command menu
   b. Back up one step in the 1-2-3 menu system
   c. Move to cell A1
   d. Edit a formula in a cell

Tutorial Assignments

1. Retrieve file T1FILE1, find the error, and correct it. (When 1-2-3 displays the list of worksheet files, press [PgDn] several times to find the worksheet file T1FILE1.) What do you think the person who created the worksheet did when entering the gross pay formula for Bramble? Print the worksheet.

2. Retrieve file T1FILE2. Why isn't total gross pay adding correctly? Correct the worksheet and print it.

3. Retrieve file T1FILE3. Why is Bramble's gross pay zero? *Hint:* Think about how labels and values are stored in 1-2-3. Correct the error and print the worksheet.

Retrieve the file T1FILE4 and do the following:

4. Juarez worked 30 hours for the week, not the 28 hours that was entered. Correct this.

5. Smith's name is actually Smythe. Change the name.

6. In cell B19, write a formula to calculate total hours worked.

7. Add a single line in cell B18 and a double line in cell B20.

Continue using file T1FILE4 to complete the following problems on federal withholding tax (FWT). FWT is the amount of money that an employer withholds from an employee's paycheck to pay for federal taxes.

8. Assume that the amount withheld from an employee's paycheck is 15 percent (.15) of gross pay. Use column E in your worksheet to display FWT. Include the column heading "FWT" in cell E12. Enter the formula for withholding tax for each employee (gross pay × .15) in cells E14, E15, E16, and E17.

9. Net pay is the gross pay less deductions (gross pay – FWT). Use column F to display the net pay for each employee. Enter the column label "Net" in cell F11 and the column label "Pay" in cell F12. Enter the net pay formula for each employee in cells F14, F15, F16, and F17.

10. Calculate the total FWT and the total net pay for all employees. Display these totals in cells E19 and F19, respectively.

11. Add single and double lines where appropriate.

12. Print the entire worksheet, including the identifying data at the top of the worksheet. Your print range is A1..F20.

13. Change cell A1 to S1FILE4.WK1. Now save your worksheet as S1FILE4.WK1.

Case Problems

1. Sales in Toyland

An article in the *Wall Street Journal* focusing on sales in the toy industry for 1990 presented the data displayed in Figure 1-45.

Toy Companies Nine-Month Sales 1990 (in millions)		
Company	**1990**	**1989**
Galoob	105	169
Hasbro	1027	993
Matchbox	140	156
Mattel	1042	878
Tonka	541	625
Tyco	334	269

Figure 1-45

Retrieve the worksheet P1TOYS and do the following:

1. Calculate total sales for the toy industry for 1989 and 1990.

2. Calculate the change in sales from 1989 to 1990. Place this result in column D. Label the column heading "Change" and use the following formula:

$$Change = 1990\ sales - 1989\ sales$$

3. Print the worksheet.

4. Save the worksheet as S1TOYS.

2. Travel Agency Survey

A travel industry association conducted a study of U.S. travel habits. The following table shows the amount of passenger miles traveled in the United States by various modes of transportation.

U.S. Travel Habits	
Mode of transportation	**Passenger miles (billions)**
Cars	1586.3
Airlines	346.5
Buses	45.2
Railroad	18.7

Figure 1-46

Retrieve the worksheet P1TRVL and do the following:

1. Enter the formula to compute total U.S. passenger miles.

2. Enter the formula to compute the percent that each mode of transportation represents of the total U.S. passenger miles. (Divide the passenger miles for each mode of transportation by total passenger miles and then multiply by 100.)

3. Print your worksheet.

4. Save your worksheet as S1TRVL.

3. A Trend Toward More Bankruptcies

Ms. Ganni is a lawyer who administers bankruptcy filings. In the last few years, she has seen a rapid increase in the number of bankruptcy cases. She states, "I know the number of bankruptcy cases I've handled has increased enormously. I don't have time for lunch anymore, much less time to analyze all the cases. We need more staff; our system is overloaded!"

As her assistant, you must help Ms. Ganni make a case to her bosses for additional resources.

Retrieve the worksheet file P1BNKRPT and do the following:

1. Calculate the total number of bankruptcies in 1989 and 1990.

2. Calculate the percent change in bankruptcies this year compared to last year for each type of bankruptcy as well as the overall percent change. The formula to calculate percent change in bankruptcies for each bankruptcy type in 1990 is:

$$\left(\frac{(Bankruptcies\ in\ 1990 - Bankruptcies\ in\ 1989)}{Bankruptcies\ in\ 1989} \right) \times 100$$

3. Print the worksheet.

4. Save the worksheet as S1BNKRPT.

Setting Up Your Copy of 1-2-3

To use your copy of 1-2-3 with these tutorials, you must set up your copy so that your data diskette filenames appear whenever you select /File Retrieve and so that the current filename appears in the lower left corner of your screen. To set up 1-2-3 correctly you must change two *global settings*, that is, two conditions that affect your copy of 1-2-3 every time you use it.

To change these settings:

❶ If you are using a *two-diskette system*, put the Systems Disk in drive A and your data diskette in drive B. If you are using a *hard-disk system*, go to Step 2.

❷ Select Worksheet Global Default (**/WGD**). The global default settings sheet appears. See Figure 1-47.

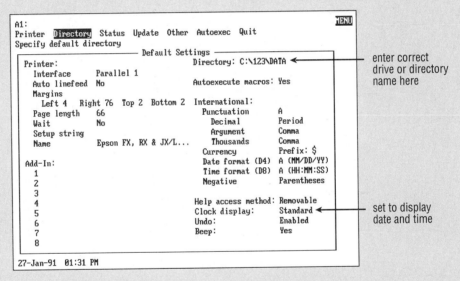

Figure 1-47
1-2-3's global default settings sheet

This settings sheet shows the settings that 1-2-3 uses each time you start 1-2-3.

❸ Select Directory (**D**).

1-2-3 prompts you to enter the letter of the drive from which you will load your data diskette files.

❹ Press **[Backspace]** to erase the current directory setting.

If you are using a *two-diskette system*, type **b:** (or the correct letter for the drive in which you have your data diskette) and press **[Enter]**.

If you are using a *hard-disk system*, type **c:\123\data** and press **[Enter]**. (If you copied your data diskette to a directory other than c:\123\data, enter the name of that directory instead.)

❺ Next select Other Clock Filename (**OCF**) to change the setting to display the filename instead of the date and time.

❻ To save these settings, select Update (**U**).

❼ To return to the worksheet, select Quit (**Q**).

Tutorial 2

Modifying a Worksheet

Pricing a Mutual Fund

Case: Allegiance Incorporated

Pauline Wu graduated last June with a degree in Finance. Today she is beginning her new job as a portfolio accountant with Allegiance Incorporated, an investment company. Pauline is very excited about getting this job, not only because Allegiance is reputed to be one of the best mutual fund companies in the United States, but also because Allegiance is known for the superior training it provides its new employees.

People who have money to invest but who do not want to manage the investment themselves invest their money with Allegiance. Allegiance employs trained professionals to manage the money in what are called mutual funds. In these funds, the money is invested in stocks, bonds, and other publicly traded securities and managed by Allegiance employees, often called portfolio managers.

For example, a portfolio manager might manage a $10 million fund that was started by selling one million shares at $10 a share to people who then become the shareholders of the fund. The manager of this fund then invests the $10 million by buying shares in companies such as IBM, AT&T, and Coca-Cola. The goal of the portfolio manager and the shareholders is that the shares purchased will increase in value so the shareholders will make money.

As a portfolio accountant, Pauline will be responsible for reporting correct information to portfolio managers so they will be able to track how well a fund is performing. One of Pauline's responsibilities in her new job is each day to calculate the value of the Balboa Equity Fund and to report this information to the national newspapers so shareholders can know the value of a share in this fund. Pauline knows that is an important responsibility. Even a minor error in her calculations could cause Allegiance to lose substantial amounts of money. She is eager to begin the new employee training program because it will help her to perform these important calculations accurately.

OBJECTIVES

In this tutorial, you will learn to:

■ Use the @SUM function

■ Change the way numbers are displayed

■ Change column widths

■ Adjust text alignments

■ Insert rows

■ Move a group of rows or columns to another worksheet area

■ Erase a group of cells

Pauline first meets the other new portfolio accountants and her training supervisor, Rochelle Osterhaut. Rochelle begins the training by discussing their daily responsibility to calculate the value of a mutual fund share. She hands out a fact sheet (Figure 2-1) that lists details about the Balboa Equity Fund. Rochelle explains that their first assignment is to use this information to calculate the value of a share of the Balboa Fund. She also reminds them that in college they probably learned that the value per share of a fund is usually called *net asset value*, or *NAV*.

```
Balboa Equity Fund    -    Fact Sheet

Mutual Fund Shares        2000

Net Asset Value            ?


Company Name        Shares Purchased        Current Price

IBM                      100                    125
Coca-Cola                 50                    42 1/4
AT&T                     100                    33 3/8
Boeing                   150                    48 1/2
```

Figure 2-1
Balboa Equity Fund
fact sheet

Rochelle explains that to calculate the NAV they must first determine the market value of each investment owned by the fund. To do this, they multiply the current price of each company share owned by the fund by the total number of shares of this company that the fund purchased. For example, Balboa Equity Fund owns 100 shares of IBM, whose current price is $125 per share. Thus, the market value of these shares in the Balboa Fund is $12,500. After the market value of each security is determined, the accountants add together the market value of each investment and other assets owned by the fund, such as cash on hand. After calculating this total they divide it by the number of shares owned by the fund's shareholders. The result is the net asset value. In other words,

$$NAV = \frac{(current\ price \times shares\ of\ company\ A\ owned\ by\ fund\,) + (current\ price \times shares\ of\ company\ B\ owned\ by\ fund\,) + \ldots}{number\ of\ shares\ of\ the\ mutual\ fund\ owned\ by\ fund's\ shareholders}$$

Pauline is eager to begin the assignment. She decides to use Lotus 1-2-3 to help make the calculations and to produce a professional-looking report. First, however, she thinks about the project; she outlines her thoughts on a planning sheet and sketches the worksheet (Figures 2-2a and 2-2b).

Figure 2-2a
Pauline's planning
sheet

My Goal:
    Calculate Net Asset Value for Balboa Equity Fund each day

What results do I want to see?
    Net Asset Value (Price/Share) of Balboa Equity Fund
    Breakdown of companies that make up the fund along with the market
    value of companies' stock

What information do I need?
    For each company stock owned by the fund:
        Name of the company
        Number of shares of the company's stock owned by fund
        Current price company's stock is selling for

What calculations will I perform?
    Calculate market value of each stock in the fund
    Calculate total value for all stock in the fund
    Calculate Net Asset Value

Figure 2-2b
Pauline's
worksheet sketch

Mutual Fund Shares

Price per share (NAV)

Company Name	# of Shares	Current Price	Market Value
XXXX	XX	XX.XXX	XXXX.XX
XXXX	XX	XX.XXX	XXXX.XX
.			
.			
.			
Totals			XXXX.XX

In this tutorial, you will create the same worksheet that Pauline creates. You will experience the power of the specialized @functions, which speed and simplify the use of formulas, learn more about entering and editing data quickly, and learn how to make changes in the appearance of the worksheet.

Retrieving the Worksheet

To retrieve the worksheet:

❶ Select /File Retrieve (**/FR**) and highlight C2FILE1.WK1. Press **[Enter]**. See Figure 2-3.

This worksheet contains the Balboa Equity Fund Portfolio data. It includes the company names and the number of shares of each company's stock that the fund purchased. It also shows the current day's stock market price of each company that is part of the Balboa Fund Portfolio. In addition, the worksheet shows the number of mutual fund shares owned by people who have invested in the Balboa Fund.

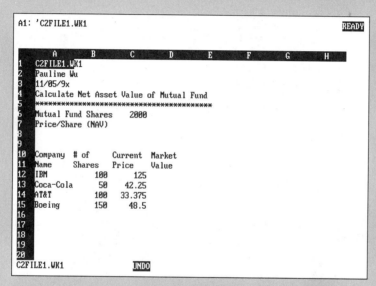

Figure 2-3
Data on Balboa
Equity Fund

Entering Formulas

Now that you have the basic data entered in the worksheet, your first step in pricing the mutual fund is to calculate the market value of each company's stock in the fund. The market value is calculated by multiplying the number of shares owned of each company's stock times the current market price of that company's stock, that is,

$$market\ value = number\ of\ shares \times current\ market\ price$$

To calculate the market value for each company:

First calculate the market value for IBM.

❶ Move the cell pointer to D12. Type **+B12*C12** and press **[↓]**.

To calculate the market value for Coca-Cola:

❷ In cell D13, type **+B13*C13** and press [↓].

To calculate the market value for AT&T:

❸ In cell D14, type **+B14*C14** and press [↓].

To calculate the market value for Boeing:

❹ In cell D15, type **+B15*C15** and press **[Enter]**. See Figure 2-4.

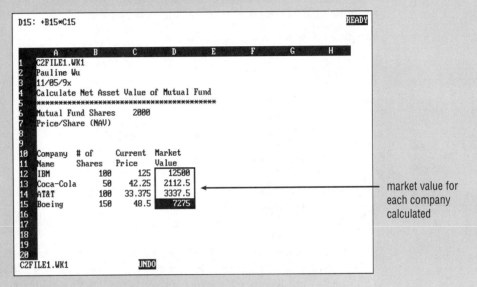

Figure 2-4

Using the @SUM Function

Now that you have calculated the market value of each company's stock in this fund, you need to calculate the total market value of the fund. The total market value of the fund is the sum of market values of all the companies in the fund, that is,

total market value = market value of IBM + market value of Coca-Cola + ...

Remember that in Tutorial 1 you summed the total gross pay by specifying the cell location of each employee's gross pay. Similarly, you could calculate the total market value by entering the formula +D12+D13+D14+D15, but this would be tedious. It would be especially tedious if the fund had perhaps 75 different companies instead of just four. To make the process much easier, you'll use 1-2-3's @SUM (pronounced "at sum") function. This function allows you to total the values in a range of cells.

What is an @Function?

A **function** is a predefined routine that performs a series of operations or calculations and then gives you a result. It can be thought of as a *predefined formula* that is built into 1-2-3.

Functions save you the trouble of creating your own formulas to perform various arithmetic tasks.

Many functions are available in 1-2-3. They are divided into eight categories: mathematical, statistical, database, financial, logical, string, date/time, and special.

Each function begins with the @ (at) symbol followed by the name of the function. The name of the function is a three-character abbreviation that suggests the purpose of the function. In parentheses following the function name, you will put any information the function needs to perform its tasks. The information in parentheses is referred to as the **arguments** of the function. Depending on the @function, the arguments may be values, references to cells or ranges, range names, formulas, and even other @functions.

The general format of a function in 1-2-3 is:

@FUNCTION(arguments)

where:

@ is the symbol that indicates that a function follows.

FUNCTION is the name of the function.

arguments represents the required information that the function needs to do its tasks.

Pauline is ready to calculate the total market value of the Balboa Equity Fund. To do this, she will use the @SUM function. Remember, the @SUM function adds a column of numbers. You specify the addresses of the first and the last cell of the column you want to add. In other words, @SUM(D12..D15) is equivalent to +D12+D13+D14+D15. The expression in parentheses, D12..D15, is the argument, representing the range of cells that will be added.

To use the @SUM function to calculate total market value:

❶ Move the cell pointer to A16 to enter the label. Type **[Space] [Space] Totals**. Press **[Enter]**.

❷ Now move the cell pointer to D16, where you will enter the formula to total the company market values.

❸ Type **@SUM(** to begin the formula. You may use either uppercase or lowercase when typing the function name SUM.

❹ Press **[↑]** to move the cell pointer to D12, the starting point for adding the market values of all companies in this fund. See Figure 2-5.

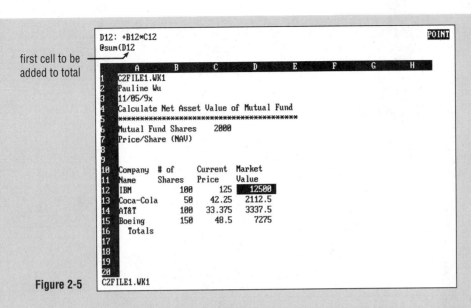

first cell to be added to total

Figure 2-5

⑤ Type **[.]** (Period) to anchor the cell. Two periods appear in the control panel to indicate that the cell is now anchored.

⑥ Press **[↓]** to highlight the range D12..D15. See Figure 2-6.

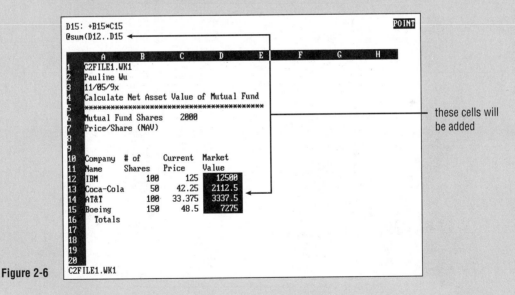

these cells will be added

Figure 2-6

⑦   Type **[)]** (Right Parenthesis) and press **[Enter]**. The calculated result, 25225, appears in cell D16. See Figure 2-7.

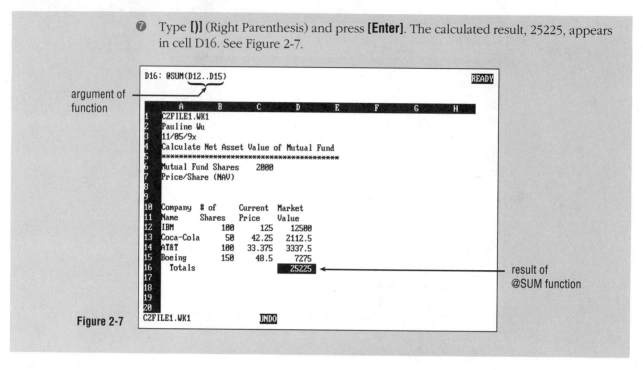

argument of function →

result of @SUM function

Figure 2-7

You have now calculated the market value for the Balboa Equity Fund.

The final calculation to determine the net asset value is to divide the total market value of the fund by the number of shares invested in the fund. In other words,

$$NAV = \frac{\text{total market value of mutual fund}}{\text{number of shares of fund owned by investors}}$$

To calculate net asset value:

❶   Move the cell pointer to C7, where the net asset value will be calculated.

❷   Type **+D16/C6** and then press **[Enter]**.

The / (Slash) symbol represents division when used in a formula.

You've now completed the calculations of the net asset value (NAV). Figure 2-8 on the next page shows the worksheet with the NAV calculated. Each share is worth $12.6125.

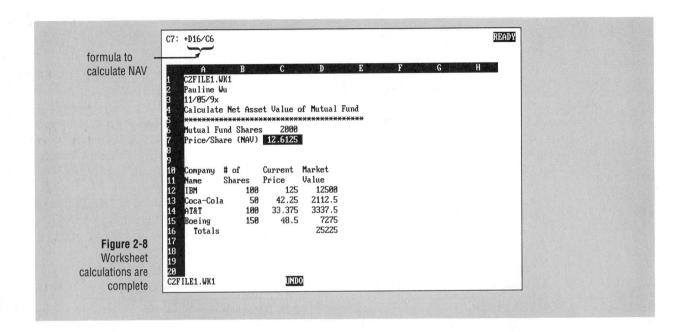

formula to
calculate NAV

Figure 2-8
Worksheet
calculations are
complete

Improving the Appearance of the Worksheet

Although Pauline has completed the calculations for pricing the mutual fund, she is not pleased with the appearance of the worksheet. For instance, the numbers in the current price and market value columns are not aligned at the decimal point. In addition, the monetary values do not show dollar signs, and the column headings are not aligned over the numbers in a column. Some improvements are needed to make the worksheet easier to read and use.

In the next several sections of this tutorial, you will learn to improve your worksheet's appearance. Figure 2-9 shows how the worksheet will look when you are finished.

Figure 2-9
Final version of
worksheet

Formatting Numbers

You probably found the numeric values in your worksheet difficult to read, because the list of current prices and market values are not aligned at the decimal point. Unless you instruct otherwise, a decimal point appears in a number only if the number has digits to the right of the decimal point. This is called the **General** format, and it is 1-2-3's default format. *Default* means that 1-2-3 automatically uses a format or setting unless you change it. Trailing zeros after the decimal are not displayed. Fortunately, you can change this by using the Format command. 1-2-3 provides several alternative formats that you can use to change the way numbers appear in your worksheet.

Figure 2-10 shows some types of numeric formatting available in 1-2-3. These formats allow you to alter the number of decimal places displayed with a number. They may include dollar signs and commas with numbers; they can place parentheses around negative numbers; and they can add percent signs to numbers representing percentages.

Format Type	Description	Examples
General	This is the default format; 1-2-3 stores numbers in this format when they are first entered.	0.5 −125
Fixed	This displays numbers to a fixed number of decimal places specified by the user.	0.50 1200.57
Currency	Numbers are preceded by dollar signs and commas are inserted after the thousands and millions places.	$1,200.57 ($125.00)
, (Comma)	Commas are inserted after the thousands and millions places. Negative numbers appear in parentheses.	1,200.57 (125.00)
Percent	This multiplies the value by 100 and inserts the percent sign to the right of the value.	50% 14.1%

Figure 2-10
Numeric formats

You can format all the cells in your worksheet using the Global Format command, which treats all the cells similarly. Or you can format a block of cells, a column, a row, or a single cell using the Range Format command. In the next steps, you will change the format of the current price and market value columns. To do this, you use the Range Format command.

To format the current prices to Currency format with three decimal places:

❶ Move the cell pointer to C12, the first cell of the Current Price column.

❷ Select /Range Format (**/RF**). The second line of the control panel lists all the formats available in 1-2-3. See Figure 2-11.

Format
commands
in 1-2-3

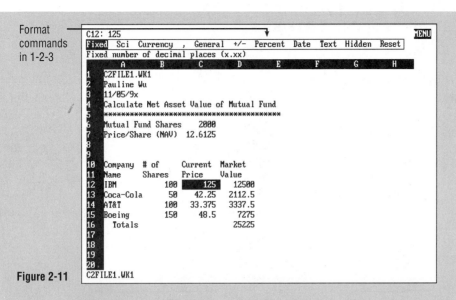

Figure 2-11

❸   Select Currency (**C**).

At this point, 1-2-3 asks you to enter the number of decimal places.

❹   Type **3** and press **[Enter]**. You chose three decimal places because stocks are bought and sold to the eighth of a dollar.

❺   At the range prompt, highlight the range C12..C15. Press **[Enter]**. See Figure 2-12.

Notice that 1-2-3 displays (C3) in the control panel, which means this cell is formatted using the currency format with three decimal places.

indicates cell is
formatted using
Currency format
with 3 decimal
places

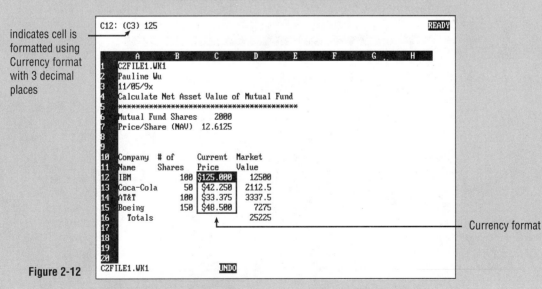

Figure 2-12

Formatting Considerations

You should be aware of the following when formatting numbers:

- If you reduce the number of decimal places of a number, 1-2-3 rounds the number that appears in the cell. For example, if you type the value 25.6273 into a cell, but decide to display the number with only two decimal places, the rounded number, 25.63, appears in the cell. If you decide to display three decimal places, the number 25.627 appears in the cell.

- For all calculations, 1-2-3 uses the value stored in the cell, rather than the value that appears in the cell. Thus, for an entry stored as 25.6273, but appearing as 25.63, 1-2-3 uses 25.6273 for all calculations.

Now let's format the market value column using Currency format with two decimal places.

To change the format of the market value column:

❶ Move the cell pointer to D12, the first cell under Market Value.

❷ Select /Range Format Currency (**/RFC**).

❸ At the prompt for the number of decimal places, press **[Enter]**. Since two decimal places is the default, it is not necessary to type 2. If you wanted zero decimal places, you would type 0 before pressing [Enter].

❹ At the range prompt, press **[↓]** to highlight the range D12..D16. Press **[Enter]**. See Figure 2-13.

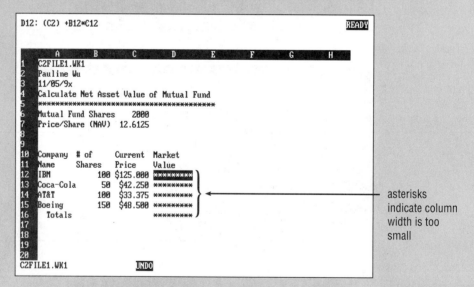

Figure 2-13

asterisks indicate column width is too small

Changing Column Widths

What happened to the values in the Market Value column? Why do asterisks appear in cells D12..D16? The asterisks indicate that the column width is not wide enough to display the values. 1-2-3 has a default width of nine characters in a cell. In this case, the asterisks indicate that the formatted market values require more than a nine-character-wide column. You must, therefore, widen the width of the Market Value column.

You can change the widths of all the columns in a worksheet at one time. We use the term **global** to describe a change that involves *all* similar items in a worksheet. You can also make a single column wider or narrower. In the next steps, you will widen a single column.

To change the width of column D:

❶ Make sure the cell pointer is in any cell in column D.

❷ Select /Worksheet Column Set-width (/**WCS**). See Figure 2-14.

preparing to change column width

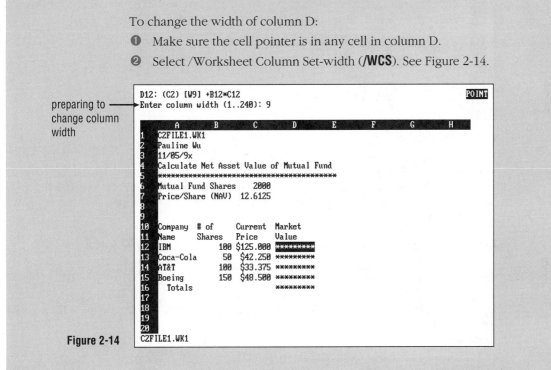

Figure 2-14

You can use two methods to enter a new column width: using the pointer-movement keys or typing a number. First, let's use the pointer-movement keys.

③ Press [→] until the column is wide enough to display all the values.

Notice how the column width increases by one character each time you press the key. See Figure 2-15.

column width is 11

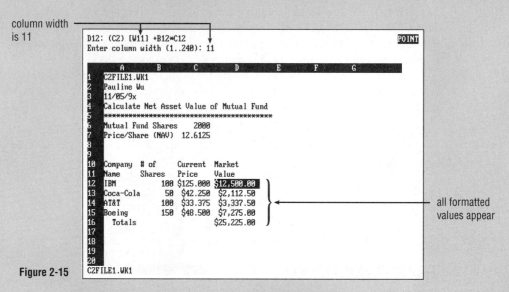

all formatted values appear

Figure 2-15

④ Press **[Enter]**.

Now let's try the second method to widen a column: typing a number. Let's widen the column to 15 characters so that it can accommodate an even larger number.

⑤ Select /Worksheet Column Set-width (**/WCS**).

⑥ Type **15** and press **[Enter]**. See Figure 2-16.

indicates cell formatted using Currency format with 2 decimal places

indicates width of column is 15 characters

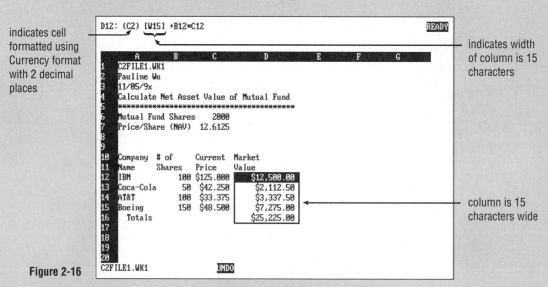

column is 15 characters wide

Figure 2-16

Notice that [W15] appears in the control panel, indicating the current width of the column is 15 characters.

Remember that all columns have a default width of nine characters. You can change the column width to accommodate labels and numbers that are longer than the column's width. Sometimes you might find nine characters too large. In such cases, you can reduce the width of a column by following the same steps you did to widen it. Just remember to choose a number less than 9.

Long Labels

Another reason to change the width of a column is to accommodate labels that are longer than nine characters. Often text entered into a cell is longer than the column's width. For example, the company name Hewlett-Packard requires more than nine characters. These text items are called **long labels.** If the cell to the right of the cell containing a long label is blank, the long label appears in the blank cell. However, if the cell to the right is not blank, then only the characters that fit into the column's current width will appear. Remember that the default column width is nine characters; thus, only the first nine characters will appear in the cell.

Let's suppose that Pauline does not want to abbreviate the names of the companies in the fund. Let's enter the full name for IBM, International Business Machines, and observe the result.

To enter a long label:

❶ Move the cell pointer to A12.

❷ Type **International Business Machines** and press **[Enter]**. Since the default column width is 9, only the first nine characters appear — Internati. Look at the control panel; notice that the entire label appears there. This indicates that 1-2-3 has stored the entire label in the cell memory, but since the width of the column is 9, only the first nine characters appear on your screen. See Figure 2-17.

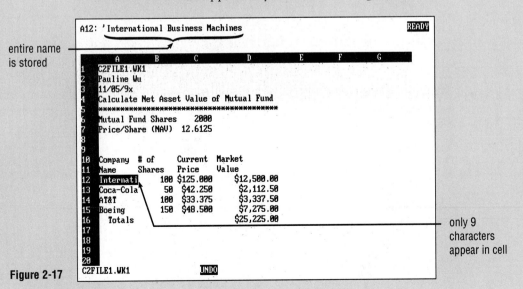

entire name is stored

only 9 characters appear in cell

Figure 2-17

Pauline wants the entire name of the company to appear, so we must increase the column width.

To increase the column width:

❶ Select /Worksheet Column Set-width (**/WCS**).

❷ Type **32** to allow enough characters for the entire name to appear on the screen.

❸ Press **[Enter]**. See Figure 2-18.

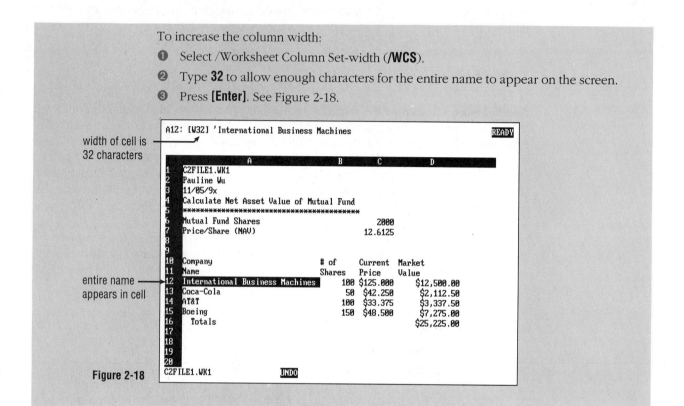

width of cell is 32 characters

entire name appears in cell

Figure 2-18

Adjusting Labels within a Cell

As you have seen, when you enter a label, 1-2-3 places it, by default, against the left edge of the cell. Such a label is said to be **left-justified** and has an apostrophe (') label prefix. You can easily change the alignment of labels to suit your needs. You can also center or right-justify labels.

Let's learn how to right-justify the labels in Pauline's worksheet.

To right-justify the column headings for the number of shares, the current price, and the market value:

❶ Move the cell pointer to B10.

❷ Select /Range Label Right (**/RLR**). See Figure 2-19. Notice that 1-2-3 automatically anchors the range at the location of the cell pointer, B10.

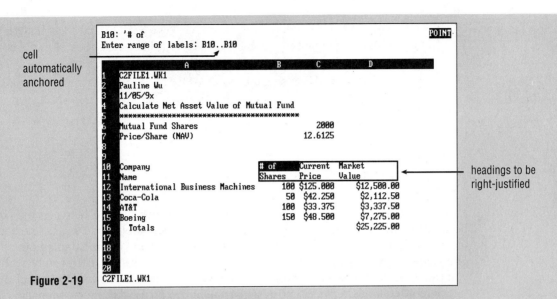

cell automatically anchored

headings to be right-justified

Figure 2-19

③ Move the [→] and [↓] keys until the cell range B10..D11 is highlighted. Press **[Enter]**. See Figure 2-20.

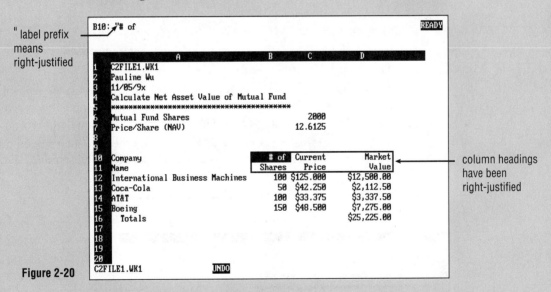

" label prefix means right-justified

column headings have been right-justified

Figure 2-20

The headings in columns B, C, and D are now right-justified.

Notice in the control panel that a " (Quote) character now precedes the label. The " character is the label prefix 1-2-3 uses to indicate a right-justified label.

To center the labels, you would select Range Label Center in Step 2.

You can also control label alignment as you type labels. For example, to center a label, type the ∧ (Caret) character (found on the [6] key) in front of any label. To right-justify a label, type a "(Quote) character in front of the label.

④ Press **[Home]** to move the cell pointer to cell A1. Type **S2FILE1** and press **[Enter]**. This changes this identifying information in cell A1 so it will be consistent with the new filename.

⑤ Save your worksheet (**/FS**), using the name S2FILE1.

Inserting Rows

You could improve the worksheet appearance by inserting a line between the column heading and the first company name. In addition, it would look better with a line between the last company name and the Totals row. But there isn't any room. Running out of room often happens when you are in the process of creating a worksheet. Fortunately, with 1-2-3 you can insert or delete one or more rows between two adjacent rows. You can also insert one or more columns between two adjacent columns. You use the Insert command to insert new rows or columns into your worksheet.

To insert a blank row between A11 and A12 in the worksheet:

① Move the cell pointer to A12, the first row that you want moved down.

② Select /Worksheet Insert Row (**/WIR**).

The prompt message "Enter row insert range: A12..A12" appears on the control panel. Since you are adding only one row, do not change the range. If you wanted to insert more rows, you would press **[↓]** for every row you wanted to insert.

③ Press **[Enter]**. 1-2-3 has inserted one blank row. All the other rows have been pushed down below the blank row. Notice also that 1-2-3 has adjusted all formula relationships. See Figure 2-21.

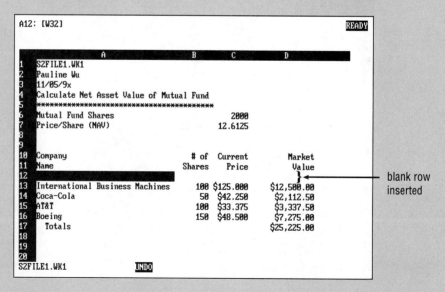

Figure 2-21

To insert a blank row after Boeing and before the Total Value row:

④ Move the cell pointer to A17.

⑤ Select /Worksheet Insert Row (**/WIR**).

⑥ Press **[Enter]**. A blank row is inserted between Boeing and the label Totals.

Now let's add some lines to improve the worksheet's appearance.

To underline the column headings:

① Move the cell pointer to A12. Type **\ –** and press **[Enter]**.

② Repeat Step 1 for cells B12, C12, and D12.

To add a row of lines to row 17:

③ Move the cell pointer to A17. Type **\ –** and press **[Enter]**.

④ Repeat Step 3 for cells B17, C17, and D17. See Figure 2-22.

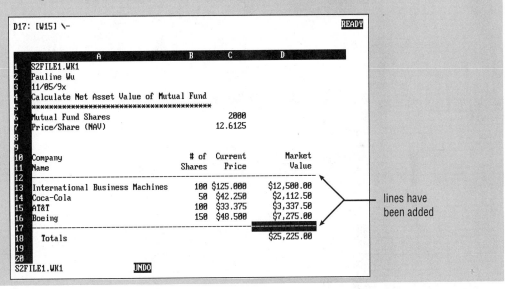

Figure 2-22

Moving Data

Pauline has made several changes that have improved the appearance of her worksheet. However, after reviewing the current worksheet, Pauline decides that she wants to make additional changes to improve it even further. First, she wants the summary data on mutual fund shares and net asset value to follow the company data. She feels the companies that make up the fund should be placed before the summary information on the NAV. (Report layout often is a matter of personal preference.) In addition, she realizes the report is actually incomplete because the company sells many different mutual funds. The worksheet does not indicate that these data are only for the Balboa Equity Fund. Also, she prices the fund at the end of each day, but the worksheet doesn't indicate the date of this report. Thus, Pauline decides to add the following two lines to the worksheet:

Balboa Equity Fund
Net Asset Value for November 5, 1990

She wants to place this title above the column headings, exactly where the Mutual Fund Shares label is now. How can she rearrange the worksheet without starting over?

Fortunately, Lotus 1-2-3 has a Move command. Its function is to move data from one part of the worksheet to another part of the same worksheet. This command is a powerful tool for creating and designing worksheets. Let's move the information on the number of shares owned and the NAV to begin in cell A19, so this information appears after the individual companies in the fund.

To move the range A6..C7 to a new location:

❶ Move the cell pointer to A6, the upper left corner of the range you want to move.

❷ Select /Move (**/M**). A6..A6 appears on the control panel as the move FROM range. The two periods mean the cell is anchored in A6. See Figure 2-23.

first cell in range to be moved —

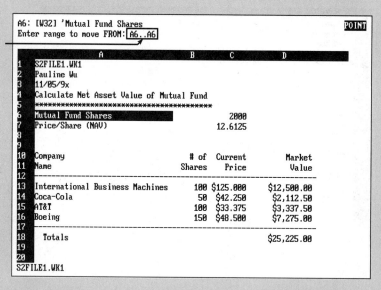

Figure 2-23

You next identify the entire range you want to move (A6 to C7):

❸ Highlight A6..C7. The highlighted area will be moved. See Figure 2-24.

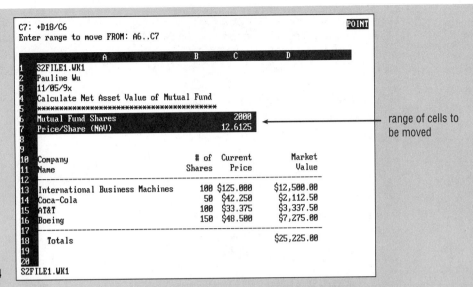

Figure 2-24

range of cells to be moved

④ Press **[Enter]**.

Now you identify the upper left corner of the new location for this block of cells:

⑤ Move the cell pointer to A19, the first cell of the move TO range. This is the cell where you want the label "Mutual Fund Shares" to begin.

⑥ Press **[Enter]**. The block of cells moves to its new location. See Figure 2-25. Notice that A6..C7 is empty.

Even if you move all or part of your worksheet, the worksheet retains all the functional relationships. 1-2-3 automatically adjusts all the formulas in the move FROM range.

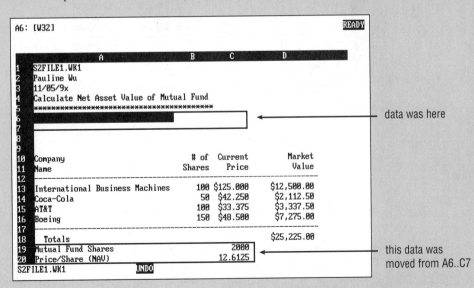

Figure 2-25

data was here

this data was moved from A6..C7

When you have completed moving the data, the cell pointer returns to the cell where you started the command.

⑦ Move the cell pointer to the cell that contains the NAV, C20, and examine the formula in the control panel. The formula is now +D18/C19. When the formula was in cell C7, the formula was +D18/C6. The formula was automatically adjusted by 1-2-3.

Now you are ready to enter the two-line title: Balboa Equity Fund and Net Asset Value for November 5, 1990.

To enter the title:

① Move the cell pointer to cell A6.

② Type **Balboa Equity Fund** and press [↓].

③ In cell A7, type **Net Asset Value for** and press [→].

④ In cell B7, type **November 5, 1990** and press [**Enter**]. See Figure 2-26.

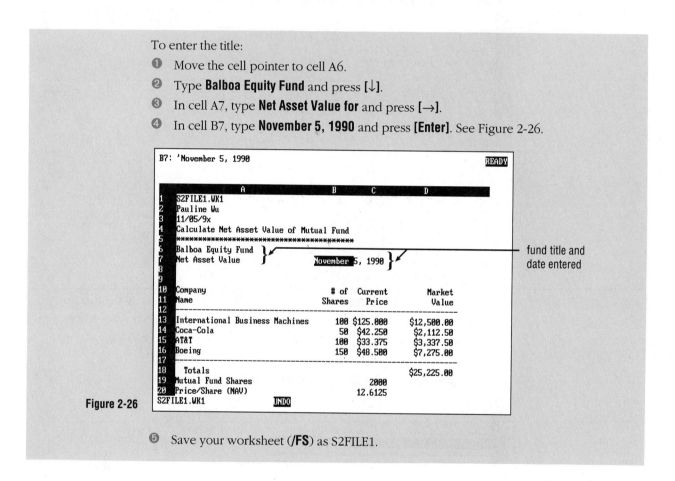

```
B7: 'November 5, 1990                                          READY

             A                    B        C         D
1 S2FILE1.WK1
2 Pauline Wu
3 11/05/9x
4 Calculate Net Asset Value of Mutual Fund
5 ***********************************************
6 Balboa Equity Fund       ⎫                              ── fund title and
7 Net Asset Value          ⎬    November 5, 1990 ⎫           date entered
8                                               ⎭
9
10 Company                         # of  Current      Market
11 Name                           Shares  Price       Value
12 ──────────────────────────────────────────────
13 International Business Machines   100 $125.000    $12,500.00
14 Coca-Cola                          50  $42.250     $2,112.50
15 AT&T                              100  $33.375     $3,337.50
16 Boeing                            150  $48.500     $7,275.00
17
18  Totals                                          $25,225.00
19 Mutual Fund Shares                      2000
20 Price/Share (NAV)                     12.6125
S2FILE1.WK1                  UNDO
```

Figure 2-26

⑤ Save your worksheet (**/FS**) as S2FILE1.

Erasing a Range of Cells

Now that the worksheet is complete, Pauline thinks about how she will use it on a daily basis. Each day, Pauline will enter the current day's prices for each company's stock. To make sure that she doesn't accidentally use a price from the previous day, she wants to erase all the prices in the current price column before she enters the prices for the current day. To erase the prices, she will use the Range Erase command.

To erase the current prices in column C:

❶ Move the cell pointer to C13, the first cell to be erased.

❷ Select /Range Erase (**/RE**). The control panel reveals the address of the current cell and prompts you to specify the range you want to erase.

❸ Press [↓] to highlight the range C13..C16. See Figure 2-27.

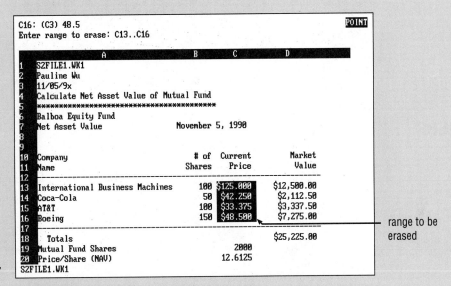

Figure 2-27

❹ Press **[Enter]**. 1-2-3 erases the entries in C13 to C16. The cell pointer returns to C13, the first cell in the range. See Figure 2-28.

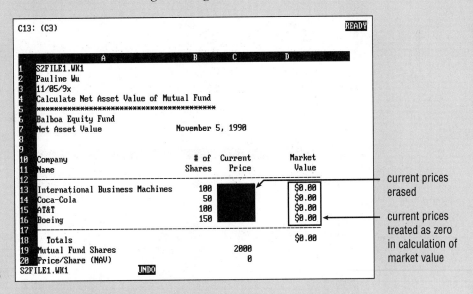

Figure 2-28

Notice that the market values are now zero. That is because their values are based on the daily prices, which are blank. 1-2-3 treats the blank cells as zero for any calculations that reference these cells.

The worksheet is now ready for Pauline to enter the prices for the next day.

❺   Save your worksheet (**/FS**) as S2FILE2.

■   ■   ■

Exercises

1. Suppose that you have a worksheet and cells F6, F7, F8, and F9 have values stored in them. Write two different formulas to calculate the total of these four cells.

2. Which formula adds six entries in row 3?
    a.   +A3+A4+A5+A6+A7+A8
    b.   @SUM(B3..E3)
    c.   @SUM(D3..I3)
    d.   +M3+N3+O3+P3

3. Suppose you type the value 1005.254 in cell A5. What format type would you select in each case to have the following values appear in the cell?
    a. $1,005.25
    b.   1,005.3
    c.   1005

4. Figure 2-29 shows a worksheet you started typing. The company name, Allied Freight, was typed in cell A3, and the address, 227 Mill St Canton Ohio 13456 was typed in B3. Why does the complete address appear in cell B3 but only Allied Fr in A3?

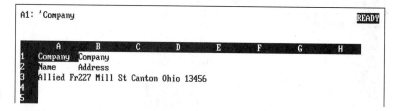

Figure 2-29

5. Figure 2-30 shows part of a worksheet. How would you improve the appearance of this worksheet? What command(s) would you use?

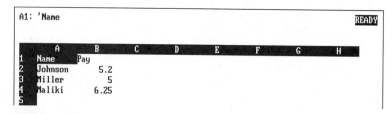

Figure 2-30

Tutorial Assignments

1. Retrieve the worksheet file T2FILE1.WK1. The formula in cell C20 is not correct. Price/Share (NAV) shows "ERR" when the worksheet is retrieved.
   a. Explain why ERR is displayed as the value for NAV.
   b. Correct the error.
   c. Print the corrected worksheet.
   d. Save the corrected worksheet as S2FILE3.

Retrieve the worksheet file T2FILE2.WK1 and do the following:

2. Adjust the labels, Mutual Fund Shares and Price/Share (NAV), so they are right-justified in their cells, A19 and A20, respectively.

3. Move the values associated with the labels in Tutorial Assignment 2 from cells C19 and C20 to B19 and B20.

4. Format NAV to two decimal places using the Currency format.

5. Print the revised worksheet. Use the print range A1..D20.

6. The worksheet is too cluttered. Move all the information in the range A6..D20 to a separate screen beginning at cell A21.

7. In cell A10 type **Press [PgDn] to view Net Asset Value Report.**

8. Save this worksheet as S2FILE4.

9. Erase the entire worksheet.

10. Retrieve the worksheet file S2FILE4.WK1.

11. Erase the current prices in the worksheet and then enter the following prices for November 6, 1990: 120.50, 43, 34.125, and 48.25. Remember to change the date in the worksheet. Print the worksheet. Save as S2FILE5.

The following exercises involve the worksheet developed in Tutorial 1. Retrieve the file T1FILE5.WK1 and do the following:

12. In cell B19, calculate total hours for all employees using the @SUM function.

13. Format the pay rate and gross pay columns to two decimal places using the Currency format.

14. A new employee, Jalecki, has been hired. Insert this name between the names Bramble and Juarez.

15. Print the revised worksheet.

16. Save the revised worksheet as S1FILE6.

Case Problems

1. Z & Z Electronics Performance Report

Craig Keifer is the general manager of the manufacturing division of Z & Z Electronics. Each year Craig prepares estimated costs for manufacturing cabinets for computers and other electronic equipment. Manufacturing costs include wages/salaries, raw materials, utilities, supplies, and other costs. Craig prepares a performance report to measure his division's performance compared to his estimate. This monthly report compares the estimated costs with the actual costs for the month just ended and the year-to-date (YTD) cumulative costs. Craig also calculates the difference between estimated and actual costs, called the *variance*, for both the monthly and cumulative periods. He does this by subtracting estimated costs from the actual costs, in other words,

$$variance \ = \ actual \ cost \ - \ estimated \ cost$$

Retrieve the P2PERFRM.WK1 worksheet. This worksheet contains the cost data for the month of March 1990, as well as cumulative costs since the beginning of the year.

1. Calculate the total costs for both the estimated and the actual cost columns (columns B, C, E, and F).

2. Calculate the variances for each cost for both monthly and year-to-date periods (columns D and G).

3. Improve the appearance of the worksheet. Add titles, lines under headings, format values, and any other changes that will make the report more readable.

4. Print your worksheet.

5. Save your worksheet as S2PERFRM.

2. Ford Motor Company Car Sales

A Ford executive is preparing a presentation for a local Chamber of Commerce. The executive asks his assistant, Steve Duncan, to prepare a 1-2-3 worksheet with Ford's sales history (units sold) from 1985 to 1988. Steve starts to summarize the data for Ford's three divisions, Ford, Mercury, and Lincoln, but he becomes ill and cannot finish the assignment. His worksheet file, P2FORD.WK1, is incomplete:

- He has not entered data for the Mercury division, which is shown in Figure 2-31. The data for the Mercury division should be placed between the Ford and the Lincoln divisions.

- Each division's sales need to be subtotaled, and then all three divisions' sales should be added to provide total sales for Ford Motor Company for each year. Only the labels for subtotals appear in the worksheet.

- Finally, the worksheet must be more professional in appearance before the executive distributes it to the Chamber of Commerce.

Mercury Division	Units Sold—Mercury Division			
	1985	**1986**	**1987**	**1988**
Topaz	73554	65498	63217	85936
Sable	879	91314	103399	118117
Cougar	118554	112812	110112	102415
Grand Marquis	134139	118364	119015	115141

Figure 2-31

Complete Steve's worksheet by doing the following:

1. Retrieve the worksheet file P2FORD.WK1.

2. Add the data for the Mercury division between the Ford and the Lincoln divisions.

3. Calculate the subtotal for each division.

4. Calculate total sales for all the divisions.

5. Improve the appearance of the worksheet. Include a title, date, and lines under the column headings, align the column headings, and make any other changes you feel are appropriate.

6. Print the worksheet.

7. Save your worksheet as S2FORD.

3. Calculating the Dow Jones Industrial Average

The Dow Jones Industrial Average (DJIA) is the best-known indicator of how stock prices fluctuate on the New York Stock Exchange (NYSE). The DJIA represents the average price of thirty large, well-known industrial corporations considered leaders in their industry. All the companies are listed on the NYSE.

Each day the DJIA is calculated by summing the closing price of each of the thirty companies and dividing by a divisor. The formula for calculating the DJIA is:

$$DJIA = \frac{sum\ of\ daily\ closing\ prices\ for\ 30\ companies}{divisor}$$

On September 5, 1990, the DJIA was 2613.14. The divisor was 0.5049.

Retrieve the file P2DOW.WK1 and do the following:

1. Finish the calculation of the DJIA (cell B43).

2. Experts suggest that changes in higher-priced stock have a greater impact on the DJIA than changes on lower-priced stock. For example, if IBM, a high-priced stock, were to increase by 10% (assume no other stock prices change), the new DJIA would change more than if Navistar, a low-priced stock, were to increase by 10%.

a.   In column C, labelled IBM Adjmt, increase IBM's price by 10% (1.10 × current price) and calculate the new DJIA (cell C43).

b.   In column D, the Navistar column, increase Navistar's price by 10% and calculate the DJIA (cell D43).

c.   Compare the new averages against the original average by calculating the percent change. Use the following formulas:

For the percent change in column C:

$$percent\ change = \frac{(IBM\ adjusted\ DJIA - original\ DJIA)}{original\ DJIA}$$

For the percent change in column D:

$$percent\ change = \frac{(Navistar\ adjusted\ DJIA - original\ DJIA)}{original\ DJIA}$$

Note that the original DJIA is in cell B43. How do these new averages compare to the original average?

3.   Format your worksheet so it is more readable. Consider formatting values, centering or right-justifying column headings, adding descriptive labels, and making any other changes you think will improve the appearance of your worksheet.

4.   Save your worksheet as S2DOW.

5.   Print your final worksheet.

Tutorial 3

Working with Larger Worksheets

Preparing a Revenue Report

Case: TriCycle Industries

Nick Theodorakis is the assistant sales manager for TriCycle Industries, a recycling center serving the tri-state area of Kentucky, Indiana, and Illinois. For the last two years, TriCycle's sales were not high enough to generate a profit. This year, however, TriCycle was profitable and came very close to achieving its sales goals.

As assistant sales manager, Nick services fifteen customer accounts, scouts for new accounts, and provides administrative assistance to the TriCycle sales manager, Kay Schilling. At the end of each quarter, Nick assists Kay in preparing a quarterly sales report. Kay then formally presents the report to top management at TriCycle's quarterly meeting.

OBJECTIVES

In this tutorial you will learn to:

- Copy contents of cells to other locations in the worksheet

- Copy relative cell references

- Copy absolute cell references

- Assign names to cell ranges

- Print using compressed type

Kay meets with Nick to discuss this quarter's report. She shows him the data she has compiled:

TriCycle Industries 1990 Revenue
(000 Omitted)

Recycled Material	First Quarter	Second Quarter	Third Quarter	Fourth Quarter
Plastics	2890	2942	3378	3837
Glass	2701	2862	2869	3601
Aluminum	2247	2282	2489	2602

Kay points out that these data represent the revenue for all four quarters of 1990. She wants to include totals and some additional information to help the top executives compare 1990 revenues to previous years. She asks Nick to create a worksheet using the data she's collected thus far and also showing the following:

- Total revenue by quarter
- Total revenue for the year 1990 by recycled material
- Total 1990 revenue
- Contribution of revenue from each material as a percentage of total 1990 revenue

Nick agrees and offers to give special attention to the appearance of the worksheet, because he knows how important this report will be. Nick spends time thinking about the project and develops a planning sheet and a sketch to assist him in completing the worksheet (Figures 3-1a and 3-1b).

My Goal:
    Prepare the Sales Report for TriCycle management

What results do I want to see?
    Sales Revenue Report including totals by quarter and recycled material
    Contribution of each recycled material to total revenue

What information do I need?
    Quarterly sales revenue for each recycled material

What calculations will I perform?
    Calculate total revenue for each quarter
    Calculate total revenue for each recycled material for the year
    Calculate total revenue for year
    Calculate percent contribution of each recycled material to total
        revenue

Figure 3-1a
Nick's planning
sheet

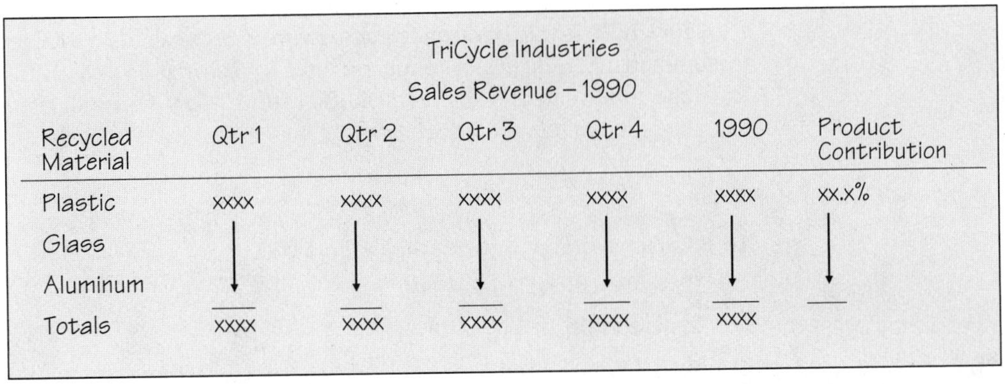

Figure 3-1b
Nick's worksheet
sketch

In this tutorial, you will use Kay's data to create Nick's report. You will learn how to copy formulas, a process that saves a great deal of time in creating a worksheet. You will also put to use several valuable 1-2-3 features, such as how to name ranges. You will also learn more about printing with 1-2-3, specifically how to use compressed type to print more data on one line.

Retrieving the Worksheet

Your first step in this tutorial is to retrieve the worksheet that Nick has started based on Kay's data.

To retrieve the worksheet:

❶   Retrieve the file C3FILE1.WK1. See Figure 3-2.

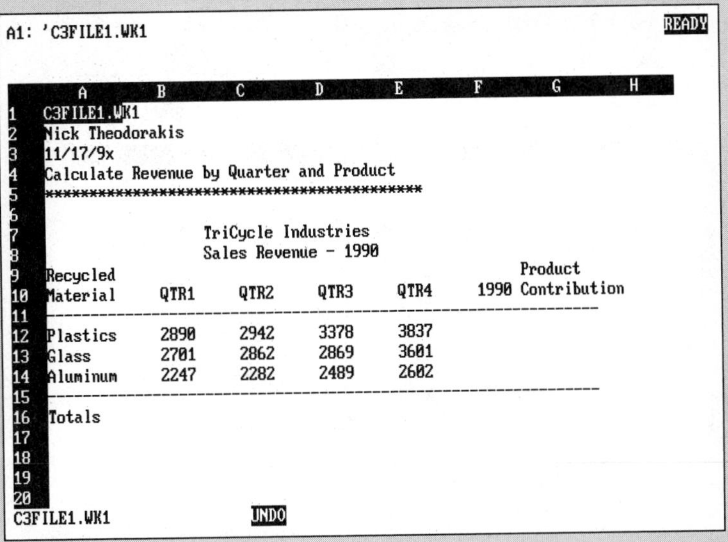

Figure 3-2
The retrieved
TriCycle worksheet
— quarterly
revenues by
recycled
material

This file contains the quarterly revenues of TriCycle Industries categorized by the material they recycle. Titles have been entered; so have revenue amounts for each material for each quarter.

How did TriCycle perform in each quarter? Let's calculate total revenues for each quarter to summarize TriCycle's revenue picture. In Tutorial 2, you used the @SUM function to calculate total market value of a mutual fund. Now you will use the @SUM function to calculate total revenue for each quarter.

To calculate total revenue for the first quarter:

❶   Move the cell pointer to B16.

❷   Type **@SUM(**

❸   Move the cell pointer to B12 and then type **[.]** (Period) to anchor the cell pointer.

❹   Press **[↓]** to highlight the range B12..B14. See Figure 3-3.

range of cells to sum

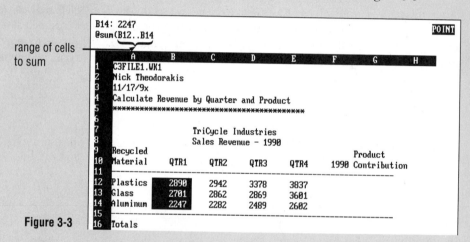

Figure 3-3

❺   Type **[)]** (Right Parenthesis) and press **[Enter]**. The total revenue in quarter 1, 7838, appears in cell B16. See Figure 3-4.

formula to calculate total revenue in quarter 1

total revenue

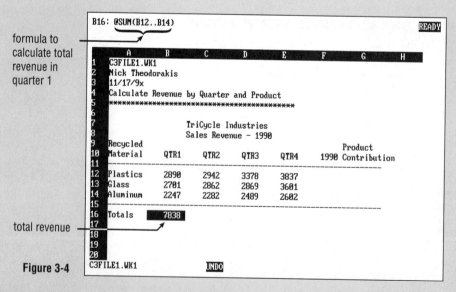

Figure 3-4

You might find it easier to type in the actual letters and numbers of the range, that is, B12..B14, instead of pointing to the cell range. If you had used this approach, Step 2 would have been

❷ Type **@SUM(B12..B14**

You would then skip Steps 3 and 4 and conclude with Step 5.

Copying Formulas

You can continue to use the @SUM function to calculate total revenue for the remaining quarters. A faster approach, however, is to use the Copy command. Experienced 1-2-3 users rely on the Copy command because it saves time and decreases the likelihood of errors. Let's calculate total revenues for quarters 2, 3, and 4 by copying the formula in cell B16 to cells C16, D16, and E16.

To copy a formula to cells C16, D16, and E16:

❶ With the cell pointer in B16, the cell whose formula will be copied, select /Copy **(/C)**.
The control panel displays B16..B16 as the copy FROM range, meaning cell B16 is to be copied to other cells. See Figure 3-5.

formula to be copied

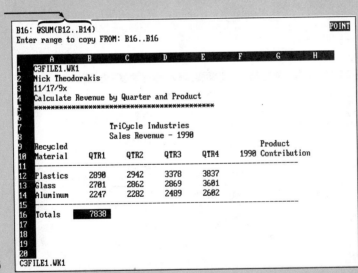

B16: @SUM(B12..B14)   POINT
Enter range to copy FROM: B16..B16

```
          A        B        C        D        E        F        G        H
1  C3FILE1.WK1
2  Nick Theodorakis
3  11/17/9x
4  Calculate Revenue by Quarter and Product
5  ****************************************************
6
7                   TriCycle Industries
8                   Sales Revenue - 1990
9  Recycled                                       Product
10 Material     QTR1     QTR2     QTR3     QTR4    1990 Contribution
11 ---------------------------------------------------
12 Plastics     2890     2942     3378     3837
13 Glass        2701     2862     2869     3601
14 Aluminum     2247     2282     2489     2602
15           -----------------------------------------
16 Totals       7838
17
18
19
20
   C3FILE1.WK1
```

Figure 3-5

❷ Press **[Enter]**, because B16 is the only cell formula you want to copy. Notice that the panel text changes and requests the range of cells to copy this formula TO. See Figure 3-6 on the next page.

formula to be copied

cell not anchored

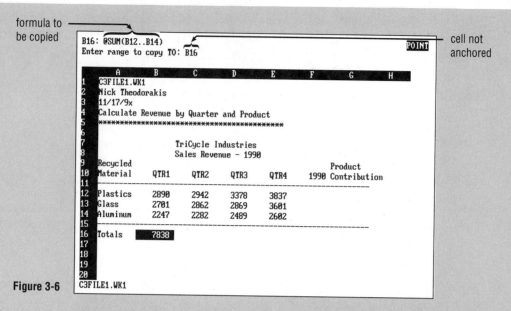

Figure 3-6 C3FILE1.WK1

❸ Move the cell pointer to C16, the first cell in the range you are copying TO.

Now anchor this cell.

❹ Press **[.]** (Period) to anchor the cell pointer. This designates C16 as the first cell in the copy TO range. See Figure 3-7.

cell anchored

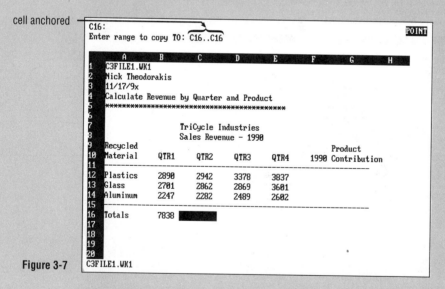

Figure 3-7 C3FILE1.WK1

❺ Press **[→]** as needed to highlight the range C16 to E16. This is the entire copy TO range. See Figure 3-8.

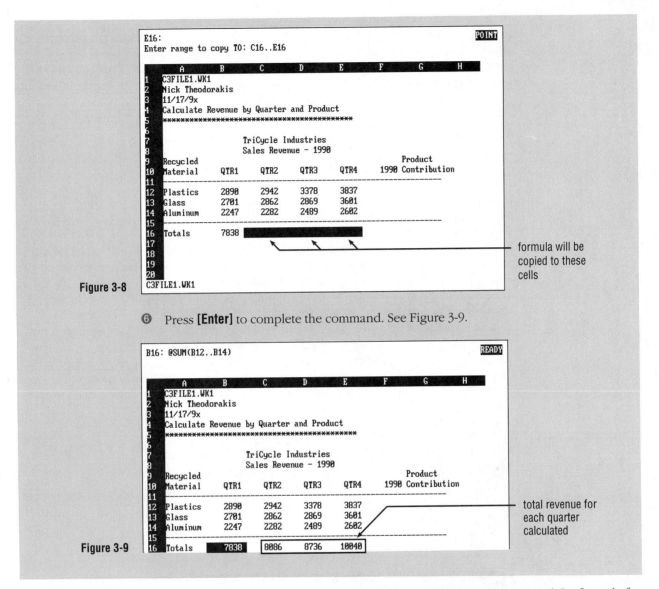

Figure 3-8

Figure 3-9

⑥   Press **[Enter]** to complete the command. See Figure 3-9.

Total revenue for each quarter has now been calculated. You entered the formula for the first quarter and then used the Copy command to copy this formula to the cell locations for quarters 2, 3, and 4.

Understanding Relative Cell References

How 1-2-3 copies a formula depends on whether you use relative cell references or absolute cell references in a formula. The concept of relative and absolute cell references is extremely important to your work with 1-2-3.

A **relative cell reference** is a cell or range of cells in a formula that 1-2-3 interprets as a location relative to the current cell. For example, in cell B16 you have the formula @SUM(B12..B14). 1-2-3 interprets this formula as "add the contents of three cells starting four cells above the formula cell." When you copy this formula to a new location, to cell C16, for example, you copy the relationship between the formula and the cell or range to which it refers. 1-2-3 automatically adjusts the addresses in the copied formulas to maintain the relationship. For example, if you copied the formula @SUM(B12..B14) to cell C16, 1-2-3 interprets the formula as "add the contents of three cells starting four cells above the formula cell"; then 1-2-3 adjusts the formula automatically to @SUM(C12..C14).

1-2-3 treats cell references as relative references unless you specify that they are absolute. You will learn about absolute cell references later in this tutorial.

Naming Ranges

Kay also wants to know how much revenue TriCycle earned from recycling each material during 1990. To calculate yearly revenue, you will continue to use the @SUM function. Instead of using cell addresses inside the @SUM function, however, you will use range names in the formulas. Whenever you are working with a large worksheet, you should use descriptive words instead of cell addresses for ranges in the formula. Descriptive words are more meaningful in a formula, since they remind you of the purpose of the calculation. 1-2-3 lets you assign descriptive names to individual cells or cell ranges. You can then use these names in place of cell references when building formulas. For example, the formula @SUM(PLASTICS) is easier to understand than @SUM(B12..E12).

Let's assign range names to the range of cells representing quarterly sales for each recycled material: plastics, glass, and aluminum. Let's also assign a range name to the range of cells representing the four quarterly totals (B16..E16).

To create a range name for revenue from plastics:

❶ Move the cell pointer to B12, the revenue from recycled plastics in the first quarter.

❷ Select /Range Name Create (**/RNC**).

❸ Type **PLASTICS** and press **[Enter]**. See Figure 3-10.

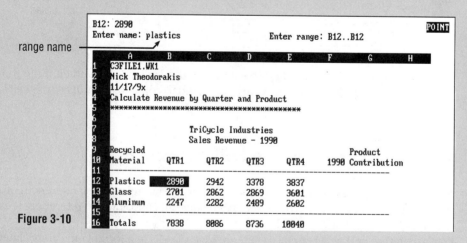

Figure 3-10

You can use lowercase or uppercase letters. 1-2-3 automatically converts lowercase to uppercase.

④ Press [→] to highlight the range B12..E12. You don't need to anchor this range, because it is automatically anchored when you use the Range Name command.

⑤ Press **[Enter]**. You have just named the range (B12..E12) PLASTICS.

Next, assign the range name GLASS to the revenue earned from recycling glass during the four quarters.

To assign the range name:

① Move the pointer to B13, the revenue from glass during the first quarter.

② Select /Range Name Create (**/RNC**).

③ Type **GLASS** and press **[Enter]**.

④ Press [→] to highlight the range B13..E13.

⑤ Press **[Enter]**. You have just named the range (B13 .. E13) GLASS.

Now, assign the range name ALUMINUM to the revenue received from recycling aluminum materials during the four quarters.

To assign the range name:

① Move the cell pointer to B14, the revenue from aluminum in the first quarter.

② Select /Range Name Create (**/RNC**).

③ Type **ALUMINUM** and press **[Enter]**.

④ Press [→] to highlight the range B14..E14.

⑤ Press **[Enter]**. You have just named the range (B14 .. E14) ALUMINUM.

Finally, assign the range name QTR_SALES to the revenue received from recycling all materials during the four quarters.

To assign the range name:

① Move the cell pointer to B16, the revenue from all products during the first quarter.

② Select /Range Name Create (**/RNC**).

③ Type **QTR_SALES** and press **[Enter]**.

Notice the use of the [_] (Underscore) to connect words; spaces and hyphens are not permitted in range names.

④ Press [→] to highlight the range B16..E16.

⑤ Press **[Enter]**. You have just named the range (B16..E16) QTR_SALES.

If you select the Range Name Create command and then realize you want to highlight a range that starts in another location, press [Esc] to unanchor the cell pointer. Then move the cell pointer to the appropriate starting cell and press [.] (Period) to reanchor the cell pointer.

Range names can be up to 15 characters long, but they cannot include spaces or the characters + * − / & { @ and # . The underscore character is often used to connect words together. Do not use range names such as Q1, because 1-2-3 will interpret Q1 as a cell location instead of a range name.

Using Named Ranges in Formulas

Now you are ready to calculate total revenue earned by TriCycle Industries during 1990. In the previous steps, you created the range names PLASTIC, GLASS, ALUMINUM, and QTR_SALES. Assigning names to a range of cells will make formulas easier to create and interpret. You can use range names in formulas two ways: by choosing the one you want from a list of the previously named ranges or by typing the name of the range directly into the formula.

To obtain a list of range names while you are entering a formula, press [F3] (NAME) to display a list of range names created in this worksheet. Highlight the range name you want, and press [Enter]. The range name is entered in the formula.

To use a range name in an @SUM formula using the [F3] key:

❶ Move the cell pointer to F12; this is the cell in which you want total revenues from plastics for 1990 to appear.

❷ Type **@SUM(**.

❸ Press **[F3]** (NAME). This function key displays a list of all range names you have created for this worksheet. See Figure 3-11.

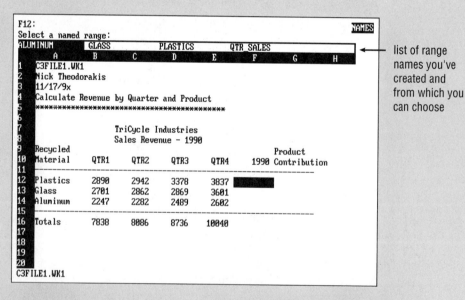

list of range names you've created and from which you can choose

Figure 3-11

④ Move the cursor to the range name you want, PLASTICS, and press **[Enter]** to select it. Your entry should now look like that in Figure 3-12.

range name you
selected for sum
function

Figure 3-12

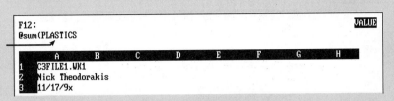

```
F12:                                                          VALUE
@sum(PLASTICS
         A       B       C       D       E       F       G       H
1  C3FILE1.WK1
2  Nick Theodorakis
3  11/17/9x
```

⑤ Continue entering the formula by typing **[)]** (Right Parenthesis).

⑥ Press **[Enter]**. 1-2-3 calculates the result, 13047, in cell F12. This is the sum of revenues earned from recycling plastics during 1990.

Alternatively, you could have typed in the range name, PLASTICS, directly after the left parenthesis in Step 2.

❷ @SUM(PLASTICS.

You would then skip Steps 3 and 4, and conclude with Step 5.
Now let's enter the formula for glass.

To use a range name in an @SUM formula using the [F3] key:

① Move the cell pointer to F13; this is the cell in which you want total revenues from glass for 1990 to appear.

② Type **@SUM(**.

③ Press **[F3]** (NAME). This function key displays a list of all range names you have created for this worksheet.

④ Move the cursor to the range name you want, GLASS, and press **[Enter]** to select it.

⑤ Type **[)]** (Right Parenthesis).

⑥ Press **[Enter]**. 1-2-3 calculates the result, 12033, in cell F13. This is the sum of revenues earned from recycling glass during 1990.

⑦ Move the cell pointer to F14. Repeat Steps 2 through 5 to enter an @SUM formula using the range name ALUMINUM to total revenue from aluminum in 1990. The result in F14 should be 9620.

⑧ Move the cell pointer to F16. Repeat Steps 2 through 5 to enter an @SUM formula using the range name QTR_SALES to total revenue from all products in 1990. The result in F16 should be 34700. See Figure 3-13 on the next page.

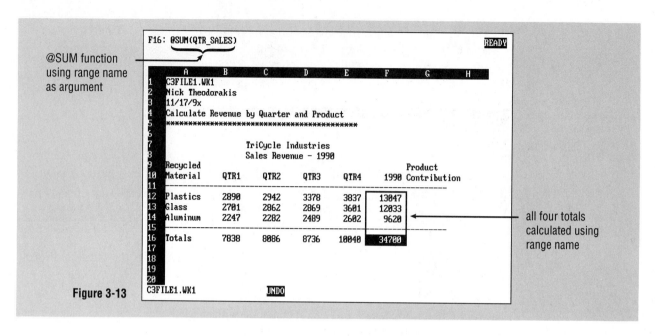

@SUM function
using range name
as argument

all four totals
calculated using
range name

Figure 3-13

If you accidentally press [Enter] before typing the right parenthesis, 1-2-3 automatically beeps and moves to EDIT mode, in which you should type [ )] (Right Parenthesis) and press [Enter].

Deleting Range Names

If you create a range name and want to delete the range, select /Range Name Delete (/RND) and press the function key [F3]. Move the menu pointer to the name you want to delete from the list and press [Enter].

Copying Formulas with Absolute References

Nick has now calculated total revenue earned by TriCycle Industries during 1990, as well as individual revenues from plastics, glass, and aluminum. Next, Nick plans to calculate each material's percentage of total 1990 revenue. To calculate each material's contribution to total revenue, you divide the 1990 revenue for each material by total company revenue for 1990.

For example,

$$percent\ contribution\ of\ plastics\ to\ total\ revenue = \frac{1990\ revenue\ for\ plastics}{total\ TriCycle\ 1990\ revenue}$$

To calculate the percent contribution of plastics:

❶ Move the cell pointer to G12.

❷ Type the formula **+F12/F16**.

❸ Press **[Enter]**. The result, 0.375994, appears in cell G12. See Figure 3-14.

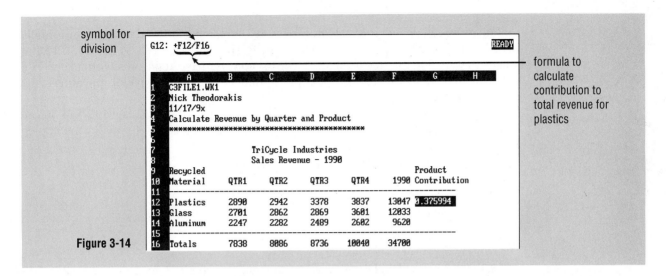

symbol for division

G12: +F12/F16

formula to calculate contribution to total revenue for plastics

Figure 3-14

Now that you have entered the formula +F12/F16 in cell G12, you can use the Copy command to copy this formula to other cells.

The steps that follow illustrate an approach that leads to incorrect results. We show these steps to demonstrate a common mistake made by many beginning students of 1-2-3, in the hopes of helping you avoid it.

To demonstrate a common mistake:

❶ Be sure the cell pointer is in G12, the cell that contains the formula to be copied. Select /Copy (**/C**). The control panel shows G12..G12 as the copy FROM range.

❷ Press **[Enter]**, since G12 is the only cell you want to copy.

❸ Move the cell pointer to G13, the first cell in the range you are copying to.

❹ Press **[.]** (Period) to anchor the cell pointer. G13 is now the first cell in the copy TO range.

❺ Highlight the range G13..G14. This is the copy TO range.

❻ Press **[Enter]** to complete the command, and notice that ERR appears in cells G13 and G14. See Figure 3-15.

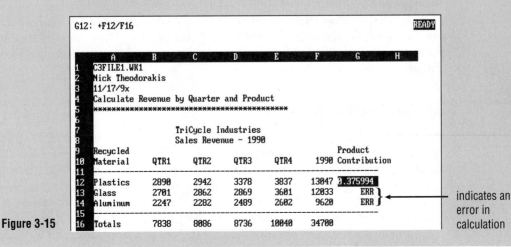

G12: +F12/F16

indicates an error in calculation

Figure 3-15

Move the cell pointer sequentially to each cell containing ERR and examine the formula in the control panel. Do you see what happened? The formula in cell G13 is +F13/F17, but what you want in G13 is the formula +F13/F16. You also have an incorrect formula in G14, +F14/F18 instead of +F14/F16. All the copied formulas have resulted in ERR appearing in the respective cells.

Why does ERR appear in these cells? When you copied the formula (+F12/F16) in cell G12, 1-2-3 assumed relative addressing and *adjusted* the cell references in the copied formula.

The following formulas resulted:

Cell	Formula
G13	+F13/F17
G14	+F14/F18

When 1-2-3 calculated the glass and aluminum contributions using the formulas in G13 and G14, it tried to divide by zero (the values below cell F16, F17 and F18, are both zero). Since division by zero is undefined, the message ERR appears in cells G13 and G14.

To calculate percent contribution of each material, you need to use the following formulas:

Recycled Material	Formula	Description
Plastic	+F12/F16	*1990 revenue for plastic* / *total TriCycle 1990 revenue*
Glass	+F13/F16	*1990 revenue for glass* / *total TriCycle 1990 revenue*
Aluminum	+F14/F16	*1990 revenue for aluminum* / *total TriCycle 1990 revenue*

Notice that the cells in the numerators vary (F12, F13, F14), while the cells in the denominators are always the same, F16. When you copy the formula for percent contribution to other cell locations, the cell addresses of the numerator should change relative to the cell formula. On the other hand, when you copy the cell address of the denominator to other cell locations, the cell address should remain unchanged. Thus, using relative referencing for the entire formula doesn't work. This is an example of a situation that requires absolute cell references.

Absolute Cell References

When you copy a formula, you sometimes want 1-2-3 to keep the original cell addresses in the copied formula. You do *not* want 1-2-3 to adjust the cell references for you. To keep the original cell or range reference constant, no matter where in the worksheet the formula is copied, you use an absolute reference. An **absolute reference** is a cell address or range name that *always* refers to the same cell, even if you copy the formula to a new location. To designate an absolute cell reference, you use [$] (Dollar Sign) to precede both the column letter and the row number or range name of the cell you want to remain unchanged. Thus,

$F$16 is an absolute cell reference, whereas F16 is a relative reference. Initially, both reference the same cell location; however, if you copy the cell location $F$16 to another cell, the cell address in the new location remains unchanged, whereas if you copy the cell location F16 to another cell, the cell address in the new location is automatically adjusted to reflect its position relative to the original cell location.

To specify absolute cell references, you can either type the $ character before the column letter and row number when you enter (or edit) a formula, or you can use another of the 1-2-3 function keys, [F4] (ABS), the Absolute key. When you press the [F4] key while in EDIT mode, 1-2-3 inserts a $ character at the cursor location in the cell address in the control panel. You could also retype the formula using the $ symbol in the appropriate places, but using the [F4] key is usually faster and helps avoid entry errors.

Before you try using the absolute reference in your formula, let's erase the incorrect formulas in cells G13 and G14 that cause ERR to be displayed.

When you type or copy an entry into the wrong cell, you can erase the contents of the cell or cells with the Range Erase command.

To erase a range of cells:

❶ Move the cell pointer to G13, the first cell to be erased.

❷ Select /Range Erase (**/RE**). The control panel reveals the address of the current cell and prompts you to specify the range you want to erase.

❸ Press [↓] to highlight the range G13 to G14.

❹ Press **[Enter]**. 1-2-3 erases the entries in G13 and G14. The cell pointer returns to G13, the first cell in the range. The formulas have been erased from cells G13 and G14. See Figure 3-16.

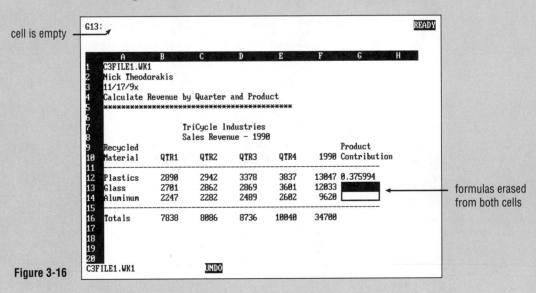

Figure 3-16

Now let's correctly calculate the contribution to total revenue from glass and aluminum.

To use [F4] (ABS) to insert absolute cell references:

❶ Move the cell pointer to G12 and press **[F2]** (EDIT) to display the formula in the control panel. Notice that +F12/F16 appears in the second line of the control panel. See Figure 3-17.

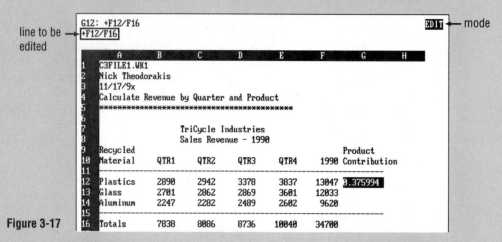

line to be edited

mode

Figure 3-17

❷ Press **[←]** until the cursor is under the F in F16. Press **[F4]** (ABS) to make the cell reference absolute. Notice that $F$16 appears in the control panel. See Figure 3-18.

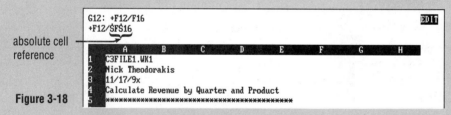

absolute cell reference

Figure 3-18

❸ Press **[Enter];** notice that the value in G12 does not change. However, a change does occur in the formula in the control panel. F16 becomes $F$16, an absolute reference. See Figure 3-19.

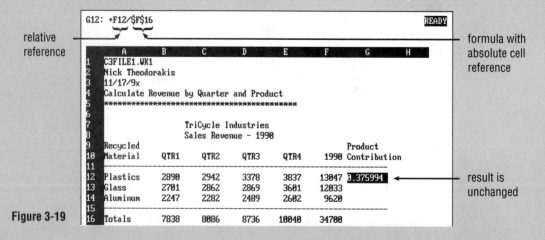

relative reference

formula with absolute cell reference

result is unchanged

Figure 3-19

Now the formula in G12 contains absolute cell references to reference total 1990 revenues and uses relative references for each material's revenue. No matter what cell you copy the formula in G12 to, the cell reference $F$16 will not change. To demonstrate this process, let's copy the formula in G12 again to see what happens.

To copy G12 to G13..G14:

❶ Make sure the cell pointer is at G12 and select /Copy (**/C**).

❷ Press **[Enter],** because G12 is the only cell you want to copy.

❸ Move the cell pointer to G13, the first cell in the range to which you are copying.

❹ Press **[.]** (Period) to anchor the cell pointer. G13 is now the first cell in the copy TO range.

❺ Highlight the range G13..G14. This is the copy TO range.

❻ Press **[Enter]** to complete the command. The percent contribution appears in cells G13 and G14. See Figure 3-20.

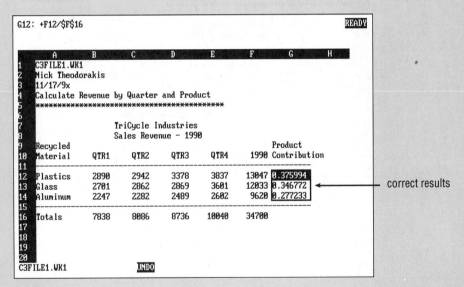

Figure 3-20

As a result of the Copy command, the following formulas appear in the control panel when you highlight cells G13 and G14:

Cell	Formula
G13	+F13/$F$16
G14	+F14/$F$16

Normally, each material's contribution to total revenue is expressed as a percentage. In the worksheet, however, these values now appear as decimals. Let's change the contribution column so that all values will appear in Percent format. Numbers will then appear as percentages, that is, whole numbers followed by percent signs (%), for example, 15%. 1-2-3 multiplies the decimal number currently in the cell by 100 so that the number becomes a whole number. For example, .05 becomes 5%.

To format a range of cells to Percent format with one decimal:
1. Make sure the cell pointer is in G12 and select /Range Format (**/RF**).
2. Select Percent (**P**).
3. Type **1** for the number of decimal places and press **[Enter]**.
4. Highlight the cells G12..G14 and press **[Enter]**. See Figure 3-21.

indicates Percent format with 1 decimal place

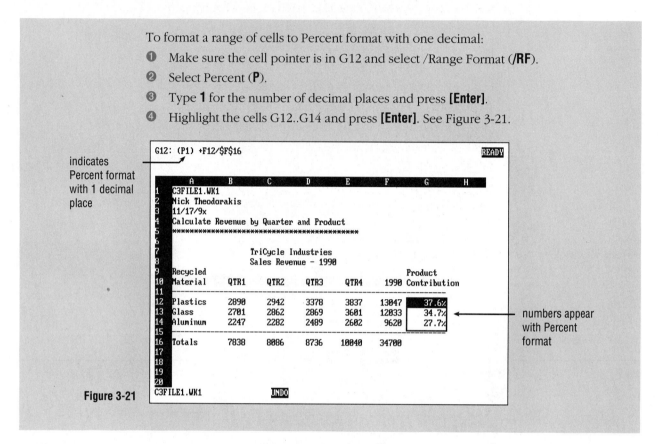

numbers appear with Percent format

Figure 3-21

The calculations are complete. All that remains is for Nick to save the worksheet and print the report.

To change the filename in cell A1 and to save the file:
1. Press **[Home]** to move the cell pointer to cell A1.
2. Type **S3FILE1.WK1**.
3. Select /File Save (**FS**). Save the worksheet as S3FILE1.WK1.

Printing with Compressed Type

Larger worksheets are often too wide to fit on one printed page. What do you do if you want to show the entire worksheet on one page for easier interpretation? You can print more data on a page by instructing your printer to use compressed type. **Compressed type** is a smaller and more compact type. As a result, your printer can accommodate a 132-character line length instead of the normal 76 characters per line.

Let's adjust the margins and enter a setup string to print with compressed type. **A setup string** is a code sent to the printer to control the characteristics of the printed output.

Many printers use the code \015 to designate compressed type. Check your printer manual, or ask your instructor or technical support person for the correct code for your printer.

To set up for compressed type:

1 Select /Print Printer (**/PP**).

2 Select Options Setup (**OS**) to choose the option to enter the code for compressed type.

3 Type **** (Backslash) **015** and press **[Enter]** to enter the setup string. \015 may not work for your printer. If it doesn't, ask your instructor or lab assistant for the correct code for your printer.

4 Select Margins (**M**) from the Options menu and then select Right (**R**). The right margin options sets the maximum number of characters that can print on one line.

5 Type **132** and press **[Enter]**. Your printer setting sheet should look similar to the one in Figure 3-22.

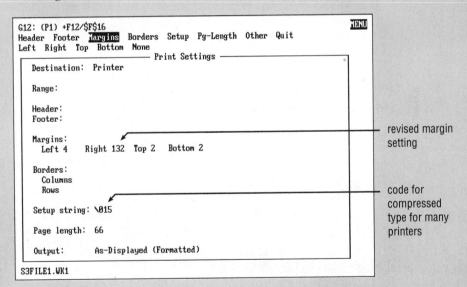

Figure 3-22

6 Select Quit (**Q**) to leave the Options menu, then select Quit (**Q**) again to leave the Print menu.

Now let's print the TriCycle revenue report. Be sure your printer is ready before you begin.

To print the TriCycle report:

❶ Select /Print Printer (**/PP**).

❷ Select Range (**R**).

❸ Move the cell pointer to A7. Press **[.]** (Period) to anchor the cell.

❹ Highlight A7..H16, the cells that contain the report, then press **[Enter]**.

❺ Select Align Go Page (**AGP**) to print the report. See Figure 3-23.

Figure 3-23
The final TriCycle
revenue report in
compressed type

```
Lotus 1-2-3 Student Business Series            Nick Theodorakis


                        TriCycle Industries
                        Sales Revenue - 1990
    Recycled                                        Product
    Material    QTR1     QTR2     QTR3     QTR4   1990 Contribution
    ------------------------------------------------------------------
    Plastics    2890     2942     3378     3837   13047     37.6%
    Glass       2701     2862     2869     3601   12033     34.7%
    Aluminum    2247     2282     2489     2602    9620     27.7%
    ------------------------------------------------------------------
    Totals      7838     8086     8736    10040   34700
```

❻ Select Quit (**Q**) to return to READY mode.

❼ Save the worksheet again as S3FILE1 (**/FS**).

Printing Checklist

Look at your printed output and check the following:

- **Headings**   Does each listing contain a heading at the top that answers the questions who, what, and where?
- **Columns**   Are all column widths correct? Do any cells contain asterisks, meaning that the values are too wide to appear in the column?
- **Margins**   Are the margins adjusted evenly?
- **Accuracy**   Is all the information correct? Are the numbers accurate? Are all words spelled correctly?
- **Lines**   Do any blank lines appear in unintended places?
- **Appearance**   Is the print legible? Do you need to install a new ribbon or make any adjustment?

Very often you will not be satisfied with your first printing of the worksheet. Fortunately, computers simplify the task of making changes. If necessary, edit your worksheet, save the changes, and print again. Do not handwrite corrections.

Exercises

1. Cell D13 contains the formula:

    +D10+D11+D12

    After copying this formula to cells E13 and F13, what will the formulas be in cells E13 and F13?

2. Suppose cell D5 contains the formula:

    +A5*$B$5+C5

    What are the absolute and relative references in this formula?

3. Suppose you copy the formula in Excercise 2 to cells D6 and D7.
    a.   What will the formula be in cell D6?
    b.   What will the formula be in cell D7?

4. Suppose cell B10 has been assigned the range name SALES and cell B11 the range name COSTS.
    a.   What formula would you enter in cell B12 to calculate profits using cell addresses?
    b.   What formula would you enter in cell B12 to calculate profits using range names?

5. Figure 3-24 shows a worksheet to calculate new salaries for employees based on a percent increase applied to all employees. The percent increase is stored in cell C3.
    Cell C8 shows the formula currently used to calculate the salary increase for Harrod.

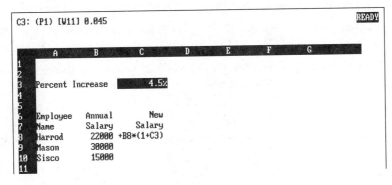

Figure 3-24

a.   Write the formulas needed in cells C9 and C10 to calculate new salaries for Mason and Sisco.
b.   If you were to copy the formula in C8 to C9 and C10, what would you do? List your steps.

Tutorial Assignments

Retrieve the worksheet T3FILE1 and do the following:

1. You want to reduce column G, Product Contribution, to a width of 6. Make this change.

2. Suppose TriCycle introduced paper recycling in the third quarter of 1990. Revenue for paper recycling was 300 in the third quarter and 400 in the fourth quarter. Include these data on the worksheet after aluminum. Be sure to adjust all formulas so the results are correct and to adjust all formats so the appearance of the worksheet is consistent.

3. Print the revised worksheet.

4. Save the worksheet as S3FILE2.

Retrieve the worksheet T1FILE6, a version of the final worksheet from Tutorial 1, and do the following:

5. Use the Copy command to copy the gross pay formula in D11 to the cells of the other employees.

6. Use the Copy command to copy the federal withholding formula (cell E11) to the cells of all other employees.

7. Use the Copy command to copy the net pay formula (cell F11) to the cells of the other employees.

8. Assign the following range names:
   a. GROSS_PAY to cells D11..D14
   b. TAXES to cells E11..E14
   c. NET_PAY to cells F11..F14

9. Calculate total gross pay, total taxes withheld, and total net pay using the @SUM function and the range names you assigned in Assignment 8.

10. Print the worksheet.

11. Save the worksheet as S1FILE7.

Retrieve the Allegiance worksheet, T2FILE3, and do the following:

12. Assign the range name FUND_SHARES to cell C19, Mutual Fund Shares, and assign the range name TOTAL_VALUE to cell D17, the total value of the mutual fund.

13. Calculate net asset value (NAV) (cell C20) using the range names in the formula instead of the cell locations.
$$NAV = \frac{TOTAL\_VALUE}{FUND\_SHARES}$$

14. Print the results using compressed type. Save your worksheet as S2FILE7.

Case Problems

1. Employee Turnover Report

Each month, the director of human resources for the public accounting firm of Armstrong, Black & Calzone turns in a report summarizing the number of employees who have left the firm. The data in this employee turnover report is valuable information to the senior partners of the firm, because they want to compare their turnover rates with previous periods and industry averages. If their rates are particularly high, they might decide to investigate the cause of the high turnover. Turnover can result from a variety of reasons, such as noncompetitive salaries, poor managers, lack of training, or poor hiring practices.

Do the following:

1. Retrieve the worksheet file P3TRNOVR.

2. Calculate the number of employees in the company.

3. Calculate the total number of employees who have left the company (number of termi-nations).

4. Calculate the rate of turnover in each department as a percentage of the number of employees in the department. Rate of turnover is calculated by using the following formula:

$$rate\ of\ turnover = \left(\frac{number\ of\ employees\ who\ left\ each\ department}{number\ of\ employees\ in\ each\ department}\right) \times 100$$

5. Calculate the rate of turnover in each department as a percentage of the number of employees in the company. Rate of turnover is calculated by using the following formula:

$$rate\ of\ turnover = \left(\frac{number\ of\ employees\ who\ left\ each\ department}{number\ of\ employees\ in\ company}\right) \times 100$$

6. Include headings, formatting, and any other changes you think will improve the appear-ance of the final report.

7. Print the worksheet.

8. Save the worksheet as S3TRNOVR.

2. Leading Restaurant Chains

The managing editor of *Restaurant Happenings*, a weekly magazine, has asked his top writer, Gene Marchand, to research and write a lead article on the sales of U.S. restaurant chains. In researching the story, Gene first determines the U.S. sales for 1988 and 1989 (in millions of dollars) and then totals the number of individual stores in 1989 for each restaurant chain. As the publishing deadline approaches, Gene asks you — the office Lotus 1-2-3 whiz — to help him with this article. Gene wants you to use 1-2-3 to calculate the following four facts:

- industry totals for sales and number of stores
- percent change in sales between 1988 and 1989 for each restaurant chain
- each restaurant's share of total industry sales in 1989
- average sales per store for each chain in 1989

Do the following for Gene:

1. Retrieve the worksheet file P3RSTAUR.WK1.

2. Calculate the four facts listed above.
   a. Calculate totals for sales in 1988, sales in 1989, and number of stores.
   b. Calculate percent change in sales for each restaurant chain by using the following formula:

$$percent\ change\ in\ sales = \left(\frac{(chain's\ 1989\ sales - chain's\ 1988\ sales)}{chain's\ 1988\ sales}\right) \times 100$$

   c. Calculate each chain's share of total industry sales in 1989 by using the following formula:

$$chain's\ share\ of\ total\ industry\ sales\ in\ 1989 = \left(\frac{chain's\ sales\ in\ 1989}{total\ industry\ sales\ in\ 1989}\right) \times 100$$

d.   Calculate the average sales per store in 1989 by using the following formula:

$$average\ sales\ per\ store\ in\ 1989 = \frac{chain's\ sales\ in\ 1989}{number\ of\ stores\ in\ chain}$$

3.   Add titles and ruled lines and format the numeric values to make the worksheet easier to read.

4.   Print the results.

5.   Save the worksheet as S3RSTAUR.

3.   Exchange Rates and Foreign Operations

As the world becomes "smaller," more and more companies operate in more than one country. A particular challenge for multinational companies is coping with doing business in different currencies. One interesting finance problem involves how to interpret financial results when different currencies are used. Typically, each country reports results in its local currency (dollar, mark, yen, franc, etc.). The challenge is to prepare a report that allows management to compare these results and accurately interpret them. Let's assume that a U.S. publishing company wants all the results of its different divisions converted to U.S. dollars.

Smithson Publishing International has divisions in England, France, Germany, and Italy. Quarterly, each division reports data on sales revenue to corporate headquarters in the U.S. where the data are combined. Each division reports its sales in its local currency (Figure 3-25).

Sales Revenue (Local Currency)				
Period	England (pound)	France (franc)	Germany (mark)	Italy (lira)
QTR1	270197	1943779	1282234	159887439
QTR2	272814	2218784	1385572	213441654
QTR3	346404	2760962	1372975	232303732
QTR4	375395	2711160	1458096	239693192

Figure 3-25

Since the data are reported in the currency of the local country, Smithson's top executives cannot accurately interpret these numbers. They cannot tell, for example, which division has the highest revenue or which division has the lowest. Thus, a staff assistant, Jim Newman, converts these foreign currencies to U.S. dollars. He collects data on exchange rates, which represent the price of one country's currency in terms of another. For example, if the exchange rate between the U.S. dollar and the British pound is 1:1.8505, for every British pound you would receive 1.8505 U.S. dollars.

Jim keeps track of the exchange rates between the U.S. and each of the four countries in which Smithson has divisions. At the end of each quarter, he enters the exchange rates into a second table (Figure 3-26).

Using these two tables, Jim can generate a third table, which shows the sales revenue for Smithson's four divisions converted to U.S. dollars.

	Exchange Rates			
Period	**England (pound)**	**France (franc)**	**Germany (mark)**	**Italy (lira)**
QTR1	1.8505	0.1672	0.5773	0.0007818
QTR2	1.7445	0.1613	0.5486	0.0007447
QTR3	1.5740	0.1413	0.5062	0.0006993
QTR4	1.6119	0.1568	0.5316	0.0007301

Figure 3-26

To convert the sales data to U.S. dollars, each quarter's sales revenue for a country is multiplied by the corresponding exchange rate. For example, in Britain, sales in the first quarter were 270,197 pounds. At the end of the first quarter, the exchange rate between the U.S. dollar and the British pound was 1:1.8505. Therefore, first-quarter sales in Britain expressed in U.S. dollars would be:

$$revenues \times exchange\ rate = converted\ amount$$

or in this case,

$$270,197 \times 1.8505 = \$500,000$$

Do the following:

1. Retrieve the worksheet named P3EXCHNG.WK1. This file contains the data shown in Figure 3-25 and Figure 3-26.

2. Create a third table that shows sales revenue expressed in U.S. dollars categorized by country and by quarter. Use the formula given above for converting currencies.

3. Also include in this table the calculation of total revenue by country.

4. Include in this table the calculation of total revenue by quarter.

5. Add titles and ruled lines, format the values, and make any other changes that will improve the appearance of the worksheet.

6. Print the three tables.

7. Save your worksheet as S3EXCHNG.

4. Salary Planning at Olmstead Corporation

The controller of Olmstead Corporation, a sports equipment manufacturer, gives each department head a worksheet containing a list of the employees in his or her department. For each employee on the worksheet, the worksheet shows name, department, performance rating for the year (1=poor, 2=fair, 3=good, 4=outstanding), and annual salary as of January 1, 1990.

Five additional column headings appear in the worksheet but show no data. These five headings are:

- *Across-the-Board Increase*: a percent increase in salary that is applied equally to each employee's current salary regardless of how they perform

- *Merit Increase*: a percent increase in salary that is awarded to an employee according to how well the employee has performed on the job

- *Total Dollar Increase*: the sum of across-the-board and merit increases

- *Total Percent Increase*: the total salary increase an employee receives expressed as a percent of current salary, in other words,

$$\left(\frac{dollar\ amount\ of\ increase}{dollar\ amount\ of\ current\ salary\ (1/1/90)} \right) \times 100 = total\ percent\ increase$$

- *New Salary (1/1/91)*: sum of current salary (1/1/90) plus total dollar increase

With this worksheet, the controller also distributed the following human resources department's guidelines concerning salary increases:

Guidelines for Salary Increases

- Each employee will receive a 2% across-the-board increase.
- Only employees with performance ratings of 3 and 4 will receive merit increases. In other words, employees who were rated 1 or 2 will not receive merit increases. Last year, the merit increases ranged from $500 to $4,000; the average was $1,800.
- An employee cannot receive a total increase greater than 20% of his/her current salary.
- Total percentage salary increase for each department can be *no more than 5%* of the total current salary for the department. For example, if current salaries in a department total $1,000,000, then $50,000 is the total amount of money available for both across-the-board and merit increases.

Assume that you are the head of a department. Do the following:

1. Retrieve the worksheet P3SALPLN.WK1.

2. Complete the worksheet by entering the formulas you need to calculate for each employee the across-the-board increase (column E), the total salary increase in dollars (column G), the total salary increase as a percent (column H), and the new salary (column I).

3. Assign merit pay to each of your employees, at your discretion. Keep in mind that:
   - Only employees with rating of 3 or 4 can receive merit increases (column C).
   - Each employee can receive a maximum 20% increase.
   - The total salary increase to your department cannot be greater than 5% of the total salaries in 1990.

   Hint: Include a section in your worksheet that will immediately show you how well you are doing toward meeting the total salary increase for your department of no more than 5 percent. You may have to adjust the merit pay you assign to certain employees several times before you meet all the requirements in the human resources guidelines.

4. Calculate department totals for the following:
   a. salaries in 1990
   b. across-the-board increases
   c. merit increases
   d. total dollar increase
   e. salaries in 1991.

5. Print your final worksheet using compressed type.

6. Save your worksheet as S3SALPLN.

Tutorial 4

Designing Professional Worksheets

Projecting Income

Case: Trek Limited

Hillary Clarke is an accountant at Trek Limited, a manufacturer of fine luggage that has been in business for 55 years. Hillary works in the controller's office and reports to the controller, Stephan Akrawi. Stephan was so impressed with Hillary's work over the 14 months she has worked for him, he selected her to attend Trek's employee development workshop series.

Today is Hillary's first day back at her regular job after attending the workshop series. She is excited about the many skills she has learned, and she tells Stephan that she'd like to use some of them immediately. She is particularly excited about the workshop called "Financial Planning Using Lotus 1-2-3," because she thinks she can use what she learned to help Stephan with some of his projects. Last year, Hillary assisted Stephan in updating Trek's Five-Year Plan, a collection of financial projections that help Trek's department managers make decisions about how to run the company. By making certain assumptions, such as that sales will increase 10% next year, the managers can plan, budget, and set goals accordingly. The plan includes the company's forecasts, or "best guesses," on what sales, expenses, and net income will be over the coming years.

In the past, Stephan prepared the plan manually, but this year Hillary wants Stephan to use Lotus 1-2-3. She points out how much more helpful the plan would be if the department managers could perform what-if analyses. Department managers could make different assumptions about the financial data to see what results those assumptions would have on the company's finances. For example, what if sales went down 10% next year instead of up? What would the results be on profits or on expenses? What if the price of

OBJECTIVES

In this tutorial you will learn to:

- Freeze titles

- Use the @IF function

- Protect cells

- Use windows

- Document a worksheet

- Print cell formulas

- Use a one-way data table

- Use the Data Fill command

cowhide increased 5% over the next two years? How would that affect the cost of manufacturing? How would it affect profits? What if analysis using Lotus 1-2-3 could help managers make better decisions. They would not have to face the drudgery of numerous recalculations; they could easily, quickly, and accurately consider different alternatives by changing the data and then having Lotus 1-2-3 recalculate the formulas and totals. Thus, managers would spend more time and creative energy on decision making because they would not have to recalculate formulas and totals every time they asked what if?

Stephan agrees with Hillary about using Lotus. He gives her the latest data that the accounting department prepared for 1990 (Figure 4-1). They agree that Hillary should design a Lotus worksheet that reflects the Trek planning process. Then together they will perform some what-if analysis and show the department managers how they can use what-if analysis with 1-2-3.

Trek Limited Income Statement

	1990	Percent of Sales
Sales	$150,000	
Variable Costs:		
Manufacturing	75,000	50%
Selling	15,000	10%
Administrative	6,000	4%
Total Variable Cost	96,000	
Fixed Costs:		
Manufacturing	10,000	
Selling	20,000	
Administrative	5,000	
Total Fixed Cost	35,000	
Net income before taxes	19,000	
Income taxes	4,750	
Net income after taxes	$14,250	

Figure 4-1
Trek's accounting
department data

Hillary spends time studying the accounting department's data and begins to create her planning sheet (Figure 4-2a). After writing down her goal and her desired results, she considers what information she needs. She knows that, generally, the sales estimate is used as the starting point for projecting income. Why? Because production and selling are geared to the rate of sales activity.

My Goal:
  Develop a worksheet that easily tests alternative scenarios to help develop
  a five-year plan for Trek Limited

What results do I want to see?
  Projected income statements for 1991 to 1995

What information do I need?
  Information that can be changed:
    Sales estimate for 1991
  Information that remains unchanged:
    Annual growth rate in sales (10%)
    Ratio of manufacturing costs to sales (50%)
    Ratio of selling costs to sales (10%)
    Ratio of administrative costs to sales (4%)
    Fixed manufacturing costs ($10)
    Fixed selling costs ($20)
    Fixed administrative costs ($5)

What calculations will I perform?
  1. sales first year = sales estimate for 1991
  2. sales subsequent years = previous year's sales × 110%
  3. variable manufacturing costs = 50% × sales estimate
  4. variable selling costs = 10% × sales estimate
  5. variable administrative costs = 4% × sales estimate
  6. total variable costs = variable manufacturing costs +
                             variable selling costs +
                             variable administrative costs
  7. total fixed costs =   fixed manufacturing costs ($10) +
                            fixed selling costs ($20) +
                            fixed administrative costs ($5)
  8. net income before taxes = sales - total variable costs - total fixed costs
  9. taxes = 25% × net income before taxes
  10. net income after taxes = net income before taxes - taxes

Figure 4-2a
Hillary's planning
sheet

Hillary decides to start her projections for 1991 sales at the same level as 1990, although she knows the managers will change this during their what-if analysis. Stephan suggests she build in a 10% increase per year in sales for 1992 to 1995. He believes sales will go up 10% annually as a result of a new line of luggage Trek Limited plans to introduce in 1991.

After looking at the sales side, Hillary turns her attention to costs. She must look at both variable and fixed costs. Variable costs are those that change in direct proportion to related volume. For instance, as sales volume goes up, variable costs such as materials, assembly labor, and sales commissions also go up. Fixed costs are costs that remain unchanged despite changes in related volume. For example, rent, property taxes, executive salaries, and insurance remain the same even when sales go up.

Once again, Hillary refers to the accounting department data in Figure 4-1. She decides to use the variable-cost percentages as the basis for calculating variable costs. For example, if sales were $200,000, the variable manufacturing costs would be calculated at 50% of sales, or $100,000. She also decides to use the fixed costs shown in the accounting data.

Next, Hillary considers the final group of calculations, net income. To calculate net income before taxes, Hillary takes the difference between sales and the total of variable and fixed costs. She assumes taxes will be 25% of net income before taxes. Finally, she calculates net income after taxes, that is, net income before taxes minus income taxes.

Figure 4-2a is Hillary's completed planning sheet. Figure 4-2b is a sketch of how she wants her worksheet to look. In this tutorial, you will use Hillary's plan and sketch to learn how to freeze titles, protect specified data, split screens, design and document your worksheet, and make use of data tables to ask what-if questions.

Figure 4-2b
Hillary's worksheet sketch

Retrieving the Worksheet

Before you follow through on Hillary's plan, you will retrieve the worksheet she built based on her planning sheet and worksheet sketch, and you will practice using the what-if capability of 1-2-3.

To retrieve the worksheet:

❶ Select /File Retrieve (**/FR**).

❷ Highlight the file C4FILE1.WK1. Press **[Enter]**.

❸ Press **[PgDn]** to view the Projected Income Statements.

This worksheet contains projected income statements for Trek Limited for the years 1991 to 1995 (Figure 4-3). All values are shown in thousands. For example, sales in 1991 are shown as 150, which represents $150,000. Also note that to simplify the numbers in this worksheet, the cells were formatted to display zero decimal places. As a result, some totals do not appear to be correct. This is because the data are rounded whenever they appear on the screen.

area of worksheet that appears on your screen →

	Trek Limited Projected Income Statement For Year Ending				
	1991	1992	1993	1994	1995
Sales	150	165	182	200	220
Variable Costs:					
Manufacturing	75	83	91	100	110
Selling	15	17	18	20	22
Administrative	6	7	7	8	9
Total Variable Costs	96	106	116	128	141
Fixed Costs:					
Manufacturing	10	10	10	10	10
Selling	20	20	20	20	20
Administrative	5	5	5	5	5
Total Fixed Costs	35	35	35	35	35
Net Income Before Taxes	19	24	30	37	44
Income Taxes	5	6	8	9	11
Net Income After Taxes	14	18	23	28	33

Figure 4-3
Contents of the entire worksheet

Demonstrating the What-If Feature

To demonstrate 1-2-3's what-if capability using Hillary's worksheet, let's suppose that you increase the sales estimate for 1991 from $150,000 (entered as 150) to $175,000 (entered as 175).

To use the what-if capability:

❶ Move the cell pointer to cell B28, sales for 1991.

❷ Type **175** and press **[Enter]**. Watch how the sales, costs, and net incomes change as a result of the change to 1991 sales. See Figure 4-4 on the next page.

changed sales estimate

calculated as a percent of sales

remains fixed

Figure 4-4

```
                              Trek Limited
                       Projected Income Statement
                            For Year Ending

                    1991      1992     1993     1994     1995
                   ------    ------   ------   ------   ------
Sales               175       193      212      233      256
Variable Costs:
    Manufacturing    88        96      106      116      128
    Selling          18        19       21       23       26
    Administrative    7         8        8        9       10
                   ------    ------   ------   ------   ------
    Total Variable Costs 112   123      136      149      164

Fixed Costs:
    Manufacturing    10        10       10       10       10
    Selling          20        20       20       20       20
    Administrative    5         5        5        5        5
                   ------    ------   ------   ------   ------
    Total Fixed Costs  35       35       35       35       35

Net Income Before Taxes 28     34       41       49       57
Income Taxes          7         9       10       12       14
                   ------    ------   ------   ------   ------
Net Income After Taxes 21      26       31       37       43
                   ======    ======   ======   ======   ======
```

Since the sales estimate for 1991 increased from 150 to 175, the variable costs, which are calculated as a percentage of sales, also increased. Net income also changed, since both sales and variable costs changed. The fixed costs, however, did not change.

The sales estimates for 1992 to 1995 also increased. Because sales are estimated to grow at 10% each year, changing the starting sales estimate for 1991 changes the sales for 1992 to 1995.

Scrolling on Large Worksheets

Notice that the entire income statement does not fit on the screen — you cannot see the information for 1995. Also, the rows that follow "Administrative" in Hillary's worksheet sketch do not appear on the screen, even though she has typed them into her worksheet. To view this information, you use the cursor-movement keys to scroll down the screen. *Scrolling* is a way to view all parts of a large worksheet that cannot fit on one screen. For example, when you scroll down, a row previously unseen appears at the bottom of the screen and a row at the top disappears.

To scroll Hillary's worksheet:

❶ Press **[PgDn]** until Net Income After Taxes appears on the screen. Note that the column headings no longer appear on the screen. See Figure 4-5.

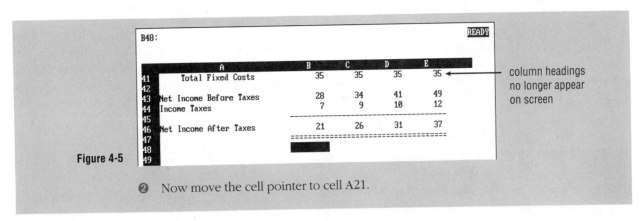

Figure 4-5

❷   Now move the cell pointer to cell A21.

The planning period for the company is 1991 to 1995, but 1995 does not appear on the screen. Let's scroll to the right to view the 1995 projections.

To scroll to the right:

❶   Press [→] until the 1995 column appears. Notice that the descriptive labels no longer appear on the left of the screen. This makes the worksheet data difficult to interpret. See Figure 4-6.

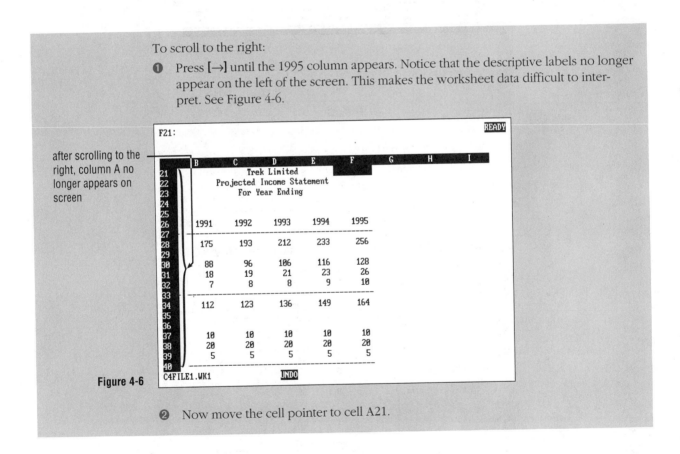

Figure 4-6

❷   Now move the cell pointer to cell A21.

Freezing Titles

As you move the cell pointer around a worksheet that is larger than the screen, you may find it difficult to remember row and column labels that may have disappeared. The Title command helps you keep your place on a large worksheet by "freezing" row and column titles on the screen; the titles remain on the screen as you move within the worksheet. The Titles command allows you to freeze rows, columns, or both. If you choose *Horizontal*, you freeze all rows above the cell pointer on the screen. If you choose *Vertical*, you freeze all columns to the left of the cell pointer. If you choose *Both*, you freeze all rows above and all columns to the left of the cell pointer. In the next steps, you freeze both the worksheet column headings and the account titles.

To freeze titles:

❶ Move the cell pointer to cell B28, the location below and to the right of the cells you want to remain on the screen.

❷ Select /Worksheet Titles (**/WT**). Your control panel should look like Figure 4-7.

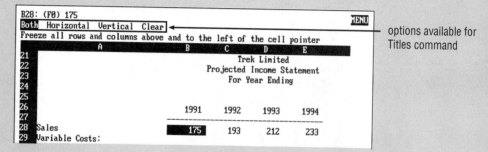

Figure 4-7

options available for Titles command

❸ Select Both (**B**) from the options available.

❹ Press [↓] to move the cell pointer to cell B47 and then [→] to move the cell pointer to cell F47. The column and row titles remain in view. See Figure 4-8.

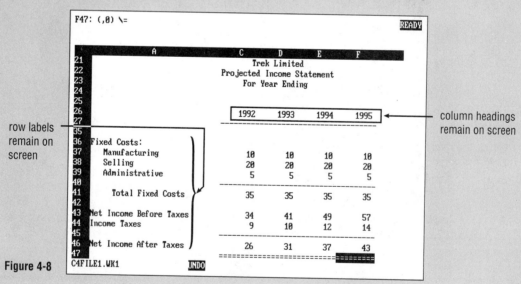

Figure 4-8

row labels remain on screen

column headings remain on screen

❺ Press **[Home]**.

Notice that the cell pointer returns to cell B28 rather than cell A1. Cell B28, the first unfrozen cell, becomes the upper left corner of the worksheet.

Unfreezing Titles

Once you freeze an area of the worksheet, you cannot move the cell pointer into that area. To make any changes to the headings or row labels, you must "unfreeze" the area before you can make those changes.

If you need to unfreeze titles, you would select the command /Worksheet Title Clear (/WTC). You would then be able to move the cell pointer into the area of the worksheet that was frozen and make the changes.

@IF Function

Now you are ready to follow Hillary's plan. The first thing Hillary wants to do is to see the effect of a poor sales year on net income. She assumes sales will be $75,000 (entered as 75) instead of $150,000 (entered as 150).

To consider the relationship between poor sales and income:

❶ Be certain the cell pointer is in cell B28.

❷ Type **75**. Press **[Enter]**.

❸ Move the cell pointer to cell B47 and look at the values in the rows for income taxes and net income after taxes. See Figure 4-9.

negative values for income taxes

Figure 4-9

Notice that income taxes appear as negative values for 1991, 1992, and 1993. This is not correct. Taxes should be zero whenever the net income before taxes is less than zero. How can we correct this?

❹ Move the cell pointer to cell B44. Look at the control panel and observe that the formula for calculating income taxes is +B43*0.25 (25% of net income before taxes). This formula is correct, as long as net income before taxes is a positive number. If net income before taxes is a negative number, the worksheet should set income taxes equal to zero, not a negative value. What went wrong? Hillary represented the relationship between net income before taxes and income taxes incorrectly when she built her worksheet.

There are many situations where the value you store in a cell depends on certain conditions, for instance:

- An employee's gross pay may depend on whether that employee worked overtime.
- A taxpayer's tax rate depends on his or her taxable income.

- A customer's charge depends on whether the size of the order entitles that customer to a discount.

In 1-2-3, the @IF function allows you to make comparisons to determine which actions 1-2-3 should take. The @IF function has the following format:

> *@IF(condition,true expression,false expression)*

The parenthetic expression can be interpreted to mean that if the condition is true, then execute the "true expression"; otherwise, execute the "false expression."

The @IF function has three components:

- A *condition* is a logical expression that represents a comparison between quantities. This comparison results in a value that is either true, indicated by a value of 1, or false, indicated by a value of 0.

- A *true expression* is a value or label stored in a cell if the condition is true.

- A *false expression* is a value or label stored in a cell if the condition is false.

An example may help to illustrate the format of an @IF function. Suppose you need to determine whether an employee earned overtime pay, that is, whether he or she worked more than 40 hours in a week. This can be expressed as:

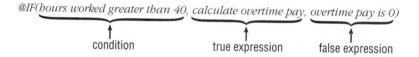

@IF(hours worked greater than 40, calculate overtime pay, overtime pay is 0)

    condition   true expression   false expression

In this example, the condition is the comparison between the hours an employee works and 40 hours. The true expression is executed if an employee works more than 40 hours; then the condition is true and overtime pay is calculated. The false expression is executed if an employee works 40 hours or less, then the condition is false and overtime pay is 0.

The most common condition, a simple condition, is a comparison between two expressions. An **expression** may be a cell or range reference, a number, a label, a formula, or another @function. Besides the expressions, a condition contains a comparison operator. A **comparison operator** indicates a mathematical comparison, such as less than or greater than. Figure 4-10 shows the comparison operators allowed in 1-2-3.

Type of Comparison	1-2-3 Symbol
Less than	<
Greater than	>
Less than or equal to	< =
Greater than or equal to	> =
Equal to	=
Not equal to	< >

Figure 4-10
Comparison
operators in 1-2-3

The comparison operator is combined with expressions to form a condition. For example, if we assume the hours worked is stored in cell D10, the condition *the number of hours worked is greater than 40* is expressed in 1-2-3 as @IF(D10>40...). Figure 4-11 illustrates several examples of conditional situations and how they can be expressed in 1-2-3.

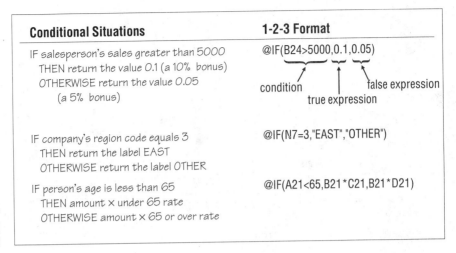

Figure 4-11
Examples of
conditional
situations

Let's now use the @IF function to correct Hillary's worksheet.

To use the @IF function to determine taxes:

❶ Make sure the cell pointer is in cell B44.

❷ Type **@IF(B43>0,0.25*B43,0)** and press **[Enter]**. See Figure 4-12.

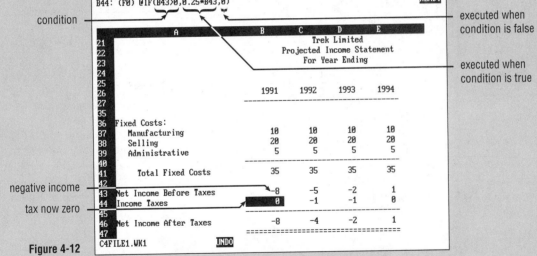

Figure 4-12

Do not include any spaces when you type this @function and be sure to separate
each component with a comma. You can interpret this function as:

IF the value in cell B43 is greater than 0
THEN return the value .25*B43 to cell B44
OTHERWISE return the value 0 to cell B44

Now let's copy this function to the cells C44 to F44 so the correct formulas to calculate income taxes for the years 1992 to 1995 can be included in the worksheet.

To copy the function to cells C44..F44:

❶ Make sure the cell pointer is in cell B44.

❷ Select /Copy (**/C**). Press **[Enter]** since you are only copying the function in cell B44.

❸ Move the cell pointer to C44 and press **[.]** to anchor the cell pointer.

❹ Highlight the range C44..F44. Press **[Enter]**.

Notice that taxes are now zero. See Figure 4-13.

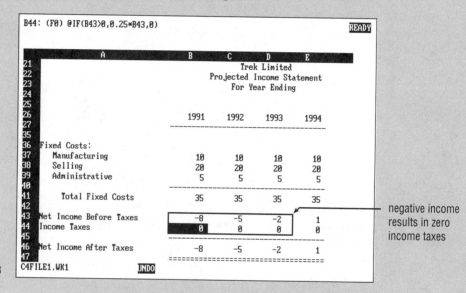

negative income results in zero income taxes

Figure 4-13

In addition to making changes to sales estimates, Hillary decides she wants to see how changes in the ratio of variable manufacturing costs to sales affects net income. To make this change, Hillary must change the formula for each cell that references variable manufacturing costs (B30, C30, D30, E30, F30). For example, she wants to change variable manufacturing costs from 50% to 52% of sales.

To change constants in a formula:

❶ Move the cell pointer to cell B30.

❷ Press **[F2]** (EDIT) to invoke the EDIT mode.

❸ Change 0.5 to 0.52 and press **[Enter]**. The formula appears in the control panel as 0.52*B28, and the variable manufacturing costs in 1991 are 39.

Now copy the formula to C30 .. F30, where the formulas for variable manufacturing costs for the years 1992 to 1995 are located.

To copy the formula to C30 .. F30:

➊ With the cell pointer in B30, select /Copy (**/C**). Press **[Enter]**.

➋ Move the cell pointer to C30. Press **[.]** to anchor the cell pointer.

➌ Highlight C30..F30. Press **[Enter]**. See Figure 4-14.

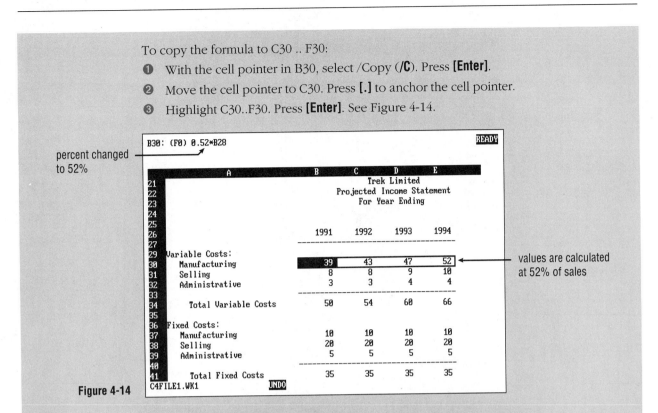

percent changed
to 52%

values are calculated
at 52% of sales

Figure 4-14

➍ Save your worksheet as S4FILE1.

To change variable selling costs from 10% to 11% requires a similar process. But is there a way to change the variable costs that takes less time and avoids the possibility of errors that can occur with so many changes? Hillary thinks about how to revise the worksheet. She realizes that the more she uses numeric constants in her formulas, the less flexibility she has if she wants to change those values. Thus, she decides to completely revise her worksheet. She prepares a new plan and worksheet sketch. Figure 4-15 on the next page shows her revised plan. Some of the major changes in this worksheet include:

- providing managers with five variables on which they can perform what-if analysis instead of one variable.
- replacing constants in formulas with range names, such as GROWTH, which reference cells in the input area.

Now you can retrieve the new worksheet that Hillary built.

My Goal:

Develop a worksheet that easily tests alternative scenarios to help develop a five-year plan for Trek Limited

What results do I want to see?

Projected income statements for 1991 to 1995

What information do I need?

Information that can be changed:

Sales estimate for 1991

Information that remains unchanged:

Annual growth rate in sales (10%)

Ratio of manufacturing costs to sales (50%)

Ratio of selling costs to sales (10%)

Ratio of administrative costs to sales (4%)

Fixed manufacturing costs ($10)

Fixed selling costs ($20)

Fixed administrative costs ($5)

What calculations will I perform?

1. sales first year = sales estimate for 1991

2. sales subsequent years = previous year's sales × 110% *(sales growth rate)*

3. variable manufacturing costs = 50% × sales estimate *(ratio of manufacturing costs to sales)*

4. variable selling costs = 10% × sales estimate *(ratio of selling costs to sales)*

5. variable administrative costs = 4% × sales estimate *(ratio of administrative costs to sales)*

6. total variable costs = variable manufacturing costs +
   variable selling costs +
   variable administrative costs

7. total fixed costs = fixed manufacturing costs ($10) +
   fixed selling costs ($20) +
   fixed administrative costs ($5)

8. net income before taxes = sales - total variable costs - total fixed costs

9. *If net income before taxes > 0 then*
   taxes = 25% × net income before taxes
   Otherwise taxes = 0

10. net income after taxes = net income before taxes - taxes

Annotations in left margin:

Hillary now wants to change this information →

Hillary will make this a conditional statement →

Figure 4-15
Hillary's revised planning sheet

To retrieve a file:

❶ Select /File Retrieve (**/FR**).

❷ Highlight C4FILE2.WK1 and press **[Enter]**.

Notice in Figure 4-16 that Hillary has divided her new worksheet into four sections. An *identification section* on the first screen consists of the filename, the person who developed the worksheet, the date the worksheet was created or last modified, and a brief description.

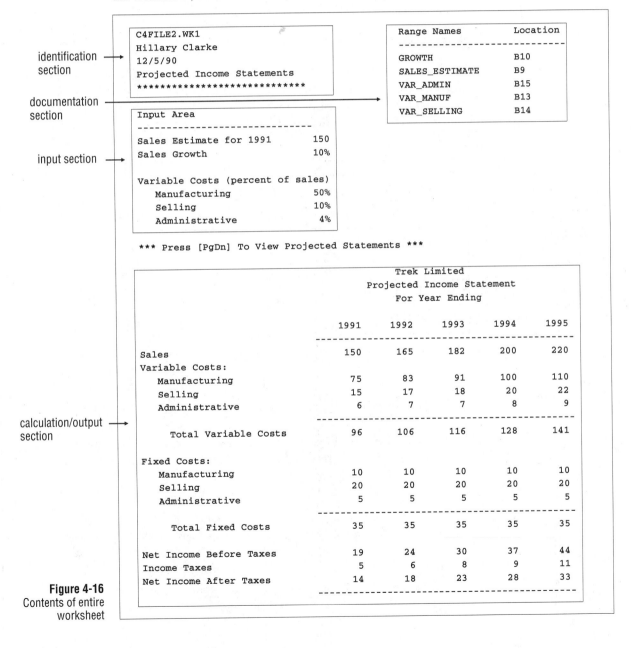

	Range Names	Location
	GROWTH	B10
	SALES_ESTIMATE	B9
	VAR_ADMIN	B15
	VAR_MANUF	B13
	VAR_SELLING	B14

```
C4FILE2.WK1
Hillary Clarke
12/5/90
Projected Income Statements
*****************************
```

identification section

documentation section

```
Input Area
-------------------------------
Sales Estimate for 1991      150
Sales Growth                 10%

Variable Costs (percent of sales)
   Manufacturing             50%
   Selling                   10%
   Administrative             4%
```

input section

*** Press [PgDn] To View Projected Statements ***

calculation/output section

	Trek Limited				
	Projected Income Statement				
	For Year Ending				
	1991	1992	1993	1994	1995
Sales	150	165	182	200	220
Variable Costs:					
Manufacturing	75	83	91	100	110
Selling	15	17	18	20	22
Administrative	6	7	7	8	9
Total Variable Costs	96	106	116	128	141
Fixed Costs:					
Manufacturing	10	10	10	10	10
Selling	20	20	20	20	20
Administrative	5	5	5	5	5
Total Fixed Costs	35	35	35	35	35
Net Income Before Taxes	19	24	30	37	44
Income Taxes	5	6	8	9	11
Net Income After Taxes	14	18	23	28	33

Figure 4-16
Contents of entire worksheet

Following the identification section is an *input section*, which lists the variables a manager at Trek can control and change in the worksheet. The manager can ask what-if questions by changing the values in the input section and then transferring these values to the output section.

The third section is the *calculation/output section*, which contains the projected income statements. Press [PgDn] to view this entire section. Press [Home] to return to A1.

The fourth section of the worksheet, a *documentation section*, contains a table of the named ranges used in this worksheet. Press [Tab] to see the table of named ranges. After you have examined the table, press [Home] to return to A1.

A Worksheet Map

A worksheet "map," similar to the one in Figure 4-17, can often accompany the worksheet to inform the user about the organization of the worksheet. Such a map is especially helpful in a large worksheet that consists of many sections. The map identifies each section and the cell range of each section. With the worksheet map, a user can quickly find different sections of a worksheet.

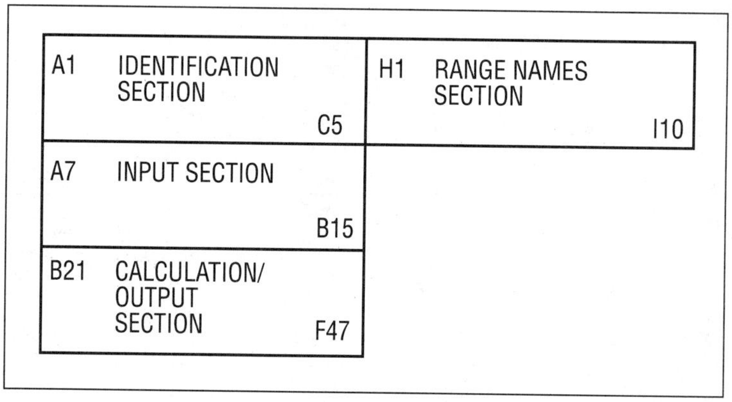

Figure 4-17
A map of Hillary's worksheet

Demonstrating What-if with the Revised Worksheet

Remember that Hillary developed this new worksheet because the previous worksheet was difficult to use for what-if–type questions. Let's try this new worksheet and see if it is any easier to use for this purpose.

To use the revised worksheet to change the variable manufacturing cost percent from 50% to 52% of sales:

❶ Use the cursor keys to move the cell pointer to cell B13.

❷ Type **52%**. Press **[Enter]**. See Figure 4-18. You could also enter the value as .52.

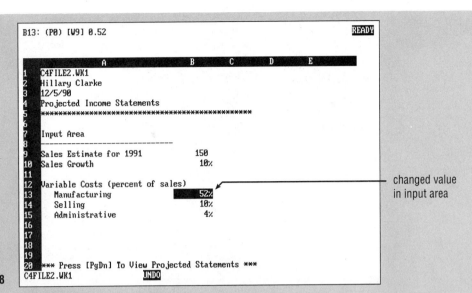

Figure 4-18

changed value
in input area

❸ Press **[PgDn]** and observe the projected income statement. See Figure 4-19. The variable manufacturing costs change from 75, 83, 91, 100, and 110 to 78, 86, 94, 104, and 114. Notice that we did not have to change formulas when we used this worksheet. When Hillary used the previous worksheet, she had to make changes to the formula every time a variable-cost percentage changed. The new worksheet is designed to transfer the input percent to the output section, where the calculations are performed.

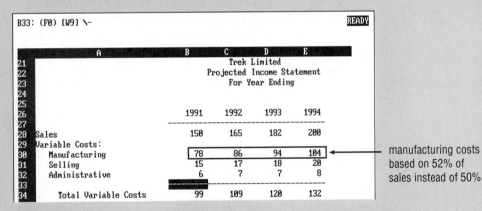

Figure 4-19

manufacturing costs
based on 52% of
sales instead of 50%

❹ Move the cell pointer to cell B30. See Figure 4-20.

no constant
in formula

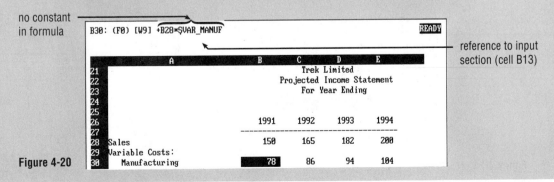

Figure 4-20

reference to input
section (cell B13)

Notice that in cell B30 the formula to calculate variable manufacturing costs uses a range name, VAR_MANUF, to reference the variable manufacturing cost percentage (cell B13). The variable manufacturing cost formula in cell B30 is (+B28*$VAR_MANUF) instead of (.5*B28), which was the formula used in the previous worksheet. Cell B28 contains the sales estimate for 1991. Now all a user has to do is change the variable manufacturing to sales percentage in the input area, and the formula in cell B30 will automatically recalculate.

Hillary thinks the revisions she has made to the worksheet will help managers more easily ask what-if questions. For example, suppose a manager wants to see what would happen if the growth rate increased from 10% to 15%.

To ask what if the growth rate for sales increased to 15%:

❶ Move the cell pointer to cell B10, the input area for the sales growth rate.

❷ Type **15%**. Press **[Enter]**. You can also enter the value as .15.

❸ Press **[PgDn]**.

Observe the results in the output section (Figure 4-21). Notice how sales in 1992 changed from 165 to 173. The revised sales estimates for 1992 also affected all the variable costs. The fixed costs, on the other hand, haven't changed. Net income before and after taxes have also changed. The increased growth rate also affects sales, variable costs, and income for 1993, 1994, and 1995.

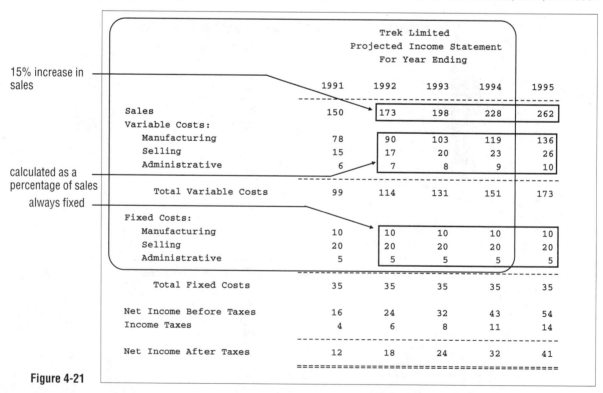

Figure 4-21

Hillary is pleased with her work and decides to ask Stephan to try the revised worksheet. But Stephan wants to ask different what-if questions. He moves the cell pointer to cell C28 in the output section and changes the sales in 1992 to 200.

Hillary explains to Stephan that all changes to the worksheet must be made in the input section, not the output section. She thinks to herself that she must prevent Stephan or other managers from inadvertently making the same mistake. She remembers from her workshop that she can protect cells. She decides first to correct the error Stephan made and then to protect the formulas in cell C28 and any other appropriate cells from being changed. Let's make the same mistake Stephan made.

To make Stephan's mistake:

❶ Move the cell pointer to cell C28. Notice the formula (1+$GROWTH)*B28 in the control panel.

❷ Type **200**. Press **[Enter]**. See Figure 4-22.

formula erased

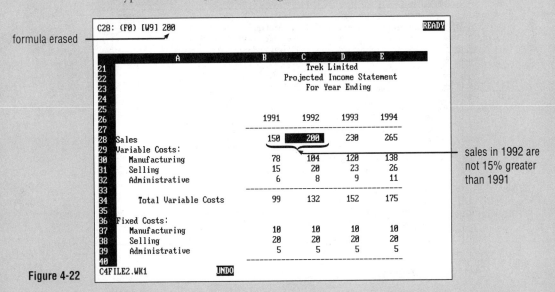

sales in 1992 are not 15% greater than 1991

Figure 4-22

Originally, cell C28 contained the formula (1+$GROWTH)*B28. When Stephan typed 200 in C28, he erased the formula and replaced it with the constant 200. The formula that was originally in this cell instructed 1-2-3 to increase sales for 1992 by the growth rate, currently 15%. Now that the formula is no longer in the cell, sales for 1992 do not reflect the anticipated 15% sales growth. Sales for 1992 are 200 and will remain 200 unless the formula is reentered in this cell.

Fortunately, Hillary is able to use the Undo feature and restore the worksheet to its previous state.

❸ Press **[Alt][F4]** (UNDO). Cell C28 now shows 173, and the formula (1+$GROWTH)*B28 appears in the control panel. If the Undo feature has not worked, type the formula (1+$GROWTH)*B28 into cell C28.

Protecting and Unprotecting Ranges

Hillary learned in her workshop that what Stephan did is a common mistake. Accidentally erasing worksheet formulas occurs often, so she learned it is a good idea to protect certain areas of a worksheet from accidental changes. She learned a combination of commands with which she can first protect an entire worksheet and then unprotect the range or ranges in which she or other users need to enter or edit data. In the steps that follow, you begin the process of protecting specific ranges in Hillary's worksheet by first protecting the entire worksheet.

To protect an entire worksheet:

❶ Select /Worksheet Global (**/WG**) to display the Global Settings sheet, as shown in Figure 4-23. Notice that the global protection default setting is "Disabled".

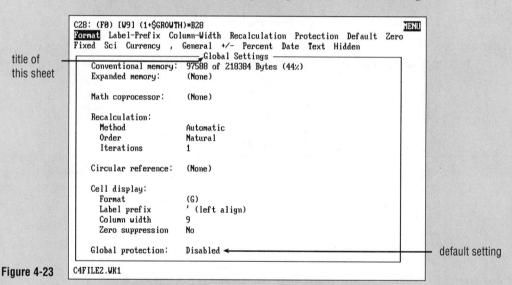

Figure 4-23

❷ Select Protection Enable (**PE**) to turn on global protection. 1-2-3 then returns to the worksheet automatically.

❸ With the cell pointer in cell C28, type **200** and press **[Enter]**. You are now prevented from making a change to that cell.

A warning beep, the ERROR indicator in the upper right corner, and the message "Protected cell" in the status line all remind you that the cell is protected. Notice the control panel. The letters PR (protected) appear in the control panel whenever the cell pointer is on a protected cell. See Figure 4-24.

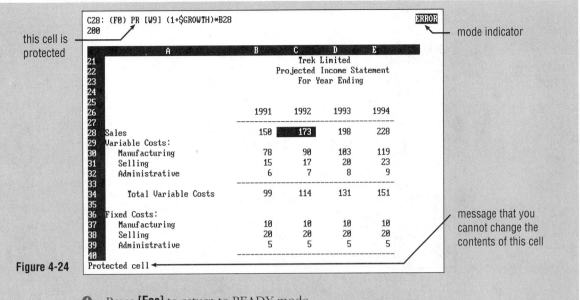

Figure 4-24

④ Press **[Esc]** to return to READY mode.

Move the cell pointer to any other cell in the worksheet and try to enter data or make a change. You'll find that you cannot make a change.

Currently every cell in the worksheet is protected. So what do you do if you need to enter values in some cell? In Hillary's worksheet, for example, we know that managers might want to ask what-if about data in cells B9 through B15. In the next steps, you will learn how to lift the protection, or unprotect, the range of cells that represents the input section of the worksheet.

To unprotect cells in a protected worksheet:

① Press **[Home]**. Then move the cell pointer to cell B9, the first cell to be unprotected.

② Select /Range Unprot (**/RU**).

③ Press **[↓]** to highlight the range B9..B15, the range of the input section.

④ Press **[Enter]**. The input area is now unprotected. See Figure 4-25 on the next page.

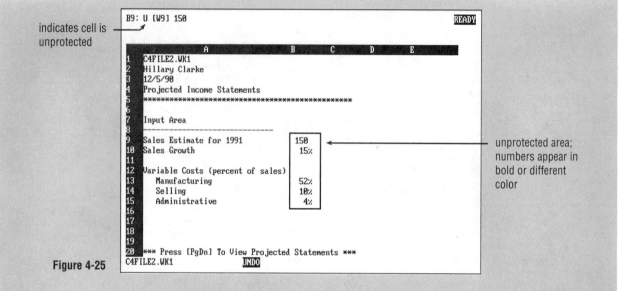

Figure 4-25

You have now lifted protection from cells B9 to B15. The only area in the worksheet where you can make entries is the input area. Notice that the control panel's first line displays U (unprotected) whenever the cell pointer is in an unprotected cell. Another indication that protection is not in effect for these cells is that the values in these cells appear in boldface or in a different color.

To see if you can enter data in the input section, let's change the variable administrative costs to 5% in cell B15.

To make a change in cell B15:

① Move the cell pointer to B15, the cell for variable administrative cost percentage.

② Type **5%** and press **[Enter]**. You can also enter this value as .05. Notice that data can now be entered in unprotected cells.

③ Press **[PgDn]** to see the results. Variable administrative costs are now 8, 9, 10, 11, and 13 for the years 1991 to 1995. See Figure 4-26.

```
B35: PR [W9]                                                        READY

           A              B       C       D        E
21                           Trek Limited
22                     Projected Income Statement
23                          For Year Ending
24
25
26                          1991    1992    1993    1994
27                        -----------------------------------
28  Sales                    150     173     198     228
29  Variable Costs:
30     Manufacturing          78      90     103     119
31     Selling                15      17      20      23
32     Administrative          8       9      10      11    <------
33                        -----------------------------------
34     Total Variable Costs  101     116     133     153
35
36  Fixed Costs:
37     Manufacturing          10      10      10      10
38     Selling                20      20      20      20
39     Administrative          5       5       5       5
40                        -----------------------------------
    C4FILE2.WK1        UNDO
```

administrative costs increase as a result of increase in administrative cost percent

Figure 4-26

If you decide to modify formulas or labels in the worksheet, remember that you will have to turn protection off. Let's try that.

To turn protection off:

❶ Select /Worksheet Global Protection (**/WGP**).

❷ Select Disable (**D**).

When you have completed the changes, you can turn protection on again by selecting /Worksheet Global Protection Enable (/WGPE). Let's keep the protection feature off for now.

Although adding protection to the worksheet is certainly an improvement, Hillary still is not satisfied. When changes are made in the input section, she has to press [PgDn] to see the results. She must then move the cell pointer back to the input section or press [PgUp] if she wants to make another change. Is there a way to have both the input and output sections appear on the screen at the same time?

Using Windows

To keep separate parts of the worksheet in view at the same time, you can use the Worksheet Window command. This command lets you view two parts of a large worksheet simultaneously. You can observe the results from one part of a worksheet while you make changes to another. You use [F6] (WINDOW) to move the cell pointer between the two windows.

In the next steps, you will split the worksheet into two windows — one for the input section and the other for the Projected Income Statement.

To split the screen into two windows:

① Press **[Home]**. Then move the cell pointer anywhere in row 8, the point where you decide to split the worksheet.

② Select /Worksheet Window Horizontal (**/WWH**). This command instructs 1-2-3 to split the screen horizontally into two windows, one above and one below the cell pointer. See Figure 4-27.

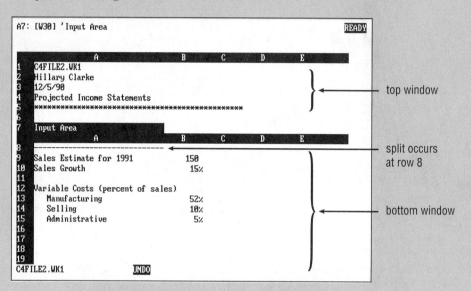

Figure 4-27

③ Press **[F6]** (WINDOW) once to move the cell pointer to the bottom window. Press the key **[F6]** (WINDOW) again to switch back to the top window.

The Window key switches the cell pointer back and forth between the two windows.

④ If necessary, adjust your view of the worksheet so the cells A9 to B15 are visible in the top window. Press **[↓]** until A9 to B15 appear in the top window. See Figure 4-28.

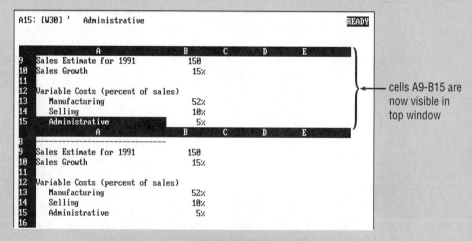

Figure 4-28

⑤ Press **[F6]** (WINDOW) again to switch the cell pointer to the bottom window. Then press **[↓]** until row 47 is visible. Your screen should be similar to Figure 4-29.

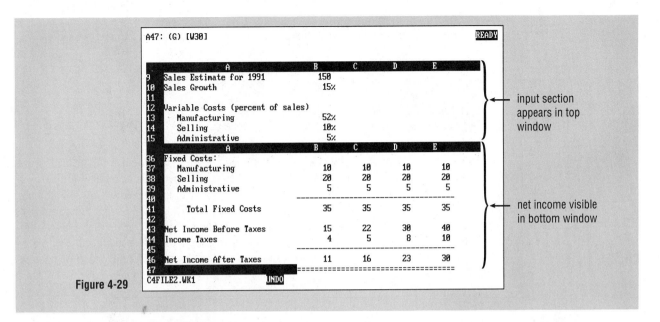

Figure 4-29

Now you can view, at the same time, part of the worksheet in the top window and part of the Projected Income Statement in the bottom window. Let's change the 1991 sales estimate to 225.

To make a change and immediately view the results:

❶ Press **[F6]** (WINDOW) to switch to the top window.

❷ Move the cell pointer to cell B9, the location for the sales estimate.

❸ Type **225** in cell B9. Press **[Enter]** and watch as the results of the change appear immediately. See Figure 4-30.

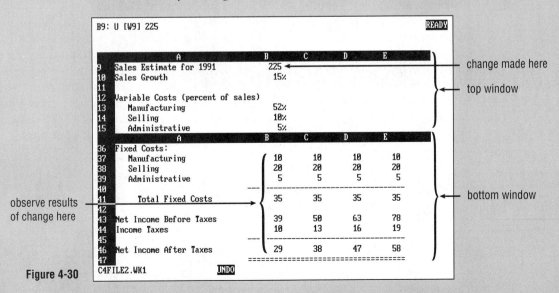

Figure 4-30

It will be easier to perform other tasks in this tutorial if you first clear the windows.

To clear the windows:

❶ Select /Worksheet Window Clear (**/WWC**).

Hillary now thinks that this worksheet is getting closer to her ideal, but she still is not completely satisfied. Each time she tries new input values, she finds herself writing down the results on a sheet of paper. She wonders if there is a way to make more than one change at a time and see the results. Hillary decides to ask an experienced 1-2-3 user at her company. She explains the problem and is told to try the Data Table command.

Before using this command, Hillary decides to set her worksheet aside. She wants to develop and experiment on a new worksheet so she does not accidentally lose or destroy her current worksheet.

To save the worksheet:

❶ Select /File Save (**/FS**). Type **S4FILE2** and press **[Enter]**.

Printing Cell Formulas

So that she will be able to come back and review the formulas in her current worksheet, Hillary prints the cell formulas that make up the current worksheet.

Printing the cell formulas is an option of the Print command. Using this option to create a printout of the cell formulas provides you with a record of the worksheet. It also allows you to see several formulas at once, thereby letting you see how formulas relate to one another. This is especailly helpful if you are trying to find a problem in your worksheet. Instead of moving from cell to cell and viewing the formula in the control panel, you have a printout of all the formulas. By attaching this printout to the usual output from your worksheet, you add valuable backup documentation for the worksheet. Let's now use the print-cell-formula option of the Print command to print the worksheet's formulas.

To print the cell formulas:

❶ Select /Print Printer Range (**/PPR**).

❷ Move the cell pointer to A28, the first cell of the print range.

❸ Press **[.]** to anchor the cell. Then highlight A28..F46 and press **[Enter]**.

The print range consists of the cells in the calculation/output area.

❹ Select Options Other Cell-Formulas (**OOC**) to cause the range to print as cell formulas rather than as values. Notice the change in the last setting, Output, in the lower left corner of the settings sheet. The settings sheet now specifies that cell formulas will be output. See Figure 4-31.

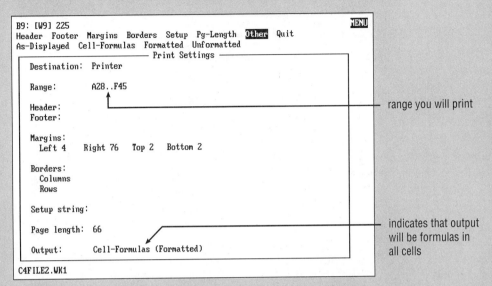

```
B9: [W9] 225                                                      MENU
Header Footer Margins Borders Setup Pg-Length  Other  Quit
As-Displayed Cell-Formulas Formatted Unformatted
                          ── Print Settings ──
   Destination:  Printer

   Range:       A28..F45

   Header:
   Footer:

   Margins:
     Left 4    Right 76   Top 2   Bottom 2

   Borders:
     Columns
     Rows

   Setup string:

   Page length:  66

   Output:       Cell-Formulas  (Formatted)

C4FILE2.WK1
```

— range you will print

— indicates that output will be formulas in all cells

Figure 4-31

⑤ Select Quit (**Q**) to leave the Options menu and return to the Print menu. Make sure the printer is ready.

⑥ Print the cell formulas. Select Align Go Page (**AGP**). 1-2-3 prints a list of the cell formulas for each cell within the specified range. See Figure 4-32.

```
Lotus 1-2-3 Student Business Series                    Hillary Clarke

A28:  (G) [W30] 'Sales
B28:  (F0) [W9] +SALES_ESTIMATE
C28:  (F0) [W9] (1+$GROWTH)*B28
D28:  (F0) [W9] (1+$GROWTH)*C28
E28:  (F0) [W9] (1+$GROWTH)*D28
F28:  (F0) [W9] (1+$GROWTH)*E28
A29:  (G) [W30] 'Variable Costs:
A30:  (G) [W30] '   Manufacturing
B30:  (F0) [W9] +B28*$VAR_MANUF
C30:  (F0) [W9] +C28*$VAR_MANUF
D30:  (F0) [W9] +D28*$VAR_MANUF
E30:  (F0) [W9] +E28*$VAR_MANUF
F30:  (F0) [W9] +F28*$VAR_MANUF
A31:  (G) [W30] '   Selling
B31:  (F0) [W9] +B28*$VAR_SELLING
C31:  (F0) [W9] +C28*$VAR_SELLING
D31:  (F0) [W9] +D28*$VAR_SELLING
E31:  (F0) [W9] +E28*$VAR_SELLING
F31:  (F0) [W9] +F28*$VAR_SELLING
A32:  (G) [W30] '   Administrative
B32:  (F0) [W9] +B28*$VAR_ADMIN
C32:  (F0) [W9] +C28*$VAR_ADMIN
D32:  (F0) [W9] +D28*$VAR_ADMIN
E32:  (F0) [W9] +E28*$VAR_ADMIN
F32:  (F0) [W9] +F28*$VAR_ADMIN
B33:  (F0) [W9] \-
```

Figure 4-32
Printout of cell formulas
(continued on next page)

```
C33:  (F0)  [W9]  \-
D33:  (F0)  [W9]  \-
E33:  (F0)  [W9]  \-
F33:  (F0)  [W9]  \-
A34:  (G)  [W30]  '      Total Variable Costs
B34:  (F0)  [W9]  +B30+B31+B32
C34:  (F0)  [W9]  +C30+C31+C32
D34:  (F0)  [W9]  +D30+D31+D32
E34:  (F0)  [W9]  +E30+E31+E32
F34:  (F0)  [W9]  +F30+F31+F32
A36:  (G)  [W30]  'Fixed Costs:
A37:  (G)  [W30]  '    Manufacturing
B37:  (F0)  [W9]  10
C37:  (F0)  [W9]  10
D37:  (F0)  [W9]  10
E37:  (F0)  [W9]  10
F37:  (F0)  [W9]  10
A38:  (G)  [W30]  '    Selling
B38:  (F0)  [W9]  20
C38:  (F0)  [W9]  20
D38:  (F0)  [W9]  20
E38:  (F0)  [W9]  20
F38:  (F0)  [W9]  20
A39:  (G)  [W30]  '    Administrative
B39:  (F0)  [W9]  5
C39:  (F0)  [W9]  5
D39:  (F0)  [W9]  5
E39:  (F0)  [W9]  5
F39:  (F0)  [W9]  5
B40:  (F0)  [W9]  \-
C40:  (F0)  [W9]  \-
D40:  (F0)  [W9]  \-
E40:  (F0)  [W9]  \-
F40:  (F0)  [W9]  \-
A41:  (G)  [W30]  '    Total Fixed Costs
B41:  (F0)  [W9]  +B37+B38+B39
C41:  (F0)  [W9]  +C37+C38+C39
D41:  (F0)  [W9]  +D37+D38+D39
E41:  (F0)  [W9]  +E37+E38+E39
F41:  (F0)  [W9]  +F37+F38+F39
A43:  (G)  [W30]  'Net Income Before Taxes
B43:  (F0)  [W9]  +B28-B34-B41
C43:  (F0)  [W9]  +C28-C34-C41
D43:  (F0)  [W9]  +D28-D34-D41
E43:  (F0)  [W9]  +E28-E34-E41
F43:  (F0)  [W9]  +F28-F34-F41
A44:  (G)  [W30]  'Income Taxes
B44:  (F0)  [W9]  @IF(B43>0,B43*0.25,0)
C44:  (F0)  [W9]  @IF(C43>0,C43*0.25,0)
D44:  (F0)  [W9]  @IF(D43>0,D43*0.25,0)
E44:  (F0)  [W9]  @IF(E43>0,E43*0.25,0)
F44:  (F0)  [W9]  @IF(F43>0,F43*0.25,0)
B45:  [W9]  \-
C45:  [W9]  \-
D45:  [W9]  \-
E45:  [W9]  \-
F45:  [W9]  \-
A46:  (G)  [W30]  'Net Income After Taxes
B46:  (F0)  [W9]  +B43-B44
C46:  (F0)  [W9]  +C43-C44
D46:  (F0)  [W9]  +D43-D44
E46:  (F0)  [W9]  +E43-E44
F46:  (F0)  [W9]  +F43-F44
```

Figure 4-32
(continued from
previous page)

Data Tables

Now let's see how Hillary can use a data table to make more than one change at a time and see the results. She decides she wants to make several changes to estimated 1991 sales and observe how those changes will affect net income before taxes.

A data table is an area of the worksheet set up to show the results a formula generates each time you change a value in that formula.

Let's illustrate this concept using a bank loan as an example. Suppose you are considering borrowing $100,000 to buy a home. The bank requires monthly payments over 25 years. What if you wanted to know how much your monthly payments would be at various interest rates, such as 9%, 10%, 11%, 12%, and 13%? To show the relationship between the monthly payments and the various interest rates, you could use a data table such as Figure 4-33.

Interest Rate	Monthly Payment
9%	839.20
10%	908.70
11%	980.11
12%	1053.22
13%	1127.84

Figure 4-33
Monthly loan payments at different interest rates

This figure shows how monthly payments increase as interest rates increase. The data table is a valuable tool because it allows you to try out several what-if questions at one time and observe their results. In the case of the monthly payments for the loan, you are saying:

What is the monthly payment *if* the interest rate is 9%?

What is the monthly payment *if* the interest rate is 10%?

What is the monthly payment *if* the interest rate is 11%?

What is the monthly payment *if* the interest rate is 12%?

What is the monthly payment *if* the interest rate is 13%?

Using a data table, you need only one formula to produce a table that shows the different results generated each time a new interest rate is substituted in the formula. When the value of only one variable in a formula is varied, the data table is referred to as a **one-way data table**.

One-Way Data Tables

The components and the layout of a one-way data table are shown in Figure 4-34 on the next page. As you can see from the figure, a one-way data table includes an **input cell** and a **table range.** The table range consists of four components: a **blank cell**, a **formula**, **input values**, and a **results area.** The data table must contain these four components and be laid out as shown in this figure.

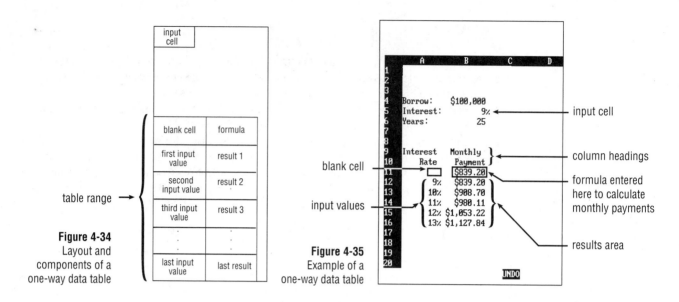

Figure 4-34
Layout and
components of a
one-way data table

Figure 4-35
Example of a
one-way data table

Figure 4-35 illustrates the components of the data table using a bank loan example. (You do not have a worksheet file for this example.) The components are defined as follows:

- The *input cell* is an unprotected cell that can be anywhere in the worksheet. It can be blank or can contain one of the input values. In the bank loan example, cell B5 is the input cell.

- The *blank cell* is a cell that does not contain data and is located at the intersection of the first row and the first column of the table range. In the bank loan example, cell A11 is considered the blank cell.

- The *formula* (or formulas) must be in the first row of the table range, starting at the second cell from the left. The formula contains a **variable**. A variable is a part of the formula for which different values can be substituted. In the bank loan example, the formula to calculate the monthly payments is in B11.

- The *input values* must be in the first column of the table range, starting immediately below the empty cell. The input values are the values that 1-2-3 substitutes for a variable whenever it performs the calculations specified in the formula. In the bank loan example, the interest rates in cells A12 to A16 are the input values that are substituted in the formula to calculate the monthly payments.

- The *results area* is the unprotected area below the formula and to the right of the input values. 1-2-3 enters the results of each calculation next to the input value it used. The results area should be blank when you first set up the data table because 1-2-3 writes over any data in this area when it calculates results. In the the bank loan example, the results area appears in cells B12 to B16.

Setting up a One-Way Data Table

Hillary now has her list of formulas and she has read how to use the Data Table command in her 1-2-3 reference manual. She draws a sketch that will help her visualize the planned changes in estimated 1991 sales and how these changes affect net income before taxes. Figure

4-36 is her handwritten sketch of how she wants her data table to look. Notice that she has followed the correct layout for a data table and has included all the required components.

		Sales	NIBT
Sales	xxx	blank cell	sales - (variable cost ratio x sales) - fixed costs
Variable cost percent	xx%	50	
Fixed cost	xx	75	
		100	
		125	
		150	Results here
		175	
		200	
		225	
		250	

Figure 4-36
Hillary's sketch for her data table

Now let's construct Hillary's data table. Begin by retrieving the file C4FILE3.WK1.

To retrieve a file:

❶ Select /File Retrieve (**/FR**). Highlight C4FILE3.WK1, and press **[Enter]**.

Your screen should now look like Figure 4-37. Notice that this file contains the input values that Hillary will use. Sales start at $50,000 (remember, the worksheets indicate the number of thousands), and variable costs are 64% of sales. Variable costs are the sum of variable manufacturing (50%), variable selling (10%), and variable administrative (4%) costs. Fixed costs are $35,000, the sum of fixed manufacturing ($10,000), fixed selling ($20,000), and fixed administrative ($5,000) costs.

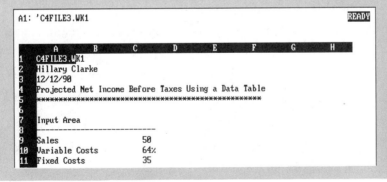

Figure 4-37
Hillary's retrieved worksheet

Your first step is to select a location in the worksheet to place the data table. The location of a data table can be any blank area of your worksheet. Let's use the cell range E8..F19.

Next, you must enter descriptive headings for the columns in the data table. Headings are *not* part of a data table, but you should enter them because they help you read the values in the data table. Hillary's sketch of the data table contains the headings you will now enter.

To enter headings for the data table:

❶ Move the cell pointer to cell **E7**. Type **"Sales** and press **[Enter]**. Notice that the label, Sales, is right-justified in the cell. That is because you typed the label prefix " (Quote) before you typed Sales.

❷ Move the cell pointer to F7 and type **"NIBT**, an abbreviation for net income before taxes. Press **[Enter]**.

Using the Data Fill Command

Now that you have entered the headings, let's enter the values in the input value section of the data table. Remember from the worksheet sketch that Hillary wants to see what will happen to NIBT as sales estimates increase in intervals of 25,000, starting at 50,000 and ending at 300,000 (remember, you type only the number of thousands, i.e., 50 for 50,000, 75 for 75,000, and so on).

You could enter each number — 50, 75, 100, and so on up to 300 — in each appropriate cell, but that would be rather time consuming. Instead you can use a new command, the Data Fill command, to enter all the sales estimates at one time into the input value section of the data table. The Data Fill command lets you enter a sequence of equally spaced values into a range of cells, either in one column or in one row. To use the Data Fill command, you first need to understand four new terms:

- **Fill range** is the range you want to fill with a series of sequential values. In Hillary's case, the fill range is E9..E19.

- **Start value** is the first value you want to enter in the fill range. In Hillary's case, 50 is the start value.

- **Step value** is the increment between the values in the sequence. Hillary wants to increase sales estimates in increments of 25.

- **Stop value** is the value you want to use as a limit for the sequence. Hillary wants her data table to stop at 300. The default limit is 8191.

To use the Data Fill command:

❶ Move the cell pointer to E9. Notice that cell E8, the first cell in the data table, is empty.

❷ Select /Data Fill (**/DF**).

Now let's enter the fill range.

❸ At cell E9, press **[.]** to anchor the range.

❹ Highlight the cells E9..E19 and press **[Enter]**.

❺ Type **50** to enter the start value and press **[Enter]**.

❻ Type **25** to enter the step value and press **[Enter]**.

❼ Type **300** to enter the stop value. Take a look at the control panel. See Figure 4-38.

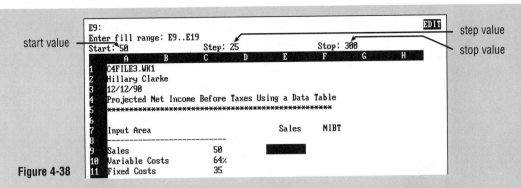

Figure 4-38

❽ Press **[Enter]**. As you do, notice that the input values appear in column E of the data table. See Figure 4-39.

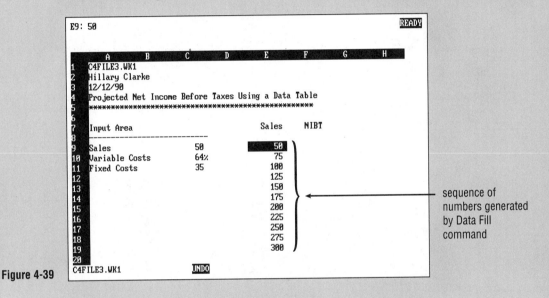

Figure 4-39

Now you should enter the formula to calculate net income before taxes (NIBT) into the formula section of the data table. Checking Hillary's sketch for her data table (Figure 4-36) you can see the formula is:

sales – (variable cost ratio × sales) – fixed costs

Be sure to enter this formula in cell F8, that is, to the right of the empty cell of the data table.

To enter the formula to calculate net income before taxes:

❶ Move the cell pointer to F8, the first row of the data table.

❷ Type **+C9–(C10*C9)–C11**. Press **[Enter]** and as you do, notice that –17, the result of the calculation of this formula, appears in F8. See Figure 4-40 on the next page.

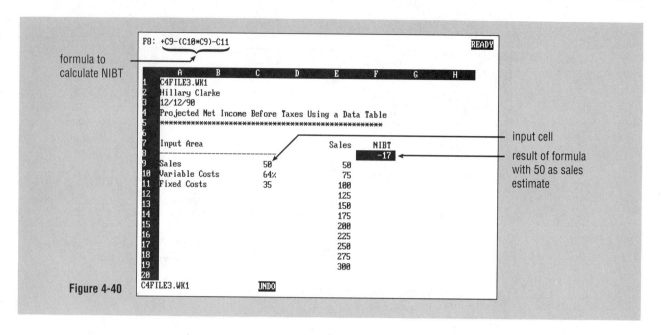

formula to calculate NIBT

input cell

result of formula with 50 as sales estimate

Figure 4-40

The components of the data table have been set up; now it's time to use the Data Table command.

To identify the cells that make up the table range of the data table:

❶ Select the command /Data Table 1 (**/DT1**) to set up a one-way data table. 1-2-3 prompts you to specify the data table range.

❷ Move the cell pointer to E8, the upper left corner of the table range.

❸ Anchor the cell by pressing **[.]**.

❹ Highlight the range E8..F19. See Figure 4-41.

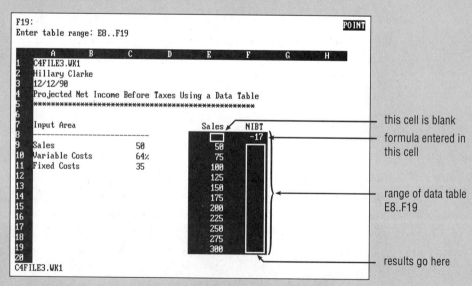

this cell is blank

formula entered in this cell

range of data table E8..F19

results go here

Figure 4-41

You have now defined the table range of the data table. Notice that the empty cell, E8, must be included in the range, but we have not included the column headings, which are in E7..F7.

❺ Press **[Enter]**.

Next, 1-2-3 prompts you to specify which cell will be the input cell. The input cell will contain the values from the input value section of the data table.

❻ Type **C9**. Press **[Enter]**. See Figure 4-42.

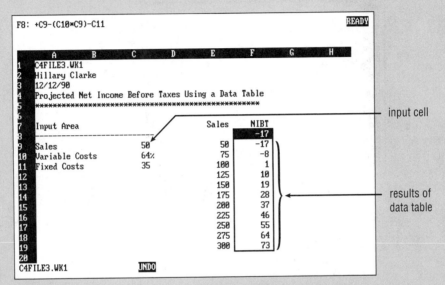

F8: +C9-(C10*C9)-C11							READY

```
           A        B        C        D        E        F        G        H
1  C4FILE3.WK1
2  Hillary Clarke
3  12/12/90
4  Projected Net Income Before Taxes Using a Data Table
5  ***************************************************
6
7  Input Area                              Sales     NIBT              ← input cell
8  -----------------------------------              -17
9  Sales              50                    50       -17
10 Variable Costs     64%                   75        -8
11 Fixed Costs        35                   100         1
12                                         125        10
13                                         150        19
14                                         175        28              ← results of
15                                         200        37                data table
16                                         225        46
17                                         250        55
18                                         275        64
19                                         300        73
20
   C4FILE3.WK1              UNDO
```

Figure 4-42

1-2-3 substitutes each value from the input section of the data table (E9..E19) into the input cell (C9), one at a time. Then using the formula in cell F8, 1-2-3 recalculates the formula using these input values and immediately displays the results in the results section of the data table (F9..F19). The data table is now complete.

❼ Save the worksheet as S4FILE3.

Data tables can provide you even greater flexibility, because you can test the sensitivity of the results to various assumptions. Suppose, for example, that you believe the variable costs will increase from 64% to 66% of sales. With data tables, all you have to do is change the variable cost in cell C10 from 64 to 66 and then press [F8] (TABLE), to recalculate the entire table. Pressing [F8] repeats the last Data Table command you selected, in this case, Data Table 1. 1-2-3 uses the previous setting for the table range and the input cell.

Now let's see how Hillary can quickly change one value using the [F8] (TABLE) key and generate 11 new forecasts of NIBT.

To use [F8] for what if analysis:

❶ Move to cell C10, type **66%**, a revised variable cost and press **[Enter]**. You can also enter the value as 66.

No changes appear in the results area.

➋   Press **[F8]** (TABLE) to recalculate the table. See Figure 4-43.

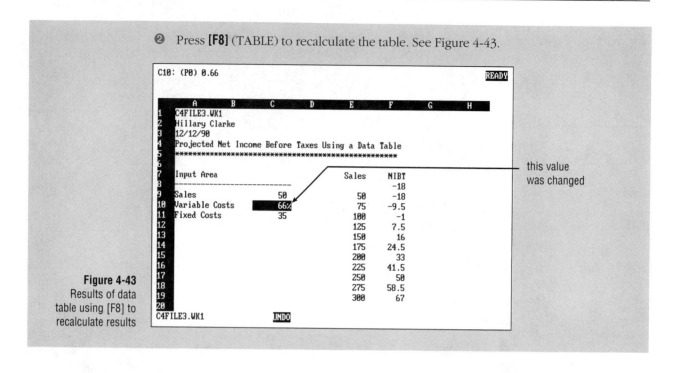

this value
was changed

Figure 4-43
Results of data
table using [F8] to
recalculate results

Exercises

1. Which of the following @IF functions would work in a 1-2-3 worksheet?
   a.   IF(D–40>0,3,7)
   b.   @IF(D4–40>0 , 3, 7)
   c.   @IFD4–40>0,3,7
   d.   @IF(D4–40>0,3,7)

2. Write an English statement that explains what this @IF function says.
   @IF(C15<0,"LOSS","PROFIT")

3. Use Figure 4-44 to write an @IF function that you could type in cell C4. This function
   should determine a salesperson's commission rate based on weekly sales. If weekly
   sales are above 10000, the commission rate is 12%; otherwise, commissions are 7.5%.

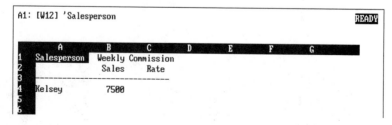

Figure 4-44

4. Use Figure 4-45 to do the following:

a. Write an @IF function that you could enter in cell D3 that checks the value in column B and places in column D the word MALE or FEMALE, depending on whether the code in column B is M (male) or F (female).

b. Write an @IF function that you could enter in cell E3 that places the phrase UNDER 21 or the phrase 21 AND OVER in the cell E3, depending on the age in column C.

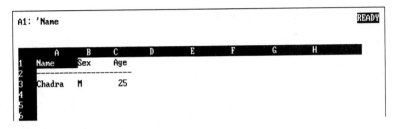

Figure 4-45

5. Identify the command you would use in the following situations:

a. You have a list of 100 customer names, addresses, and phone numbers. As you scroll down the worksheet, the column headings disappear from the screen.

b. Users of the worksheet keep erasing formulas accidentally.

c. You want an efficient way to do what-if analysis.

d. You want to see two different parts of a large worksheet at the same time.

e. You want to number cells in column A of your worksheet 1 to 500 without typing each number.

Tutorial Assignments

Before you begin these Tutorial Assignments, check your Lotus 1-2-3 data diskette. Be sure you have space to save the additional worksheet files you'll create in these assignments (at least 40,000 bytes). If not, save your files as appropriate to another formatted diskette.

Retrieve the worksheet file T4FILE1 and do the following:

1. Split the screen so you can observe sales and all variable costs in the top window and net income before taxes, income taxes, and net income after taxes in the bottom window.

2. Change sales for 1991 to 160.

3. Save the worksheet as S4FILE4.

4. Clear the split screen.

5. Change the formula for variable administrative costs to 5% of sales for all five years.

6. Save the worksheet as S4FILE5.

Retrieve the worksheet T4FILE2 and do the following:

7. Scroll the worksheet to find the net income after taxes for 1991 to 1995.

8. Unfreeze the worksheet so you can move to the Input section of the worksheet.

9. Change the variable administrative costs from 4% to 5% (enter as either .05 or 5%).

10. Print the projected income statement using compressed type.

11. Save the worksheet as S4FILE6.

Retrieve the worksheet file T4FILE3 and do the following:

12. Change the fixed costs from 35 to 45 and recalculate the data table. Print your results.

13. Reduce the variable costs from 64% to 60% and recalculate the data table. Print the results.

14. Save the worksheet as S4FILE7.

Retrieve the worksheet file from Tutorial 2, T2FILE4, and do the following:

15. Protect the worksheet so the only cells that can be changed are the daily stock prices, cells C12..C15.

16. Attempt to type 125 in cell B12 (you should not be able to). Enter the following prices in cells C12 to C15: 130, 40, 30, and 50, respectively. Save your worksheet as S2FILE8.

Case Problems

1. Price Breaks at PC Outlet

PC Outlet, a personal computer mail order company, wants to increase commercial orders by offering attractive discounts to customers who purchase in large quantities. One machine, a 386-MHz PC, is being sold at $1,630 per machine for purchases of 25 or fewer machines. If the customer orders 26 or more machines, each machine costs $1,480.

PC Outlet gives price quotes over the phone. Each customer service/sales operator has a 1-2-3 worksheet at his or her desk. Whenever a customer calls with a large order, the operator enters the order size into the worksheet and 1-2-3 calculates the total price (price per unit × order size), taking into account whether the discount applies.

Do the following:

1. Develop a worksheet based on the above information.

2. Enter a customer who orders five PCs. Print your results. Then enter a second customer who orders 30 PCs. Print your results.

3. What if PC Outlet decides to lower the price for orders above the break point? Now, if an order totals 26 or more, the price per unit is $1,430. The design of your worksheet should easily accommodate this type of change. Print your results using the data in Step 2 above.

4. What if PC Outlet lowers the break point for the quantity discount from 26 to 21 units? If an order totals 21 or more, the price per unit is $1,430. The design of your worksheet should easily accommodate this type of change. Print your results using the data in Step 2 above.

5. Save your worksheet as S4PRICE.

6. Print the cell formulas of your worksheet.

2. Loan Repayment Schedule

Occasionally, businesses need to borrow money for new buildings, equipment, or other large purchases. If a business takes out a term loan, it must pay back the loan in installments over a specified period of time.

For example, assume Lockwood Enterprises borrows $10,000, payable over five years, at an interest rate of 16% per year on the unpaid balance. Each month Lockwood pays $243.18 to cover principal and interest. The principal is the amount of the loan still unpaid, and the interest is the amount paid for the use of the money.

Figure 4-46 is a partial repayment schedule that shows the monthly payments broken out into principal repaid (amount borrowed) and interest paid. If this table were carried out for 60 months (5 years × 12 months per year, or the life of the loan), it would show a remaining balance of 0 at the conclusion of the 60-month period.

Payment Number	Monthly Payment	Interest[1]	Principal[2] Repayment	Remaining Balance
0	0.00	0.00	0.00	10000.00
1	243.18	133.33	109.85	9890.15
2	243.18	131.87	111.31	9778.84
...				
60	243.18	3.20	239.98	0[3]

[1] Interest is equal to the monthly interest rate, .013333 (16% divided by 12 months), times the remaining balance from the previous period. For example, in month 1, interest equals $133.33 (.013333 × 10000). In month 2, interest equals $131.87 (.013333 × 9890.15).

[2] Principal repayment for each period is equal to the monthly payment ($243.18) minus the interest for the period. For example, in month 2, the monthly payment ($243.18) minus the interest ($131.87) equals the principal repaid ($111.31).

[3] Because of rounding, the result will not be exactly zero.

Figure 4-46

Do the following:

1. Develop a worksheet that prepares a complete loan payment schedule for this loan. At the bottom of the payment schedule, calculate the total payments and the total interest.

2. Print the repayment schedule.

3. Save your worksheet as S4LOAN.

4. What if the interest rate is 16.5%? The monthly payment is $245.85. Print a new repayment schedule.

3. Predicting Demand for Mars Automobiles

Lynette Spiller, an economist working at HN Motor Company headquarters, has developed the following formula to estimate demand for HN's new line of Mars automobiles:

$$D \quad = \quad 100,000 - 100P + 2,000N + 50I - 1,000G + 0.2A$$

where

D	=	demand for Mars automobiles (in units)
P	=	price of Mars automobile (in dollars)
N	=	population in United States (in millions)
I	=	disposable income per person (in dollars)
G	=	price of gasoline (cents per gallon)
A	=	advertising expenses by HN for Mars (in dollars)

The senior managers at HN are considering raising the price of Mars, but before they do, they want to determine how increasing the price will affect demand for this car. They ask Lynette to show how increasing the price in $100 increments from $10,000 to $11,000 will affect demand for the Mars.

Assume the following values when estimating demand:

N	=	250
I	=	$14,000
G	=	140 cents
A	=	$1,000,000

Do the following:

1. Design a worksheet using the Data Table command to solve this problem. The data table should include a column for possible car prices beginning at $10,000, increasing in $100 increments to $11,000. The second column should show the demand for cars at each price.

2. Print your results.

3. Save your worksheet as S4MARS.

4. What if gasoline prices are $1.75 (enter as 175 cents) per gallon? Rerun the worksheet using the new price of gasoline. Print your results.

5. What if gasoline prices are $1.75 a gallon and the advertising budget is increased to $1,500,000? Print your results.

6. Save the worksheet as S4MARS1.

4. Production Planning at QuikNails

QuikNails Manufacturing, makers of artificial fashion fingernails, anticipates selling 42,000 units of QuikNails in May. Currently, the company has 22,000 units ready in inventory. The QuikNails plant will produce the additional product (20,000 units) during April to have enough product to meet the sales forecast for May. In addition to meeting May's sales forecast, the plant manager wants to have 24,000 units of QuikNails in inventory at the end of May for anticipated sales at the beginning of June. Thus, the QuickNails production requirement for April is the sum of the QuikNails units necessary to meet May sales estimates (20,000) plus the units needed to meet the desired ending inventory level (24,000).

The major ingredient needed to produce QuikNails is a chemical called Zinex. Assume the production department needs three gallons of Zinex to make one unit of QuikNails. Currently, the company has an inventory of 100,000 gallons of Zinex. The plant will use all of this raw material to meet its production requirement for April. It also needs 110,000 gallons of Zinex on hand at the end of April for production in May.

Sally Dolling is in charge of inventory control for both raw materials and finished products. She needs to inform senior management and the purchasing manager how much Zinex is required for the current and future materials production. As Sally's assistant, you will develop a spreadsheet to help calculate the number of gallons of Zinex that she should tell the purchasing manager to buy in April for QuikNails to meet the production requirements. You decide to adapt the form that Sally has been using to develop her estimate for production and material requirements (Figure 4-47).

QuikNails Production:	Units
Monthly sales estimate for QuikNails	xxxx
Less QuikNails currently in inventory	.
Production needed to meet sales forecast	.
Plus QuikNails needed at end of month	.
Total QuikNails production requirement	xxxx
Zinex Purchases:	Gallons
Zinex needed to meet QuikNails production requirement	xxxx
Less Zinex currently in inventory	.
Purchases of Zinex required to meet QuikNails production	.
Plus desired level of Zinex at end of month	.
Total Purchases of Zinex	xxxx

Figure 4-47

Design your spreadsheet so you can easily test alternative plans, such as different sales estimates and different inventory levels for QuikNails and Zinex.

Do the following:

1. Design a worksheet to calculate the production requirements of QuikNails and the amount of Zinex to purchase for the QuikNails manufacturing division. Use the form in Figure 4-47 as a guide in developing your worksheet.

2. Print the results.

3. Print the cell formulas.

4. Save your worksheet as S4NAILS.

5. What if the sales estimates of QuikNails for May is revised to 50,000 units? Print your revised results. What if the sales estimate for May is 30,000 units? Print your revised results.

Tutorial 5

Creating and Printing Graphs

Automobile Industry Sales: A Four-year Summary

OBJECTIVES

In this tutorial you will learn to:

■ Start 1-2-3 and PrintGraph from the Access menu

■ Create pie, line, bar, and stacked bar graphs

■ Add titles, legends, and axis formatting

■ Name and save graph settings

■ Save graphs for printing

■ Customize and use PrintGraph to print saved graphs

Case: McAuliffe & Burns

Carl Martinez majored in human resources in college and was particularly interested in labor relations. Thus, he was delighted when he landed a job as a staff assistant with McAuliffe & Burns (M&B), a leading consulting firm in Washington, D.C. M&B specializes in consulting to unions on labor relations issues.

When Carl began at M&B, his computer skills were not as polished as those of the other staff assistants. He knew how to use a word processor, but his spreadsheet skills were limited. But after M&B sent him to a two-day workshop on Lotus 1-2-3, Carl used Lotus 1-2-3 daily to prepare analyses for M&B's senior consultants. Over time, Carl's skills with Lotus 1-2-3 improved dramatically, and he was promoted to a staff associate.

In his new job, Carl is working for three senior consultants on a project for the United Auto Workers (UAW) union. Leaders of the UAW hired M&B to help them prepare testimony for upcoming Congressional committee hearings that will investigate whether the U.S. should establish import quotas for foreign cars.

Carl's first task is to research all automobile sales in the U.S. and gather data on unit sales by year and by company. After he gathers the data and creates a worksheet, Carl decides that he could present the data more effectively if he used the graphics function of Lotus 1-2-3. Carl is convinced that the data will make more of an impact on the Congressional subcommittee members if the UAW leaders show graphic representations of trends and markets. Carl plans to use a bar graph to show trends and a pie chart to show market shares. Figure 5-1a on the next page shows Carl's planning sheet for preparing his graphs. Figure 5-1b on the next page shows his sketches of the graphs he wants to create with 1-2-3.

Figure 5-1a
Carl's planning
sheet

My Goal:
  Prepare graphs showing market shares and trends of automobile sales
  in U.S. from 1985 - 1988

What results do I want to see?
  Bar graphs of sales from 1985 - 1988
  Pie chart showing market shares for 1988

What information do I need?
  Number of cars sold by year for General Motors, Ford, Chrysler, Honda,
  Toyota, and Nissan

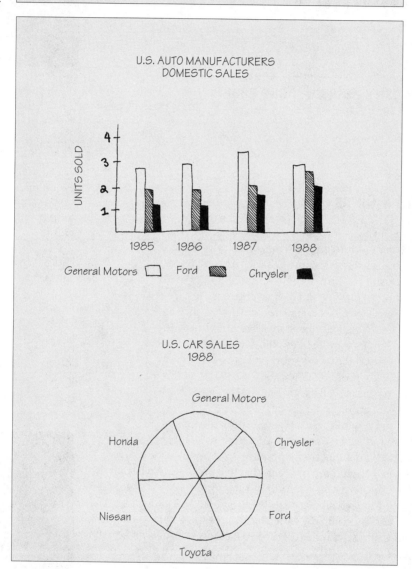

Figure 5-1b
Carl's sketches of
the graphs

This tutorial leads you through Carl's process of using graphs to analyze auto sales in the U.S. After starting 1-2-3 from the Access menu, you will create a series of graphs to learn which type of graph is best suited to your data. Finally, you will print the graphs.

Introduction to Graphics

In business, graphics are used to represent one or more data series in a more visually appealing and easily understood format. A **data series** is a single set of data represented by a line, a bar, or a pie. For example, a data series may include:

- Sales of a product by quarter (one data series)
- Sales of three products by quarter (three data series)
- Daily stock prices of a company over the past month (one data series)
- Daily stock prices of two companies over the past month (two data series)

With your computer and 1-2-3, you can create graphs that will help you communicate your ideas quickly and easily. Lotus 1-2-3 includes a variety of graphs: bar graphs, line graphs, stacked bar graphs, pie charts, and XY graphs.

A **bar graph** consists of a series of vertical or horizontal bars. Each bar in the chart represents a single value from a set of values. The length or height of each bar is determined by the size of each value relative to all the other values. A bar graph is used to compare related data items during one time period or over a few time periods, such as four quarters. Bar graphs use the x axis, or horizontal axis, to classify data over regions, over time, over products, and so on. The vertical, or y axis, shows the quantity you are measuring, such as dollars, units sold, weight, or number of employees. For example, revenue at TriCycle Industries (Tutorial 3) could be represented by a bar graph that shows the relationship of sales of recycled materials by quarter (Figure 5-2a).

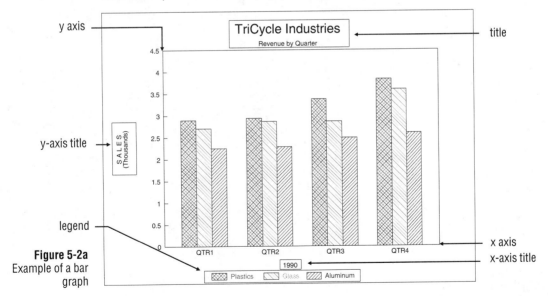

Figure 5-2a
Example of a bar graph

A **line graph** represents data with points and connects these points with a straight line. Line graphs are effective at showing trends in data over time. Each line represents one set of data, such as the daily stock prices of IBM. A line graph is a better choice than a bar graph to present a large number of data points over time. Figure 5-2b on the next page uses a line graph to show quarterly revenue for each recycled material at Tricycle Industries.

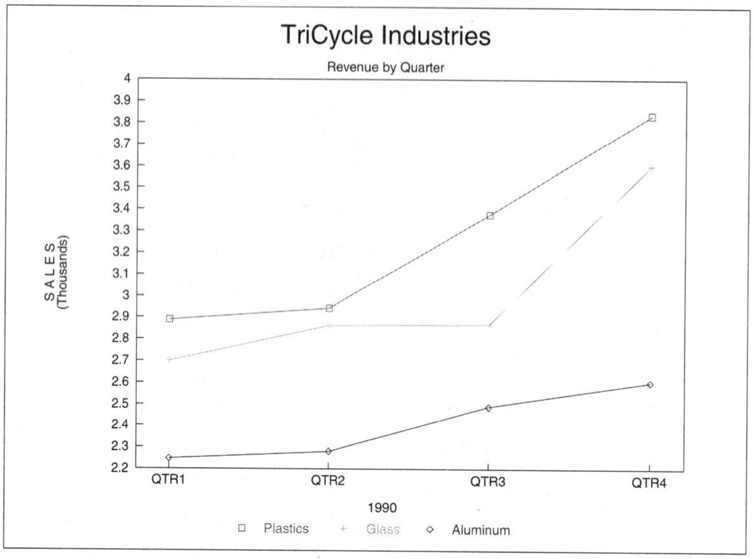

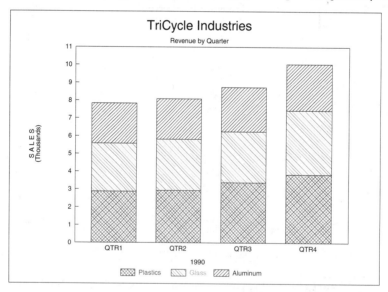

Figure 5-2b
Example of a line
graph

Stacked bar graphs show related data values on top of one another. These graphs show the components of several wholes. They are used to emphasize several totals and a breakdown of their components. For example, sales of each recycled material at TriCycle for the first quarter would appear on one bar, one on top of the other (Figure 5-2c). A second bar would represent the same data for the second quarter. A third and fourth bar would show the sales of the last two quarters. This graph can compare total sales over several quarters, while also identifying the components that make up each quarterly total.

Figure 5-2c
Example of a
stacked bar graph

Pie charts are useful for showing how each value contributes to the whole. For example, the total 1990 sales at TriCycle are divided among plastic, glass, and aluminum (Figure 5-2d), each represented by a slice of the whole. The size of a slice depends on its component's value relative to the whole. When you want to express your data as percentages, consider using pie charts. You can emphasize one or more slices by using a cut, or "exploded," slice to draw the viewer's attention.

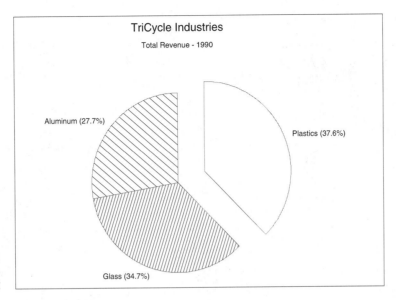

Figure 5-2d
Example of a pie
chart

XY graphs, also called scatter graphs, show relationships between two variables. This graph shows how a change in one variable relates to another variable. For example, sales management at TriCycle graphed the relationship between the amount of waste in tons and sales revenue at TriCycle (Figure 5-2e). We will not cover XY graphs in this tutorial, but Lotus 1-2-3 can produce XY graphs.

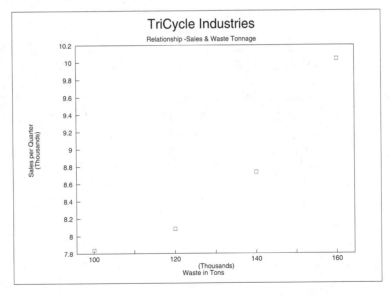

Figure 5-2e
Example of an XY
graph

Starting 1-2-3 from the Access Menu

Whenever you plan to print graphs, you should start 1-2-3 differently from how you've started it in Tutorials 1 through 4. In this tutorial, you will print graphs, so you have to learn how to start 1-2-3 from the Access menu. By starting from the Access menu, you can move directly to PrintGraph once you are ready to print your graphs.

To start 1-2-3 from the Access menu:

❶ If you are using 1-2-3 on a *hard-disk system*, be sure the directory that contains the 1-2-3 program files is the current directory. Type **cd\123** and press **[Enter]**. If 123 is not the name of your directory, type the correct name instead. Then proceed to Step 2.

If you are running 1-2-3 on a *two-disk system*, insert the 1-2-3 System Disk in drive A and your Lotus 1-2-3 data diskette in drive B. Type **a:** and press **[Enter]**. If you are not using drive A for the System Disk, type the correct drive letter instead.

❷ Type **lotus** and press **[Enter]**. The Access system menu appears. See Figure 5-3.

use to print
graphs

```
1-2-3  PrintGraph  Install  Exit
Use 1-2-3


                        1-2-3 Access System
                        Copyright  1986, 1989
                     Lotus Development Corporation
                        All Rights Reserved
                      Release 2.2 Student Edition

        The Access system lets you choose 1-2-3, PrintGraph or the
        Install program, from the menu at the top of this screen.  If
        you're using a two-diskette system, the Access system may prompt you to
        change disks.  Follow the instructions below to start a program.

        o  Use → or ← to move the menu pointer (the highlighted rectangle
           at the top of the screen) to the program you want to use.

        o  Press ENTER to start the program.

        You can also start a program by typing the first character of its name.

        Press HELP (F1) for more information.
```

Figure 5-3
Access menu

From this menu, you can choose 1-2-3, PrintGraph, Install, or Exit.

❸ Highlight 1-2-3 and press **[Enter]**. A blank worksheet appears on your screen. If you start from the Access system, you are returned to the Access system menu when you quit 1-2-3. From now on in the tutorials, start 1-2-3 from either the operating system prompt or the Access system.

Creating a Bar Graph

Now let's retrieve one of Carl's worksheets that contains the number of cars sold in the U.S. from 1985 to 1988.

To retrieve this file:

❶ Retrieve the file C5FILE1.WK1. See Figure 5-4.

```
A1: [W18] 'C5FILE1.WK1                                          READY

           A              B          C          D          E
1   C5FILE1.WK1
2   Carl Martinez
3   12/23/90
4   Create graph showing market share & trends
5   **********************************************
6
7                        Automobile Sales in US
8                          Unit Sales by Year
9
10                     1985       1986       1987       1988
11  ------------------------------------------------------------
12  General Motors   3,179,488  3,359,326  2,968,978  3,182,404
13  Ford             1,161,321  1,334,731  1,397,060  1,510,130
14  Chrysler           405,272    467,962    547,916    765,883
15  Toyota             575,345    588,909    612,621    644,763
16  Nissan             579,262    554,102    611,365    471,981
17  Honda              536,792    602,758    608,819    662,138
18
19
20
    C5FILE1.WK1              UNDO
```

Figure 5-4
Carl's worksheet showing total car sales by manufacturer by year

Notice that the data in this worksheet contain the number of cars sold annually in the US from 1985 through 1988, broken down by manufacturer.

According to Carl's sketch, one of the graphs he wants to create is a bar graph showing car sales by manufacturer. Before creating the bar graph, you first need to learn about the Graph menu and the graph settings sheet.

To create any graph in 1-2-3, you must use the Graph command. This command reveals the **graph settings sheet,** in which you specify what data you want to graph and how you want to graph them. As you use the menu options available from the Graph command, 1-2-3 updates the graph settings sheet.

To create a graph, you must specify the following:

- The type of graph you want
- The range of cells that represent the labels for the x axis
- The data series you plan to use in the graph

Carl plans first to compare graphically total units sold by U.S. manufacturers (General Motors, Ford, Chrysler) over a four-year period (1985 to 1988) and then to compare these total U.S. units to units sold in the U.S. by Japanese manufacturers. Let's start by creating a bar graph of General Motors' data that shows unit sales over a four-year period.

To create a bar graph of cars sold by General Motors:

❶ Select /Graph (**/G**). 1-2-3 displays the graph settings sheet.

❷ Select Type (**T**) and then select Bar (**B**) to indicate the type of graph you want to create — a bar graph. See Figure 5-5 on the next page.

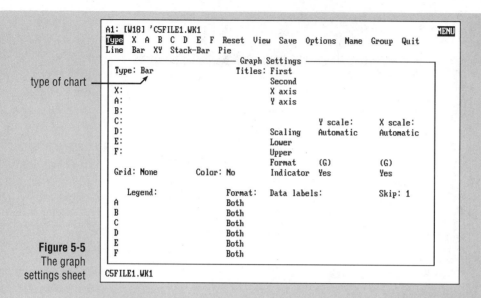

type of chart

Figure 5-5
The graph
settings sheet

Next, specify the X data range, the worksheet range that contains the *labels* you want to place along the *x axis* (horizontal axis). Recall from Carl's sketch (Figure 5-1b) that you are using the years 1985, 1986, 1987, and 1988 as the x-axis labels.

❸ Select X to specify the X data range. 1-2-3 reveals Carl's worksheet.

❹ Move the cell pointer to cell B10, the first label to appear on the x axis. Press **[.]** (Period) to anchor the cell. Then highlight the range B10..E10 and press **[Enter]** to specify the X data range.

Now use the same method to specify the first data series, sales of General Motors cars from 1985 to 1988, to appear in the graph. The first data series is assigned to the A data range of your 1-2-3 graph menu.

❺ Select A to specify the A data range from the Graph menu. Move the cell pointer to B12, the cell containing General Motors sales data for l985. Press **[.]** to anchor the cell. Highlight B12..E12. See Figure 5-6a.

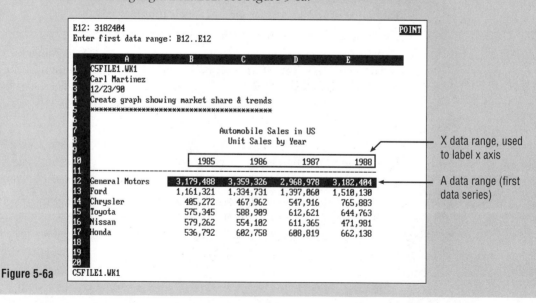

X data range, used to label x axis

A data range (first data series)

Figure 5-6a

⑥ Press **[Enter]**.

The graph settings sheet now indicates the graph type and the X and A ranges you specified. See Figure 5-6b. You can graph up to six data series at one time. 1-2-3 uses the letters A through F to represent these data series.

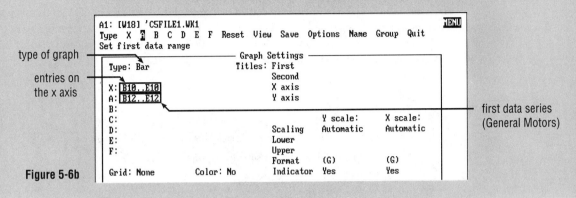

type of graph

entries on
the x axis

Figure 5-6b

first data series
(General Motors)

Viewing the Current Graph

After you have chosen your graph type and specified the data ranges, you can view the graph on the screen.

To view the graph while in the Graph menu:

❶ Select View (**V**). The graph appears on the screen. See Figure 5-7.

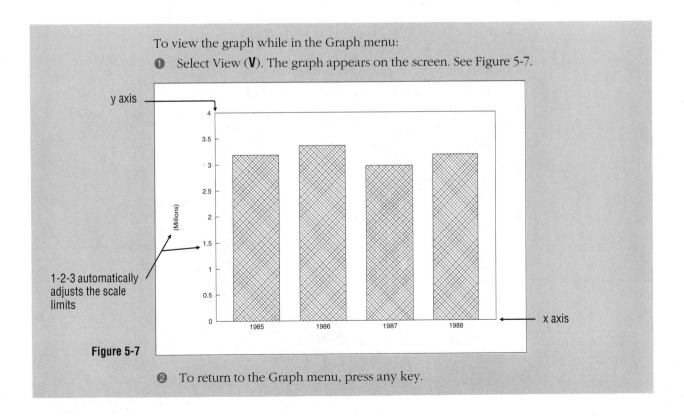

y axis

1-2-3 automatically
adjusts the scale
limits

x axis

Figure 5-7

❷ To return to the Graph menu, press any key.

Now let's leave the Graph menu and return to the worksheet.

❸   Select Quit (**Q**). Now you are in READY mode.

In 1-2-3, the graph that appears on the screen when you enter the View command is called the **current graph**. When 1-2-3 is in READY mode, you can also use [F10] (GRAPH) to display the current graph directly from the worksheet. This feature allows you to change data in your worksheet and quickly see the results graphically.

To view the current graph by using the function key [F10]:

❶   Make sure 1-2-3 is in READY mode. Check the upper right corner of your screen.

❷   Press **[F10]** (GRAPH). The current graph appears.

❸   Press any key to return to the worksheet.

If you press [F10] (GRAPH) when there is no graph type, A data range, or X data range specified in the settings sheet, your screen will become blank. If that happens, press any key to return to the worksheet.

Adding Multiple Variables

Following Carl's plan, let's continue developing the graph by returning to the Graph menu and then adding the unit sales for Ford and Chrysler, that is, the B and C data ranges, to the bar graph.

To add the B and C data ranges to the bar graph:

❶   Select /Graph (**/G**) to return to the Graph menu. The second data series, cars sold by Ford, will be assigned to the second, or B, data range.

❷   Select B to specify the B data range from the Graph menu.

❸   Move the cell pointer to B13, the cell containing Ford sales data for 1985. Press **[.]** (Period) to anchor the cell. Highlight B13..E13. Press **[Enter]**.

The graph settings sheet now indicates the graph type and the X, A, and B ranges you have specified.

Now specify the third, or C, data range, sales of Chrysler cars from 1985 to 1988.

❹   Select C, for the C data range, from the Graph menu. You will assign the data for Chrysler to this range.

Move the cell pointer to B14, the cell containing Chrysler sales data for 1985. Press **[.]** (Period) to anchor the cell. Highlight B14..E14 and press **[Enter]**.

The graph settings sheet now indicates the graph type and the X, A, B, and C ranges you have specified. See Figure 5-8.

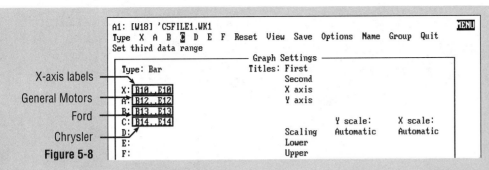

X-axis labels
General Motors
Ford
Chrysler
Figure 5-8

⑤ To view the current appearance of the graph, select View (**V**) from the Graph menu. See Figure 5-9.

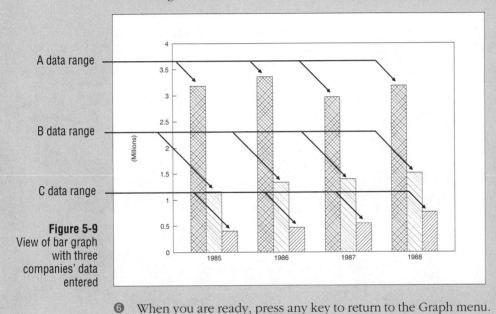

A data range

B data range

C data range

Figure 5-9
View of bar graph
with three
companies' data
entered

⑥ When you are ready, press any key to return to the Graph menu.

Experimenting with Different Graph Types

Some types of graphs may be more appropriate for your data than others. You can experiment with different types of graphs by simply selecting another graph type from the Graph menu. You can display the same data in different forms and see which form best presents the information. Let's illustrate this by changing the graph you just created to a line graph and then to a stacked bar graph.

To change graph type to a line graph:
① Select Type Line (**TL**) and then select View (**V**). The data appear as a line graph. See Figure 5-10 on the next page.

1-2-3 automatically scales the values along the y axis based on the values from the three data series (A, B, and C data ranges). For example, in 1985 General Motors sold 3,179,488 cars. On the y axis, this is shown as 3.2 million. 1-2-3 has automatically scaled this data and added the label "Millions" to the y axis. This automatic scaling occurs for bar and stacked bar graphs, as well.

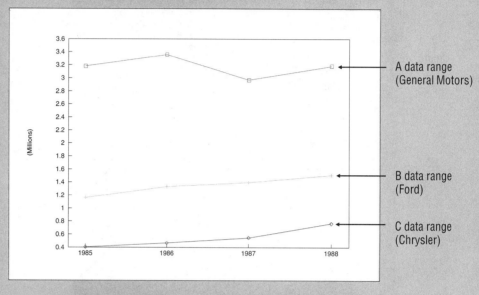

Figure 5-10
View of Carl's data as a line graph

❷   Press any key to return to the Graph menu.

Now let's see how a stacked bar graph displays the data.

To display a stacked bar graph:

❶   Select Type and Stack-Bar (**TS**).

❷   Select View (**V**). See Figure 5-11.

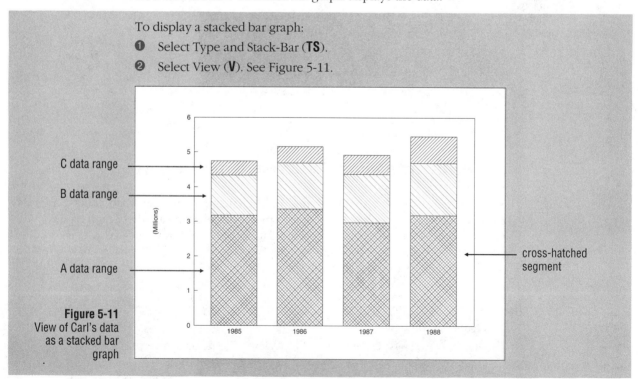

Figure 5-11
View of Carl's data as a stacked bar graph

1-2-3 displays the data as a stacked bar graph. This graph has a single bar for every value in the X data range, that is, a bar for each year. Each bar is made up of cross-hatched segments. Each segment of a bar represents the sales that each manufacturer contributed to total domestic sales in that year. Each bar viewed as a whole shows the total domestic sales in each year.

❸ Press any key to return to the Graph menu.

Carl decides that the relationship between the different companies over the small number of time periods can best be shown by a bar graph. Let's return the graph settings to a bar graph.

To return the graph settings sheet to a bar graph:

❶ Select Type Bar (**TB**).

❷ Select View (**V**). The bar graph appears on your screen.

❸ When you are ready, press any key to return to the Graph menu.

Carl decides not to try another popular type of graph, the pie chart, because it is not appropriate for the type of data with which he is working — data over time. A pie chart is more appropriate to show the relationship of the sales of each automobile company to total sales for a single year. You will create pie charts later in this tutorial.

Adding Titles and Legends

The current form of Carl's graph is difficult to interpret. What information does his graph represent? It has no title or labels to help anyone viewing the graph interpret the information. With 1-2-3, you can include a one- or two-line title and also label your x and y axes. Titles can be up to 39 characters.

Which bar in the graph represents General Motors sales? Ford sales? Chrysler sales? When you graph multiple data series, you should add a legend to identify the various lines on a line graph, the bars on a bar graph, or the segments on a stacked bar graph. The legend appears at the bottom of a graph. You can add a legend of up to 19 characters for each data series.

Now you will add titles and legends to the bar graph you've created.

To add titles and legends:

❶ From the Graph menu, select Options Titles First (**OTF**) to indicate you are entering the *first* line of the title.

❷ Type **U.S. Auto Manufacturers**, the title of Carl's graph, and then press **[Enter]**.

❸ Select Titles Second (**TS**) to indicate you are entering the second line of the title.

❹ Type **Domestic Sales** for the second line of the graph, then press **[Enter]**.

Now enter the legend for each car company.

❺ Select Legend A (**LA**) from the Graph menu. Then type **General Motors** to specify the legend for the A data range. Press **[Enter]** to enter the legend setting.

❻ Select Legend B (**LB**) and type **Ford** for the legend for the B data range. Press **[Enter]**.

❼ Select Legend C (**LC**) and type **Chrysler** for the legend for the C data range. Press **[Enter]**. See Figure 5-12.

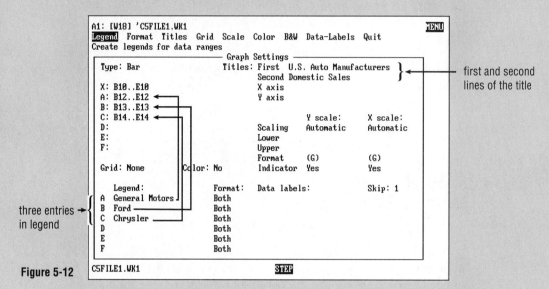

Figure 5-12

❽ Select Quit (**Q**) to leave the Options menu.

❾ Select View (**V**) to display the graph with the title and the legend. See Figure 5-13.

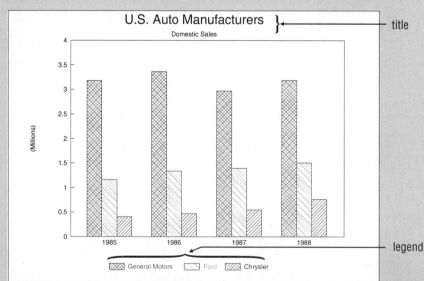

Figure 5-13
View of Carl's bar graph with title and legend

❿ Press any key to return to the Graph menu.

Adding Axis Titles

You can add titles for both the horizontal (x) and the vertical (y) axes. Currently 1-2-3 indicates that the values on the y axis are in the millions. Millions of what? You can also add an axis title to improve the description of the y axis. The next step shows you how.

To add a y-axis title:

❶ From the Graph menu, choose Options Titles Y axis (**OTY**).

❷ Type **UNITS SOLD**, being sure to leave a space between each letter. Press **[Enter]**.

❸ Select Quit (**Q**) to return to the Graph menu.

❹ Select View (**V**) to see the revised graph. See Figure 5-14.

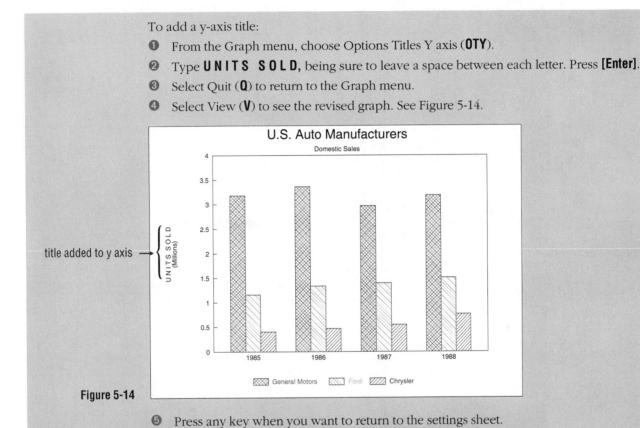

Figure 5-14

❺ Press any key when you want to return to the settings sheet.

❻ Select Quit (**Q**) to leave the Graph menu.

Naming the Current Graph

Carl plans to create several graphs within his worksheet. To have more than one graph available within your worksheet, you must assign a name to each graph. If you name this bar graph now, 1-2-3 stores all the settings needed to create this graph. Then whenever you want, you can view the graph without having to specify all the settings again.

Let's learn how to create named graphs in 1-2-3 by naming this bar graph BAR_BIG3. Note that the bar graph is the current graph, because it is the one you have most recently entered.

To name the current graph:

❶ Select /Graph Name Create (**/GNC**). The graph settings sheet appears on the screen, showing the settings that will be assigned to the named graph.

Figure 5-15a illustrates the current worksheet in the computer's memory.

You can enter a name of up to 15 characters. As with range names, spaces within a name and certain characters are not allowed. It's often a helpful reminder to include the type of graph in the name you choose.

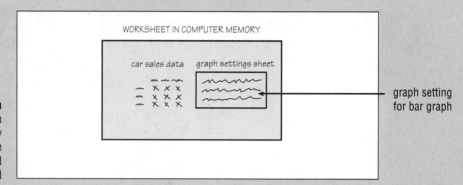

Figure 5-15a
Worksheet in memory immediately before /Graph Name Create command executed

❷ Type **BAR_BIG3** as the name of the graph and press **[Enter]**. You won't see any change in the settings sheet; this name does not appear on the settings sheet, but it does store the information found on the graph settings sheet as part of the worksheet. Figure 5-15b shows that the current graph settings are now named BAR_BIG3 and stand as part of the worksheet within the computer's memory.

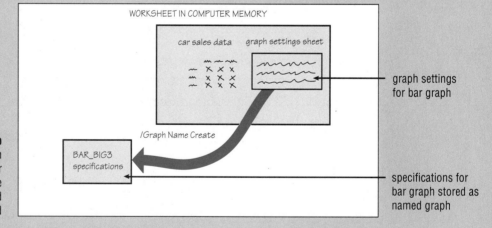

Figure 5-15b
Worksheet in memory after /Graph Name Create command executed

❸ Select Quit (**Q**) to leave the Graph menu and return to Ready mode. It is important to realize that when you name a graph you have not saved the graph specification to disk. You have only modified the worksheet in the computer memory. To include a named graph as part of a worksheet file on disk, you must use the File Save command.

❹ Save the worksheet file, which includes the named graph BAR_BIG3, as S5FILE1.WK1.

Now when you save your worksheet, each graph setting for the named graphs is saved as part of the worksheet. If you haven't named a graph, the settings for that graph will not be saved as part of the worksheet file. For example, earlier in the tutorial you created a line graph and a stacked bar graph. You did not, however, create a named graph for either of these graphs. Therefore, they were not saved as part of S5FILE1.WK1. See Figure 5-15c.

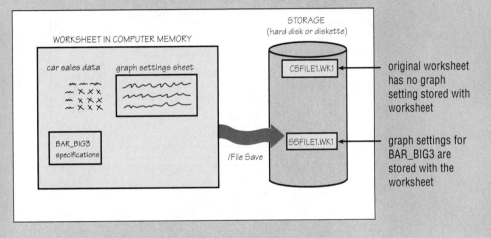

Figure 5-15c
Worksheet stored on Data Disk after /File Save command executed

Resetting Graph Settings

Once you have named a graph, you can define another graph. First, you may need to erase some or all of the current graph settings. You can erase the graph settings for the current graph by using the Graph Reset command.

To erase *all* the current graph settings:

❶ Select /Graph Reset (**/GR**). See Figure 5-16 on the next page.

You can reset each setting individually, or you can reset the entire graph.

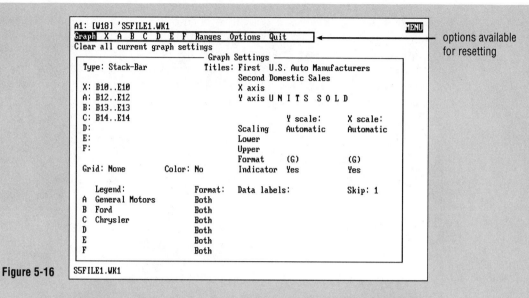

A1: [W18] 'S5FILE1.WK1   MENU
Graph X A B C D E F Ranges Options Quit   ←——— options available
Clear all current graph settings   for resetting
                        ┌─── Graph Settings ───┐
   Type: Stack-Bar   Titles: First U.S. Auto Manufacturers
                                    Second Domestic Sales
   X: B10..E10   X axis
   A: B12..E12   Y axis U N I T S   S O L D
   B: B13..E13
   C: B14..E14   Y scale: X scale:
   D: Scaling   Automatic   Automatic
   E: Lower
   F: Upper
                               Format   (G)   (G)
   Grid: None   Color: No   Indicator   Yes   Yes

      Legend: Format: Data labels: Skip: 1
   A General Motors   Both
   B Ford   Both
   C Chrysler   Both
   D   Both
   E   Both
   F   Both

Figure 5-16   S5FILE1.WK1

❷   Select Graph (**G**) to erase all the graph settings.

The current settings disappear from the graph settings sheet. See Figure 5-17.

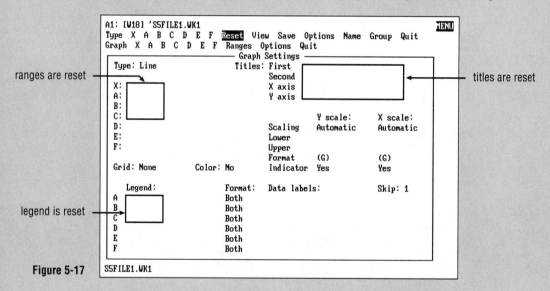

A1: [W18] 'S5FILE1.WK1   MENU
Type X A B C D E F Reset View Save Options Name Group Quit
Graph X A B C D E F Ranges Options Quit
                        ┌─── Graph Settings ───┐
   Type: Line   Titles: First ┌──────────────┐
ranges are reset ———   Second │   │ ——— titles are reset
   X: ┌──────────┐   X axis │   │
   A: │   │   Y axis └──────────────┘
   B: │   │
   C: │   │   Y scale: X scale:
   D: │   │   Scaling   Automatic   Automatic
   E: │   │   Lower
   F: └──────────┘   Upper
                              Format   (G)   (G)
   Grid: None   Color: No   Indicator   Yes   Yes

      Legend: Format: Data labels: Skip: 1
   A ┌──────────┐   Both
   B │   │   Both
legend is reset —→ C │   │ Both
   D │   │   Both
   E └──────────┘   Both
   F   Both

Figure 5-17   S5FILE1.WK1

❸   Select View (**V**). No graph appears because there are no current graph settings.

❹   Press any key to return to the graph settings sheet.

Even though the graph settings are cleared from the screen, the settings for BAR_BIG3 are still stored in memory as part of the worksheet. These settings are available by retrieving the named graph BAR_BIG3.

Retrieving a Named Graph

You were not able to view the bar graph after you erased the graph settings. However, since you have named your graph, the settings are still part of the worksheet. You can display the bar graph by selecting it from a list of named graph settings.

To view a named graph:

❶ Select Name Use (**NU**). 1-2-3 displays the names of all the different graph settings that are part of this worksheet. In this case, only one graph name appears because you have named only one so far in this tutorial.

❷ Highlight BAR_BIG3. Press **[Enter]** to view the graph. The bar graph appears on the screen. 1-2-3 has retrieved the graph settings for BAR_BIG3 that were stored as part of the worksheet and entered them as the current graph settings.

❸ Press any key. The graph settings sheet now contains the settings for the bar graph. See Figure 5-18.

❹ Select Quit (**Q**) to return to the worksheet.

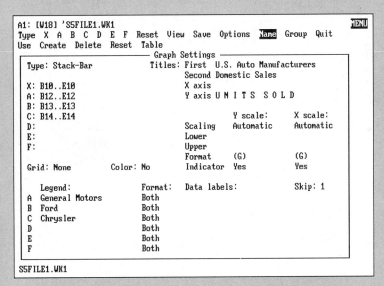

Figure 5-18
Current settings
for bar graph

Creating a Pie Chart

Now that Carl has looked at automobile sales over time, he decides to focus on sales in a single year — 1988, the last year for which he has complete data. A pie chart is a useful way to visualize data for an entire year, because pie charts typically represent the relative contribution of each part to the whole. The larger the slice, the greater that part's percentage of the whole. When you create a pie chart, you need:

- The set of values that represent the slices of the pie
- The set of labels that identify each slice of the pie chart

Before you can enter the settings for the pie chart, you must erase the bar graph settings.

To erase the current graph settings:

❶ Select /Graph (**/G**). Notice that the settings for the bar graph are the current settings.

❷ Select Reset Graph (**RG**). This erases the settings for the bar graph. See Figure 5-19.

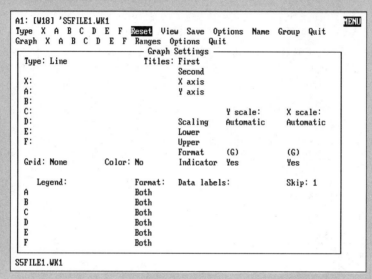

Figure 5-19
Graph settings
erased

Selecting the A Range

Now Carl can begin to enter the settings for the pie chart.

To create a pie chart for the number of cars sold in 1988:

❶ Select Type Pie (**TP**). The pie chart becomes the current graph type. The A data range is used to indicate the set of values that represent the slices of the pie.

❷ Select A, the range representing the set of values in the pie chart.

❸ Move the cell pointer to E12, number of cars sold by General Motors for 1988, and press **[.]** to anchor the cell. Highlight E12..E17 and press **[Enter]**. See Figure 5-20.

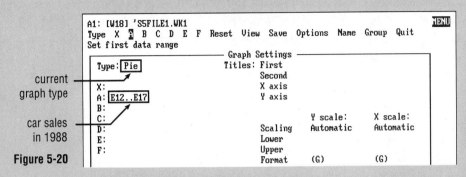

current
graph type

car sales
in 1988

Figure 5-20

❹ Select View (**V**) to view the status of your graph. See Figure 5-21.

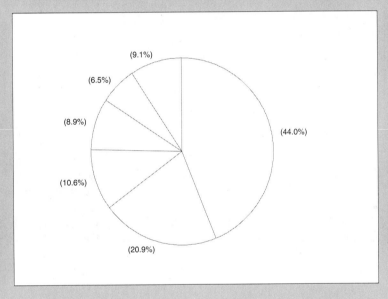

Figure 5-21
A view of Carl's
unlabelled
pie chart

Selecting the X range

As you view the graph, you cannot tell which car manufacturer is represented by which slice. Thus, you need to specify in the X range the labels that describe each slice. You will use the names of the car manufacturers in column A of the worksheet as the labels for the slices of the pie chart.

To label each pie slice:

❶ Press any key to return to Graph menu.

❷ Select X.

❸ Move the cell pointer to A12, the cell holding the label General Motors. Press **[.]** to anchor the cell. Highlight A12..A17. Press **[Enter]**. Note that the labels in the X range correspond to the elements in the A range, that is, the first label in the X range will be the label of the first slice in the A range, and so on.

❹ Press View (**V**) to view the pie chart. See Figure 5-22. Now you can identify each slice in the pie chart with a manufacturer.

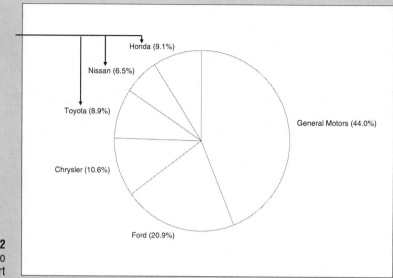

Figure 5-22
Labels added to
Carl's pie chart

❺ When you are ready, press any key to return to the Graph menu.

To help readers interpret your pie chart, you should add titles describing the pie chart. 1-2-3 allows you to include two title lines to the pie chart. Recall that Carl's sketch of the pie chart had a two-line title:

U.S. CAR SALES
1988

To add titles to the pie chart:

❶ Select Options Titles First (**OTF**) to add the first line of the title.

❷ Type **U.S. CAR SALES**, then press **[Enter]**.

❸ Select Titles Second (**TS**) to add the second line of the title.

❹ Type **1988** and press **[Enter]**.

❺ Select Quit (**Q**) to leave the Options menu.

❻ Select View (**V**) to see the title you have added to the graph. See Figure 5-23.

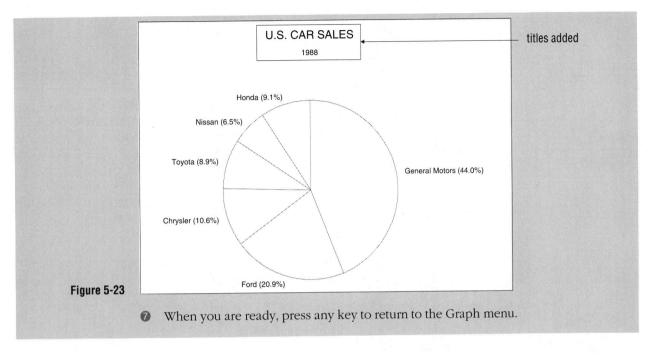

Figure 5-23

❼ When you are ready, press any key to return to the Graph menu.

Let's now assign a name to the pie chart so its settings will be stored with the worksheet.

To assign a name to the pie chart:

❶ Select Name Create (**NC**).

❷ Type **PIE_88**, a descriptive name for this chart. Press **[Enter]**. Figure 5-24 shows that the current graph settings are now nameed PIE_88 and stored as part of the work-sheet in the computer's memory.

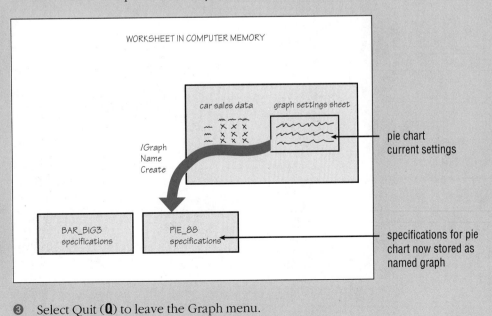

Figure 5-24
Worksheet in
computer memory
after /Graph Name
Create command
executed

❸ Select Quit (**Q**) to leave the Graph menu.

Selecting the B Range

To make the pie chart easier to read, shading (cross-hatched patterns) can be added to each slice of the pie chart. You use the B data range to add shading to your pie chart. The B data range is set up in your worksheet to correspond to the elements in the A data range. Each cell in the B range is associated with one cell in the A range. In each cell of the B range, you can enter a number between 1 and 7. 1-2-3 associates these numbers, when used in the B range of the graph settings for a pie chart, with different cross-hatched patterns. A value of 0, 8, or blank assigned to cells in the B range indicates you do not want shading in the associated slice.

Let's use cells F12 to F17 to enter the shading codes. The first cell, F12, will identify General Motors. The second cell, F13, will identify Ford. The final cell, F17, will identify Honda. In this graph you will assign shading to the slices for General Motors, Chrysler, and Nissan.

To assign cross-hatched pattern codes for slices of the pie chart:

❶ Move the cell pointer to cell F12, type **1,** and then press **[Enter]**. This code will assign a pattern to the General Motors' slice.

❷ Move the cell pointer to cell F14, type **2,** and then press **[Enter]**. This code will assign a pattern to Chyrsler's slice.

❸ Move the cell pointer to cell F16, type **3**, and then press **[Enter]**. This code will assign a pattern to Nissan's slice. See Figure 5-25.

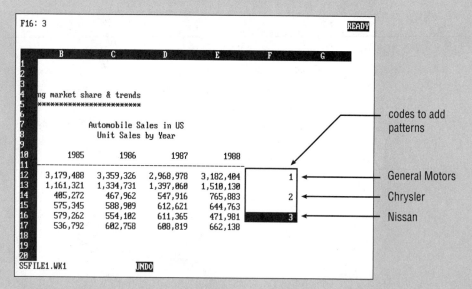

Figure 5-25

Notice that the cells identifying Ford (cell F13), Toyota (cell F15), and Honda (cell F17) are blank. 1-2-3 interprets these blank cells as zero, and no cross-hatched pattern will fill these slices of the pie chart. We have intentionally left these cells blank, because too many cross-hatched patterns make it difficult to distinguish slices.

For the shading to be included in the pie chart, the B range must be included in the graph settings.

To define the B range in the graph settings:

❶ Select /Graph B (**/GB**).

❷ Move the cell pointer to cell F12, the cell that corresponds to the first cell of the A data range. Press [**.**] to anchor the cell. Then highlight the range F12..F17 and press [**Enter**]. The B range is now included in the graph settings. See Figure 5-26.

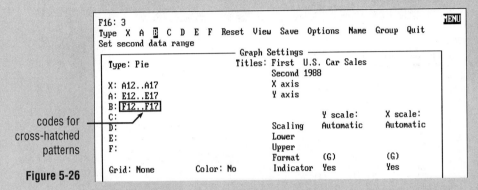

codes for cross-hatched patterns

Figure 5-26

Be sure to highlight all cells in this range even though some may be blank. The B data range *must* contain the same number of cells as the pie chart's A data range.

❸ Select View (**V**) to display the new pie chart. See Figure 5-27.

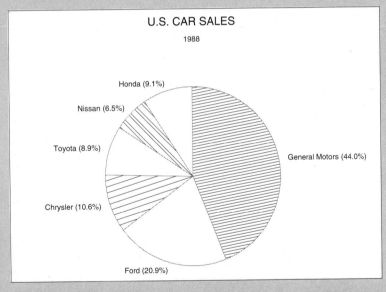

Figure 5-27
Pie chart with shading

❹ When you are ready, press any key to return to the Graph menu.

You can call even more attention to a slice of the pie chart by "exploding" it, that is, separating it from the rest of the pie. In 1-2-3, you indicate that a slice is to be exploded by adding 100 to whatever the value is in the B range. For example, if the value is 2, you would enter 102 in the B range.

The next steps show you how to set up and use the B data range for exploding pie slices. Let's explode the slice representing Chrysler.

First, leave the graph menu:

❶ Select Quit (**Q**) to return to the worksheet.

❷ Move the cell pointer to F14, type **102,** and press **[Enter]**. See Figure 5-28.

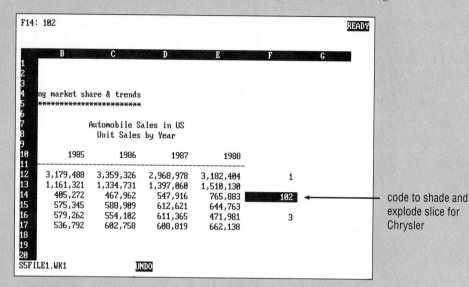

code to shade and explode slice for Chrysler

Figure 5-28

❸ Press **[F10]** (GRAPH) to view the pie chart. See Figure 5-29.

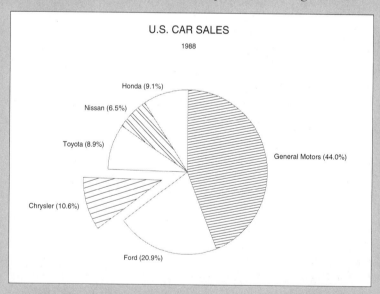

Figure 5-29
Pie chart with shading and "exploded" slice

❹ When you are ready, press any key to return to READY mode.

Let's now assign a name to the pie chart so its settings will be stored with the worksheet.

To assign a name to the pie chart:

❶ Select /Graph Name Create (**/GNC**).

❷ Type **PIE_88S**. Press **[Enter]**. Figure 5-30 shows that the current graph settings are now named PIE_88S and are stored as part of the worksheet in the computer's memory.

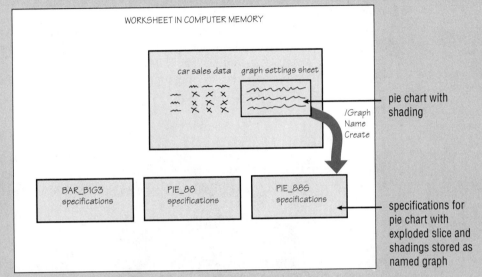

Figure 5-30
Worksheet in computer memory after /Graph Name Create command executed

❸ Select Quit (**Q**) to leave the Graph menu.

❹ Select /File Save (**/FS**), press **[Enter],** and select Replace (**R**). The current worksheet replaces the previous version of S5FILE1.WK1. This saved worksheet now includes three named graphs: BAR_BIG3, PIE_88, and PIE_88S. See Figure 5-31.

The use of the B range for shading and exploding slices applies to pie charts only. For other graph types, the B range is used for data. Except for this special use of the B range, pie charts use only the X and A ranges.

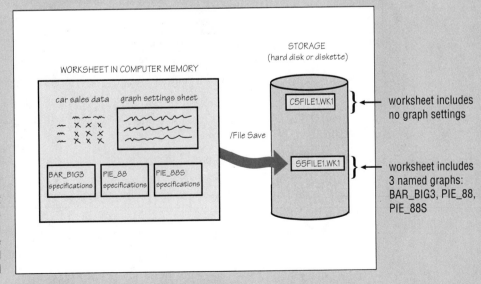

Figure 5-31
Current worksheet replaces S5FILE1.WK1 on Data Disk after /File Save command executed

Saving Graphs for Printing

In the previous section, you learned how to transform Carl's data into graphs. In this section, you will print two of the graphs you created and named. To print a graph, you must take two steps: (1) save the graphs for printing with the Graph Save command and (2) print the graph with the Lotus PrintGraph program.

You must use a special command — the Graph Save command — to save a graph that you want to print. Saving the worksheet by using /File Save only saves *named* graphs for later *viewing*, but not for printing. The /File Save command does *not* create the type of files the PrintGraph program needs to print a graph. To save a graph for printing, you *must use the Graph Save command*. In the next steps, you learn how to save graphs specifically for printing.

To save a graph for printing:

❶ Select /Graph Name Use (**/GNU**) to list the named graphs. Next, retrieve PIE_88, the chart you will print.

❷ Highlight **PIE_88**. Press **[Enter]**. The first pie chart you created and named appears on the screen.

❸ Press any key to return to the Graph menu. The graph settings for the pie chart appear in the graph settings sheet. See Figure 5-32.

shading and exploded part no longer part of the settings

Figure 5-32

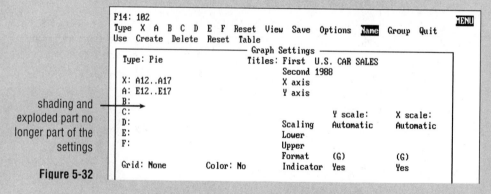

❹ Select Save (**S**) from the Graph menu. Only the current graph can be saved for printing.

Enter a name for the graph file. DOS limits the filename to eight characters, as it does for worksheet names.

❺ Type **PIE_US88** and press **[Enter]**.

1-2-3 saves the graph in a file named PIE_US88.PIC; it automatically adds the extension .PIC. Each graph that you want to print must be saved as a separate .PIC file. See Figure 5-33.

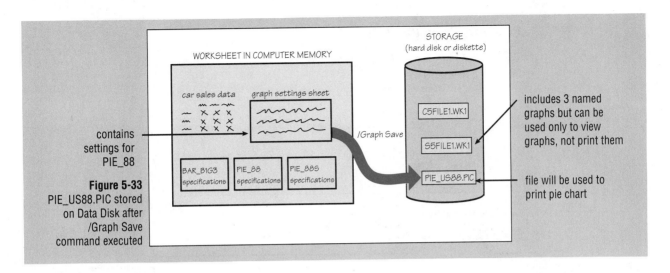

contains settings for PIE_88

Figure 5-33
PIE_US88.PIC stored on Data Disk after /Graph Save command executed

includes 3 named graphs but can be used only to view graphs, not print them

file will be used to print pie chart

Now let's save the bar graph so you can also print it.

To save the bar graph for printing:

❶ Select Name Use (**NU**) from the Graph menu. Next, retrieve BAR_BIG3, the bar graph you will print.

❷ Highlight BAR_BIG3. Press **[Enter]**. The bar graph appears on your screen, and the graph settings for the bar graph are now the current graph settings.

❸ Press any key to return to the Graph menu.

❹ Select Save (**S**).

❺ Type the graph filename **BAR_US**. See Figure 5-34. 1-2-3 saves the graph in a file named BAR_US.PIC.

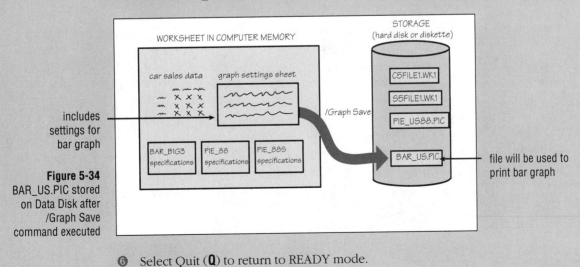

includes settings for bar graph

Figure 5-34
BAR_US.PIC stored on Data Disk after /Graph Save command executed

file will be used to print bar graph

❻ Select Quit (**Q**) to return to READY mode.

Finding Your PIC Files

To check what graph (.PIC) files are on your disk or in your data directory, you can use the File List commands.

To display a list of the .PIC files:

❶   Select /File List Graph (**/FLG**). See Figure 5-35. A list of the files that have the extension .PIC extension appears.

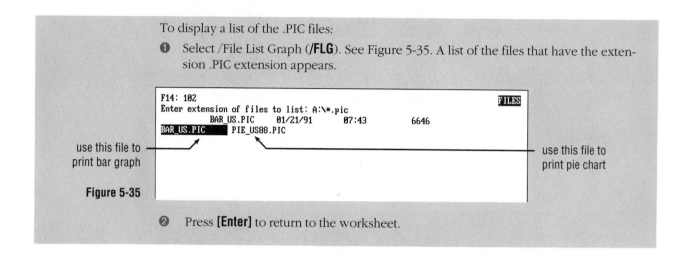

use this file to print bar graph

Figure 5-35

use this file to print pie chart

❷   Press **[Enter]** to return to the worksheet.

Using PrintGraph

The **PrintGraph** program is a separate program that comes with 1-2-3 to enable you to print graphs. With PrintGraph, you can print any graph you have previously saved with the Graph Save command.

To start PrintGraph:

❶   Select /Quit Yes (**QY**) to quit 1-2-3 and display the Access menu. If you are using a *hard-disk system*, skip to Step 4. If you are using a *two-disk system*, you must first leave the Access system before you start PrintGraph.

❷   For two-disk users *only*: insert your DOS disk in drive A. Then select Exit (**E**) to leave the Access system.

❸   For two-disk system users *only*: insert the PrintGraph disk in drive A and type **lotus**.

❹   Select PrintGraph (**P**) from the Access menu. The menu of PrintGraph commands appears at the top of the screen, and the current settings of PrintGraph appear below. Your screen should look similar to Figure 5-36.

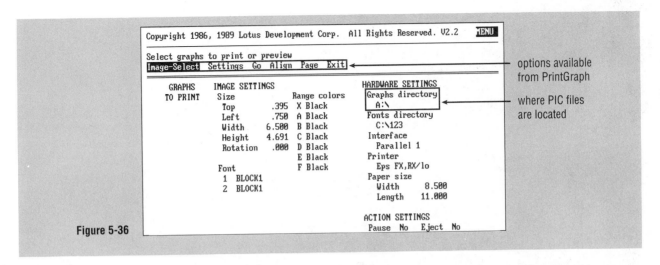

```
Copyright 1986, 1989 Lotus Development Corp.  All Rights Reserved. V2.2   MENU

Select graphs to print or preview
Image-Select  Settings  Go  Align  Page  Exit

        GRAPHS     IMAGE SETTINGS                  HARDWARE SETTINGS
       TO PRINT    Size              Range colors  Graphs directory
                    Top      .395    X Black          A:\
                    Left     .750    A Black        Fonts directory
                    Width   6.500    B Black          C:\123
                    Height  4.691    C Black        Interface
                    Rotation .000    D Black          Parallel 1
                                     E Black        Printer
                   Font              F Black          Eps FX,RX/lo
                    1  BLOCK1                        Paper size
                    2  BLOCK1                          Width    8.500
                                                       Length  11.000

                                                    ACTION SETTINGS
                                                     Pause  No  Eject  No
```

options available
from PrintGraph

where PIC files
are located

Figure 5-36

If this is the first time you have ever started PrintGraph, the program assumes that your graph (.PIC) files and font (.FNT) files are located either on a PrintGraph Disk in drive A or, if you are using a hard-disk system, in your 1-2-3 directory. **Fonts** are the typefaces used to print the graph text.

Look at the rightmost column of the PrintGraph settings sheet at the entries under Graphs directory and Fonts directory. You might need to adjust the disk/directory information for your Graph and Font directories and be sure your printer is specified properly. If necessary, ask your instructor or technical support person for assistance. The next steps show you how to change the PrintGraph settings in case the current settings are not correct for your system. Once you make and save these changes, you will not need to go through these steps again unless you make a change in your system.

To adjust the default PrintGraph settings, you first must specify the directory that contains the graph (.PIC) files so PrintGraph knows where to find your graphs:

❶   Select Settings Hardware Graphs-Directory (**SHG**).

❷   Enter the name of the directory or drive where you saved your graph files.

If you are using a *two-disk system*, type **b:** (or the name of the drive that contains your data) and press **[Enter]**.

If you are using a *hard-disk system*, type **c:\123\data** if you keep the data files on the hard disk or **a:** (or the name of the directory or drive that contains your data) if you keep the files on a diskette in drive A. Then press **[Enter]**.

Next, specify the directory that contains the font (.FNT) files. PrintGraph needs to access these files to print your graphs.

❸   Select Fonts-Directory (**F**).

❹   Enter the name of the directory or drive where the fonts are stored.

If you are using a *two-disk system*, type **a:** or the letter for the drive with the Print-Graph disk. Press **[Enter]**.

If you are using a *hard-disk system*, type **c:\123** or the name of the directory that contains the 1-2-3 and PrintGraph programs. Press **[Enter]**.

Finally, select a graphics printer to print your graphs.

❺ Select Printer (**P**) to display a list of installed printers.

❻ Follow the on-screen instructions. Press [↓] or [↑] to highlight the printer you want to use. Press **[Space]** to mark your selection. Then press **[Enter]**. The # sign indicates the printer that you have selected for printing your graphs.

If you have a choice of low and high density, choose low density so your graphs will print more quickly. If you select high density, the quality of the graph will improve, but the graph will take longer to print.

❼ Select Quit (**Q**) to leave the Hardware menu and return to the PrintGraph menu.

❽ Select Save (**S**) to save these settings so they will appear automatically the next time you run PrintGraph.

These settings will remain as the current PrintGraph settings if you decide to print your graphs now.

Now you are ready to print the two graphs you saved as PIC files.

To print a single graph:

❶ Select Image-Select (**I**) from the PrintGraph menu to display an alphabetized list of all the graphs that have been saved for printing. See Figure 5-37.

PIC files —

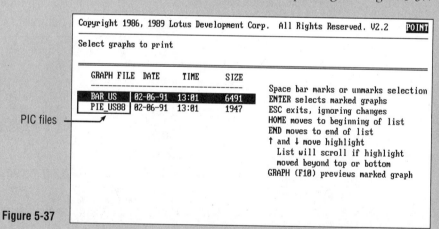

Figure 5-37

These are the files that you created with the Graph Save command and that 1-2-3 stored with a .PIC extension. Each file stores the description of one graph.

❷ Highlight BAR_US. Then press **[Space]** to mark your selection. The # sign indicates that a graph has been selected for printing. See Figure 5-38.

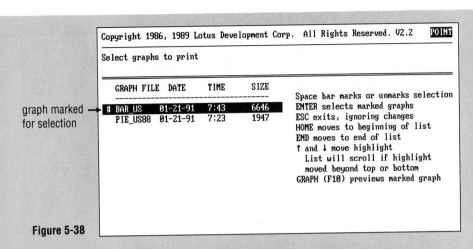

graph marked
for selection

Figure 5-38

If you change your mind about which graph to select, you can press [Space] to unmark the selection.

❸ Press **[F10]** (GRAPH) to preview the graph. The bar graph appears on your screen. You should always preview a graph before you print it to make sure you have selected the graph you want to print. Press any key to leave the preview and return to the Select Graph to Print screen.

❹ Press **[Enter]** to complete the selection process and return to the PrintGraph menu. Notice that a filename appears under the "Graphs to Print" section of the settings sheet. See Figure 5-39.

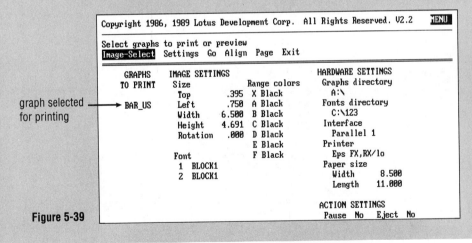

graph selected
for printing

Figure 5-39

⑤ Check that your printer is ready. Then select Align Go (**AG**) to print the first graph. See Figure 5-40.

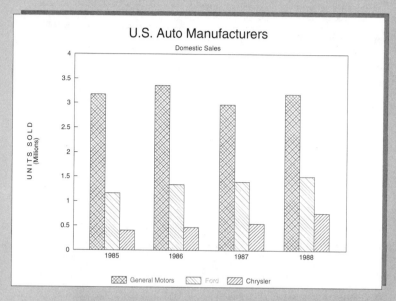

Figure 5-40

⑥ Select Page (**P**) to advance the printer to the top of the next page.

You can also print more than one graph on a page at a time.

To print more than one graph on a page:

❶ Select Image-select (**I**).

❷ Highlight the graph file PIE_US88. Press **[Space]** to mark the file PIE_US88 with a # sign. Then press **[Enter]**.

Now two graphs are selected for printing. See Figure 5-41. If your printer uses single sheets, go to Step 5.

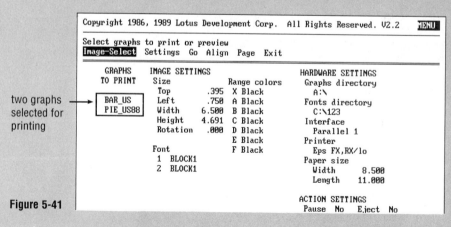

Figure 5-41

③ Select Settings Image Size Half (**SISH**) to print each of these images on half a page.

④ Select Quit (**Q**) three times to return to the PrintGraph menu.

⑤ Select Align Go and Page (**AGP**) to print the two graphs. See Figure 5-42.

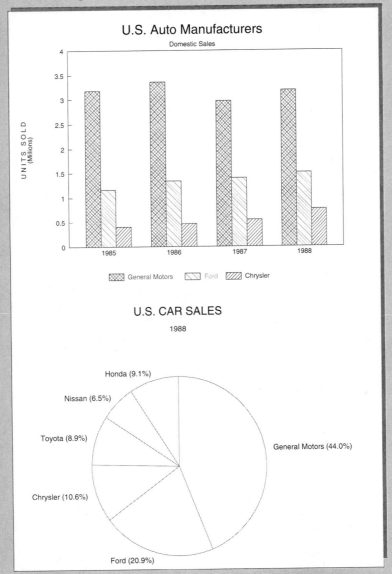

Figure 5-42

⑥ Select Exit Yes (**EY**) to leave PrintGraph. You are now at the Access menu.

⑦ Select Exit (**E**) to leave the Access menu and return to DOS.

Exercises

1. Use Figure 5-43 to identify the following components of a graph:
    a. type of graph
    b. x-axis labels
    c. y-axis titles
    d. legend
    e. title
    f. x-axis title
    g. data series for projected sales

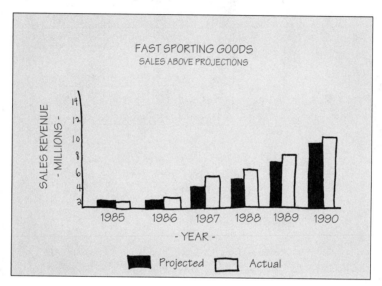

Figure 5-43

Retrieve the worksheet T5GRDEMO and do the following:

2. Save this worksheet as S5GRDEMO.

3. Make the named graph PIE1 the current graph.

4. Change the value for first-quarter revenue of plastics from 2890 to 4890.

5. View the pie chart again. Did the appearance of the graph change? If yes, how did it change?

6. Make the named graph BAR the current graph. Is this graph based on the original data from the worksheet or the new data you entered in Exercise 4?

7. Save this worksheet as S5GRDEMO.

8. Erase the worksheet from the screen.

9. On your Lotus 1-2-3 data diskette is the file T5PIE.PIC, which contains the pie chart that you viewed in Exercise 3. If you were to print T5PIE.PIC, would the graph reflect the original data in the worksheet or the data after the change you made to the worksheet data in Exercise 4?

10. If you were to retrieve the worksheet S5GRDEMO.WK1 and view the graph named PIE1, would the pie chart be based on the original data or the revised data from Exercise 4?

Tutorial Assignments

Before you begin these Tutorial Assignments, check your Lotus 1-2-3 data diskette. Be sure you have space to save the additional worksheet files you'll create in these assignments (at least 30,000 bytes). If not, save your files as appropriate to another formatted diskette.

Retrieve worksheet T5FILE1.WK1 and do the following:

1. Create a pie chart that illustrates the market share of each of the six auto manufacturers for 1987.

2. Include a title on the pie chart.

3. Explode the slice that represents Honda.

4. Name this graph PIE_87.

5. Save this graph as a .PIC file. Use the name PPIE_87.

6. Reset all the graph settings in this worksheet.

7. Prepare a bar graph showing the three Japanese companies' sales from 1985 to 1988.

8. Add a title and a legend to this graph.

9. Name this graph BAR_JPN.

10. Save this graph as a .PIC file. Use the name PBAR_JPN.

11. Change the graph to a stacked bar graph.

12. Name this graph STK_JPN.

13. Save this graph as a .PIC file. Use the name PSTK_JPN.

14. Save your worksheet as S5FILE2.

15. Print the graph file PPIE_87 on a separate page.

16. Print the graph files PBAR_JPN and PSTK_JPN on the same page.

Case Problems

1. Graphing Health Maintenance Organizations' Membership Data

Medical costs have risen dramatically over the last 10 to 15 years. Health maintenance organizations (HMOs) were created as an alternative to traditional health insurance to help decrease medical costs. HMOs provide a range of comprehensive health care services to people who pay an enrollment fee and become members. By joining an HMO, a member gains access to a team of doctors 365 days a year. Employers, labor unions, government agencies, and consumer groups often provide this type of medical coverage for their employees.

Figure 5-44 shows a table of the enrollment in HMO programs by major insurer.

Enrollment in HMOs	
Insurer	**Millions of members**
Blue Cross	15.5
Cigna	3.6
Aetna	2.5
Metropolitan	2.4
Prudential	2.2
Travelers	1.6

Figure 5-44

Use the data in Figure 5-44 to do the following:

1. Construct a pie chart.
2. Explode the Aetna segment.
3. Add appropriate titles and labels.
4. Create the named graph PIE_HMO.
5. Save your worksheet as S5HMO.
6. Save the pie chart as a .PIC file. Use the name PPIE_HMO.
7. Print the pie chart.

2. Graphing Data on Cellular Telephone Subscribers and Revenues

Many people are using cellular telephones more and more in their business and personal lives. Figure 5-45 shows the changes in the number of cellular telephone subscribers in the U.S. and the revenue they generated from 1985 through 1990.

U.S. Cellular Telephones

	1985	1986	1987	1988	1989	1990
Subscribers	200	500	1000	1600	2700	4300
Revenue	1500	4500	5000	8000	13500	21000

Figure 5-45

Create a worksheet file from the table above and do the following:

1. Create a line chart that shows the growth in number of subscribers and revenues from 1985 through 1990.

2. Enter appropriate titles and legends.

3. Create the named graph LINE_TELE for the line chart.

4. Graph this same data using a bar graph. Create the named graph BAR_TELE for the bar graph.

5. Save your worksheet as S5TELE.

6. Save each graph setting as a .PIC file. Save the line chart as PLNE_TEL and the bar graph as PBAR_TEL.

7. Print the line chart and the bar graph.

3. Using Line Charts to Analyze Stock Prices

Levon Smith, a stock analyst for the firm of Morris-Sorensen, specializes in recommending what computer industry stock investors should buy. Levon wants to analyze indexes and stock prices at the end of each month for 1990 to identify any trends. He has collected month-end data (Figure 5-46) on the following indexes and companies: Standard & Poor's 500 stock index, computer industry stock index, IBM, Digital Equipment Corporation, Cray Research, and Apple Corporation.

	S&P 500	Computer Index	Digital Equipment	IBM	Apple	Cray Research
Jan	297	205	118	130	44	64
Feb	289	213	120	130	37	61
Mar	295	195	104	121	34	60
Apr	310	189	97	116	40	59
May	321	191	90	114	49	59
Jun	318	190	86	115	50	58
Jul	346	195	90	116	40	56
Aug	351	193	105	120	45	55
Sep	349	181	104	119	46	54
Oct	340	170	84	110	50	45
Nov	346	164	84	101	47	42
Dec	353	190	80	102	45	40

Figure 5-46
Selected
month-end index
and stock prices

Retrieve the worksheet P5STOCK.WK1 and do the following:

1. Create a line chart of the month-end Standard & Poor's 500 and computer industry indexes. Remember to include a title and a legend. Name this graph LINE_MARKET.

2. Create a second line chart that includes the month-end stock prices for IBM, Digital, Cray Research, and Apple so Levon can observe the trend in stock prices for these companies. Remember to include a title and a legend. Name this graph LINE_COMPANY.

3. Save your worksheet as S5STOCK.

4. Save each line chart as a .PIC file. Save the first line graph as PLNE_MRK and the second graph as PLNE_CMP.

5. Print the graphs.

4. The U.S. Airline Industry

During the 1980s, U.S. airline companies consolidated into eight major carriers. With growth of international travel expected to exceed domestic U.S. travel in the 1990s, these eight major carriers are scrambling to increase their number of international routes. Figure 5-47 shows passenger revenues generated by international routes from 1985 through 1989 for each carrier. These numbers are rounded to the nearest million.

Passenger Revenues International Routes					
Carrier	**1985**	**1986**	**1987**	**1988**	**1989**
American	400	472	672	884	1858
Continental	249	319	526	743	843
Delta	216	227	410	634	742
Northwest	936	1094	1362	1767	2051
Pan Am	2197	1806	2088	2353	2154
TWA	1369	872	1123	1294	1321
UAL	114	802	1112	1514	1780

Figure 5-47
Passenger revenues

Figure 5-48 shows the amount of net income these eight carriers earned from their international routes from 1985 through 1989. These numbers are rounded to the nearest thousand.

Net Income International Routes					
Carrier	**1985**	**1986**	**1987**	**1988**	**1989**
American	7438	6650	−10911	−866	8723
Continental	13196	31238	46247	125272	83013
Delta	11722	8386	32028	58686	18104
Northwest	36862	49313	77146	114318	167207
Pan Am	302913	−157149	13142	−70600	−165392
TWA	−18021	−24852	49210	133499	−6051
UAL	−23662	−36840	11715	163313	100507

Figure 5-48

Retrieve the worksheet P5AIRLN.WK1. The worksheet contains Figures 5-47 and 5-48. Use the data to do the following:

1. Prepare a bar graph that illustrates passenger revenue for American, TWA, and UAL from 1985 through 1989. Remember to include appropriate titles and legends. Name this graph BAR_REV.

2. Prepare a stacked bar graph showing the same data as Problem 1. Name this graph STK_REV.

3. Prepare a bar graph comparing net income for these three companies. Name this graph BAR_INC.

4. Prepare a pie chart of passenger revenues for each carrier during 1985. Name this graph PIE_85. Remember to include appropriate titles.

5. Prepare a second pie chart with similar data for 1989. Name this graph PIE_89. Remember to include appropriate titles.

6. Save your worksheet as S5AIRLN.

7. Save the named graphs as separate .PIC files.

8. Print your graphs.

Tutorial 6

Using a Database

A Customer/Accounts Receivable Database

Case: Medi-Source Inc.

Medi-Source Inc. distributes supplies to hospitals, medical laboratories, and pharmacies throughout the United States. Files of all Medi-Source customers and accounts receivable data are available to department managers on the company's mainframe computer.

Joan Glazer, the manager of the credit and collection department, was recently reviewing these data and noticed that the outstanding balance of several Massachusetts and Rhode Island customers appeared to be higher than that of the average Medi-Source customer, which is approximately $6,000. She wants to study the accounts in these two states more carefully.

Joan asks Bert Spivak, the manager of the information systems department, to prepare several reports to help her analyze the data. Bert tells her that he and his programming staff are backed up on projects and will not be able to help her for four to six weeks. He suggests instead that he retrieve the Rhode Island and Massachusetts data from the mainframe database and provide her with a Lotus 1-2-3 file. Then she can analyze the data herself. Joan thinks this is a great idea. Bert says he'll have the data to her in two days.

While waiting for the data, Joan thinks about the analysis she will do. She decides to plan her project and makes a list of her goals, output, input and calculations (Figure 6-1a on the next page). Joan realizes the worksheet will be large and will include several sections. As a part of her planning, she develops a sketch to help organize the overall structure of the worksheet (Figure 6-1b on the next page).

OBJECTIVES

In this tutorial you will learn to:

- Define the terms *field, record, file,* and *database*

- Sort a database

- Use statistical functions: @AVG, @MAX, @MIN

- Find records that match specified criteria

- Extract records that match specified criteria

- Use database statistical functions

My Goals:
    Review the Rhode Island and Massachusetts customer database to
    determine whether balances owed by customers in those states are higher
    than average Medi-Source customers

What results do I want to see?
    List records in database by:
        customer name
        outstanding balance
        state and within state by outstanding balance
    List customers with outstanding balances above Medi-Source average
    Report showing summary statistics for RI and MA customers
    Report of outstanding balance by state

What information do I need?
    Subset of Medi-Source database – all RI and MA customer records

What calculations will I perform?
    Total outstanding balance
    Average outstanding balance
    Maximum outstanding balance
    Minimum outstanding balance
    Count number of customers

Figure 6-1a
Joan's planning
sheet

RI & MA Database
~~~~ ~~~~~~ ~~
~~~ ~~~~ ~~~~~
~~~ ~~~~ ~~~~~.

•

•

•

Criteria Range

Output Range

Summary Report
RI and MA Customers
Medi-Source

	Outstanding Balance
Total	xxxx
Average	xxxx
Maximum	xxxx
Minimum	xxxx
Count	xxxx

Outstanding Balance
by State
Medi-Source

	RI	MA
Total	xx	xx
Average	xx	xx

Figure 6-1b
Joan's worksheet
sketch

In this tutorial, you will learn some new database terms, learn how to arrange data into a meaningful order through sorting, search a database to locate and extract records that meet specific criteria, and use database statistical functions to perform statistical analysis on selected records within the database.

Introduction to File Concepts

Before you retrieve the Medi-Source file, you need to understand important terms that are critical to understanding and using computerized databases. These terms are field, record, file, and database.

A **field** is an attribute (characteristic) of some object, person, or place. For example, each item of data that Medi-Source tracks is referred to as a field or a data element. Customer #, customer name, balance customer owes, and year-to-date sales represent attributes about a customer (Figure 6-2).

Figure 6-2
Fields in Medi-Source's customer database

Customer ID
Customer Name
Address
City
State
Zip
Type of business
Credit limit
Balance owed
Year-to-date sales
Date of last sale

Related fields are grouped together to form a **record**, a collection of attributes describing a person, place, or thing. All the data about a customer, such as Bristol Pharmacy, are referred to as a record. The Bristol Pharmacy record consists of data fields such as customer #, customer name, and balance customer owes (Figure 6-3). If Medi-Source has 1,500 customers, then the company will have 1,500 records.

field names

record

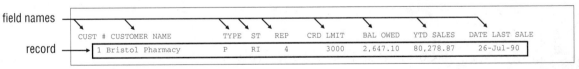

CUST #	CUSTOMER NAME	TYPE	ST	REP	CRD LMIT	BAL OWED	YTD SALES	DATE LAST SALE
1	Bristol Pharmacy	P	RI	4	3000	2,647.10	80,278.87	26-Jul-90

Figure 6-3
Bristol Pharmacy's record

A collection of related records is called a **data file**. The 1,500 customer records at Medi-Source, viewed in their entirety, represent the customer data file. Figure 6-4 shows a few of the records from the data file.

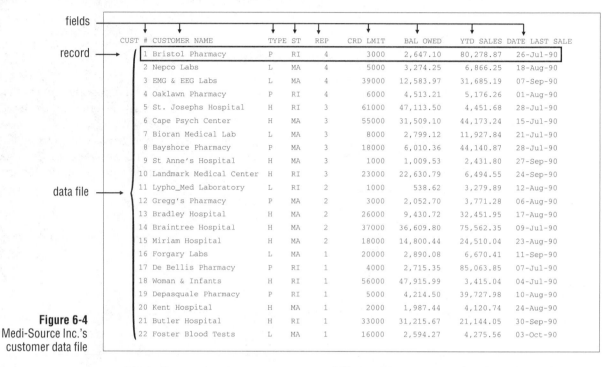

Figure 6-4
Medi-Source Inc.'s
customer data file

Typically, companies maintain many different files to store related customer data. One file stores the basic customer data; a second file stores data on each outstanding invoice; a third file tracks each payment made by a customer; a fourth file tracks customer orders that have not yet been shipped. These four files may be thought of as the customer database. Thus, a **database** is a collection of logically related files.

At Medi-Source, the credit and collection department is working with only one data file. Thus, our database in this tutorial consists of just one data file. Spreadsheet software works well when you are processing records from a single file such as this one. But when you must process data from multiple files, other software packages process the data more effectively than spreadsheets. These other software packages are referred to as **database packages.**

Retrieving the Worksheet

To retrieve the Medi-Source database:

❶ Retrieve the file C6FILE1.WK1 from your Lotus 1-2-3 data diskette. See Figure 6-5.

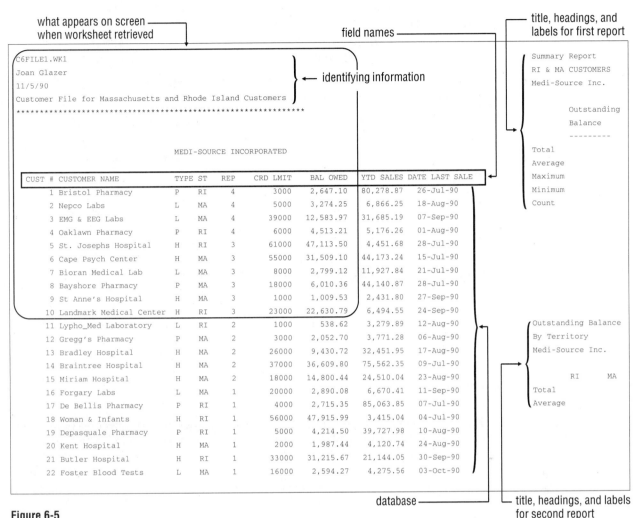

what appears on screen ———
when worksheet retrieved

field names ———

title, headings, and
labels for first report

```
C6FILE1.WK1
Joan Glazer                                          }  ← identifying information
11/5/90
Customer File for Massachusetts and Rhode Island Customers
**************************************************************

                        MEDI-SOURCE INCORPORATED


 CUST # CUSTOMER NAME        TYPE ST  REP   CRD LMIT   BAL OWED   YTD SALES DATE LAST SALE
      1 Bristol Pharmacy      P   RI   4      3000     2,647.10   80,278.87   26-Jul-90
      2 Nepco Labs            L   MA   4      5000     3,274.25    6,866.25   18-Aug-90
      3 EMG & EEG Labs        L   MA   4     39000    12,583.97   31,685.19   07-Sep-90
      4 Oaklawn Pharmacy      P   RI   4      6000     4,513.21    5,176.26   01-Aug-90
      5 St. Josephs Hospital  H   RI   3     61000    47,113.50    4,451.68   28-Jul-90
      6 Cape Psych Center     H   MA   3     55000    31,509.10   44,173.24   15-Jul-90
      7 Bioran Medical Lab    L   MA   3      8000     2,799.12   11,927.84   21-Jul-90
      8 Bayshore Pharmacy     P   MA   3     18000     6,010.36   44,140.87   28-Jul-90
      9 St Anne's Hospital    H   MA   3      1000     1,009.53    2,431.80   27-Sep-90
     10 Landmark Medical Center H RI   3     23000    22,630.79    6,494.55   24-Sep-90
     11 Lypho_Med Laboratory  L   RI   2      1000       538.62    3,279.89   12-Aug-90
     12 Gregg's Pharmacy      P   MA   2      3000     2,052.70    3,771.28   06-Aug-90
     13 Bradley Hospital      H   MA   2     26000     9,430.72   32,451.95   17-Aug-90
     14 Braintree Hospital    H   MA   2     37000    36,609.80   75,562.35   09-Jul-90
     15 Miriam Hospital       H   MA   2     18000    14,800.44   24,510.04   23-Aug-90
     16 Forgary Labs          L   MA   1     20000     2,890.08    6,670.41   11-Sep-90
     17 De Bellis Pharmacy    P   RI   1      4000     2,715.35   85,063.85   07-Jul-90
     18 Woman & Infants       H   RI   1     56000    47,915.99    3,415.04   04-Jul-90
     19 Depasquale Pharmacy   P   RI   1      5000     4,214.50   39,727.98   10-Aug-90
     20 Kent Hospital         H   MA   1      2000     1,987.44    4,120.74   24-Aug-90
     21 Butler Hospital       H   RI   1     33000    31,215.67   21,144.05   30-Sep-90
     22 Foster Blood Tests    L   MA   1     16000     2,594.27    4,275.56   03-Oct-90
```

Summary Report
RI & MA CUSTOMERS
Medi-Source Inc.

          Outstanding
          Balance

Total
Average
Maximum
Minimum
Count

Outstanding Balance
By Territory
Medi-Source Inc.

          RI   MA
Total
Average

database ———

title, headings, and labels
for second report

Figure 6-5
Joan's initial worksheet

Notice that each *row* in the database represents a customer record. The first row of the database, row 10, contains the **field names**. Field names are labels that identify the fields in a database as needed, and they *must* be in the first row of any database you use in 1-2-3.

❷ Press **[PgDn]** and **[Tab]** as needed to view the entire file.

❸ Press **[Home]** to return to cell A1.

The field names in the customer database are:

Field	Description
CUST #	Unique identification number assigned to each customer
CUSTOMER NAME	Name of each customer
TYPE	Code indicating the type of business, for example, P = Pharmacy, L = Laboratory, and H = hospital
ST	State abbreviation: RI = Rhode Island; MA = Massachusetts
REP	ID of the sales representative assigned to make sales calls on this customer
CRD LMIT	Maximum amount of credit the customer is allowed
BAL OWED	Amount of money customer currently owes Medi-Source
YTD SALES	Total sales to customer since the beginning of the year
DATE LAST SALE	Date of the last sales transaction with this customer

Now that you are familiar with the Medi-Source customer file, you are ready to manipulate the file.

Sorting Data

The Data Sort command lets you arrange the file in an order that you specify. For instance, you could arrange your data alphabetically by customer name or numerically by the amount of money the customer owes to Medi-Source.

Before performing the data sort, you need to understand three terms related to sorting data in 1-2-3: data range, primary key, and secondary key.

Data-Range

The **data range** represents the records in the database you want to sort. This range usually includes all the records in the database. The data range does *not* include the field names of the columns, because the field names are merely labels and not part of the data you want to sort. You *must* be sure to include *all* the fields (columns) for the records you specify in the data range; otherwise, you will alter the relationships among data fields in the database.

Primary Key

A field that determines the order in which you sort the database is called a **sort key**. The **primary key** (primary sort key) represents the field (column) you want 1-2-3 to use to determine the new order for the database records. For example, if you want 1-2-3 to arrange the data by the amount customers owe Medi-Source, the primary key is the field balance owed (BAL OWED).

Secondary Key

The **secondary key** (secondary sort key) represents a second field (column) to determine the sort order within the primary sort key field. For example, you might select type of customer as the primary sort key, and customer name as the secondary sort key. Thus, you could sort the data by customer type (such as hospital, lab, pharmacy) and within each customer type alphabetically by customer name. To explain this example further, all the hospital customers appear first in alphabetical order, followed by an alphabetized list of laboratory customers, and finally the pharmacy customers appear arranged in alphabetical order.

Sorting Using the Primary Key

Joan wants to sort the data alphabetically by customer name. Ordering the data by customer name will make it easier for her to locate a customer than will the current order of the database, which is by customer number.

To sort a data file by customer name:

❶ Select /Data Sort (**/DS**), and the sort settings sheet appears. See Figure 6-6.

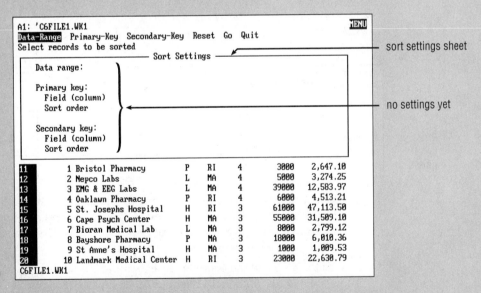

Figure 6-6

The settings sheet indicates the settings for the data range, the primary key, and the secondary key. Currently there are no settings.

Now identify the area of the worksheet to be sorted, which 1-2-3 refers to as the data range.

❷ Select Data Range (**D**). The worksheet appears on your screen.

❸ Move the cell pointer to the first cell in the data range, A11, and press **[.]** to anchor the cell. Highlight A11..I32 and press **[Enter]**. See Figure 6-7 on the next page.

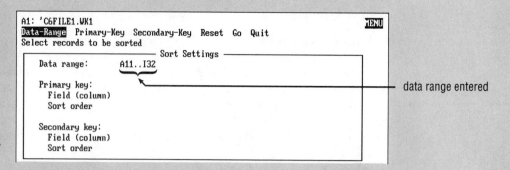

Figure 6-7

data range entered

1-2-3 enters A11..I32 as the data range on the settings sheet. Remember that field names are not part of the data range and that every column in your database should be included in the data range.

Joan wants to sort the data by customer name. Next, specify customer name as the primary sort key.

④ Select Primary-Key (**P**). Move the cell pointer to the first record in the customer field, cell B11, the customer name field, and press **[Enter]**.

Actually you can move the cell pointer to any cell in column B to indicate that the primary sort key is customer name.

Next you specify the sort order.

⑤ Type **A** to specify ascending sort order and press **[Enter]**. See Figure 6-8.

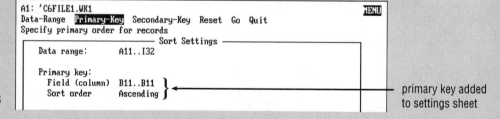

Figure 6-8

primary key added to settings sheet

Ascending order for labels means arranging the data alphabetically from A to Z and numerically from lowest to highest number. Descending order for labels means arranging the data alphabetized backward from Z to A and numerically from highest to lowest number.

⑥ Select Go (**G**) to sort the data file. When sorting is completed, your screen should show the records alphabetized by customer name. See Figure 6-9.

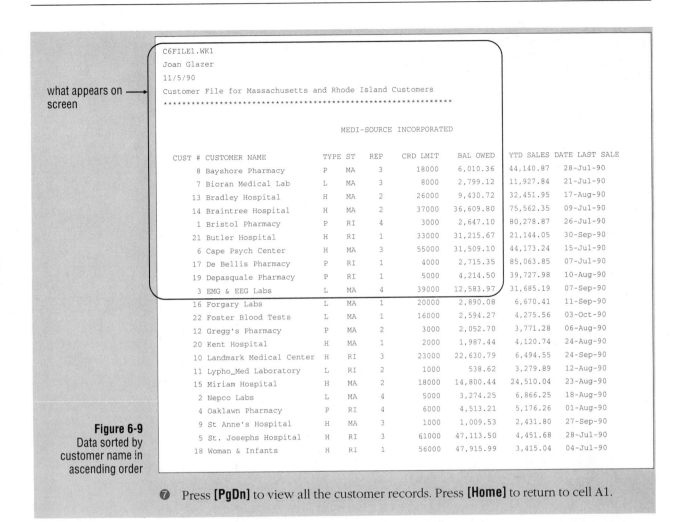

what appears on screen →

```
C6FILE1.WK1
Joan Glazer
11/5/90
Customer File for Massachusetts and Rhode Island Customers
*****************************************************************

                        MEDI-SOURCE INCORPORATED


CUST #  CUSTOMER NAME          TYPE ST  REP   CRD LMIT   BAL OWED   YTD SALES DATE LAST SALE
     8  Bayshore Pharmacy       P   MA   3      18000     6,010.36  44,140.87  28-Jul-90
     7  Bioran Medical Lab      L   MA   3       8000     2,799.12  11,927.84  21-Jul-90
    13  Bradley Hospital        H   MA   2      26000     9,430.72  32,451.95  17-Aug-90
    14  Braintree Hospital      H   MA   2      37000    36,609.80  75,562.35  09-Jul-90
     1  Bristol Pharmacy        P   RI   4       3000     2,647.10  80,278.87  26-Jul-90
    21  Butler Hospital         H   RI   1      33000    31,215.67  21,144.05  30-Sep-90
     6  Cape Psych Center       H   MA   3      55000    31,509.10  44,173.24  15-Jul-90
    17  De Bellis Pharmacy      P   RI   1       4000     2,715.35  85,063.85  07-Jul-90
    19  Depasquale Pharmacy     P   RI   1       5000     4,214.50  39,727.98  10-Aug-90
     3  EMG & EEG Labs          L   MA   4      39000    12,583.97  31,685.19  07-Sep-90
    16  Forgary Labs            L   MA   1      20000     2,890.08   6,670.41  11-Sep-90
    22  Foster Blood Tests      L   MA   1      16000     2,594.27   4,275.56  03-Oct-90
    12  Gregg's Pharmacy        P   MA   2       3000     2,052.70   3,771.28  06-Aug-90
    20  Kent Hospital           H   MA   1       2000     1,987.44   4,120.74  24-Aug-90
    10  Landmark Medical Center H   RI   3      23000    22,630.79   6,494.55  24-Sep-90
    11  Lypho_Med Laboratory    L   RI   2       1000       538.62   3,279.89  12-Aug-90
    15  Miriam Hospital         H   MA   2      18000    14,800.44  24,510.04  23-Aug-90
     2  Nepco Labs              L   MA   4       5000     3,274.25   6,866.25  18-Aug-90
     4  Oaklawn Pharmacy        P   RI   4       6000     4,513.21   5,176.26  01-Aug-90
     9  St Anne's Hospital      H   MA   3       1000     1,009.53   2,431.80  27-Sep-90
     5  St. Josephs Hospital    H   RI   3      61000    47,113.50   4,451.68  28-Jul-90
    18  Woman & Infants         H   RI   1      56000    47,915.99   3,415.04  04-Jul-90
```

Figure 6-9
Data sorted by customer name in ascending order

❼ Press **[PgDn]** to view all the customer records. Press **[Home]** to return to cell A1.

Joan also planned to sort the customer data by balance owed, with customers having the largest outstanding balance appearing first, that is, in descending order. That way Joan can quickly identify the customers that have the highest outstanding balance.

To sort a data file in descending order by balance owed:

❶ Select /Data Sort (**/DS**). 1-2-3 displays the sort settings sheet.

Since the range of cells to be sorted was previously entered and still appears in the sort settings sheet, you do not have to select the data range again.

The next step is to change the primary sort key from customer name to balance owed (BAL OWED).

❷ Select Primary-Key (**P**). Move the cell pointer to cell G11, or any cell in the BAL OWED column, and press **[Enter]**.

❸ Type **D** to specify descending sort order and press **[Enter]**. See Figure 6-10 on the next page.

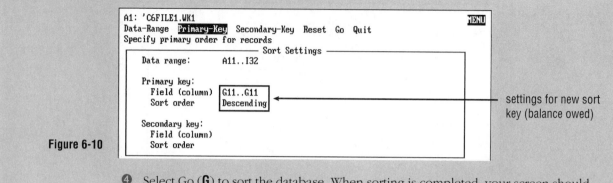

Figure 6-10

④ Select Go (**G**) to sort the database. When sorting is completed, your screen should look like Figure 6-11. Notice that the customer having the highest balance owed appears first. The customer with the lowest balanced owed is last.

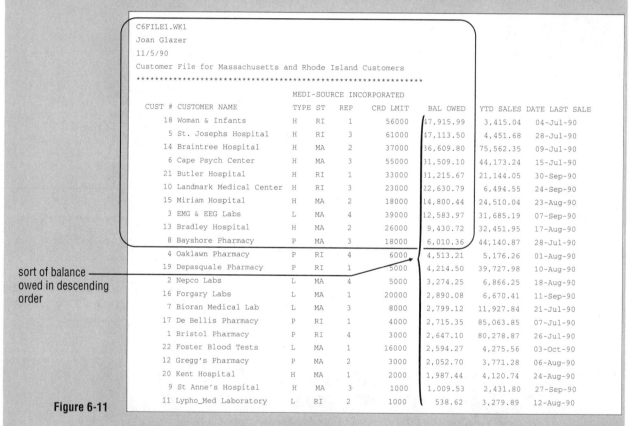

sort of balance owed in descending order

Figure 6-11

⑤ Press **[PgDn]** to view all the customer records. When you are finished viewing the records, press **[Home]** to return to cell A1.

Sorting Using a Secondary Key

You can organize data on more than one sort key. For example, Joan wants to organize the customers by state, and within each state, from highest balance owed to lowest balance owed. This will allow Joan to see which customers in each state owe the most to Medi-Source.

To sort a file on two sort keys:

❶ Select /Data Sort (**/DS**), and the sort settings sheet appears.

Since the range of cells to be sorted was previously entered and still appears in the sort settings sheet, you do not have to select the data range again.

Next specify state as the primary sort key.

❷ Select Primary-Key (**P**). Move the cell pointer to cell D11, the ST field, and press **[Enter]**.

❸ Type **A** to specify ascending sort order and press **[Enter]**.

Now specify balance owed as the secondary sort key.

❹ Select Secondary-Key (**S**). Move the cell pointer to cell G11, the BAL OWED field, and press **[Enter]**.

❺ Press **[Enter]** if D (descending) already appears as the sort order for BAL OWED. If A appears, type D and press **[Enter]**.

❻ Select Go (**G**) to sort the data file. See Figure 6-12.

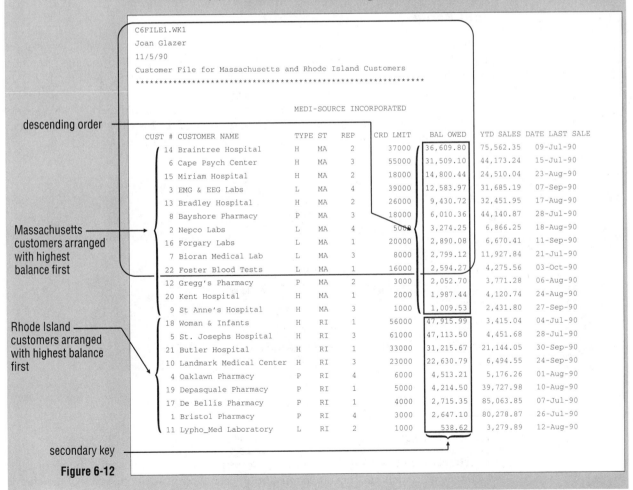

Figure 6-12

Notice that all Massachusetts customers are grouped together, followed by all customers from Rhode Island. Within each state, the customer records are arranged by balance owed, with customers having the highest balance appearing first. Joan observes that the hospital customers from both states have large outstanding balances.

Data Query Command — Finding Records

Now that Joan has sorted the data, she wants to examine specific customer accounts. While sorting the data, she noticed that customers in the hospital category have outstanding balances that are high compared to customers in the lab and pharmacy categories. So, she decides to examine these accounts first.

The Data Query command lets 1-2-3 select records that match certain criteria and finds (highlights) or extracts (copies) these records without examining every record in the database. Before 1-2-3 can find a record in the database, you must specify an input range and set up a criteria range. Let's discuss what we mean by these two ranges.

Input Range

An **input range** is the range of data, *including field names*, to be searched as part of the query. When you specify an input range to use with any Data Query command, you must include the field names as part of the range. This is unlike the data range in the Data Sort command, which does *not* include the field names.

You can assign a range name to represent the input range, although 1-2-3 does not require that you do this to execute the Data Query command. This will allow you to specify the database without having to remember the exact cell locations of your database.

To assign a range name to the database:

❶ Move the cell pointer to cell A10, the upper left corner of the database. Remember when you use the Data Query command, you must include the field names in the input range.

❷ Select /Range Name Create (**/RNC**).

❸ Type the name **DATABASE** and press **[Enter]**.

❹ Highlight the database cells A10..I32. Press **[Enter]**. The range name DATABASE has been assigned to this range of cells.

Again, note that the range includes the field names and the data records.

Criteria Range

The **criteria range** is a small area in your worksheet where you describe the records for which you are searching. This range must be at least two rows. The first row of the criteria range contains some or all of the field names from the database. The field names in the criteria range must be identical to the database field names. The rows below the field names in the criteria range include the search criteria.

The criteria range is often established below the database. Let's use cells A35 to I36. In the first row of the criteria range, you must enter the criteria field names. Since these names must be *identical* to the database field names, it is best to copy the database field names to the criteria range, so no difference can occur between the database field names and the criteria field names.

To copy the database fields names to the criteria range:

❶ Make sure the cell pointer is in cell A10, the location of the first database field name to be copied.

❷ Select /Copy (**/C**).

❸ Highlight A10..I10 and press **[Enter]**.

❹ Now move the cell pointer to cell A35, the location where you will place the field names for the criteria range. Then press **[Enter]**.

❺ Move the cell pointer to cell A35, so you can see that the database field names have been copied to the criteria range. See Figure 6-13.

```
C6FILE1.WK1
Joan Glazer
11/5/90
Customer File for Massachusetts and Rhode Island Customers
****************************************************************

                              MEDI-SOURCE INCORPORATED


CUST #  CUSTOMER NAME        TYPE  ST   REP    CRD LMIT    BAL OWED    YTD SALES DATE LAST SALE
    14  Braintree Hospital    H    MA    2       37000    36,609.80   75,562.35  09-Jul-90
     6  Cape Psych Center     H    MA    3       55000    31,509.10   44,173.24  15-Jul-90
    15  Miriam Hospital       H    MA    2       18000    14,800.44   24,510.04  23-Aug-90
     3  EMG & EEG Labs        L    MA    4       39000    12,583.97   31,685.19  07-Sep-90
    13  Bradley Hospital      H    MA    2       26000     9,430.72   32,451.95  17-Aug-90
     8  Bayshore Pharmacy     P    MA    3       18000     6,010.36   44,140.87  28-Jul-90
     2  Nepco Labs            L    MA    4        5000     3,274.25    6,866.25  18-Aug-90
    16  Forgary Labs          L    MA    1       20000     2,890.08    6,670.41  11-Sep-90
     7  Bioran Medical Lab    L    MA    3        8000     2,799.12   11,927.84  21-Jul-90
    22  Foster Blood Tests    L    MA    1       16000     2,594.27    4,275.56  03-Oct-90
    12  Gregg's Pharmacy      P    MA    2        3000     2,052.70    3,771.28  06-Aug-90
    20  Kent Hospital         H    MA    1        2000     1,987.44    4,120.74  24-Aug-90
     9  St Anne's Hospital    H    MA    3        1000     1,009.53    2,431.80  27-Sep-90
    18  Woman & Infants       H    RI    1       56000    47,915.99    3,415.04  04-Jul-90
     5  St. Josephs Hospital  H    RI    3       61000    47,113.50    4,451.68  28-Jul-90
    21  Butler Hospital       H    RI    1       33000    31,215.67   21,144.05  30-Sep-90
    10  Landmark Medical Center H  RI    3       23000    22,630.79    6,494.55  24-Sep-90
     4  Oaklawn Pharmacy      P    RI    4        6000     4,513.21    5,176.26  01-Aug-90
    19  Depasquale Pharmacy   P    RI    1        5000     4,214.50   39,727.98  10-Aug-90
    17  De Bellis Pharmacy    P    RI    1        4000     2,715.35   85,063.85  07-Jul-90
     1  Bristol Pharmacy      P    RI    4        3000     2,647.10   80,278.87  26-Jul-90
    11  Lypho_Med Laboratory  L    RI    2        1000       538.62    3,279.89  12-Aug-90

CUST #  CUSTOMER NAME        TYPE  ST   REP    CRD LMIT    BAL OWED    YTD SALES DATE LAST SALE
```

input range (includes field names)

first row of criteria range

Figure 6-13

Now enter the search criteria into the second row of the criteria range. Joan is searching for all hospital customers. To search for an exact match, enter the value you are searching for exactly as it appears in the database. Enter the value below the appropriate field name in the criteria range.

To enter the search criteria to find hospital customers:

❶ Move the cell pointer to cell C36, the location in the criteria range that stores the search criteria for the type of customer.

❷ Type **H** and press **[Enter]**. See Figure 6-14.

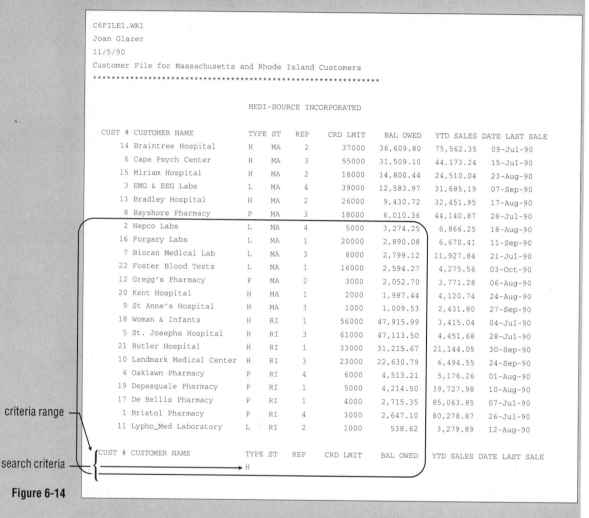

```
C6FILE1.WK1
Joan Glazer
11/5/90
Customer File for Massachusetts and Rhode Island Customers
***********************************************************************

                           MEDI-SOURCE INCORPORATED

CUST # CUSTOMER NAME          TYPE ST   REP   CRD LMIT   BAL OWED    YTD SALES DATE LAST SALE
    14 Braintree Hospital      H    MA    2     37000    36,609.80   75,562.35  09-Jul-90
     6 Cape Psych Center       H    MA    3     55000    31,509.10   44,173.24  15-Jul-90
    15 Miriam Hospital         H    MA    2     18000    14,800.44   24,510.04  23-Aug-90
     3 EMG & EEG Labs          L    MA    4     39000    12,583.97   31,685.19  07-Sep-90
    13 Bradley Hospital        H    MA    2     26000     9,430.72   32,451.95  17-Aug-90
     8 Bayshore Pharmacy       P    MA    3     18000     6,010.36   44,140.87  28-Jul-90
     2 Nepco Labs              L    MA    4      5000     3,274.25    6,866.25  18-Aug-90
    16 Forgary Labs            L    MA    1     20000     2,890.08    6,670.41  11-Sep-90
     7 Bioran Medical Lab      L    MA    3      8000     2,799.12   11,927.84  21-Jul-90
    22 Foster Blood Tests      L    MA    1     16000     2,594.27    4,275.56  03-Oct-90
    12 Gregg's Pharmacy        P    MA    2      3000     2,052.70    3,771.28  06-Aug-90
    20 Kent Hospital           H    MA    1      2000     1,987.44    4,120.74  24-Aug-90
     9 St Anne's Hospital      H    MA    3      1000     1,009.53    2,431.80  27-Sep-90
    18 Woman & Infants         H    RI    1     56000    47,915.99    3,415.04  04-Jul-90
     5 St. Josephs Hospital    H    RI    3     61000    47,113.50    4,451.68  28-Jul-90
    21 Butler Hospital         H    RI    1     33000    31,215.67   21,144.05  30-Sep-90
    10 Landmark Medical Center H    RI    3     23000    22,630.79    6,494.55  24-Sep-90
     4 Oaklawn Pharmacy        P    RI    4      6000     4,513.21    5,176.26  01-Aug-90
    19 Depasquale Pharmacy     P    RI    1      5000     4,214.50   39,727.98  10-Aug-90
    17 De Bellis Pharmacy      P    RI    1      4000     2,715.35   85,063.85  07-Jul-90
     1 Bristol Pharmacy        P    RI    4      3000     2,647.10   80,278.87  26-Jul-90
    11 Lypho_Med Laboratory    L    RI    2      1000       538.62    3,279.89  12-Aug-90

CUST # CUSTOMER NAME          TYPE ST   REP   CRD LMIT   BAL OWED    YTD SALES DATE LAST SALE
                               H
```

criteria range

search criteria

Figure 6-14

1-2-3 considers lowercase and uppercase characters the same in the criteria range.

You can also assign a range name to the criteria range, although you do not have to do so to use the Data Query command. This allows you to specify the location of the criteria range without remembering the cell locations of this range.

To assign the range name SEARCH to the criteria range:

❶ Move the cell pointer to A35, the upper left corner of the criteria range.

❷ Select /Range Name Create (**/RNC**).

❸ Type **SEARCH** and press **[Enter]**. Highlight the criteria range A35..I36. Press **[Enter]**. Now the criteria range A35..I36 has the name SEARCH.

❹ To document that this range of cells is the criteria range, move the cell pointer to cell A34, type **Criteria Range**, and press **[Enter]**. See Figure 6-15.

```
C6FILE1.WK1
Joan Glazer
11/5/90
Customer File for Massachusetts and Rhode Island Customers
*********************************************************************

                         MEDI-SOURCE INCORPORATED

   CUST # CUSTOMER NAME        TYPE ST  REP  CRD LMIT   BAL OWED   YTD SALES DATE LAST SALE
       14 Braintree Hospital    H    MA   2    37000   36,609.80  75,562.35  09-Jul-90
        6 Cape Psych Center     H    MA   3    55000   31,509.10  44,173.24  15-Jul-90
       15 Miriam Hospital       H    MA   2    18000   14,800.44  24,510.04  23-Aug-90
        3 EMG & EEG Labs        L    MA   4    39000   12,583.97  31,685.19  07-Sep-90
       13 Bradley Hospital      H    MA   2    26000    9,430.72  32,451.95  17-Aug-90
        8 Bayshore Pharmacy     P    MA   3    18000    6,010.36  44,140.87  28-Jul-90
        2 Nepco Labs            L    MA   4     5000    3,274.25   6,866.25  18-Aug-90
       16 Forgary Labs          L    MA   1    20000    2,890.08   6,670.41  11-Sep-90
        7 Bioran Medical Lab    L    MA   3     8000    2,799.12  11,927.84  21-Jul-90
       22 Foster Blood Tests    L    MA   1    16000    2,594.27   4,275.56  03-Oct-90
       12 Gregg's Pharmacy      P    MA   2     3000    2,052.70   3,771.28  06-Aug-90
       20 Kent Hospital         H    MA   1     2000    1,987.44   4,120.74  24-Aug-90
        9 St Anne's Hospital    H    MA   3     1000    1,009.53   2,431.80  27-Sep-90
       18 Woman & Infants       H    RI   1    56000   47,915.99   3,415.04  04-Jul-90
        5 St. Josephs Hospital  H    RI   3    61000   47,113.50   4,451.68  28-Jul-90
       21 Butler Hospital       H    RI   1    33000   31,215.67  21,144.05  30-Sep-90
       10 Landmark Medical Center H  RI   3    23000   22,630.79   6,494.55  24-Sep-90
        4 Oaklawn Pharmacy      P    RI   4     6000    4,513.21   5,176.26  01-Aug-90
       19 Depasquale Pharmacy   P    RI   1     5000    4,214.50  39,727.98  10-Aug-90
       17 De Bellis Pharmacy    P    RI   1     4000    2,715.35  85,063.85  07-Jul-90
        1 Bristol Pharmacy      P    RI   4     3000    2,647.10  80,278.87  26-Jul-90
       11 Lypho_Med Laboratory  L    RI   2     1000      538.62   3,279.89  12-Aug-90

Criteria Range
   CUST # CUSTOMER NAME        TYPE ST  REP  CRD LMIT   BAL OWED  YTD SALES DATE LAST SALE
```

added documentation

criteria range

Figure 6-15

Finding Records Using a Constant

Now that you have set up the input and criteria ranges, you can use the Data Query command to find (highlight) all hospital customers. The Find command is used to activate the search of the database records, finding each record that satisfies the criteria you specified in the criteria range.

To find hospital customers in the database:

❶   Select /Data Query (**/DQ**). The query settings sheet appears. See Figure 6-16.

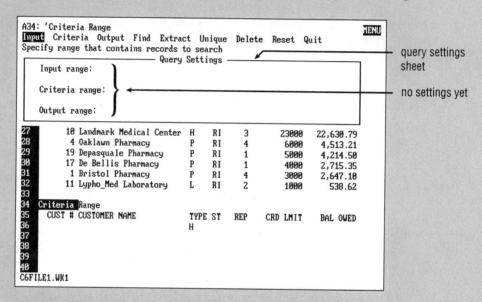

Figure 6-16

This sheet describes the ranges 1-2-3 will use to perform the data query operations. Currently, none of the query settings are defined.

To use the Find command, you must specify the locations of the input and criteria ranges. First, let's specify the input range.

❷   Select INPUT (**I**) to indicate the range of cells you want to search.

Enter the name of the input range.

❸   Type **DATABASE** and press **[Enter]**.

DATABASE, the range name you assigned to cells A10..I32, appears in the query settings sheet.

Next, specify the criteria range.

❹   Select Criteria (**C**) to indicate the range of cells that contains the search criteria.

Enter the name of the criteria range.

❺   Type **SEARCH** and press **[Enter]**.

SEARCH, the range name you assigned to your criteria range, that is, cells A35..I36, appears in the query settings sheet. See Figure 6-17.

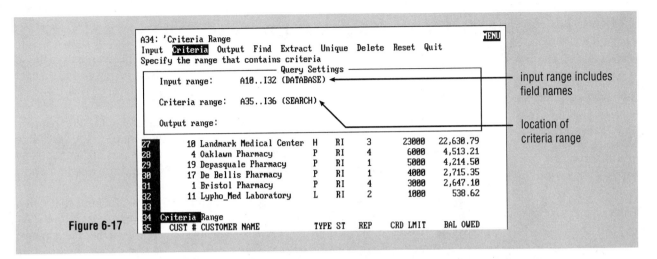

```
A34: 'Criteria Range                                          MENU
Input  Criteria  Output  Find  Extract  Unique  Delete  Reset  Quit
Specify the range that contains criteria
                    ┌─── Query Settings ───┐
    Input range:       A10..I32 (DATABASE)                          input range includes
                                                                    field names
    Criteria range:    A35..I36 (SEARCH)

    Output range:

27        10 Landmark Medical Center   H   RI   3    23000    22,630.79
28         4 Oaklawn Pharmacy          P   RI   4     6000     4,513.21
29        19 Depasquale Pharmacy       P   RI   1     5000     4,214.50
30        17 De Bellis Pharmacy        P   RI   1     4000     2,715.35
31         1 Bristol Pharmacy          P   RI   4     3000     2,647.10
32        11 Lypho_Med Laboratory      L   RI   2     1000       538.62
33
34  Criteria Range
35  CUST # CUSTOMER NAME               TYPE ST  REP  CRD LMIT  BAL OWED
```

location of
criteria range

Figure 6-17

Now use the Find command to highlight the records that meet the search criteria.

To find all hospital customers:

❶ Select Find **(F)**.

1-2-3 highlights the first record that matches the criteria of TYPE equal to H. See Figure 6-18.

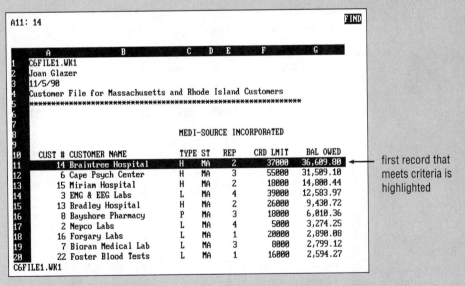

```
A11: 14                                                         FIND

     A           B          C    D    E        F         G
1  C6FILE1.WK1
2  Joan Glazer
3  11/5/90
4  Customer File for Massachusetts and Rhode Island Customers
5  ************************************************************
6
7
8                    MEDI-SOURCE INCORPORATED
9
10 CUST # CUSTOMER NAME            TYPE ST  REP  CRD LMIT  BAL OWED
11      14 Braintree Hospital       H   MA   2    37000    36,609.80      first record that
12       6 Cape Psych Center        H   MA   3    55000    31,509.10      meets criteria is
13      15 Miriam Hospital          H   MA   2    18000    14,800.44      highlighted
14       3 EMG & EEG Labs           L   MA   4    39000    12,583.97
15      13 Bradley Hospital         H   MA   2    26000     9,430.72
16       8 Bayshore Pharmacy        P   MA   3    18000     6,010.36
17       2 Nepco Labs               L   MA   4     5000     3,274.25
18      16 Forgary Labs             L   MA   1    20000     2,890.08
19       7 Bioran Medical Lab       L   MA   3     8000     2,799.12
20      22 Foster Blood Tests       L   MA   1    16000     2,594.27
   C6FILE1.WK1
```

Figure 6-18

❷ Press [↓] to find the next hospital customer. Continue to press [↓] to find all hospital customers.

You can also press [↑] to search the database in the other direction. 1-2-3 will beep when you try to move beyond the first or the last matching record.

❸ Press **[Esc]** or **[Enter]** to return to QUERY mode.

❹ Quit **(Q)** to return to READY mode.

Finding Records Using a Search Formula

Remember that the average customer's outstanding balance is $6,000. This average was based on customers from all states in which Medi-Source does business. Now Joan wants to identify Rhode Island and Massachusetts customers who owe more than the average Medi-Source customer.

This query requires a search formula be included beneath the BAL OWED field name in the criteria range. When entering a formula as a criterion, begin the formula with a plus sign (+). Follow the plus sign with the cell address of the *first record* that appears immediately under the field name in the input range. Next in the formula is a comparison operator and a value to compare against the cell address.

In the following steps, you will enter the search formula, +G11>6000. This is the search criteria to find all customers who owe more than $6,000.

First, erase the search criteria from the previous query that still appears in the criteria range.

To erase the search criteria from row 36:

❶ Move the cell pointer to the second line of the criteria range, cell A36.

❷ Select /Range Erase (**/RE**).

❸ Highlight A36..I36 and press **[Enter]**. The row that stores the search criteria is now erased.

Now enter the new search criteria:

❹ Move the cell pointer to cell G36.

❺ Type **+G11>6000** and press **[Enter]**. See Figure 6-19.

search formula ⎯⎯⎯⎯⎯⎯⎯⎯

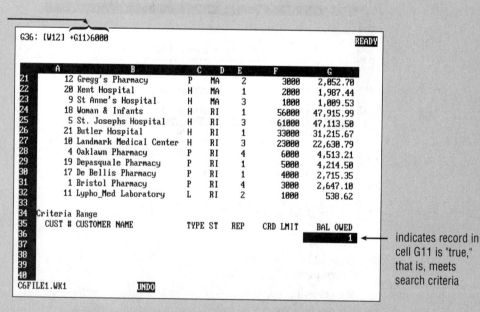

Figure 6-19

indicates record in cell G11 is "true," that is, meets search criteria

Remember, you must place the + sign in front of the cell address; otherwise, 1-2-3 will treat the condition as a label. Also remember that you *must reference the first database cell* following the field name in the column you are searching.

Notice that a 1 appears in cell G36. When a condition containing a search formula is assigned to a cell in the criteria range, a 0 or a 1 will appear. The value in G36, the cell with the formula +G11>6000, depends on the value in cell G11. If the value in cell G11 is greater than 6,000, then the condition is true, and a 1 appears. If the condition is false, a 0 appears.

You can choose to have the formula appear in the criteria range instead of the value 0 or 1. This is often done because the formula is more meaningful than a 1 or a 0. To display the formula in the cell, you use the Range Format Text command.

To display the formula in the cell:

❶ Make sure the cell pointer is at G36.

❷ Select /Range Format Text (**/RFT**).

❸ Highlight G36..G36 and press **[Enter]**. The formula for the search criteria now appears in cell G36. See Figure 6-20.

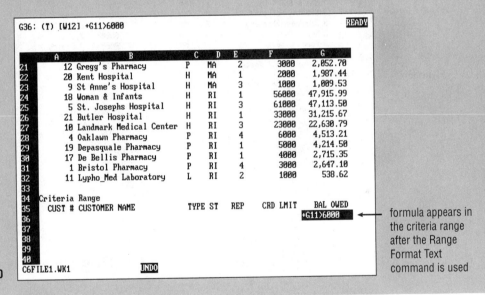

Figure 6-20

Now Joan uses the Data Query Find command to highlight all customers with a balance above $6,000.

To use the Data Query Find command:

❶ Select /Data Query (**/DQ**).

The same input and criteria ranges appear on the query settings sheet that were used earlier in the tutorial. Since you defined the input and criteria ranges when you searched for hospital customers, you do not need to define these ranges again.

Once the input and criteria ranges are defined, you can search the database records by choosing the Find command.

❷ Select Find (**F**).

1-2-3 highlights the first record with an outstanding balance greater than 6,000. See Figure 6-21.

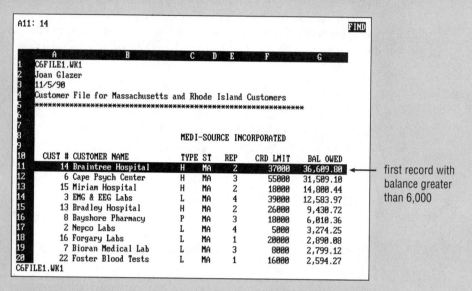

Figure 6-21

first record with balance greater than 6,000

❸ Press [↓] to find the next matching record in the database.

Continue to press [↓] to find all customers with a balance above $6,000. 1-2-3 will beep when you try to move beyond the last matching record.

❹ Press [**Esc**] and then Quit (**Q**) to return to READY mode.

Data Query Command — Extracting Records

Joan has been using the Data Query Find command to highlight (locate) all records that meet the search criteria. Now she wants to copy customer records with balances greater than $6,000 to a different part of the worksheet. In this separate area of the worksheet, she wants to list only those records that have balances above $6,000. This will make it easier for Joan to print or perform calculations on these records.

The Data Query Extract command lets you copy all records from the input range that match specific criteria in the criteria range to a location in the worksheet called the output range.

Before you use the Data Query Extract command, you must define the input range, the criteria range, and the output range.

Input Range

The input range identifies the database 1-2-3 will search. This range includes the field names in addition to the records of the database. You specify this range by using the Input option of the Data Query command. The input range was defined when the Find command was used earlier in the tutorial, so you do not need to enter it again.

Criteria Range

The criteria range specifies the criteria you want to use to extract records from the database. You specify the criteria range by using the Criterion option of the Data Query command. Joan wants to extract records of customers with balances above $6,000. Since the search criteria are the same as those used earlier in this tutorial, you do not have to enter the search criteria again.

Output Range

The **output range** is an area of the worksheet where records from the input range that meet the search criteria are copied. The first row of the output range must contain field names that are identical to field names in the input range. The Extract command copies all matching records into the output range beginning in the row below the field names of the output range. Since the Extract command erases all data values that were previously in these cells, it's best to choose an area of your worksheet that contains no data for the placement of the output range. Let's begin the output range in row 40.

When you define an output range, you usually specify the row with the field names as the range of the output range. 1-2-3 uses as many rows below the output range as it needs to copy the records to this area.

To copy the field names to row 40, the first row of the output range:

1. Move the cell pointer to cell A10.
2. Select /Copy (**/C**).
3. Highlight cells A10..I10, then press **[Enter]**.
4. Move the cell pointer to A40 and press **[Enter]**. The database field names appear in row 40.
5. Move the cell pointer to A40 to see the copied field names.
6. Move the cell pointer to A39, type **Output Range**, and then press **[Enter]**. This label helps identify this area of the worksheet. See Figure 6-22 on the next page.

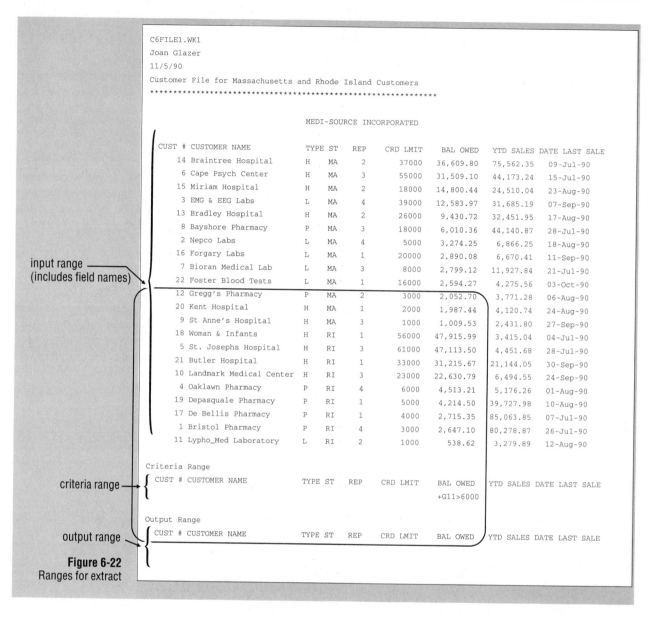

```
C6FILE1.WK1
Joan Glazer
11/5/90
Customer File for Massachusetts and Rhode Island Customers
******************************************************************

                        MEDI-SOURCE INCORPORATED

CUST # CUSTOMER NAME            TYPE ST   REP   CRD LMIT    BAL OWED    YTD SALES DATE LAST SALE
    14 Braintree Hospital        H   MA    2      37000    36,609.80   75,562.35   09-Jul-90
     6 Cape Psych Center         H   MA    3      55000    31,509.10   44,173.24   15-Jul-90
    15 Miriam Hospital           H   MA    2      18000    14,800.44   24,510.04   23-Aug-90
     3 EMG & EEG Labs            L   MA    4      39000    12,583.97   31,685.19   07-Sep-90
    13 Bradley Hospital          H   MA    2      26000     9,430.72   32,451.95   17-Aug-90
     8 Bayshore Pharmacy         P   MA    3      18000     6,010.36   44,140.87   28-Jul-90
     2 Nepco Labs                L   MA    4       5000     3,274.25    6,866.25   18-Aug-90
    16 Forgary Labs              L   MA    1      20000     2,890.08    6,670.41   11-Sep-90
     7 Bioran Medical Lab        L   MA    3       8000     2,799.12   11,927.84   21-Jul-90
    22 Foster Blood Tests        L   MA    1      16000     2,594.27    4,275.56   03-Oct-90
    12 Gregg's Pharmacy          P   MA    2       3000     2,052.70    3,771.28   06-Aug-90
    20 Kent Hospital             H   MA    1       2000     1,987.44    4,120.74   24-Aug-90
     9 St Anne's Hospital        H   MA    3       1000     1,009.53    2,431.80   27-Sep-90
    18 Woman & Infants           H   RI    1      56000    47,915.99    3,415.04   04-Jul-90
     5 St. Josephs Hospital      H   RI    3      61000    47,113.50    4,451.68   28-Jul-90
    21 Butler Hospital           H   RI    1      33000    31,215.67   21,144.05   30-Sep-90
    10 Landmark Medical Center   H   RI    3      23000    22,630.79    6,494.55   24-Sep-90
     4 Oaklawn Pharmacy          P   RI    4       6000     4,513.21    5,176.26   01-Aug-90
    19 Depasquale Pharmacy       P   RI    1       5000     4,214.50   39,727.98   10-Aug-90
    17 De Bellis Pharmacy        P   RI    1       4000     2,715.35   85,063.85   07-Jul-90
     1 Bristol Pharmacy          P   RI    4       3000     2,647.10   80,278.87   26-Jul-90
    11 Lypho_Med Laboratory      L   RI    2       1000       538.62    3,279.89   12-Aug-90

Criteria Range
 CUST # CUSTOMER NAME           TYPE ST   REP   CRD LMIT    BAL OWED   YTD SALES DATE LAST SALE
                                                          +G11>6000

Output Range
 CUST # CUSTOMER NAME           TYPE ST   REP   CRD LMIT    BAL OWED   YTD SALES DATE LAST SALE
```

input range
(includes field names)

criteria range

output range

Figure 6-22
Ranges for extract

Although it is not required to extract records, you can assign a range name to the output range A40..I40. This allows you to specify the output range without remembering the cell locations.

To assign the range name HIGH_BALANCE to the output range:

❶ Move the cell pointer to the first field name in the output range, cell A40.

❷ Select /Range Name Create (**/RNC**).

❸ Type **HIGH_BALANCE** and press **[Enter]**.

❹ Highlight the field names of the output range, A40..I40, then press **[Enter]**.
   The output range has the name HIGH_BALANCE.

Before you can use the Data Query Extract command, you must specify the input, criteria, and output ranges.

Since the input and criteria ranges were specified earlier in this tutorial, you do not need to enter them again. However, the output range has not been specified.

To specify the output range for the Data Query command:

❶ Select /Data Query (**/DQ**).

❷ Select Output (**O**), press **[F3]** (NAME), and highlight the range name HIGH_BALANCE, which is the output range. Press **[Enter]**. See Figure 6-23. The cell locations of the output range now appear in the query settings sheet.

```
A40: "CUST #                                                    MENU
Input  Criteria  Output  Find  Extract  Unique  Delete  Reset  Quit
Specify the range to which extracted records are copied
                          ┌── Query Settings ──────────────┐
    Input range:      A10..I32 (DATABASE)

    Criteria range:   A35..I36 (SEARCH)

    Output range:     A40..I40 (HIGH_BALANCE)  ◄─────────┘        output range now
                                                                  part of settings
27        10 Landmark Medical Center  H   RI   3    23000   22,630.79
28         4 Oaklawn Pharmacy         P   RI   4     6000    4,513.21
29        19 Depasquale Pharmacy      P   RI   1     5000    4,214.50
30        17 De Bellis Pharmacy       P   RI   1     4000    2,715.35
31         1 Bristol Pharmacy         P   RI   4     3000    2,647.10
32        11 Lypho_Med Laboratory     L   RI   2     1000      538.62
33
34  Criteria Range
35     CUST # CUSTOMER NAME           TYPE ST  REP  CRD LMIT  BAL OWED
36                                                           +G11>6000
37
38
39  Output Range
40     CUST # CUSTOMER NAME           TYPE ST  REP  CRD LMIT  BAL OWED
C6FILE1.WK1
```

Figure 6-23

Extracting Records

Now that the input, criteria, and output ranges are specified, you can use the Extract command. Joan wants to extract customer records with an outstanding balance above $6,000.

To extract records with a balance above $6,000:

❶ Select Extract (**E**).

   1-2-3 copies to the output range all records from the database that meet the search formula you entered, in this case, customers whose balance is greater than $6,000.

❷ Select Quit (**Q**) to return to READY mode.

❸ Move the cell pointer to A53 and view all the extracted records. See Figure 6-24. Notice that 1-2-3 has extracted only the records that meet the criteria, that is, only those customers whose outstanding balance is greater than 6,000.

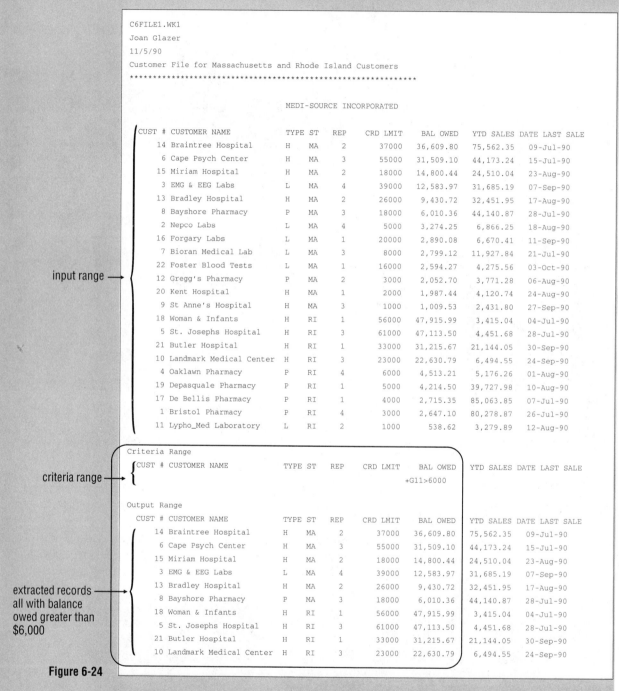

```
C6FILE1.WK1
Joan Glazer
11/5/90
Customer File for Massachusetts and Rhode Island Customers
****************************************************************

                        MEDI-SOURCE INCORPORATED

CUST # CUSTOMER NAME        TYPE ST   REP   CRD LMIT    BAL OWED   YTD SALES DATE LAST SALE
    14 Braintree Hospital    H    MA    2     37000    36,609.80   75,562.35   09-Jul-90
     6 Cape Psych Center     H    MA    3     55000    31,509.10   44,173.24   15-Jul-90
    15 Miriam Hospital       H    MA    2     18000    14,800.44   24,510.04   23-Aug-90
     3 EMG & EEG Labs        L    MA    4     39000    12,583.97   31,685.19   07-Sep-90
    13 Bradley Hospital      H    MA    2     26000     9,430.72   32,451.95   17-Aug-90
     8 Bayshore Pharmacy     P    MA    3     18000     6,010.36   44,140.87   28-Jul-90
     2 Nepco Labs            L    MA    4      5000     3,274.25    6,866.25   18-Aug-90
    16 Forgary Labs          L    MA    1     20000     2,890.08    6,670.41   11-Sep-90
     7 Bioran Medical Lab    L    MA    3      8000     2,799.12   11,927.84   21-Jul-90
    22 Foster Blood Tests    L    MA    1     16000     2,594.27    4,275.56   03-Oct-90
    12 Gregg's Pharmacy      P    MA    2      3000     2,052.70    3,771.28   06-Aug-90
    20 Kent Hospital         H    MA    1      2000     1,987.44    4,120.74   24-Aug-90
     9 St Anne's Hospital    H    MA    3      1000     1,009.53    2,431.80   27-Sep-90
    18 Woman & Infants       H    RI    1     56000    47,915.99    3,415.04   04-Jul-90
     5 St. Josephs Hospital  H    RI    3     61000    47,113.50    4,451.68   28-Jul-90
    21 Butler Hospital       H    RI    1     33000    31,215.67   21,144.05   30-Sep-90
    10 Landmark Medical Center H  RI    3     23000    22,630.79    6,494.55   24-Sep-90
     4 Oaklawn Pharmacy      P    RI    4      6000     4,513.21    5,176.26   01-Aug-90
    19 Depasquale Pharmacy   P    RI    1      5000     4,214.50   39,727.98   10-Aug-90
    17 De Bellis Pharmacy    P    RI    1      4000     2,715.35   85,063.85   07-Jul-90
     1 Bristol Pharmacy      P    RI    4      3000     2,647.10   80,278.87   26-Jul-90
    11 Lypho_Med Laboratory  L    RI    2      1000       538.62    3,279.89   12-Aug-90

Criteria Range
CUST # CUSTOMER NAME        TYPE ST   REP   CRD LMIT    BAL OWED   YTD SALES DATE LAST SALE
                                                        +G11>6000

Output Range
CUST # CUSTOMER NAME        TYPE ST   REP   CRD LMIT    BAL OWED   YTD SALES DATE LAST SALE
    14 Braintree Hospital    H    MA    2     37000    36,609.80   75,562.35   09-Jul-90
     6 Cape Psych Center     H    MA    3     55000    31,509.10   44,173.24   15-Jul-90
    15 Miriam Hospital       H    MA    2     18000    14,800.44   24,510.04   23-Aug-90
     3 EMG & EEG Labs        L    MA    4     39000    12,583.97   31,685.19   07-Sep-90
    13 Bradley Hospital      H    MA    2     26000     9,430.72   32,451.95   17-Aug-90
     8 Bayshore Pharmacy     P    MA    3     18000     6,010.36   44,140.87   28-Jul-90
    18 Woman & Infants       H    RI    1     56000    47,915.99    3,415.04   04-Jul-90
     5 St. Josephs Hospital  H    RI    3     61000    47,113.50    4,451.68   28-Jul-90
    21 Butler Hospital       H    RI    1     33000    31,215.67   21,144.05   30-Sep-90
    10 Landmark Medical Center H  RI    3     23000    22,630.79    6,494.55   24-Sep-90
```

input range →

criteria range →

extracted records all with balance owed greater than $6,000 →

Figure 6-24

❹ Save your worksheet as S6FILE1.

Using @AVG, @MIN, @MAX, @COUNT Statistical Functions

According to her plan, Joan also wants to create two reports. The first report will show summary statistics for all Rhode Island and Massachusetts customers. She wants this report to include a count of the number of customers, the total and the average balance owed, and the highest and lowest balances owed for all customers. She wants the second report to show the total and the average balances owed separately for Rhode Island and Massachusetts customers.

To prepare the first report, you will use several statistical functions that perform calculations on a range of numbers. The statistical functions used in this report are summarized in Figure 6-25.

Function	Description	Example
@AVG(range)	Calculates the average of the range	@AVG(G11..G20)
@COUNT(range)	Calculates the number of nonblank cells in the range	@COUNT(G11..G20)
@MAX(range)	Determines the largest value in the range	@MAX(G11..G20)
@MIN(range)	Determines the smallest value in the range	@MIN(G11..G20)
@SUM(range)	Calculates the sum of the range	@SUM(G11..G20)

Figure 6-25
Statistical functions

To work more easily with the statistical functions, let's first assign a range name, OWED, to the group of cells representing the balance owed.

To assign the range name OWED:
1. Move the cell pointer to G11, the first cell containing a balance owed value.
2. Select /Range Name Create (**/RNC**).
3. Type **OWED** and press **[Enter]**. Highlight G11..G32 and press **[Enter]**.
   The range name, OWED, has been assigned to the cells G11..G32.

Let's now prepare Joan's first report, which calculates the sum, the average, the minimum, and the maximum balance owed for all customers in the database. Place this report in the range N1 to P10. The headings and labels for the report have already been entered in the worksheet.

Now calculate the statistics for the report.

To enter the @functions:

First, to calculate the total amount owed by all RI and MA customers:

❶ Move the cell pointer to cell O8, type **@SUM(OWED)**, and press **[Enter]**. The total owed is 291056.50.

To calculate the average owed by all RI and MA customers:

❷ Move the cell pointer to cell O9, type **@AVG(OWED)**, and press **[Enter]**. The average owed is 13229.84.

To calculate the maximum amount owed by RI and MA customers:

❸ Move the cell pointer to cell O10, type **@MAX(OWED)**, and press **[Enter]**. The maximum owed is 47915.99.

To calculate the minimum amount owed by RI and MA customers:

❹ Move the cell pointer to cell O11, type **@MIN(OWED)**, and press **[Enter]**. The lowest balance is 538.62.

Finally, to count the number of customers in the database:

❺ Move the cell pointer to O12, type **@COUNT(OWED)**, and press **[Enter]**. There are 22 customers. See Figure 6-26.

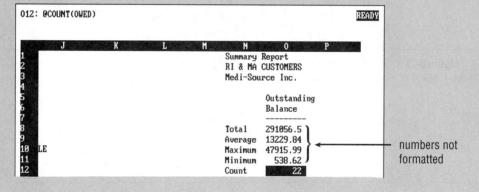

Figure 6-26
Joan's first report

The statistics for the report are completed. The appearance of the report, however, can be improved. Specifically, the values in O8..O11 can be formatted using Currency format.

To improve the appearance of the report using Currency format:

❶ Move the cell pointer to O8.

❷ Select /Range Format Currency (**/RFC**).

❸ Type **0** for the number of decimal places and press **[Enter]**.

   With balances this large, Joan believes numbers rounded to the nearest whole number are appropriate.

❹ Highlight O8..O11. Press **[Enter]**.

Your worksheet should look like Figure 6-27. Notice the cell O12 is not included in the range because count does not represent a dollar quantity.

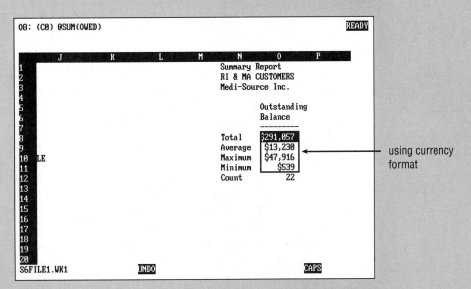

```
O8: (C0) @SUM(OWED)                                              READY

         J          K          L          M          N          O          P
1                                                      Summary Report
2                                                      RI & MA CUSTOMERS
3                                                      Medi-Source Inc.
4
5                                                      Outstanding
6                                                      Balance
7                                                      ──────────
8                                                Total    $291,057
9                                                Average   $13,230         ◄──────  using currency
10  LE                                           Maximum   $47,916                  format
11                                               Minimum      $539
12                                               Count         22
13
14
15
16
17
18
19
20
    S6FILE1.WK1                    UNDO                              CAPS
```

Figure 6-27

Joan is satisfied with the first report. She notices that the average outstanding balance for Rhode Island and Massachusetts customers is $13,230, more than twice the Medi-Source company average.

Before she begins her next task, Joan saves the worksheet.

⑤   Save your worksheet as S6FILE1.WK1.

Understanding Database @Functions

In addition to the report already developed, Joan wants a report that shows the total and average outstanding balances by state. One approach to calculating these statistics is to use the database functions available in 1-2-3.

Lotus 1-2-3 has seven database @functions: @DAVG, @DSUM, @DMAX, @DMIN, @DCOUNT, @DSTD, and @DVAR. Each function calculates a value based on records in the database that match criteria in the criteria range. The database @functions differ from the corresponding statistical @functions, because the database @functions calculate statistics *only* for the records in a database that match the criteria you specify. For example, you used @AVG to calculate the average balance owed for all the records in the database. You will use @DAVG to calculate the average balance owed for only those records that meet the criteria of RI customers.

All of the database @functions have the same format, which is:

@function(input range,offset,criteria range)

---

where:

@function is one of the following: @DAVG, @DSUM, @DCOUNT, @DMAX, @DMIN, @DSTD, @DVAR and each database function consists of three arguments:

Input range — the range that contains the database, including the field names in the range definition. The range can be specified as a range name or as cell addresses.

Offset — the position number of the column in the database that is to be summed, averaged, counted, etc. 1-2-3 assigns the first field in the database the offset number 0, the second field the offset number 1, and so on. For example, CUTS # is the first column in the database and has the offset number 0; CUSTOMER NAME is the second column, so it has the offset number 1; and BAL OWED is the seventh column in the database, so it has the offset number 6.

Criteria range — an area of your worksheet where you specify the search criteria to determine which records you will use in the calculations.

Figure 6-28 summarizes the 1-2-3 database functions.

Function Name	Description	Example
@DAVG	Averages the values in the offset column that meet specified criteria	@DAVG(A11..G32,6,T25..T26)
@DSUM	Sums the values in the offset column that meet specified criteria	@DSUM(A11..G32,6,T25..T26)
@DMAX	Determines the largest value in the offset column that meets specified criteria	@DMAX(A11..G32,6,T25..T26)
@DMIN	Determines the smallest value in the offset column that meets specified criteria	@DMIN(A11..G32,6,T25..T26)
@DCOUNT	Counts the number of records in which the values in the offset column meet specified criteria	@DCOUNT(A11..G32,6,T25..T26)
@DSTD	Calculates the standard deviation of the values in the offset column that meet specified criteria	@DSTD(A11..G32,6,T25..T26)
@DVAR	Calculates the variance of the values in the offset column that meet the specified criteria	@DVAR(A11..G32,6,T25..T26)

Figure 6-28
Database functions

Using Database @Functions

Joan wants to calculate separate statistics for Rhode Island and Massachusetts customers. She wants to know if there is a difference between the total and the average amount owed by customers in each state.

To calculate these statistics, you will use the database @functions @DSUM and @DAVG. Each function requires an input range, an offset range, and a criteria range.

The input range identifies the records to use in calculations. You already defined this range earlier in the tutorial. The input range includes cells A10..I32 and has been assigned the name DATABASE.

You set up separate criteria ranges for each group of records on which you are performing calculations.

Let's first set up a criteria range at S25..S26 to use when you search for Rhode Island customers:

❶ Move the cell pointer to cell D10, the field name that is to be copied to the criteria range.

❷ Select /Copy (**/C**) and press **[Enter]**.

❸ Type **S25** and press **[Enter]**. The label ST is copied to cell S25.

❹ Move the cell pointer to S26, the second row of the criteria range.

❺ Type **RI** and press **[Enter]**. The criteria range for RI customers is complete.

Notice that the criteria range includes only one database field name. The criteria range does not have to include all field names in the database. It needs to include only the field names you intend to search.

Next, set up a separate criteria range at T25..T26 to search for customers in Massachusetts:

❶ Move the cell pointer to S25 to copy the field name to the second criteria range.

Now copy the label ST to cell T25.

❷ Select /Copy (**/C**) and press **[Enter]**.

❸ Type **T25** and press **[Enter]**. The label ST appears in cell T25.

❹ Move the cell pointer to T26, the second row of the criteria range.

❺ Type **MA** and press **[Enter]**. The criteria range for specifying MA customers is complete. See Figure 6-29.

Figure 6-29

criteria range for Rhode Island customers

criteria range for Massachusetts customers

Now that you have defined the input and criteria ranges, let's determine the offset number for the balance owed field.

To determine the offset number for balance owed:

❶ Move the cell pointer to cell A10, the first field in the database.

❷ Starting with 0 for the CUST # field, count the columns to determine the offset number for column G, BAL OWED. Your answer should be 6. See Figure 6-30.

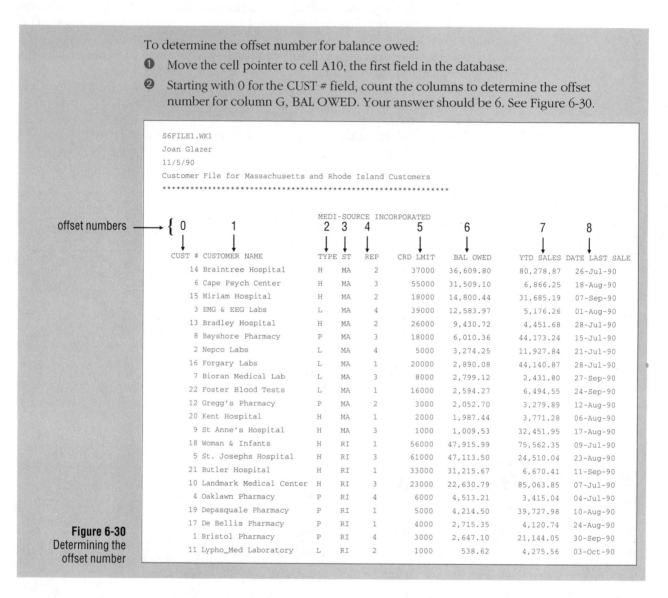

Figure 6-30
Determining the offset number

Let's put this second report in cells N21 to O25. The headings and descriptive labels for the report have already been entered in the worksheet. Now let's use the database @functions to complete the report.

To use database @functions to calculate the statistics:

❶ Press [F5] (GOTO), type **N21**, and press [Enter]. The cell pointer is now in the section of the worksheet where you will calculate the Outstanding Balance by State Report. See Figure 6-31.

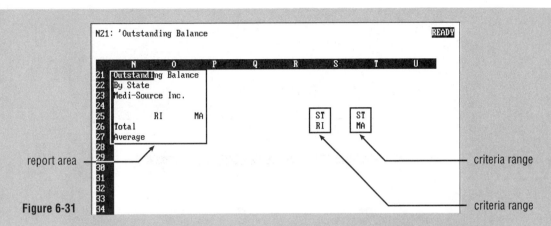

Figure 6-31

report area ──→

criteria range
criteria range

② Move the cell pointer to cell O26, under the cell labelled RI.

③ Type **@DSUM(DATABASE,6,S25..S26)** and press **[Enter]** to calculate the total balance owed for Rhode Island customers. The total 163504.7 appears on the screen.

④ Move the cell pointer to cell O27.

⑤ Type **@DAVG(DATABASE,6,S25..S26).** Press **[Enter]** to calculate the average balance owed by Rhode Island customers. The average balance owed is $18,167.19. See Figure 6-32.

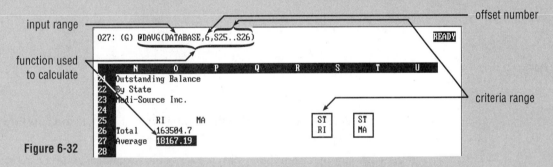

Figure 6-32

input range ──→
offset number
function used to calculate ──→
criteria range

⑥ Move the cell pointer to cell P26, under the cell labelled MA.

⑦ Type **@DSUM(DATABASE,6,T25..T26)**. Press **[Enter]** to calculate the total balance owed by all Massachusetts customers. Massachusetts customers owe 127551.70.

⑧ Move the cell pointer to cell P27.

⑨ Type **@DAVG(DATABASE,6,T25..T26).** Press **[Enter]** to calculate the average balance owed by Massachusetts customers. On average, Massachusetts customers owe 9811.25.

The statistics for the report are complete. The appearance of the report, however, can be improved. Specifically, the values in O26..P27 can be formatted using Currency format.

To improve the appearance of the report, using Currency format:

① Move the cell pointer to O26.

❷ Select /Range Format Currency (/**RFC**).

❸ Type **0** and press **[Enter]**.

❹ Highlight O26..P27. Press **[Enter]**.

Your worksheet should look like Figure 6-33.

Figure 6-33
Joan's calculated
information about
Rhode Island and
Massachusetts
customers

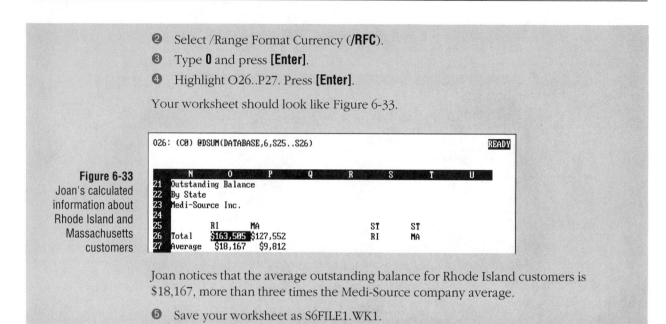

Joan notices that the average outstanding balance for Rhode Island customers is $18,167, more than three times the Medi-Source company average.

❺ Save your worksheet as S6FILE1.WK1.

Exercises

1. The customer database that you used in this tutorial, C6FILE1.WK1, contains how many fields? How many records?

2. To sort the customer names in Z to A order, you would use which sorting option?

3. List the steps you would follow to locate Kent Hospital in the customer database using the Find command.

4. List the steps you would follow to extract all Rhode Island customers using the Extract command.

5. What @function would you use to calculate the following statistics:
   a. The average sales for the year for sales representative #4
   b. The highest balance owed by all customers in the database
   c. The number of pharmacies in the database

6. If you had used the database statistical function @DAVG(DATABASE,7,T25..T26) in this tutorial, what statistic would you be calculating?

Tutorial Assignments

Before you begin these Tutorial Assignments, check your Lotus 1-2-3 data diskette. Be sure you have space to save the additional worksheet files you'll create in these assignments (at least 85,000 bytes). If not, save your files as appropriate to another formatted diskette.

Retrieve the worksheet T6FILE1.WK1 and do the following:

1. Sort the database by year-to-date (YTD) sales with the customer having the lowest YTD sales appearing first. Save the file as S6FILE2.

2. Sort the database in descending order using the field TYPE (type of customer) as the primary sort key. Save the file as S6FILE3.

3. Arrange the customer database by type of customer (ascending order) and, within type of customer, arrange the accounts in alphabetical order by customer name. Print the sorted records.

Use the Data Query command for Assignments 4 through 7.

4. Copy the database field names to the first row of criteria range, row 40.

5. Query the database to find all customers located in Rhode Island (code = RI). Save the worksheet as S6FILE4.

6. Query the database to find all customers with average YTD sales above $50,000. Save the worksheet as S6FILE5.

7. Query the database to extract and print all customers assigned to sales representative #4. Set up an output range beginning at row 50. Save the worksheet as S6FILE6.

Use statistical functions for Assignments 8 and 9:

8. Calculate the average YTD sales for all records in the database. Place the result in cell O8.

9. Calculate the maximum YTD sales using all the records in the database. Place the result in cell O9. Save your current worksheet as S6FILE7.

Complete Assignments 10 through 12 using the database statistical function @DAVG. Three criteria ranges have been partially set up in cells R25, S25, and T25.

10. Calculate the average outstanding balance for hospitals. Complete the criteria range in R25..R26. Place your result in cell O27.

11. Calculate the average outstanding balance for labs. Complete the criteria range in S25..S26. Place your result in cell O28.

12. Calculate the average outstanding balance for pharmacies. Complete the criteria range in T25..T26. Place your result in cell O29.

13. Print this Outstanding Balance Report by Type of Customer.

14. Save your worksheet as S6FILE8.

Case Problems

1. Human Resource Database

The human resource department of a small furniture manufacturer has developed a human resource database. The field names in this database are:

Field	Description
EMP#	Employee number
LNAME	Last name
FNAME	First name
BIRTH	Date of birth (yyyymmdd)
SEX	Code for sex (M = male; F = female)
MAR	Code for marital status (Y = married; N = not married)
DEP	Number of dependents
ANNSAL	Annual salary
HIREDT	Date employee hired (yyyymmdd)
XMPT	Exempt employee (X = exempt; N = nonexempt)
MED	Code for medical plan (F = family plan; I = individual plan; N = not on medical plan)
401K	401K retirement plan (Y = making contributions to plan; N = not making contributions to plan)
DIV	Division where employee works
JOBTITLE	Job title
PER	Payment method (H = hourly; M = monthly)

Retrieve the worksheet P6PERSNL and do the following:

1. Sort and print the database alphabetically by last name.

2. Sort and print the database by hire date.

3. Sort and print the database by division and, within division, by salary in descending order.

4. Find all employees that have the family medical plan. The code is F.

5. Find all employees with one or more dependents.

6. Extract and print the records of all married employees.

7. Print a summary report showing salaries categorized by sex. Format the report as sketched in Figure 6-34.

	Females	Males
Average	$ xxxx	$ xxxx
Maximum	$ xxxx	$ xxxx
Minimum	$ xxxx	$ xxxx
Count	xxxx	xxxx

Figure 6-34

8. Save your worksheet as S6PERSNL.

2. The Top 50 U.S. Companies

Every year, a leading business magazine publishes a list of the 50 largest U.S. companies and presents financial data about them.

Retrieve the worksheet P6TOP50. The field names in the file containing these data are:

Field	Description
COMPANY	Name of company
INDUSTRY	Industry code
SALES	Sales revenue for the year
PROFITS	Net income
ASSETS	Total assets
EQUITY	Portion of assets owned by stockholders
MKT VAL	Market value of company

Do the following:

1. Sort and print the database alphabetically by company.

2. Sort and print the database arranged by sales, with the company with the highest sales appearing first.

3. Calculate rate of return (ROR) for each company. The formula is:

$$ROR = \frac{Profit}{Equity}$$

Place this new field in column H and label the column ROR. Format using the Percent format with one decimal place.

4. Sort the database by ROR, with the company having the highest rate of return appearing first. *Hint:* Think about your data range.

5. Print the database, which now includes the rate of return field.

6. Extract and print all companies in the computer industry (industry code = 6).

7. Prepare and print a summary report comparing the average, maximum, and minimum sales for companies in the oil industry (code = 17) versus companies in the aerospace industry (code = 1). Format the report as sketched in Figure 6-35.

Top 50 U.S. Companies
Industry Comparison

	Oil	Aerospace
Average sales	$ xxx	$ xxx
Minimum sales	xxx	xxx
Maximum sales	xxx	xxx

Figure 6-35

8. Save your worksheet as S6TOP50.

3. Inventory of Microcomputer Software

A company that sells microcomputer software just completed its annual physical inventory prior to preparing its financial statement. The data from this inventory was entered into a 1-2-3 worksheet.

Retrieve the worksheet P6SFTWRE. The field names for this inventory database include:

Field	Description
ITEM #	Unique number to identify each product
TITLE	Name of product
CAT	Category of software
COST	Cost to company per unit
QOH	Number of packages on hand (in inventory)
QOO	Number of package on order
PRICE	Retail price of software package
YTD SALES	Year-to-date sales

The codes for the category of software (CAT) are:

CO	=	Communications
DP	=	Desktop publishing
DB	=	Database
GR	=	Graphics
SP	=	Spreadsheet
WP	=	Word processing
UT	=	Utility

Do the following:

1. Print a list of current software products arranged by category and, within category, alphabetized by title.

2. Find the software products that have one or more units on order.

3. Extract and print the database (DB) software products.

4. Add two columns to the worksheet, Inventory Value — Cost (column I) and Inventory Value — Retail (column J). Calculate and print the total cost value and the total retail value of all inventory items. (*Hint:* You can use the following formulas: Inventory Value — Cost = QOH × COST and Inventory — Retail = QOH × PRICE.)

5. Calculate and print the total retail value of the inventory by software category. Be sure your report has a separate total for each of the seven category codes listed above. Format this report as sketched in Figure 6-36.

Inventory - Retail Value
By Software Category

	Total Value
Communication	xxxx
Desktop Publishing	xxxx
Database	xxxx
Graphics	xxxx
Spreadsheet	xxxx
Word Processing	xxxx
Utility	xxxx
Total	$

Figure 6-36

6. Prepare a pie chart illustrating the same data that were calculated in Assignment 5. Create a PIC file named PIESOFT.

7. Save your worksheet as S6SFTWRE.

8. Print the pie chart PIESOFT.

Tutorial 7

Creating and Using Macros

OBJECTIVES

In this tutorial you will learn to:

■ Plan a macro

■ Create a macro

■ Execute a macro

■ Edit and debug a macro

■ Use LEARN mode

Case: Krier Marine Services Revisited

Remember Vince Diorio from Tutorial 1? He is the part-time employee at Krier Marine Services who helped Mrs. Krier create a worksheet for her employee payroll. Vince, in his senior year at the University of Rhode Island, will graduate next month and begin working as a programmer for a nearby major insurance company. He knows that Mrs. Krier will continue to use the worksheet he created and that she is nervous about using it without him around to help her.

Vince has recently been using macros to become a more productive user of 1-2-3. To him, macros are stored keystrokes. For example, he created a macro to print a worksheet. With this macro, he saves himself the time and the trouble of making 15 keystrokes every time he wants to print a worksheet. He presses only two keys, and Lotus 1-2-3 automatically prints the payroll worksheet. Vince knows that Mrs. Krier, in addition to printing the worksheet, will need to save the payroll worksheet at the end of each payroll period. He decides, therefore, that creating a macro to save the worksheet will be useful. Vince also plans to create a macro to create range names, because he frequently assigns range names to use with macros as well as for other 1-2-3 functions.

Vince decides to show Mrs. Krier his macro for printing and plans to create additional macros to make it easier for her to use the payroll worksheet. He prepares his planning sheet (Figure 7-1 on the next page) before beginning the revision of the worksheet.

My Goal:
To simplify the use of the payroll worksheet to Mrs. Krier by creating macros.

What results do I want to see?
Weekly payroll report

What information do I need?
Payroll data
Macro data

What macros do I want?
Print worksheet
Save worksheet
Name Ranges
Format columns using Currency

Figure 7-1
Vince's planning
sheet

In this tutorial, you will first run a macro from the payroll worksheet. Then you will add several macros to this worksheet. This involves planning, placing, entering, naming, and documenting each macro. Next, you will execute each macro. You will also use an alternative approach to create macros, the LEARN mode. Finally, you will learn how to find errors in macros using the STEP mode and how to correct them.

What Are Macros?

A **macro** is a series of keystrokes and special commands stored in a worksheet as cell entries. You can run a macro whenever you want to use it. Macros are most often created to automate frequently used Lotus 1-2-3 tasks, such as printing a worksheet, naming a range, saving a worksheet, or formatting cells. Thus, macros save time. They also help less sophisticated users of 1-2-3 by making the worksheet easier to use.

A macro can be used to carry out a simple task and save a few keystrokes, such as a macro to print a worksheet, or it can be used to help prevent typing or keystroke errors. For example, you can avoid errors by creating a macro that automatically moves the cell pointer to specified cells in a worksheet and automatically enters the date and time. Otherwise, you would have to move the cell pointer to the cells where you want to enter the date and time and then enter this information. A macro can also be designed to accomplish a series of more complex and repetitive tasks, such as preparing a weekly report that (1) lists all receivables over 30 days old, (2) sorts the list alphabetically by account, and then (3) prints three copies using compressed print — all in one macro — all automatically!

Retrieving the Worksheet

Vince has been using macros to make his work at Krier Marine Services more productive. For instance, he developed a print macro to simplify the printing of the Krier Marine Services payroll. Let's retrieve the payroll worksheet and run Vince's print macro.

To retrieve the worksheet and run the macro:

❶ Select /File Retrieve (**/FR**).

❷ Move the menu pointer to C7FILE1.WK1 and press **[Enter]**. See Figure 7-2.

```
C7FILE1.WK1
Vince Diorio
10/10/9x
Calculating Krier Payroll
***************************

Krier Marine Services Payroll
Week Ending 10/15/9x

Employee    Hours    Pay    Gross
Name        Worked   Rate    Pay
------------------------------------
Bramble       15       7      105
Juarez        28       5      140
Smith         40       7      280
Diorio        22       5      110
                                ---------
Totals                          635
                                =========
```

area of worksheet reserved for macros

```
MACRO AREA

Name    Macro      Description
---------------------------
\P      /pp        print the payroll worksheet
        ra8.d20~   specifies print range
        agpq       align, go, page, quit
```

Figure 7-2
Vince's initial
worksheet

Vince named his printing macro \P and saved it with this worksheet. The \P macro automates printing of the payroll worksheet.

❸ Turn your printer on and make sure it's ready to print.

❹ Press **[Alt][P]** to run the macro named \P.

To run a macro that begins with \ (Backslash), you press the [Alt] key in place of the backslash.

❺ The macro automatically prints the payroll worksheet. See Figure 7-3.

```
Krier Marine Services Payroll
Week Ending 10/15/9x

Employee    Hours    Pay    Gross
Name        Worked   Rate    Pay
------------------------------------
Bramble       15       7      105
Juarez        28       5      140
Smith         40       7      280
Diorio        22       5      110
                                ---------
Totals                          635
                                =========
```

Figure 7-3
Printout of Vince's
worksheet using
his print macro

Now let's look at the section of the worksheet where the print macro, \P, is located.

To examine the \P macro:

❶ Press **[F5]** (GOTO), type **I21**, and press **[Enter]** to move the cell pointer to the area of the worksheet where Vince plans to store the macros. See Figure 7-4. Vince has labelled cell I21 MACRO AREA to identify this section of the worksheet.

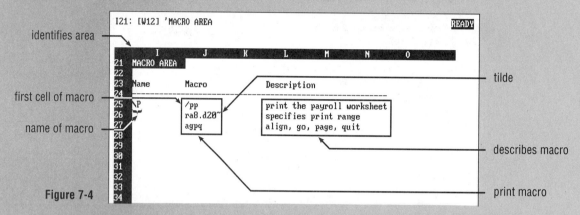

Figure 7-4

❷ Move the cell pointer to cell J25. Here you find the first cell of the actual macro, that is, the stored keystrokes. The complete macro is found in cells J25, J26, and J27. The print macro is a series of keystrokes stored as a label. This macro contains the following stored keystrokes:

/pp	(cell J25)	/print printer
ra8.d20~	(cell J26)	Range A8..D20 press [Enter]
agpq	(cell J27)	Align Go Page Quit

To run a macro, you must assign a range name to it. Vince has assigned the name \P to his print macro.

The keystroke [Enter] is represented in a macro by the ~ (Tilde). On many keyboards, this key is found in the upper left corner of the keyboard, to the left of the "1" key.

❸ Move the cell pointer to cell I25. In this cell, Vince has entered the name of the print macro. By including the name of the macro next to the stored keystrokes, he can easily identify the name assigned to the macro.

❹ Move the cell pointer to cell L25, the first line of the description of the macro. The entire description is found in cells L25, L26, and L27. Like cell I25, these cells serve to document the macro.

As you have seen, the print macro automatically prints the payroll worksheet. This saves Vince some time and allows others who may be less familiar with 1-2-3 commands to print the worksheet.

Special Keys

Before you create your own macros, you need to know one more thing about them. Some keys require a special entry to represent the actual keystroke in the macro. As we've just seen, for example, the ~ (Tilde) represents the [Enter] key in Vince's print macro.

Function keys, cursor-movement keys, and other special keys are represented by the name of the key enclosed in braces. For instance, to represent pressing the right arrow key in a macro, you would type {right}. To represent pressing the [Home] key, you would type {home}. Figure 7-5 shows what you should enter in a macro to represent function keys, cursor-movement keys, and other special keys.

Action	Macro entry
	Cursor-movement keys
Move cursor up one row	{up} or {u}
Move cursor down one row	{down} or {d}
Move cursor left one column	{left} or {l}
Move cursor right one column	{right} or {r}
Jump to cell A1	{home}
Jump to intersection of first blank and non-blank cell	{end} + (Arrow macro key)
Jump up 20 rows	{pgup}
Jump down 20 rows	{pgdn}
Move left one screen	{bigleft}
Move right one screen	{bigright}
	Function keys
F2; edit current cell	{edit}
F3; list range names in POINT mode	{name}
F4; relative, absolute	{abs}
F5; move cursor to specified cell	{goto}
F6; switch between windows	{window}
F7; repeat last /Data Query command	{query}
F8; repeat last /Data Table command	{table}
F9; recalculate the worksheet	{calc}
F10; display current graph	{graph}
	Other special keys
Press the [Enter] key	~
Press the [Esc] key	{esc}
Press the [Backspace] key	{bs}
Press the [Delete] key	{del}
Cause a pause in running of macro	{?}

Figure 7-5
Special keys used
for macro
keystrokes

Creating the Macro

It takes time to plan and develop macros, but they can save you a great deal of time and effort.

The process of developing a macro involves several steps:

- Planning the macro
- Placing the macro
- Entering the macro
- Naming the macro
- Documenting the macro
- Running and testing the macro
- Debugging or correcting any problems
- Saving the worksheet that includes the macro

Planning the Macro

One way to plan a macro is to write down on paper the keystrokes as you type them. For example, whenever Vince saves the Krier Payroll worksheet, he presses the following keys:

Keystrokes	Action
/	To call the command menu
F	To select the File command
S	To select the Save command Prompt appears: "Enter name of file to save: filename"
[Enter]	
	Prompt appears: "Cancel Replace Backup"
R	To select Replace to update file

Thus, Vince writes these keystrokes on a piece of paper:

/FS[Enter]R

This is the macro Vince wants to develop.

Placing the Macro

After planning the macro, you are ready to enter it. First, however, you must decide where to place it in the worksheet. The location of a macro should be in a part of the worksheet that will not be affected by changes made in the rest of the worksheet. One recommendation for the placement of macros is in an unused section of your worksheet, below and to the right of the current worksheet entries. Thus, your macros are not stored in an area that is likely to have data copied to it, nor in an area in which you might insert or delete rows (Figure 7-6).

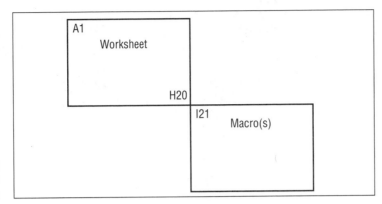

Figure 7-6
Where to place
macros

Vince has decided to enter the macros in an area beginning at cell I21. He has placed the label, MACRO AREA, in this cell to identify this area of the worksheet.

Entering the Macro

You can enter a macro in two different ways:

- By typing the keystrokes that represent the task (macro) as a series of labels directly into the worksheet cells
- By having 1-2-3 automatically record your keystrokes as you perform the task. You use the LEARN mode, explained later in this tutorial, to do this.

A macro is stored in a cell just like a number, a letter, or a formula. However, a macro *must* be entered as a label. Thus, you begin a macro with a label prefix, usually the ['] (Apostrophe), and enter the macro in a column of one or more cells. Although a cell can hold up to 240 keystrokes (all 240 keystrokes won't appear in the cell unless the column width is increased, but they are stored in the cell), it is easier to understand a macro if only a small number of related keystrokes are entered in a cell.

Vince has planned his macro. He knows what keystrokes he needs to enter and where to place them. He is now ready to enter the save macro by typing it in cell J29.

To enter the macro worksheet:

❶ Move the cell pointer to cell J29, the location of the keystrokes for this macro.

❷ Type **'/ fs~r** and press **[Enter]**. The macro's keystrokes appear in cell J29. See Figure 7-7.

first character in
macro is apostrophe

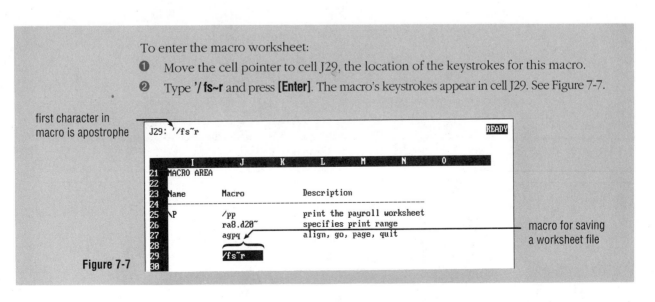

macro for saving
a worksheet file

Figure 7-7

Since macros are entered as labels, the first entry for a macro is a label prefix. If you do not begin the macro with a label prefix, the 1-2-3 command menu will appear on the screen. If this happens, press [Esc] and retype the macro with an apostrophe as the first character.

If you type the macro keystrokes incorrectly, just reenter the keystrokes.

Leave a blank cell below the last macro instruction to indicate the end of the macro.

Naming the Macro

Before you execute a macro, you must assign a range name to it. You can assign two types of range names to a macro:

- A \ (Backslash) and a single letter, such as \P
- A range name consisting of up to 15 characters

With either approach, you give the macro its name by using the Range Name Create (/RNC) command.

When you name a macro, you assign the range name to only the *first* cell of the macro. This is because 1-2-3 reads down the column of macro instructions until it reaches an empty cell; thus, you need name only the first cell.

Vince used the first type of name mentioned (Backslash plus a letter) to name his print macro (\P). For the macros you create in this tutorial, you will use the second approach, a range name with up to 15 characters. Although names such as \P are somewhat simpler to use, they can also be more difficult to remember. If you have several macros in a worksheet, you might forget which letter executes a particular task. By using a more descriptive name, you will be able to remember more about what your macro does.

Vince decides to name this macro SAVEPAY; he feels this name should make the macro easy to remember.

To name the save macro SAVEPAY:

❶ Be sure the cell pointer is in cell J29, the first cell containing the macro. Select /Range Name Create (**/RNC**).

❷ Type the range name **SAVEPAY** and press **[Enter]**.

❸ Press **[Enter]** to indicate you want to assign the name SAVEPAY to cell J29.

There is no need to assign every cell in the macro to the range name. 1-2-3 will automatically move to the next cell below the current cell in the macro until it finds a blank cell, which indicates the end of the macro.

Documenting the Macro

Whenever you create a macro, a good habit is to include a label containing the macro's name in a cell to the *left* of the macro so you can easily see the name when you examine the macro. It is also a good idea to enter a short description of the macro's function to the *right* of the macro. In this way, you can see at a glance what the macro does. Documenting a macro is not required to make it work, but it is a good habit to develop because some macros can be quite complex and difficult to read. Good macro documentation will save you time and help you avoid confusion.

Let's document Vince's save macro:

① Move the cell pointer to cell I29 and type the label **SAVEPAY**. Press **[Enter]**.

② Move the cell pointer to cell L29 and type **saves a worksheet file**, then press **[Enter]**. See Figure 7-8.

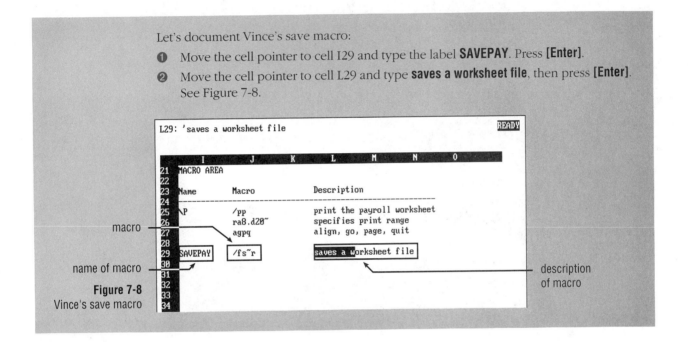

Figure 7-8
Vince's save macro

Running and Testing the Macro

Once you have entered and named your macro, you can run it. How you issue the command to run a macro depends on the type of name you assigned to the macro.

- If you named the macro with a backslash and a letter, you press the [Alt] key while pressing the letter of the macro name. You used this approach to run the print macro.

- If you named the macro with a range name of up to 15 characters, you use [Alt][F3] (RUN) and select the name of the macro you want to execute from a list of names that appears on the control panel.

When you run a macro, 1-2-3 reads the macro keystrokes starting with the first cell of the macro. When all the keystrokes in the first cell have been run, 1-2-3 continues reading down the column of cells, executing all keystrokes in each cell. It continues this process until it encounters an empty cell, which 1-2-3 interprets as the end of the macro.

As a general rule, you should save your worksheet prior to running your macro for the first time. This is a good habit to develop because *running a macro with an error could damage a worksheet.*

Now let's save the current version of the worksheet before you test the macro you just entered.

To save your worksheet as S7FILE1:

❶ Press **[Home]** to move the cell pointer to cell A1.

❷ Type **S7FILE1.WK1** and press **[Enter]**, to change the identifying information in the worksheet.

❸ Select /File Save (**/FS**).

❹ Type **S7FILE1** and press **[Enter]**. The worksheet is saved.

Now you can test the macro to see if it is working correctly.

To run the SAVEPAY macro :

❶ Press **[Alt][F3]** (RUN). See Figure 7-9. A list of range names appears in the control panel.

Figure 7-9

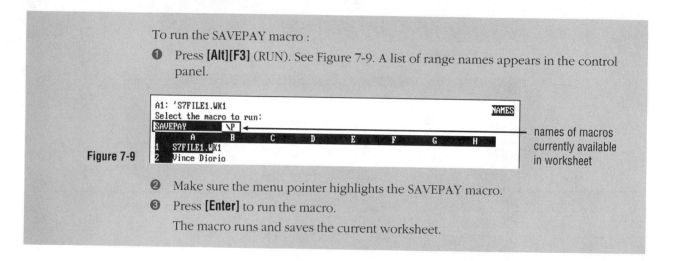

names of macros currently available in worksheet

❷ Make sure the menu pointer highlights the SAVEPAY macro.

❸ Press **[Enter]** to run the macro.

The macro runs and saves the current worksheet.

Interrupting a Macro

If you need to interrupt a macro during execution, press [Ctrl][Break]. 1-2-3 returns you immediately to READY mode. If the ERROR mode indicator flashes in the upper right corner of your screen when you press [Ctrl][Break], press [Esc]. This clears the error and returns you to READY mode.

Editing a Macro

Don't be surprised if your macro doesn't work the first time you execute it. When you typed the macro, you may have forgotten a tilde, included spaces, or entered the wrong command. The process of eliminating such errors is called **debugging**. If an error message appears when you run a macro, press [Esc] to return to READY mode. Then correct the macro by moving the cell pointer to the cell that contains the macro and do one of the following:

- Type over the current macro.
- Edit the cell of the macro that contains the error by pressing [F2] (EDIT) and changing the necessary keystrokes.

Creating Interactive Macros

Vince also planned to create a macro to create range names, because he frequently assigns range names to use with macros as well as for other 1-2-3 functions. He writes down the keystrokes required for assigning a range name to a range of cells:

Keystrokes	Action
/	To call the command menu
R	To select the Range command
N	To select the Name command
C	To select the Create command Prompt appears "Enter name"
Type range name	
[Enter]	1-2-3 prompts for range
Highlight range	
[Enter]	Indicates end of Range Name command

In looking over his notes, Vince realizes that the macro must pause to allow him to type the range name and the cells that represent the range. You can create macros that prompt you to enter data, enter a range name, or select a 1-2-3 command, and then the macro continues to run. A macro that pauses during its run is called an **interactive macro**.

To create an interactive macro, you use the Pause command, which is represented by {?}. You can enter {?} anywhere in your macro instruction. When 1-2-3 reads the {?} command, it temporarily stops the macro from running so you can manually enter a range name, move the cell or menu pointer, complete part of a command, or enter data for the macro to process. The macro continues to run when you press [Enter].

When you use {?} in a macro, you must complete the cell entry with a ~ (Tilde). This instructs 1-2-3 to continue running the macro after you press [Enter].

Vince writes down the keystrokes required for the range name macro:

/RNC{?}~{?}~

This interactive macro selects /Range Name Create. At the first {?} command, the macro pauses so you can specify the name of the range. When you press [Enter], the macro continues to run. The macro encounters another {?} command and pauses again. This time, you highlight the range of cells included in the range name. Press [Enter] again, to indicate that you want to end the pause. 1-2-3 then encounters the tilde and executes [Enter] to store the range. The macro is then complete.

To enter an interactive macro:

❶ Move the cell pointer to the macro area, cell J31, the location where you will enter the interactive macro.

❷ To enter the macro, type **'/rnc{?}~{?}~** and press **[Enter]**. See Figure 7-10 on the next page.

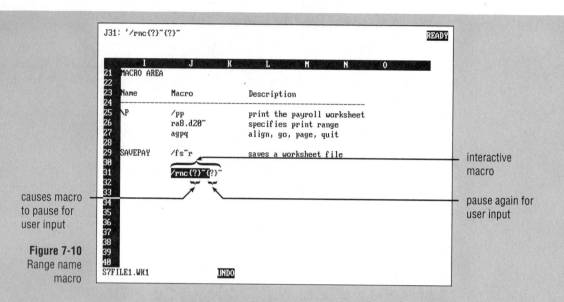

Figure 7-10
Range name
macro

Now name the macro NAMEARANGE. You will select the Range Name Create command instead of using the NAMEARANGE macro, because you are still in the process of creating the NAMEARANGE macro.

❸ With the cell pointer at cell J31, Select /Range Name Create (**/RNC**). Type **NAMEARANGE** and press **[Enter]**.

❹ Press **[Enter]** to assign the range name to cell J31.

Let's document the macro with a name and a description of what it does.

❺ Move the cell pointer to cell I31, type **NAMEARANGE**, and press **[Enter]**.

❻ Move the cell pointer to cell L31, type **assign range name to a range of cells** and press **[Enter]**. See Figure 7-11.

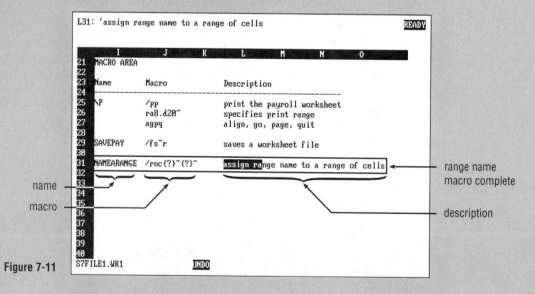

Figure 7-11

The NAMEARANGE macro is now complete.

Let's determine if the macro works properly. Again you need to save the current version of the worksheet before you run the new macro for the first time. Use the SAVEPAY macro you created earlier in the tutorial to save your worksheet.

To save your worksheet using the SAVEPAY macro:

❶ Press **[Alt][F3]** and highlight SAVEPAY from the list of range names listed on the control panel. Press **[Enter]**. The current version of the worksheet has been saved.

You are now ready to test the NAMEARANGE macro, but first let's do something that will save us time as we work through this tutorial. Since this is a tutorial on macros, we'll be going to the macro area frequently. Let's assign the name MACROS to cell I21, so you can use this name with the GOTO key [F5] to move directly to the macro area from any point in the worksheet.

To run the NAMEARANGE macro:

❶ Move the cell pointer to cell I21.

❷ Press **[Alt][F3]** and highlight NAMEARANGE from the list of range names listed in the control panel. Press **[Enter]**. See Figure 7-12.

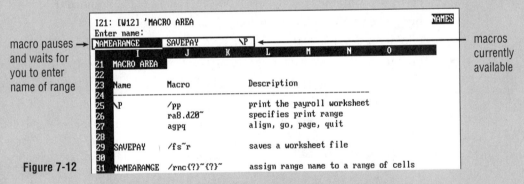

Figure 7-12

The macro begins to run. When 1-2-3 encounters the {?} command, the macro stops running, and the prompt "Enter name" appears in the control panel.

Notice that the status indicator CMD appears at the bottom of the screen whenever a macro is interrupted.

Now enter the range name.

❸ Type **MACROS**. Press **[Enter]**.

The macro pauses, waiting for you to highlight the range of cells for the range name.

❹ Press **[Enter]** since the range of the macro is a single cell, I21.

The macro continues to run until 1-2-3 encounters a blank cell, at which point it stops.

Let's verify that the NAMEARANGE macro worked properly.

To test the NAMEARANGE macro:

❶ Press **[Home]** to move the cell pointer to cell A1.

❷ Press **[F5]** (GOTO), type **MACROS**, and press **[Enter]**.

The cell pointer should now be at cell I21.

LEARN Mode

Vince wants to create a macro that he can use to format any column of data to Currency format with two decimal places.

As we mentioned earlier, Vince could type this macro directly into worksheet cells or he could use 1-2-3's LEARN mode. In LEARN mode, 1-2-3 automatically records the keystrokes as it performs a sequence of 1-2-3 operations. The keystrokes are captured in a separate area of the worksheet called the **learn range**. Vince can then name the learn range and execute it as a macro whenever he chooses.

Let's use LEARN mode to create Vince's macro to format a column. When you use the LEARN mode to create a macro, you must follow these steps:

- Decide where in the worksheet you want to put the learn range. The learn range must be a single column, long enough to contain all the keystrokes of the macro.
- Specify the learn range, using the Worksheet Learn Range command.
- Turn on LEARN mode to start recording all keystrokes.
- Perform the task you want 1-2-3 to record.
- Turn off LEARN mode to stop recording keystrokes.
- Assign a range name to the first cell in the learn range.
- Run the macro.

Now let's follow these steps and use the LEARN mode to create a macro that will format a column of numbers in Vince's worksheet.

First, Vince decides to place the learn range in cells J33 to J38.

To specify the learn range and record the macro:

❶ Move the cell pointer to cell J33 and select /Worksheet Learn Range (**/WLR**).

❷ Press **[.]** to anchor the cell. Highlight the range J33..J38 and press **[Enter]**. The learn range is now defined.

❸ Move the cell pointer to cell C14, the point where you want to begin formatting the values.

Follow the next steps carefully because once you turn on LEARN mode, every keystroke you make will be recorded. For example, if you press [Backspace] several times to correct typing errors, 1-2-3 will record the [Backspace] keystrokes.

Now turn LEARN Mode on:

❹ Press **[Alt][F5]** (LEARN) to turn on LEARN mode. Notice that the status indicator LEARN appears at the bottom of your screen. See Figure 7-13.

Figure 7-13

```
 8 ▌Krier Marine Services Payroll
 9 ▌Week Ending 10/15/9x
10 ▌
11 ▌Employee      Hours     Pay     Gross
12 ▌Name          Worked    Rate     Pay
13 ▌──────────────────────────────────────
14 ▌Bramble        15        7      105
15 ▌Juarez         28        5      140
16 ▌Smith          40        7      280
17 ▌Diorio         22        5      110
18 ▌                               ────────
19 ▌Totals                          635
20 ▌                               ========
S7FILE1.WK1                    UNDO LEARN
```

→ indicates LEARN mode is on

The next step is to perform the tasks you want to record.

⑤ Select /Range Format Currency (**/RFC**) and press **[Enter]**. Press **[End]** [↓] and press **[Enter]**. The column is now formatted using the currency format. See Figure 7-14.

Figure 7-14

```
 8 ▌Krier Marine Services Payroll
 9 ▌Week Ending 10/15/9x
10 ▌
11 ▌Employee      Hours     Pay     Gross
12 ▌Name          Worked    Rate     Pay
13 ▌──────────────────────────────────────
14 ▌Bramble        15      $7.00    105
15 ▌Juarez         28      $5.00    140
16 ▌Smith          40      $7.00    280
17 ▌Diorio         22      $5.00    110
18 ▌                               ────────
19 ▌Totals                          635
20 ▌                               ========
S7FILE1.WK1                    UNDO LEARN
```

→ performed formatting task while LEARN mode is on

Now you should turn off LEARN mode to stop recording the keystrokes.

⑥ Press **[Alt][F5]** (LEARN) to turn off LEARN mode. Notice that the status indicator LEARN no longer appears on the screen.

⑦ Press **[Enter]** so the recorded keystrokes appear in the learn range. Move the cell pointer to cell J33, the first cell in the learn range, to view the keystrokes that 1-2-3 has recorded. See Figure 7-15.

represents [↓]

LEARN indicator disappears

Figure 7-15

```
29 ▌SAVEPAY    /fs~r              saves a worksheet file
30 ▌
31 ▌NAMEARANGE /rnc{?}~{?}~       assign range name to a range of cells
32 ▌
33 ▌          /rfc~{END}{D}~
34 ▌
35 ▌
36 ▌
37 ▌
38 ▌
39 ▌
40 ▌
S7FILE1.WK1                    UNDO  [    ]
```

→ keystrokes captured during LEARN mode

If the macro looks correct, the next step is to specify a range name for it. On the other hand, if the macro needs corrections, you can edit it as you would any other cell. Note that the {End} {D} symbol moves the cell pointer down the column to the intersection of a blank and not-blank cell.

Let's name the macro CURRENCY2 using the NAMEARANGE macro.

To name and document the macro:

❶ With the cell pointer in cell J33, press **[Alt][F3]** and highlight NAMEARANGE from the list of range names on the control panel. Press **[Enter]**.

❷ Type **CURRENCY2** and press **[Enter]** to enter the range name.

❸ Press **[Enter]** to assign the range name to the first cell of the learn range.

Now let's document the macro.

❹ Move the cell pointer to cell I33. Type **CURRENCY2**, then press [**Enter**]. Move the cell pointer to cell L33. Type **format range of cells to currency** and press [**Enter**]. See Figure 7-16.

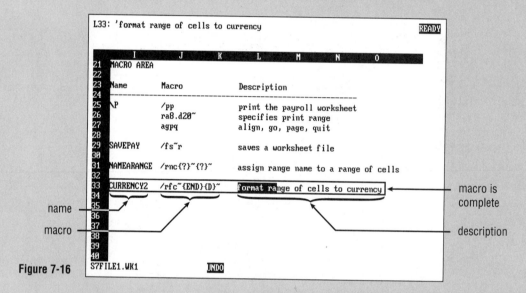

Figure 7-16

If you now wanted to create another macro using LEARN mode, you would have to reset the learn range to another range of cells (/Worksheet Learn Range); otherwise, the new macro would be added to the end of the existing macro.

Finally, let's run the CURRENCY2 macro to see if it works.

To run the macro:

❶ Move the cell pointer to cell D14.

❷ Press **[Alt][F3]** and highlight CURRENCY2 from the list of range names on the control panel. Press **[Enter]**.

The gross pay values appear in the Currency format.

❸ Save your worksheet as S7FILE1 using the SAVEPAY macro.

Using STEP Mode to Debug a Macro

The first time you run a macro, it may not work as you intended. In a simple macro, you can easily identify errors by comparing the keystrokes in the worksheet with the keystroke entries you planned. In large macros, however, it is more difficult to identify errors, so Lotus 1-2-3 has a special feature to help you in debugging macros. This feature, called **STEP mode**, allows you to run a macro one keystroke at a time.

To demonstrate the use of STEP mode, let's run the SAVEPAY macro in STEP mode. First, we'll modify the SAVEPAY macro so it is intentionally incorrect; then we'll see how STEP mode can help us find the error.

To modify the SAVEPAY macro and intentionally enter an error:

➊ Move the cell pointer to cell J29, the location of the SAVEPAY macro.

➋ Type **'/f~s~r** and press **[Enter]**. See Figure 7-17.

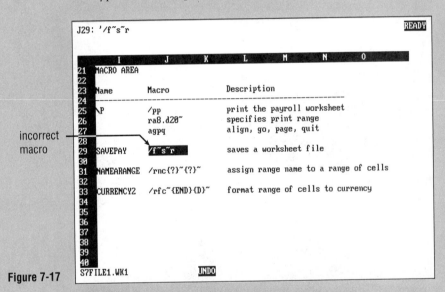

incorrect macro

Figure 7-17

Notice that a ~ (Tilde) appears between F and S. The correct macro is '/FS~R.

Let's try to use this modified SAVEPAY macro.

To run the incorrect SAVEPAY macro:

❶ Press **[Alt][F3]** (Run) and highlight SAVEPAY from the list of range names on the control panel. Press **[Enter]**. See Figure 7-18.

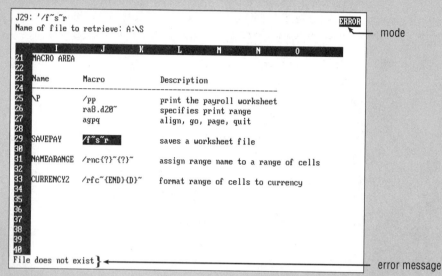

Figure 7-18
Attempt to run
SAVEPAY macro

Notice that the mode indicator in the upper right corner has changed to ERROR and is blinking. This indicates something is wrong with your macro. In addition, the message appearing in the status line says that the "File does not exist."

❷ Press **[Esc]** to clear the error condition and return to READY mode.

What happened? Why did the macro stop running? If the reason is not obvious to you from looking at the macro keystrokes, you can use STEP mode to help debug the macro.

To use STEP mode:

❶ Press **[Alt][F2]** (Step). This turns STEP mode on. See Figure 7-19. Notice that the STEP indicator appears in the status line at the bottom of the screen.

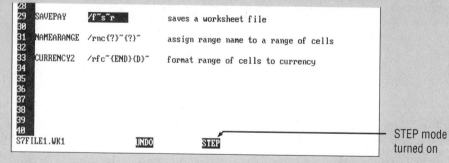

Figure 7-19

To run a macro in STEP mode, you press any key to run the macro one keystroke at a time. This way, you can see each step the macro takes and perhaps determine the problem with the macro.

Now rerun the macro:

❷ Press **[Alt][F3]** (Run) and highlight SAVEPAY from the list of range names on the control panel. Press **[Enter]**. See Figure 7-20.

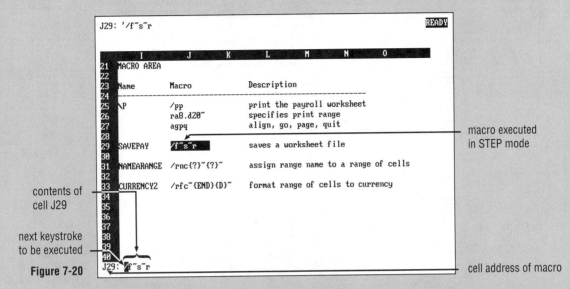

Figure 7-20

The cell address that contains the macro appears on the status line, along with the contents of that cell. The keystroke to be executed the next time you press a key is highlighted.

❸ Press **[Space]**. This executes the first keystroke of the macro, the / (Slash). See Figure 7-21.

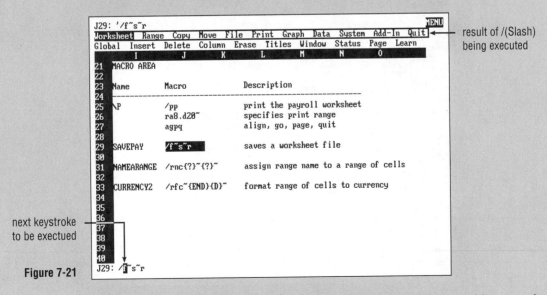

Figure 7-21

Notice that the Command menu appears in the control panel. In addition, in the status line, the keystroke that will be executed next, F, is highlighted.

❹ Press **[Space]** once more. This executes the next keystroke in the macro. See Figure 7-22.

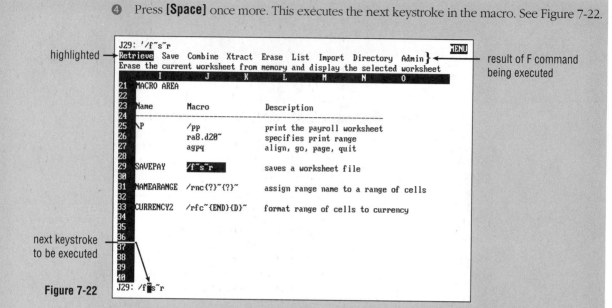

highlighted →

result of F command being executed →

next keystroke to be executed →

Figure 7-22

The File command from the Command menu is selected, and the File command options appear on the control panel. The Retrieve command is highlighted. Also notice that the ~ (Tilde) in the status line is highlighted. This is the next keystroke to be executed.

❺ Press **[Space]** once again. This runs the ~, that is, the [Enter] keystroke. See Figure 7-23. Since the Retrieve command was highlighted in the control panel, pressing [Enter] executes Retrieve rather than Save. The prompt "Name of the file to retrieve" appears in the control panel. Notice that the next keystroke to be executed, S, is highlighted in the status line.

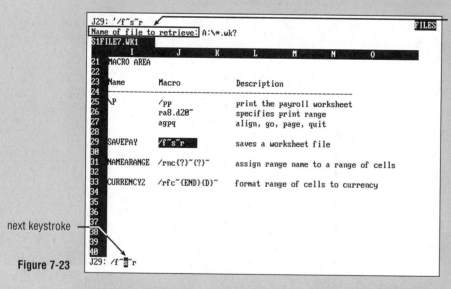

Retrieve command executed as a result of erroneous ~ (Tilde)

next keystroke →

Figure 7-23

❻ Press **[Space]** again. S is entered as the name of the file to retrieve. See Figure 7-24.

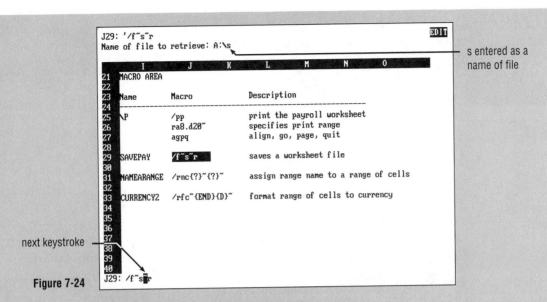

Figure 7-24

next keystroke

s entered as a name of file

The status line indicates the ~ (Tilde) will be the next keystroke to be executed.

❼ Press **[Space]**. 1-2-3 interprets the ~ as the [Enter] keystroke and attempts to retrieve a file named S. See Figure 7-25.

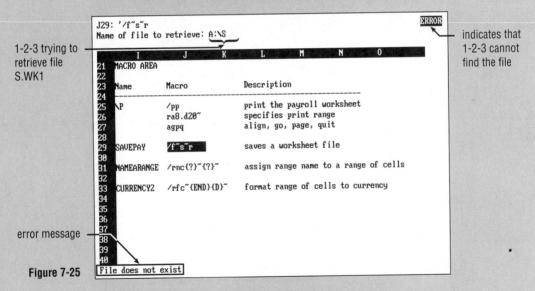

Figure 7-25

1-2-3 trying to retrieve file S.WK1

indicates that 1-2-3 cannot find the file

error message

1-2-3 doesn't find the file S.WK1 on your data diskette. The ERROR indicator appears in the upper right corner of your screen, and the error message "File does not exist" appears in the status line.

❽ Press **[Esc]** to clear the error message and return to READY mode.

Once your worksheet is in READY mode, you can edit the macro.

❾ Be sure the cell pointer is in cell J29. Type **'/FS~R** and press **[Enter]** to correct the macro.

You are still in STEP mode, which means if you attempt to run another macro, 1-2-3 will continue to run the macro one keystroke at a time.

⑩ Press **[Alt][F2]** (Step). This turns STEP mode off. Now the macros will run normally. The status indicator STEP disappears from the status line.

The Final Worksheet

As a final step in preparing the worksheet for Mrs. Krier, Vince decides to create a section of the worksheet that will guide Mrs. Krier and other users through the various options of the worksheet. This section will also provide instructions that walk a user through the various steps to run these options. Figure 7-26a shows Vince's sketch of the instruction section he plans to enter into his worksheet. Figure 7-26b shows his revised worksheet map.

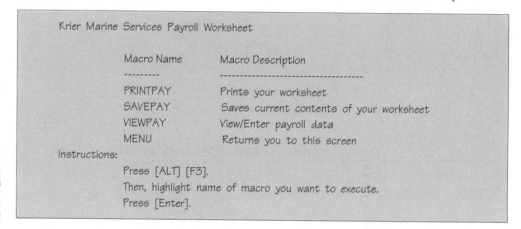

Figure 7-26a
Vince's sketch of the instruction section

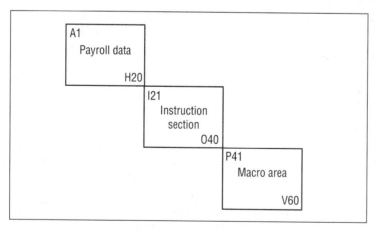

Figure 7-26b
Vince's revised worksheet map

To retrieve Vince's revised worksheet:

❶ Select /File Retrieve (**/FR**).

❷ Highlight C7FILE2 and press **[Enter]**. See Figure 7-27. The instruction screen appears immediately upon retrieval of the worksheet. This way, the first thing a user sees when retrieving the worksheet will be instructions on how to use the worksheet.

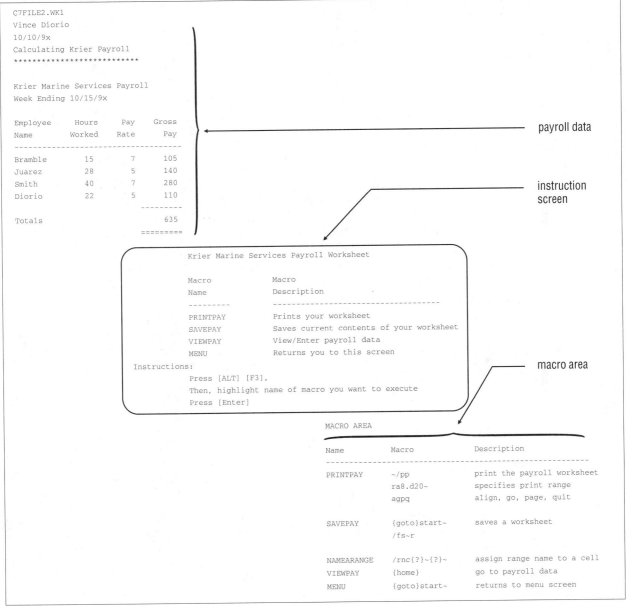

```
C7FILE2.WK1
Vince Diorio
10/10/9x
Calculating Krier Payroll
****************************


Krier Marine Services Payroll
Week Ending 10/15/9x

Employee      Hours     Pay    Gross
Name          Worked    Rate   Pay
------------------------------------

Bramble        15        7      105
Juarez         28        5      140
Smith          40        7      280
Diorio         22        5      110
                                ---------
Totals                          635
                                =========
```
payroll data

instruction
screen

```
        Krier Marine Services Payroll Worksheet


        Macro          Macro
        Name           Description
        ---------      ----------------------------------
        PRINTPAY       Prints your worksheet
        SAVEPAY        Saves current contents of your worksheet
        VIEWPAY        View/Enter payroll data
        MENU           Returns you to this screen
Instructions:
        Press [ALT] [F3],
        Then, highlight name of macro you want to execute
        Press [Enter]
```

macro area

```
        MACRO AREA

        Name       Macro          Description
        -----------------------------------------------------
        PRINTPAY   ~/pp           print the payroll worksheet
                   ra8.d20~       specifies print range
                   agpq           align, go, page, quit

        SAVEPAY    {goto}start~   saves a worksheet
                   /fs~r

        NAMEARANGE /rnc{?}~{?}~   assign range name to a cell
        VIEWPAY    {home}         go to payroll data
        MENU       {goto}start~   returns to menu screen
```

Figure 7-27
Vince's final worksheet

Vince has made some modifications to the worksheet. For instance, the print macro is named PRINTPAY instead of /P. He also has added a macro named MENU that returns the user to the instruction screen from any location in the worksheet.

Let's try out the revised worksheet.

To view the payroll data:

❶ Press **[Alt][F3]** (Run), highlight VIEWPAY, and press **[Enter]**. The payroll worksheet appears.

To return to the instruction screen:

❷ Press **[Alt][F3]** (Run), highlight MENU, and press **[Enter]**. The instruction screen reappears.

Vince is satisfied with the worksheet and is ready to show Mrs. Krier how to use the macros he's created.

Exercises

1. What keystrokes are used to do the following?
   a. Run a macro
   b. Turn STEP mode on and off
   c. Turn LEARN mode on and off

2. What do you use in a macro to represent the following?
   a. Pressing the [Enter] key
   b. A pause in the running of a macro
   c. Pressing [F5] (GOTO) key
   d. The [↑] key

3. What do the following macros do?
   a. {goto}MACROS~ (Note: MACROS is a range name)
   b. /rff{?}~{?}~
   c. /rfc2~{end}{down}~
   d. /c~{down}~
   e. /ppoocqq

Tutorial Assignments

Before you begin these Tutorial Assignements, check your Lotus 1-2-3 data diskette. Be sure you have space to save the additional worksheet files you'll create in these assignments (at least 30,000 bytes). If not, save your files as appropriate to another formatted diskette.

Retrieve the worksheet T7FILE1.WK1. This worksheet contains the four macros created in this tutorial. Make the following additions or modifications to the macro area.

1. First, save this worksheet as S7FILE2.

2. Modify the SAVEPAY macro so the cell pointer moves to cell A1 before the worksheet is saved. Save the worksheet using the revised SAVEPAY macro. What is the purpose of moving the cell pointer to cell A1 before saving the worksheet?

3. Whenever you run the macro SAVEPAY, it replaces the previously saved payroll worksheet with the current worksheet, thereby erasing any record of the earlier pay period.

a.   Modify the SAVEPAY macro again so that you can enter the filename during execution of the SAVEPAY macro. Be sure that this macro pauses to allow you to assign a new worksheet name to the current worksheet before saving the worksheet.

b.   Use the SAVEPAY macro and save the worksheet as S7FILE3.

4.   Each week, Vince retrieves the payroll worksheet and before entering the new hours worked for each employee, he erases the Hours Worked column from the previous pay period.

a.   Use the typing method to create a macro that erases a range of cells.

b.   Name this macro ERASECELLS.

c.   Document the macro.

d.   Save your worksheet as S7FILE3.

e.   Run the ERASECELLS macro and then enter the following hours for Bramble, Juarez, Smith, and Diorio, respectively: 20, 35, 35, and 10.

5.   Create a macro as follows:

a.   Use LEARN mode to develop a macro to format a range of cells using Currency format with zero decimal places.

b.   Name this macro CURRENCY0.

c.   Document the macro.

d.   Save the worksheet as S7FILE3.

e.   Format the Gross Pay and Pay Rate columns using this macro.

6.   Create a macro as follows:

a.   Use LEARN mode to create a macro to set print settings to compressed print. (Remember to change the learn range before you create this macro). This macro will set the right margin to 132 and the setup string to the code for compressed print used by your printer. For many printers, the setup string for compressed print is \015.

b.   Name this macro COMPRSPRINT.

c.   Document the macro.

d.   Save the worksheet as S7FILE3.

e.   Run the COMPRSPRINT macro. Check the print settings sheet to determine if your macro worked properly.

7.   Create a macro as follows:

a.   Use the typing method to create a macro that sets the print settings to normal print. This macro will set the right margin to 76 and the setup string to the code for normal print used by your printer. For many printers, the setup string for normal print is \018.

b.   Name this macro NORMPRINT.

c.   Document the macro.

d.   Save the worksheet as S7FILE3.

e.   Run the NORMPRINT macro. Check your print settings sheet to determine if your macro worked properly.

8.   Print the payroll worksheet using compressed type. First, run the COMPRSPRINT macro and then the print (\P) macro.

9.   Print the payroll worksheet using normal type. First, run the NORMPRINT macro and then the print (\P) macro.

Retrieve worksheet file T7FILE2. This worksheet has two new macros in addition to the four that were originally in the T7FILE1 worksheet.

10. The first new macro, COLWIDTH, located in cell J35, is supposed to change the column width. It doesn't work properly.

a.   Run the macro.

b.   Correct the macro.

c.   Run the corrected macro to increase the column width in column I from 12 to 15 characters.

11. The second macro, DELARANGE, located in cell J37, is supposed to allow you to select a range name to delete. When it runs, an error occurs.
    a. Run the macro.
    b. Correct the macro so it deletes a range name.
    c. Run the corrected macro and delete the range name /P.
    d. Use the NAMEARANGE macro in the worksheet to assign the macro in cell J25 the name PRINTPAY.
    e. Print the worksheet using the PRINTPAY macro.
    f. Make the appropriate changes to the documentation in the macro documentation.
    g. Print the worksheet using the macro PRINTPAY.

12. Save your worksheet as S7FILE4. Do not use the SAVE macro to save this file.

Case Problems

1. Reporting on Word Processing Software

A marketing research firm has compiled data on the number of units the top six word processing software packages have shipped worldwide during 1989 (Figure 7-29).

Product	Units Shipped
WordPerfect	1,400,000
Microsoft Word	500,000
WordStar	345,000
Display Write	300,000
Professional Write	250,000
Multimate	200,000

Figure 7-29

1. Create a worksheet using the data from Figure 7-29.

2. Prepare a report that includes all the products and has the following format:

	Add title	
Product	Units shipped	Market share
XXXXXXXXXXX	XXXXX	XX.X%
XXXXXXXXXXX	XXXXX	XX.X%
.	.	.
.	.	.
.	.	.
Total Units	XXXXX	

3. Create a pie chart of shipments by product. Name the graph PIE_SHIP.

4. Create a bar graph of shipments by product. Name the graph BAR_SHIP.

5. Create a macro to print the report. Name the macro PRINT.

6. Create a macro to view the pie chart. Name the macro PIEWP.

7. Create a macro to view the bar graph. Name the macro BARWP.

8. Include within your worksheet an instruction section that will help anyone who uses the macros in this worksheet. This section should be the first screen that appears when a user retrieves the worksheet.

9. Save your worksheet as S7WORD.

10. Use the macro PRINT to print the report from Problem 2 above.

2. Tutorial 2 Revisited

Retrieve the worksheet P2FUND, the final version of the Balboa Mutual Fund worksheet from Tutorial 2, and do the following:

1. Modify the worksheet so that the first screen includes the following:

Macro name	Description
ERASERANGE	Erase a column
PRINTFUND	Print fund report
SAVEFUND	Save the worksheet
RETURN	Return to this screen
[Place instructions on how to run a macro here]	

2. Create a macro to erase the prices from the Current Prices column. You should be able to select (highlight) the range of cells to erase. Name the macro ERASERANGE.

3. Create a macro to print the Mutual Fund Report. Name the macro PRINTFUND.

4. Create a macro to save the worksheet. You should be able to name the worksheet that you are saving. Name the macro SAVEFUND.

5. Create a macro to return the instruction screen.

6. Enter the Current Prices for November 12, 1990. The current prices for that day were:

IBM	127
Coca-Cola	44
AT&T	35
Boeing	45

First, use your macro to erase the Current Price column. Then enter the new prices. Remember to also change the date.

7. Print the Net Asset Value report for November 12, 1990, using your print macro.

8. Save your file as S2FUND using your save macro.

3. Tutorial 6 Revisited

Retrieve the worksheet P6CUST, the final version of the Customer database of Rhode Island and Massachusetts customers from Tutorial 6. Let's modify this worksheet to include macros to do the following:

- View the statistical summary report for Rhode Island and Massachusetts customers
- View the outstanding balance report by state
- Sort the database
- Print the database

Do the following:

1. Modify the worksheet so that the first screen includes the following:

Macro name	Description
REPORT1	Go to Summary Report
REPORT2	Go to Outstanding Balances by state
SORT	Sort database by field you select
PRINT	Print all records in database
RETURN	Return to this screen
[Place instructions on how to run a macro here]	

2. Create a macro to go to the first report in this worksheet. This is the summary report that shows total, average, maximum, and minimum outstanding balances for all Rhode Island and Massachusetts customers (cells N1..O12).

3. Create a macro to go to the second report in this worksheet. This report shows the outstanding balances by state (cells N21..P27).

4. Create a macro that sorts the data file on any primary sort key that you choose and also lets you select the sort order (ascending or descending). Be sure that all other steps in the sort macro are done automatically.

5. Create a macro to print the database. Run this macro.

6. Create a macro to return to the instruction screen. Run this macro.

7. Save your worksheet as S6CUST.

8. Use the SORT macro to sort the worksheet by YTD Sales in descending order.

9. Print the database.

10. Remember to document all your macros.

11. Prepare a worksheet map.

Additional Cases

Additional Case 1:
Preparing an Invoice for Island Influences

Natalie Ryad moved to Barbados a few years ago and opened Island Influences, a gift gallery featuring the works of Caribbean artists. Their works evoke the flavor of the islands through paintings on plates, mugs, glasses, coasters, and other giftware.

Natalie's business has done quite well, but customers continue to ask her if she has a mail order catalog from which they could order gifts. After studying the catalog business concept, Natalie decides to develop a mail order business to supplement her retail business. She believes sales will come from people who have visited Barbados and her shop and who want to purchase additional giftware without returning to the island.

As the catalog orders begin to come in, Natalie manually processes the mail orders (customers use forms included in the catalogs). She calculates the amount of each item ordered, adds the island tax and shipping costs, and then totals the final amount owed. But after 13 months, the catalog business represents 23 percent of Natalie's total sales. She decides it is time to computerize.

Natalie will use Lotus 1-2-3 to help her prepare invoices. Actually, she will create an invoice **template,** a preformatted worksheet that contains the labels and formulas needed to process an invoice but that does not include any values. Natalie will enter the values when she prepares an invoice for each customer. She will enter formulas into the template so that as she enters the customer's order, 1-2-3 will automatically perform

In this case you will do the following:

- Format a worksheet to improve its appearance
- Create a template
- Protect worksheet cells
- Use the @IF function
- Develop a print macro

calculations for the invoice. These calculations will include the dollar amount of each item ordered, the total amount of all items ordered, tax, shipping charges, and the total amount owed.

Figure 1a shows the invoice template that Natalie sketched and Figure 1b shows the calculations she plans to perform for each order. The boxed numbers are guides to help you relate Natalie's sketch to the calculations.

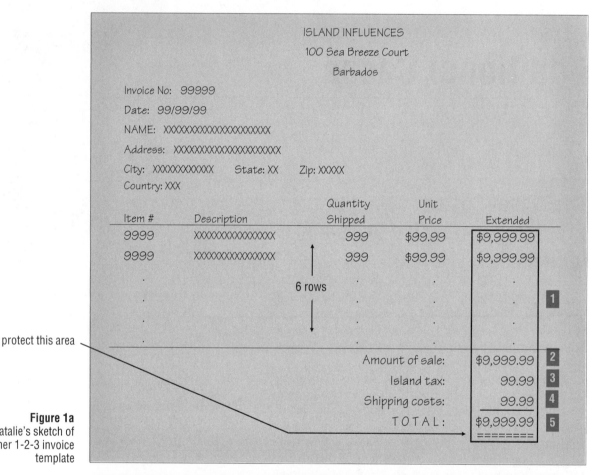

Figure 1a
Natalie's sketch of her 1-2-3 invoice template

protect this area

ISLAND INFLUENCES
100 Sea Breeze Court
Barbados

Invoice No: 99999

Date: 99/99/99

NAME: XXXXXXXXXXXXXXXXXXXX

Address: XXXXXXXXXXXXXXXXXXX

City: XXXXXXXXXXX   State: XX   Zip: XXXXX

Country: XXX

Item #	Description	Quantity Shipped	Unit Price	Extended
9999	XXXXXXXXXXXXXXX	999	$99.99	$9,999.99
9999	XXXXXXXXXXXXXXX	999	$99.99	$9,999.99

6 rows

1

Amount of sale: $9,999.99   2
Island tax: 99.99   3
Shipping costs: 99.99   4
TOTAL: $9,999.99   5

Figure 1b
Calculations Natalie plans for her invoice template

1. extended price   **1**   =   unit price × quantity shipped
    Six rows for items ordered. Enter this formula six times.

2. amount of sale = SUM (of the extended price column)
    Enter formula to add all six rows in the column

3. island tax = 7% × amount of sale   **2**

4. shipping cost =   if amount of sale less than $100
                           shipping cost = $15
                      otherwise
                           shipping cost = $25

5. TOTAL =   **5**   amount of sale   **2**   + tax   **3**   + shipping   **4**

Do the following:

1. Begin your worksheet by entering the labels for the invoice template. Adjust column widths if necessary. The placement of the labels and their corresponding values do not have to match Natalie's sketch exactly.

2. Enter the formulas in Figure 1b into your worksheet.

3. Format the following columns or cells as Currency with two decimal places:
    a. unit price
    b. extended price
    c. amount of sale
    d. Island tax
    e. shipping charges
    f. total sales

4. Protect the worksheet so that the cell pointer cannot enter any cell whose value is determined by a formula.

5. Develop a macro to print the invoice. Name the macro PRINT_INVOICE.

6. Save the worksheet template as S1INVC1.

7. Process the sales order shown in Figure 2.

Figure 2
Sales order received by Island Influences

ISLAND INFLUENCES
Catalog Order Form

Ordered by:
Martin Felsap
123 Archway St
Atlanta, Ga 97812

Item#	Description	Qty	Unit Price
64	Island Scene Mug 12 oz	6	12.00

a. Retrieve the preformatted worksheet file S1INVC1 from Assignment 6 above.
b. Enter the data from Mr. Felsap's order form into the invoice template. This will be invoice number 1078 and use today's date. Note how the calculations are automatically calculated as you enter the data.
c. Print the invoice using the macro you created in Assignment 5, above.

Additional Case 2:
Bidding for a Contract with the U.S. Navy

Quidnesset Shipyard has completed a prototype of a new submarine. The Navy, impressed with the prototype, asks Quidnesset to bid on a contract to build 10 additional submarines.

As a member of the cost accounting group at Quidnesset Shipyard, you have accumulated the following information about what it will cost to build the new submarines (Figure 1).

Since labor represents such a large portion of the cost, Quidnesset management wants an accurate estimate of labor hours so they can submit a realistic and competitive bid to the Navy. They believe that they should allow for the learning process as workers and management build

> **In this case you will do the following:**
>
> ■ Use exponents in a formula
>
> ■ Create a one-way data table
>
> ■ Prepare and print a report
>
> ■ Create a named graph
>
> ■ Print a graph
>
> ■ Ask *what-if* questions about the completed worksheet

each submarine. The amount of time required to build the second submarine will probably be less than the first, the third submarine will require less time than the second, and in general the time to build each additional sub will decrease. As workers continue to gain experience, their dexterity on repetitive tasks should improve. Also, as the managers become more familiar with building the submarines, they should be able to schedule work more efficiently.

Figure 1

Direct materials (per sub)	$1,000,000
Direct labor and overhead	
(100,000 hours @ $50/hour)	$5,000,000
Total Cost	$6,000,000

One approach to how you can estimate the reduced time needed to build each submarine is to use what is called the *learning curve*. This is a mathematical formula to calculate how labor hours per unit manufactured decline as the units of output increase. A popular learning curve formula is:

$$m = ax^b$$

where

m = time to produce the last single unit
x = number of units produced (x is 1, or x is 2, x is 3, . . . x is 11)
a = time required to produce the prototype unit
b = rate of learning

Quidnesset Shipyards uses an 80-percent learning curve to estimate the number of direct labor hours to complete each submarine. For example, as the quantity of units produced is *doubled*, from say the second submarine to the fourth submarine, the time needed to produce the fourth submarine is 80 percent of the time needed to produce the second submarine.

The parameters Quidnesset Shipyard uses in the learning curve formula are:

x = 1, 2, 3, 4, 5, 6, 7, 8, 9, 10, 11

b = −.3219 (where b is the precalculated number for an 80% learning curve)

a = 100000

Do the following:

1. Use the Data Table command to develop a table that displays the number of hours required to produce the first submarine (the prototype), the second submarine, the third, and so on, until you reach the eleventh. In this table, have the first column list x, the number of units produced (x = 1, x = 2, x = 3, etc.). Have the second column list the hours required to build each corresponding submarine in the first column.

    Hint: When x = 1, the formula calculates that it will take 100000 hours to build the prototype. Thus, when you create this data table, what you are really interested in is the time it would take to build the second to the eleventh submarines.

    When x = 2, the formula calculates that it will takes approximately 80000 hours to build the second submarine.

    In 1-2-3, the characters you use to represent an exponent is ^. For example, you would enter 4^2 as 4^2.

2. Use the results from Assignment 1, above, to calculate the cost of assembling each submarine. Use Figure 2-1 to construct a formula for cost estimation.

3. Prepare and print the report as sketched in Figure 2.

Figure 2

Quidnesset Shipyards Cost Estimate		
Submarine	Hours	Cost
2	xxx	$xxxx
3	xxx	xxxx
. . .	. . .	. . .
11	xxx	xxxx
Totals	xxx	$xxxx

4. Create a line graph of the number of hours it takes to build each submarine. Name the graph LINEHOUR.

5. Save your worksheet as S2SUBS.

6. Create a PIC file for your line graph named LNHRS.PIC. Print your graph.

7. What if, due to a union renegotiation of wages, the direct labor and overhead costs increase to $52 per hour? Rerun your model and print out a second report using the format in Assignment 3, above.

Additional Case 3:
Budgeting for Employee Benefits at BranCo International

Salaries and other forms of employee compensation, such as benefits, are one of a company's major human resource expenditures. The cost of employee benefits often represents 30 percent to 35 percent of an employee's total compensation; thus, company managers must carefully budget to pay for employee benefits.

Manula Abba, vice president of administration for BranCo International, has asked you to help her calculate the annual human resources budget. You agree to help and begin by retrieving the employee worksheet, P3PERSL.WK1. This file contains BranCo employee data as a 1-2-3 database.

The field names in the employee database are shown in Figure 1.

In this case you will do the following:

- Work with a 1-2-3 database

- Use @IF function

- Add new variables to a worksheet

- Sort records

- Create and print one detail and one summary report

- Create several macros

- Create one graph

- Ask *what-if* questions about the completed worksheet

BranCo's Benefits Program

Manula wants you to first study carefully the BranCo benefits package. It includes:

- a medical plan for employees and their dependents
- a group life insurance plan
- a 401K retirement plan
- worker's compensation
- contributions to social security
- federal unemployment insurance
- state unemployment insurance

Field	Description
EMP#	employee number
LNAME	last name
FNAME	first name
BIRTH	date of birth (yyyymmdd)
SEX	code for sex (M = male; F = female)
MAR	code for marital status (Y = married; N = not married)
DEP	number of dependents
ANNSAL	annual salary
HIREDT	date employee hired (yyyymmdd)
XMPT	exempt employee (X = exempt; N = nonexempt)
MED	code for medical plan (F = family plan; I = individual plan; N = no medical plan)
401K	401K retirement plan (Y = contributing to plan; N = not contributing to plan)
DIV	division in which employee works
JOBTITLE	job title
PER	payment method (H = hourly; M = monthly)

Figure 1

Medical Plan

BranCo provides medical insurance for its employees through an insurance company. This insurance company charges two premiums, one for individual employees and one for employees with families (dependents). The company pays 80 percent of the cost of this medical insurance and the employee pays 20 percent. The total monthly premiums are: *Hint:* This calculation requires an @IF function embedded or nested within an @IF function.

Individual	$195 per month
Family	$250 per month
No coverage	$ 0

Employees who have other medical insurance, such as with their spouses' employers, can choose no coverage at BranCo.

Group Life Insurance

BranCo pays entirely for group life insurance. The annual fee is $1.70 per $1000 of coverage. The benefit for employees varies, depending on whether the employee is exempt (not eligible for overtime pay) or nonexempt (eligible for overtime pay). An exempt employee's benefit is two times his or her annual salary; a nonexempt employee's benefit is one and one-half times his or her annual salary excluding overtime. For example, if an exempt employee's annual salary is $34,200, then the insurance coverage is $68,400 (2 × $34,200); the premium paid by the company to cover this employee is $116.28 ($1.70 × 68.4).

401K Retirement Plan

To help employees save for their retirement, the company provides a 401K plan. Employees can contribute up to 5 percent of their pretax salaries to the savings plan, and the money they contribute is not taxable until they withdraw it at retirement. In addition, the company matches what an employee contributes dollar for dollar up to the first 3 percent of the participating employee's salary. The code Y in the 401K field in the employee database indicates employees who participate in the plan. For the purposes of this budget, Manula wants you to assume all participating employees will contribute the maximum allowed.

Worker's Compensation

BranCo is required by law to provide this benefit. It is an insurance that pays the medical bills of workers injured on the job. The workers compensation premium is based on a fee of $4.68 per $1,000 of annual salary. For example, if an employee earns $40,400, then the firm pays a premium of $189.07 per year for this employee ($4.68 × 40.4).

FICA Taxes (Social Security)

FICA taxes, also called Social Security, are paid equally by the employee and the employer. The employee's share is withheld from his or her paycheck, and BranCo pays an equal share to each employee's FICA account. For 1990, Social Security tax for each employee was 7.65% of the first $50,400 the employee earned. For example, if an employee earns $30,000, then the FICA tax is $2,295 (.0765 × 30000). BranCo also must pay $2,295 to this employee's account. As another example, if an employee earns $60,000, then the FICA tax is $3,855.60 (.0765 × 50400). No FICA tax is applied to the amount an employee earns over $50,400. The employee and BranCo each must pay $3,855.60 toward the employee's FICA account.

Federal Unemployment Tax (FUTA)

BranCo, like other employers, must pay an unemployment tax equal to 6.2 percent of the first $7,000 of each employee's annual salary. FUTA tax is paid only by the employer.

State Unemployment Tax (SUTA)

Employers pay an unemployment tax to the state equal to 3 percent of the first $7,000 of each employee's annual salary. SUTA is paid only by the employer.

Creating the Worksheet

After studying the details of the benefits program at BranCo, you begin by sketching the final employee benefits budget for 1990 (Figure 2).

```
┌─────────────────────────────────────────────┐
│              BranCo Corporation             │
│           Employee Benefits Budget          │
│                                             │
│                      1990                   │
│   Programs           Amount                 │
│   ─────────────────────────────────         │
│                                             │
│   Medical plan        $xxxx                 │
│   Life insurance       xxxx                 │
│   401K plan            xxxx                 │
│   Worker's comp        xxxx                 │
│   FICA taxes           xxxx                 │
│   FUTA                 xxxx                 │
│   SUTA                 xxxx                 │
│                                             │
│   Total benefits      $xxxxx                │
│                                             │
│   Note: The budget for employee benefits rep-│
│   resents expenditures made only by the com-│
│   pany, not by the employees.               │
│                                             │
└─────────────────────────────────────────────┘
```

Figure 2

You realize that before you can develop a final budget showing the company's costs per benefit, you must add additional columns to the employee database to calculate each employee's individual benefits.

Do the following:

1. Retrieve the worksheet, P3PERSL.WK1 and expand the employee database to include seven additional columns, one for each benefit. Calculate the cost of each benefit for each employee by incorporating the appropriate formulas described for each benefit.

    Hint: Consider setting up an input section in your worksheet that references the variables in the benefits formulas. Then, if the formulas change, you won't have to reenter the formulas for each employee.

2. Set up an output area in your worksheet for the Benefits Summary Report; then create the Benefits Summary Report.

3. Create a macro to print the Benefits Summary Report. Name the macro PRINT_BENEFIT.

4. Use the data from the Benefits Summary Report to create a graph comparing the cost of each benefit. Choose a graph that you feel will most appropriately show the comparison of the costs. Name your graph BENEFITS.

5. Create a macro that will allow Manula to view this graph easily and quickly. Name the macro VIEWGRAPH.

6. Create a second report, entitled Detailed Employee Benefits Report. This report should show the total compensation (salaries plus benefits) for each employee. Include the following columns: employee last name, salary, each benefit (seven columns), total benefits (sum of previous seven columns), and total compensation (salary plus total benefits). Include totals for the columns when appropriate. Arrange the employee records by division and, within division, alphabetically by last name. *Hint:* Use the Data Query Extract command to retrieve the columns you need for the Detailed Employee Benefits Report.

7. Create a macro to print the Detailed Employee Benefits Report. Name the macro PRINT_DETAIL.

8. Print the Detailed Employee Benefits Report using the macro PRINT_DETAIL.

9. Print the Benefits Summary Report using the macro PRINT_BENEFIT.

10. Save your worksheet as S3PERSL1.

11. What if, due to rising costs for medical insurance, BranCo management increases employees' share of medical insurance payments from 20 percent to 30 percent?
    a. What cost savings are achieved by increasing the employees' share of medical insurance payments?
    b. Print this Benefits Summary Report.
    c. Save your worksheet as S3PERSL2.

12. What if Congress revises the tax laws for 1991, and the new law affects the payments employees and employers make to FICA taxes? Suppose the new law calculates FICA taxes as shown in Figure 3.

If salary is	Then FICA is
less than or equal to $53,400	7.65% × annual salary
greater than $53,400 but less than or equal to $125,000	$4,085.10 + (annual salary − 53,400) × 1.45%
greater than $125,000	$5,123.30

Figure 3

Remember that 7.65% and 1.45% can also be entered as .0765 and .0145, respectively.

   a. Revise the FICA calculation in your worksheet based on this new Federal tax law.
   b. How much more will BranCo have to pay in FICA taxes as a result of the new law?
   c. Print the Benefits Summary Reports.
   d. Save your worksheet as S3PERSL3.

Part Four

■   ■   ■

dBASE III PLUS Tutorials

Tutorial 1

An Introduction to Database Concepts and dBASE III PLUS

OBJECTIVES

In this tutorial you will learn to:

- Define the terms *field*, *record*, *file*, and *database*

- Load dBASE

- Identify the components of the Assistant screen

- Use Assistant mode

- Get help while in Assistant mode

- Switch from Assistant mode to dot prompt mode

- Quit dBASE

Case: Wells & Martinez Advertising Agency — The Need for Computerization

Three years ago Nancy Wells and Martin Martinez founded the Wells & Martinez Advertising Agency (W&M) in Sante Fe, New Mexico. Their initial goal was to plan, prepare, and place advertising and other promotions for small to mid-sized local companies. Like many new, struggling businesses, W&M has experienced limited initial success providing advertising services to a few key clients. Their current client list includes a fashion boutique, a furniture designer, a caterer, a law firm, an automobile dealership, an insurance agency, and the town of Sante Fe's tourism board.

Recently, in an effort to attract more clients, Nancy and Martin launched an aggressive marketing campaign that focused on their agency's strengths — creativity, flexibility, and reasonable rates. The campaign generated increased interest among local companies, but, more important, it also attracted attention from several regional companies.

The prospect of increasing the size of their client list is both good news and bad news for Nancy and Martin. They have a limited budget and only six employees to help run the operations and creative activities of the agency. In addition the day-to-day administration of W&M is time consuming. Nancy and Martin recognize that if they don't improve their own and their employees' efficiency W&M might not be able to handle new business.

Martin directs the creative activities of W&M. He is responsible for generating advertising ideas and converting those ideas into print and broadcast messages. As the head of this part of W&M, Martin is primed and ready for the impending growth.

Nancy manages the administrative and production side of the agency. She has been struggling with the manual business systems that handle the billing, payroll, and general bookkeeping. Nancy knows that W&M has outgrown these basic systems, which she established three years ago; she expects to run into even more difficulty with possible new business.

Martin and Nancy have identified several problems with their current system. They are concerned about cash flow and that billings to clients are not always mailed promptly. Martin and Nancy have no way of knowing whether clients are being charged correctly or whether a specific job is profitable. In addition, their systems to track the various jobs and job-related expenses are inadequate. Finally, they know that the manual systems often supply erroneous information.

Nancy and Martin realize that computerization is the way to solve these administrative problems. But because of the cost of their recent marketing campaign, they cannot afford a computerized software package specifically designed for advertising agencies. They put their heads together and try to come up with a solution. If only they themselves knew about computers. Then Nancy remembers that Esther Wong, a recent business college graduate she hired 10 months ago, is familiar with accounting and microcomputer software. Nancy and Martin decide to talk to Esther and ask her to help them develop a computerized system in house.

Esther is flattered that Nancy and Martin have asked her to help, and she sets to the task immediately. She begins her analysis by first evaluating how work flows within W&M. She interviews Nancy, Martin, and the other employees to better understand how the advertising jobs are initiated, tracked, and billed.

After studying the work flow and discussing ways to improve the business systems, Esther outlines a possible solution. She presents her ideas to Nancy, Martin, and other staff members; they discuss her proposal, make several modifications, and then agree to create three files. First, a Clients file will store each client's identification code (ID), the names of the client companies, the names of the contacts at the client companies, and the clients' main telephone numbers. Second, a Jobs file will store information about each job that a client has authorized W&M to complete. The jobs file will include job numbers, client identification, brief descriptions of the jobs, due dates, and estimates of the costs to the clients. The third file, the Expenses file, will include for each expense the ID of the client to be charged; the job number; the billing category, which describes the expense, such as creative meeting, typesetting, copywriting, and so on; the date; the amount; and a brief explanation. Esther decides to use dBASE III PLUS to create and maintain these files and thus computerize W&M.

Introduction to Database Concepts

Before you work along with Esther and begin the W&M database system, you need to understand a few important terms and concepts.

How Data Are Organized

Stored data, computerized or not, are commonly organized into a structure, or hierarchy, which starts at the bottom with fields and then builds to records, files, and then databases (Figure 1-1). This organization of data helps you to process and retrieve information.

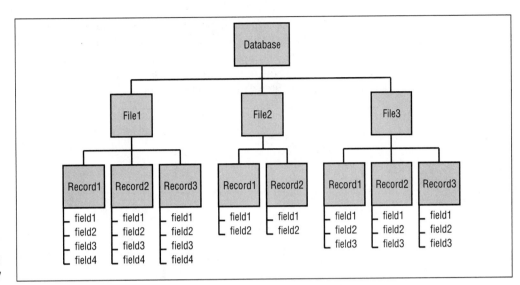

Figure 1-1
Data hierarchy

First, let's look at a field. A **field,** also called a **data item** or a **data element**, is a characteristic of an object, person, place, or thing. For example, the client identification number, client name, client phone number, and name of contact person are fields that W&M wants to track for each client. Each field has a value. The *value of a field* is its specific contents. For example, the value of the field "phone number" might be (419)783-6210, and the value of the field "contact person" might be Gunther Williams.

If we group related fields together, they form what is known as a record. A **record** is a collection of data elements that describe an event, person, or object. For example, a complete client record at W&M consists of the following group of four related fields: client identification, client name, name of contact person, and phone number (Figure 1-2).

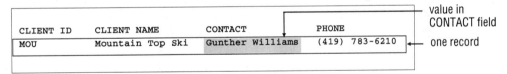

Figure 1-2
A client record

A collection of related records is called a **file**. At W&M, the nine client records collectively represent a file, in this case, the agency's clients file. Each record within the file contains the same four fields, but the data values in those fields vary from record to record. Figure 1-3 shows the complete W&M file CLIENT.

CLIENT ID	CLIENT NAME	CONTACT	PHONE	
MOU	Mountain Top Ski	Gunther Williams	(419) 783-6210	← record 1
VIK	Viking Auto Group	Jeff Serito	(505) 984-9216	← record 2
ALE	Alexander Insurance	Paul Alexander	(505) 883-9222	← record 3
SAN	Santa Fe Tourist Center	Liddy Posada	(505) 986-5555	← record 4
ORI	Origins	Gary Higgins	(505) 988-0733	← record 5
Fat	Fat Wheels Bicycle Tours	Helen Carson	(505) 994-2432	← record 6
CEL	Celebrity Catering	Linda Randall	(505) 883-9922	← record 7
EYE	Eyes Have It	Sandy Alonso	(505) 780-2277	← record 8
IMA	Images	Wendy Falchetti	(505) 898-1286	← record 9

Figure 1-3
W&M CLIENT file

Typically a company maintains several different files to store related data. A **database** is a collection of related files. For example, at W&M Esther's system will include a file to store basic data about clients, a second file to store data about each client's job on which W&M is working, and a third file to track the expenses incurred by W&M as they work on those jobs. These three related files can be thought of as W&M's database (Figure 1-4).

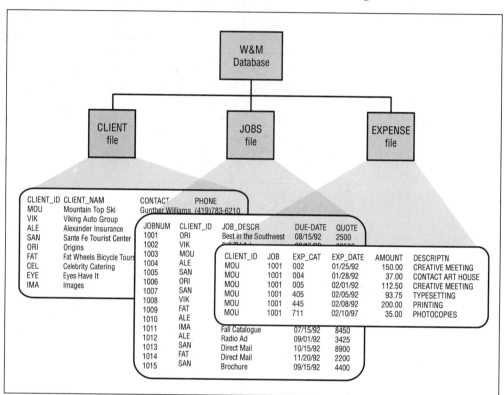

Figure 1-4
W&M's database

Database Management Systems

To create and manage its database, a company often purchases a database management system. A **database management system** (DBMS) is the software that lets you enter, maintain, manipulate, retrieve, and output data from a database.

A DBMS works as an "intermediary," that is, it serves as an interface between a database and the users who are seeking data from that database (Figure 1-5). A DBMS allows you to retrieve information from a database and to store data in a database conveniently and efficiently. Specifically a DBMS does the following:

- It creates the structure of the database files. In other words, it defines the fields in a record.

- It facilitates the initial loading of data into the database and enables you to update the database by adding, deleting, and modifying records.

- It allows you to ask questions by using query language and report generator software. A **query language** lets you obtain immediate responses to questions you ask about information in the database. You specify what you are looking for, and the DBMS searches the database and gives you the answers. The emphasis of a query is on quick response rather than well-designed output. A **report generator** allows you to develop professional looking reports by including page numbers, report titles, column headings, and totals as part of the output.

- It provides a mechanism to protect the database from damage and unlawful use.

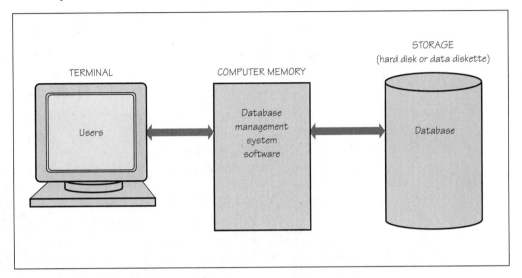

Figure 1-5
A database
management
system

An Introduction to dBASE III PLUS

dBASE III PLUS, marketed by Borland International, is a DBMS package used to create, maintain, and manipulate database files. Currently it is one of the most widely used database software packages for IBM and compatible microcomputers. For the rest of this tutorial you will learn about different ways to use dBASE III PLUS, and you will practice two of those methods. This practice will equip you for Tutorials 2 through 7, so you can work with Esther as she creates a DBMS for W&M.

dBASE Modes

When you use dBASE III PLUS (referred to hereafter simply as dBASE), you can instruct the DBMS to do what you want in one of three ways. First, you can use a menu-driven approach, called **Assistant mode**. This mode provides you with a menu of choices and guides you in the development of dBASE commands. With Assistant mode you do not need an in-depth understanding of the dBASE commands. Second, you can type in commands using dBASE's **Command mode**, or **dot prompt mode**. In this mode, you are presented with a blank screen except for a period (a dot) that appears near the bottom of the screen. The cursor is positioned after the period, which indicates that dBASE is ready for you to type your command. Third, you can store commands in a program file and use dBASE's **Program mode**. You can then execute those commands by issuing a single command. In this text, you will use Assistant mode and dot prompt mode.

Assistant mode is easy to understand because it includes the most frequently used dBASE commands. Because this mode is easier and less intimidating for beginners than dot prompt mode, you will use Assistant mode in the first three tutorials. After you become more proficient in dBASE, we will switch to dot prompt mode, which you will find faster and more flexible, for part of Tutorial 4, and all of Tutorials 5, 6, and 7.

Starting dBASE

Before you begin to practice using Assistant mode and dot prompt mode, you must first load dBASE into computer memory. If you are using your own computer and you have not already installed dBASE, see *Installing dBASE III PLUS*, instructions that accompanied the dBASE disks.

To start dBASE:

❶ Before you start dBASE, make sure you have the dBASE III PLUS data diskette ready. If you haven't already created the dBASE III PLUS data diskette, follow the instructions on page 79.

❷ If you are using a *two-diskette system*, insert the first dBASE diskette in drive A and your data diskette in drive B. Type **a:** and press **[Enter]**.

If you are using a *hard-disk system*, put your data diskette in drive A. Type **cd\dbase** and press **[Enter]**.

If you are using a network system, check with your technical support person for instructions on how to start dBASE and in which drive to put your data diskette.

This makes the directory that contains the dBASE program files the current directory.

❸ At the DOS prompt, type **dbase** and press **[Enter]**.

The dBASE copyright and license agreement screen appears. See Figure 1-6.

```
              dBASE III PLUS  version 1.0  IBM/MSDOS DEMO
        Copyright (c) Ashton-Tate 1984, 1985, 1986.  All Rights Reserved.
            dBASE, dBASE III, dBASE III PLUS, and Ashton-Tate
                    are trademarks of Ashton-Tate


       You may use the dBASE III PLUS software and  printed materials in
       the dBASE III PLUS software package under the terms  of the dBASE
       III  PLUS  Software License Agreement.   In summary, Ashton-Tate
       grants you a paid-up,  non-transferable,  personal license to use
       dBASE III PLUS on one  microcomputer or workstation.   You do not
       become the owner of  the package,  nor do  you have  the right to
       copy or alter the software or printed materials.  You are legally
       accountable  for any violation of  the License  Agreement  or of
       copyright, trademark, or trade secret laws.




    Command Line    <B:>
       Press ↵ to assent to the License Agreement and begin dBASE III PLUS.
```

Figure 1-6
dBASE copyright and license agreement screen

❹ If you have a 5¼-inch, two-diskette system, insert the second dBASE diskette in drive A and press **[Enter]**.

dBASE is now loaded into computer memory. See Figure 1-7a.

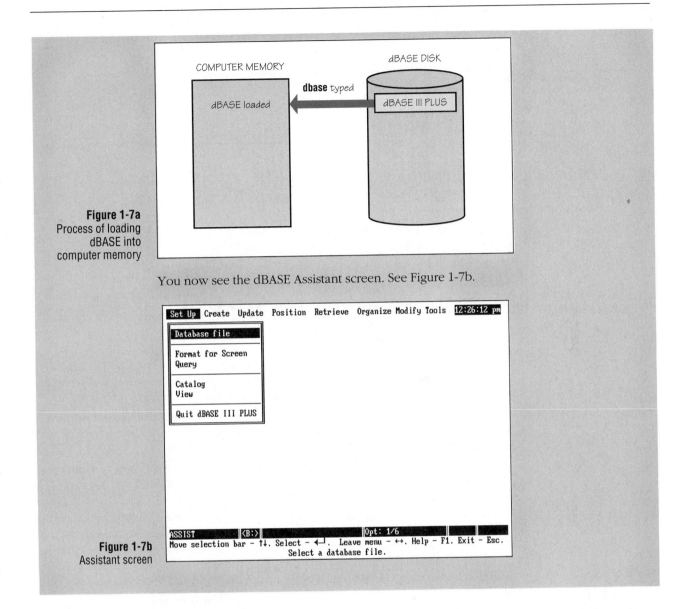

Figure 1-7a
Process of loading
dBASE into
computer memory

You now see the dBASE Assistant screen. See Figure 1-7b.

Figure 1-7b
Assistant screen

The dBASE Assistant Screen

The Assistant screen is the screen you work from when you are in Assistant mode. Understanding this screen will help you use dBASE more effectively. The Assistant screen consists of the following six components, which are shown in Figure 1-8.

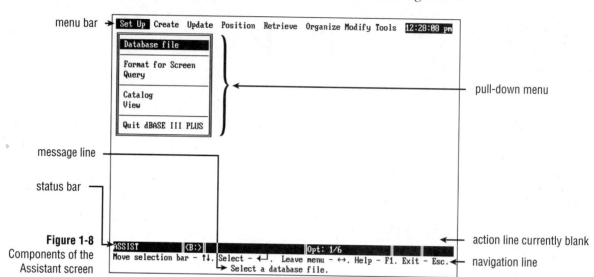

Figure 1-8
Components of the
Assistant screen

- Menu bar   The top line of the Assistant screen is called the **menu bar**. This line identifies the main options available from the Assistant screen. For example, if you select the *Set Up* option, you can then set up a database file or the format of your screen.

- Pull-down menus   Each option on the menu bar has its own **pull-down menus**. A different pull-down menu appears when each menu option from the menu bar is highlighted.

- Status bar   The highlighted line near the bottom of the screen is called the **status bar**. It is divided into six sections, each displaying current information about various aspects of dBASE's status. The first section displays the command that is being executed; the second section indicates the disk drive where dBASE looks for the database and other files; the third section identifies the database filename (if one is in use); if a file is in use, the fourth section lists the number of records in the database file; the fifth section indicates whether [INS] ([Insert]) is on; and the sixth section indicates whether [CAPS] ([Caps Lock]) and/or [NUM] ([Num Lock]) is on.

- Action line   The line above the status bar, the **action line**, shows the development of the dBASE command that you are building.

- Navigation line   The next to the last line on the Assistant screen is the **navigation line**. This line tells you how to move between menu items on the menu bar and how to select items from the pull-down menus.

- Message line   The last line of the screen is the **message line**. This line tells you what the current selection in the pull-down menu will do.

Overview of the Menu Bar Options

In dBASE's Assistant mode, you begin each activity by selecting an option from the menu bar. When you first enter Assistant mode, the *Set Up* option is highlighted. You can then continue with the *Set Up* option or select another option. You select another option by pressing [←] or [→] to move the **selection cursor**, or **highlight**, to that option.

To view the options on the Assistant screen:

❶ Press [→] to move the selection cursor to the *Create* option on the menu bar. See Figure 1-9. You use this option to create different types of dBASE files.

option highlighted

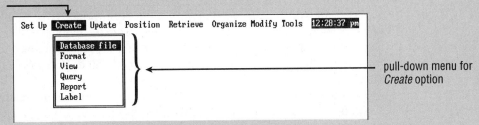

Figure 1-9

pull-down menu for *Create* option

❷ Press [→] to move the selection cursor to the *Update* option. See Figure 1-10. You use the options in this pull-down menu to add, delete, and modify records, in other words, keep the database current.

option highlighted

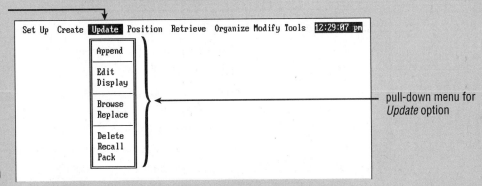

Figure 1-10

pull-down menu for *Update* option

You can also select an option on the menu bar by typing the first letter of the menu option name.

❸ Type **t** to move directly to the *Tools* option. See Figure 1-11.

option highlighted

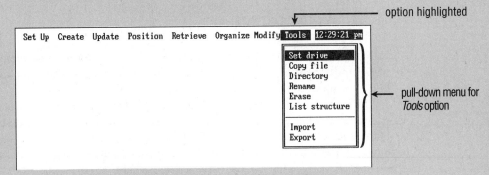

Figure 1-11

pull-down menu for *Tools* option

Now let's return to the *Set Up* option.

❹ Press [→] to move the selection cursor to the *Set Up* option. Notice how the selection cursor "wraps around" to the first menu option on the menu bar when you move past the last option.

As you moved the selection cursor, you probably noticed that each option on the menu bar has its own set of options that "pulls down" from the menu bar. If you wanted to choose an option from a pull-down menu, you would use [↑] or [↓] to move the selection cursor to that option. The option you chose would be highlighted. You would then press [Enter] to select your option.

As you moved the selection cursor through the menu bar and read the list of choices in each pull-down menu, you may have wondered what it means to "Format for Screen Query" or what "Tools" are. Right now the menu bar and the pull-down menu options may seem vague, but don't worry. As you work through the tutorials in this book, you will learn through your own hands-on experience what many of these options and pull-down menus can do to help you build an effective database. For now, Figure 1-12 will give you an overview of what you can do from the Assistant screen.

Menu Option	Description
Set Up	Uses different files that have already been created
Create	Creates new database or other type of files
Update	Updates your database by adding, changing, and removing records
Position	Moves to specific records in your database
Retrieve	Selects and displays all or part of your database
Organize	Arranges your database in a specific order
Modify	Changes any files you have created
Tools	Copies, lists, renames, and erases any files

Figure 1-12
Description of
menu bar options

Using Assistant Mode

Now that you have a basic understanding of database terms and concepts and are familiar with the dBASE Assistant screen, you are ready to work with Esther as she uses dBASE to build the Wells & Martinez database.

First let's look at some work Esther has already completed. She has created a clients file and entered the client data, which consist of each client's company name and ID, the name of the contact person at each client company, and each client's main telephone number. To familiarize you more with the Assistant screen, let's access W&M's clients file.

Before you can retrieve data from a database file, you must open the database file. To open the database file CLIENT, you would select the option *Database file* from the Set Up menu.

To open a database file:

❶ Make sure the *Set Up* option on the menu bar is highlighted. You will see that the option *Database file* is also highlighted. Press **[Enter]** to select the *Database file* option. Another pull-down menu listing disk drive options appears, as shown in Figure 1-13. Don't be concerned if the disk drive options listed on your screen differ from those in Figure 1-13.

option selected ➡️

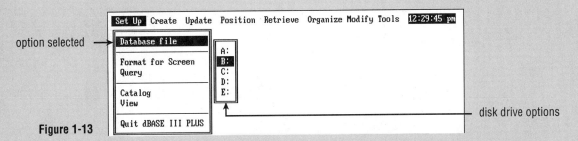

disk drive options

Figure 1-13

Now tell dBASE on what disk drive you have stored the database file CLIENT.

❷ If you have a *two-diskette system*, move the selection cursor to B: and press **[Enter]**.

If you have a *hard-disk system*, make sure the selection cursor is pointing to A: and press **[Enter]**.

You will see a list of all database files stored on this drive. This list is called a **database file submenu**. The extension DBF following the filename stands for "database file." See Figure 1-14.

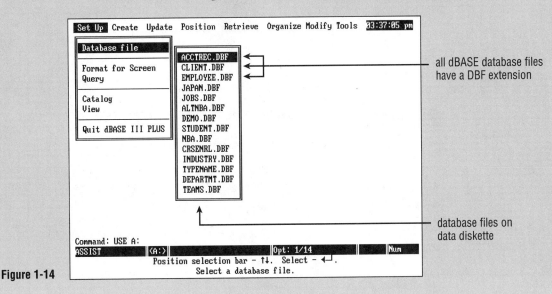

all dBASE database files have a DBF extension

database files on data diskette

Figure 1-14

❸ Use [↓] to move the selection cursor to CLIENT.DBF and press **[Enter]**. See Figure 1-15.

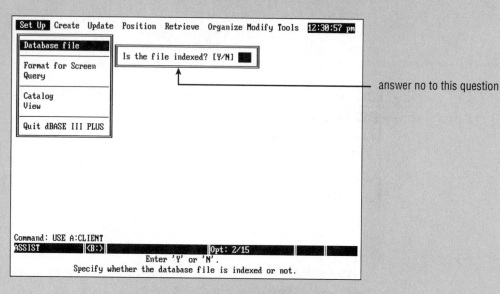

answer no to this question

Figure 1-15

❹ You will see the prompt "Is the file indexed? [Y/N]."

Do not concern yourself with what this prompt means. For now type **n** for "no." The Set Up menu appears again. See Figure 1-16.

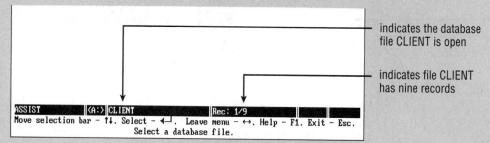

indicates the database file CLIENT is open

indicates file CLIENT has nine records

Figure 1-16

Notice that the status bar, near the bottom of the screen, indicates that the database file CLIENT is now open. The status bar also shows that there are nine records in this file.

Now that you have opened the file, you can access the data in the file. Let's look at the data that Esther has put in the W&M clients file.

To list the data in the file CLIENT:

❶ Press [→] to select the *Retrieve* option from the menu bar. You will see *List* highlighted on the pull-down menu. See Figure 1-17.

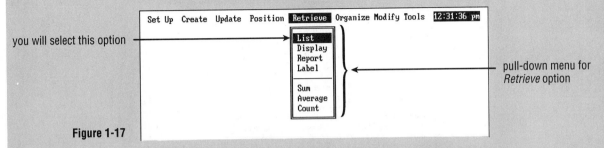

you will select this option

pull-down menu for *Retrieve* option

Figure 1-17

❷ Press **[Enter]** to select the *List* option. A submenu appears indicating the options available. See Figure 1-18.

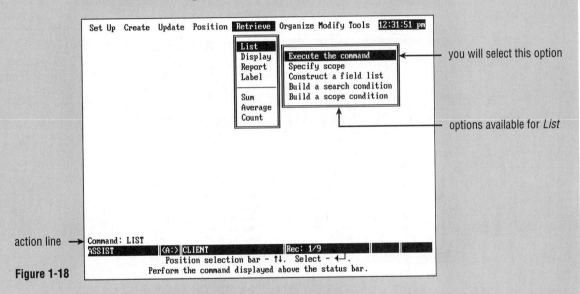

you will select this option

options available for *List*

action line

Figure 1-18

Notice that the action line shows the command LIST. As you select menu options from the Assistant screen, dBASE automatically builds the command that you would have typed if you were using the dot prompt mode.

❸ Press **[Enter]** to select the option *Execute the command*.

You will see a prompt asking if you want a printout of your results. See Figure 1-19.

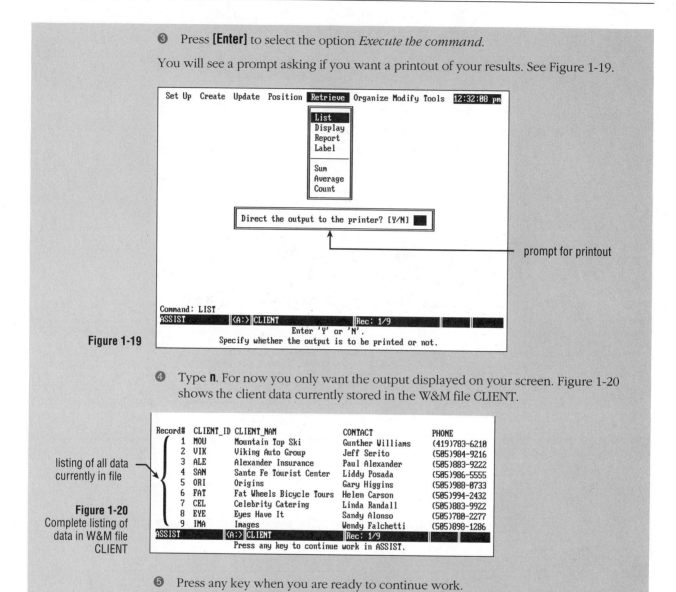

Figure 1-19

prompt for printout

❹ Type **n**. For now you only want the output displayed on your screen. Figure 1-20 shows the client data currently stored in the W&M file CLIENT.

listing of all data currently in file

Figure 1-20
Complete listing of data in W&M file CLIENT

❺ Press any key when you are ready to continue work.

You are returned to the Assistant screen.

If you find yourself in trouble, you can cancel a step at any point by pressing [Esc]. Occasionally you may press [Esc] when the selection cursor is positioned on one of the menu bar options. If you do this, you will leave Assistant mode and go to dot prompt mode. Don't panic! Just type **assist** and press [Enter] or press [F2] to return to Assistant mode.

Getting Help in Assistant Mode

While in Assistant mode, you may need help understanding or using one of the options. To get additional information on any highlighted option, press the function key [F1]. For example, let's get more information on the *List* option.

To get help:

❶ With the selection cursor on *List*, press **[F1]**. See Figure 1-21.

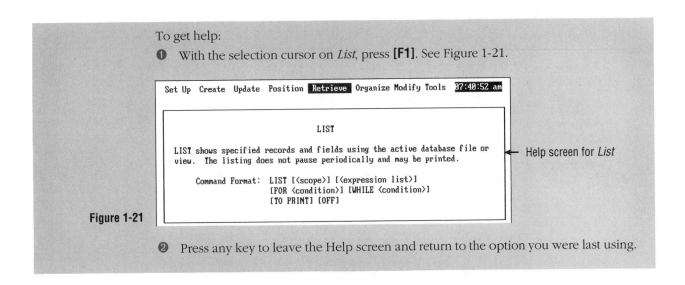

Figure 1-21

Help screen for *List*

❷ Press any key to leave the Help screen and return to the option you were last using.

Using Dot Prompt Mode

Now that you have had some experience with Assistant mode, let's use the dot prompt mode to list the Wells & Martinez database file CLIENT. As we discussed earlier in this tutorial, the dot prompt mode requires you to enter commands.

First you need to learn how to switch dBASE from Assistant mode to dot prompt mode.

To switch from Assistant mode to dot prompt mode:

❶ Press **[Esc]** to switch to dot prompt mode. The Assistant screen is erased, and a dot, called the **dot prompt**, appears near the lower left of your screen. See Figure 1-22. The dot prompt indicates that dBASE is waiting for you to type a dBASE command.

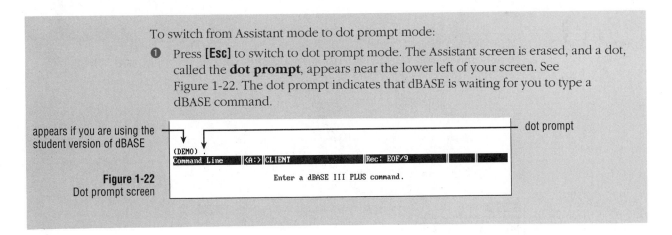

appears if you are using the student version of dBASE

dot prompt

Figure 1-22
Dot prompt screen

Since you opened the file CLIENT while you were in Assistant mode, you can now list all the clients in that database file.

To list all the clients:

❶ Type **list** and press **[Enter]**. dBASE displays the clients currently stored in the W&M database file CLIENT. See Figure 1-23 on the next page.

dBASE command to list
all clients

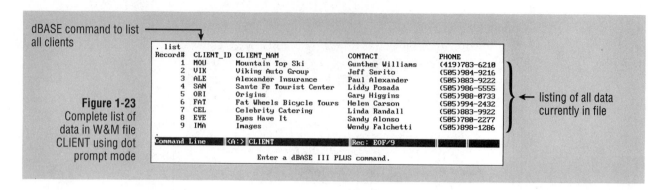

Figure 1-23
Complete list of
data in W&M file
CLIENT using dot
prompt mode

listing of all data
currently in file

That's all you will do in dot prompt mode for now. Let's leave dBASE.

Quitting dBASE

You have now completed Tutorial 1. Because you will be working in Assistant mode for the first four tutorials, you should know how to leave or quit dBASE from that mode.

You can switch from dot prompt mode to Assistant mode at any time by using the Assist command. Let's do that now.

To switch to Assistant mode:

❶ Type **assist** and press **[Enter]**. The Assistant screen appears.

You can also use the function key [F2] (ASSIST) to return to Assistant mode from dot prompt mode.

To quit dBASE, you use the *Quit dBASE* option from the *Set Up* option of the menu bar.

To quit dBASE:

❶ If necessary move the selection cursor to the *Set Up* option or type **s**.

❷ Press [↓] to highlight the option *Quit dBASE III PLUS*. See Figure 1-24. Select this option by pressing **[Enter]**. You are returned to the DOS prompt.

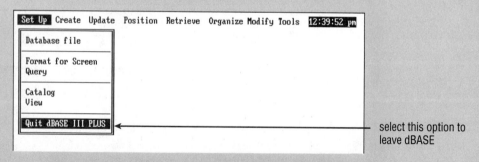

Figure 1-24

select this option to
leave dBASE

The *Quit* option closes all open files. *Be careful! If you turn your machine off before you issue the Quit option, you might lose any new data you typed this session.*

       ■   ■   ■

Exercises

1. Define the following terms:
    a. field
    b. record
    c. file
    d. database
    e. database management system

Use the data in Figure 1-25 to answer Exercises 2 through 6.

Library Card Holders

Card No.	Name	Street	City	State
2456	Ellery	17 Finch Rd.	Newport	RI
4687	Hemkin	1 Brook St.	Portsmith	RI
7991	Becker	323 High St.	Fall River	MA
9123	Drovsky	PO Box #12	Newport	RI

Books on Loan

Card No.	Book No.	Due Date
4687	12-32115	7/11/93
4687	18-23444	7/11/93
7991	17-23999	7/15/93
4687	22-95321	7/16/93
2456	14-11223	7/16/93

Figure 1-25

2. What are the fields in the library database?

3. How many fields are in the file BOOKS ON LOAN?

4. Identify the fields in the file LIBRARY CARD HOLDERS.

5. How many records are there in the file LIBRARY CARD HOLDERS?

6. The head librarian requests a list of all library cardholders. What option in the Assistant menu would you select to provide this information?

7. At the DOS prompt what do you type to load dBASE III PLUS?

8.   In Assistant mode what do you do to:
   a.   quit dBASE?
   b.   get to dot prompt mode?

9.   In dot prompt mode what command do you use to get to the Assistant screen?

10. In Assistant mode what do you do to use the Help feature?

Tutorial Assignments

Load dBASE and do the following:

1.   From the *Set Up* option in Assistant mode, open the database file DEMO.DBF.

2.   List on the screen the contents of this file.

3.   Print the contents of this file.

4.   Switch from Assistant mode to dot prompt mode.

5.   While in dot prompt mode, list on the screen the contents of this file.

6.   Switch from dot prompt mode to Assistant mode.

7.   Quit dBASE.

Tutorial 2

Creating a Database File Structure

OBJECTIVES

In this tutorial you will learn to:

■ Design the structure of a database file

■ Create a dBASE database file

■ Enter data into a dBASE database file

■ List the structure of a dBASE database file

■ Modify the structure of a dBASE database file

Case: Wells & Martinez — Creating the File Structure for WMJOBS

Early one morning Martin receives a phone call from Phyllis Higgins. Phyllis and her husband, Gary, are the owners of Origins, a Southwest fashion boutique, and have been W&M clients since Martin and Nancy started the agency. Phyllis tells Martin that she and Gary are very excited about their new line of Southwest fashion denim clothing for men and women and that they want W&M to develop an ad campaign to launch the new line. Later that day Martin tells Nancy about this new business from Origins. They decide that Martin and his creative team will put together a campaign plan. As soon as he has an outline of the plan, Martin will give the outline to Nancy, so she can estimate the costs of the job. They agree to have both the campaign plan and the cost estimate finalized and ready to present to Gary and Phyllis in two weeks.

Two weeks later Martin and Nancy meet with Phyllis and Gary Higgins and present the plan and the estimate. The Higginses are impressed and authorize W&M to begin work on the campaign — "Best in the Southwest" — immediately. They sign W&M's standard job authorization form, which authorizes Martin to begin working on the campaign and acknowledges the probable costs as Nancy has estimated them.

When Nancy returns to the office, she meets with Esther and tells her that she wants to begin the new database system with the Origins campaign. She asks Esther what to do first. Esther tells Nancy that she needs a copy of the job authorization form, which summarizes key information about a new job and which must be filled out before any expenses can be charged to that particular job (Figure 2-1). Before the new database system this form would have been filed for future reference; now Esther will enter the data on the form into a file she will create and name WMJOBS.

Wells & Martinez Ad Agency
Job Authorization Form   **No. 1001**

Client: Origins

Address: 220 Canyon Road
Sante Fe, New Mexico

Description: Best in the Southwest

Quote: $2,500   **Due Date:** August 15, 1992
Accepted: *Phyllis Higgins*   **Date:** June 1, 1992

Figure 2-1
W&M job
authorization form

Esther has carefully studied the manual system that W&M had been using. She knows what type of information Martin and Nancy need about their clients, the individual jobs, and the costs of the jobs. She has also reviewed database design principles, which she learned in her courses at school, and the rules for designing a dBASE database.

Based on her study and review, Esther recognizes that the database system she is designing must track each job that W&M does for each client. For example, if next week Gary and Phyllis authorize W&M to begin an advertising campaign on Origins' new line of formal wear, someone at W&M would have to fill out another job authorization form. They could not use the same form that Nancy filled out for the "Best in the Southwest" campaign. Having a separate authorization form for each job will allow Martin and Nancy to track each job by its due date and to track costs *by job* rather than *by client*. They will be able to keep a closer watch over their costs for each job and to see how actual costs compare to Nancy's original estimates.

Esther decides to create a database file, which she names WMJOBS, in which she will store all the data on all the job authorization forms. Each record in the WMJOBS file will include an individual job's number, client ID, description, due date, and cost estimate.

Esther has already created the CLIENT file so that Nancy and Martin can track specific data about each client. In this tutorial you will create W&M's second file, the WMJOBS database file.

Guidelines for Designing a Database File

Before you use any database software, you should plan and design the database you are going to build. If you plan first, your database is more likely to meet the goals for the new system.

When you design a database, you should follow these basic design principles:

- **Identify the type of information users will need from the database**. This will help you decide which data elements to track. For example, Martin and Nancy need information on their clients, the jobs their clients have authorized them to work on, and the costs for completing each job.

- **Group logically related fields in the same file**. For example, the fields that contain the client ID, the client's name, the contact's name, and the client's phone number are characteristics that describe clients and are included in the CLIENT file.

- **Include a common field in each related file (if your application has more than one file)**. Use this field to act as a connector when you need to combine data from related files. For example, the field CLIENT_ID is included in both the CLIENT and WMJOBS files and can be used to relate records in both files.
- **Avoid data redundancy**. Include data elements in a way that eliminates the need to enter the same information many times in many files. For example, Esther did not include company name, contact name, or phone number in the WMJOBS file. She already stores these data in the CLIENT file.

As you design a database file, for each field in a record you must:

- Assign a unique field name to identify the field
- Specify a maximum number of characters
- Assign a specific type of data — character, numeric, date, logical, or memo — to be stored in each field

Rules for Creating a dBASE Database File

As you design a database file, you must decide on the fields that are included in a record, the amount of space allotted to each field, and the type of data to be stored in each field. This information makes up the **file structure**. Later, when you are ready to develop the system, you must also consider the rules of the database software you will use. In our case, dBASE has rules for naming files and fields and for handling data input to the files. Let's look at these rules.

Naming Files

It is always a good habit to choose descriptive names for your files that will help you identify their contents. For example, Esther's choices of CLIENT and WMJOBS are appropriate because the names help identify the data she plans to put into the files.

In dBASE a filename can contain up to eight letters, numbers, and/or special characters, such as _ - $ % &. Esther's choices follow these rules.

Naming Fields

You've already seen that each file is made up of records. For example, the WMJOBS file consists of a record for each job that W&M undertakes. Each of these records is made up of fields, and you must name each field. A **field name** describes the data stored in each field. Esther has named the fields in the CLIENT file CLIENT_ID, CLIENT_NAM, CONTACT, and PHONE. Field names help you work more easily with the data in a file.

Rules for naming fields in dBASE are as follows:

- A field name can be up to 10 characters long.
- A field name must start with a letter.
- A field name can consist of letters, numbers, and the underscore character but must *not* include spaces or hyphens. The underscore is used to connect words. For example, CLIENT_ID is permitted, but CLIENT-ID and CLIENT ID are not.

Data Types

For each field dBASE requires that you assign a **data type**, that is, the type of data a field can contain. Each field can store only one data type. You can choose from the following dBASE data types:

- A **character data type** stores any sequence of letters, digits, blank spaces, and special characters, such as + - % $ &. The maximum width for a character field is 254 characters. In our W&M example, the client's company name and the contact person's name would be stored in character data type fields. Fields that contain a sequence of digits that do not represent a quantity, such as zip codes or telephone numbers, are typically stored as character-type data.

- A **numeric data type** stores values that are negative or positive, integer or decimal. The only characters permitted within a numeric field are the digits 0 to 9, a decimal point (.), and a sign (+ or -). No commas, parentheses, or dollar signs are permitted. You assign the numeric data type to fields that can be used in calculations. For example, the cost estimate for a job would be a numeric field.

- A **date data type** stores any valid date. Normally dates are entered and displayed in *mm/dd/yy* format, where *mm* represents a two-digit month, *dd* represents a two-digit day of the month, and *yy* represents the last two digits of the year. Dates stored using the date data type can be used in calculations. For example, say the due date is 30 days after the job was authorized. This due date can be computed by adding 30 to the date the job authorization form was signed. A date can also be stored as a character data type, but then that field cannot be used in calculations.

- A **logical data type** represents values as either true or false. An entry of T or t (for true) or Y or y (for yes) represents a true value, while F or f (for false) or N or n (for no) represents a false value. For example, in an EMPLOYEE file the field US_CITIZEN would store the value true (T, t, Y, or y) if the employee were a U.S. citizen or false (F, f, N, or n) if the employee were not a citizen.

- A **memo data type** stores large blocks of descriptive text. Though similar to the character data type, the memo data type is used when a field will contain a large amount of text. For example, an abstract of a book or a medical diagnosis would be stored as a memo data type.

Field Widths

When you use dBASE, you must indicate the number of characters, or the **width**, for each field. dBASE reserves a specified amount of space for each field. For some fields, deciding the width is a straightforward process. For example, Wells & Martinez uses the first three letters of a company's name as the client identification, so the width is 3. On the other hand, the job description field must be based on Esther's knowledge of the data. She knows that job titles vary in length but that most titles are shorter than Origins' "Best in the Southwest" description. Accordingly she has chosen a width of 25 characters, which allows each job description entry to be meaningful.

Numeric fields must be long enough to hold the largest possible number that will be stored in them, including a decimal point if the number has a fractional part and a sign if the number is negative. For example, W&M's cost estimate is always quoted to the nearest dollar. The largest estimate W&M has made so far is $32,500. Esther, however, has chosen a width of 6 to allow for estimates as large as $999,999. She has specified 0 for the number of decimal places because W&M cost estimates do not need decimal numbers.

The widths of logical, date, and memo fields are predefined by dBASE. For the logical data type the width is 1, for the date data type the width is 8, and for the memo data type the width is 5,000. Figure 2-2 summarizes the maximum widths of all dBASE data types.

Data Type	Maximum Width
Character	254
Date	8
Logical	1
Numeric	19
Memo	5,000

Figure 2-2
Widths of dBASE
data types

Preparing a File Layout Sheet

When you design a file for a computer system, you should document the structure of the records you will include in the file. For example, Esther sketched the structure of the WMJOBS file on a file layout sheet. A **file layout** is a document that describes the field name, the data type, and the length of every field in a record. The file layout sheet that Esther developed for the WMJOBS file is shown in Figure 2-3.

WMJOBS File

Field Name	Data Type	Width	Decimal
JOBNUM	Character	4	
CLIENT_ID	Character	3	
JOB_DESCR	Character	25	
DUE_DATE	Date	8	
QUOTE	Numeric	6	0

Figure 2-3
File layout for
WMJOBS file

How did Esther decide on this file layout? The first field, the job number, comes from the job authorization form, which is preprinted with a four-digit job number (Figure 2-1). Because these numbers will not be used for calculations, Esther did not need to use a numeric data type. Instead, she selected the character data type and assigned JOBNUM as the field name.

W&M uses the first three letters of the client's company name as the client identification. Esther named the client identification field CLIENT_ID. Because an ID always will be three letters, the data type is character and the length is 3.

Deciding the width of the job description field required Esther to make a judgment based on her knowledge of the data. The job descriptions vary in length, but none is longer than 25 characters. So Esther assigned the third field a width of 25, a field name of JOB_DESCR, and the data type character.

The fourth field is the date a project is due. In this field Esther stores dates in *mm/dd/yy* format. The field name is DUE_DATE, the data type is date, and the width is 8.

Esther chose numeric as the data type for the cost estimate because W&M personnel will use this field for calculations. As you've already seen, she knows that a numeric field must be long enough to hold the largest possible number that will be stored in it. W&M's cost estimates are always quoted to the nearest dollar, with the largest estimate so far being $32,500. Although no quote in the past has needed more than five digits, Esther chose a width of 6 in anticipation of larger projects. With a width of 6, dBASE can store quotes as large as $999,999. Esther specified 0 for the number of decimal places, because cost estimates are made to the nearest dollar. The field name is QUOTE, the data type is numeric, the width is 6, and the number of decimal places is 0.

Creating a Database File

Esther has documented the structure of the WMJOBS file in the file layout sheet. To define the structure of each database file in dBASE, Esther will use the *Create* option from the Assistant screen. She will enter the information on the file layout sheet into dBASE. Let's try it.

To create the database file named WMJOBS:

❶ Load dBASE and be sure you're in Assistant mode.

❷ Move the selection cursor to the *Create* option on the menu bar. See Figure 2-4.

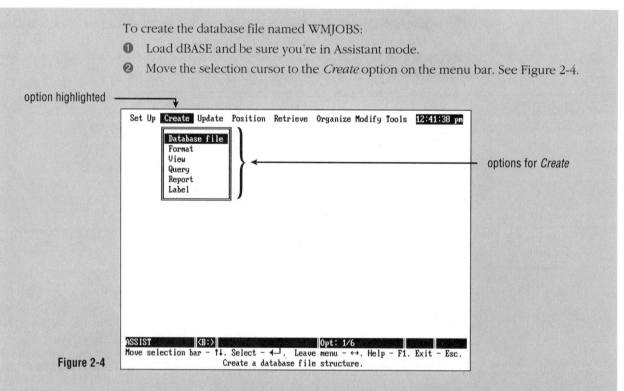

Figure 2-4

Do not confuse the *Create* option with the *Set Up* option. Remember, you use the *Create* option when you are creating a file the *first* time. You use the options from the Set Up pull-down menu (except the *Quit dBASE* option) only *after* a file has already been created.

❸ Make sure the *Database file* option on the pull-down menu is highlighted. Press **[Enter]**. See Figure 2-5.

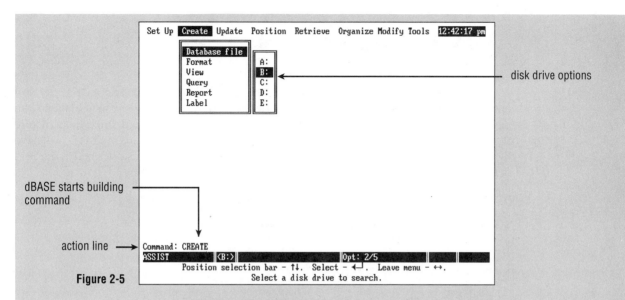

dBASE starts building command

action line →

Figure 2-5

Notice that the command CREATE appears on the action line. As you make menu selections from the Assistant screen, dBASE starts to build the command. As you work through the next two steps, watch how the entire dBASE command appears. Each option you select adds a portion of the command to the action line.

④ Now, select the drive where you want the database file stored.

If you are using a *two-diskette system*, move the selection cursor to B: and press **[Enter]**.

If you are using a *hard-disk system*, move the selection cursor to A: and press **[Enter]**.

dBASE opens a small window and prompts you for the name of the database file.

⑤ Type **wmjobs**. See Figure 2-6. Press **[Enter]**. The complete dBASE command you just built in Assistant mode is CREATE A:WMJOBS.

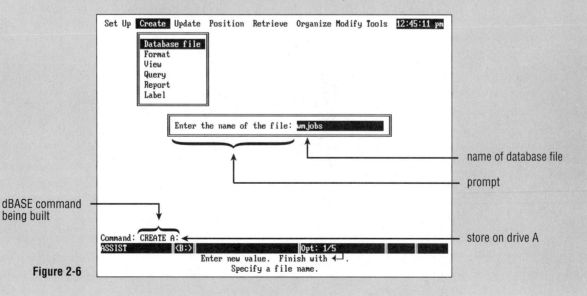

dBASE command being built

Figure 2-6

dBASE is now in field entry mode, where you will define the fields that will be in each record of the file.

Figure 2-7 shows the **field definition screen**, which automatically appears after you enter a filename. For each field you enter its **definition**, which includes the field name, the data type, and the width. After completing this screen, you will have defined the structure of the WMJOBS file. Once you have defined the structure, all like records in this file will have the same fields, and each field will have the same length and data type as defined in the field definition screen.

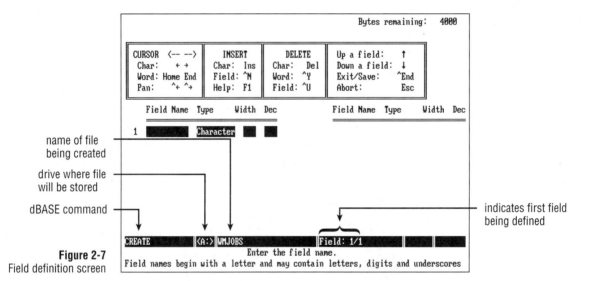

Figure 2-7
Field definition screen

You will recall that Esther plans to have five fields for each record in the WMJOBS file: job number, client identification, job description, due date, and quote. Esther uses the information from the file layout she created to help her define each field for the WMJOBS file.

The first field in the file layout sheet (Figure 2-3) is job number. Let's define this field.

To define the JOBNUM field:

❶ Type **jobnum** and press **[Enter]**. See Figure 2-8. You can type the field name in either uppercase or lowercase, but it will always appear on screen in uppercase. The field name JOBNUM appears in uppercase, and the cursor moves to the Type column.

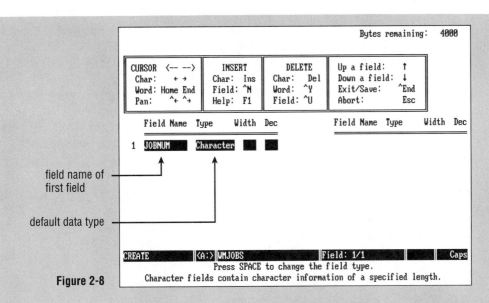

field name of
first field

default data type

Figure 2-8

Esther's file layout shows that JOBNUM will be used to store character data. Because the job numbers will not be used for calculations, a numeric data type is not needed. Esther selects the character data type.

❷ Press **[Enter]** to select the character data type for the JOBNUM field. The cursor advances to the Width column.

If you do not select a specific data type, the default is character data type. That is, unless you instruct it otherwise, dBASE assumes a field's data type is character.

Now enter the width, that is, the maximum number of characters the field can store. You enter the field widths only for character and numeric fields. For fields defined as logical, date, and memo, the widths are predefined by dBASE. The JOBNUM field is character data type, and, as Figure 2-3 shows, its width is 4.

❸ Type **4** and press **[Enter]** to enter the width. See Figure 2-9.

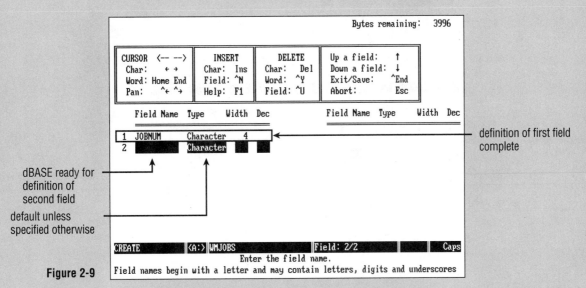

dBASE ready for
definition of
second field

default unless
specified otherwise

definition of first field
complete

Figure 2-9

Notice that the cursor did not advance to the "Dec" column. This is because we defined JOBNUM as a character field, and "Dec" is used only with numeric fields. The definition of the first field is complete, and the cursor advances to the next row. dBASE waits for you to enter the definition of the second field.

In Esther's file layout client identification is the second field in the WMJOBS record. Esther has named this field CLIENT_ID, the data type is character, and the length is 3. Let's define this second field.

To define the client identification field:

❶ Type **client_id** and press **[Enter]**. The cursor automatically moves to the Type column.

Esther plans to use the first three letters of the company name as the client ID, so she selects character as the data type for the CLIENT_ID field.

❷ Press **[Enter]** to select the character data type for the CLIENT_ID field.

Now enter the width, that is, the maximum number of characters the field can store. As Figure 2-3 shows, the width of the CLIENT_ID field is 3.

❸ Type **3** and press **[Enter]**. See Figure 2-10.

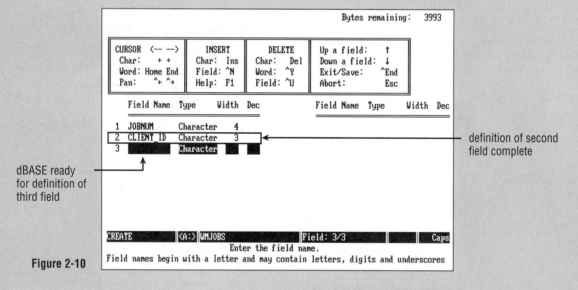

Figure 2-10

You have now completed the definition of the second field. The cursor advances to the next row, where you will enter the definition of the third field.

The third field is the job description. Again referring to the file layout in Figure 2-3, you can see that the field name is JOB_DESCR, the data type is character, and the width is 25. You will discover that the entries for this field are similar to the entries for the first two fields. Let's enter the information now.

To enter the job description field:

❶ Enter the information for this field as it is shown in Figure 2-3. Your screen should look like Figure 2-11.

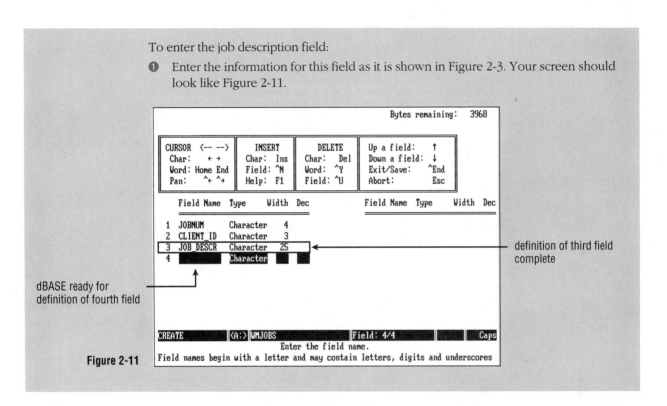

definition of third field complete

dBASE ready for definition of fourth field

Figure 2-11

The fourth field is the date the project is due. According to Esther's file layout, the field name is DUE_DATE, the data type is date, and the width is 8. Let's enter the due date field.

To enter the due date field:

❶ Type **due_date** and press **[Enter]**. The cursor moves to the Type column.

Up until now you have selected only character data types, but this field requires a date data type. To change the data type, press the spacebar to move through the five available data types. When the data type you want is displayed, press [Enter] to select it. Alternatively, you can select a data type by entering the first letter of the data type name: C, for character; N, for numeric; D, for date; L, for logical; or M, for memo. For now, select the date data type by pressing the spacebar.

❷ Press **[Spacebar]** twice, then press **[Enter]** to select the date data type. The value of 8 is automatically entered as the width of the DUE_DATE field, and the cursor advances to the next field. See Figure 2-12.

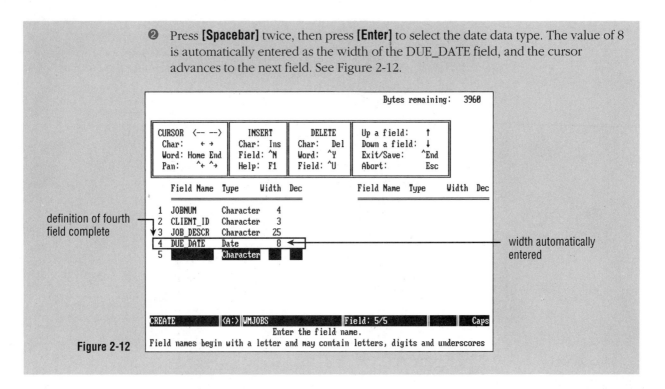

definition of fourth
field complete

width automatically
entered

Figure 2-12

The fifth field represents the W&M quote to the client. Figure 2-3 shows that the field name is QUOTE, the data type is numeric, the width is 6, and the number of decimal places is 0.

To enter the QUOTE field:

❶ Type **quote** and press **[Enter]**. The cursor moves to the Type column.

Esther has chosen numeric as the data type because W&M personnel will use the QUOTE field for calculations.

This time let's select the data type by typing the first letter.

❷ Type **n** to select numeric data type. The cursor moves to the Width column.

❸ Type **6** for width and press **[Enter]**. The cursor moves to the decimal place column.

The only time the cursor moves to the decimal (Dec) column is when you choose the numeric data type. You must tell dBASE how many decimal places following the decimal point you want reserved for each number stored. Because W&M makes quotes only to the nearest whole dollar, Esther has chosen no decimal places for this field.

④ Type the number **0** (zero) and press **[Enter]**. See Figure 2-13.

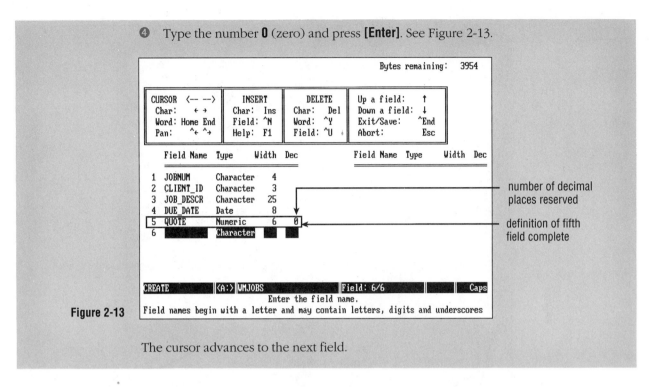

Figure 2-13

The cursor advances to the next field.

Now that you have specified the name of the database file and defined each field, the structure of the WMJOBS file is complete. Look over your screen. It should be identical to Figure 2-13.

Correcting Errors

If you make an error while dBASE is displaying the field definition screen, you can press any key except [Enter]. You then will be able to correct the field definitions. The upper portion of your screen will display information on how to move from field definition to field definition. Figure 2-14 on the next page summarizes the keystroke combinations that you can use to edit the field definition screen.

Keystroke	Action
Cursor	
[→] [←]	Moves cursor one character to the right or the left
[Home]	Moves cursor to previous field definition word
[End]	Moves cursor to next field definition word
[Ctrl][→]	Moves cursor one field definition to the right
[Ctrl][←]	Moves cursor one field definition to the left
Insert	
[Ins]	Switches between insert and overtype modes for insertion or correction
[Ctrl][N]	Inserts a blank field definition line above current cursor position
Delete	
[Del]	Deletes the character the cursor is on
[Ctrl][Y]	Deletes all characters in the field definition where cursor is currently positioned
[Ctrl][U]	Deletes the entire field definition where cursor is currently positioned
Miscellaneous	
[↑] [↓]	Moves cursor to previous or next field
[Ctrl][End]	Saves the dBASE file structure and exits file creation mode
[Esc]	Aborts file creation mode without saving file
[F1]	Help

Figure 2-14
Keystrokes for
editing field
definition screen

Saving the Database File Structure

When you have finished defining all the fields, you must indicate your intention to save the file structure by typing [Ctrl][End].

To save the file structure:

❶ Press **[Ctrl][End]**. See Figure 2-15.

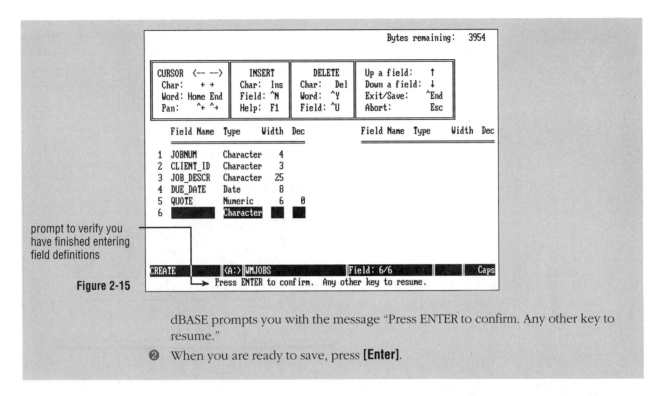

```
                                                    Bytes remaining:   3954

┌─────────────────┬──────────────┬──────────────┬─────────────────────┐
│ CURSOR  <-- -->│    INSERT    │    DELETE    │ Up a field:      ↑  │
│ Char:    ← →   │ Char:   Ins  │ Char:   Del  │ Down a field:    ↓  │
│ Word: Home End │ Field:  ^N   │ Word:   ^Y   │ Exit/Save:     ^End │
│ Pan:    ^← ^→  │ Help:   F1   │ Field:  ^U   │ Abort:          Esc │
└─────────────────┴──────────────┴──────────────┴─────────────────────┘

      Field Name  Type    Width  Dec        Field Name  Type    Width  Dec
      ──────────────────────────────        ──────────────────────────────
   1  JOBNUM      Character   4
   2  CLIENT_ID   Character   3
   3  JOB_DESCR   Character  25
   4  DUE_DATE    Date        8
   5  QUOTE       Numeric     6    0
   6              Character


CREATE          |<A:>|WMJOBS            Field: 6/6                    Caps
          └──→  Press ENTER to confirm.  Any other key to resume.
```

prompt to verify you have finished entering field definitions

Figure 2-15

dBASE prompts you with the message "Press ENTER to confirm. Any other key to resume."

❷ When you are ready to save, press **[Enter]**.

dBASE saves the database file to the disk you designated in the *Database file* option. You already entered the filename WMJOBS when you used the *Create* option. dBASE automatically adds a DBF extension to the filename (similar to the way Lotus 1-2-3 adds WK1 to worksheet files you save). Thus, your database file is stored on your data diskette as WMJOBS.DBF.

Figure 2-16 shows conceptually what takes place when you save a database file. Before you press [Enter] to save the database file, WMJOBS.DBF is not stored on your data diskette; it is stored only in computer memory (Figure 2-16a).

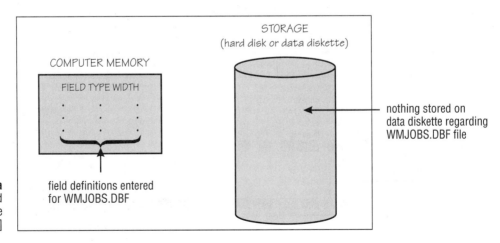

Figure 2-16a
CREATE command in process before pressing [Ctrl] [End]

field definitions entered for WMJOBS.DBF

nothing stored on data diskette regarding WMJOBS.DBF file

When you press [Enter] after the prompt to confirm that you intend to save your file, WMJOBS.DBF is stored on your data diskette. At this point, no records are stored in the database file, only the database file structure (Figure 2-16b).

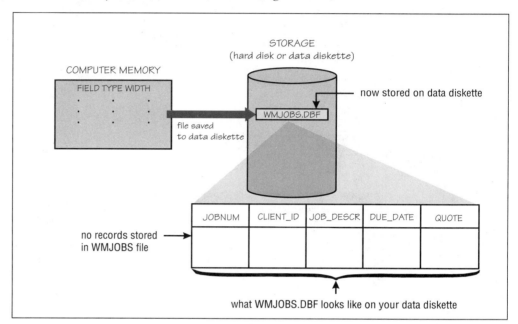

Figure 2-16b
After pressing
[Ctrl][End] and
[Enter] to save file
structure

Notice that dBASE displays the prompt "Input data records now? (Y/N)" (Figure 2-17). In the next steps you will respond to this prompt and you can then enter data into the WMJOBS file.

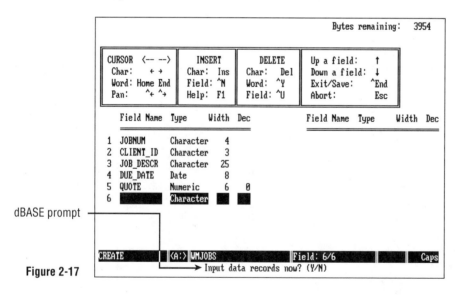

Figure 2-17

Entering Data into the WMJOBS File

Now that Esther has created the WMJOBS file, defined its fields, and saved it, she is ready to enter the data for the Origins job recently approved by the Higginses. Esther has a copy of the job authorization form Nancy filled out for the Origins "Best in the Southwest" job (Figure 2-1). Esther begins to enter the data.

To enter data into the database file:

❶   The prompt "Input data records now? (Y/N)" should still be on your screen. Type **y** to indicate you are ready to enter data. You are now in dBASE's data entry mode. A blank record form appears on the screen. See Figure 2-18. You will use this form to enter the data for each job. Notice that the field names you defined for the WMJOBS file appear on the screen. Next to each name are highlighted spaces equal to the width of each field as you defined it.

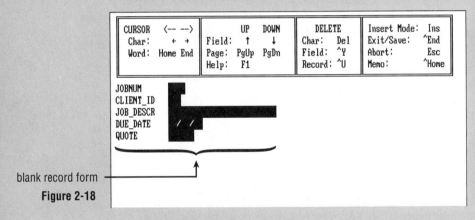

blank record form —
Figure 2-18

Let's use Figure 2-1 to enter the data for the "Best in the Southwest" job that Origins has authorized W&M to begin.

The job authorization form shows that the job is number 1001.

❷   With the cursor in the JOBNUM field, type **1001**. The cursor automatically advances to the CLIENT_ID field.

If the data fill all the spaces in the field, the computer will beep, and the cursor will automatically advance to the next field. If the entry does not fill the field, you must press [Enter] to move to the next field.

❸   With the cursor at the CLIENT_ID field, type **ORI** (be sure to use uppercase), the client identification for Origins.

The entry of character data is **case sensitive**. This means that entries are stored *exactly* as you type them. For example, if you enter the CLIENT_ID for Origins as ori, it is stored in lowercase — it is *not* changed to uppercase and stored as ORI.

The cursor is now positioned at the JOB_DESCR field.

❹ Type **Best in the Southwest** and press **[Enter]**. The cursor advances to the DUE_DATE field. See Figure 2-19.

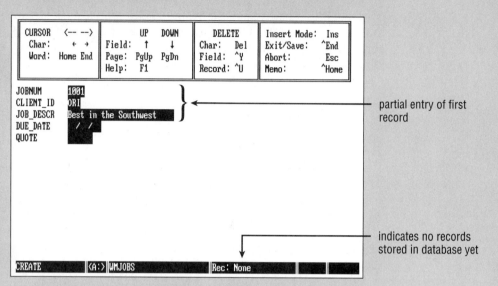

partial entry of first record

indicates no records stored in database yet

Figure 2-19

The form shows that the job due date is August 15, 1992 (8/15/92).

❺ Type **081592**. Because dBASE requires a two-digit month, you must enter 08 for August, not 8. (If the due date were August 2, you would also need to enter two digits for the day, 02).

The cursor advances to the QUOTE field. The estimate for the job is $2,500.

❻ Type **2500**, but do not press [Enter] yet. See Figure 2-20.

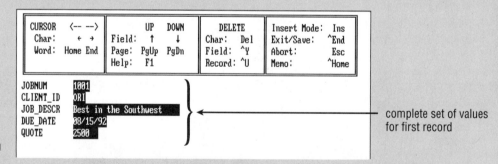

complete set of values for first record

Figure 2-20

dBASE always right-justifies (aligns on the right) a value in a numeric field after you press [Enter]. If you work with a numeric field that contains decimal values, be sure to type a decimal point *before* you enter the decimal digits.

❼ Press **[Enter]**. A new blank record form appears. See Figure 2-21.

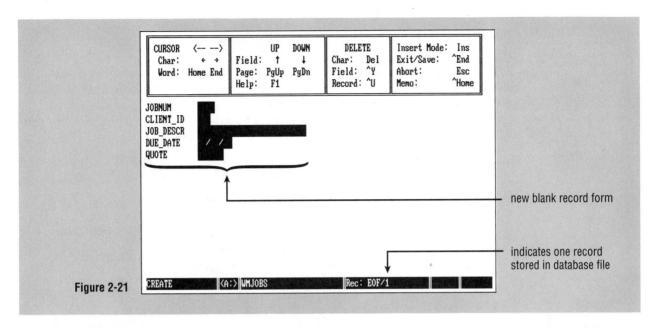

CURSOR	<-- -->		UP	DOWN		DELETE		Insert Mode:	Ins
Char:	← →	Field:	↑	↓		Char:	Del	Exit/Save:	^End
Word:	Home End	Page:	PgUp	PgDn		Field:	^Y	Abort:	Esc
		Help:	F1			Record:	^U	Memo:	^Home

JOBNUM
CLIENT_ID
JOB_DESCR
DUE_DATE   / /
QUOTE

— new blank record form

— indicates one record stored in database file

CREATE   ‹A:› WMJOBS   Rec: EOF/1

Figure 2-21

dBASE automatically saves the first record, record number 1, to the WMJOBS file. Figure 2-22 illustrates the contents of the WMJOBS file on your data disk after you have entered the first record.

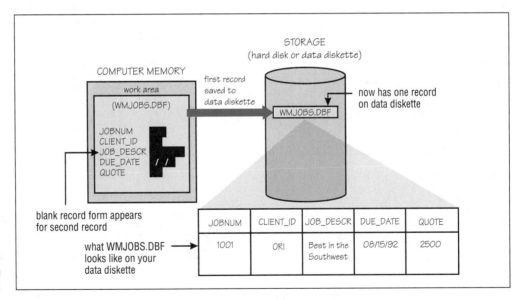

Figure 2-22
After entry of the first record

Since this is the only record we have so far for the WMJOBS file, we are ready to stop the data entry process.

To exit data entry mode:

❶ With the cursor in the first position of a blank first field (JOBNUM), press **[Enter]**. dBASE exits the data entry mode and returns to the Assistant screen.

Viewing the Database File Structure

Esther wants to verify that the database file structure has been created as she specified in the file layout sheet. To do this, she will select the *List structure* option from the Tools pull-down menu. This option allows her to view the structure of a database file. You may also find this option helpful if you forget a field name or what data type you assigned to a particular field.

To view the file structure:

❶ Select the *Tools* option from the menu bar. See Figure 2-23.

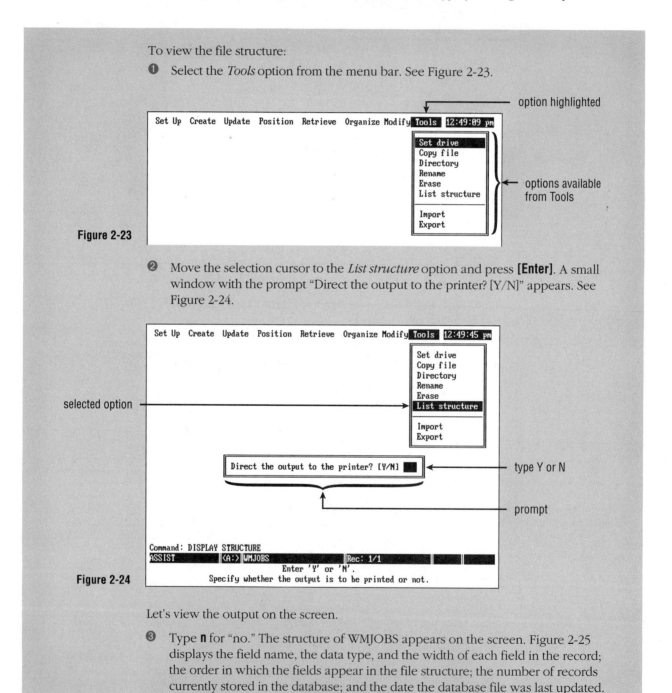

Figure 2-23

❷ Move the selection cursor to the *List structure* option and press **[Enter]**. A small window with the prompt "Direct the output to the printer? [Y/N]" appears. See Figure 2-24.

Figure 2-24

Let's view the output on the screen.

❸ Type **n** for "no." The structure of WMJOBS appears on the screen. Figure 2-25 displays the field name, the data type, and the width of each field in the record; the order in which the fields appear in the file structure; the number of records currently stored in the database; and the date the database file was last updated.

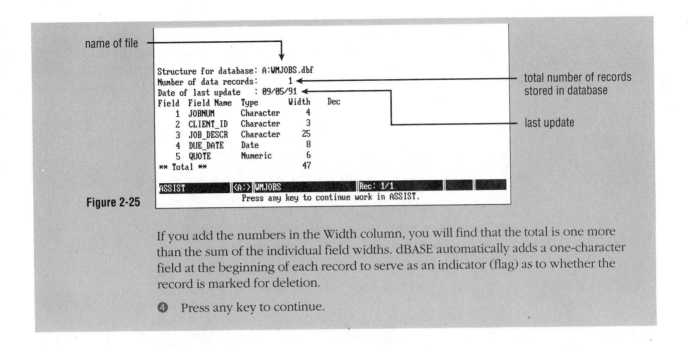

name of file

total number of records
stored in database

last update

Figure 2-25

```
Structure for database: A:WMJOBS.dbf
Number of data records:      1
Date of last update   : 09/05/91
Field  Field Name  Type       Width    Dec
    1   JOBNUM      Character      4
    2   CLIENT_ID   Character      3
    3   JOB_DESCR   Character     25
    4   DUE_DATE    Date           8
    5   QUOTE       Numeric        6
** Total **                      47
ASSIST          <A:> WMJOBS                    Rec: 1/1
                Press any key to continue work in ASSIST.
```

If you add the numbers in the Width column, you will find that the total is one more than the sum of the individual field widths. dBASE automatically adds a one-character field at the beginning of each record to serve as an indicator (flag) as to whether the record is marked for deletion.

④   Press any key to continue.

Modifying the Database File Structure

Now that Esther has created, saved, and viewed the WMJOBS database file, she is proud of herself and thinks her work is done. As she walks down the hall to get herself a cold drink, she passes Nancy and Martin in the hall; they are talking about how many jobs W&M has completed this month. Esther immediately thinks to herself, "Oh, no! What if Nancy or Martin want a list of completed jobs or of jobs in process? I have no way to retrieve that information from the database." Esther realizes that her WMJOBS file has no field to enable her to distinguish between completed jobs and ongoing jobs. What can she do? She then remembers that dBASE has an option that allows her to change the file structure. Esther gets her cold drink and returns to her office to change the file structure of the WMJOBS file.

Referring to her file layout, she decides to add a field named STATUS after the QUOTE field (Figure 2-26). The STATUS field will use the code C to indicate if a job is complete or the code I if the job is in process, that is, incomplete.

Figure 2-26
Revised file layout
for WMJOBS file

WMJOBS File			
Field Name	**Data Type**	**Width**	**Decimal**
JOBNUM	Character	4	
CLIENT_ID	Character	3	
JOB_DESCR	Character	25	
DUE_DATE	Date	8	
QUOTE	Numeric	6	0
STATUS	Character	1	

Perhaps the data you originally planned for your database are not adequate to handle a particular business problem. Or perhaps a field is not long enough to store certain data values. You can use the *Modify Database file* option in dBASE to change the structure of the file. This option allows you to add and delete fields and change a field's name, width, or data type. This is the option Esther will use to modify the structure of the WMJOBS file and add the field STATUS.

To modify the database file named WMJOBS:

❶ Move the selection cursor to the *Modify* option on the menu bar. See Figure 2-27.

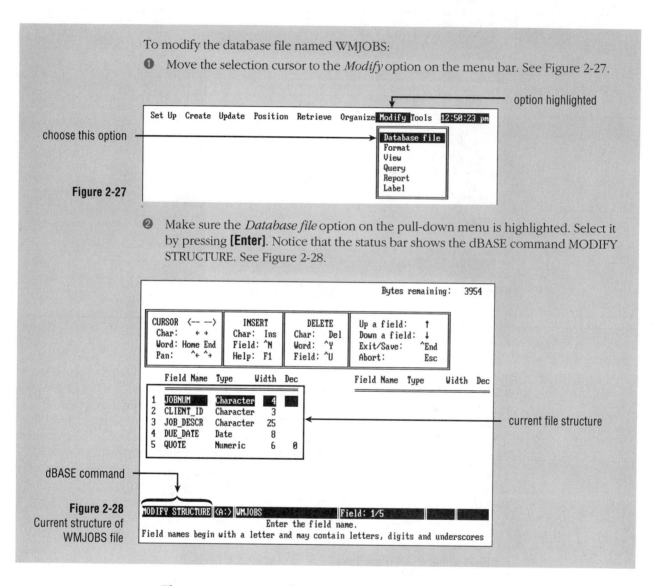

choose this option

option highlighted

Figure 2-27

❷ Make sure the *Database file* option on the pull-down menu is highlighted. Select it by pressing **[Enter]**. Notice that the status bar shows the dBASE command MODIFY STRUCTURE. See Figure 2-28.

current file structure

dBASE command

Figure 2-28
Current structure of WMJOBS file

The current structure of the WMJOBS file appears on the field definition screen. Now you can add the new field.

To add a new field:

❶ Move the cursor past field 5 to field 6, the first blank field.

Enter the name of the new field.

❷   Type **status** and press **[Enter]**. The cursor advances to the Type column. See Figure 2-29.

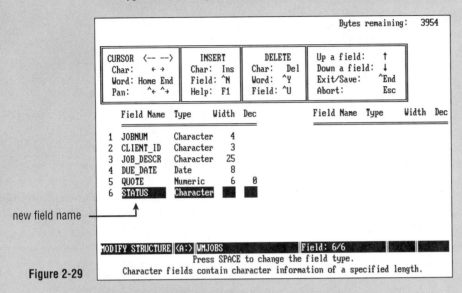

new field name ──→

Figure 2-29

Now enter the data type.

❸   Press **[Enter]** to accept the character data type for this field. The cursor advances to the Width column.

Next enter the width.

❹   Type **1** and press **[Enter]**. The cursor advances to the next row.

You have just inserted a new field in the WMJOBS file. Look over your screen. It should be identical to Figure 2-30. If it is not, move to the STATUS field and make the appropriate corrections.

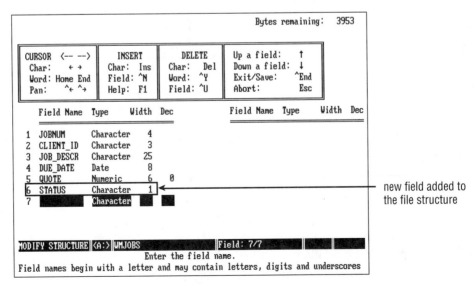

new field added to the file structure

Figure 2-30

Now let's save the modified database file structure.

To save the database file structure:

❶ Press **[Ctrl][End]**.

Notice that dBASE prompts "Press Enter to confirm. Any other key to resume."

When you are ready to save, you press [Enter]. Let's save the file structure now.

❷ Press **[Enter]**. This saves the database file structure to your data diskette. dBASE automatically *writes over* the original database file and replaces it with the modified database file. You have stored the file as WMJOBS.DBF.

Figure 2-31 shows what has taken place on your data diskette. You stored WMJOBS.DBF on your data diskette, but you changed its structure from the original database file. Your new version includes the field STATUS. Let's take a look.

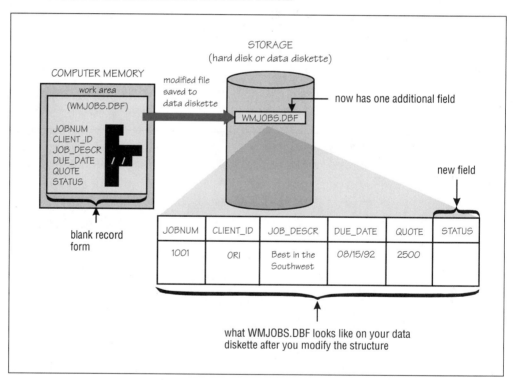

Figure 2-31
After modifying the
WMJOBS file
structure

You will recall that the *List structure* option lets you view the structure of a database file. Let's see if the structure of the WMJOBS file has changed. This time let's get a hard copy.

To print the file structure:

❶ Select the *Tools* option from the menu bar.

❷ Move the selection cursor to the *List structure* option and press **[Enter]**. You see a small window with the prompt "Direct the output to the printer? [Y/N]."

Let's send the output to the printer.

❸ Make sure the printer is turned on and ready.

❹ Type **y**. You see the structure of WMJOBS on your screen and receive a hard copy at your printer. See Figure 2-32.

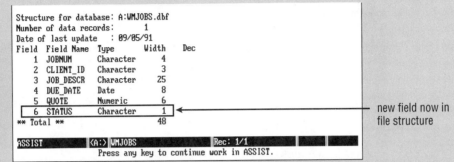

Figure 2-32
Current structure of WMJOBS file

Notice that the new field is now part of the database file structure.

❺ Press any key to return to the Assistant screen.

After changing the structure of the file WMJOBS, the value in the new field, STATUS, is blank. To change this value to "C" or "I," you would use dBASE options found among the menu choices in the *Update* option. Let's turn next to Tutorial 3, where you'll learn how to update database files.

■   ■   ■

Exercises

1. Which of the following are valid dBASE filenames? For those names that are not valid, give the reason why.
   a. SALES HISTORY
   b. SALES92
   c. 92SALES
   d. SALESHISTORY
   e. SALES

2. Which of the following are valid dBASE field names? For those names that are not valid, give the reason why.
   a. CUST#
   b. CUSTOMER_NUMBER
   c. CUSTOMER
   d. CUST:NUM
   e. CUST92
   f. 1STQTR
   g. QTR 1
   h. CUST_NUM
   i. CUSTNUM

3. Give an example of the values that can be entered for each of the following data types:
   a. logical
   b. date
   c. character
   d. numeric
   e. memo

4. What is the default data type?

5. Jim defines a phone number with a width of 7, using a numeric data type. Frank defines a phone number with a width of 14, using a character data type. How would each enter phone numbers? Give an example of a phone number that Jim would enter. Give an example of a phone number that Frank would enter.

6. If *field names* in dBASE are limited to 10 characters or less, how can you have a client named "Mountain Top Ski" stored in the database?

7. What file extension does dBASE use for database files?

8. Does the DOS command DIR help you determine if dBASE database files are stored on your data diskette? Explain.

9. When would you want to use the *List Structure* option?

10. Suggest a field name, a data type, and a width for each field in the invoice file shown in Figure 2-33.

Field Description

Invoice number (highest number is 4300)

Customer name (longest name is "Orlando Sand and Gravel Company")

Date of invoice

Amount of invoice (highest amount is $850.68)

Eligible for sales tax (y/n)

Figure 2-33

Use the record layout in Figure 2-34 to answer Exercises 11 through 16. The layout describes data on the faculty at a local college. The fields include a faculty identification number, faculty name, department, phone extension, and annual salary.

Field Name	Data Type	Width	Decimal
FID	Numeric	5	
FNAME	Character	15	
DEPT	Character	4	
EXTENSION	Character	4	
SALARY	Numeric	5	0

Figure 2-34

11. Use the CREATE command to enter the definition of the faculty file using the file layout, but *do not* save the file. Name the database file FACULTY.

12. At the "Press ENTER to confirm. Any other key to resume" prompt, press any key except [Enter] and make the following modifications to the field definitions:
    a. Change the first field, FID, to FACULTY_ID and the data type to character.
    b. Change FNAME to FACNAME.
    c. Delete the EXTENSION field from the record.
    d. Change the width of the SALARY field to 6.

13. Save the FACULTY database file on your data diskette. Do not enter any faculty data to the file.

14. Print the file structure.

15. Modify the file structure to include a new field, the faculty member's hire date. The field name is HIRE_DATE, and the data type is date.

16. Print the file structure after the file has been modified.

Refer to Figure 2-35, which shows the structure of a database file, to answer Exercises 17 through 19.

```
Structure for database: A:student.dbf
Number of data records:      10
Date of last update   : 09/14/91
Field  Field Name  Type        Width    Dec
    1  SID         Character      3
    2  SNAME       Character     10
    3  SEX         Character      1
    4  MAJOR       Character      3
    5  GPA         Numeric        4       2
** Total **                      22
```

Figure 2-35

17. What is the name of the database file?

18. Identify each field.

19. How many records are currently stored in this file?

Tutorial Assignments

Esther decides to create an EXPENSES file, the third database file in the W&M database system. Each record in this file will represent an expense that W&M has incurred for a client, and each expense will be assigned to a specific expense category. Figure 2-36 shows the record layout for this file.

Field Description	Field Name	Data Type	Width	Decimal
Client ID	CLIENT_ID	Character	3	
Job number	JOBNUM	Character	4	
Billing category	CAT	Character	3	
Date of expense	DATE_EXP	Date	8	
Amount of expense	AMOUNT	Numeric	7	2

Figure 2-36

1. Create the database file and store it on your data diskette. Name the file EXPENSES.

2. After you have created the EXPENSES database file, add the data in Figure 2-37 to the file.

	Record 1	Record 2
CLIENT_ID	ORI	ORI
JOBNUM	1001	1001
CAT	002	004
DATE_EXP	02/01/92	02/02/92
AMOUNT	150.00	37.50

Figure 2-37

3. Print the structure of the EXPENSES database file.

4. Modify the EXPENSES file structure to include an additional field. Name this field DESCRIPTN and give it the data type character and a width of 30.

5. Print the modified structure of the EXPENSES database file.

Case Problems

1. Biggs & Hang Investment Corporation

Biggs & Hang Investment Corporation (B&H Corp.) is an investment company located in San Francisco. Lavel Simpson, an executive assistant, notices that many of his manager's clients are asking for information on Japanese companies. Lavel suggests to his manager that B&H begin evaluating the investment potential of several companies listed on the Tokyo Stock Exchange. With his manager's approval, Lavel begins to compile a database of financial data about these companies.

The design of his database is shown in the file layout in Figure 2-38.

Field Description	Field Name	Data Type	Width	Decimal
Company ID	COMP_ID	Character	4	
Company name	COMP_NAME	Character	30	
Industry code	IND_CODE	Character	1	
Description	DESCRPT	Character	60	
Total assets	ASSETS	Numeric	10	0
Sales	SALES	Numeric	10	0
Profits	PROFIT	Numeric	10	0
Shares outstanding	OUT_SHRS	Numeric	10	0

Figure 2-38

Do the following:

1. Create a database file named INVEST and store the file on your data diskette.

2. After you have created the INVEST file, add the record in Figure 2-39 to the database.

COMP_ID	7267
COMP_NAME	Honda Motor
IND_CODE	A
DESCRPT	Automobile and motorcycle manufacturer
ASSETS	1,370,582
SALES	3,852,905
PROFITS	210,000
OUT_SHRS	967,393

Figure 2-39

3. Print the structure of the INVEST database file.

4. Add two new fields to the end of the database file. First, add the company's highest price on the Tokyo Stock Exchange during the year. The field name is HIGH_PRICE, the data type is numeric, the length is 10, and the number of decimal places is 0. Second, add the company's lowest price on the Tokyo Stock Exchange during the year. The field name is LOW_PRICE, the data type is numeric, the length is 10, and the number of decimal places is 0.

5. Print the modified structure of the INVEST database file.

2. Medi-Source Inc.

Medi-Source Inc. distributes supplies to hospitals, medical laboratories, and pharmacies throughout the United States. Files of all Medi-Source customers and accounts receivable data are available to department managers on the company's mainframe computer.

Upon a recent review of the files, Joan Glazer, the manager of the credit and collection department, notices that the outstanding balances of several Massachusetts and Rhode Island customers appear to be higher than that of the average Medi-Source customer, which is approximately $6,000. She decides to study the accounts in these two states more carefully.

Joan asks Bert Spivak, manager of the information systems department, to prepare several reports to help her analyze the data. Bert tells Joan that he and his programming staff are backed up on projects and will not be able to help her for four to six weeks. He suggests instead that he retrieve the Rhode Island and Massachusetts data from the mainframe database and provide her with a dBASE file, which she can analyze herself. Joan thinks this is a great idea. Bert says he'll have the data to her in two days.

Figure 2-40 shows the layout of the Medi-Source customer database file.

Field Name	Description	Data Type	Width	Decimal
CUSTID	A unique identification number assigned to each customer	Character	2	
CUSTNAME	Name of customer	Character	25	
TYPE	Code indicating type of business, e.g., P=Pharmacy, L=Laboratory, H=Hospital	Character	1	
STATE	Code of state: RI=Rhode Island, MA=Massachusetts	Character	2	
REP	ID of sales rep assigned to customer	Character	1	
CRD_LIMIT	Maximum amount of credit customer is allowed	Numeric	6	0
BAL_OWED	Amount customer currently owes Medi-Source	Numeric	9	2
YTD_SALES	Total sales to customer since beginning of year	Numeric	9	2

Figure 2-40

Do the following:

1. Create the database file and name the file CUST.

2. Add two records. You make up the sample data.

3. Print the file structure of CUST.

4. Modify the structure of the CUST file to include a field for the date of the last sale. Insert the field after the YTD_SALES field and use the field name DATE_LSTSL and the date data type.

5. Print the modified file structure of CUST.

3. Appleton & Drake Electrical Supply Company

Terry Rossati has worked at Appleton & Drake Electrical Supply Company for six months in the human resources (HR) department. He is amazed at the company's need for better and more up-to-date information about its employees. He knows he could be much more efficient and effective in his job if his department could be computerized.

Terry and his HR assistant can use the company payroll database that was created and is maintained by the accounting office. But because this database was originally designed for accounting purposes, it is not helpful for HR needs. For example, Terry cannot get the payroll database to do something as simple as list the employees alphabetically by last name. The payroll system stores employees' first and last names in one field with first names entered first, as they would appear on payroll checks.

Terry needs to develop computerized Equal Employment Opportunity reports for the federal government; timely performance and salary review due date reports (each employee is reviewed on the anniversary of his/her date of hire); internal telephone directory reports; and marital status reports (to check eligibility for certain health benefits).

Currently Terry and his assistant must put together all these reports either manually or with partial information from the payroll system. When he does use the payroll system, Terry must still manipulate and recalculate the data before he can obtain the information he needs. Terry makes several requests to the data processing manager, Alice Austic, for help. But Alice tells him that her staff is too busy on other projects and will have no time this year to help the human resources department.

Terry decides to assign Cheryl Muldoon, a recent business school graduate, to work with him to develop a human resources information system. Cheryl studied database concepts and dBASE in school.

After studying the requirements of the human resources department, Cheryl designs an employee file and creates the employee file layout shown in Figure 2-41.

Description	Field Name	Data Type	Width	Decimal
Employee number	EMP_NUM	Character	3	
Last name	LNAME	Character	15	
First name	FNAME	Character	10	
Sex (F/M)	SEX	Character	1	
Married (Y/N)	MAR	Character	1	
Number of dependents	DEP	Numeric	2	0
Annual salary	ANNSAL	Numeric	6	0
Department*	DEPT	Character	3	

* Codes are: SAL = Sales, COR = Corporate, ENG = Engineering

Figure 2-41

Do the following:

1. Create the database file EMP using the employee file layout.

2. Add two employees to the file using the data shown in Figure 2-42.

	Record 1	Record 2
EMP_NUM	129	130
LNAME	Phelps	Leung
FNAME	Fred	Margaret
SEX	M	F
MAR	N	Y
DEP	0	2
ANNSAL	35000	39000
DEPT	SAL	COR

Figure 2-42

3. Print the structure of the EMP database file.

4. Modify the structure of the database file to include a field for the employee's hire date. Insert this field between the fields DEP and ANNSAL. Use HIRE_DATE as the field name and DATE as the data type.

5. Print the modified file structure of the EMP database file.

4. National Basketball Association

Instructor's note: You can use one of two DBF files with this case. NBA.DBF contains 28 records. ALTNBA.DBF contains 100 records. If students use ALTNBA.DBF, they must use the commercial version of dBASE III PLUS.

Sharman Durfee is working as a summer intern at the National Basketball Association (NBA) headquarters in New York City. The NBA office receives numerous requests every day for information from sportswriters, TV announcers, team owners, agents, and other interested parties. Sharman's assignment is to set up a database of players' salaries to help NBA staff provide accurate information quickly and with little effort.

After studying the problem, she comes up with the file layout shown in Figure 2-43.

Field Description	Field Name	Data Type	Width	Decimal
Team ID	TEAM	Character	3	
Player's first name	FNAME	Character	12	
Player's last name	LNAME	Character	15	
Salary	SALARY	Numeric	10	0

Figure 2-43

Do the following:

1. Create the database file and name it PLAYER.

2. Add the data in Figure 2-44 to the file.

	Record 1	Record 2
TEAM	BOS	CHI
FNAME	Larry	Michael
LNAME	Bird	Jordan
SALARY	1,500,000	2,500,000

Figure 2-44

3. Print the structure of the database file.

4. A writer has expressed interest in seeing if there are salary differences by position. Modify the structure of the PLAYER database file to include a new field that represents the position an athlete plays. Use the codes shown in Figure 2-45 to represent the positions.

Code	Position
C	Center
F	Forward
G	Guard

Figure 2-45

Insert this field between the fields LNAME and SALARY. Name the new field POS and assign it a character data type and a width of 1.

5. Print the modified file structure.

Tutorial 3

Keeping the Database Current

Case: Wells & Martinez — Updating the CLIENT and JOBS Files

Three weeks have passed since Esther created the JOBS file and added the first record. During this time she has entered all the data from W&M's job authorization forms into the database. Esther has also started to document the database by placing copies of the CLIENT and JOBS file structures in a folder for easy reference (Figures 3-1a and 3-1b on the next page).

Today is the second Friday of the month, the day on which Nancy and Martin hold a staff meeting to let the employees know what's going on at W&M.

The meeting starts on time, and as usual Martin begins with any good news or success stories. He is happy to announce that W&M's marketing campaign for new clients has brought in two new clients: a local restaurant chain, Taco Heaven, and a retail shop that specializes in custom-made down comforters, Peaches & Ice. Esther jots a note to herself; after the meeting she must talk to Martin and get the information she needs to add these two clients to the database.

The next portion of the meeting is devoted to an update of the status of the various jobs in progress. The creative team discusses several of the larger jobs, sharing with everyone the nature of the various campaigns and their progress. Martin announces with pride that the job for Images — a 20-page, full-color fall catalogue — was completed this week on schedule. He tells the group that two days ago Sledge Hill Printers delivered 2,000 catalogues to the mailing house. Esther pulls out her notes; she can change the JOBS file to show that the Images job has been completed.

OBJECTIVES

In this tutorial you will learn to:

- Open a database file

- Add records to a database file using the *Append* option

- Edit records in a database file using the *Edit* option or the *Browse* option

- Mark records for deletion using the *Edit* option or the *Delete* option

- Recall records marked for deletion using the *Recall* option

- Permanently remove records from a database file using the *Pack* option

- Make a backup copy of a database file using the *Copy* option

```
Structure for database: A: CLIENT.dbf
Number of data records: 10
Date of last update: 09/18/91
Field   Field Name  Type        Width Dec
  1     CLIENT_ID   Character      3
  2     CLIENT_NAM  Character     25
  3     CONTACT     Character     20
  4     PHONE       Character     13
**Total**                        62
```

Figure 3-1a
File structure for CLIENT file

```
Structure for database: A: JOBS.dbf
Number of data records: 20
Date of last update: 09/18/91
Field  Field Name   Type       Width Dec
  1    JOBNUM       Character      4
  2    CLIENT_ID    Character      3
  3    JOB_DESCR    Character     25
  4    DUE_DATE     Date           8
  5    QUOTE        Numeric        6
  6    STATUS       Character      1
**Total**                        48
```

Figure 3-1b
File structure for JOBS file

Martin then tells the group that despite their efforts, one of their clients, Eyes Have It, a specialty eyeglass store, has gone out of business. Esther makes another note — this time to delete Eyes Have It from the database.

Finally Martin asks if there are any other announcements. Nancy doesn't have any announcements, but she wonders if anyone has heard recently from Gunther Williams, W&M's contact person at Mountain Top Ski. Ann Lightfeather responds that the owner of Mountain Top Ski called yesterday and told her that Gunther had resigned and Victor Juarez is taking over his job. Nancy thanks Ann and asks Esther to update the database, but Esther is already adding this note to her list of things to do.

When the meeting is over, Esther asks Martin to write down the contacts and the phone numbers for Taco Heaven and Peaches & Ice and get that information to her as soon as he can. About 30 minutes later, Martin drops by her office and hands her a note (Figure 3-2).

Figure 3-2
Data on W&M's
new clients

> Esther, new client info:
>
> Client name: Peaches & Ice
> Contact: Alice Beaumont
> Phone: (505) 728-5176
>
> Client name: Taco Heaven
> Contact: Bert Clinton
> Phone: (505) 728-1295

Updating Database Files

What do all of the tasks on Esther's list have in common? They affect the accuracy of the data in the W&M database. W&M, like any other business, must keep the contents of its database files up-to-date and accurate so the output from those files is meaningful and helpful in making business decisions. **File maintenance** — the adding, changing, and deleting of records — is a basic function you must perform when you have a DBMS. In this tutorial, you will learn how to use a variety of dBASE commands to update database files.

Opening a Database File

Esther is ready to add the two new clients to the CLIENT file. However, before she can update this or any other database file, she must first open the specific file she wants to update. The dBASE command USE tells dBASE to find a specific database file on your data diskette and to set aside a small portion of computer memory as a work area for that database file. This process is called *opening* the file.

When you open a file, dBASE does not display the data on the screen, as it does a Lotus 1-2-3 or WordPerfect file. You must first select other dBASE options before you can update, display, print, or manipulate records in a database file.

In Tutorial 1 Esther created the CLIENT database file and entered the client data. Let's load dBASE, open the CLIENT file, and add the new clients to the file. To open the CLIENT database file, you select the option *Database file* from the Set Up menu of the Assistant screen.

To open the CLIENT database file:

① With the selection cursor positioned on the *Set Up* option of the menu bar, you will see that the option *Database file* is highlighted. Press **[Enter]** to select the *Database file* option. A pull-down menu appears listing the disk drive options. See Figure 3-3.

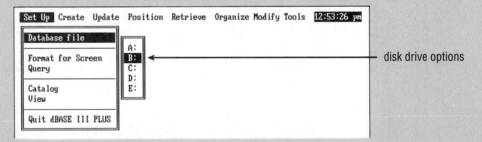

Figure 3-3

You need to tell dBASE on which disk drive you have stored the CLIENT database file.

② If you have a *two-diskette system*, move the selection cursor to B: and press **[Enter]**.

If you have a *hard disk*, make sure the selection cursor is pointing to A: and press **[Enter]**.

A list of all database files stored on the selected drive appears. See Figure 3-4.

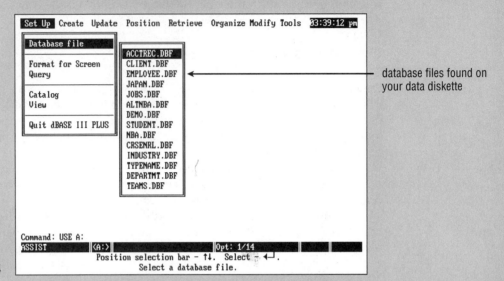

database files found on your data diskette

Figure 3-4

❸ Move the selection cursor to CLIENT.DBF and press **[Enter]**. See Figure 3-5.

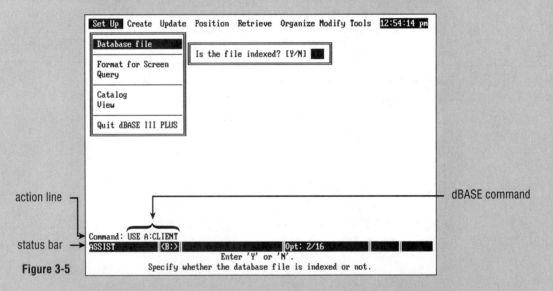

action line

status bar

dBASE command

Figure 3-5

Notice the command USE A:CLIENT on the action line. A prompt also appears asking whether the file is indexed. This prompt, which you first saw in Tutorial 1, appears every time you open a dBASE database file in Assistant mode. You may be wondering what "indexed" means. Indexing is an option in dBASE that allows you to put records in a particular order, such as alphabetical or numerical. You will learn more about indexing later. For now, every time you see this prompt, answer "no."

❹ Type **n** for no.

You have now opened the database. The Set Up menu returns to the Assistant screen.

Look at the status bar in Figure 3-6. The information you see there indicates that the file is open. One message tells you that you are working in drive A and that you have opened the file named CLIENT. In the section labeled "Rec:" the message 1/9 means that dBASE is looking at the first record out of a total of nine records in the database file.

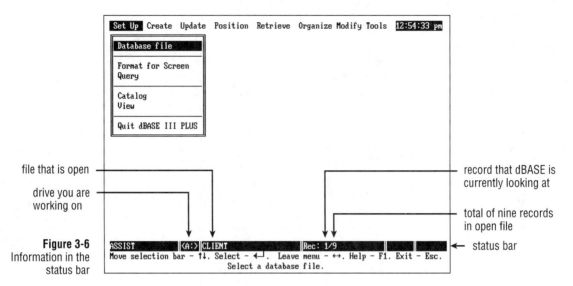

file that is open

drive you are working on

record that dBASE is currently looking at

total of nine records in open file

status bar

Figure 3-6
Information in the status bar

Figure 3-7 will help you visualize what happens when you open a database file. Figure 3-7a illustrates the situation after you have loaded dBASE but have not opened a database file. No link exists between dBASE and any of the database files on your data diskette. Thus, you cannot update, list, or manipulate the records in any database file.

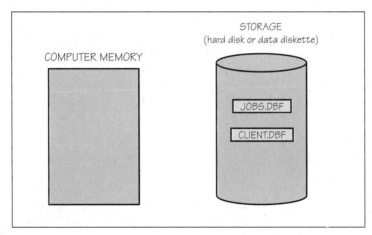

Figure 3-7a
No files opened

Figure 3-7b shows what happens after you open the CLIENT database file. dBASE has found your file on the data diskette and set aside a portion of the computer's memory as a work area for the data in this file. The arrows between the work area in memory and the CLIENT file in storage indicate the CLIENT file is open. You can now update, list, and manipulate records in this file using dBASE.

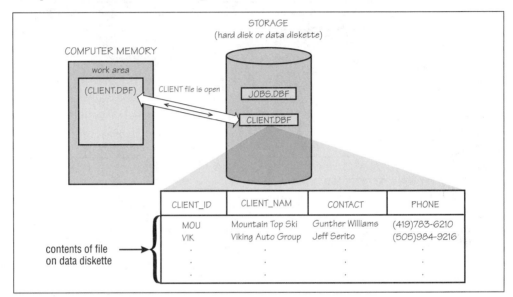

Figure 3-7b
CLIENT.DBF file
open

Adding Records to a Database File

Now that you have opened the CLIENT file, you can add the two new client records to it by using the *Append* option. As its name suggests, this option appends, or adds, new records to the end of a database file. When you use the *Append* option, dBASE allows you to enter data, and a blank input form appears on the screen. The input form guides you as you enter the data values for the new record.

Let's add the new client records to the database file using the the *Append* option of the Update menu.

To add a new record to the CLIENT database file:

❶ Move the selection cursor to the *Update* option on the menu bar.

❷ Move the selection cursor to highlight the *Append* option and press **[Enter]**.

You are now in dBASE's data entry mode. A blank record form appears on the screen. See Figure 3-8. Notice that the form contains the field names Esther defined for the CLIENT file. An input area equal to the field's width follows each name. You use this form to enter the data values for each client. Before you enter any data, the cursor is always in the first position of the first field.

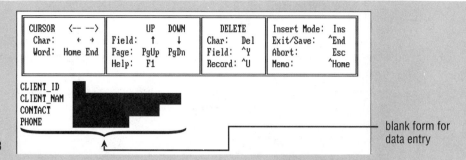

Figure 3-8

blank form for
data entry

Let's enter the data that Martin gave Esther for the new client, Peaches & Ice. See Figure 3-2.

❸ With the cursor positioned at the CLIENT_ID field, type in uppercase **PEA**, the client
ID that W&M will use for Peaches & Ice. The computer beeps and the cursor
advances to the CLIENT_NAM field.

As you enter the data for this record, keep in mind the following guidelines:

- The entry of character data is *case sensitive*, which means that uppercase and
lowercase letters are stored exactly as you type them. For example, if you entered
the CLIENT_ID for Peaches & Ice as "pea", it would be stored in lowercase; it would
not be changed to uppercase and stored as "PEA".

- If the data you enter fill all the positions in the field, the computer will beep, and the
cursor will automatically advance to the next field of the current record or to the first
field of the next record (if the cursor is in the last field of the current record).

- If the data you enter do not fill the field, you must press [Enter] to move to the next field.

- If you enter an illegal character in a field, such as a letter in a numeric field, the computer
will beep and your entry will not appear. In that case just type a valid character.

- If you notice a typing error, you can move between fields within a given record by
using [↑] or [↓]. You can then modify the contents of a field by typing over what
you previously entered in the field.

Figure 3-9 summarizes the keystroke combinations you can use whenever you enter data.
You probably will not use them all right now, but they are listed here for your convenience
and possible future use.

Keystroke	Function
[←] [→]	Moves the cursor one character to the left or the right
[↑] [↓]	Moves the cursor to the previous or next field in record
[PgUp][PgDn]	Moves the cursor to the previous or next record in database
[Ins]	Switches between insert and replacement modes
[Del]	Deletes the character the cursor is on
[Ctrl][End]	Saves all appended records, including the current record, and returns you to the Assistant screen or the dot prompt
[Esc]	Returns you to the Assistant screen or the dot prompt without saving the current record

Figure 3-9
Keystroke
combinations for
the *Append* option

Next let's enter the client's name.

To enter the client's name:

❶ With the cursor in the CLIENT_NAM field, type **Peaches & Ice** and press **[Enter]**. Note that the cursor advances to the CONTACT field.

Next enter the name of the contact person.

❷ Type **Alice Beaumont** and press **[Enter]**. See Figure 3-10. The cursor advances to the PHONE field.

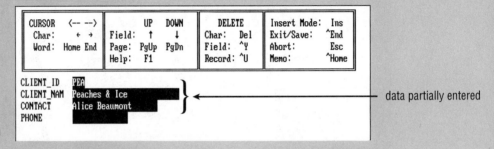

Figure 3-10

data partially entered

❸ Type **(505)728-5176**. See Figure 3-11. The computer beeps, and a new blank record form appears.

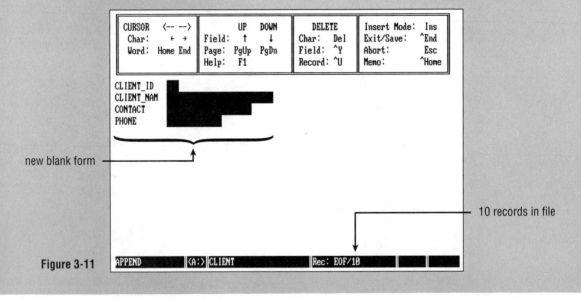

new blank form

10 records in file

Figure 3-11

If you want to return to the record you just typed, press [PgUp] and the record will reappear. To correct any errors, move the cursor to the appropriate field and make your changes. When you are happy with what you see, press [PgDn] to return to the blank data entry form. Figure 3-12 illustrates the contents of the CLIENT file on your data diskette after you entered the complete Peaches & Ice record. dBASE automatically saves the Peaches & Ice record, the tenth client, as record number 10 in the CLIENT file. Notice that the status bar indicates a total of 10 records (Figure 3-11). dBASE automatically assigns consecutive numbers, starting with 1, to the records you store in a database file. Thus, the first record you enter is record number 1, the second record is record number 2, and so on. You just added Peaches & Ice to the nine records already in the CLIENT file, so this record was assigned record number 10.

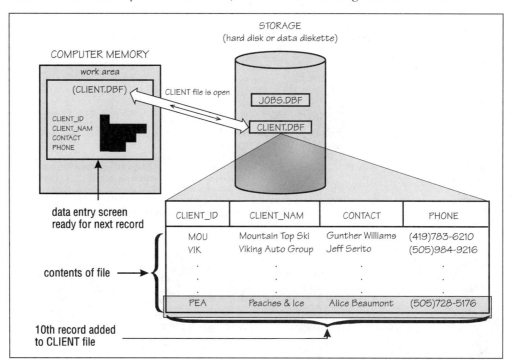

Figure 3-12

The Record Pointer

dBASE keeps track of its place in the database file with a record pointer. The **record pointer** stores in the computer's memory the record number of the record that dBASE is currently "looking at." For example, 1/10 in the status bar means that dBASE is currently looking at the first of 10 records in a file. This record is called the **current record**. It is important for you to know about the concept of current records, because some dBASE commands process only the current record or begin processing at the current record.

Sometimes in the status bar you will see the letters EOF followed by a slash and a number. EOF is an abbreviation that means that the current record is the *end of the file*. EOF appears each time you add a record to a database file, because dBASE always appends a record to the *end* of a file.

Adding Another Record

Now that you have entered data into the last field of the Peaches & Ice record, a blank record form appears. You can now enter data for the second new client.

To enter the data for the second new client:
❶   Type **TAC** in the CLIENT_ID field.
❷   Enter the remainder of the data for Taco Heaven found in Figure 3-2.

Leaving the Data Entry Screen

After you have entered data into the last field of the Taco Heaven client record, the status bar indicates that a total of 11 records are stored in the CLIENT file. A new blank record form appearing on the screen is your indication that the record you just entered has been appended to the CLIENT file. Now that you have entered the new records, how do you leave the data entry mode?

To leave data entry mode:

❶ With the cursor on the first position of the first field of the new blank record, press **[Enter]** or press **[Esc]**. This causes you to exit data entry mode and return to the Assistant screen.

Now let's list all the clients currently stored in the Wells & Martinez CLIENT database to make sure that the new records have been added.

To list the clients in the CLIENT file:

❶ Select the *Retrieve* option from the menu bar. You will see *List* highlighted on the pull-down menu.

❷ Press **[Enter]** to select the *List* option. A submenu appears indicating the options available.

❸ Press **[Enter]** to choose the option *Execute the command.*

❹ You do not want a hard copy of the file, so type **n** when you see the prompt "Direct the output to the printer? [Y/N]." Figure 3-13 shows how the data in the W&M CLIENT file should appear on your screen.

two new records

Figure 3-13
Contents of W&M
CLIENT file

11 records in file

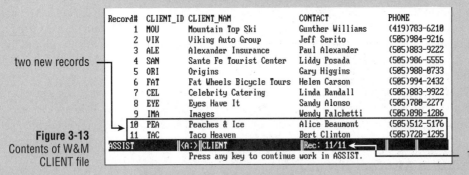

```
Record#  CLIENT_ID CLIENT_NAM              CONTACT           PHONE
      1  MOU       Mountain Top Ski        Gunther Williams  (419)783-6210
      2  VIK       Viking Auto Group       Jeff Serito       (505)984-9216
      3  ALE       Alexander Insurance     Paul Alexander    (505)883-9222
      4  SAN       Sante Fe Tourist Center Liddy Posada      (505)986-5555
      5  ORI       Origins                 Gary Higgins      (505)988-0733
      6  FAT       Fat Wheels Bicycle Tours Helen Carson     (505)994-2432
      7  CEL       Celebrity Catering      Linda Randall     (505)883-9922
      8  EYE       Eyes Have It            Sandy Alonso      (505)788-2277
      9  IMA       Images                  Wendy Falchetti   (505)898-1286
     10  PEA       Peaches & Ice           Alice Beaumont    (505)512-5176
     11  TAC       Taco Heaven             Bert Clinton      (505)728-1295
ASSIST        <A:> CLIENT               Rec: 11/11
              Press any key to continue work in ASSIST.
```

Seeing that the two new clients are currently in the file confirms that you did, in fact, enter those two records. Also notice that the first column displays the record number that dBASE has assigned to each record.

❺ Press any key when you are ready to continue.

Changing Records

Esther consults the list she made at the staff meeting. Since she already has the CLIENT database file open, she checks for any other changes she needs to make to this file. As she scans the list, she notices that she needs to delete Gunther Williams as the contact person for Mountain Top Ski and replace him with Victor Juarez.

Esther can use either the *Edit* or the *Browse* option to make a change like this. In some ways the choice of one option over the other is simply a matter of preference. As you will soon see, each option offers an advantage. With the *Edit* option, you focus on all the relevant information for one record. With the *Browse* option, you see several records displayed at once. Let's try both so you can decide which you prefer.

The *Edit* Option

You use the *Edit* option when you want to view one record at a time. The *Edit* option places you in Edit mode. You use the same data entry form to enter changes to an existing record that you used when you originally entered the record. The only difference is that the values of the *current* record appear in the form.

You use the *Edit* option of the Update menu to change the field contents of a record. Let's use this *Edit* option now to replace "Gunther Williams" with "Victor Juarez."

To change data in a record:

❶ Move the selection cursor to the *Update* option on the menu bar. See Figure 3-14.

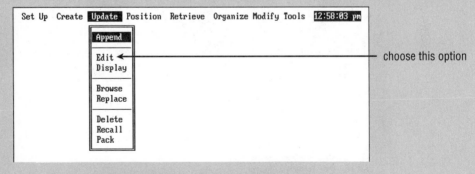

Figure 3-14

❷ Move the selection cursor to the *Edit* option and press **[Enter]**.

You are now in dBASE's Edit mode. The *Edit* option has displayed the current record, Taco Heaven, which is the eleventh record. See Figure 3-15 on the next page. But Taco Heaven is not the record you want to change. You can move to the next record by using [PgDn] or to the previous record by using [PgUp].

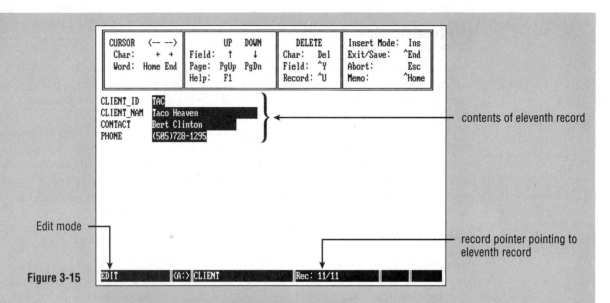

Edit mode

contents of eleventh record

record pointer pointing to eleventh record

Figure 3-15

Now let's retrieve the Mountain Top Ski record, the record you want to edit.

❸ With the cursor positioned at the CLIENT_ID field, press **[PgUp]** until you see the Mountain Top Ski record displayed.

If you happen to return to the Assistant screen as you search for Mountain Top Ski, return to Step 2 and try again.

You can change the contents of any field by moving the cursor to the appropriate field and entering the changes. Let's try it.

❹ Press **[↓]** to move the cursor to the CONTACT field. Replace "Gunther Williams" by typing **Victor Juarez** over it. Then type three spaces to erase the remaining letters. Press **[Enter]**. See Figure 3-16.

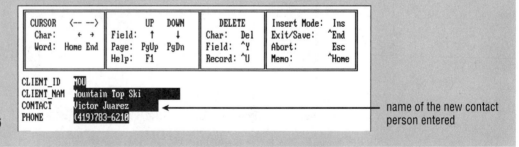

name of the new contact person entered

Figure 3-16

You can use the same keystrokes in Edit mode that you used in Append mode to make changes to the data. Refer to Figure 3-9 for a summary of these keystrokes.

To exit Edit mode at any time, press [Ctrl][End]. dBASE saves the changes and returns you to the Assistant screen.

Now let's save the changes to the CLIENT file.

To save the changes to the CLIENT file:

❶ Press **[Ctrl][End]**. You are returned to the Assistant menu.

If you do not want your changes saved to the database file, press [Esc] instead of [Ctrl][End].

Now let's list all the clients currently stored in the W&M database to see the changes you made to the CLIENT file.

To list the clients in the CLIENT file:

❶ Press **[→]** to select the *Retrieve* option from the menu bar. Notice that *List* is highlighted on the pull-down menu.

❷ Press **[Enter]** to select the *List* option. A submenu appears indicating the options available.

❸ Press **[Enter]** to select the option *Execute the command*.

❹ Since you do not need a hard copy of this file, type **n** when you see the prompt "Direct the output to the printer? [Y/N]." Your screen displays the client data currently stored in the W&M CLIENT file. See Figure 3-17.

```
                                                          new contact

Record#  CLIENT_ID CLIENT_NAM            CONTACT          PHONE
      1  MOU       Mountain Top Ski      Victor Juarez    (419)783-6210
      2  VIK       Viking Auto Group     Jeff Serito      (505)984-9216
      3  ALE       Alexander Insurance   Paul Alexander   (505)883-9222
      4  SAN       Sante Fe Tourist Center Liddy Posada   (505)986-5555
      5  ORI       Origins               Gary Higgins     (505)988-0733
      6  FAT       Fat Wheels Bicycle Tours Helen Carson  (505)994-2432
      7  CEL       Celebrity Catering    Linda Randall    (505)883-9922
      8  EYE       Eyes Have It          Sandy Alonso     (505)780-2277
      9  IMA       Images                Wendy Falchetti  (505)898-1286
     10  PEA       Peaches & Ice         Alice Beaumont   (505)512-5176
     11  TAC       Taco Heaven           Bert Clinton     (505)728-1295
ASSIST              <A:> CLIENT            Rec: 1/11
                    Press any key to continue work in ASSIST.
```

Figure 3-17

Notice that the new contact person, Victor Juarez, appears in the Mountain Top Ski company record.

❺ Press any key when you are ready to continue.

The *Browse* Option

Esther consults her list again. She decides next to update the JOBS[*] file to show that the Images fall catalogue job has been completed. This time she'll use the *Browse* option.

Unlike the *Edit* option, which lets you view only one record at a time, the *Browse* option lets you view several records at once. In Browse mode, you can see up to 17 records at one time, one record per line. (If a record is more than 80 characters wide — the screen's width — you have to scroll left and right to view the other fields.) You can use the *Browse* option to edit, delete, and add records to the currently open database file. Figure 3-18 summarizes the keystrokes you can use in Browse mode.

Keystroke	Function
[←] [→]	Moves the cursor one character to the left or the right
[Home] [End]	Moves the cursor one field to the left or the right
[↓] [↑]	Moves highlight to previous or next record
[PgUp] [PgDn]	Scrolls one screen up or down
[Ctrl][→]	Scrolls one field to right
[Ctrl][←]	Scrolls one field to left
[Ctrl] [U]	Marks or unmarks current record for deletion
[Ctrl][End]	Saves all appended and edited records and returns you to the Assistant screen or dot prompt
[Esc]	Saves all edited and appended records except the current one and returns you to the Assistant screen or dot prompt

Figure 3-18
Keystroke combinations for the *Browse* option

Let's use the *Browse* option to change the status of Images' fall catalogue from in process (I) to completed (C). The CLIENT file is currently open, but you need to change a record in the JOBS file. Therefore, you must close the CLIENT file and open the JOBS file.

To open the JOBS database file:

❶ Move the selection cursor to the *Set Up* option of the menu bar. The option *Database file* is highlighted. Press **[Enter]** to select the *Database file* option. A pull-down menu listing disk drive options appears.

Now tell dBASE on what disk drive you have stored the JOBS database file.

❷ If you have a *two-diskette system*, move the selection cursor to B: and press **[Enter]**.

If you have a *hard disk*, make sure the selection cursor is pointing to A: and press **[Enter]**.

---

[*]   In this tutorial you will use the database file JOBS.DBF in place of WMJOBS.DBF, which you created in Tutorial 2. Whereas the WMJOBS.DBF file has only 1 record, the JOBS.DBF file has 20 records and is the updated version of the file. It contains all of the jobs that Esther has entered into the W&M database.

A list of all database files stored on the specified drive appears.

❸ Move the selection cursor to JOBS.DBF and press **[Enter]**.

Notice that the command USE A:/JOBS now appears on the action line.

❹ Type **n** when you see the prompt "Is the file indexed? [Y/N]."

The JOBS database file is now open, and the Set Up menu again appears.

Look at the status bar (Figure 3-19). You will see information that indicates that the JOBS file is open, the current drive is A, the open file is JOBS, the total number of records in JOBS is 20, and the current record number is 1.

new file opened

current drive

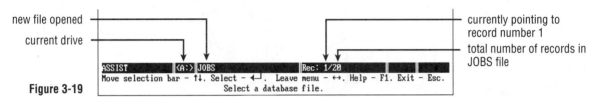

Figure 3-19

currently pointing to
record number 1

total number of records in
JOBS file

To help you visualize what has just occurred, look at Figure 3-20. Figure 3-20a illustrates the situation before you opened the JOBS database file, when the CLIENT database file was open. You were able to update, list, and manipulate the records in the CLIENT file.

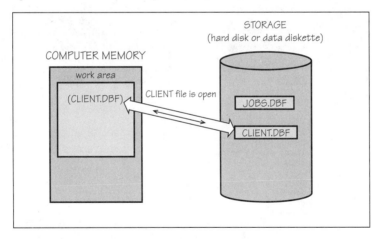

Figure 3-20a
CLIENT file open

Figure 3-20b shows what happened after you opened the JOBS database file. Now you have a link between the work area in the computer's memory and the JOBS file on your data diskette. You can update, list, and manipulate records in the JOBS file. However, you can no longer access any data in the CLIENT file.

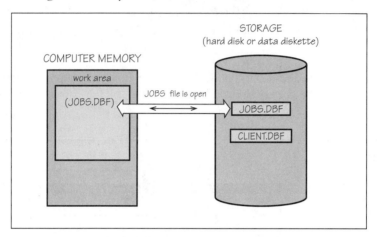

Figure 3-20b
JOBS file open

Let's select the *Browse* option to change the job's status.

To use the *Browse* option:

❶   Move the selection cursor to the *Update* option. See Figure 3-21.

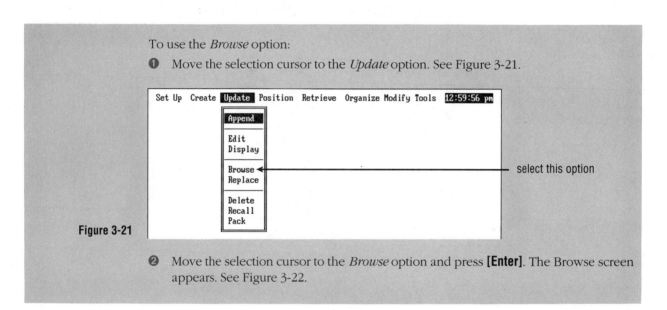

Figure 3-21

❷   Move the selection cursor to the *Browse* option and press **[Enter]**. The Browse screen appears. See Figure 3-22.

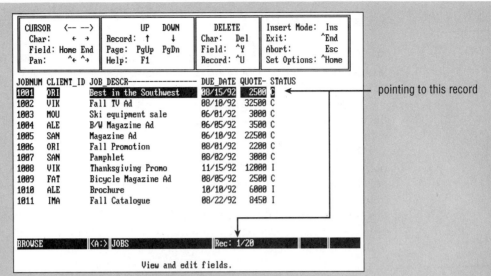

Figure 3-22
The Browse screen

⬤ If the status bar is not pointing to record 1, press **[PgUp]** or **[↑]** until the status bar indicates record 1. If you are at record 1, you are ready for the next step.

⬤ With the cursor in the JOBNUM field, press **[End]**. You will see that the cursor moves one field to the right each time you press [End]. Try it again.

⬤ Press **[Home]**. The cursor moves one field to the left. Try it again. Now return the cursor to the JOBNUM field.

⬤ Press **[↓]** until you have highlighted job number 1011, Fall Catalogue.

⬤ Press **[End]** until the cursor is positioned on the STATUS field. Type uppercase **C** to change the job status to "completed." See Figure 3-23. The cursor advances to the next record.

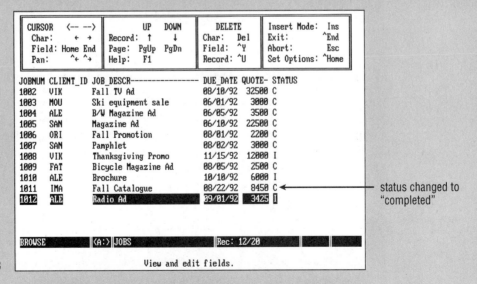

Figure 3-23

⬤ Press **[Ctrl][End]**. You have now saved your changes to the JOBS file and returned to the Assistant screen.

Deleting Records

Esther has now completed three of the four items on her list. All that remains for her to do is to delete Eyes Have It from the CLIENT file. Because the company has gone out of business, this record is no longer needed.

To permanently delete a record from a database file, you take two steps: (1) you "mark" the record for deletion, then (2) you "pack" the database file. First let's discuss marking a record for deletion.

When you **mark** a record, you make the record ready for permanent removal. You have not yet physically removed the record from the database file during this step. You can still edit, list, and include in statistical calculations, among other dBASE actions, records marked for deletion.

Let's perform the first step in deleting Eyes Have It from the database file by marking this record for deletion. Currently you have the JOBS file open. However, the record you want to delete is in the CLIENT file. Thus, you must open the CLIENT file again.

To open the CLIENT file:

❶ Move the selection cursor to the *Set Up* option of the menu bar and open the CLIENT file. After you complete this task, the status bar indicates that the CLIENT file is open and that a total of 11 records are in the open file, CLIENT. See Figure 3-24.

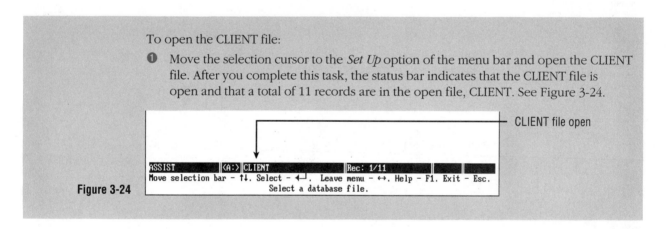

Figure 3-24

Marking Records for Deletion Using the *Edit* Option

You can use the *Delete*, *Edit*, or *Browse* option to mark a record for deletion. The *Edit* and *Browse* options may be better for marking a single record; however, if you are marking a group of related records for deletion, the *Delete* option will accomplish that task faster.

Esther decides to use the *Edit* option to mark the Eyes Have It record for deletion, because it allows her to see the contents of the record and verify that she has the correct record before she marks it for deletion.

To mark a record for deletion using the *Edit* option:

❶ Move the selection cursor to the *Update* option on the menu bar.

❷ Move the selection cursor to the *Edit* option and press **[Enter]**. The current record is Mountain Top Ski. See Figure 3-25.

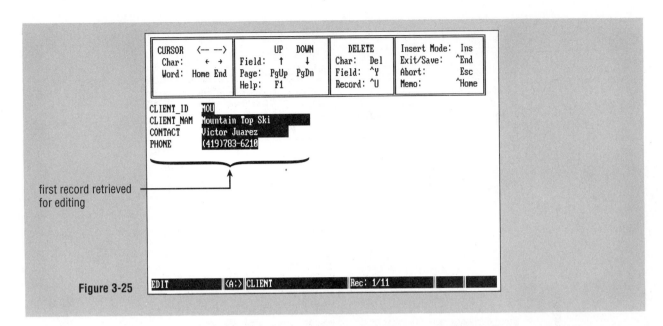

first record retrieved
for editing

Figure 3-25

Next you would scroll through the CLIENT file, using [PgDn], until you found the record you wanted to delete. But what would happen if you made a mistake and accidentally marked the wrong record for deletion? Let's *intentionally* mark a wrong record for deletion. You'll do this by making Origins the current record and then, while in Edit mode, using the keystroke combination [Ctrl][U] to mark it for deletion.

To mark the Origins record for deletion:

❶ Press [PgDn] until Origins is the current record. See Figure 3-26.

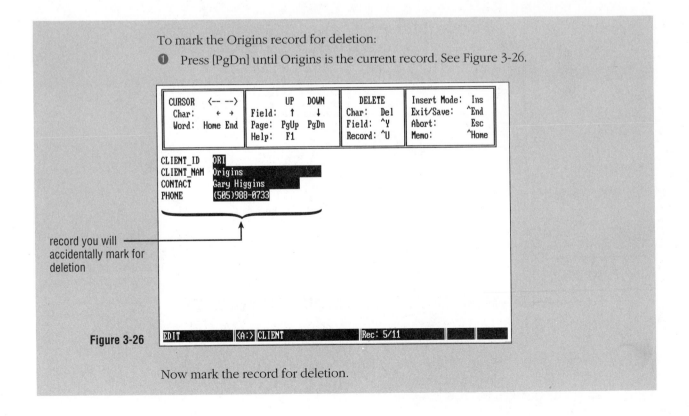

record you will
accidentally mark for
deletion

Figure 3-26

Now mark the record for deletion.

❷   Press **[Ctrl][U]**. The status bar now shows "Del". See Figure 3-27. This means that the current record is marked for deletion.

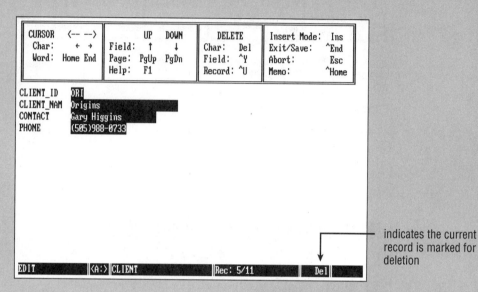

indicates the current record is marked for deletion

Figure 3-27

[Ctrl][U] is a **toggle**, that is, it acts like an on/off switch. If you press [Ctrl][U] one time, the record is marked for deletion. Press the keystroke combination a second time, and the record is no longer marked for deletion; press it again, and the record is marked for deletion; and so on.

❸   Press **[Ctrl][U]** again. "Del" no longer appears on the status bar. See Figure 3-28. The current record is not marked for deletion.

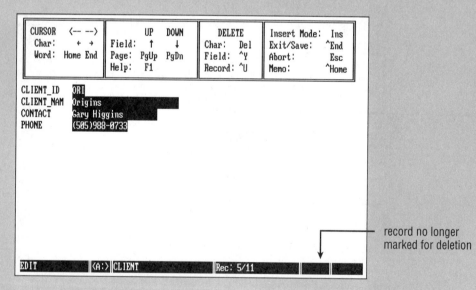

record no longer marked for deletion

Figure 3-28

Now let's mark the record for deletion again.

❹   Press **[Ctrl][U]**. Notice that "Del" appears on the status bar. The record is again marked for deletion.

Let's leave Edit mode with the Origins record marked for deletion.

⑤ Press **[Ctrl][End]**. You return to the Assistant screen.

Now let's list all the clients currently stored in the Wells & Martinez CLIENT file to see if the record Origins is marked for deletion. When you use the *List* option, any record marked for deletion appears with an asterisk (*) to the left of its first field.

To list the clients in the CLIENT file:

① Move the selection cursor to the *Retrieve* option on the menu bar and select the *List* option. The client data currently stored in the W&M CLIENT file appears. See Figure 3-29. As you can see, the record you marked for deletion, Origins, is "marked" with an asterisk to the left of the first field in the record. Also note from the listing that the record number for this company is 5.

indicates record is
marked for deletion

```
Record#  CLIENT_ID CLIENT_NAM              CONTACT          PHONE
       1  MOU       Mountain Top Ski        Victor Juarez    (419)783-6210
       2  VIK       Viking Auto Group       Jeff Serito      (505)984-9216
       3  ALE       Alexander Insurance     Paul Alexander   (505)883-9222
       4 ↓SAN       Sante Fe Tourist Center Liddy Posada     (505)986-5555
       5 *ORI       Origins                 Gary Higgins     (505)988-0733
       6  FAT       Fat Wheels Bicycle Tours Helen Carson    (505)994-2432
       7  CEL       Celebrity Catering      Linda Randall    (505)883-9922
       8  EYE       Eyes Have It            Sandy Alonso     (505)780-2277
       9  IMA       Images                  Wendy Falchetti  (505)898-1286
      10  PEA       Peaches & Ice           Alice Beaumont   (505)512-5176
      11  TAC       Taco Heaven             Bert Clinton     (505)728-1295
ASSIST        <A:> CLIENT                   Rec: 5/11
              Press any key to continue work in ASSIST.
```

Figure 3-29

② Press any key when you are ready to continue.

Remember, the Origins record is marked for deletion in error. Now you need to learn how to "unmark" a record.

The *Recall* Option

As you did with the Origins record, sometimes you might accidentally mark a record for deletion or you might need to "remove" a record from the file yet have it accessible in the event circumstances change and you need it to be unmarked. In such cases you can use the *Recall* option to "unmark" a record marked for deletion. The *Recall* option removes the "mark for deletion" from one or more records.

Remember that you accidentally marked the Origins record for deletion, and that its record number is 5. Now let's use the *Recall* option to unmark this record.

To use the *Recall* option:

① Move the selection cursor to the *Update* option of the menu bar.

② Move the selection cursor to the *Recall* option. See Figure 3-30.

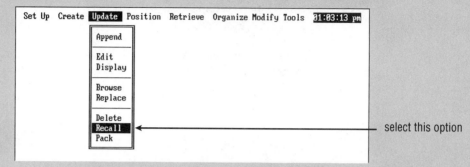

Figure 3-30

select this option

③ Press **[Enter]**. A submenu appears indicating the options available for the *Recall* option. See Figure 3-31.

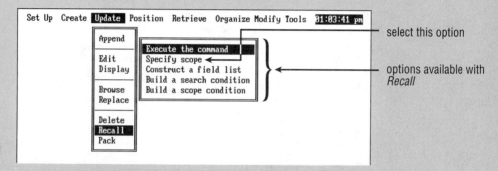

Figure 3-31

select this option

options available with *Recall*

④ Move the selection cursor to the option *Specify scope* and press **[Enter]**. A menu of scope options appears. See Figure 3-32.

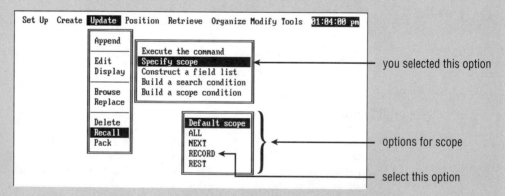

Figure 3-32

you selected this option

options for scope

select this option

Remember, the record number for Origins is 5.

⑤ Move the selection cursor to RECORD and press **[Enter]**.

A prompt appears asking you to "Enter a numeric value." This means you should enter the record number of the record you want to unmark. In this case, the record number is 5.

⑥ Type **5** and press **[Enter]**. The dBASE command in the action line is RECALL RECORD 5. See Figure 3-33.

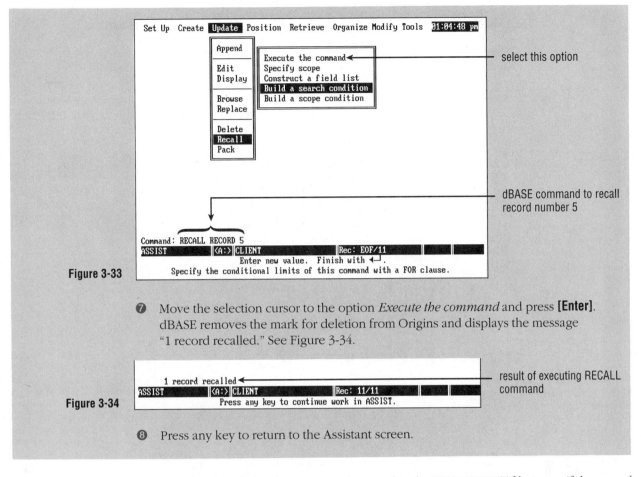

Figure 3-33

⑦ Move the selection cursor to the option *Execute the command* and press **[Enter]**. dBASE removes the mark for deletion from Origins and displays the message "1 record recalled." See Figure 3-34.

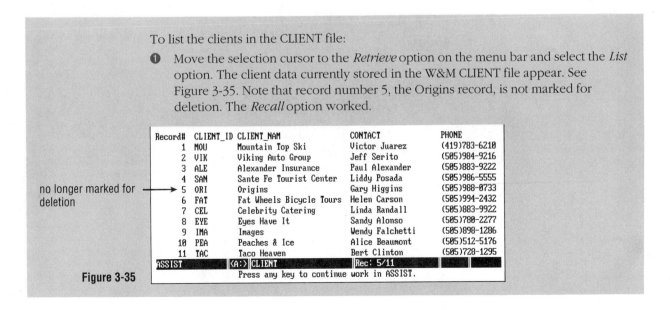

Figure 3-34

⑧ Press any key to return to the Assistant screen.

Now let's list all the clients currently stored in the W&M CLIENT file to see if the record Origins is still marked for deletion.

To list the clients in the CLIENT file:

① Move the selection cursor to the *Retrieve* option on the menu bar and select the *List* option. The client data currently stored in the W&M CLIENT file appear. See Figure 3-35. Note that record number 5, the Origins record, is not marked for deletion. The *Recall* option worked.

Figure 3-35

Marking Records for Deletion Using the *Delete* Option

Now let's mark the correct record for deletion, Eyes Have It. We could use the *Edit* option again, but this time let's use another option that will accomplish the same thing.

The *Delete* option marks one or several records for deletion. For example, if you wanted to delete all the jobs for a particular client in the JOBS file, you could use the *Delete* option.

Let's use the *Delete* option to mark the record Eyes Have It, record number 8, for deletion.

To use the *Delete* option to mark a record:

❶   Move the selection cursor to the *Update* option.

❷   Move the selection cursor to *Delete*. See Figure 3-36.

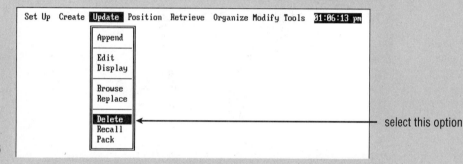

Figure 3-36   select this option

❸   Press **[Enter]**. Another submenu appears indicating the options available with the *Delete* option. See Figure 3-37.

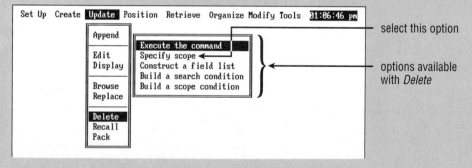

Figure 3-37   select this option
                                                                              options available
                                                                              with *Delete*

Now find the record you want to mark for deletion.

❹   Move the selection cursor to the option *Specify scope* and press **[Enter]**. A menu of scope options appears. See Figure 3-38.

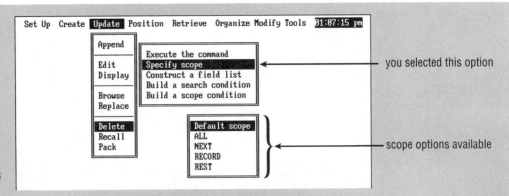

you selected this option

scope options available

Figure 3-38

⑤ Move the selection cursor to RECORD and press **[Enter]**.

A prompt appears asking you to "Enter a numeric value."

The record number for Eyes Have It is 8. Now enter the record number of the record you want to mark, in this case, the number 8.

⑥ Type **8** and press **[Enter]**. See Figure 3-39. Notice that the dBASE command in the action line is DELETE RECORD 8.

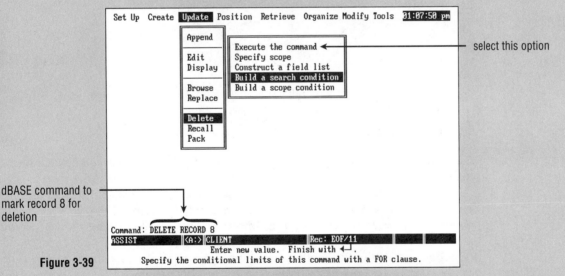

select this option

dBASE command to mark record 8 for deletion

Figure 3-39

⑦ Move the selection cursor to the option *Execute the command* and press **[Enter]**.

dBASE displays the message "1 record deleted"; however, it has only *marked* the appropriate record for deletion, not deleted it. See Figure 3-40.

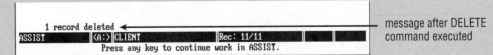

message after DELETE command executed

Figure 3-40

⑧ Press any key to return to the Assistant menu.

To make sure that Eyes Have It is marked for deletion, let's list all the clients currently stored in the W&M CLIENT file.

To list the clients in the CLIENT file:

❶ Select the *Retrieve* option on the menu bar, then select the *List* option. The data currently stored in the W&M CLIENT file appear on the screen. See Figure 3-41.

Record#	CLIENT_ID	CLIENT_NAM	CONTACT	PHONE
1	MOU	Mountain Top Ski	Victor Juarez	(419)783-6210
2	VIK	Viking Auto Group	Jeff Serito	(505)984-9216
3	ALE	Alexander Insurance	Paul Alexander	(505)883-9222
4	SAN	Sante Fe Tourist Center	Liddy Posada	(505)986-5555
5	ORI	Origins	Gary Higgins	(505)988-0733
6	FAT	Fat Wheels Bicycle Tours	Helen Carson	(505)994-2432
7	CEL	Celebrity Catering	Linda Randall	(505)883-9922
8	*EYE	Eyes Have It	Sandy Alonso	(505)780-2277
9	IMA	Images	Wendy Falchetti	(505)898-1286
10	PEA	Peaches & Ice	Alice Beaumont	(505)512-5176
11	TAC	Taco Heaven	Bert Clinton	(505)728-1295

ASSIST   ⟨A:⟩ CLIENT   Rec: 8/11

Press any key to continue work in ASSIST.

indicates record marked for deletion

Figure 3-41

Eleven records appear on the screen, with an asterisk before the record Eyes Have It. Thus, you have used the *Delete* option to mark this record for deletion.

❷ Press any key to return to the Assistant screen.

Now let's learn how to permanently remove a record from the database file.

The *Pack* Option

When we first discussed removing records from a file, we said that removing a record is actually a two-step process: first you must mark the record to be deleted, then you must pack it. You have already learned that marking a record does not permanently delete the record. You can use the *Recall* option to recover a marked record. When you are ready to *permanently* remove a record, you use the *Pack* option. *You cannot recover (Recall) a marked record once you remove it with the Pack option.*

Before you use the *Pack* option, be certain that you have marked the correct records for deletion. Use the *List* option to see which, if any, records are marked. Remember, an asterisk (*) precedes each record marked for deletion. If you are using the *Browse* option, you will know a record is marked for deletion if "Del" appears in the status bar when the record is highlighted.

To remove marked records permanently:

❶ Move the selection cursor to the *Update* option on the menu bar.

❷ Move the selection cursor to the *Pack* option. See Figure 3-42. Press **[Enter]**.

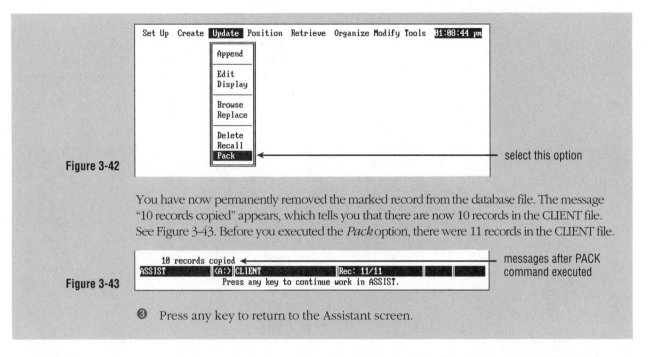

Figure 3-42

select this option

You have now permanently removed the marked record from the database file. The message "10 records copied" appears, which tells you that there are now 10 records in the CLIENT file. See Figure 3-43. Before you executed the *Pack* option, there were 11 records in the CLIENT file.

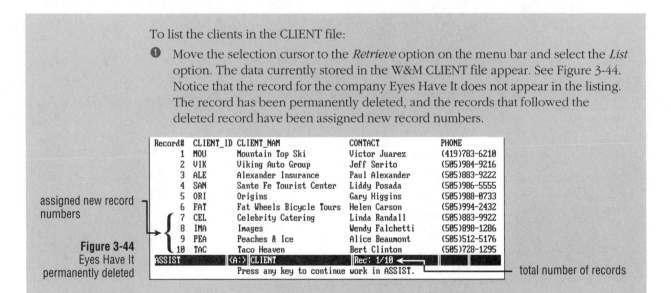

messages after PACK
command executed

Figure 3-43

❸ Press any key to return to the Assistant screen.

To verify that the record is no longer in the CLIENT file, let's list the file one last time.

To list the clients in the CLIENT file:

❶ Move the selection cursor to the *Retrieve* option on the menu bar and select the *List* option. The data currently stored in the W&M CLIENT file appear. See Figure 3-44. Notice that the record for the company Eyes Have It does not appear in the listing. The record has been permanently deleted, and the records that followed the deleted record have been assigned new record numbers.

assigned new record
numbers

Figure 3-44
Eyes Have It
permanently deleted

total number of records

Copying a Database File

Esther has completed the updating tasks she planned for today, but before she quits dBASE, she knows she must make copies of the updated database files. The process of making a duplicate copy of each database file is called **backing up** the database file. Esther does this to protect her data in case the original database file is lost, stolen, damaged, or destroyed. The backup file can then be used in place of the original file.

In dBASE you use the *Copy* option to create a new database with a file structure identical to that of the currently open database file. You can copy some or all of the records in a file to the backup file.

To make a backup of all records in the currently opened file:

❶ Highlight the *Organize* option on the menu bar.

❷ Move the selection cursor to the *Copy* option and press **[Enter]**. See Figure 3-45. A pull-down menu appears listing the disk drive options. You need to tell dBASE on what disk drive you want to store the duplicate copy of the CLIENT database file.

select this option ─────────

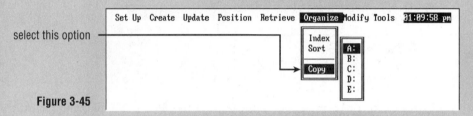

Figure 3-45

❸ If you have a *two-diskette system*, move the selection cursor to B: and press **[Enter]**.

If you have a *hard disk*, make sure the selection cursor is pointing to A: and press **[Enter]**.

A prompt appears asking you to enter a filename for the backup file. See Figure 3-46.

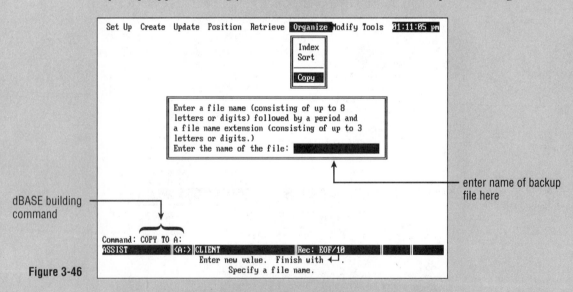

enter name of backup file here

dBASE building command ─────────

Figure 3-46

❹ Type **clientbk** and press **[Enter]**. A submenu appears indicating the options available for the *Copy* option.

⑤ Press **[Enter]** to choose the option *Execute the command*. The message "10 records copied" appears on the screen. The database file named CLIENTBK.DBF is now saved. Figure 3-47 illustrates the stored backup file.

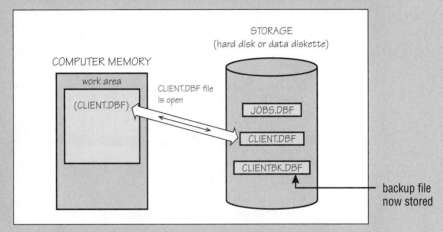

Figure 3-47
Hard disk or data
diskette after backup

If you store a backup file to the same diskette as the original file, the name of the backup file must be different from the original filename. Esther adds the letters BK, an abbreviation for backup, to the original name of the file to help her easily identify her backup files.

⑥ Press any key to continue.

To verify that you have a duplicate copy of your CLIENT database file, let's open the backup file from your data diskette and list the contents.

To open the database file CLIENTBK.DBF:

① Move the selection cursor to the *Set Up* option on the menu bar and open the CLIENTBK.DBF file. After you complete this task, the status bar indicates that the CLIENTBK file is open and that a total of 10 records are in the open file, CLIENTBK. See Figure 3-48.

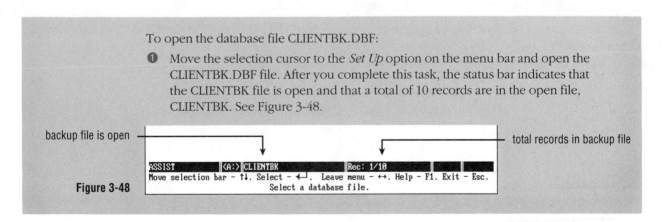

Figure 3-48

Now list the contents of the backup file.

❷ Move the selection cursor to the *Retrieve* option on the menu bar and select the *List* option. The data currently stored in the backup file appear on the screen. See Figure 3-49.

Figure 3-49

```
Record#  CLIENT_ID  CLIENT_NAM                CONTACT          PHONE
      1  MOU        Mountain Top Ski          Victor Juarez    (419)783-6210  ⎫
      2  VIK        Viking Auto Group         Jeff Serito      (505)984-9216  ⎪
      3  ALE        Alexander Insurance       Paul Alexander   (505)883-9222  ⎪
      4  SAN        Sante Fe Tourist Center   Liddy Posada     (505)986-5555  ⎪
      5  ORI        Origins                   Gary Higgins     (505)988-0733  ⎬ ← records in
      6  FAT        Fat Wheels Bicycle Tours  Helen Carson     (505)994-2432  ⎪    backup file
      7  CEL        Celebrity Catering        Linda Randall    (505)883-9922  ⎪
      8  IMA        Images                    Wendy Falchetti  (505)898-1286  ⎪
      9  PEA        Peaches & Ice             Alice Beaumont   (505)512-5176  ⎪
     10  TAC        Taco Heaven               Bert Clinton     (505)728-1295  ⎭
ASSIST          <A:>|CLIENTBK          |Rec: 1/10
                Press any key to continue work in ASSIST.
```

Quitting dBASE

Now that you have backed up the CLIENT file, you have finished this dBASE tutorial. You are ready to use the *Quit* option to leave dBASE. When you execute the *Quit* option, dBASE automatically closes all open files. If the open database file is not properly closed, you may not be able to access all the data in the database file when you attempt to open the file again.

To quit dBASE:

❶ Select the *Set Up* option from the menu bar.

❷ Move the highlight to the option *Quit dBASE III PLUS*. Press **[Enter]**. You are now at the DOS prompt.

You have now completed Tutorial 3.

■   ■   ■

Exercises

1. What information on the Assistant screen tells you which database file is open?

2. What line on the Assistant screen tells you how many records are stored in the open database file?

3. What two options on the Assistant screen can you use to determine if any records are marked for deletion? How does each of these options let you know whether any records are marked for deletion?

4.   What is the difference between the *Edit* option and the *Browse* option?

5.   After you mark a record for deletion, what option permanently removes a record from a database file?

6.   What is the purpose of the *Recall* option?

7.   What option from the Assistant screen would you select to make a backup database file?

Use the file layout in Figure 3-50 to answer Exercises 8 and 9. Assume employee 101 has skills in Lotus 1-2-3 (code = LOT123) and dBASE III PLUS (code = DBASE3).

Field	Data Type	Width
EMPLOY_ID	Character	3
SKILL1_CD	Character	6
SKILL2_CD	Character	6
SKILL3_CD	Character	6

Figure 3-50

8.   Sketch the blank data entry form that you would see if you selected the *Append* option from the Update menu.

9.   Fill in the sketch from Exercise 8 using the data for employee 101.

Use the file layout in Figure 3-51 to answer Exercises 10 and 11. Assume employee 101 has skills in Lotus 1-2-3 (code = LOT123) and dBASE III PLUS (code = DBASE3).

Field	Data Type	Width
EMPLOY_ID	Character	3
SKILL_CD	Character	6

Figure 3-51

10.   Sketch the blank data entry form that you would see if you selected the *Append* option from the Update menu.

11.   How would you enter the data for employee 101? *Hint:* You need to add more than one record.

Tutorial Assignments

Instructor's note: The figures of the screens in Tutorial 4 reflect the updates to the CLIENT and JOBS files that students make in these assignments.

For the W&M CLIENT database file, do the following file maintenance tasks:

1.   Open the database file.

2.   Print the file structure.

3. Add the record shown in Figure 3-52.

CLIENT_ID	MAM
CLIENT_NAM	Mama Lee's Pizza
CONTACT	Emma Lee
PHONE	(505)984-3245

Figure 3-52

4. Correct the phone number for Celebrity Catering from (505)883-9922 to (800)884-2321.

5. Mark the client Viking Auto Group for deletion.

6. Print the CLIENT file.

7. Recall Viking Auto Group.

8. Print the CLIENT file.

For the JOBS database file do the following file maintenance tasks:

9. Open the JOBS database file.

10. Print the file structure.

11. Add the four records shown in Figure 3-53. Remember, when you're ready to leave the APPEND process press either [Enter] or [Esc] with the cursor on the first position of the first field of a blank record form. *Do not press [Ctrl] [End] to leave the APPEND process after you have moved to a blank record form.*

	Record 1	Record 2	Record 3	Record 4
JOBNUM	1021	1022	1023	1024
CLIENT_ID	ALE	MAM	TAC	PEA
JOB_DESCR	B/W magazine ad	Newspaper ad	TV ad	Brochure
DUE_DATE	11/10/92	12/01/92	12/15/92	11/30/92
QUOTE	6600	5300	14000	11000
STATUS	I	I	I	I

Figure 3-53

12. Print all the records in the JOBS file.

13. Make a backup copy of the JOBS file. Name the file JOBSBK.DBF.

14. Print the file structure of the backup file JOBSBK.DBF.

Case Problems

1. Biggs & Hang Investment Corporation

Do the following file maintenance tasks with the database file JAPAN.

1. Open the database file JAPAN.DBF.

2. Print the file structure.

3. Add the two records shown in Figure 3-54.

	Record 1	Record 2
COMP_ID	7272	7269
COMP_NAME	Yamaha Motor	Suzuki Motor
IND_CODE	A	A
DESCRPT	world's 2nd largest motorcycle manufacturer	world's 3rd largest motorcycle manufacturer
ASSETS	285833	551611
SALES	592559	982573
PROFITS	34933	27796
OUT_SHRS	230198	408612
HIGH_PRICE	1430	1040
LOW_PRICE	961	660

Figure 3-54

4. Change the PROFITS field from 210000 to 200585 for Honda Motor.

5. Mark the client Honda Motor for deletion.

6. Print all the records in the file.

7. Recall Honda Motor.

8. Print all the records in the file.

9. Make a backup copy of the database file JAPAN.DBF. Name the file JAPANBK.DBF.

10. Print the file structure of the backup file you created in Problem 9.

2. Medi-Source Inc.

For the database file ACCTREC do the following file maintenance tasks:

1. Open the database file ACCTREC.DBF.

2. Print the file structure.

3. Add the two records shown in Figure 3-55.

	Record 1	Record 2
CUSTID	24	25
CUSTNAME	Rogers Hospital	Elmwood Pharmacy
TYPE	H	P
STATE	RI	MA
REP	4	4
CRD_LIMIT	15000	5000
BAL_OWED	0	0
YTD_SALES	0	0
DATE_LSTSL	no date	no date

Figure 3-55

4. Change the sales rep number for Bayshore Pharmacy from 3 to 1.

5. Mark the customer Forgary Labs for deletion.

6. Print the ACCTREC file.

7. Recall the record marked for deletion.

8. Print the ACCTREC file.

9. Make a backup copy of the database file ACCTREC.DBF. Name the file ACCTRBK.DBF.

10. Print the file structure of the backup file you created in Problem 9.

3. Appleton & Drake Electrical Supply Company

For the database file EMPLOYEE do the following file maintenance tasks:

1. Open the database file EMPLOYEE.DBF.

2. Print the file structure.

3. Add the two records shown in Figure 3-56.

	Record 1	**Record 2**
EMP_NUM	129	130
LNAME	Appleton	Lucas
FNAME	Kathy	Mark
SEX	F	M
MAR	Y	N
DEP	0	0
HIRE_DATE	6/2/92	8/15/92
ANNSAL	29000	27500
DEPT	ENG	SAL

Figure 3-56

4. Change Janet Krause's salary from 25800 to 27200.

5. Mark employee Nora Chin for deletion.

6. Print the file.

7. Recall Nora Chin.

8. Print the file.

9. Make a backup copy of the database file EMPLOYEE. Name the file EMPLOYBK.DBF.

10. Print the file structure of the backup file you created in Problem 9.

4. National Basketball Association

For the database file NBA do the following file maintenance tasks:

1. Open the database file NBA.DBF.

2. Print the file structure.

3. Add the two records shown in Figure 3-57.

	Record 1	**Record 2**
TEAM	PHI	PHI
FNAME	CHARLES	JOHNNY
LNAME	BARKLEY	DAWKINS
POS	F	G
SALARY	2900000	1500000

Figure 3-57

4. KIKI VANDEWEGHE is the correct spelling of the player's name, not KIKI VANEWEGHE. Correct the name.

5. Mark DENNIS RODMAN's record for deletion.

6. Print the file.

7. Recall DENNIS RODMAN's record.

8. Print the file.

9. Make a backup copy of the database file NBA.DBF. Name the file NBABK.DBF.

10. Print the file structure of the backup file you created in Problem 9.

Tutorial 4

Querying the Database

Case: Wells & Martinez — Retrieving Information from the W&M Database

One morning Esther finds on her desk a note from Nancy saying, "Need a printout of all W&M clients." Nancy explains in her note that she wants to give this list to potential clients who want to contact current clients for references on W&M's work. As Esther begins to work on Nancy's request, Martin pops in and asks for a list of all unfinished jobs. He says he needs it by noon that day. Then during coffee break Nancy finds Esther and makes another request — this time for completed jobs having a quote over $5,000. She wants Esther to include only the client ID, the job number, and the quote in the printout. Nancy also asks her if it is possible to calculate the number of jobs W&M has completed, the total amount of the quotes for all completed jobs, and the average quote for the completed jobs. Esther replies that she can use dBASE's statistical commands to do that. Nancy is pleased to hear this and asks to have the information on her desk by the end of the day.

As Esther walks back to her office, she thinks to herself that it would take hours to search the files manually to get this kind of information and to do the calculations and lists. She then realizes the value of dBASE's querying capability and statistical options.

OBJECTIVES

In this tutorial you will learn to:

- Direct records to the screen or to a printer using the LIST and the DISPLAY commands

- Select only the fields you want to see in your output

- Build a conditional expression for selecting records that meet certain criteria

- Use the statistical commands COUNT, SUM, and AVERAGE

Introduction to Queries

Information systems are developed to provide information to help solve business problems. As computer professionals create these systems, they try to anticipate all the questions that managers may want answered from the data in a database, and try to develop reports that can be produced on a regular basis. In spite of their efforts, however, computer professionals cannot anticipate all the questions that managers will ask.

When existing reports cannot answer their questions, dBASE users rely on the query facility of a DBMS. The query facility allows users to enter English-like commands to access the database and retrieve the records that will answer their questions. In this tutorial you will use the dBASE query options to develop the queries Esther needs to answer Nancy and Martin's requests for information.

Using the *List* Option

Nancy has asked Esther for a list of all W&M clients. Esther plans to use the *List* option to answer Nancy's request. But remember, a database file must be open before you can update, list, or perform calculations on any data in the file. So load dBASE as before and then let's open the file CLIENT.

To open the file CLIENT:

❶   With the selection cursor positioned on the *Set Up* option on the menu bar, you will see that the option *Database file* is highlighted. Press **[Enter]** to select the *Database file* option. A pull-down menu appears listing disk drive options. See Figure 4-1.

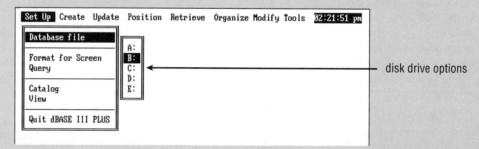

Figure 4-1

You need to tell dBASE on which disk drive you have stored the database file CLIENT.

❷   If you have a *two-diskette system*, move the selection cursor to B: and press **[Enter]**.

If you have a *hard disk*, make sure the selection cursor is pointing to A: and press **[Enter]**.

A list of all database files stored on the selected drive appears. See Figure 4-2.

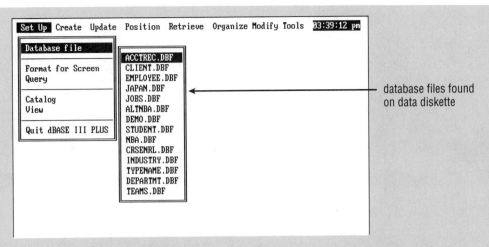

database files found
on data diskette

Figure 4-2

❸ Move the selection cursor to CLIENT.DBF and press **[Enter]**. The command USE A:CLIENT appears on the action line. A prompt asking you whether the file is indexed also appears. See Figure 4-3.

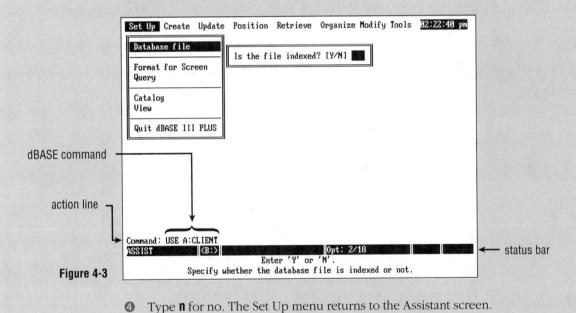

dBASE command

action line

status bar

Figure 4-3

❹ Type **n** for no. The Set Up menu returns to the Assistant screen.

You have now opened the file. The status bar indicates that the file CLIENT contains a total of 11 records. Now that the file CLIENT is open, you can prepare the list of clients for Nancy.

To list the clients in the file CLIENT:

❶ Press **[→]** to select the *Retrieve* option from the menu bar. *List* will be highlighted on the pull-down menu.

❷   Press **[Enter]** to select the *List* option. A submenu appears indicating the available options.

Notice that the command LIST appears on the action line. dBASE is building the command as you use the Assistant screen.

❸   Press **[Enter]** to select the option *Execute the command.* A prompt appears asking if you want a printout of your results. See Figure 4-4.

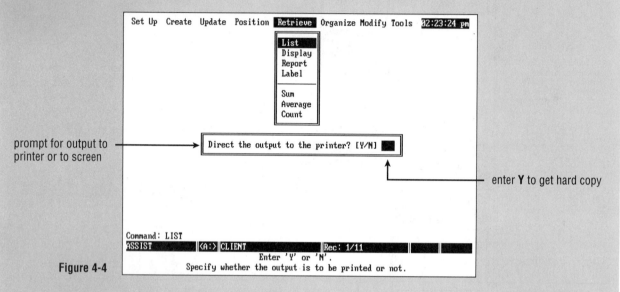

prompt for output to printer or to screen

enter **Y** to get hard copy

Figure 4-4

If you wanted to view the results only on the screen, you would answer no. Let's print the results.

❹   Make sure your printer is turned on.

❺   Type **y** for yes. Figure 4-5 shows how your printout of the data in the W&M CLIENT file should look.

Record#	CLIENT_ID	CLIENT_NAM	CONTACT	PHONE
1	MOU	Mountain Top Ski	Victor Juarez	(419)783-6210
2	VIK	Viking Auto Group	Jeff Serito	(505)984-9216
3	ALE	Alexander Insurance	Paul Alexander	(505)883-9222
4	SAN	Sante Fe Tourist Center	Liddy Posada	(505)986-5555
5	ORI	Origins	Gary Higgins	(505)988-0733
6	FAT	Fat Wheels Bicycle Tours	Helen Carson	(505)994-2432
7	CEL	Celebrity Catering	Linda Randall	(800)884-2321
8	IMA	Images	Wendy Falchetti	(505)898-1286
9	PEA	Peaches & Ice	Alice Beaumont	(505)512-5176
10	TAC	Taco Heaven	Bert Clinton	(505)728-1295
11	MAM	Mama Lee's Pizza	Emma Lee	(505)984-3245

Figure 4-5
Printout of data in
CLIENT file

❻   Press any key when you are ready to continue.

Selecting the Field Names

As Esther looks over the printout, she remembers that Nancy wants to use it as a reference list for prospective clients. She realizes that Nancy needs only the client name, the contact person, and the telephone number for each client. A prospective client doesn't need to know a reference's client ID. Esther can easily make this change in the output by retrieving *selected* fields. All she needs to do is instruct dBASE to list only the fields that she designates. Let's do this now.

To list only the client name, contact person, and telephone number fields from the file CLIENT:

❶ Press **[Enter]** to select the *List* option. Again you see a submenu indicating the available options. See Figure 4-6.

Figure 4-6

Now select the option that allows you to designate the fields you want displayed.

❷ Move the selection cursor to the option *Construct a field list* and press **[Enter]**.

A submenu listing all the fields in the file CLIENT appears in a box on the Assistant screen, with the first field name highlighted. A box containing a description of the highlighted field appears in the middle of the screen. See Figure 4-7.

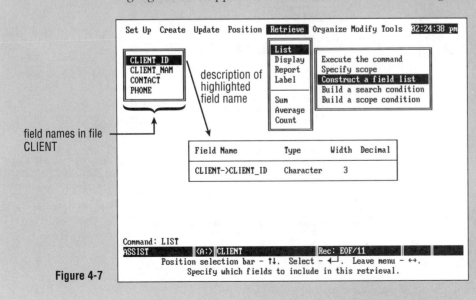

Figure 4-7

Next you need to select the fields you want displayed.

❸   Move the selection cursor to CLIENT_NAM and press **[Enter]**.

CLIENT_NAM appears on the action line just after the word LIST. dBASE automatically highlights the next field name in the list of field names and displays the definition of the highlighted field in a box in the center of the screen. See Figure 4-8.

building dBASE command

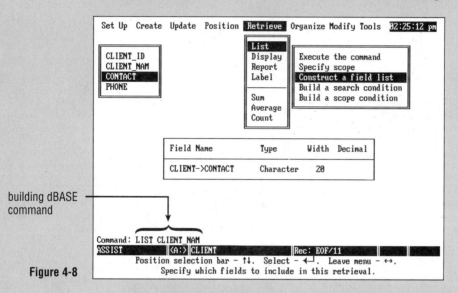

Figure 4-8

❹   Make sure the selection cursor is highlighting the field name CONTACT and press **[Enter]**. On the action line, CONTACT is displayed next to CLIENT_NAM as part of the LIST command. See Figure 4-9. The highlight automatically advances to the next field name.

building dBASE command

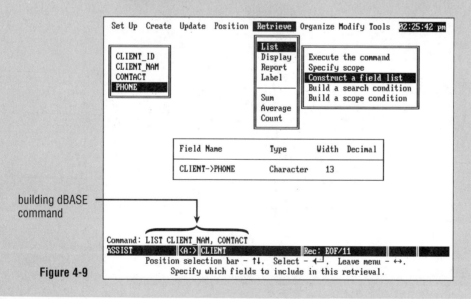

Figure 4-9

⑤ Make sure the selection cursor is highlighting the field name PHONE and press **[Enter]**. PHONE appears next to CONTACT as part of the LIST command. See Figure 4-10.

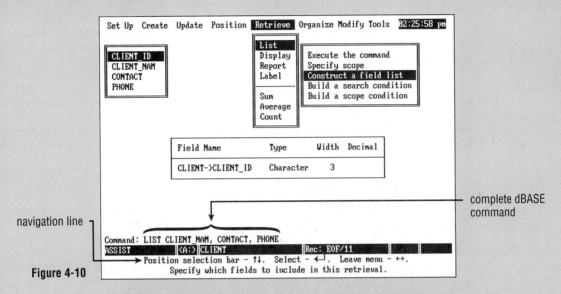

navigation line ⌐

Figure 4-10

complete dBASE command

⑥ Now that you have selected the fields you want to print out, press **[→]** to exit the field list submenu and return to the pull-down menu of options for *List*. Notice that the navigation line, near the bottom of the Assistant screen, displays your keystroke options. See Figure 4-10.

⑦ Move the selection cursor to the option *Execute the command* and press **[Enter]**.

Because Nancy wants a printout of the client data, you now have to send the results to the printer.

⑧ Make sure your printer is turned on.

⑨ Type **y** when you see the prompt "Direct the output to the printer? [Y/N]." You have now created the list that Nancy can give to prospective clients. See Figure 4-11.

```
Record#   CLIENT_NAM              CONTACT            PHONE
      1   Mountain Top Ski        Victor Juarez      (419)783-6210
      2   Viking Auto Group       Jeff Serito        (505)984-9216
      3   Alexander Insurance     Paul Alexander     (505)883-9222
      4   Sante Fe Tourist Center Liddy Posada       (505)986-5555
      5   Origins                 Gary Higgins       (505)988-0733
      6   Fat Wheels Bicycle Tours Helen Carson      (505)994-2432
      7   Celebrity Catering      Linda Randall      (800)884-2321
      8   Images                  Wendy Falchetti    (505)898-1286
      9   Peaches & Ice           Alice Beaumont     (505)512-5176
     10   Taco Heaven             Bert Clinton       (505)728-1295
     11   Mama Lee's Pizza        Emma Lee           (505)984-3245
```

Figure 4-11
Printout of
selected fields
from CLIENT file

⑩ Press any key when you are ready to continue.

Search Conditions

Now that Esther has finished her first task for Nancy, she turns her attention to Martin's request, which she must accomplish by noon. She knows Martin wants to see a listing only of jobs in process, not of jobs that have been completed. How, Esther thinks, can I get this information from the database? To solve that problem, she must form a condition. Let's explore this concept.

Simple Conditions

A **condition** is the criterion that determines whether a record will be selected. For example, in this case, Esther wants records selected if they meet the condition that a job is still in process.

A condition is expressed in dBASE by a **conditional expression**, which has the following format:

expression   relational operator   expression

The first expression in a conditional expression is usually a field name. The **relational operator** is a mathematical comparison of the two expressions, such as less than, greater than, equal to, and so forth. Figure 4-12 lists the relational operators allowed in dBASE.

Comparison	dBASE Symbol
Less than	<
Greater than	>
Less than or equal to	<=
Greater than or equal to	>=
Equal to	=
Not equal to	<>

Figure 4-12
dBASE relational operators

The second expression in a conditional expression is usually a field name or a constant. To form a conditional expression, you combine the relational operator with the two expressions. In our example, jobs that are "in process" are assigned a code of I in the STATUS field. Thus, you'd write the conditional expression in dBASE as:

STATUS = 'I'

When your criterion for determining if a record is selected contains only one conditional expression, it is referred to as a **simple condition**.

Now that you know how to form a conditional expression, how would you use it in dBASE? To select certain records based on a condition, as in Martin's example, you would include a conditional expression in the LIST command. dBASE tests each record in the database file based on the conditional expression to determine whether to select that record. In other words, for each record, dBASE asks whether the conditional expression is true or false. When the conditional expression is true, the record is displayed; when the conditional expression is false, the record is not displayed. For example, if the code in the STATUS field in the first record in the file JOBS is I, then your conditional expression STATUS = 'I' is true (I is equal to I), and the record is displayed. If the status for the second record is C, then your conditional expression STATUS = 'I' is false (C is not equal to I), and the record is not displayed.

Now let's see how Esther can construct Martin's query using dBASE's Assistant screen. To list all the jobs with an "in process" status, you must first open the file JOBS. Your copy of the file CLIENT should still be open. When you open a new file, in this case, JOBS, dBASE automatically closes the previously open file, in this case, CLIENT.

To open the file JOBS:

➊ As you have done before, open the file JOBS.DBF.

Look at the status bar. It indicates your current drive and that the open file, JOBS, has a total of 24 records. See Figure 4-13. (The total number of records in your file JOBS may be different if you did not add the records in the Tutorial Assignments at the end of Tutorial 3.)

JOBS file open

your current drive
might be different

24 records in the file

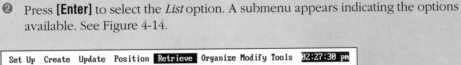

```
ASSIST           |<A:>||JOBS                    |Rec: 1/24
Move selection bar - ↑↓. Select - ←┘.  Leave menu - ↔. Help - F1. Exit - Esc.
                         Select a database file.
```

Figure 4-13

Now let's print the data that Martin wants, the jobs that are in process.

To print the jobs in process:

➊ Press **[→]** to select the *Retrieve* option from the menu bar. You will see *List* highlighted on the pull-down menu.

➋ Press **[Enter]** to select the *List* option. A submenu appears indicating the options available. See Figure 4-14.

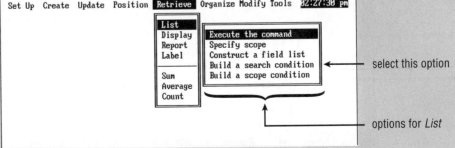

```
Set Up  Create  Update  Position  Retrieve  Organize Modify Tools  02:27:30 pm
                                   List
                                   Display    Execute the command
                                   Report     Specify scope
                                   Label      Construct a field list
                                              Build a search condition    ◄──── select this option
                                   Sum        Build a scope condition
                                   Average
                                   Count                                  ◄──── options for List
```

Figure 4-14

Now you must specify the records you want to retrieve.

③ Move the selection cursor to the option *Build a search condition* and press **[Enter]**. A list of field names for JOBS is displayed in a submenu on the Assistant screen, and a description of the highlighted field name appears in the middle of the sceen. See Figure 4-15.

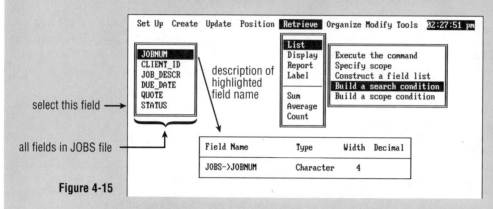

Figure 4-15

④ Since you want to search the STATUS field, move the selection cursor to STATUS and press **[Enter]**. A menu of relational operators appears. See Figure 4-16.

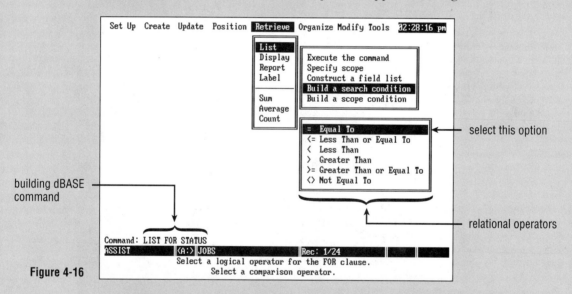

Figure 4-16

⑤ With the selection cursor highlighting the option = *Equal to*, press **[Enter]**.

dBASE prompts you to enter a character value without the quotes. See Figure 4-17.

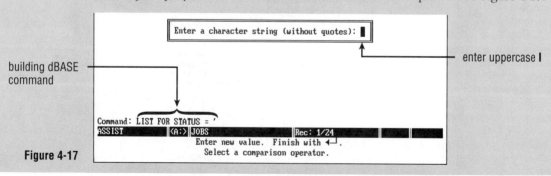

Figure 4-17

6 Type uppercase **I**, the code for "in process." A list of condition options appears. See Figure 4-18.

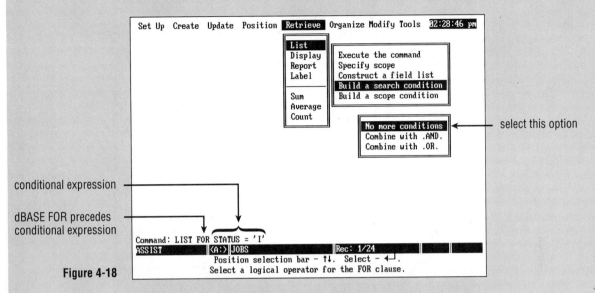

conditional expression ⎯⎯⎯

dBASE FOR precedes
conditional expression ⎯⎯⎯

select this option ⎯⎯⎯

Figure 4-18

7 Because there is only one condition, select the option *No more conditions* and press **[Enter]**.

You have now constructed the conditional expression. Look at the action line above the status bar and you will see the dBASE command

LIST FOR STATUS = 'I'

8 Move the selection cursor to the option *Execute the command* and press **[Enter]**. See Figure 4-19.

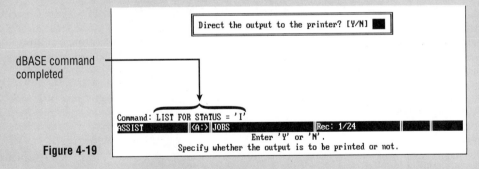

dBASE command
completed ⎯⎯⎯

Figure 4-19

Since we want a printout of this list, let's print the results.

9 Make sure your printer is turned on, then type **y** for yes. dBASE prints out the jobs in the W&M JOBS file with a status equal to I. See Figure 4-20.

```
Record#   JOBNUM  CLIENT_ID  JOB_DESCR              DUE_DATE  QUOTE  STATUS
      8   1008    VIK        Thanksgiving Promo     11/15/92  12000  I
     10   1010    ALE        Brochure               10/10/92   6000  I
     12   1012    ALE        Radio Ad               09/01/92   3425  I
     13   1013    SAN        Direct Mail            10/15/92   8900  I
     14   1014    FAT        Direct Mail            11/20/92   2200  I
     15   1015    SAN        Brochure               09/15/92   4400  I
     16   1016    IMA        Magazine Ad            10/15/92  10000  I
     17   1017    CEL        Flyer                  09/20/92    850  I
     18   1018    VIK        TV ads                 01/15/93  35700  I
     19   1019    SAN        Festival campaign      09/12/92   8900  I
     20   1020    FAT        Mail order catalogue   10/10/92   9400  I
     21   1021    ALE        B/W magazine ad        11/10/92   6600  I
     22   1022    MAM        Newspaper ad           12/01/92   5300  I
     23   1023    TAC        TV ad                  12/15/92  14000  I
     24   1024    PEA        Brochure               11/30/92  11000  I
```

Figure 4-20
Printout of jobs in process

10 Press any key when you are ready to continue.

Compound Conditions

Now that Esther has printed Martin's list of jobs in process, she turns her attention to Nancy's request for a list of all completed jobs that had quotes greater than $5,000. The query for Martin was a simple condition, and Esther had to search the database with only one condition. For many situations, that will be all you need to query when you use dBASE. However, there will be times when you need to search a database for data based on two or more simple conditions. This is the case with Nancy's query about completed jobs quoted at more than $5,000. In this situation, you use **logical operators** to combine the simple conditions. In dBASE the logical operators are as follows:

.AND.   Processes all records for which all conditions are true

.OR.   Processes all records for which at least one condition is true

Two or more simple conditions combined by a logical operator form a **compound condition**. The general form of a compound condition is

conditional expression	*logical operator*	*conditional expression*

For example, Nancy's query as a compound condition would be

If the job is completed AND *the quote is greater than $5,000*

When you use a simple conditional expression, dBASE evaluates the condition as either true or false; true results in the record being displayed, and false results in the record not being displayed. The same is true with compound conditions. dBASE evaluates a compound condition as either true or false; true results in the record being displayed, and false results in the record not being displayed.

In dBASE you would write Nancy's query in the form of a compound condition as

STATUS = 'C' .AND. QUOTE > 5000

You would use the logical operator .AND. because for a job to appear on Nancy's list *both* conditions have to be met.

If Nancy wanted a list of jobs that either have been completed *or* had a quote over $5,000, Esther would express this logic in dBASE as

STATUS = 'C' .OR. QUOTE > 5000

Here Esther would use the logical operator .OR. because for a job to be listed it would have to meet at least one of the conditions.

Using Dot Prompt Mode

Before you answer Nancy's request, you are going to switch from Assistant mode to dot prompt mode. You are making this switch because some dBASE commands and command extensions are available only in dot prompt mode. Also, you will find dot prompt mode much quicker. For these reasons, you will use dot prompt mode from now on to enter the dBASE commands in this book.

To switch from Assistant mode to dot prompt mode:

❶ Press **[Esc]** to move to dot prompt mode. The Assistant screen is erased, and a dot, called the **dot prompt**, appears near the lower left of your screen. See Figure 4-21. The dot prompt indicates that dBASE is waiting for you to type a dBASE command.

appears in student version of dBASE III PLUS

```
(DEMO) .                                                                    ─── dot prompt
Command Line    <A:> JOBS              Rec: EOF/24        Ins
                        Enter a dBASE III PLUS command.
```

Figure 4-21

You will recall from Tutorial 1 that the dot acts as a prompt ready to accept the commands you type. The commands instruct dBASE to perform various tasks. For a command to work correctly, you must follow the rules, or **syntax**, of the dBASE language. In this book whenever we introduce a dBASE command, we show the command's syntax within a box. In these boxes, dBASE command words are shown in uppercase, although you can type them in either uppercase or lowercase. When you use these commands, however, you must spell the words *exactly* as they appear in the syntax boxes. Other information you need to supply is included in the boxes in lowercase. Optional parts of the command are shaded. You include or omit the optional parts of a command, depending on what you are trying to accomplish.

Now let's use dot prompt mode to answer Nancy's query to list all the completed W&M jobs with a quote over $5,000. The syntax for the LIST command that includes a condition is

> LIST   *field names*   FOR *condition*

When you include a FOR condition, dBASE displays only those records that meet the condition. Also, when you specify field names after the word LIST, the output includes only the fields listed in the command rather than all fields in the record.

You will build a compound condition by constructing each simple condition and then combining the simple conditions with the logical operator **.AND.** . The two simple conditions are STATUS = 'C' and QUOTE > 5000.

To list all the completed jobs with quotes over $5,000:

❶ At the dot prompt type **list client_id, jobnum, quote for status = 'C' .and. quote > 5000** and press **[Enter]**. See Figure 4-22. Remember to type an uppercase C for the status code. Otherwise no records will be retrieved.

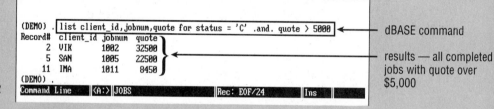

Figure 4-22

The output shows only completed jobs having a quote over $5,000.

Esther finds the column of record numbers in the output distracting. In Assistant mode, she has no choice; record numbers are always displayed. In dot prompt mode, she has the opportunity to remove the record numbers from the output by typing OFF after the LIST command. The syntax for the version of the LIST command that removes the numbers from the output is

> LIST OFF   *field names*   FOR *condition*

You can type OFF anywhere after the word LIST, but most dBASE users place it immediately after the word LIST.

Let's try it.

To remove the record number from the listing:

❶ At the dot prompt type **list off client_id, jobnum, quote for status = 'C' .and. quote > 5000** and press **[Enter]**. The record numbers are now excluded from the output. See Figure 4-23.

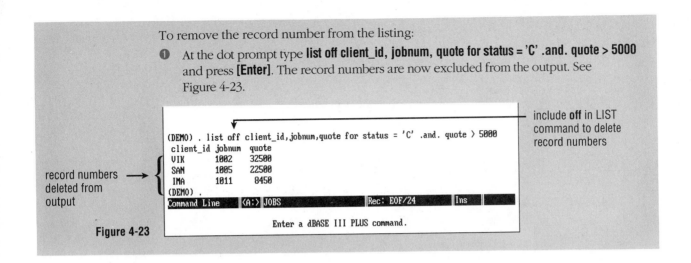

record numbers deleted from output →

include **off** in LIST command to delete record numbers

Figure 4-23

Now Esther is ready to send the output to the printer. She needs to add TO PRINT to the LIST command. The syntax for the LIST command that sends results to the printer is as follows:

LIST OFF *field names* FOR *condition* TO PRINT

Esther could retype the previous command and add TO PRINT to it, but that would mean retyping over 50 keystrokes. Fortunately, dBASE provides a way for Esther to reduce the number of keystrokes she has to make to print the results of her query.

The History Buffer

Whenever you use dBASE, your 20 most recent commands are stored in a **history buffer**, or storage area, within the computer's memory (Figure 4-24). Thus, you can recall these commands, rather than reentering them at the keyboard.

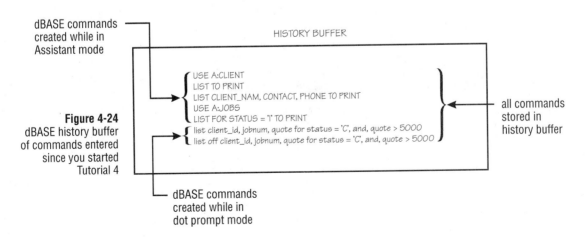

dBASE commands created while in Assistant mode

Figure 4-24
dBASE history buffer of commands entered since you started Tutorial 4

HISTORY BUFFER

USE A:CLIENT
LIST TO PRINT
LIST CLIENT_NAM, CONTACT, PHONE TO PRINT
USE A:JOBS
LIST FOR STATUS = 'I' TO PRINT
list client_id, jobnum, quote for status = 'C', and, quote > 5000
list off client_id, jobnum, quote for status = 'C', and, quote > 5000

all commands stored in history buffer

dBASE commands created while in dot prompt mode

Instead of retyping the LIST command, therefore, Esther can recall that command from the history buffer. Let's try it.

To reexecute a command from the history buffer:

❶ At the dot prompt press [↑]. The previous command appears at the dot prompt. See Figure 4-25. You simply press [↑] or [↓] to display the commands one at a time at the dot prompt. When a command is displayed, you can reexecute it by pressing **[Enter]** or you can modify the command before executing it. To edit the command, move the cursor to the position where you want to insert or delete characters and make your changes. Then press **[Enter]** to execute the revised command.

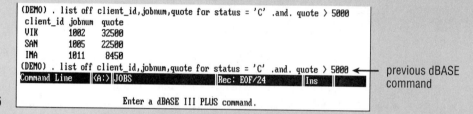

previous dBASE command

Figure 4-25

You can recall any commands you built in Assistant mode, but you must use dot prompt mode to recall them.

Now modify Esther's last command so the output goes to the printer.

To modify the command at the dot prompt:

❶ Press [→] to move to the end of the command.

Now enter your revision.

❷ Type **to print**. Your revised command is complete. See Figure 4-26.

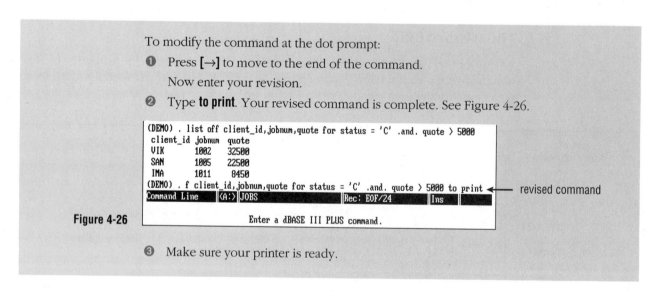

revised command

Figure 4-26

❸ Make sure your printer is ready.

4 Press **[Enter]**.

The optional clause TO PRINT in the LIST command sends the output to your printer. See Figure 4-27. You will also see the jobs displayed on the screen.

Figure 4-27
Printout of
completed jobs
having a quote over
$5,000

```
client_id jobnum   quote
  VIK      1002    32500
  SAN      1005    22500
  IMA      1011     8450
```

Esther has now finished the list of all completed jobs having a quote over $5,000, and gives the printed report to Nancy.

The DISPLAY Command

So far you have used the LIST command to display records in a database file. The LIST command works well if you have no more than 20 records to view. But if the output contains more than 20 records, when you use the LIST command the data on the screen will scroll without stopping until the entire file has been displayed. This makes it difficult to view the data. Thus, if your output consists of more than 20 records, use the LIST command only to print your output.

To view more than 20 records on the screen, use the DISPLAY command. The syntax of the DISPLAY command is

DISPLAY ALL   *field names*

When you use ALL with the DISPLAY command, dBASE sends all the records to the screen one screenful at a time and then pauses. To view the next screenful of data, you press any key.

Esther knows that W&M currently has more than 20 jobs in its JOBS file. So she decides to use the DISPLAY command to query the database. Let's view all the jobs currently stored in the W&M JOBS file.

To use DISPLAY to view all the jobs in the JOBS file:

1 At the dot prompt type **display all** and press **[Enter]**.

You will see the first screenful of records from the JOBS file displayed. See Figure 4-28 on the next page.

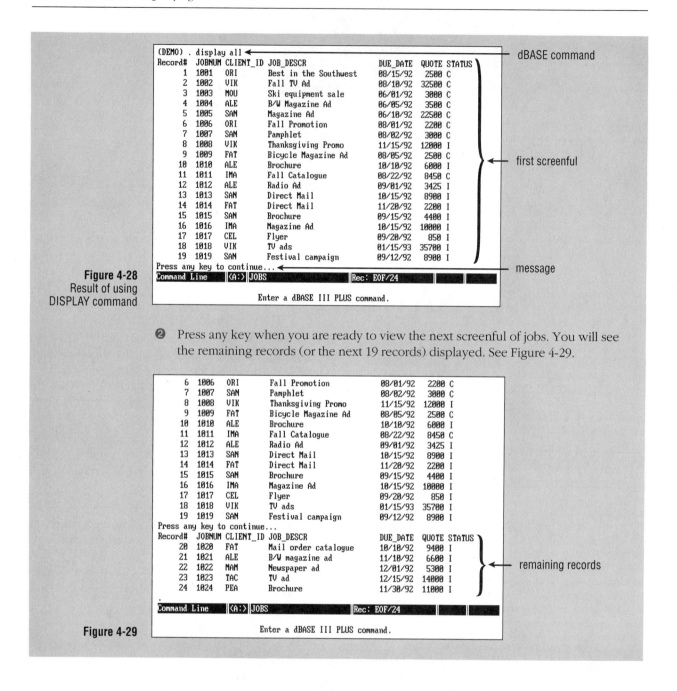

Figure 4-28
Result of using
DISPLAY command

```
(DEMO) . display all ◄──────────────────────────── dBASE command
Record#  JOBNUM CLIENT_ID JOB_DESCR           DUE_DATE QUOTE STATUS
     1   1001   ORI      Best in the Southwest  08/15/92  2500 C
     2   1002   VIK      Fall TV Ad             08/10/92 32500 C
     3   1003   MOU      Ski equipment sale     06/01/92  3000 C
     4   1004   ALE      B/W Magazine Ad        06/05/92  3500 C
     5   1005   SAN      Magazine Ad            06/10/92 22500 C
     6   1006   ORI      Fall Promotion         08/01/92  2200 C
     7   1007   SAN      Pamphlet               08/02/92  3000 C
     8   1008   VIK      Thanksgiving Promo     11/15/92 12000 I
     9   1009   FAT      Bicycle Magazine Ad    08/05/92  2500 C   ◄── first screenful
    10   1010   ALE      Brochure               10/10/92  6000 I
    11   1011   IMA      Fall Catalogue         08/22/92  8450 C
    12   1012   ALE      Radio Ad               09/01/92  3425 I
    13   1013   SAN      Direct Mail            10/15/92  8900 I
    14   1014   FAT      Direct Mail            11/20/92  2200 I
    15   1015   SAN      Brochure               09/15/92  4400 I
    16   1016   IMA      Magazine Ad            10/15/92 10000 I
    17   1017   CEL      Flyer                  09/20/92   850 I
    18   1018   VIK      TV ads                 01/15/93 35700 I
    19   1019   SAN      Festival campaign      09/12/92  8900 I
Press any key to continue... ◄──────────────────────── message
Command Line   <A:> JOBS              Rec: EOF/24
           Enter a dBASE III PLUS command.
```

② Press any key when you are ready to view the next screenful of jobs. You will see the remaining records (or the next 19 records) displayed. See Figure 4-29.

```
     6   1006   ORI      Fall Promotion         08/01/92  2200 C
     7   1007   SAN      Pamphlet               08/02/92  3000 C
     8   1008   VIK      Thanksgiving Promo     11/15/92 12000 I
     9   1009   FAT      Bicycle Magazine Ad    08/05/92  2500 C
    10   1010   ALE      Brochure               10/10/92  6000 I
    11   1011   IMA      Fall Catalogue         08/22/92  8450 C
    12   1012   ALE      Radio Ad               09/01/92  3425 I
    13   1013   SAN      Direct Mail            10/15/92  8900 I
    14   1014   FAT      Direct Mail            11/20/92  2200 I
    15   1015   SAN      Brochure               09/15/92  4400 I
    16   1016   IMA      Magazine Ad            10/15/92 10000 I
    17   1017   CEL      Flyer                  09/20/92   850 I
    18   1018   VIK      TV ads                 01/15/93 35700 I
    19   1019   SAN      Festival campaign      09/12/92  8900 I
Press any key to continue...
Record#  JOBNUM CLIENT_ID JOB_DESCR           DUE_DATE QUOTE STATUS
    20   1020   FAT      Mail order catalogue   10/10/92  9400 I
    21   1021   ALE      B/W magazine ad        11/10/92  6600 I
    22   1022   MAM      Newspaper ad           12/01/92  5300 I   ◄── remaining records
    23   1023   TAC      TV ad                  12/15/92 14000 I
    24   1024   PEA      Brochure               11/30/92 11000 I
.
Command Line   <A:> JOBS              Rec: EOF/24
           Enter a dBASE III PLUS command.
```

Figure 4-29

Using the COUNT, SUM, and AVERAGE Commands

Finally Esther is ready to tackle Nancy's last request. Nancy believes that W&M's jobs have become more sophisticated and that quotations have become larger. To validate her hunch, Nancy has asked Esther to calculate the number of completed jobs, the total amount of the quotes for the completed jobs, and the average quote for those jobs.

Esther knows she can calculate statistical information such as totals, averages, and counts on all or selected records in a database file. To do this, she will use COUNT, AVERAGE, and SUM, the dBASE commands that calculate statistics on numeric fields.

The COUNT Command

The COUNT command tallies, or counts, and displays either the number of records in a database file or all the records that satisfy a condition. The syntax for the COUNT command is

COUNT   FOR *condition*

In our example, Nancy wants to know the number of completed jobs.

To calculate the number of completed jobs:

❶ At the dot prompt type **count for status = 'C'** and press **[Enter]**.

The message "9 records" is displayed on the screen, indicating that there are nine completed jobs. See Figure 4-30.

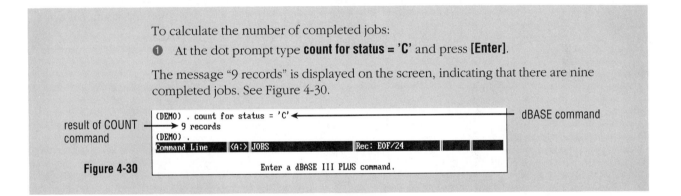

result of COUNT command

dBASE command

Figure 4-30

```
(DEMO) . count for status = 'C'
         9 records
(DEMO) .
Command Line    <A:> JOBS                    Rec: EOF/24
              Enter a dBASE III PLUS command.
```

The SUM Command

The SUM command adds one or more numeric fields and displays the total for all the records in a database file or for all the records that satisfy a specified condition. The syntax for the SUM command is

SUM   *numeric fields*   FOR *condition*

In our example, Nancy wants to know the total quotes for completed jobs.

To calculate the sum of the quotes for completed jobs:

❶ At the dot prompt type **sum quote for status = 'C'** and press **[Enter]**.

The total of the quotes for the nine completed jobs is $80,150. See Figure 4-31.

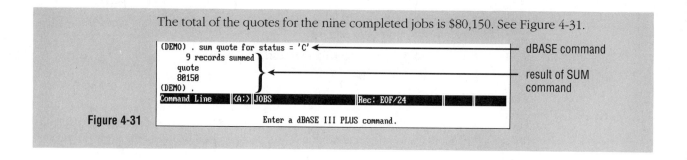

Figure 4-31

The AVERAGE Command

The AVERAGE command calculates the arithmetic average of one or more numeric fields for all the records in a database file or for the records that satisfy a specified condition. The syntax for the AVERAGE command is

AVERAGE *numeric fields*   FOR *condition*

In our example, Nancy wants to know the average amount of quotes on completed jobs.

To calculate the average quote for all completed jobs:

❶ At the dot prompt type **average quote for status = 'C'** and press **[Enter]**.

The screen shows that nine records were included in computing the average, $8,906. See Figure 4-32.

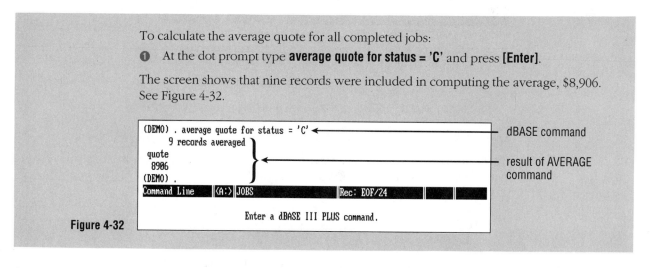

Figure 4-32

Esther has now calculated the number of completed jobs, the total quote amount of those jobs, and the average quote. She gives this information to Nancy (Figure 4-33).

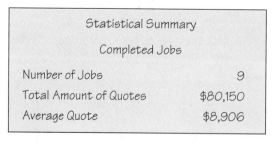

Figure 4-33

Exercises

1. How do you switch from Assistant mode to dot prompt mode?

2. Explain the difference between the LIST command and the DISPLAY ALL command.

3. Identify the general term that describes each of the following:
   a. <
   b. .OR.
   c. JOBNUM = '1234'

4. Explain what each of the following queries means:
   a. LIST FOR QUOTE > 3000 .AND. QUOTE <= 4000
   b. LIST FOR QUOTE <= 3000 .OR. QUOTE > 4000
   c. LIST FOR JOBNUM > '1010' .AND. QUOTE >= 4000

5. Given the conditional expression QUOTE <= 3500, indicate whether the result is true or false for each of the values of QUOTE shown in Figure 4-34.

Value of Quote	Result
0	
2000	
3500	
5000	

Figure 4-34

6. Given the conditional expression QUOTE > 4000 .AND. CLIENT_ID = 'ORI', indicate whether the result is true or false for each of the values of QUOTE and CLIENT_ID that appears in Figure 4-35.

Value of Quote	Value of CLIENT_ID	Result
6000	ORI	
2000	ALP	
4000	ORI	
5000	ORI	
4000	ALP	
4001	ALP	

Figure 4-35

Use the file layouts shown in Figure 4-36 for an employee skills database to do Exercises 7 and 8.

File Layout 1		
Field	**Type**	**Width**
EMP_ID	Character	3
EMP_NAME	Character	30
SKILL1_CD	Character	6
SKILL2_CD	Character	6
SKILL3_CD	Character	6

File Layout 2		
Field	**Type**	**Width**
EMP_ID	Character	3
EMP_NAME	Character	30
SKILL_CODE	Character	6

Figure 4-36

7. For each layout, write the query needed to find all employees who have experience using Lotus 1-2-3 (skill code LOT123). *Hint:* You need two different queries.

8. For each layout, write the query needed to find all employees who have experience using Lotus 1-2-3 (skill code LOT123) or dBASE III PLUS (skill code DBASE3). *Hint:* You need two different queries.

9. What is the difference between the COUNT command and the SUM command?

Tutorial Assignments

Use the file CLIENT to complete Assignments 1 through 4.

1. Open the file CLIENT.

2. List the structure of the database file and send the output to the printer.

3. For all clients, list the fields CLIENT_NAM and PHONE and send the output to the printer.

4. For the client Origins, list the CLIENT_NAM and PHONE and send the output to the printer.

Use the JOBS database to complete Assignments 5 through 12.

5. Open the file JOBS.

6. List the structure of the database file and send the output to the printer.

7. For all jobs still in process (status is I), print the fields CLIENT_ID, JOB_DESCR, and DUE_DATE.

8. For all Mountain Top Ski (MOU) jobs, print the fields CLIENT_ID, JOB_DESCR, QUOTE, and STATUS.

9. For all jobs with a status code of C or having a quote above $10,000, print the fields CLIENT_ID, STATUS, and QUOTE.

10. How many jobs are in process (status is I)?

11. For jobs in process, calculate the total quote.

12. For jobs in process, calculate the average quote.

Case Problems

1. Biggs & Hang Investment Corporation

Do the following:

1. Open the file JAPAN.

2. List the structure of the database file and send the output to the printer.

3. For all companies, print the company name, the industry code, sales, and the profits.

4. For all companies in the automobile industry (code = A), print the company ID, the company name, the industry code, the sales, and the profits.

5. For all companies with sales above 1,000,000 Yen, print the company ID, the company name, the industry code, the sales, assets, and the profits.

6. For all companies with sales above 2,500,000 Yen and profit above 300,000 Yen, print the company name, the industry code, the sales, and the profits.

7. Use the SUM, AVERAGE, and COUNT commands to fill in the table shown in Figure 4-37.

Industry Summary

	Auto	Electronic
Total sales		
Average sales		
Number of companies		

Figure 4-37

2. Medi-Source Inc.

Do the following:

1. Open the file ACCTREC.

2. List the structure of the database file and send the output to the printer.

3. For all customers, print the customer name, the type of customer, and the balance owed.

4. For all customers who are in the hospital (code = H) industry, print the customer name, the type of customer, the state, and the balance owed.

5. For all customers whose balance owed is more than $6,000, print the customer ID, the customer name, the type of customer, and the balance owed.

6. For all Rhode Island (RI) customers whose outstanding balance is greater than $6,000, print the customer name, the type of customer, and the balance owed.

7. Use the SUM, AVERAGE, and COUNT commands to fill in the table shown in Figure 4-38.

Customer Summary by State

	RI	MA
Total owed		
Average owed		
Number of customers		

Figure 4-38

3. Appleton & Drake Electrical Supply Company

Do the following:

1. Open the file EMPLOYEE.

2. List the structure of the database file and send the output to the printer.

3. For all employees, print the last name, first name, sex, department, and salary.

4. For all female employees, print the last name, first name, sex, department, and salary.

5. For all female employees earning $35,000 or more, print the last name, first name, sex, and salary.

6. For all employees who are either in the SALES department (code = SAL) or married (code = Y), print the last name, first name, department, sex, and salary.

7. For all male employees earning $50,000 or less, print the last name, first name, and salary.

8. Use the SUM, AVERAGE, and COUNT commands to fill in the table shown in Figure 4-39.

Statistical Summary by Department

	Dept COR	Dept SAL	Dept ENG
Number of employees			
Total salaries			
Average salaries			

Figure 4-39

4. National Basketball Association

Do the following:

1. Open the file NBA.

2. List the structure of the database file and send the output to the printer.

3. For all players, print the team ID, the player's full name, his position, and his salary.

4. For all players playing center (code = C), print the team ID, the player's full name, his position, and his salary.

5. For all players earning over $1 million, print the team ID, the player's full name, his position, and his salary.

6. For all players who are members of the LA Lakers (code = LAK) or the Chicago Bulls (code = CHI), print the team ID, the player's full name, his position, and his salary.

7. For all guards (code = G) earning under $500,000, print the team ID, the player's full name, his salary, and his position.

8. Use the AVERAGE and COUNT commands to fill in the table shown in Figure 4-40.

Summary by Position

	Guards	Forwards	Centers
Number of players			
Average salary			

Figure 4-40

9. Use the SUM command to fill in the table shown in Figure 4-41.

Total Salary by Team

Team	Total Salary
Chicago Bulls	
LA Lakers	
NY Knicks	

Figure 4-41

Tutorial 5

Sorting and Indexing the Database

Case: Wells & Martinez — Sorting the JOBS File

The next day Esther arrives at work to find another note from Nancy on her desk. Nancy wants to know the status of all the jobs in the database, in other words, which jobs are in progress and which have been completed. Esther realizes that if she simply lists the JOBS file, she can easily provide this information to Nancy. She quickly lists the file to the printer and takes the printout to Nancy's office (Figure 5-1 on the next page).

As Nancy looks over the list, she shakes her head and apologizes for not making her needs clear. She explains to Esther that she wants the list to help her determine how many jobs W&M has completed for each client and how many jobs are in progress for each client. Thus, Nancy says, this list would be more helpful if the jobs are arranged by client. Esther tells her not to worry — she can quickly and easily produce the list Nancy wants by using dBASE's SORT command.

Nancy is relieved and asks Esther if she would also be able to produce two more lists: one showing all jobs arranged by quote from highest to lowest and another showing all jobs for each client in order by due date. Esther assures Nancy that these two reports also will be easy to create using the SORT command.

OBJECTIVES

In this tutorial you will learn to:

■ Sort records in both dot prompt mode and Assistant mode

■ Sort records in ascending and descending order

■ Sort records on more than one sort key

■ Index records in both dot prompt mode and Assistant mode

■ Create an index file

■ Open existing index files

■ Add records with indexes open

■ List records using an index

■ Change the master index

```
Record#   JOBNUM  CLIENT_ID  JOB_DESCR              DUE_DATE  QUOTE  STATUS
      1   1001    ORI        Best in the Southwest  08/15/92   2500  C
      2   1002    VIK        Fall TV Ad             08/10/92  32500  C
      3   1003    MOU        Ski equipment sale     06/01/92   3000  C
      4   1004    ALE        B/W Magazine Ad        06/05/92   3500  C
      5   1005    SAN        Magazine Ad            06/10/92  22500  C
      6   1006    ORI        Fall Promotion         08/01/92   2200  C
      7   1007    SAN        Pamphlet               08/02/92   3000  C
      8   1008    VIK        Thanksgiving Promo     11/15/92  12000  I
      9   1009    FAT        Bicycle Magazine Ad    08/05/92   2500  C
     10   1010    ALE        Brochure               10/10/92   6000  I
     11   1011    IMA        Fall Catalogue         08/22/92   8450  C
     12   1012    ALE        Radio Ad               09/01/92   3425  I
     13   1013    SAN        Direct Mail            10/15/92   8900  I
     14   1014    FAT        Direct Mail            11/20/92   2200  I
     15   1015    SAN        Brochure               09/15/92   4400  I
     16   1016    IMA        Magazine Ad            10/15/92  10000  I
     17   1017    CEL        Flyer                  09/20/92    850  I
     18   1018    VIK        TV ads                 01/15/93  35700  I
     19   1019    SAN        Festival campaign      09/12/92   8900  I
     20   1020    FAT        Mail order catalogue   10/10/92   9400  I
     21   1021    ALE        B/W magazine ad        11/10/92   6600  I
     22   1022    MAM        Newspaper ad           12/01/92   5300  I
     23   1023    TAC        TV ad                  12/15/92  14000  I
     24   1024    PEA        Brochure               11/30/92  11000  I
```

Figure 5-1
Esther's printout of
the JOBS file

Introduction to Sorting

You can rearrange data in a specific order through a process called **sorting**. As Nancy knows, records arranged in a particular order can make a report more meaningful.

To sort a file, you first must identify the **sort key**, which is the field that will be used to order the records in the file. For example, Esther wants to sort the JOBS file by client; thus, CLIENT_ID will be the sort key. To sort the file by due date, then DUE_DATE would be the sort key. Sort keys can be numeric, character, or date fields.

You sort records in either ascending or descending order. Ascending means increasing order, and descending means decreasing order. For example, if you sort the JOBS database file in ascending order by job number, the record with the lowest job number will be the first record in the sorted file. The record with the highest job number will be the last record. When the sort key is a character field, ascending order means A through Z, and descending means Z through A. For example, if you sort the JOBS file in ascending order by client ID, the records in the sort file will be in alphabetical order, A to Z. When the sort key is a field that is defined with a date data type, ascending means earliest date to latest date, and descending means latest date to earliest date.

Sort keys can be unique or nonunique. Sort keys are **unique** if the value of the sort key field for each record is different. For example, the job numbers you use in the JOBS file are unique sort keys, because each job has a different job number. Sort keys are **nonunique** if more than one record can have the same value in the sort key field. For example, the client ID in the JOBS file is nonunique because the same client can have more than one job.

When you use a nonunique sort key, dBASE groups together all records with the same value and lists the groups in either ascending or descending order. Within a group the records can be in any order. As Figure 5-2 shows, if you sorted the JOBS file by client ID, all records for Alexander Insurance Company (ALE) would be listed before all job records for Celebrity Catering (CEL), which would be listed before all job records for Fat Wheels Bicycle Tours (FAT), and so on.

JOBNUM	CLIENT_ID	JOB_DESCR	DUE_DATE	QUOTE	STATUS
1004	ALE	B/W Magazine Ad	06/05/92	3500	C
1010	ALE	Brochure	10/10/92	6000	I
1012	ALE	Radio Ad	09/01/92	3425	I
1021	ALE	B/W magazine ad	11/10/92	6600	I
1017	CEL	Flyer	09/20/92	850	I
1009	FAT	Bicycle Magazine Ad	08/05/92	2500	C
1014	FAT	Direct Mail	11/20/92	2200	I
1020	FAT	Mail order catalogue	10/10/92	9400	I
1011	IMA	Fall Catalogue	08/22/92	8450	C
1016	IMA	Magazine Ad	10/15/92	10000	I
1022	MAM	Newspaper ad	12/01/92	5300	I
1003	MOU	Ski equipment sale	06/01/92	3000	C
1001	ORI	Best in the Southwest	08/15/92	2500	C
1006	ORI	Fall Promotion	08/01/92	2200	C
1024	PEA	Brochure	11/30/92	11000	I
1005	SAN	Magazine Ad	06/10/92	22500	C
1007	SAN	Pamphlet	08/02/92	3000	C
1013	SAN	Direct Mail	10/15/92	8900	I
1015	SAN	Brochure	09/15/92	4400	I
1019	SAN	Festival campaign	09/12/92	8900	I
1023	TAC	TV ad	12/15/92	14000	I
1002	VIK	Fall TV Ad	08/10/92	32500	C
1008	VIK	Thanksgiving Promo	11/15/92	12000	I
1018	VIK	TV ads	01/15/93	35700	I

Figure 5-2
JOBS file sorted by
client ID

To arrange the records in each group in a certain sequence, you must specify a second sort key field. For example, you could arrange the jobs in alphabetical order by client ID and then for each client ID in descending order by quote. In that case, you would use two sort keys to sort the JOBS file: a primary sort key (CLIENT_ID) and a secondary sort key (QUOTE). The result of such a sort would look like Figure 5-3 on the next page.

```
JOBNUM  CLIENT_ID  JOB_DESCR              DUE_DATE   QUOTE  STATUS
1021    ALE        B/W magazine ad        11/10/92    6600  I
1010    ALE        Brochure               10/10/92    6000  I
1004    ALE        B/W Magazine Ad        06/05/92    3500  C
1012    ALE        Radio Ad               09/01/92    3425  I
1017    CEL        Flyer                  09/20/92     850  I
1020    FAT        Mail order catalogue   10/10/92    9400  I
1009    FAT        Bicycle Magazine Ad    08/05/92    2500  C
1014    FAT        Direct Mail            11/20/92    2200  I
1016    IMA        Magazine Ad            10/15/92   10000  I
1011    IMA        Fall Catalogue         08/22/92    8450  C
1022    MAM        Newspaper ad           12/01/92    5300  I
1003    MOU        Ski equipment sale     06/01/92    3000  C
1001    ORI        Best in the Southwest  08/15/92    2500  C
1006    ORI        Fall Promotion         08/01/92    2200  C
1024    PEA        Brochure               11/30/92   11000  I
1005    SAN        Magazine Ad            06/10/92   22500  C
1013    SAN        Direct Mail            10/15/92    8900  I
1019    SAN        Festival campaign      09/12/92    8900  I
1015    SAN        Brochure               09/15/92    4400  I
1007    SAN        Pamphlet               08/02/92    3000  C
1023    TAC        TV ad                  12/15/92   14000  I
1018    VIK        TV ads                 01/15/93   35700  I
1002    VIK        Fall TV Ad             08/10/92   32500  C
1008    VIK        Thanksgiving Promo     11/15/92   12000  I
```

Figure 5-3
JOBS file sorted by client ID and within client ID by quote

The SORT Command

Esther needs to redo the job status listing for Nancy. This time she will use the SORT command to sort the jobs by client ID before she prints the report. The syntax for the SORT command is

SORT ON *primary sort key field* TO *filename*

When you use the SORT command, dBASE copies records from the currently open database file to a new database file. The records in the copied file are physically rearranged according to the primary sort key field. When you use the SORT command, dBASE creates a new database file with the same structure and the same number of records as the original file. The only difference between the two files is that the records are arranged in a different sequence.

Now let's use the SORT command to arrange the records in the JOBS file by client ID. Before you sort, be sure the database file you want to sort is open. So after you load dBASE, and switch to the dot prompt mode, be sure dBASE knows in which drive your data diskette is located.

Now let's open the JOBS file using dot prompt mode.

To open a file using the USE command:

❶ At the dot prompt type **use jobs** and press **[Enter]**.

The status bar indicates that the JOBS database file is now open and has a total of 24 records. See Figure 5-4.

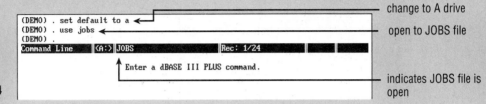

Figure 5-4

Once you have opened the database file, you can issue the SORT command. Since you want to arrange the data alphabetically by client ID, CLIENT_ID is the sort key and the sort order is ascending. You will store the sorted data in a file named SORT1.

To sort the database file:

❶ At the dot prompt type **sort on client_id to sort1** and press **[Enter]**.

You type the field name of the sort key after the command word ON. dBASE assumes the sort order is ascending unless you tell it otherwise.

The new filename is SORT1. Remember, the filename you select must be no more than eight characters in length and consist only of letters, numbers, and the special characters such as _ - $ & %. dBASE saves the new database file on your data diskette and automatically adds the extension DBF to the filename.

Notice on your screen the message "100% sorted 24 Records sorted". Also notice that the status bar shows that the open file is still JOBS. See Figure 5-5.

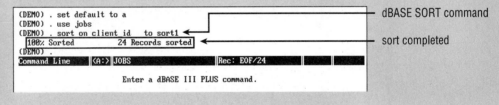

Figure 5-5

What has happened? Figure 5-6a shows your data diskette after you opened the JOBS file, but before you issued the SORT command.

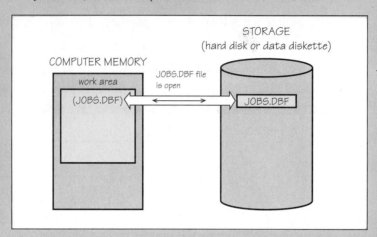

Figure 5-6a

Figure 5-6b shows the contents of your data diskette after the sort. You now have a second file on your data diskette named SORT1.DBF, which is the same as JOBS.DBF except that the records are in sorted sequence.

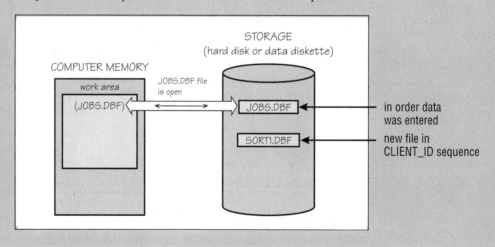

Figure 5-6b

The SORT command does not display the contents of the sorted file on the screen. To view the sorted file, Esther must list or display that file. Esther decides to print the contents of the sorted file to see what has happened.

To print the database file:
❶ At the dot prompt type **list to print** and press **[Enter]**.

Esther is surprised by the results. Her records are not sorted but are in the same order in which they were originally entered (Figure 5-7). What did she do wrong? Esther made a common mistake when using the SORT command. Remember, the open file is still JOBS, and the JOBS file was not rearranged. Esther listed the contents of the JOBS file, not the SORT1 file. Esther should have first opened the database file SORT1 and then issued the LIST command.

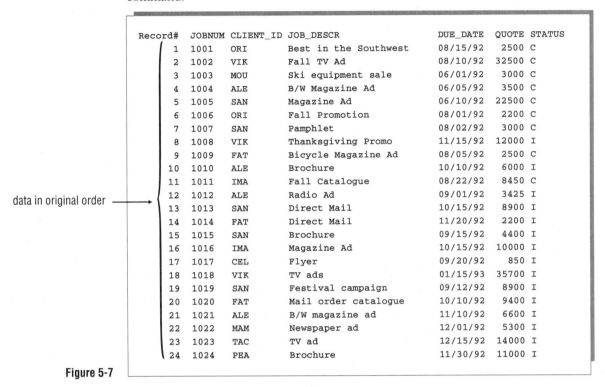

```
Record#  JOBNUM  CLIENT_ID  JOB_DESCR              DUE_DATE  QUOTE  STATUS
      1  1001    ORI        Best in the Southwest  08/15/92   2500  C
      2  1002    VIK        Fall TV Ad             08/10/92  32500  C
      3  1003    MOU        Ski equipment sale     06/01/92   3000  C
      4  1004    ALE        B/W Magazine Ad        06/05/92   3500  C
      5  1005    SAN        Magazine Ad            06/10/92  22500  C
      6  1006    ORI        Fall Promotion         08/01/92   2200  C
      7  1007    SAN        Pamphlet               08/02/92   3000  C
      8  1008    VIK        Thanksgiving Promo     11/15/92  12000  I
      9  1009    FAT        Bicycle Magazine Ad    08/05/92   2500  C
     10  1010    ALE        Brochure               10/10/92   6000  I
     11  1011    IMA        Fall Catalogue         08/22/92   8450  C
     12  1012    ALE        Radio Ad               09/01/92   3425  I
     13  1013    SAN        Direct Mail            10/15/92   8900  I
     14  1014    FAT        Direct Mail            11/20/92   2200  I
     15  1015    SAN        Brochure               09/15/92   4400  I
     16  1016    IMA        Magazine Ad            10/15/92  10000  I
     17  1017    CEL        Flyer                  09/20/92    850  I
     18  1018    VIK        TV ads                 01/15/93  35700  I
     19  1019    SAN        Festival campaign      09/12/92   8900  I
     20  1020    FAT        Mail order catalogue   10/10/92   9400  I
     21  1021    ALE        B/W magazine ad        11/10/92   6600  I
     22  1022    MAM        Newspaper ad           12/01/92   5300  I
     23  1023    TAC        TV ad                  12/15/92  14000  I
     24  1024    PEA        Brochure               11/30/92  11000  I
```

data in original order

Figure 5-7

Let's try it the correct way.

To open the SORT1 file:

❶ At the dot prompt type **use sort1** and press **[Enter]**.

Now the status bar indicates that the file SORT1 is open (Figure 5-8). Remember that dBASE automatically closes the JOBS file at the same time it opens the SORT1 file.

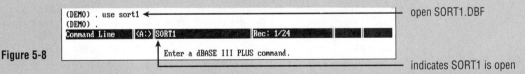

```
(DEMO) . use sort1 ◄─────────────────────────────────── open SORT1.DBF
(DEMO) .
Command Line    ‖<A:>‖SORT1              ‖Rec: 1/24 ‖       ‖     ‖
                    Enter a dBASE III PLUS command.
```

indicates SORT1 is open

Figure 5-8

Figure 5-9 on the next page shows a diagram of how the dBASE work area and the data diskette now look. Notice the link between the dBASE work area and the file SORT1.DBF. You can also see that there is no link between the work area and the JOBS database file, which has been closed.

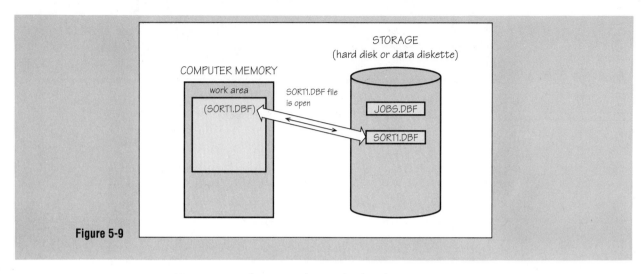

Figure 5-9

Is SORT1.DBF sorted in ascending order by client ID? Let's see.

To print SORT1.DBF:

❶ At the dot prompt type **list to print** and press **[Enter]**.

At last Esther gets the results she wants — a list of W&M jobs arranged by client ID (Figure 5-10). She puts the report aside and turns her attention to Nancy's second request.

Record#	JOBNUM	CLIENT_ID	JOB_DESCR	DUE_DATE	QUOTE	STATUS
1	1012	ALE	Radio Ad	09/01/92	3425	I
2	1010	ALE	Brochure	10/10/92	6000	I
3	1004	ALE	B/W Magazine Ad	06/05/92	3500	C
4	1021	ALE	B/W magazine ad	11/10/92	6600	I
5	1017	CEL	Flyer	09/20/92	850	I
6	1020	FAT	Mail order catalogue	10/10/92	9400	I
7	1014	FAT	Direct Mail	11/20/92	2200	I
8	1009	FAT	Bicycle Magazine Ad	08/05/92	2500	C
9	1011	IMA	Fall Catalogue	08/22/92	8450	C
10	1016	IMA	Magazine Ad	10/15/92	10000	I
11	1022	MAM	Newspaper ad	12/01/92	5300	I
12	1003	MOU	Ski equipment sale	06/01/92	3000	C
13	1006	ORI	Fall Promotion	08/01/92	2200	C
14	1001	ORI	Best in the Southwest	08/15/92	2500	C
15	1024	PEA	Brochure	11/30/92	11000	I
16	1015	SAN	Brochure	09/15/92	4400	I
17	1007	SAN	Pamphlet	08/02/92	3000	C
18	1005	SAN	Magazine Ad	06/10/92	22500	C
19	1019	SAN	Festival campaign	09/12/92	8900	I
20	1013	SAN	Direct Mail	10/15/92	8900	I
21	1023	TAC	TV ad	12/15/92	14000	I
22	1018	VIK	TV ads	01/15/93	35700	I
23	1002	VIK	Fall TV Ad	08/10/92	32500	C
24	1008	VIK	Thanksgiving Promo	11/15/92	12000	I

Figure 5-10
JOBS file arranged
by client ID

Sorting in Descending Order

Now Esther wants to arrange W&M's jobs by quote, with the highest quote appearing first. To do this, she must sort the quote data in descending order.

The command syntax for sorting data in descending order is the same as shown before except that /D is placed after the sort key field.

> SORT ON *primary sort key field*   /D   TO *filename*

Esther knows she needs to sort the file JOBS on the sort key QUOTE and that the sort order is descending. She will name the file that stores the sorted data SORT2.DBF.

Let's open the JOBS file and sort in descending order.

To open the JOBS file and sort in descending order:

❶   At the dot prompt type **use jobs** and press **[Enter]**.

Now sort the file.

❷   At the dot prompt type **sort on quote/d to sort2** and press **[Enter]**.

Since you want the records arranged in descending order, you typed /d after the field name QUOTE. Remember, if no code follows the field name, dBASE assumes you want the records arranged in ascending order.

You have completed the sort, again with 24 records sorted. See Figure 5-11. You now have another file on your data diskette named SORT2.DBF, in which the records are arranged in descending order by quote.

sort completed →   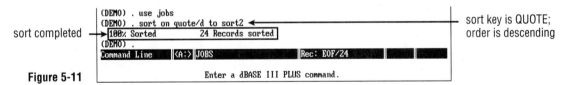   — sort key is QUOTE; order is descending

Figure 5-11

It is important to remember that when you use the SORT command, *each file you create requires additional disk space*. If your database file is large, you may run out of disk space.

Let's see the results of this sort. Remember, you first have to open the file that contains the sorted data. Currently the JOBS file is open.

To open the SORT2 database file and print its contents:

❶   At the dot prompt type **use sort2** and press **[Enter]**.

Now print the contents of the SORT2 file.

❷   At the dot prompt type **list to print** and press **[Enter]**. See Figure 5-12 on the next page.

jobs arranged in descending order by quote

```
Record#   JOBNUM  CLIENT_ID JOB_DESCR              DUE_DATE  QUOTE STATUS
      1   1018    VIK       TV ads                 01/15/93  35700 I
      2   1002    VIK       Fall TV Ad             08/10/92  32500 C
      3   1005    SAN       Magazine Ad            06/10/92  22500 C
      4   1023    TAC       TV ad                  12/15/92  14000 I
      5   1008    VIK       Thanksgiving Promo     11/15/92  12000 I
      6   1024    PEA       Brochure               11/30/92  11000 I
      7   1016    IMA       Magazine Ad            10/15/92  10000 I
      8   1020    FAT       Mail order catalogue   10/10/92   9400 I
      9   1013    SAN       Direct Mail            10/15/92   8900 I
     10   1019    SAN       Festival campaign      09/12/92   8900 I
     11   1011    IMA       Fall Catalogue         08/22/92   8450 C
     12   1021    ALE       B/W magazine ad        11/10/92   6600 I
     13   1010    ALE       Brochure               10/10/92   6000 I
     14   1022    MAM       Newspaper ad           12/01/92   5300 I
     15   1015    SAN       Brochure               09/15/92   4400 I
     16   1004    ALE       B/W Magazine Ad        06/05/92   3500 C
     17   1012    ALE       Radio Ad               09/01/92   3425 I
     18   1007    SAN       Pamphlet               08/02/92   3000 C
     19   1003    MOU       Ski equipment sale     06/01/92   3000 C
     20   1001    ORI       Best in the Southwest  08/15/92   2500 C
     21   1009    FAT       Bicycle Magazine Ad    08/05/92   2500 C
     22   1014    FAT       Direct Mail            11/20/92   2200 I
     23   1006    ORI       Fall Promotion         08/01/92   2200 C
     24   1017    CEL       Flyer                  09/20/92    850 I
```

Figure 5-12
Printout of
SORT2 file

Esther has completed Nancy's second request. She has printed the list of jobs arranged by quote in descending order, and she puts it with the other report. She now focuses on Nancy's third request.

Using Primary and Secondary Sort Keys

Nancy wants to see a list of all jobs by client and for each client by due date. Esther needs to rearrange the JOBS database file so that the jobs for each client are grouped together and within each group the jobs are arranged by due date. This type of sort requires a primary and a secondary sort key.

The syntax of the SORT command using primary and secondary keys is

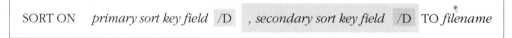

SORT ON *primary sort key field* /D , *secondary sort key field* /D TO *filename*

The order in which you list the sort key fields is important. The first field name is the **primary sort key**, and the second field is the **secondary sort key**. You must use a comma to separate the primary sort key from the secondary sort key.

Let's sort the original database file again. First, open the JOBS file.

To open the JOBS file and sort using a primary and a secondary key:

❶ At the dot prompt type **use jobs** and press **[Enter]**.

Now sort the file. Because we want to sort by client and within client by due date, CLIENT_ID is the primary sort key and DUE_DATE is the secondary sort key.

❷   At the dot prompt type **sort on client_id, due_date to sort3** and press **[Enter]**.

You have completed the sort, again with 24 records sorted (Figure 5-13). This time the data in SORT3.DBF are arranged by client ID and within client ID by due date.

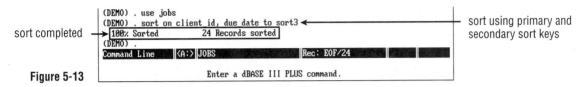

sort completed →

sort using primary and secondary sort keys

Figure 5-13

Let's see the results of this sort. Remember, you first have to open the file that contains the sorted data. Currently the JOBS file is open, so let's open the SORT3 file.

To open the SORT3 file:

❶   At the dot prompt type **use sort3** and press **[Enter]**.

❷   At the dot prompt type **list to print** and press **[Enter]**.

You have now arranged the records by client ID and within each client ID by due dates, with the earliest due dates first (Figure 5-14).

sorted by due date within client

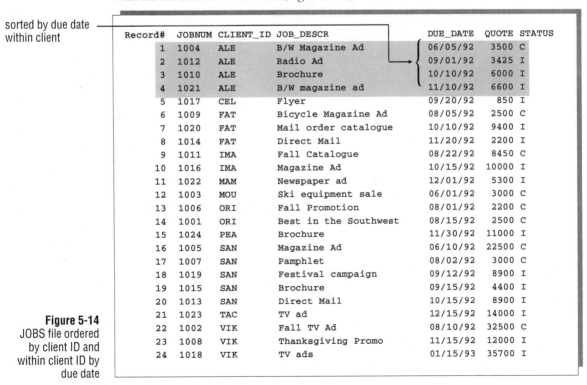

Record#	JOBNUM	CLIENT_ID	JOB_DESCR	DUE_DATE	QUOTE	STATUS
1	1004	ALE	B/W Magazine Ad	06/05/92	3500	C
2	1012	ALE	Radio Ad	09/01/92	3425	I
3	1010	ALE	Brochure	10/10/92	6000	I
4	1021	ALE	B/W magazine ad	11/10/92	6600	I
5	1017	CEL	Flyer	09/20/92	850	I
6	1009	FAT	Bicycle Magazine Ad	08/05/92	2500	C
7	1020	FAT	Mail order catalogue	10/10/92	9400	I
8	1014	FAT	Direct Mail	11/20/92	2200	I
9	1011	IMA	Fall Catalogue	08/22/92	8450	C
10	1016	IMA	Magazine Ad	10/15/92	10000	I
11	1022	MAM	Newspaper ad	12/01/92	5300	I
12	1003	MOU	Ski equipment sale	06/01/92	3000	C
13	1006	ORI	Fall Promotion	08/01/92	2200	C
14	1001	ORI	Best in the Southwest	08/15/92	2500	C
15	1024	PEA	Brochure	11/30/92	11000	I
16	1005	SAN	Magazine Ad	06/10/92	22500	C
17	1007	SAN	Pamphlet	08/02/92	3000	C
18	1019	SAN	Festival campaign	09/12/92	8900	I
19	1015	SAN	Brochure	09/15/92	4400	I
20	1013	SAN	Direct Mail	10/15/92	8900	I
21	1023	TAC	TV ad	12/15/92	14000	I
22	1002	VIK	Fall TV Ad	08/10/92	32500	C
23	1008	VIK	Thanksgiving Promo	11/15/92	12000	I
24	1018	VIK	TV ads	01/15/93	35700	I

Figure 5-14
JOBS file ordered by client ID and within client ID by due date

Figure 5-15 shows your data diskette after the three sorts have been completed. You now have four DBF files that contain job data. JOBS.DBF is the original database file arranged in the order in which you entered the data. SORT1.DBF contains the job records arranged by client ID. SORT2.DBF contains the records arranged by quote in descending order. Finally SORT3.DBF contains the job records arranged by client ID and within client IDs by due date.

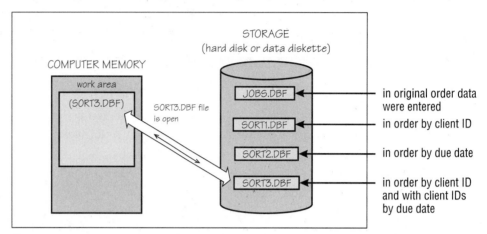

Figure 5-15

Case: Wells & Martinez — Indexing the JOBS File

Esther has now completed Nancy's three requests, which she delivers to Nancy. As she is walking back down the hall, Martin calls her into his office. He is very excited about a new job he has just landed, and he gives Esther a completed job authorization form. Mountain Top Ski, he announces, has decided to advertise their annual Christmas Weekend Getaway by having W&M launch a big ad campaign in the Sunday newspaper. Esther knows that Martin has been trying to land this job for weeks, so she heartily congratulates him.

As Esther leaves his office, Martin asks her to enter the data from the job authorization form and then print a listing of all jobs by due date so he can include this new job somewhere in the work schedule. Esther thinks about what this means. She has just created three new .DBF files for Nancy's lists: SORT1.DBF, SORT2.DBF, and SORT3.DBF. Will she have to sort the data again?

Esther realizes every time she adds a record to the JOBS file, such as for the new Mountain Top Ski job, the data in SORT1.DBF, SORT2.DBF, and SORT3.DBF are no longer consistent with the data in the JOBS file. She would have to sort each file again before she could print the data from the files; otherwise, the output would not be current. In addition, sorting requires a lot of disk space. A file equal to the size of the original file is created for each sort that uses a different sort key. Esther thinks about an alternative approach. She recalls that indexing saves disk space, requires less time to maintain, and is more flexible. She decides to use indexing with the JOBS file.

Introduction to Indexing

When you sorted the records in the JOBS file, you physically rearranged the records and stored them in a second file. When you use indexing, you do not physically rearrange the data in the database file. Instead, you create *another* file, called an **index file**, that controls the sequence in which the records in the database file will be processed.

In some ways an index file is similar to the index in a book. An index is a list of items included in a book. It lists the items in alphabetical order and for each item includes the page number(s) where the item can be found. In dBASE an index file contains a list of items found in another place, a database file. An index file stores one record for each record in the database file. For each record the file has two fields: an indexing field and a location field. The **indexing field** stores the field you want the database ordered by. The **location field** stores the record numbers of the records in the database file, thus serving as a "pointer" to the records in the database file.

When you index in dBASE, you arrange the records in the index file in a particular order based on the values in the indexing field. Thus, you "sort" the index file rather than the database file. dBASE uses the index file along with the database file to arrange the data in the sequence you specify. You can index any field, and you can have several index files related to one database file.

Figure 5-16 illustrates the relationship between a database file and an index file. This figure shows the JOBS database file and an index file that uses CLIENT_ID as the indexing field. Notice that the index file is a separate file ordered alphabetically by client ID that has one record for each database record. Each record in the index file "points" to a database record.

CLIENT.NDX

client_id	Record #
ALE	4
ALE	10
ALE	12
ALE	21
CEL	17
FAT	9
FAT	14
FAT	20
IMA	11
IMA	16
MAM	22
MOU	3
ORI	1
ORI	6
PEA	24
SAN	5
SAN	7
SAN	13
SAN	15
SAN	19
TAC	23
VIK	2
VIK	8
VIK	18

indexing field
location field

JOBS.DBF

Record#	JOBNUM	CLIENT_ID	JOB_DESCR	DUE_DATE	QUOTE	STATUS
1	1001	ORI	Best in the Southwest	08/15/92	2500	C
2	1002	VIK	Fall TV Ad	08/10/92	32500	C
3	1003	MOU	Ski equipment sale	06/01/92	3000	C
4	1004	ALE	B/W Magazine Ad	06/05/92	3500	C
5	1005	SAN	Magazine Ad	06/10/92	22500	C
6	1006	ORI	Fall Promotion	08/01/92	2200	C
7	1007	SAN	Pamphlet	08/02/92	3000	C
8	1008	VIK	Thanksgiving Promo	11/15/92	12000	I
9	1009	FAT	Bicycle Magazine Ad	08/05/92	2500	C
10	1010	ALE	Brochure	10/10/92	6000	I
11	1011	IMA	Fall Catalogue	08/22/92	8450	C
12	1012	ALE	Radio Ad	09/01/92	3425	I
13	1013	SAN	Direct Mail	10/15/92	8900	I
14	1014	FAT	Direct Mail	11/20/92	2200	I
15	1015	SAN	Brochure	09/15/92	4400	I
16	1016	IMA	Magazine Ad	10/15/92	10000	I
17	1017	CEL	Flyer	09/20/92	850	I
18	1018	VIK	TV ads	01/15/93	35700	I
19	1019	SAN	Festival campaign	09/12/92	8900	I
20	1020	FAT	Mail order catalogue	10/10/92	9400	I
21	1021	ALE	B/W magazine ad	11/10/92	6600	I
22	1022	MAM	Newspaper ad	12/01/92	5300	I
23	1023	TAC	TV ad	12/15/92	14000	I
24	1024	PEA	Brochure	11/30/92	11000	I

points to record in database

Figure 5-16
Relationship between an index file and a database file

Why use an index file? Why not just sort? Indexing offers three advantages over sorting. First, indexing is more flexible, because a separate index file is created for each field you want to sort. Thus, by maintaining several index files *at one time*, you can process the database in a number of different ways. Second, since you are not creating duplicate copies of the database file, indexing takes less disk space. And third, indexing is the only way you can use certain dBASE commands.

Now that you know some of the basic requirements and uses of indexing, let's learn how to index a file.

The INDEX Command

You do not automatically create an index file when you create a database file. You must use the INDEX command to create each index file.

The syntax of the INDEX command is

> INDEX ON *indexing field* TO *filename*

To index, you specify the field on which you want to sequence the database file. This field is the **index key** or the **indexing field**. For example, to arrange the jobs by client, you would use CLIENT_ID as the indexing field. Any character, numeric, or date field in the database file can be your indexing field. The INDEX command creates an index file based on the indexing field and assigns the filename specified in the INDEX command to the index file. dBASE automatically adds the extension NDX to the index file's filename.

Esther decides that she first wants to index the JOBS file on the client ID. She decides to create an index file, which she will name CLIENT. She will use CLIENT_ID as the indexing field.

Before she can create an index file, Esther first must open the related database file.

To open the JOBS database file and create an index file:

❶ At the dot prompt type **use jobs** and press **[Enter]**.

Now create an index file named CLIENT using the indexing field CLIENT_ID.

❷ At the dot prompt type **index on client_id to client** and press **[Enter]**.

You will see the message "100% indexed   24 Records indexed" (Figure 5-17). You have created a new file, an index file that is stored on your data diskette as CLIENT.NDX. Remember, the extension NDX identifies the file as an index file and is automatically assigned by dBASE when the index file is stored on your data diskette. Also remember not to confuse this file with the database file CLIENT.DBF.

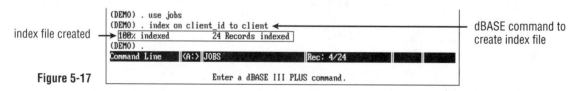

index file created

dBASE command to create index file

Figure 5-17

Now you are ready to print the contents of the database file.

To print the records:

❶ At the dot prompt type **list to print** and press **[Enter]**.

Notice that records are arranged alphabetically by client ID (Figure 5-18). The LIST command uses the index file CLIENT.NDX to determine the order in which the JOBS.DBF file will be listed.

```
Record#  JOBNUM  CLIENT_ID  JOB_DESCR              DUE_DATE   QUOTE  STATUS
     4   1004    ALE        B/W Magazine Ad        06/05/92    3500  C
    10   1010    ALE        Brochure               10/10/92    6000  I
    12   1012    ALE        Radio Ad               09/01/92    3425  I
    21   1021    ALE        B/W magazine ad        11/10/92    6600  I
    17   1017    CEL        Flyer                  09/20/92     850  I
     9   1009    FAT        Bicycle Magazine Ad    08/05/92    2500  C
    14   1014    FAT        Direct Mail            11/20/92    2200  I
    20   1020    FAT        Mail order catalogue   10/10/92    9400  I
    11   1011    IMA        Fall Catalogue         08/22/92    8450  C
    16   1016    IMA        Magazine Ad            10/15/92   10000  I
    22   1022    MAM        Newspaper ad           12/01/92    5300  I
     3   1003    MOU        Ski equipment sale     06/01/92    3000  C
     1   1001    ORI        Best in the Southwest  08/15/92    2500  C
     6   1006    ORI        Fall Promotion         08/01/92    2200  C
    24   1024    PEA        Brochure               11/30/92   11000  I
     5   1005    SAN        Magazine Ad            06/10/92   22500  C
     7   1007    SAN        Pamphlet               08/02/92    3000  C
    13   1013    SAN        Direct Mail            10/15/92    8900  I
    15   1015    SAN        Brochure               09/15/92    4400  I
    19   1019    SAN        Festival campaign      09/12/92    8900  I
    23   1023    TAC        TV ad                  12/15/92   14000  I
     2   1002    VIK        Fall TV Ad             08/10/92   32500  C
     8   1008    VIK        Thanksgiving Promo     11/15/92   12000  I
    18   1018    VIK        TV ads                 01/15/93   35700  I
```

JOBS file arranged in ascending order by client ID

Figure 5-18

Creating a Second Index File

Esther next concentrates on Martin's request for a list of all jobs ordered by their due dates. To do this, she needs to create a second index file, named DATEDUE, using DUE_DATE as the indexing field.

To create an index file:

❶ At the dot prompt type **index on due_date to datedue** and press **[Enter]**.

dBASE displays the message "100% indexed   24 Records indexed" (Figure 5-19). dBASE stores this new index file on your data diskette as DATEDUE.NDX. When you execute the INDEX command, dBASE automatically closes any open index file (in this case, CLIENT.NDX) and opens the index file that you just created.

index file created

create index file using DUE_DATE as indexing field

```
(DEMO) . index on due_date to datedue
100% indexed        24 Records indexed
(DEMO) .
Command Line    |<A:> JOBS                    |Rec: 3/24
                Enter a dBASE III PLUS command.
```

Figure 5-19

Figure 5-20a illustrates the relationship between your dBASE work area and the database and index files on your data diskette. As you can see, the JOBS file is open. In addition, you now have two index files on your data diskette (CLIENT.NDX and DATEDUE.NDX). The open index file is the last one you created, DATEDUE.NDX. The other index file, CLIENT.NDX, is closed.

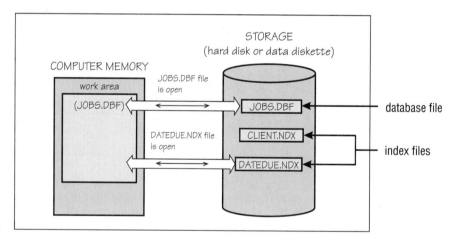

Figure 5-20a

Figure 5-20b illustrates the contents of each index file and its relationship to the JOBS database file.

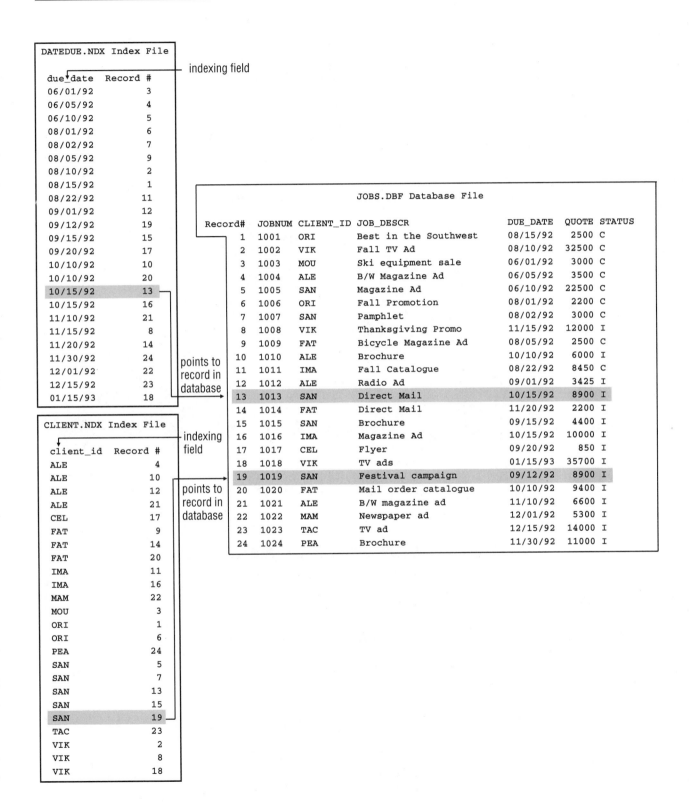

Figure 5-20b
Relationship between index files and database file

Opening Existing Index Files

Before preparing the list of jobs by due date for Martin, Esther knows she must update the JOBS file by adding the new job for Mountain Top Ski. If Esther opens the index files along with the database file, dBASE will automatically update the open index files when she updates the database file. But if Esther updates the database file and the index files are not open, dBASE cannot update the index files. So Esther now needs to open the JOBS file and its associated index files. To do this, she will execute the USE command.

The syntax of the USE command that opens a database file and its associated indexes is

USE *filename*   INDEX *index filename1, index filename2,…index filename7*

When you open a database file, you can open up to seven associated index files. You open the index files by placing the index filenames after the command word INDEX and separating the index filenames with commas. The first index filename you list is called the **master index**. The master index is considered the *active index* and is used to control the sequence of the file's records. All the other index files are open but inactive — they can be updated if changes are made to the database file, but they do not control the sequence of the records.

Let's open the JOBS file and its associated index files and make CLIENT the master (active) index.

To open the JOBS file and its associated index files:

❶   At the dot prompt type **use jobs index client,datedue** and press **[Enter]**.

You have opened the database file JOBS along with the associated index files CLIENT and DATEDUE (Figure 5-21). Because you placed CLIENT first, it is the master index. Thus, the sequence of output will be based on the CLIENT index.

Figure 5-21

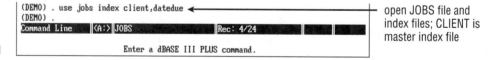

```
(DEMO) . use jobs index client,datedue ←──────────────┬──  open JOBS file and
(DEMO) .                                               │    index files; CLIENT is
Command Line    ‖<A:>‖JOBS                 ‖Rec: 4/24‖  │    master index file
              Enter a dBASE III PLUS command.
```

Why include the DATEDUE index in the USE command? So it will be updated, along with the CLIENT index file, if records are added, edited, or deleted to the JOBS database file. Remember, only *opened* indexes are updated when a database is updated.

The relationship between the work area and the database and index files is illustrated in Figure 5-22. The JOBS file is open. In addition, the CLIENT and DATEDUE index files are open. CLIENT.NDX is the active, or master index, while DATEDUE.NDX is open but inactive.

Adding Records with Index Files Open

You will recall from Tutorial 3 that you use the APPEND command to add records to a database file. Esther now needs to enter the new Mountain Top Ski record to the JOBS file. She uses the job authorization form that Martin has filled out (Figure 5-23).

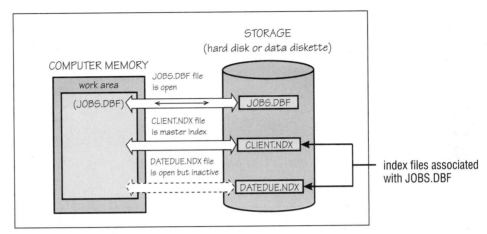

Figure 5-22

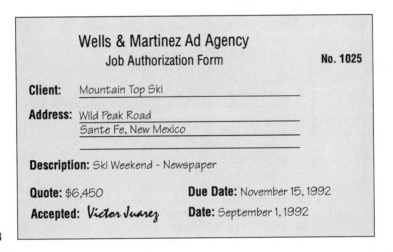

Figure 5-23

To add a new record to the JOBS database file:

❶   At the dot prompt type **append** and press **[Enter]**.

You can now enter data. As you have seen before, a blank record form appears on the screen. You use this form to enter the data values for each job. Refer to Figure 5-23 to enter the data for the new Mountain Top Ski job.

Remember, when you're ready to leave the APPEND process press either [Enter] or [Esc] with the cursor on the first position of the first field of a blank record form.

After you have entered the data into the last field of the job record form, a new blank record form appears on your screen. You have no new records to enter, so you can leave data entry mode by pressing [Enter] or [Esc]. *Do not press [Ctrl][End] to leave the APPEND process after you have moved to a blank record form.* dBASE saves the Mountain Top Ski record, the twenty-fifth record in the JOBS file. Notice that the status bar indicates a total of 25 records. Figure 5-24 on the next page shows the contents of the JOBS database file and the CLIENT.NDX and DATEDUE.NDX index files after you have entered the new job record.

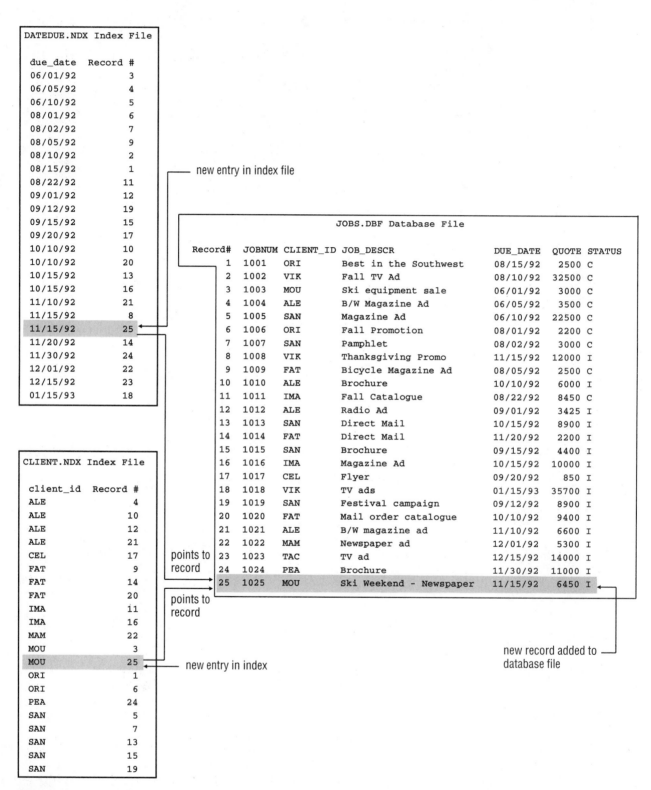

```
DATEDUE.NDX Index File

due_date    Record #
06/01/92         3
06/05/92         4
06/10/92         5
08/01/92         6
08/02/92         7
08/05/92         9
08/10/92         2
08/15/92         1
08/22/92        11
09/01/92        12
09/12/92        19
09/15/92        15
09/20/92        17
10/10/92        10
10/10/92        20
10/15/92        13
10/15/92        16
11/10/92        21
11/15/92         8
11/15/92        25
11/20/92        14
11/30/92        24
12/01/92        22
12/15/92        23
01/15/93        18
```

— new entry in index file

```
JOBS.DBF Database File

Record#  JOBNUM  CLIENT_ID  JOB_DESCR                DUE_DATE   QUOTE  STATUS
      1   1001   ORI        Best in the Southwest    08/15/92    2500   C
      2   1002   VIK        Fall TV Ad               08/10/92   32500   C
      3   1003   MOU        Ski equipment sale       06/01/92    3000   C
      4   1004   ALE        B/W Magazine Ad          06/05/92    3500   C
      5   1005   SAN        Magazine Ad              06/10/92   22500   C
      6   1006   ORI        Fall Promotion           08/01/92    2200   C
      7   1007   SAN        Pamphlet                 08/02/92    3000   C
      8   1008   VIK        Thanksgiving Promo       11/15/92   12000   I
      9   1009   FAT        Bicycle Magazine Ad      08/05/92    2500   C
     10   1010   ALE        Brochure                 10/10/92    6000   I
     11   1011   IMA        Fall Catalogue           08/22/92    8450   C
     12   1012   ALE        Radio Ad                 09/01/92    3425   I
     13   1013   SAN        Direct Mail              10/15/92    8900   I
     14   1014   FAT        Direct Mail              11/20/92    2200   I
     15   1015   SAN        Brochure                 09/15/92    4400   I
     16   1016   IMA        Magazine Ad              10/15/92   10000   I
     17   1017   CEL        Flyer                    09/20/92     850   I
     18   1018   VIK        TV ads                   01/15/93   35700   I
     19   1019   SAN        Festival campaign        09/12/92    8900   I
     20   1020   FAT        Mail order catalogue     10/10/92    9400   I
     21   1021   ALE        B/W magazine ad          11/10/92    6600   I
     22   1022   MAM        Newspaper ad             12/01/92    5300   I
     23   1023   TAC        TV ad                    12/15/92   14000   I
     24   1024   PEA        Brochure                 11/30/92   11000   I
     25   1025   MOU        Ski Weekend - Newspaper  11/15/92    6450   I
```

points to record

points to record

new record added to database file

```
CLIENT.NDX Index File

client_id   Record #
ALE              4
ALE             10
ALE             12
ALE             21
CEL             17
FAT              9
FAT             14
FAT             20
IMA             11
IMA             16
MAM             22
MOU              3
MOU             25
ORI              1
ORI              6
PEA             24
SAN              5
SAN              7
SAN             13
SAN             15
SAN             19
```

— new entry in index

Figure 5-24
Contents of index files and database file after new record is added to JOBS file

Now let's see how the JOBS file looks. We should see that the new record is included and that the file is sequenced by the master index, CLIENT.

To list the JOBS file:

❶ At the dot prompt type **list to print** and press **[Enter]**.

The listing includes the new record you added to the file (Figure 5-25). Notice that although the new Mountain Top Ski record is the last record in the database file, the new record is in the thirteenth position of the printout. This is because CLIENT.NDX is the master index.

new record

master index is
CLIENT.NDX;
records arranged in
ascending order by
client ID

Record#	JOBNUM	CLIENT_ID	JOB_DESCR	DUE_DATE	QUOTE	STATUS
4	1004	ALE	B/W Magazine Ad	06/05/92	3500	C
10	1010	ALE	Brochure	10/10/92	6000	I
12	1012	ALE	Radio Ad	09/01/92	3425	I
21	1021	ALE	B/W magazine ad	11/10/92	6600	I
17	1017	CEL	Flyer	09/20/92	850	I
9	1009	FAT	Bicycle Magazine Ad	08/05/92	2500	C
14	1014	FAT	Direct Mail	11/20/92	2200	I
20	1020	FAT	Mail order catalogue	10/10/92	9400	I
11	1011	IMA	Fall Catalogue	08/22/92	8450	C
16	1016	IMA	Magazine Ad	10/15/92	10000	I
22	1022	MAM	Newspaper ad	12/01/92	5300	I
3	1003	MOU	Ski equipment sale	06/01/92	3000	C
25	1025	MOU	Ski weekend - Newspaper	11/15/92	6450	I
1	1001	ORI	Best in the Southwest	08/15/92	2500	C
6	1006	ORI	Fall Promotion	08/01/92	2200	C
24	1024	PEA	Brochure	11/30/92	11000	I
5	1005	SAN	Magazine Ad	06/10/92	22500	C
7	1007	SAN	Pamphlet	08/02/92	3000	C
13	1013	SAN	Direct Mail	10/15/92	8900	I
15	1015	SAN	Brochure	09/15/92	4400	I
19	1019	SAN	Festival campaign	09/12/92	8900	I
23	1023	TAC	TV ad	12/15/92	14000	I
2	1002	VIK	Fall TV Ad	08/10/92	32500	C
8	1008	VIK	Thanksgiving Promo	11/15/92	12000	I
18	1018	VIK	TV ads	01/15/93	35700	I

Figure 5-25

The SET ORDER TO Command

What if you wanted to print the JOBS file in due date sequence? This is what Esther needs to give to Martin. Can you change the master index? Yes, you can. You can change the master index by executing the USE command again, placing the DATEDUE index first. In this case, the USE command would appear as follows:

USE JOBS INDEX DATEDUE,CLIENT

Another way you can change the master index is to use the SET ORDER TO command. The syntax for this command is

> SET ORDER TO *position number*

dBASE assigns each index file a number, beginning with 1, in the order in which the index name appears in the USE statement. For example, in the statement

USE JOBS INDEX CLIENT,DATEDUE

the index file CLIENT is assigned the number 1 and the index file DATEDUE is assigned the number 2.

Now let's use the SET ORDER TO command to change the master index to DATEDUE.

To change the master index:

❶ At the dot prompt type **set order to 2** and press **[Enter]**.

The index file in position 2, DATEDUE, is now the master index (Figure 5-26).

message indicating new master index →

command to switch master index

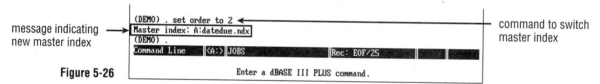

```
(DEMO) . set order to 2
Master index: A:datedue.ndx
(DEMO) .
Command Line    <A:> JOBS                      Rec: EOF/25
                Enter a dBASE III PLUS command.
```

Figure 5-26

Figure 5-27 illustrates the relationship between the work area and the database and index files after the SET ORDER TO command is executed. The active file is now DATEDUE.NDX.

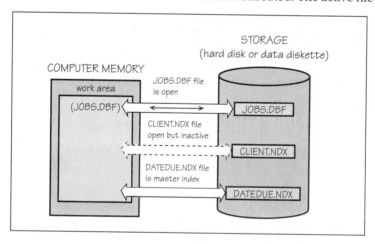

Figure 5-27

Let's verify that DATEDUE.NDX is the master index by printing the contents of JOBS and observing the order in which the records are displayed.

To list the JOBS file:

❶ At the dot prompt type **list to print** and press **[Enter]**. See Figure 5-28.

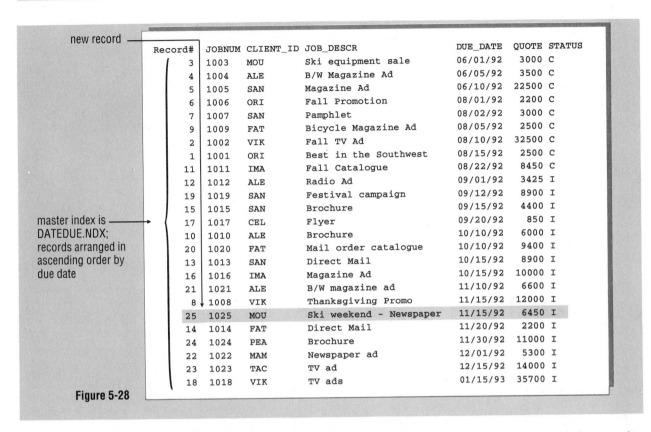

new record

Record#	JOBNUM	CLIENT_ID	JOB_DESCR	DUE_DATE	QUOTE	STATUS
3	1003	MOU	Ski equipment sale	06/01/92	3000	C
4	1004	ALE	B/W Magazine Ad	06/05/92	3500	C
5	1005	SAN	Magazine Ad	06/10/92	22500	C
6	1006	ORI	Fall Promotion	08/01/92	2200	C
7	1007	SAN	Pamphlet	08/02/92	3000	C
9	1009	FAT	Bicycle Magazine Ad	08/05/92	2500	C
2	1002	VIK	Fall TV Ad	08/10/92	32500	C
1	1001	ORI	Best in the Southwest	08/15/92	2500	C
11	1011	IMA	Fall Catalogue	08/22/92	8450	C
12	1012	ALE	Radio Ad	09/01/92	3425	I
19	1019	SAN	Festival campaign	09/12/92	8900	I
15	1015	SAN	Brochure	09/15/92	4400	I
17	1017	CEL	Flyer	09/20/92	850	I
10	1010	ALE	Brochure	10/10/92	6000	I
20	1020	FAT	Mail order catalogue	10/10/92	9400	I
13	1013	SAN	Direct Mail	10/15/92	8900	I
16	1016	IMA	Magazine Ad	10/15/92	10000	I
21	1021	ALE	B/W magazine ad	11/10/92	6600	I
8	1008	VIK	Thanksgiving Promo	11/15/92	12000	I
25	1025	MOU	Ski weekend - Newspaper	11/15/92	6450	I
14	1014	FAT	Direct Mail	11/20/92	2200	I
24	1024	PEA	Brochure	11/30/92	11000	I
22	1022	MAM	Newspaper ad	12/01/92	5300	I
23	1023	TAC	TV ad	12/15/92	14000	I
18	1018	VIK	TV ads	01/15/93	35700	I

master index is DATEDUE.NDX; records arranged in ascending order by due date

Figure 5-28

Notice that the listing includes the new record you added to the file. Although this record is the last record in the database file, it is the twentieth record in the listing by due date. Having the listing ordered by due date and not client ID demonstrates that DATEDUE.NDX is the master index. Esther has now completed the report for Martin. She takes this output to his office.

Sorting and Indexing in Assistant Mode

So far in this tutorial you have learned how to sort and index database files using dot prompt mode. You may be wondering if you could have accomplished these same tasks in Assistant mode. In most cases you could.

To illustrate the use of sorting and indexing in Assistant mode, let's arrange the jobs by status, that is, listing all completed jobs before jobs that are still in process.

Sorting in Assistant Mode

Let's sort the records in the JOBS file by status. STATUS is the sort key, and SORT4.DBF is the new database file.

To sort all records in the currently open file:

❶ Switch from dot prompt mode to Assistant mode by pressing **[F2]** or typing **Assist** and pressing **[Enter]**.

❷   Move the selection cursor to the *Organize* option on the menu bar.

❸   Move the selection cursor to *Sort*. See Figure 5-29. Press **[Enter]**.

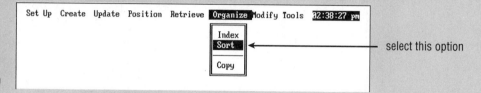

Figure 5-29

A boxed submenu listing all the fields in the JOBS file appears on the Assistant screen. The first field in this list of field names is highlighted, and a box describing the highlighted field appears in the middle of the screen. See Figure 5-30.

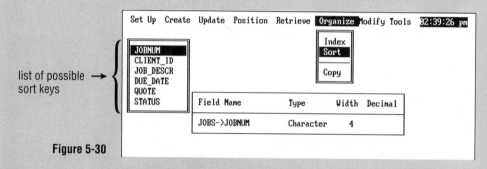

Figure 5-30

Next select the field that is to be the primary sort key.

❹   Move the selection cursor to STATUS and press **[Enter]**.

"STATUS" appears on the action line just after the command words "SORT ON." See Figure 5-31. If you needed a secondary sort key, you would select it now.

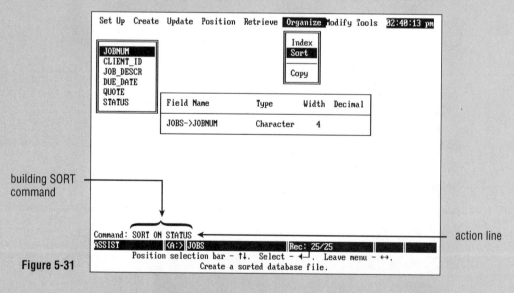

Figure 5-31

❺   Since we need only a primary sort key for this sort, press **[→]** to exit the field-list submenu and to return to the pull-down menu of options for *Sort*.

Next tell dBASE on what disk drive you want to store the sorted copy of the JOBS database file.

❻ If you have a *two-diskette system*, move the selection cursor to B: and press **[Enter]**.

If you have a *hard disk*, make sure the selection cursor is pointing to A: and press **[Enter]**.

A prompt appears asking you to enter a filename for the sorted file.

❼ Type **sort4** and press **[Enter]**. See Figure 5-32.

enter **SORT4**

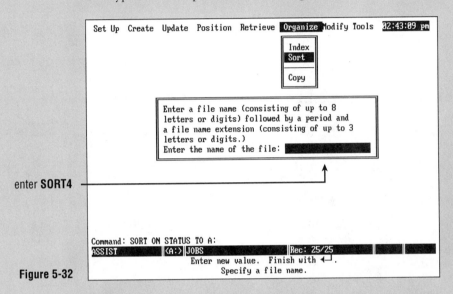

Figure 5-32

The message "100% Sorted   25 Records sorted" appears on your screen. See Figure 5-33. A fourth sorted file, SORT4.DBF, is stored on your data diskette.

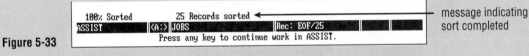

message indicating sort completed

Figure 5-33

❽ Press any key to continue.

Indexing in Assistant Mode

Now let's create an index file named STATUSX, using STATUS as the indexing field.

To index all records in the currently open file:

❶ Move the selection cursor to the *Index* option of *Organize* and press **[Enter]**.

A prompt appears asking you to enter the index key for the index file. See Figure 5-34 on the next page.

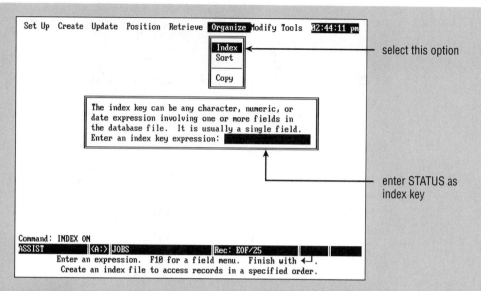

Figure 5-34

❷   Type **status** and press **[Enter]**.

Now that you have selected the index key, you need to tell dBASE on what disk drive you want to store the index file.

❸   If you have a *two-diskette system*, move the selection cursor to B: and press **[Enter]**.

If you have a *hard disk*, make sure the selection cursor is pointing to A: and press **[Enter]**.

A prompt appears asking you to enter a filename for the index file. See Figure 5-35.

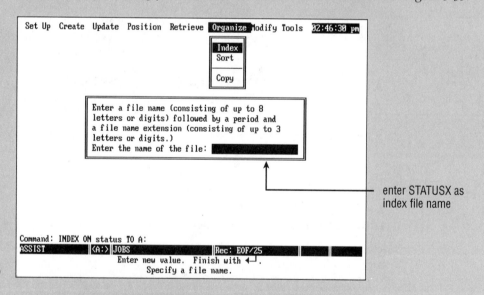

Figure 5-35

❹   Type **statusx** and press **[Enter]**.

The message "100% indexed   25 Records indexed" appears on your screen. See Figure 5-36. A fourth index file, STATUSX.NDX, is now stored on your data diskette.

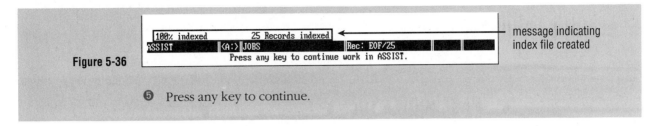

Figure 5-36

message indicating
index file created

❺ Press any key to continue.

Remember to quit dBASE before you turn off your computer.

These two examples of using Assistant mode to sort and index show you an alternative way to manipulate the data in a database. Whether you use Assistant mode or dot prompt mode is often a matter of personal preference. As you become more experienced using dBASE, you will discover which mode you prefer to use to accomplish specific tasks.

■   ■   ■

Summary Table of Database Files and Associated Index Files

This table lists all the database files and their associated index files used in this book. You can refer to this table to help you recall information you will need to work through Tutorial 5 as well as the Case Problems for Tutorials 5, 6, and 7 and the Additional Cases.

Database (dbf)	Index File (ndx)	Indexing Field
CLIENT	CLNAMEX	CLIENT_NAM
	CONTACTX	CONTACT
JOBS	CLIENT	CLIENT_ID
	DATEDUE	DUE_DATE
	STATUSX	STATUS
JAPAN	JPINDX1	COMP_NAME
	JPINDX2	PROFITS
	JPINDX3	IND_CODE
ACCTREC	MEDINDX1	CUSTNAME
	MEDINDX2	YTD_SALES
	MEDINDX3	TYPE
EMPLOYEE	EMPINDX1	SEX
	EMPINDX2	ANNSAL
	EMPINDX3	LNAME
	EMPINDX4	DEPT
NBA	NBAINDX1	LNAME
	NBAINDX2	POS
	NBAINDX3	TEAM
CITIES	CITINDX1	city name
	CITINDX2	region
HOUSING	HSEINDX1	owner's last name
	HSEINDX2	town

Exercises

1. Suppose you find a file on your data diskette named TITLE.NDX. What type of a file is this?

2. What file extension does a sorted file have?

The database file structure for INVENTRY.DBF contains the five fields shown in Figure 5-37.

Field Description	Field Name
Part Number	PARTID
Part Name	PART_NAME
Warehouse location	LOC
Quantity on hand	QOH
Cost per unit	COST

Figure 5-37

Based on INVENTRY.DBF, write the dBASE commands for Exercises 3 through 7.

3. Sort by part name in ascending order to a file named SORT1.

4. Sort by quantity on hand in ascending order to a file named SORT2.

5. Sort by warehouse location and within warehouse location by part name to a file named SORT3.

6. Index by part name to a file named INDEX1.

7. Index by warehouse location to a file named INDEX2.

Assume for Exercises 8 through 11 that a database file named STUDENT is opened with the following USE command:

    USE STUDENT INDEX LASTNAME, MAJOR, SEX

8. How many index files are open?

9. If you executed a LIST command, how would the student records be sequenced?

10. If you want to sequence the STUDENT file by major, what must you do?

11. Why are three index files open if only one index file controls the sequencing of records?

12. Assume you have a database file named CONTACTS.DBF that contains three fields: NAME, CITY, and STATE. Figure 5-38 contains a sample of the contents of this file.

Name	City	State
Mike Franklin	Lincoln	NB
Heather Ennu	Tallahasee	FL
Ellen Jenks	Aberdeen	SD

Figure 5-38

Can you sort these data alphabetically by last name? If you can, provide the SORT command required. If not, what is the problem?

Tutorial Assignments

In the following Tutorial Assignments you can use the LIST STRUCTURE command if you cannot remember the field names in an open database file.

Open the W&M CLIENT database file and do the following:

1. Sort by client name in alphabetical order to a file named SORT5.

2. Print the contents of the sorted file.

3. Print the client data in the order in which the data were entered.

4. Index by client name in alphabetical order to a file name CLNAMEX.

5. Print the CLIENT file in alphabetical order using your index.

6. Print the CLIENT file in the order in which it was entered.

7. Index by contact name to a file named CONTACTX.

8. Print the CLIENT file using CONTACTX. What do you observe about your output?

Open the JOBS file and do the following:

9. Sort by status and within status by quote. Arrange status in ascending order and quote in descending order. Name the sorted file SORT6.

10. Print the contents of the file SORT6.

Case Problems

In the following Case Problems you can use the LIST STRUCTURE command if you cannot remember the field names in an open database file.

1. Biggs & Hang Investment Company

Do the following:

1. Open the JAPAN database file.

2. Sort the companies in the file by sales with highest sales first. Name the sorted file JPSORT1.

3. Use JPSORT1 to print a ranking of the companies by sales. Include company name, industry code, and sales in your listing.

4. Sort the companies by industry and within industry by company name. Name the sorted file JPSORT2.

5. Use JPSORT2 to print a listing by industry. Include industry code, company name, assets, sales, and profits.

6. Use the JAPAN.DBF to create an index named JPINDX1 using company name as the indexing field.

7. Print a list of all companies in the automobile industry (industry code = A) in alphabetical order by company name. Include company name, sales, profits, and high price in your listing.

8. Use JAPAN.DBF to create an index named JPINDX2 using profit as the indexing field.

9. Calculate the average profit for all companies in the database. See Tutorial 4 for calculating averages. Print a list of all companies that had profits below the average, with companies having smallest profits first. Include company name and profits in your listing.

2. Medi-Source Inc.

Do the following:

1. Open the file named ACCTREC.DBF.

2. Sort the file by customer name. Name the sorted file MEDSORT1.

3. Use MEDSORT1 to print a list of customers in alphabetical order. Include customer name, industry type, state, balance owed, and year-to-date sales.

4. Sort the customers by industry type and within industry type by balance owed with highest balance owed first. Name the sorted file MEDSORT2.

5. Use MEDSORT2 to print a listing by industry type. Include industry type, customer name, state, and balance owed.

6. Use the ACCTREC.DBF to create an index named MEDINDX1 using customer name as the indexing field.

7. Print a list of all companies in the hospital industry (industry code = H) in alphabetical order by customer name. Include customer name, credit limit, and balance owed.

8. Use ACCTREC.DBF to create an index named MEDINDX2 using YTD_SALES as the indexing field.

9. Print a list of customers ordered by year-to-date sales using MEDINDX2. Include customer name, industry type, year-to-date sales, and balance owed.

3. Appleton and Drake Electrical Supply Company

Do the following:

1. Open the file named EMPLOYEE.DBF.

2. Sort the employees by their last names. Name the sorted file EMPSORT1.

3. Use EMPSORT1 to print a list of employees in alphabetical order. Include employee first and last name, sex, department, and salary.

4. Sort the employees by department and within department by last name. Name the sorted file EMPSORT2.

5. Use EMPSORT2 to print a listing by department. Include department, employee first and last name, and salary.

6. Use the EMPLOYEE.DBF file to create an index named EMPINDX1 using sex as the indexing field.

7. Print a list of all employees ordered by sex. Include each employee's first and last name, sex, department, and salary.

8. Use EMPLOYEE.DBF to create an index named EMPINDX2 using salary as the indexing field.

9. Print a list of employees earning less than the company average. Include each employee's first and last name, department, sex, and salary. You will need to calculate the average salary first. See Tutorial 4.

4. National Basketball Association

Do the following:

1. Open the NBA database file.

2. Sort the records into alphabetical sequence using the player's last name as your sort key. Name the sorted file NBASORT1.

3. Use the sorted file, NBASORT1, to print an alphabetical listing of all players. Include the following fields: last name, first name, team, and salary.

4. Sort the NBA file by team and within team by salary (highest salary first) to a database file named NBASORT2.

5. Use the sorted file, NBASORT2, to print the team, last name, first name, and salary for players earning over $1,000,000.

6. Use the NBA database file to create an index file named NBAINDX1, using last name as the indexing field.

7. Print the NBA data in alphabetical order using your index file. Include each player's first and last name, team, and salary in your output.

8. Use the NBA database file to create an index file named NBAINDX2, using position as the indexing field.

9. Print the NBA file ordered by position. Include all fields from the database in your printout.

Tutorial 6

Using the Report Generator

Case: Wells & Martinez — Generating the Jobs Status Monthly Report

Nancy has called Esther into her office to discuss the W&M database. She thanks Esther for the work Esther has been doing and tells her how helpful the database has been.

Nancy then says that the jobs status listing has been so helpful that she wonders if Esther could update and print it regularly, perhaps once a month. Esther immediately recognizes that what Nancy is asking for is a report and that her request provides the perfect opportunity for Esther to use dBASE's report generator. Esther suggests that they discuss the design and format of the report to make it as useful as possible. Nancy agrees, and Esther begins to ask questions about the report and how it will be used. After 45 minutes they have decided that the report will:

- Be issued monthly
- Be dated so Nancy will know which printout is the latest
- Include a title that describes its contents, so Nancy can easily distinguish it from other reports
- Contain column headings that are more descriptive than those Esther used on the last job status printout
- Omit record numbers; Nancy often confuses them with job numbers
- Omit the status column; Nancy wants only the completed jobs listed
- Total the quotes column, so Nancy can better track W&M's monthly cash flow.

Esther takes this list and begins work.

Designing Reports

When Esther first developed the job status listing for Nancy, she paid little attention to the format. She wanted to answer Nancy's requests without delay, so she did what most people do when they query a database — produced the printout quickly, without concern for the appearance of the output. Thus, the headings were not as descriptive as they could have been, the printout was not titled, and other useful report features that make printed reports easy to read were also omitted.

Printed reports must provide information succinctly, clearly, and correctly. Before working at the computer, you should take the time to plan the report and its format. Ask yourself these general questions whenever you are planning a report:

- What information do I need?
- How much detail do I want to include? Do I need to display every record or only summary totals?
- How should I present the data? In columns? As a chart? As a graph?
- How often will the report be prepared?

As part of your planning process you should prepare a report layout sheet. A **report layout sheet** is a sketch of your report, which you can prepare on plain paper, graph paper, or special printer spacing charts. Figure 6-1 is the report layout that Esther prepared after her meeting with Nancy.

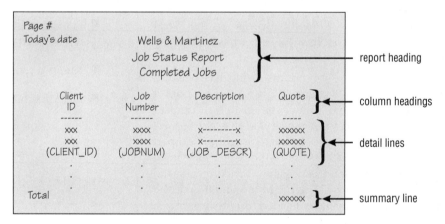

Figure 6-1
Esther's report
layout sheet

Your report layout sheet should address the following questions:

- What items should be included in the report?
- Where on the report should each field be located?
- What report and column headings should be included?
- How should the records be ordered?
- Which groups of records should be subtotaled?
- Which fields should be totaled?

You can use a series of *X*s in the print positions to represent the fields. If you have room, include the name of the field in parentheses under the *X*s, as Esther did on her report layout sheet. For long fields you can do as Esther did for the field JOB_DESCR — put two *X*s connected by a line. You typically put only one or two lines on the report layout sheet to represent multiple lines that will contain the same type of information.

Esther's report contains several types of lines typical of many reports: heading lines, detail lines, and summary lines. **Heading lines** are usually printed at the top of each page to describe the nature of the data in your report. Column heading lines describe the columns of output. **Detail lines** are in the body of the report and provide detailed information about the results of processing. Typically you print one detail line for each record in the database. **Summary lines**, which are usually at the end of a report, give the totals of numbers from the detail lines.

You can use dBASE's report generator to build a report step by step. Using the report generator gives a report a professional appearance, including features such as the date on which you printed the report, page numbers, report titles, column headings, and totals.

Let's start by creating a report format file.

Creating the Report Format File

Let's work with Esther as she uses the report generator to create W&M's Job Status Report. You've already seen Esther's sketch of how she thought the report should look (Figure 6-1). The next step is to create the **report format file**. The report format file contains a report's definition, that is, its titles, headings, columns, and fields.

Before you can create the report definition, you first must open the JOBS file.

To get started:
❶ Load dBASE, switch to dot prompt mode, set the default drive, and open the JOBS database file.

Now you are ready to create the report format file, which contains the definition of the report. You use the CREATE REPORT command to create a report format file. The syntax of this command is

CREATE REPORT *reportname*

When you use the CREATE REPORT command, the dBASE report generator steps you through the building of a column-oriented report. The result is a report format file, which contains the definition of the report and which is stored on your data diskette as the report name you choose. dBASE automatically adds the extension FRM to a report name.

Let's start Esther's report. We'll name the report JOBSTAT.

To begin creating the report:
❶ At the dot prompt type **create report jobstat** and press **[Enter]**.

You now see the Report Format screen (Figure 6-2). Notice that the top line of this screen has a menu bar with five options: *Options, Groups, Columns, Locate,* and *Exit.* These five options have pull-down menus that do the following:

- The Options submenu establishes the overall appearance and the physical characteristics for each page of the report.
- The Groups submenu divides the report into groups of related records.
- The Columns submenu specifies the contents, the heading, and the width of every column.
- The Locate submenu lets you quickly access individual columns when you want to revise a report.
- The Exit submenu saves or abandons the report format file.

menu bar

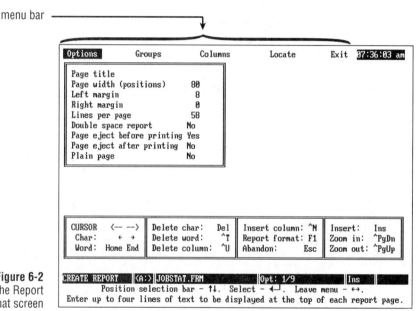

Figure 6-2
The Report
Format screen

Defining Overall Page Characteristics

When you first enter the Create Report screen, the Options menu is open. The Options menu allows you to specify page headings, page width, left and right margins, number of lines per page, and double- or single-line spacing. Figure 6-3 gives a detailed description of what each menu item on the Options menu does. Take some time now to familiarize yourself with the important information, such as defaults and ranges, in Figure 6-3.

Page title	Up to four lines of text can be specified. The title is printed at the top of each page.
Page width	The maximum number of characters permitted in one line. Default is 80, range is 1 to 500.
Left margin	Number of spaces between the left edge of the paper and the first printed character. Default is 8.
Right margin	Number of spaces between the right edge of the paper and the last allowed character on the line. Default is 0.
Lines per page	Number of printed lines per page. Default is 58, range is 30 to 100.
Double space report	If double spaced, report prints one blank line between each record. Default is no, or single spacing.
Page eject before printing	Advance paper to top of next page before printing first record. Default is yes.
Page eject after printing	Eject one blank page after printing last record. Default is no.
Plain page	If yes, page numbers and system date are not printed. Title is printed on first page only. Default is no.

Figure 6-3
Items on the
Options menu

Now let's assign a page title for this report. According to her report layout sheet, Esther wants the following three-line page title:

Wells & Martinez
Job Status Report
Completed Jobs

To enter the page title:

❶ When you enter the Report Format screen, the Options menu is open and the *Page title* option highlighted. Press **[Enter]** to select this option.

A triangle appears before the entry area for the page title. A text window also appears; this is where you enter the title of the report. See Figure 6-4. You can enter up to four lines of text in the text window.

triangle indicating
entry area open

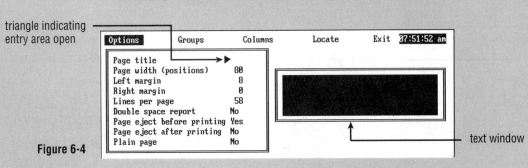

Figure 6-4

text window

Now let's enter the three-line page title.

❷ Type **Wells & Martinez** and press **[Enter]**. The cursor advances to the next line.

❸ Type **Job Status Report** and press **[Enter]**. The cursor advances to the next line.

❹ Type **Completed Jobs** and press **[Enter]**. See Figure 6-5. You have completed the page title.

Figure 6-5

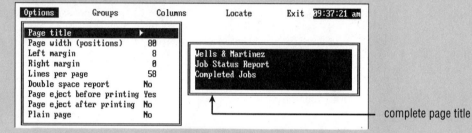

complete page title

❺ Press **[Ctrl][End]** to return to the Report Format screen. Alternatively you can press **[↓]** until you return to the Report Format screen.

Notice that the first eight characters of the page title appear in the Page title entry area. See Figure 6-6.

Figure 6-6

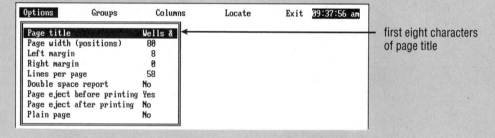

first eight characters of page title

Eight other page-characteristic options are available in the Options menu. Let's accept the dBASE settings (the defaults) for page width, left and right margins, lines per page, spacing, ejection, and page. You have now completed entering the basic page characteristic information. Let's move to the Columns menu.

Defining Columns in a Report

You are now ready to enter the body of the report: the contents, the heading, and the width for each column. Let's begin by defining the first column of the report, client ID.

To define the client ID column:

❶ Move the selection cursor to the *Columns* option on the menu bar. The box near the top of the screen describes the information you need to specify each column. See Figure 6-7.

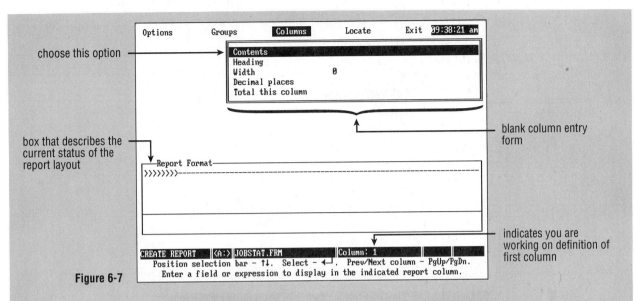

choose this option

box that describes the current status of the report layout

blank column entry form

indicates you are working on definition of first column

Figure 6-7

2 Press **[Enter]** to select the *Contents* option. A triangle appears before the Contents entry area, indicating that the entry area is open. See Figure 6-8. In this area you need to enter the field name for this column.

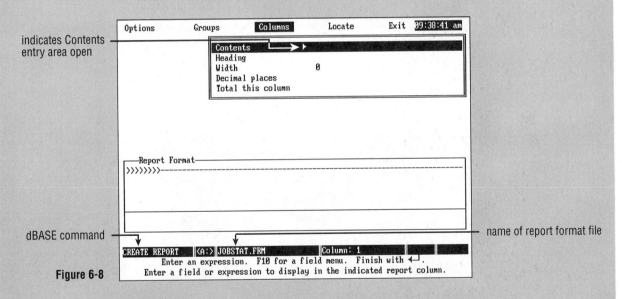

indicates Contents entry area open

dBASE command

name of report format file

Figure 6-8

You can enter the field name immediately following the triangle.

❸   Type **client_id** and press **[Enter]**. See Figure 6-9. The triangle disappears from the entry area, and the entry area is closed.

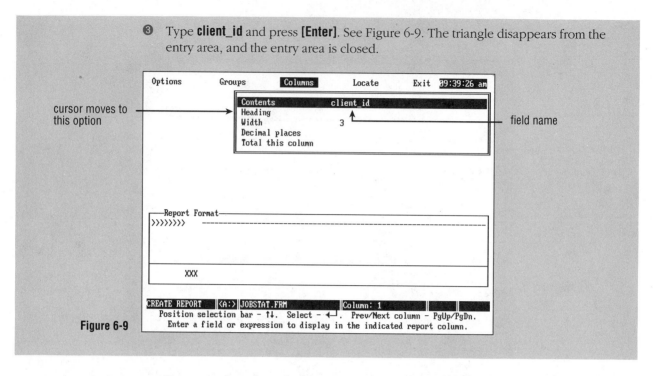

cursor moves to this option

field name

Figure 6-9

Next enter the column heading. According to her report layout sheet (Figure 6-1), Esther plans a three-line column heading:

CLIENT
  ID
- - - - - -

To enter the column heading:

❶   Move the selection cursor to the *Heading* option and press **[Enter]**.

A triangle appears in the Heading entry line, and a window appears on the right side of your screen. You will enter your column heading in the window. A column heading can be up to four lines.

Now enter the heading.

❷   Type **CLIENT** and press **[Enter]**. Notice that the cursor advances to the second line.

❸   Type **[Space] [Space] ID** and press **[Enter]**. The cursor advances to the third line.

❹   Type - - - - - - and press **[Enter]**. See Figure 6-10.

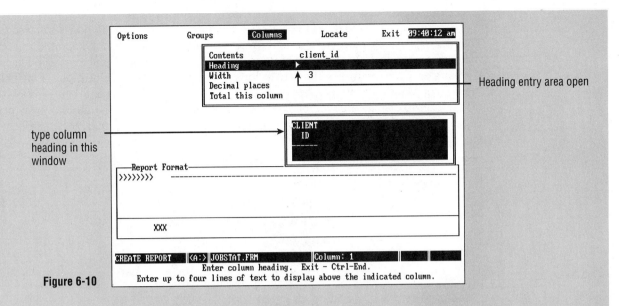

Figure 6-10

You have completed the heading.

⑤ Press **[Ctrl] [End]** to return to the Heading line. Alternatively you can press **[↓]** until the cursor returns to the Heading line. The heading appears in the Heading entry area with semicolons separating the text lines. See Figure 6-11. dBASE automatically inserted a semicolon every time you pressed [Enter].

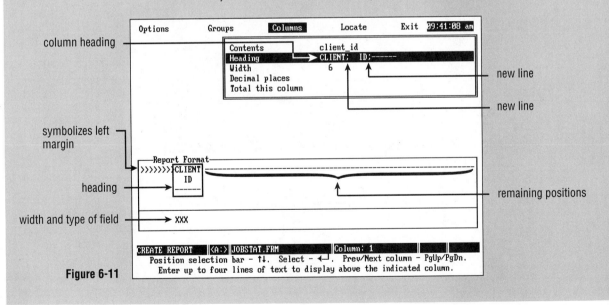

Figure 6-11

Next you enter the width for each column. dBASE automatically enters a number for this item: either the width of the field or the number of characters in the column heading, whichever is larger. You can change the width of the column heading; however, in this case, the width is acceptable because a W&M client ID is never more than three characters wide.

The next two options, *Decimal places* and *Total this column*, apply only to numeric fields. Thus, you have completed the definition of the first column.

Next let's discuss the Report Format box, near the bottom of the Report Format screen. This box displays the current status of the report layout. For instance, the Report Format box now displays on the output line in its upper portion the margins, the column headings, and the number of remaining positions. In its lower portion it displays the locations of the fields. The row of *X*s indicates where the client IDs will appear. Figure 6-12 shows the symbols that dBASE uses to display the type of data in each column of a report. The number of symbols corresponds to the number of positions that the data cover. For example, >>>>> indicates a left margin of five spaces; XXX indicates a field of three characters.

>	Left margin
<	Right margin
-	Remaining output position
X	Character field
9	Numeric field that will not be totaled
#	Numeric field that will be totaled
mm/dd/yy	Date field
.L.	Logical field

Figure 6-12
Format codes used
in Report Format box

Now you are ready to define the second column, job number.

To define the job number column:

❶ Press **[PgDn]**. This keystroke erases the previous entry, and a blank column entry form appears. See Figure 6-13. Notice that the column number in the status bar has changed to 2.

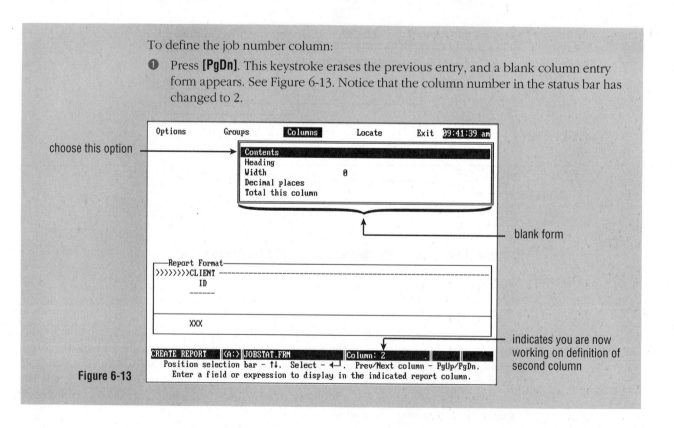

choose this option

blank form

indicates you are now working on definition of second column

Figure 6-13

To move to the next column, press [PgDn]. To revise any entry in the previous column, press [PgUp].

❷ Be sure the option *Contents* is highlighted and press **[Enter]**. A triangle appears, indicating that dBASE is waiting for you to enter a field name for this column.

If you've forgotten the name, press the function key [F10] to get a list of all the field names in the open database file.

❸ Press **[F10]**. A list of field names appears on your screen. See Figure 6-14.

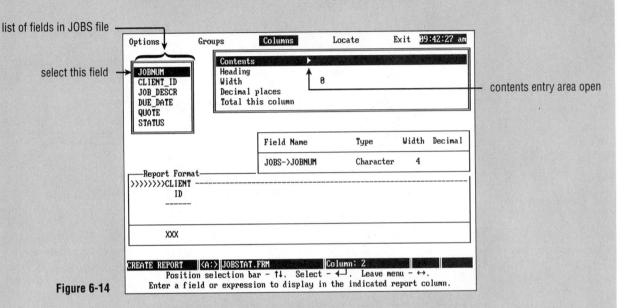

list of fields in JOBS file ⎯

select this field ⎯

contents entry area open

Figure 6-14

❹ Select JOBNUM and press **[Enter]**. The field name you selected appears in the Contents entry area. See Figure 6-15.

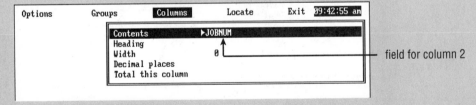

field for column 2

Figure 6-15

❺ Press **[Enter]** to indicate this is the correct entry. Notice that the triangle disappears, indicating that the Contents entry area is closed. You have selected the field for the second column.

Now you need to enter the three-line column heading:

Job
Number
- - - - - -

To enter the column heading:

❶   Move the selection cursor to the *Heading* option and press **[Enter]**. A triangle and the heading window appear, indicating that dBASE is waiting for you to enter the heading.

Now enter the heading.

❷   Type **[Space] JOB** and press **[Enter]**.

❸   Type **NUMBER** and press **[Enter]**.

❹   Type - - - - - - and press **[Enter]**.

You have completed the column heading for the second column. See Figure 6-16.

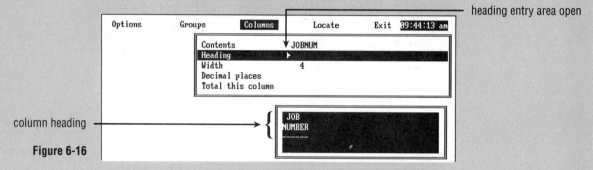

column heading
Figure 6-16

❺   Press **[Ctrl][End]** to indicate you have completed the column heading. You return to the Columns menu. Notice that the three-line heading for the second column now appears in the Report Format box, with a field width of four characters. See Figure 6-17.

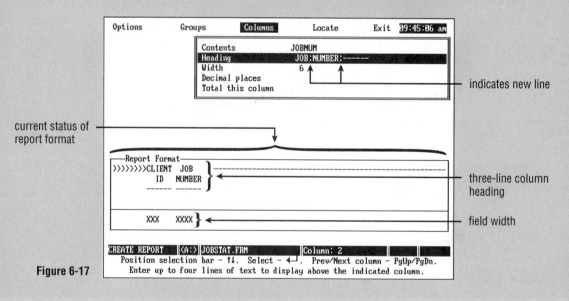

current status of report format

Figure 6-17

You have now completed the information needed for the second column. You are ready to enter information for the third column, job description.

To define the third column:

1. Press **[PgDn]** to move to a blank column form.
2. Press **[Enter]**. A triangle appears on the Contents line.
3. Press **[F10]** to get a listing of all fields in the JOBS database file.
4. Move the selection cursor to JOB_DESCR and press **[Enter]**.

    The third field name now appears in the Contents entry area. See Figure 6-18.

Figure 6-18

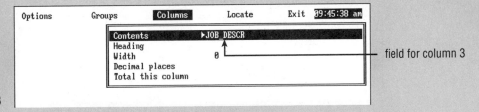

5. Press **[Enter]** to accept this entry. The triangle disappears.

Now enter the heading for the JOB_DESCR field.

To enter the column heading:

1. Move the selection cursor to the *Heading* option and press **[Enter]**. A triangle appears in the Heading entry area, and the heading window also appears.
2. In the window type **DESCRIPTION** and press **[Enter]**.

    In Esther's report layout sheet (Figure 6-1), you can see that next you should enter a blank line followed by a line of hyphens. Let's intentionally omit these two lines from the heading so later you can learn how to modify the report format.
3. Press **[Ctrl][End]** to return to the column options screen.

    Notice that the Report Format box shows a one-line heading for the third column and a field width of 25 characters. See Figure 6-19 on the next page.

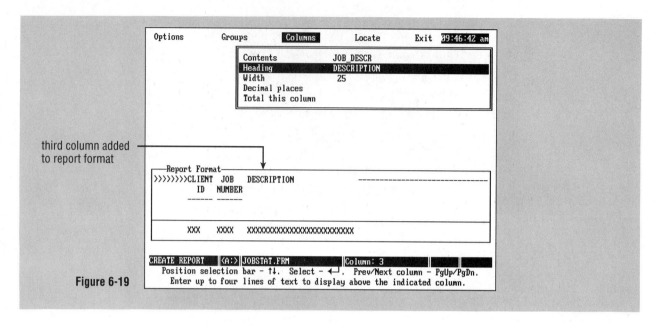

third column added
to report format

Figure 6-19

Now move on to the last column, quote.

To enter the fourth column:

❶ Press **[PgDn]**. A blank column form appears.

Now select the *Contents* option.

❷ With the *Contents* option highlighted, press **[Enter]**.

Now enter the field name.

❸ Type **quote** and press **[Enter]**.

Now enter the column heading.

❹ Move the selection cursor to *Heading* and press **[Enter]**.

❺ Type **QUOTE** and press **[Enter]**.

❻ Press **[Enter]** to insert a blank line.

❼ Type **-----** and press **[Enter]**. You have completed the heading.

❽ Press **[Ctrl][End]** to return to the *Heading* option. See Figure 6-20.

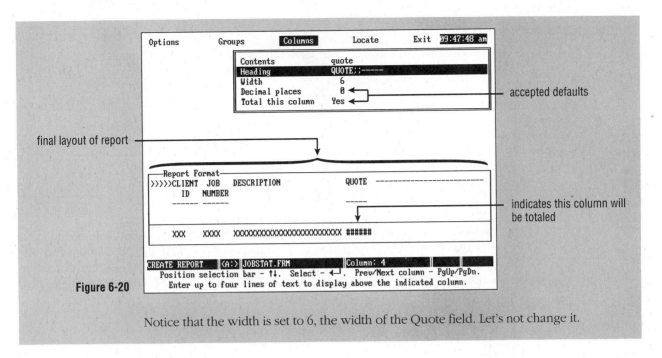

final layout of report

accepted defaults

indicates this column will be totaled

Figure 6-20

Notice that the width is set to 6, the width of the Quote field. Let's not change it.

Because QUOTE is a numeric field, you must define the last two options of the *Columns* option, *Decimal places* and *Total this column*. You defined a specific number of decimal places for this field when you first created the JOBS file in Tutorial 2, so dBASE automatically sets the number of decimal places equal to that number. You can change the number of decimal places by pressing [Enter] and typing a new number. In this case, zero decimal places is acceptable.

You also have the option to *Total this column*; the default is yes. If you do not want to total this column, you must change the answer to no. Esther's layout sheet indicates that you do want to total this column, so you can accept the default. You have now completed the definition of the fourth column.

Let's review the Report Format box in Figure 6-20. The upper portion displays the margins, column headings, and remaining positions. In the lower portion of the Report Format box the location of each field is displayed. The row of *X*s indicates where client ID, job number, and description fields will appear. The symbol # appearing in the QUOTE column indicates that that column will be totaled. If you weren't going to total this column, the symbol 9 would appear, indicating no totals for this numeric column. For now, let's ignore the missing underline for the Description column. If you need to make corrections, use [PgUp] to move to any column and enter your changes.

You are now ready to save the report format file.

To save the report format file:

❶ Press [→] to move the selection cursor to the *Exit* option on the menu bar. You have two options: *Save* and *Abandon*. See Figure 6-21.

Options	Groups	Columns	Locate	Exit 09:48:20 am

Save
Abandon ◄──────── choose this option

Figure 6-21

❷ With the *Save* option highlighted, press **[Enter]**. You are returned to the dot prompt.

Remember that when you began to create this report you named this file JOBSTAT. You have just saved the report definition to a file named JOBSTAT.FRM; dBASE automatically assigned the extension FRM to the file stored on your data diskette. Figure 6-22 illustrates the contents of your data diskette. In addition to DBF and NDX files, your data diskette now contains FRM files, which are report format files.

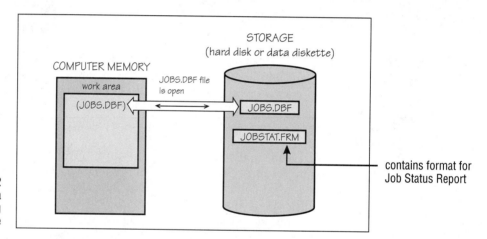

Figure 6-22
Contents of data
diskette after saving
report format file

To leave the *Columns* option without saving the report format file, select the *Abandon* option from the Exit menu. dBASE will ask if you are sure you do not want to save the report format file. If you answer yes, you will be returned to the Assistant screen or dot prompt mode and dBASE will not save your report format file.

In this case, you have saved the report format file and are ready to learn how to output the report.

Viewing a Report

You used the CREATE REPORT command to develop the report format file, which defines the Job Status Report. To actually print or display the report, you must use the REPORT FORM command. The syntax of the REPORT FORM command is

REPORT FORM *reportname*   FOR *condition*   TO PRINT

When you execute the REPORT FORM command, the records from the open database file merge with the report format file to generate a report that is sent to the printer or the screen. The REPORT FORM command displays all records in the database unless you include the FOR clause. If you include the FOR clause, then only the records that meet the specified condition are included in your report.

In this case, Esther wants only those jobs that have been completed to appear in the report. Esther is anxious to see the report. Let's view it.

To view the report:

❶ At the dot prompt type **report form jobstat for status = 'C'** and press **[Enter]**. Be sure you enter the status code as uppercase C.

The report appears only on the screen because you did not include TO PRINT in the command. When you executed the command, dBASE accessed the report format file JOBSTAT.FRM from your data diskette, merged it with the data in the open database file, JOBS, for those records that met the condition "status is complete," and then displayed the report. See Figure 6-23.

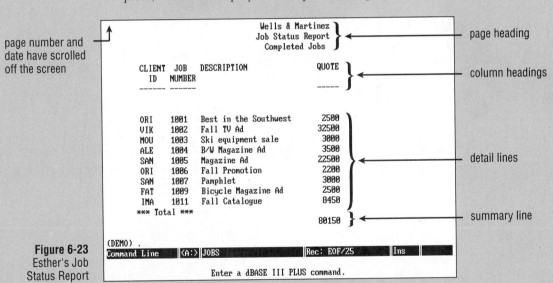

page number and date have scrolled off the screen

page heading

column headings

detail lines

summary line

Figure 6-23
Esther's Job
Status Report

Notice that the page number and the date at the top of the report scrolled off the screen. The page title followed by the column headings and then the detail lines appear next. At the end of the report is the summary line.

Esther is not completely satisfied with the appearance of the report. First, she notices that the page title is not centered; it's too far to the right. Second, the underline for the Description column is missing. Third, the jobs are not ordered by client, as she would like. Before she gives the report to Nancy, Esther decides to modify the report to make it look more professional. Figure 6-24 on the next page identifies the changes Esther plans to make.

needs to be centered

add missing
underline

order by client

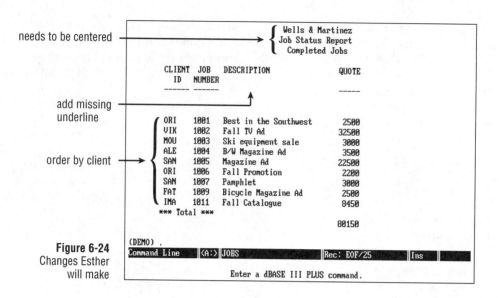

Figure 6-24
Changes Esther
will make

Modifying a Report

You can modify a report format file by executing the MODIFY REPORT command. The syntax for this command is

MODIFY REPORT *reportname*

When you execute the MODIFY REPORT command, dBASE retrieves the specified report format file and makes the definition of the report available via the same screen you used when you created the report form.

To modify the report:

❶ At the dot prompt type **modify report jobstat** and press **[Enter]**. The report format screen appears. See Figure 6-25.

first eight characters
of title page

current page width

current settings for page
characteristics

dBASE command

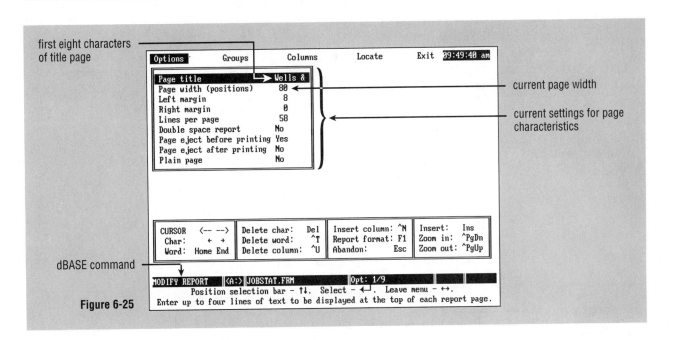

Figure 6-25

The first change Esther wants to make is to center the page title. You can see from the settings that the dBASE report generator centers a page title based on a default page width of 80 positions. Esther's report, however, required a width of approximately 55 positions. Thus, she must change the page width to 55 to center the page title. Let's try it.

To change the page width:

❶ Move the selection cursor to the *Page width* option and press **[Enter]**. A triangle indicates that the Page width entry area is open.

Now enter the page width.

❷ Type **55** and press **[Enter]**. You have changed the page width to 55. See Figure 6-26.

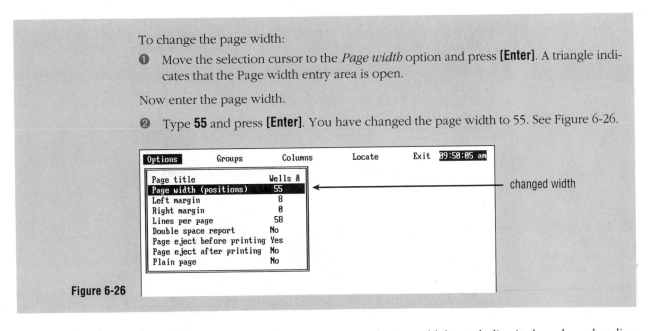

changed width

Figure 6-26

The second change Esther wants to make is to add the underline in the column heading for description. First, you must retrieve the Description column. If you can recall the field name for the column, you can quickly access individual column definitions by using the *Locate* option from the menu bar.

To retrieve the column definition:

❶ Move the selection cursor to the *Locate* option on the menu bar. A list of field names for the columns in the report appears in a pull-down menu. See Figure 6-27.

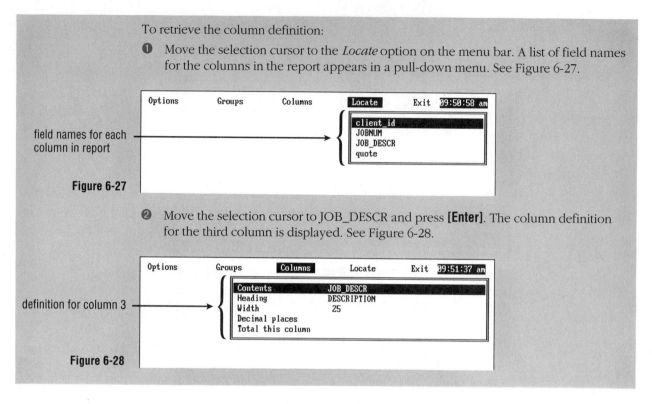

field names for each
column in report

Figure 6-27

❷ Move the selection cursor to JOB_DESCR and press **[Enter]**. The column definition for the third column is displayed. See Figure 6-28.

definition for column 3

Figure 6-28

Now adjust the heading for the third column.

To adjust the heading:

❶ Move the selection cursor to the Heading line and press **[Enter]**. A triangle appears, and the heading window also appears with the current heading text on the screen. See Figure 6-29.

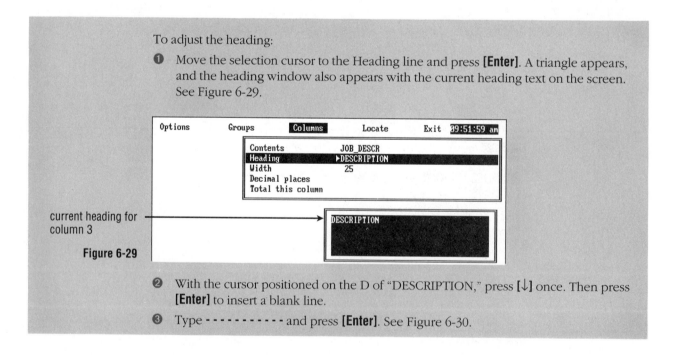

current heading for
column 3

Figure 6-29

❷ With the cursor positioned on the D of "DESCRIPTION," press **[↓]** once. Then press **[Enter]** to insert a blank line.

❸ Type - - - - - - - - - - - and press **[Enter]**. See Figure 6-30.

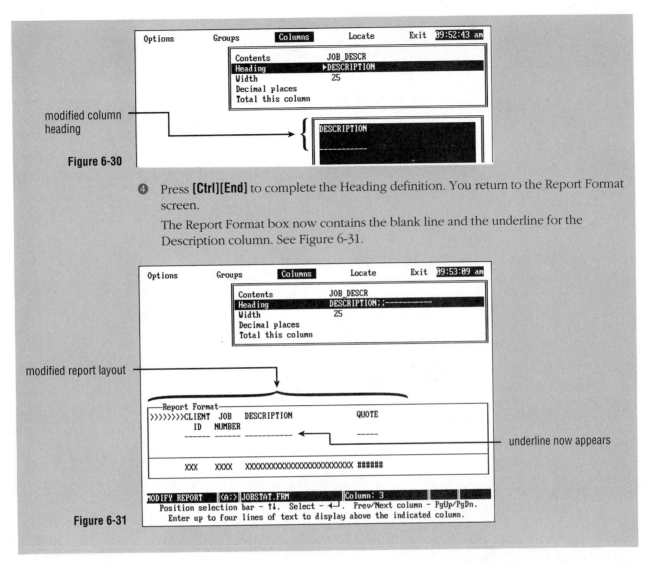

modified column heading

Figure 6-30

④ Press **[Ctrl][End]** to complete the Heading definition. You return to the Report Format screen.

The Report Format box now contains the blank line and the underline for the Description column. See Figure 6-31.

modified report layout

underline now appears

Figure 6-31

Now that you have modified the report format file, you must save it.

To save the report format file:

① Move the selection cursor to the *Exit* option on the menu bar.

② With the *Save* option highlighted, press **[Enter]** to return to the dot prompt. You have "written over" the report format file on your data diskette, and the original version is no longer available.

Before printing the report, Esther still needs to order the data alphabetically by client ID. How can she do this? Remember that indexes can be used to control the order in which records are processed. In Tutorial 5 Esther created the index file CLIENT.NDX, which was associated with the JOBS database file. She could, therefore, open the index file CLIENT.NDX and output the records by client ID. Let's do that now.

To open the index file along with the JOBS file:

❶ At the dot prompt type **use jobs index client** and press **[Enter]**.

You have now opened the index file CLIENT, which allows you to display the report in alphabetical order.

Let's view the report.

To view the report:

❶ At the dot prompt type **report form jobstat for status = 'C'** and press **[Enter]**. See Figure 6-32.

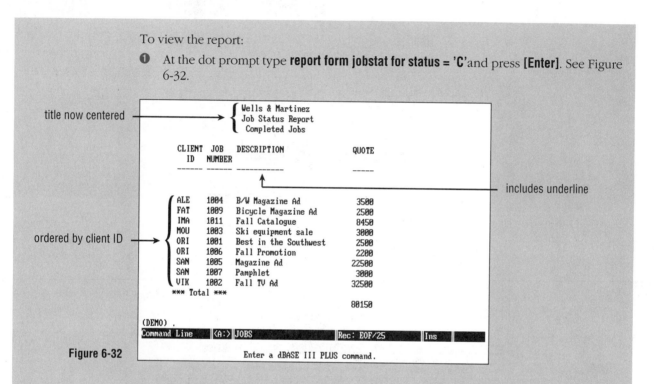

title now centered

includes underline

ordered by client ID

Figure 6-32

```
                    Wells & Martinez
                    Job Status Report
                    Completed Jobs

        CLIENT  JOB   DESCRIPTION              QUOTE
          ID   NUMBER
        ------ ------ -----------              -----

         ALE   1004   B/W Magazine Ad          3500
         FAT   1009   Bicycle Magazine Ad      2500
         IMA   1011   Fall Catalogue           8450
         MOU   1003   Ski equipment sale       3000
         ORI   1001   Best in the Southwest    2500
         ORI   1006   Fall Promotion           2200
         SAN   1005   Magazine Ad              22500
         SAN   1007   Pamphlet                 3000
         VIK   1002   Fall TV Ad               32500
       *** Total ***

                                              80150

    (DEMO) .
    Command Line    <A:> JOBS          Rec: EOF/25        Ins
                        Enter a dBASE III PLUS command.
```

This is the same command that produced the report in Figure 6-23 except that the report format file has been modified and the index file CLIENT is open with the database file JOBS.

The appearance of the report has improved. The page title is centered, and the column heading for description is underlined. Also the records have been reordered by client, which does not improve the appearance but does make the report easier for Nancy to use.

Esther is now ready to print a hard copy. Instead of typing the command, she recalls the last command from the history buffer.

To obtain the previous command from the history buffer:

❶ At the dot prompt press **[↑]**. The previous command appears at the dot prompt. See Figure 6-33.

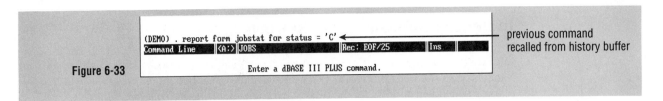

Figure 6-33

previous command
recalled from history buffer

Now let's modify this command so the output goes to the printer.

To modify the command at the dot prompt:

❶ Press [→] to move to the end of the command.

Now enter your revision.

❷ Type **to print**. The revised command is complete. See Figure 6-34.

added to command

```
(DEMO) . report form jobstat for status = 'C' to print
Command Line    |<A:>||JOBS                    |Rec: EOF/25     ||Ins ||
                   Enter a dBASE III PLUS command.
```

Figure 6-34

❸ Make sure your printer is ready.

❹ Press **[Enter]**, and the report prints. See Figure 6-35.

```
Page No.       1
10/18/91
                    Wells & Martinez
                    Job Status Report
                     Completed Jobs

CLIENT  JOB    DESCRIPTION              QUOTE
  ID    NUMBER
------  ------ -----------              -----


ALE     1004   B/W Magazine Ad           3500
FAT     1009   Bicycle Magazine Ad       2500
IMA     1011   Fall Catalogue            8450
MOU     1003   Ski equipment sale        3000
ORI     1001   Best in the Southwest     2500
ORI     1006   Fall Promotion            2200
SAN     1005   Magazine Ad              22500
SAN     1007   Pamphlet                  3000
VIK     1002   Fall TV Ad               32500
*** Total ***
                                        80150
```

Figure 6-35
The printed Job
Status Report

Esther gives the printed report to Nancy.

Including Subtotals in a Report

Later that day Esther finds the Job Status Report back on her desk with a brief note from Nancy saying she likes the report but wants to make a few changes. Nancy would like the report to include a subtotal of the quotes for each client.

To create a report with subtotals, you total one or more numeric fields for a group of records that have a common value in a specified field. For example, Nancy wants to total the quotes for all records that have the same client ID. To develop a report with subtotals, you need to process the records in sequence according to the field on which the records will be grouped. The field that determines how the records are grouped is called the **control field**. In this case, client ID is the control field. This means that to subtotal by client, all the job records for ALE (Alexander Insurance), for example, will be processed before any records for CEL (Celebrity Caterers).

To calculate a subtotal for the first group of records, those with the client ID ALE, dBASE adds together the quotes of all ALE records. The sum is the subtotal for the group ALE. A subtotal is displayed or printed when the value in the control field changes. In other words, when the client ID changes from ALE to CEL, dBASE displays or prints a subtotal for all previous records that have the client ID value ALE. The term **control break** is used to describe when the value in the control field changes. When a control break occurs, a subtotal for the group of records just processed is displayed. This type of report, one that groups records by control field and includes subtotals, is called a **control break report**.

Modifying the Report

In response to Nancy's request, Esther prepares another report layout sheet to help her plan the revised report (Figure 6-36). In addition to including subtotals in the revised Job Status Report, she also decides to remove the client ID column from the report. Esther realizes that this column is no longer necessary because dBASE will automatically include the client ID as a heading before each group of clients.

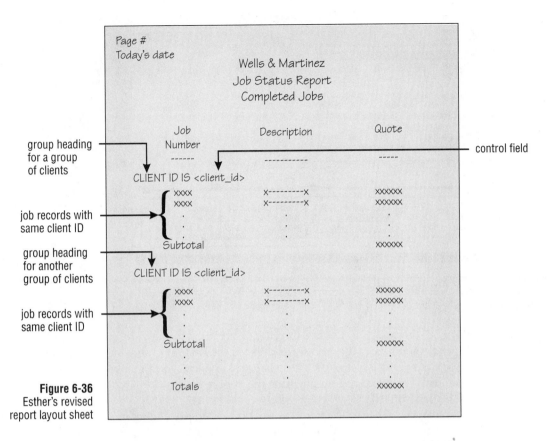

Figure 6-36
Esther's revised
report layout sheet

Esther is now ready to modify the current report format file.

To modify the report format file JOBSTAT.FRM:

❶ At the dot prompt type **modify report jobstat** and press **[Enter]**. The Report Format
screen appears. See Figure 6-37 on the next page.

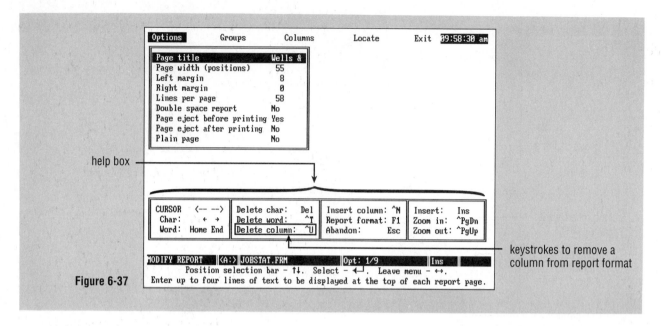

Figure 6-37

First, Esther wants to remove the client ID column from the report format. How do you remove a column from a report format file? At the bottom of the Report Format screen is a help box of editing keystrokes. These keystrokes allow you to make changes to the report format file. To delete a column from the report format, you would use the keystroke combination [Ctrl][U].

To remove the client ID column from the report format, Esther must retrieve the definition of the client ID column. Remember, you can quickly access individual column definitions from a report format file by using the *Locate* option from the menu bar. Let's try it.

To retrieve the column definition:

❶ Move the selection cursor to the *Locate* option. A list of field names for each column of the report appears in a pull-down menu.

❷ Select CLIENT_ID and press **[Enter]**. The column definition for the first column appears. Notice that the client ID appears as the first column in the Report Format box at the bottom of the screen. See Figure 6-38.

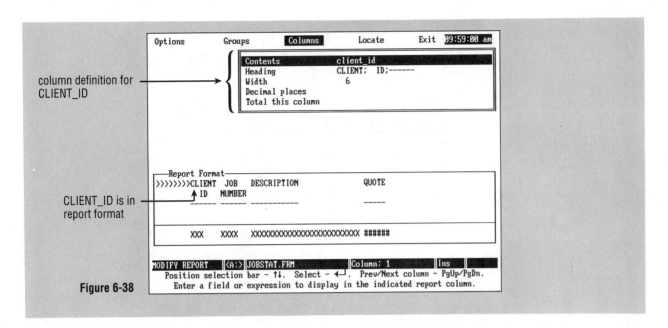

column definition for CLIENT_ID

CLIENT_ID is in report format

Figure 6-38

Now remove the client ID column from the report.

To remove a column from the report format:

❶ Press **[Ctrl][U]**. Look at the Report Format box — the client ID column is no longer a part of the report format. See Figure 6-39.

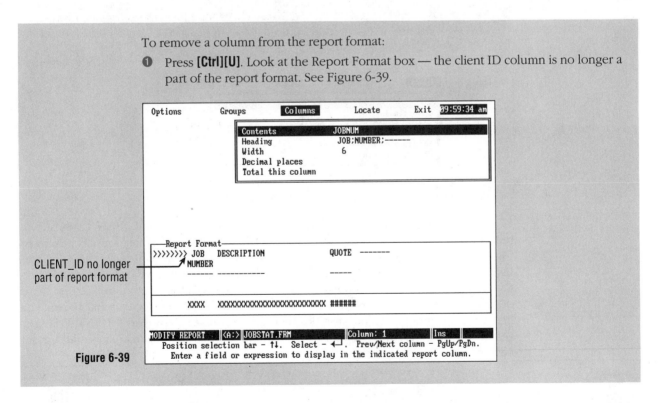

CLIENT_ID no longer part of report format

Figure 6-39

Esther is ready to modify the report format so the records in the report are grouped by client ID. The Groups menu in the Report Format screen allows you to group records by a particular field (a control field) in the database file and to accumulate subtotals for groups of records.

To group records in a report format:

❶ Move the selection cursor to the *Groups* option on the menu bar. A pull-down menu appears. See Figure 6-40.

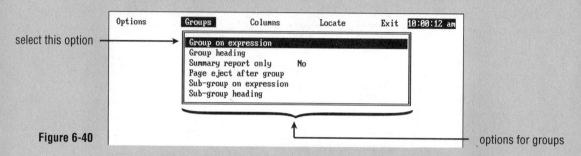

select this option ⟶

Figure 6-40

options for groups

To specify the field on which the report format file will group records, you use the option *Group on expression*.

❷ With the option *Group on expression* highlighted, press **[Enter]**. A triangle appears, indicating that the entry area is open.

Now enter the name of the field on which to group the records. The control field is CLIENT_ID.

❸ Type **client_id** and press **[Enter]**. See Figure 6-41. This closes the entry area for the *Group on expression* option. Alternatively you can press [F10] to get a list of fields and then select the field you want to use to group the records.

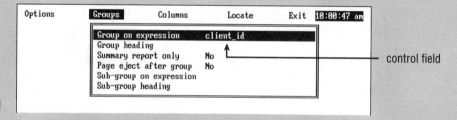

control field

Figure 6-41

Now Esther is ready to add a group heading to the report format. dBASE automatically precedes each group of records with the value of the control field for that group. For example, dBASE will place ALE on a separate line before the group of records for the Alexander Insurance Company (ALE), CEL on a separate line before the group of records for Celebrity Caterers (CEL), and so on. To place a label before the value of the control field to better describe the group of records, you use the *Group heading* option. For example, to make the line before the group of records for Alexander Insurance Company read "CLIENT ID is ALE," you would add a group heading to the definition of the report format. Let's add a group heading now.

To add a group heading:

❶ Move the selection cursor to the option *Group heading* and press **[Enter]**. A triangle indicates that the entry area is open.

Now enter the group heading.

❷ Type **CLIENT ID =** and press **[Enter]**. This closes the entry area for the *Group heading* option. See Figure 6-42.

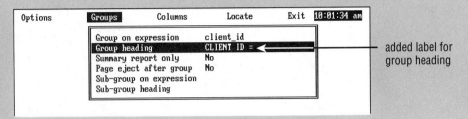

Figure 6-42

Several other options are available in the Groups menu. For example, if you wanted to prepare a summary report containing only subtotals for each group, you could answer *yes* to the option *Summary report only*. If you wanted to print each group on a separate page, you could answer *yes* to the option *Page eject after group*. But in this case let's leave the remaining options at their default values.

Now that you have completed the modifications of the report format file, you must save it.

To save the report format file:

❶ Move the selection cursor to *Exit* on the menu bar.

❷ With the *Save* option highlighted, press **[Enter]**. You have written over the report format file on your data diskette, and your previous version is no longer available.

Printing the Report

When printing or viewing a control break report, you must order the database file by the control field for the records to be grouped. Therefore, before Esther prints the report, she must open an index file whose indexing field is the same as the field on which the report will be grouped. When Esther opened the JOB file, she also opened the CLIENT index file, so she is ready to print the modified report.

Instead of retyping the command, Esther recalls the REPORT FORM command from the history buffer.

To obtain the command from the history buffer:

❶ At the dot prompt press **[↑]** until the REPORT FORM command appears. See Figure 6-43 on the next page.

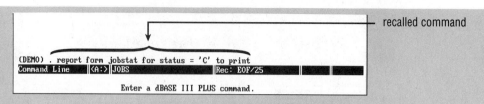

recalled command

Figure 6-43

```
(DEMO) . report form jobstat for status = 'C' to print
Command Line    <A:> JOBS              Rec: EOF/25
                Enter a dBASE III PLUS command.
```

Now execute the command.

❷ Press **[Enter]** to direct the final version of the report to the printer. See Figure 6-44.

```
Page No.      1
10/18/91
                    Wells & Martinez
                    Job Status Report
                    Completed Jobs


   JOB    DESCRIPTION              QUOTE
 NUMBER
 ------  -----------              -----


** CLIENT ID = ALE
  1004   B/W Magazine Ad           3500
** Subtotal **
                                   3500


** CLIENT ID = FAT
  1009   Bicycle Magazine Ad       2500
** Subtotal **
                                   2500


** CLIENT ID = IMA
  1011   Fall Catalogue            8450
** Subtotal **
                                   8450


** CLIENT ID = MOU
  1003   Ski equipment sale        3000
** Subtotal **
                                   3000


** CLIENT ID = ORI
  1001   Best in the Southwest     2500
  1006   Fall Promotion            2200
** Subtotal **
                                   4700


** CLIENT ID = SAN
  1005   Magazine Ad              22500
  1007   Pamphlet                  3000
** Subtotal **
                                  25500


** CLIENT ID = VIK
  1002   Fall TV Ad               32500
** Subtotal **
                                  32500

*** Total ***

                                  80150
```

Figure 6-44
Final version of
W&M Job Status
Report

Esther looks over the report and sees that the records are printed in groups based on the values in the control field client ID. She has met Nancy's requirements, so she delivers the report.

Creating, Modifying, and Viewing Reports in Assistant Mode

So far in this tutorial you have used dot prompt mode to create, modify, and output reports. You also could have accomplished these same tasks in Assistant mode.

Creating a Report Format File in Assistant Mode

Let's first create a report format file.

To create a report format file:

❶ Switch from dot prompt mode to Assistant mode by pressing **[F2]** or typing **assist**. Remember to open the database file before you create the report format file.

❷ Move the selection cursor to the *Create* option on the menu bar.

❸ Highlight the *Report* option and press **[Enter]**. A pull-down menu listing the disk drive options appears.

❹ Highlight the drive where you want to store the report format file and press **[Enter]**.

A prompt appears asking you to enter a filename for the report format file. See Figure 6-45.

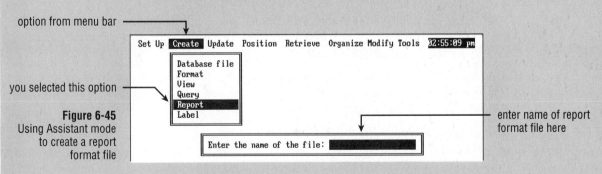

option from menu bar

you selected this option

Figure 6-45
Using Assistant mode to create a report format file

Set Up **Create** Update Position Retrieve Organize Modify Tools `02:55:09 pm`

Database file
Format
View
Query
Report
Label

Enter the name of the file:

enter name of report format file here

❺ Type **practice** and press **[Enter]**. The Report Format screen appears. (This is the same screen you have been using throughout this tutorial.)

Because you are familiar with the Report Format screen, we will not develop another report. Leave this screen without saving the report format file.

To leave the Report Format screen without saving the file:

❶ Press **[→]** to move the selection cursor to the *Exit* option on the menu bar.

❷ Highlight the *Abandon* option and press **[Enter]**.

❸ Type **y** to verify that you want to leave without saving the file. You return to the Assistant screen.

Modifying a Report Format File in Assistant Mode

In Assistant mode you can use the *Modify menu* option to change a report format file.

To modify a report format file in Assistant mode:

❶ Move the selection cursor to the *Modify* option on the menu bar.

❷ Highlight the *Report* option and press **[Enter]**. A pull-down menu listing the disk drive options appears.

❸ Select the drive where your report format files are stored.

A list of stored report format files appears. See Figure 6-46.

report format files on
your data diskette

option from menu bar

```
Set Up  Create │Update  Position  Retrieve  Organize│Modify│Tools  02:56:33 pm

                      ┌─────────────┐ ┌──────────────┐
                      │ STATUS1.FRM │ │Database file │
                      │ STATUS2.FRM │ │Format        │
                      │ JOBSTAT.FRM │ │View          │
                      └─────────────┘ │Query         │
                                      │Report        │ ◄──── you selected this option
                                      │Label         │
                                      └──────────────┘
```

Figure 6-46
Using Assistant mode
to modify a report
format file

❹ Highlight JOBSTAT.FRM and press **[Enter]**. The Report Format screen containing the definition of the Job Status Report appears. This is the same Report Format screen you have used throughout this tutorial.

Because you have modified the Job Status Report in this tutorial, we will not modify the report again. You can leave the Report Format screen without modifying the report format file you just retrieved.

❺ Select *Abandon* from the the *Exit* menu option.

Printing or Viewing Reports in Assistant Mode

To print or display a report in Assistant mode, you must use the *Retrieve* menu option.

To view a report in Assistant mode:

❶ Move the selection cursor to the *Retrieve* option on the menu bar.

❷ Highlight the *Report* option and press **[Enter]**. A pull-down menu listing the disk drive options appears.

③ Select the drive where your report format files are stored.

A list of stored report format files appears. See Figure 6-47.

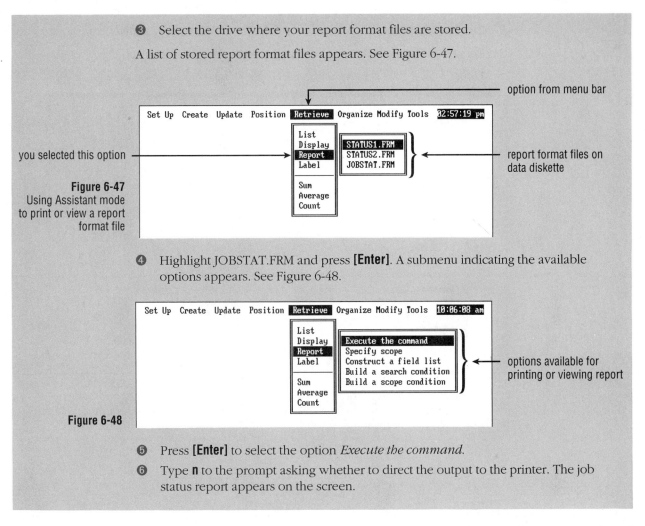

you selected this option ——

Figure 6-47
Using Assistant mode
to print or view a report
format file

Figure 6-48

④ Highlight JOBSTAT.FRM and press **[Enter]**. A submenu indicating the available options appears. See Figure 6-48.

⑤ Press **[Enter]** to select the option *Execute the command.*

⑥ Type **n** to the prompt asking whether to direct the output to the printer. The job status report appears on the screen.

You have now created, viewed, and modified a report using both dot prompt mode and Assistant mode.

■   ■   ■

Exercises

1. If you see the file extension FRM on your data diskette, what do you know about this file?

2. What command do you use to develop a report form?

3. What command do you use to change a report form?

4. What command do you use to display a report?

5. What command do you use to print a report?

6. What is meant by the term *control break report?*

7. To include subtotals in a report, you would use what options from the Create Report screen?

8. To include subtotals in a report, how must your data be organized?

9. Figure 6-49 is an inventory report created with the dBASE report generator.

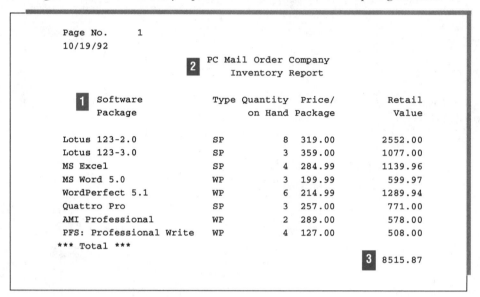

```
Page No.      1
10/19/92
                              PC Mail Order Company
                         2       Inventory Report

          1  Software          Type Quantity  Price/        Retail
             Package                on Hand  Package        Value

          Lotus 123-2.0          SP         8  319.00       2552.00
          Lotus 123-3.0          SP         3  359.00       1077.00
          MS Excel               SP         4  284.99       1139.96
          MS Word 5.0            WP         3  199.99        599.97
          WordPerfect 5.1        WP         6  214.99       1289.94
          Quattro Pro            SP         3  257.00        771.00
          AMI Professional       WP         2  289.00        578.00
          PFS: Professional Write WP        4  127.00        508.00
          *** Total ***
                                                     3  8515.87
```

Figure 6-49

a. What option from the report format screen produced the item numbered 1?
b. What option from the report format screen produced the item numbered 2?
c. What option from the report format screen produced the item numbered 3?

10. Figure 6-50 is a revised inventory report also created with the dBASE report generator.

```
        Page No.      1
        10/19/92
                               PC Mail Order Company
                                 Inventory Report

                 Software           Quantity  Price/           Retail
                 Package            on Hand  Package            Value

     1  ** Software Category: SP
         Lotus 123-2.0                  8    319.00            2552.00
         Lotus 123-3.0                  3    359.00            1077.00
         MS Excel                       4    284.99            1139.96
         Quattro Pro                    3    257.00             771.00
         ** Subtotal **

                                                               5539.96


         ** Software Category: WP
         MS Word 5.0                    3    199.99             599.97
         WordPerfect 5.1                6    214.99            1289.94
         AMI Professional               2    289.00             578.00
         PFS: Professional Write        4    127.00             508.00
         ** Subtotal **

                                                               2975.91

         *** Total ***

                                                               8515.87
```

Figure 6-50

a. What option from the report format screen produced the item numbered 1?
b. Notice the column Retail Value has a subtotal but that the column Price/Package does not. What option from the report format screen was used to subtotal the retail value but not the price/package?

Tutorial Assignments

Use the CLIENT file to complete Assignments 1 and 2.

1. Use the report layout sheet shown in Figure 6-51 and the CLIENT database file to create a report format file. Name the report format file CLREPT.

```
Page #
Date
                    Wells & Martinez
                      Client List

    Client Name      Contact Person      Phone

    X-----------X    X------------X      X------X
    X-----------X    X------------X      X------X

         .                .                .
         .                .                .
         .                .                .
```

Figure 6-51

2. Use the report format file CLREPT and print W&M's clients in alphabetical order. If you did not create the index file CLNAMEX.NDX in the Tutorial Assignments for Tutorial 5, create it now. The indexing field is CLIENT_NAM.

Open JOBS.DBF and use the report format file STATUS1.FRM on your data diskette to answer Assignments 3 through 6.

3. Use STATUS1.FRM and the JOBS database file to print a report for each completed job having a quote under $10,000.

4. Modify STATUS1 to include a fifth column for the field STATUS. Also remove the line "Completed Jobs" from the page heading.

5. Print the revised report in alphabetical order by client ID for all jobs. Use the index file CLIENT.NDX.

6. Print the revised report in alphabetical order by client ID for all jobs having a quote between $5,000 and $15,000.

Open JOBS.DBF and CLIENT.NDX and use the report format file STATUS2.FRM on your data diskette to answer Assignments 7 through 10.

7. Use STATUS2.FRM to print a report by client for all completed jobs having a quote greater than or equal to $2,000.

8. Modify STATUS2.FRM to include a fourth column with the heading DUE DATE. Also remove the line "Completed Jobs" from the page heading.

9. Print the revised report for all jobs.

10. Print the revised report for all jobs having a quote between $5,000 and $15,000.

Case Problems

1. Biggs and Hang Investment Company

Do the following:

1. Use the report layout sheet in Figure 6-52 and the JAPAN database file to create the report format file JPRPT1.

```
Page #
Date
                        Japanese Companies
                        Financial Data - 1990

Company        Ind       Sales        Profits        Assets

X------X        X        XXXXXX       XXXXXX         XXXXXX
X------X        X        XXXXXX       XXXXXX         XXXXXX

                          .            .              .
                          .            .              .
                          .            .              .
Total                    XXXXXX       XXXXXX         XXXXXX
```

Figure 6-52

Use the report format file JPRPT1 to complete Assignments 2 through 4.

2. Print JPRPT1 in alphabetical order by company. Use the index file JPINDX1.NDX.

3. Print JPRPT1 with the companies ordered by industry. Create an index file named JPINDX3.NDX.

4. Print JPRPT1 for companies with profits above 100,000 Yen ordered by industry.

5. Use the report layout sheet shown in Figure 6-53 to modify JPRPT1.

```
Page #
Date
                      Japanese Companies
                      Financial Data - 1990

Company      Sales          Profits        Assets

Industry - <IND>
X------X     XXXXXX         XXXXXX         XXXXXX
X------X     XXXXXX         XXXXXX         XXXXXX

   .            .              .              .
   .            .              .              .
   .            .              .              .
Subtotal     XXXXXX         XXXXXX         XXXXXX
Industry - <IND>
X------X     XXXXXX         XXXXXX         XXXXXX
X------X     XXXXXX         XXXXXX         XXXXXX

   .            .              .              .
   .            .              .              .
   .            .              .              .
Subtotal     XXXXXX         XXXXXX         XXXXXX
Total        XXXXXX         XXXXXX         XXXXXX
```

Figure 6-53

6. Use the modified JPRPT1 to print the companies with subtotals by industry.

7. Use the report layout sheet in Figure 6-54 and the JAPAN database file to create the report format file JPRPT2.

```
Page #

Date

                    Japanese Companies
                    Financial Data - 1990

Company          Ind        High           Low
Name                        Price          Price
_____
X------X          X        XXXXXX         XXXXX

X------X          X        XXXXXX         XXXXX

    .             .           .              .
    .             .           .              .
    .             .           .              .
```

Figure 6-54

8. Print JPRPT2 for all companies in alphabetical order.

9. Print JPRPT2 for all companies whose high price is at least one-and-one-half times their low price, and arrange the companies in alphabetical order.

2. Medi-Source Inc.

Do the following:

For Assignments 1, 2, and 3, open the ACCTREC database file and the MEDINDX1.NDX index file.

1. Use the ACCTREC database file and the report layout in Figure 6-55 to prepare a report format file named MEDRPT1.

```
Page #

Date

                  Medi-Source Inc.
                  Outstanding Balances

Customer        Type        State       Balance
Name                                    Owed
_____
X--------X       X          XX         XXXXX.XX

X--------X       X          XX         XXXXX.XX

    .            .           .              .
    .            .           .              .
    .            .           .              .

Total                                  XXXXX.XX
```

Figure 6-55

Use the MEDRPT1 report format file to complete Assignments 2 and 3.

2. Print the outstanding balances report for all customers with the customers in alphabetical order. Use the index file MEDINDX1.NDX.

3. Print the outstanding balances report for only those customers that have outstanding balances over $15,000. Arrange the customers in alphabetical order.

4. Use the report layout sheet in Figure 6-56 and the ACCTREC database file to create a report format file named MEDRPT2. The control field is TYPE (type of business).

Figure 6-56

```
Page #
Date
                        Medi-Source Inc.
                      Outstanding Balances
                       By Type of Business
Customer              State        Balance
Name                               Owed
_____
Type of business <TYPE>

X--------X             XX           XXXXX.XX
X--------X             XX           XXXXX.XX

        .              .                .
        .              .                .
        .              .                .

Subtotal                            XXXXX.XX
Type of business <TYPE>

X--------X             XX           XXXXX.XX
X--------X             XX           XXXXX.XX

        .              .                .
        .              .                .
        .              .                .

Subtotal                            XXXXX.XX
Total                               XXXXX.XX
```

5. Using TYPE as the indexing field, create the index file MEDINDX3.

Use the MEDRPT2 report format file to complete Assignments 6, 7, and 8.

6. Print MEDRPT2 for all customers.

7. Print MEDRPT2 for customers who are not in the hospital industry (industry code = H).

8. Print MEDRPT2 for customers whose outstanding balance is over $5,000.

3. Appleton and Drake Supply Company

Do the following:

1. Use the report layout sheet in Figure 6-57 and the EMPLOYEE database file to create the report format file EMPRPT1.

```
Page #
Date

                    Appleton & Drake
                    Employee Report

Last Name        Dept        Sex        Salary

X---------X      XXX          X          XXXXX

X---------X      XXX          X          XXXXX

        .          .          .            .
        .          .          .            .
        .          .          .            .

Total                                    XXXXX
```

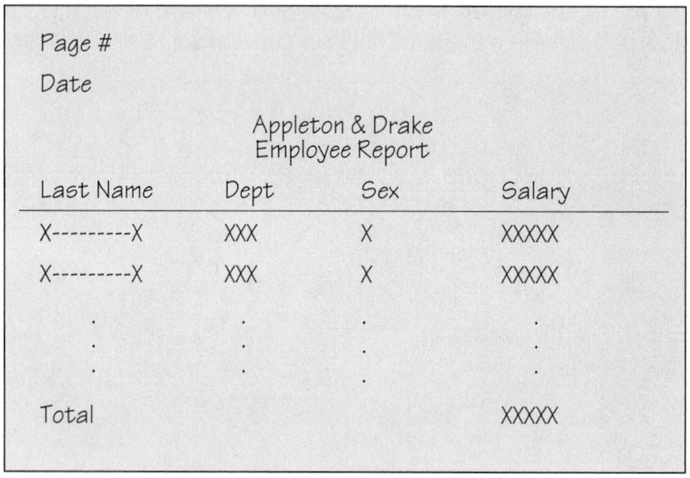

Figure 6-57

Use the report format file EMPRPT1 to complete Assignments 2 through 5.

2. Print an alphabetized list of all employees. To do this you need to create an index file named EMPINDX3.NDX, using LNAME as the indexing field.

3. Print a list of employees in alphabetical order for employees in the Corporate department (department code = COR).

4   Modify EMPRPT1 to include a third page-heading line, Salary Summary.

5. Print the modified EMPRPT1 report for all employees earning under $30,000. Order the data by department. To do this you need to create an index file named EMPINDX4.NDX, using DEPT as the indexing field.

6. Use the report layout sheet in Figure 6-58 and the EMPLOYEE database file to create the report format file EMPRPT2. The control field is DEPT.

```
Page #
Date
                      Appleton & Drake
                      Employee Report
                       By Department
     Last Name              Sex         Salary

     Department <DEPT>

     X---------X             X          XXXXX
     X---------X             X          XXXXX
           .                 .             .
           .                 .             .
           .                 .             .

     Subtotal                           XXXXX

     Department <DEPT>

     X---------X             X          XXXXX
     X---------X             X          XXXXX

           .                 .             .
           .                 .             .
           .                 .             .

     Subtotal                           XXXXX
     Total                              XXXXX
```

Figure 6-58

Use report format file EMPRPT2 to complete Assignments 7 and 8.

7. Print EMPRPT2 for all employees.

8. Print EMPRPT2 for all employees earning over $35,000.

4. National Basketball Association

Do the following:

1. Use the report layout sheet in Figure 6-59 on the next page and the NBA database file to create the report format file NBARPT1.

```
Page #
Date
                              NBA Salary Report
    Last Name        First Name        Team          Pos        Salary
    X--------X       X---------X        XXX           X          XXXXXXXX
    X--------X       X---------X        XXX           X          XXXXXXXX
        .                .               .             .              .
        .                .               .             .              .
        .                .               .             .              .
    Total                                                        XXXXXXXX
```

Figure 6-59

Use the report format file NBARPT1 to complete Assignments 2 and 3.

2. Print an alphabetized list of all players. If you did not create the index file NBAINDX1.NDX in the case problems for Tutorial 5, create it now. The indexing field is LNAME.

3. Print an alphabetized list of all players who play the position of forward (position code is F) or guard (position code is G).

4. Use the report layout sheet in Figure 6-60 and the NBA database file to create the report format file NBARPT2. The control field is TEAM. Create an index file named NBAINDX3.NDX, using TEAM as the indexing field.

```
Page #
Date
                          NBA Salary Report By Team
    Last Name        First Name        Pos              Salary
    Team <teamname>
    X--------X       X---------X        X                XXXXXX
    X--------X       X---------X        X                XXXXXX
        .                .               .                   .
        .                .               .                   .
        .                .               .                   .
    Subtotal                                             XXXXXXX
    Team <teamname>
    X--------X       X---------X        X                XXXXXX
    X--------X       X---------X        X                XXXXXX
        .                .               .                   .
        .                .               .                   .
        .                .               .                   .
    Subtotal                                             XXXXXXX
    Total                                                XXXXXXX
```

Figure 6-60

Use NBARPT2 to complete Assignments 5 and 6.

5. Print a report by team.

6. Print a report by team for players earning over $1 million.

Tutorial 7

Linking Database Files

Case: Wells & Martinez — Linking the JOBS File and the CLIENT File

Esther has just returned from the monthly staff meeting, when Martin comes into her office and asks for help. He tells Esther that he has been teaching himself dBASE so he can query the database himself and not always bother her with requests. However, he has encountered a problem he cannot solve. Martin wants to modify the Due Date Report for jobs in process. He now wants the report to provide all the information about a job and the client in one place. Specifically he wants to get a listing that includes the full name of the client, the due dates and quotes for all the jobs in progress for each client, and the name and phone number of the contact person for each client. He knows that all the information is in the database, but no one file contains all this information. He asks Esther what he should do.

Esther quickly examines the contents of the JOBS file; she points out to Martin that this file contains the jobs' due dates and quotes. She then lists the CLIENT file and notes that the remaining information he wants — client name, contact person, and phone number — are in that file. Esther explains to Martin that he can get the information he wants in one listing by linking the two files.

OBJECTIVES

In this tutorial you will learn to:

■ Open files in separate work areas

■ Move from one work area to another

■ Link two database files

■ Print data from two database files

■ Check the status of your work areas

■ Close all open files

■ Create a view file

■ Use a view file

Introduction to Linking Files

So far in this book you have queried the database and created reports by retrieving data from only one database file at a time. But what if answering a query or creating a report requires data from two or more files? For example, for Esther to display the listing that Martin needs, she must use data from both the CLIENT and the JOBS database files.

A common way to retrieve data from two files is to link them. You can link two database files if the files have a common field. For example, because both the CLIENT and the JOBS files include the field CLIENT_ID, you can link them.

The SELECT Command

You know from earlier tutorials that whenever you are working with a file and you open a second file, dBASE automatically closes the first file. Until now you have opened only one database file at a time, with the USE command. By using the SELECT command and assigning each database file to a separate work area, you can open up to 10 database files at one time. The work areas are numbered 1 through 10 (Figure 7-1). Whenever you opened a database file with the USE command, dBASE placed the database file in a work area. Since you never specified a work area, dBASE automatically placed the database file in work area 1.

COMPUTER MEMORY

work area 1   work area 2   work area 3   work area 4   work area 5

work area 6   work area 7   work area 8   work area 9   work area 10

Figure 7-1
Ten work areas
available in dBASE

What happens when you issue the USE command to open the CLIENT and then the JOBS database files in work area 1? First, when you issue the USE CLIENT command, the CLIENT file is opened in work area 1 (Figure 7-2a).

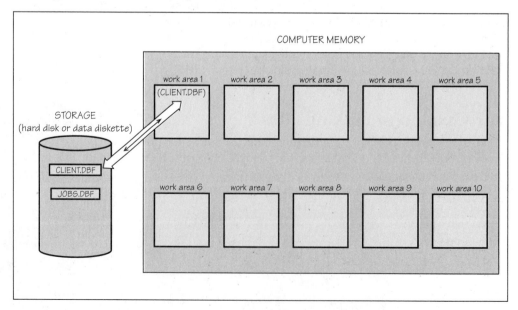

COMPUTER MEMORY

STORAGE
(hard disk or data diskette)

work area 1   work area 2   work area 3   work area 4   work area 5
(CLIENT.DBF)

CLIENT.DBF

JOBS.DBF

work area 6   work area 7   work area 8   work area 9   work area 10

Figure 7-2a
After USE CLIENT
command issued

When you then issue the USE JOBS command, the JOBS file is opened in work area 1, and the CLIENT file is closed (Figure 7-2b). Thus, once you open the JOBS file, you lose access to the CLIENT file.

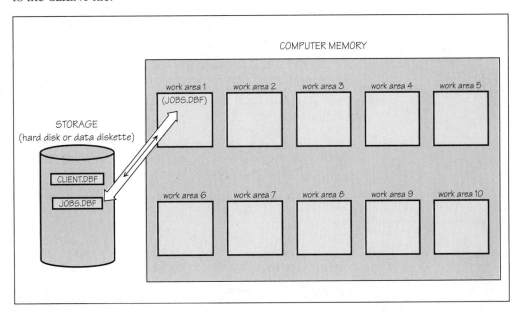

Figure 7-2b
After USE JOBS
command issued

To open a second database file without closing the first database file, you use the USE command but you also switch from one work area to another by using the SELECT command. With the SELECT command you can open each file in a separate work area. The syntax for the SELECT command is

SELECT *work area number*

When you use the SELECT command, dBASE designates the specified work area as the currently selected work area. A file open in the currently selected work area is called the **active file**. All dBASE commands access data from the file in the currently selected work area. Database files in other work areas remain open but are "inactive," which means that the dBASE commands cannot access the data in those files. You can have up to 10 database files open in 10 work areas at one time, but *only one* file can be active.

To have more than one database file open at the same time, you must open each database file in a separate work area. To do this, you first select the work area and then open the file. In other words you use the SELECT command first, then the USE command.

Let's see what happens when you use this method to open two database files. Load dBASE, then switch to dot prompt mode. Let's suppose Esther decides to put CLIENT in work area 1 and JOBS in work area 2.

To assign CLIENT.DBF to work area 1:

❶ At the dot prompt type **select 1** and press **[Enter]**. Work area 1 is now the currently selected work area.

Open CLIENT.DBF.

❷ At the dot prompt type **use client** and press **[Enter]**. You have opened the CLIENT database file in work area 1. CLIENT.DBF is the active database file.

Let's list the database file to verify it is in the currently selected work area.

❸ At the dot prompt type **list** and press **[Enter]**. The data from the CLIENT file appear. See Figure 7-3.

open CLIENT file →

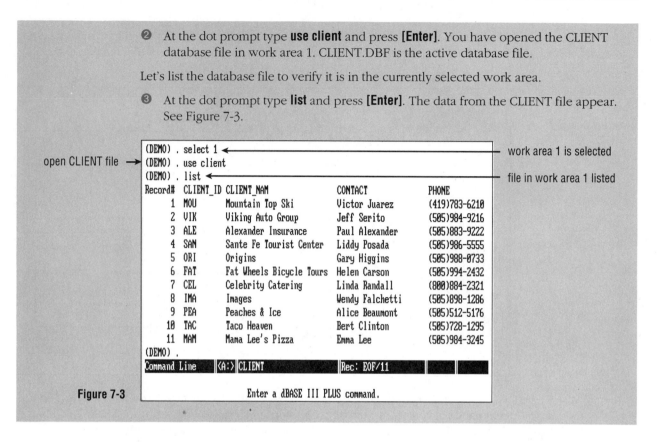

work area 1 is selected

file in work area 1 listed

```
(DEMO) . select 1  ◄
(DEMO) . use client
(DEMO) . list  ◄
Record#  CLIENT_ID CLIENT_NAM            CONTACT           PHONE
      1  MOU       Mountain Top Ski      Victor Juarez     (419)783-6210
      2  VIK       Viking Auto Group     Jeff Serito       (505)984-9216
      3  ALE       Alexander Insurance   Paul Alexander    (505)883-9222
      4  SAN       Sante Fe Tourist Center Liddy Posada    (505)986-5555
      5  ORI       Origins               Gary Higgins      (505)988-0733
      6  FAT       Fat Wheels Bicycle Tours Helen Carson   (505)994-2432
      7  CEL       Celebrity Catering    Linda Randall     (800)884-2321
      8  IMA       Images                Wendy Falchetti   (505)898-1286
      9  PEA       Peaches & Ice         Alice Beaumont    (505)512-5176
     10  TAC       Taco Heaven           Bert Clinton      (505)728-1295
     11  MAM       Mama Lee's Pizza      Emma Lee          (505)984-3245
(DEMO) .
Command Line   |<A:>|CLIENT              |Rec: EOF/11
                        Enter a dBASE III PLUS command.
```

Figure 7-3

Now let's open JOBS in work area 2. To open a database file in a separate work area, you first select a different work area. Let's do what Esther does and select work area 2.

To assign JOBS.DBF to work area 2:

❶ At the dot prompt type **select 2** and press **[Enter]**. Notice that the status bar no longer indicates a file is open. See Figure 7-4. This is because you selected work area 2 as the currently selected work area, but you have not yet opened a file in this work area.

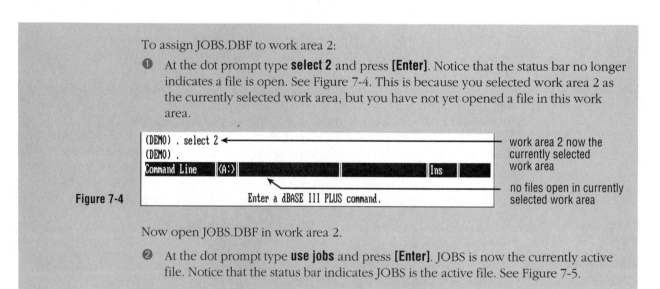

work area 2 now the currently selected work area

no files open in currently selected work area

```
(DEMO) . select 2  ◄
(DEMO) .
Command Line   |<A:>|                              |Ins|
                        Enter a dBASE III PLUS command.
```

Figure 7-4

Now open JOBS.DBF in work area 2.

❷ At the dot prompt type **use jobs** and press **[Enter]**. JOBS is now the currently active file. Notice that the status bar indicates JOBS is the active file. See Figure 7-5.

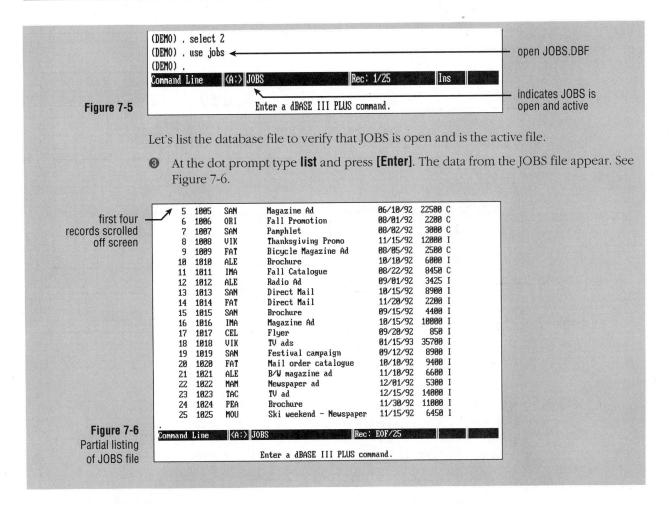

```
(DEMO) . select 2
(DEMO) . use jobs  ◄───────────────────────────── open JOBS.DBF
(DEMO) .
┌─────────────┬───────┬────────────────────┬───────────┬─────────┐
│Command Line │‖<A:>‖ │JOBS                │Rec: 1/25  │‖Ins ‖   │
└─────────────┴───────┴────────────────────┴───────────┴─────────┘
                            │                              ◄───── indicates JOBS is
              Enter a dBASE III PLUS command.                     open and active
```

Figure 7-5

Let's list the database file to verify that JOBS is open and is the active file.

❸ At the dot prompt type **list** and press **[Enter]**. The data from the JOBS file appear. See Figure 7-6.

```
first four ─────►   5  1005  SAN   Magazine Ad           06/10/92  22500 C
records scrolled    6  1006  ORI   Fall Promotion        08/01/92   2200 C
off screen          7  1007  SAN   Pamphlet              08/02/92   3000 C
                    8  1008  VIK   Thanksgiving Promo     11/15/92  12000 I
                    9  1009  FAT   Bicycle Magazine Ad    08/05/92   2500 C
                   10  1010  ALE   Brochure              10/10/92   6000 I
                   11  1011  IMA   Fall Catalogue         08/22/92   8450 C
                   12  1012  ALE   Radio Ad               09/01/92   3425 I
                   13  1013  SAN   Direct Mail           10/15/92   8900 I
                   14  1014  FAT   Direct Mail           11/20/92   2200 I
                   15  1015  SAN   Brochure              09/15/92   4400 I
                   16  1016  IMA   Magazine Ad           10/15/92  10000 I
                   17  1017  CEL   Flyer                 09/20/92    850 I
                   18  1018  VIK   TV ads                01/15/93  35700 I
                   19  1019  SAN   Festival campaign      09/12/92   8900 I
                   20  1020  FAT   Mail order catalogue  10/10/92   9400 I
                   21  1021  ALE   B/W magazine ad       11/10/92   6600 I
                   22  1022  MAM   Newspaper ad          12/01/92   5300 I
                   23  1023  TAC   TV ad                 12/15/92  14000 I
                   24  1024  PEA   Brochure              11/30/92  11000 I
                   25  1025  MOU   Ski weekend - Newspaper 11/15/92 6450 I
┌─────────────┬───────┬────────────────────┬───────────┬─────────┐
│Command Line │‖<A:>‖ │JOBS                │Rec: EOF/25│‖     ‖   │
└─────────────┴───────┴────────────────────┴───────────┴─────────┘
              Enter a dBASE III PLUS command.
```

Figure 7-6
Partial listing
of JOBS file

To help you visualize what has just occurred, look at Figure 7-7 on the next page. You opened the CLIENT database file in work area 1 and the JOBS database file in work area 2, as shown in the figure. The solid lines indicate that the JOBS file is the active file. You can access, update, and manipulate records in work area 2, the currently selected work area. The dotted lines indicate that the CLIENT file is open but the file is inactive. You cannot access the data in this work area unless you make it the currently selected work area. You change the currently selected work area by using the SELECT command again. Let's change the currently selected work area from area 2 to area 1.

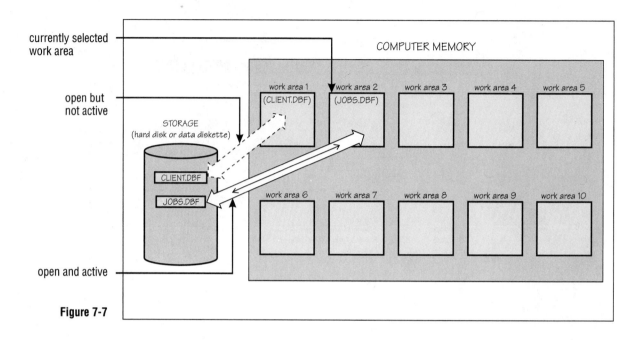

currently selected work area

open but not active

STORAGE (hard disk or data diskette)

open and active

Figure 7-7

To change the currently selected work area:

❶ At the dot prompt type **select 1** and press **[Enter]**. You have now made work area 1 the currently selected work area. Notice that the status bar indicates CLIENT is the active file. See Figure 7-8.

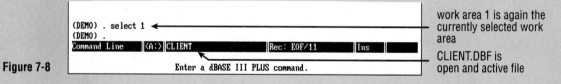

Figure 7-8

work area 1 is again the currently selected work area

CLIENT.DBF is open and active file

Figure 7-9 illustrates the change in active files. The dotted lines that now connect work area 2 with the JOBS file indicate it's open but inactive. Solid lines connect work area 1 to CLIENT because it is now the active file.

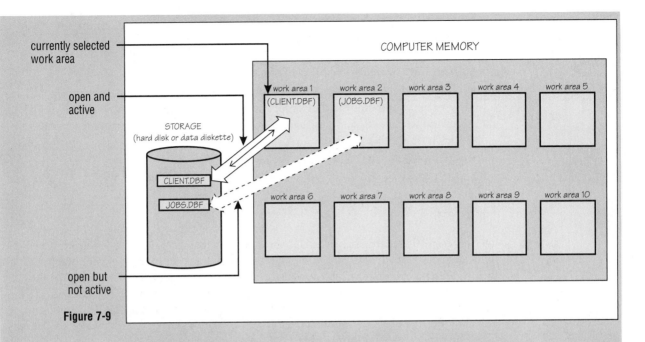

currently selected work area

open and active

STORAGE (hard disk or data diskette)

COMPUTER MEMORY

work area 1 (CLIENT.DBF)   work area 2 (JOBS.DBF)   work area 3   work area 4   work area 5

CLIENT.DBF

JOBS.DBF

work area 6   work area 7   work area 8   work area 9   work area 10

open but not active

Figure 7-9

Let's list the database file to verify that you can now access the CLIENT file.

❷ At the dot prompt type **list** and press **[Enter]**. The data from the CLIENT file appear. See Figure 7-10. Thus, you can access the CLIENT data without opening the CLIENT file again. Work area 1 is now the currently selected work area, and any dBASE commands you issue will access the file opened in that area until you select another work area. dBASE maintains separate record pointers for each work area. As dBASE moves from record to record in the active database file, movement of the record pointer there has no effect on the record pointer in any other work area. When you switch from one work area to another, dBASE uses the record pointer of the work area you select to process the database file in that work area.

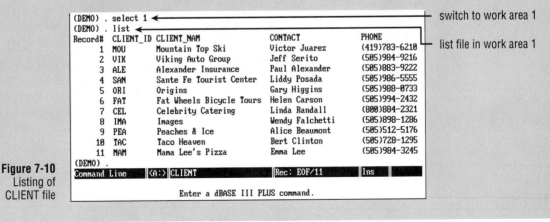

switch to work area 1

list file in work area 1

Figure 7-10 Listing of CLIENT file

Let's summarize our discussion of work areas and the SELECT command:

- dBASE allows up to 10 work areas, which are numbered 1 through 10.
- In each work area you can open one database file.
- Only one database file is active at one time, although as many as 10 database files can be open at one time. The most recently executed SELECT command determines the currently selected work area. If no SELECT command is issued, then work area 1 is the currently selected work area.
- Each work area has a separate record pointer.

The SET RELATION Command

You will recall that Martin has asked Esther to list data from two files in one report. You might think she could use the SELECT command to switch back and forth between the two open files. But this method cannot display data from two files in one listing — as Figure 7-9 showed, these files are open but there is no relationship between them. They are not linked. How can Esther link the two files? The answer is she can use the SET RELATION command.

The SET RELATION command establishes a relationship between two open database files. The syntax for this command is

> SET RELATION TO *common field* INTO *open database file*

You use the SET RELATION command to define a relationship between two open database files. Specifically you use this command to establish a link between the records in the active database file and the records in a second database file in another work area. To link the database files, you must have a field common to both database files. For example, the CLIENT_ID field is common to both the JOBS and the CLIENT files (Figure 7-11). Once these files are linked, you can perform such tasks on the two files as listing fields from both files as though they come from one file.

Whenever you issue the SET RELATION command, you must follow certain rules. To demonstrate these rules, let's use the example of Martin's request for a listing that requires Esther to link the JOBS file and the CLIENT file.

- You must select the work area *from* which you are linking; this is the **source database**. The source database is the file you want processed. In our example the source database is the JOBS file, since Martin wants a list of all jobs still in progress. The source database must be in the *currently selected* work area when you issue the SET RELATION command.

```
                              CLIENT.DBF


Record#   CLIENT_ID  CLIENT_NAM          CONTACT          PHONE
      1   MOU        Mountain Top Ski    Victor Juarez    (419)783-6210
      2   VIK        Viking Auto Group   Jeff Serito      (505)984-9216
      3   ALE        Alexander Insurance Paul Alexander   (505)883-9222
      4   SAN        Sante Fe Tourist Center Liddy Posada (505)986-5555
      5   ORI        Origins             Gary Higgins     (505)988-0733
      6   FAT        Fat Wheels Bicycle Tours Helen Carson (505)994-2432
      7   CEL        Celebrity Catering  Linda Randall    (800)884-2321
      8   IMA        Images              Wendy Falchetti  (505)898-1286
      9   PEA        Peaches & Ice       Alice Beaumont   (505)512-5176
     10   TAC        Taco Heaven         Bert Clinton     (505)728-1295
     11   MAM        Mama Lee's Pizza    Emma Lee         (505)984-3245
```

common field

```
                              JOBS.DBF


Record#  JOBNUM  CLIENT_ID  JOB_DESCR              DUE_DATE  QUOTE STATUS
      1   1001   ORI        Best in the Southwest  08/15/92   2500 C
      2   1002   VIK        Fall TV Ad             08/10/92  32500 C
      3   1003   MOU        Ski equipment sale     06/01/92   3000 C
      4   1004   ALE        B/W Magazine Ad        06/05/92   3500 C
      5   1005   SAN        Magazine Ad            06/10/92  22500 C
      6   1006   ORI        Fall Promotion         08/01/92   2200 C
      7   1007   SAN        Pamphlet               08/02/92   3000 C
      8   1008   VIK        Thanksgiving Promo     11/15/92  12000 I
      9   1009   FAT        Bicycle Magazine Ad    08/05/92   2500 C
     10   1010   ALE        Brochure               10/10/92   6000 I
     11   1011   IMA        Fall Catalogue         08/22/92   8450 C
     12   1012   ALE        Radio Ad               09/01/92   3425 I
     13   1013   SAN        Direct Mail            10/15/92   8900 I
     14   1014   FAT        Direct Mail            11/20/92   2200 I
     15   1015   SAN        Brochure               09/15/92   4400 I
     16   1016   IMA        Magazine Ad            10/15/92  10000 I
     17   1017   CEL        Flyer                  09/20/92    850 I
     18   1018   VIK        TV ads                 01/15/93  35700 I
     19   1019   SAN        Festival campaign      09/12/92   8900 I
     20   1020   FAT        Mail order catalogue   10/10/92   9400 I
     21   1021   ALE        B/W magazine ad        11/10/92   6600 I
     22   1022   MAM        Newspaper ad           12/01/92   5300 I
     23   1023   TAC        TV ad                  12/15/92  14000 I
     24   1024   PEA        Brochure               11/30/92  11000 I
     25   1025   MOU        Ski weekend - Newspaper 11/15/92  6450 I
```

Figure 7-11
Common field is
CLIENT_ID

- The database file *to* which you are linking must be open in a separate work area. This database file, called the **target database,** is where you "look up" related records. In our example the CLIENT file is the target database, since we are looking up the full client name, the contact name, and the phone number based on a client ID from a record in the JOBS file.

- Both the source and the target database files must have a field in common. This is called the **link field**. In our example CLIENT_ID is the link field.

- For the source and the target files to be related, you must open the target database file with an index file whose indexing field is the link field. In our example you must open an index file associated with the CLIENT file whose indexing field is CLIENT_ID. This enables dBASE to look up records in the target file (CLIENT) given a CLIENT_ID from a record in the source file (JOBS).

Establishing a Link between Two Database Files

As stated in the list of rules on linking files, to link two files you must open the target file (in this case, CLIENT) with an index file whose index field is the link field (in this case, CLIENT_ID). If such an index file doesn't exist on your data diskette, you must create one. No index file does currently exist, so let's create one and name it CLNTX.

Before you create the index file, check the status bar to make sure that CLIENT.DBF is the active database file. If it is not, use the SELECT command to switch work areas so CLIENT.DBF is the active file. Now create the index file.

To create an index file named CLNTX:

❶ At the dot prompt type **index on client_id to clntx** and press **[Enter]**. You will see the message "100% indexed   11 Records indexed." You have created a new index file that is stored on your data diskette as CLNTX.NDX.

Index files are a common area of confusion in dBASE. For instance, you may be wondering why you need two index files, CLIENT.NDX (which you created in Tutorial 5) and CLNTX.NDX, to order database files? Why can't you use just CLIENT.NDX?

CLIENT.NDX is an index file associated with the JOBS.DBF file, while CLNTX.NDX is an index file associated with the CLIENT.DBF database file. To order the records in the JOBS file by client ID, you would use the CLIENT.NDX index file. To order the records in the CLIENT database file by client ID, you would use the CLNTX.NDX index file.

Before you link the JOBS and the CLIENT files, you must be sure the source database is the active file. The JOBS file is the source database; currently this file is open but inactive. Let's switch work areas so JOBS becomes the active file.

To switch work areas:

❶ At the dot prompt type **select 2** and press **[Enter]**. You have selected work area 2. Notice that the status bar indicates JOBS is the active file.

Now create the link between the two database files by issuing the SET RELATION command.

❷ At the dot prompt type **set relation to client_id into client** and press **[Enter]**. See Figure 7-12.

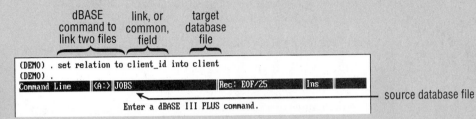

Figure 7-12

source database file

Nothing happens on your screen, but by issuing the SET RELATION command, you have linked the JOBS database file to the CLIENT database file based on the common field CLIENT_ID.

Figure 7-13 illustrates what has just occurred. You opened the CLIENT database and its associated CLNTX index file in work area 1 and the JOBS database file in work area 2. Now you have two open files. The dotted arrow between work area 1 and CLIENT.DBF in storage indicates that the file is open but inactive. The solid arrow between work area 2 and JOBS.DBF indicates the file is open and active. The open-ended lines between work area 1 and work area 2 indicate you have linked the two open database files.

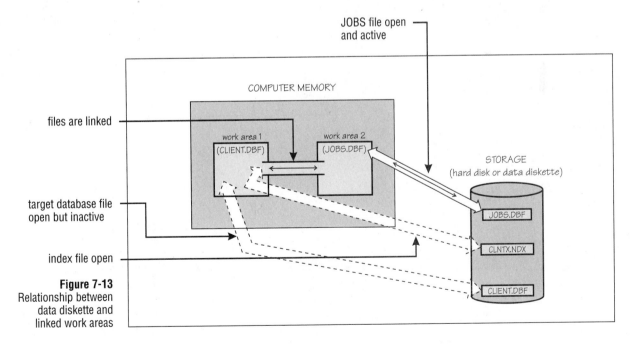

Figure 7-13
Relationship between data diskette and linked work areas

dBASE does not inform you if the SET RELATION command successfully linked the two files, but you can examine the status of the current dBASE environment by issuing the DISPLAY STATUS command. This command provides you with information about the status of your work areas and open files. The syntax of this command is

DISPLAY STATUS   TO PRINT

The DISPLAY STATUS command shows the following information for each work area:

- the number of the work area
- the name of the open database file
- the names of all open index files and their indexing fields
- information regarding related database files

Let's issue the DISPLAY STATUS command to identify the open database and index files and any established relationships.

To view the status of all work areas:

❶ At the dot prompt type **display status** and press **[Enter]**. A screen shows, among other things, that the CLIENT file is open in work area 1 and that CLNTX is the open index file, with CLIENT_ID the indexing field. The screen also shows that work area 2 is the "currently selected" work area, that JOBS is the open database file, and that JOBS is related to the CLIENT file through the link field CLIENT_ID. See Figure 7-14.

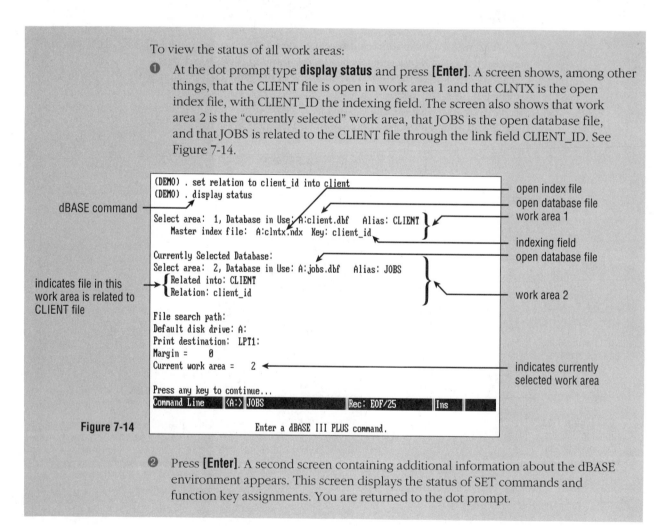

Figure 7-14

❷ Press **[Enter]**. A second screen containing additional information about the dBASE environment appears. This screen displays the status of SET commands and function key assignments. You are returned to the dot prompt.

Now that you have verified that the files are open and linked correctly, you can create the listing that Martin wants.

Listing Data from Linked Database Files

Once you have established a link between two files, you can use the LIST or the DISPLAY command to include field names from both files in one listing. Before you learned how to use the SET RELATION command, you could list data from only one file. Now you can prepare the information Martin wants: a list that includes client name, contact name, phone number, due date, and quote for all ongoing jobs at Wells & Martinez.

To display or print data from linked files, you must identify the fields in the open but inactive database file (CLIENT.DBF, in this case), so dBASE knows in what work area to find these fields. You do this by placing the filename in front of the field name; in other words, you are *qualifying* the field name with the filename. The syntax for qualifying a field name is:

---

filename->field name

You enter the arrow symbol, [->], with two keystrokes: a hyphen [-] followed by a greater-than symbol [>]. These two symbols together indicate that the field name belongs to the preceding filename. It allows you to refer to a field that is not in the active file in the same command in which you specify field names that are from the active file. Fields from the active file do not need to be qualified.

To display data from the linked files:

❶ At the dot prompt type **list off client->client_nam, client->contact, client->phone, due_date, quote for status = 'I' to print** and press **[Enter]**.

Notice that you qualified the fields from the inactive file, CLIENT.DBF, by placing the filename and the arrow symbol (CLIENT->) in front of the field name. Remember, you must qualify all field names that are not in the active file, so dBASE knows from what database file the fields come. For example, CLIENT->CONTACT identifies the CONTACT field in the CLIENT file.

Figure 7-15 on the next page is a listing of all jobs with STATUS equal to I. Notice that it includes fields from both the JOBS file (DUE_DATE and QUOTE) and the CLIENT file (CLIENT_NAM, CONTACT, and PHONE).

from CLIENT.DBF			from JOBS.DBF	
client->client_nam	client->contact	client->phone	due_date	quote
Viking Auto Group	Jeff Serito	(505)984-9216	11/15/92	12000
Alexander Insurance	Paul Alexander	(505)883-9222	10/10/92	6000
Alexander Insurance	Paul Alexander	(505)883-9222	09/01/92	3425
Sante Fe Tourist Center	Liddy Posada	(505)986-5555	10/15/92	8900
Fat Wheels Bicycle Tours	Helen Carson	(505)994-2432	11/20/92	2200
Sante Fe Tourist Center	Liddy Posada	(505)986-5555	09/15/92	4400
Images	Wendy Falchetti	(505)898-1286	10/15/92	10000
Celebrity Catering	Linda Randall	(800)884-2321	09/20/92	850
Viking Auto Group	Jeff Serito	(505)984-9216	01/15/93	35700
Sante Fe Tourist Center	Liddy Posada	(505)986-5555	09/12/92	8900
Fat Wheels Bicycle Tours	Helen Carson	(505)994-2432	10/10/92	9400
Alexander Insurance	Paul Alexander	(505)883-9222	11/10/92	6600
Mama Lee's Pizza	Emma Lee	(505)984-3245	12/01/92	5300
Taco Heaven	Bert Clinton	(505)728-1295	12/15/92	14000
Peaches & Ice	Alice Beaumont	(505)512-5176	11/30/92	11000
Mountain Top Ski	Victor Juarez	(419)783-6210	11/15/92	6450

Figure 7-15
Printout of
linked files for
Martin

How does dBASE include fields from both files in your output? The record pointers and the index file of the target file hold the answer. You will recall that the record pointer stores the record number of the current record. As the record pointer in the active database file moves to a different job record, the record pointer for the target file is automatically repositioned to the corresponding record in the CLIENT file. Figure 7-16 illustrates how dBASE links one record in the JOBS file with its corresponding record in the CLIENT file. In this figure the record pointer for the JOBS file is pointing to record 7, which is job number 1007. The client ID for this record is SAN. dBASE searches the index file, CLNTX.NDX, for a record that matches the client ID value from the JOBS file. When dBASE finds a match, the record pointer from the corresponding column in the index file is used as the record pointer for CLIENT.DBF. Thus, the record pointer for CLIENT.DBF points to record number 4, the Sante Fe Tourist Center record. Now you can list fields from record number 7 of the JOBS file and record number 4 of the CLIENT file as though they came from one record.

The VIEW File

Esther realizes that if Martin wants her to use these two linked files again she will have to open the files and set up the relationships all over. In other words, she must type the following five dBASE commands:

```
SELECT 1
USE CLIENT INDEX CLNTX
SELECT 2
USE JOBS
SET RELATION TO CLIENT_ID INTO CLIENT
```

Esther decides to create a view file to save her time in the future. A **view file** saves all the current information about the open database and index files, their associated work areas, and the relationships among the files. A view file simplifies the process of opening files and establishing relationships, not to mention the task of remembering the syntax needed to link files.

```
                                    JOBS.DBF

          Record#   JOBNUM CLIENT_ID JOB_DESCR              DUE_DATE  QUOTE STATUS
                1   1001   ORI       Best in the Southwest  08/15/92   2500 C
                2   1002   VIK       Fall TV Ad             08/10/92  32500 C
                3   1003   MOU       Ski equipment sale     06/01/92   3000 C
                4   1004   ALE       B/W Magazine Ad        06/05/92   3500 C
                5   1005   SAN       Magazine Ad            06/10/92  22500 C
                6   1006   ORI       Fall Promotion         08/01/92   2200 C
                7   1007   SAN       Pamphlet               08/02/92   3000 C
                8   1008   VIK       Thanksgiving Promo     11/15/92  12000 I
                9   1009   FAT       Bicycle Magazine Ad    08/05/92   2500 C
               10   1010   ALE       Brochure               10/10/92   6000 I
               11   1011   IMA       Fall Catalogue         08/22/92   8450 C
               12   1012   ALE       Radio Ad               09/01/92   3425 I
               13   1013   SAN       Direct Mail            10/15/92   8900 I       work
               14   1014   FAT       Direct Mail            11/20/92   2200 I       area 1
               15   1015   SAN       Brochure               09/15/92   4400 I
               16   1016   IMA       Magazine Ad            10/15/92  10000 I
               17   1017   CEL       Flyer                  09/20/92    850 I
               18   1018   VIK       TV ads                 01/15/93  35700 I
               19   1019   SAN       Festival campaign      09/12/92   8900 I
               20   1020   FAT       Mail order catalogue   10/10/92   9400 I
               21   1021   ALE       B/W magazine ad        11/10/92   6600 I
               22   1022   MAM       Newspaper ad           12/01/92   5300 I
               23   1023   TAC       TV ad                  12/15/92  14000 I
               24   1024   PEA       Brochure               11/30/92  11000 I
               25   1025   MOU       Ski weekend - Newspaper 11/15/92  6450 I
```

dBASE "looks up"
corresponding
CLIENT_ID in
CLNTX.NDX

```
       CLNTX.NDX

 client_id  Record#
 ALE          3
 CEL          7
 FAT          6
 IMA          8
 MAM         11
 MOU          1
 ORI          5
 PEA          9
 SAN          4
 TAC         10
 VIK          2
```

```
                                    CLIENT.DBF

         Record#  CLIENT_ID CLIENT_NAM          CONTACT          PHONE
              1   MOU       Mountain Top Ski    Victor Juarez    (419)783-6210
              2   VIK       Viking Auto Group   Jeff Serito      (505)984-9216
              3   ALE       Alexander Insurance Paul Alexander   (505)883-9222
              4   SAN       Sante Fe Tourist Center Liddy Posada (505)986-5555
  points    5   ORI       Origins             Gary Higgins     (505)988-0733
  to        6   FAT       Fat Wheels Bicycle Tours Helen Carson (505)994-2432    work
  record    7   CEL       Celebrity Catering  Linda Randall    (800)884-2321    area 2
              8   IMA       Images              Wendy Falchetti  (505)898-1286
              9   PEA       Peaches & Ice       Alice Beaumont   (505)512-5176
             10   TAC       Taco Heaven         Bert Clinton     (505)728-1295
             11   MAM       Mama Lee's Pizza    Emma Lee         (505)984-3245
```

Figure 7-16

Creating a View File

The syntax to create a view file is

CREATE VIEW *view filename* FROM ENVIRONMENT

You issue the view file command *after* you have opened all the required files and issued the appropriate SET RELATION command. The view file is saved on your data diskette, and dBASE automatically adds the extension .VUE to the view filename. The view file contains information about the dBASE environment, that is, which database and index files are open and what relationships exist among them.

Before we create Esther's view file, let's look at the current status of dBASE to see what you will be saving in the view file.

To view the current status of dBASE:

❶ At the dot prompt type **display status** and press **[Enter]**. A screen appears that shows, among other things, that in work area 1 CLIENT is the open database file and CLNTX is the open index file, with CLIENT_ID the indexing field. Information about the related files and open index files in each work area also appears. See Figure 7-17.

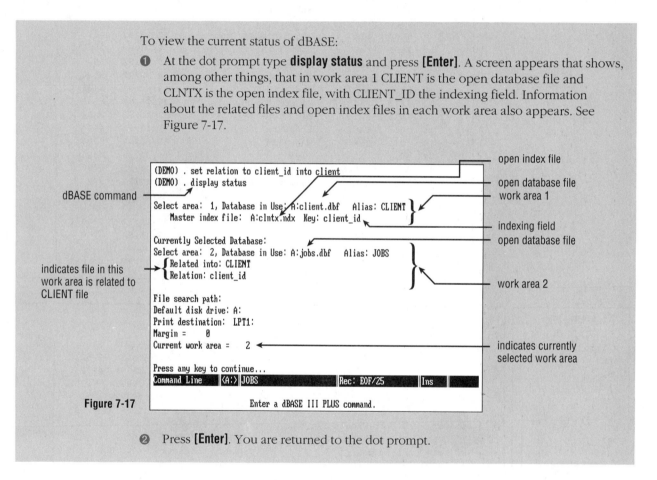

Figure 7-17

❷ Press **[Enter]**. You are returned to the dot prompt.

Now create a view file of this dBASE environment. Name the view file CLNTJB, for "clientjobs."

To create a view file:

❶ At the dot prompt type **create view clntjb from environment** and press **[Enter]**. See Figure 7-18. Although nothing on your screen indicates that a view file has been created, dBASE has stored the view file on your data diskette.

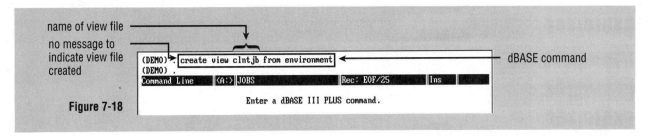

name of view file

no message to
indicate view file
created

Figure 7-18

(DEMO) . `create view clntjb from environment` ← dBASE command
(DEMO) .
Command Line   ‖<A:>‖JOBS   ‖Rec: EOF/25   ‖‖Ins ‖‖
                    Enter a dBASE III PLUS command.

As Figure 7-19 illustrates, you now have on your data diskette a new file named CLNTJB.VUE that contains all the information you need to open work areas, database files, and index files and to establish relationships among them.

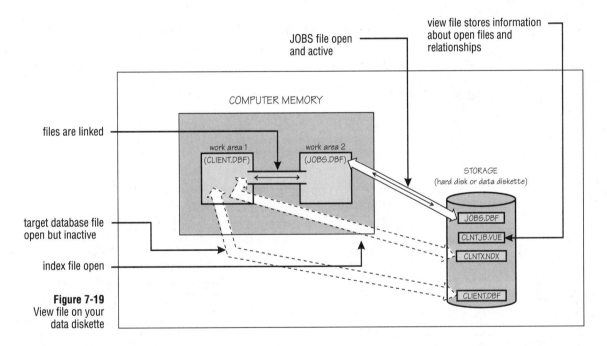

JOBS file open
and active

view file stores information
about open files and
relationships

files are linked

target database file
open but inactive

index file open

Figure 7-19
View file on your
data diskette

COMPUTER MEMORY

work area 1
(CLIENT.DBF)

work area 2
(JOBS.DBF)

STORAGE
(hard disk or data diskette)

JOBS.DBF
CLNTJB.VUE
CLNTX.NDX
CLIENT.DBF

Using a View File

Once you have created a view file, you can retrieve it with a single command. You can open a view file at any time with the SET VIEW command. The syntax of this command is

SET VIEW TO *view filename*

The SET VIEW command opens the view file and restores the dBASE environment to the state dBASE was in when the view file was created. The appropriate database files and their associated index files are placed in their assigned work areas, and the relationship among the files is reestablished.

To see how the SET VIEW command works, first make sure that the CLIENT and the JOBS files are open in separate work areas, that the index file CLNTX is open, and that the two files are linked. Next close all open files so you can verify that the SET VIEW command has returned you to the same dBASE environment you have now.

The CLOSE ALL command closes all open database and index files in all work areas. The syntax for this command is

CLOSE ALL

To close all open files:

❶ At the dot prompt type **close all** and press **[Enter]**. Notice that the status bar indicates no file is open. See Figure 7-20.

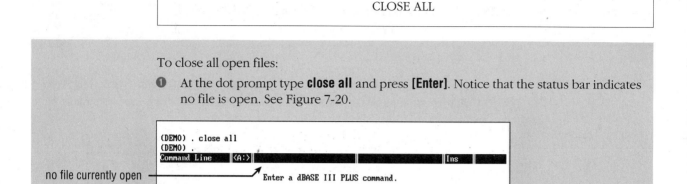

no file currently open

Figure 7-20

Now let's issue the DISPLAY STATUS command again to verify that all the files have been closed.

To see the current status of the work areas:

❶ At the dot prompt type **display status** and press **[Enter]**. The screen indicates that no files are open. See Figure 7-21.

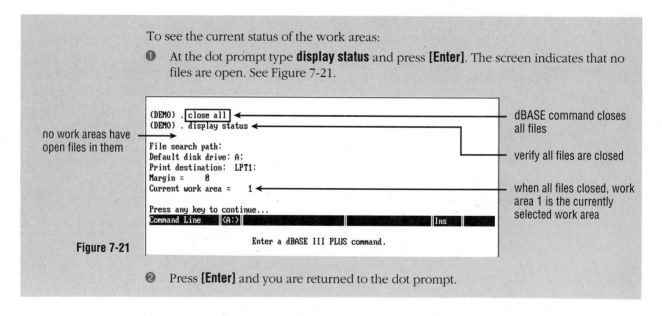

no work areas have open files in them

dBASE command closes all files

verify all files are closed

when all files closed, work area 1 is the currently selected work area

Figure 7-21

❷ Press **[Enter]** and you are returned to the dot prompt.

You are ready to use the SET VIEW command to open the files and set the relationships.

To open a view file:

❶ At the dot prompt type **set view to clntjb** and press **[Enter]**. The only change on your screen is that JOBS now appears in the status bar. See Figure 7-22.

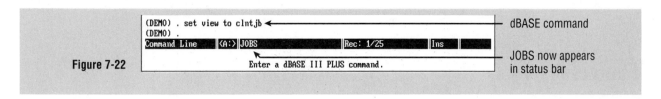

Figure 7-22

dBASE command

JOBS now appears
in status bar

Let's verify that the dBASE environment is now the same as when you created the
view file.

To see the current status of the work areas:

❶ At the dot prompt type **display status** and press **[Enter]**. A screen appears that shows,
among other things, that in work area 1 CLIENT is the open database file and
CLNTX is the open index file, with CLIENT_ID the indexing field. In addition JOBS
is the active file, and is linked to the CLIENT file. See Figure 7-23.

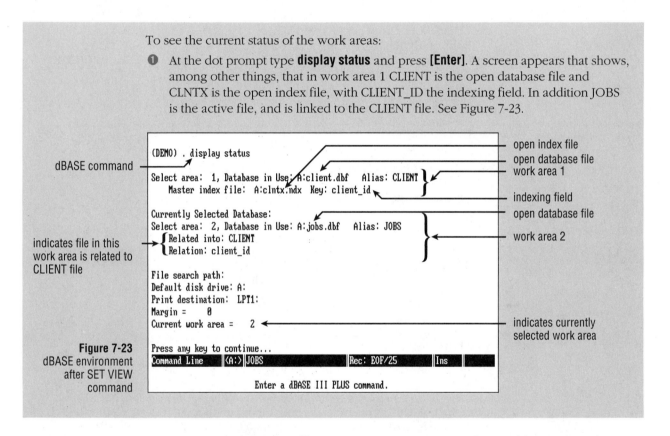

dBASE command

indicates file in this
work area is related to
CLIENT file

Figure 7-23
dBASE environment
after SET VIEW
command

open index file
open database file
work area 1

indexing field
open database file

work area 2

indicates currently
selected work area

You can see how view files save time. More important they enable you to easily query
a complex set of related files.

Now that the files are linked, you can print the due date query just as you did earlier in
the tutorial. When you're finished, quit dBASE.

Linking Files in Assistant Mode

You may be wondering if you can link files in Assistant mode. The answer is yes. You can
create a view file by selecting the *Create View* option in the Assistant screen. This option
begins a menu-driven procedure that eventually creates a view file. Unfortunately this option
does not guide you easily through the steps required to create a view file. You will find it
easier to link files in dot prompt mode.

■   ■   ■

Exercises

1. Below are four sets of dBASE commands. For each set of commands, first indicate the work area number and the active file in that work area after all commands are executed, and second, the database file that would be listed.

   a. USE VENDORS
       USE PURCHASE
       USE VENDORS
       LIST

   b. SELECT 1
       USE VENDORS
       SELECT 2
       USE PURCHASE
       LIST

   c. SELECT 1
       SELECT 2
       USE PURCHASE
       SELECT 1
       LIST

   d. SELECT 2
       USE VENDORS
       SELECT 1
       USE PURCHASE
       LIST
       SELECT 1
       LIST

2. What dBASE command closes all database and index files?

Use the following sequence of dBASE commands to answer Exercises 3 through 6.

       SELECT 1
       USE PUBLISHR INDEX PUBID
       SELECT 2
       USE BOOKS
       SET RELATION TO PUB_ID INTO PUBLISHR

3. Which database files are linked?

4. What is the source database?

5. What is the target database?

6. What is the link field?

Use Figures 7-24 and 7-25 to answer Exercises 7 through 9. They present information about customers (CUST.DBF) and their outstanding invoices (INVOICES.DBF). The CUST.DBF file has an associated index file named CUSTX that uses CUST_ID as the indexing field. The source database is INVOICE and the target database is CUST.

Layout of CUSTOMER File — One Record per Customer		
CUST_ID	Character	3
CUST_NAME	Character	25
ADDRESS	Character	20
CITY	Character	20
STATE	Character	2
ZIP	Character	5

Figure 7-24

Layout of INVOICE File — One Record for Each Invoice

INVOICE_NO	Character	5
CUST_ID	Character	3
INVCE_DTE	Date	8
INVCE_AMT	Numeric	8 2 (decimals)

Figure 7-25

7. Write the sequence of dBASE commands needed to link these two files.

8. Write the dBASE command to create a view file named CUSTINVC.

9. Write the dBASE command to print all invoices in the INVOICE file. Include customer name, invoice date, and amount.

For additional hands-on practice linking database files, complete Exercises 10 through 15. Figures 7-26 and 7-27 show the record layouts of two database files that list students (STUDENT.DBF) and the courses in which they are enrolled (CRSENRL.DBF). These files are on your data diskette. The STUDENT file has an associated index file named STUDNTID that uses SID as the indexing field. The source database file is CRSENRL, and the target database is STUDENT.

Layout of STUDENT File — One Record per Student

SID	Character	3
LAST_NAME	Character	10
SEX	Character	1
MAJOR	Character	3
GPA	Numeric	4 2 (decimals)

Figure 7-26

Layout of CRSENRL File — One Record for Each Course Student Enrolled in

CRSNBR	Character	6
SID	Character	3
GRADE	Character	1

Figure 7-27

10. Type the sequence of dBASE commands that will link the two files.

11. Print the students enrolled in the course FIN601. Include last name, major, course number, and grade in the listing.

12. Create a view file named STUCRS.

13. Close all the files.

14. Open the view file.

15. Print the students who have received a grade of A in any course. Include the student's last name and the course number.

Tutorial Assignments

1. Link the JOBS database file and the CLIENT database file using dot prompt mode. Remember to open the associated index file, CLNTX.NDX.

For each of the following listings, include these fields: client name, job number, job description, due date, quote, and status.

2. Print all jobs in the JOBS file.

3. Print all completed jobs.

4. Print all jobs with a quote over $5,000.

5. Close all files and print the status of dBASE.

6. Open the view file CLNTJB.

7. Print the status of dBASE after the view file has been opened.

8. Print client name, job number, job description, due date, and status for all jobs in the JOBS file.

Case Problems

In the following problems you can use the LIST STRUCTURE command if you cannot remember the field names in an open database file. Also you can refer to the table of database files and associated index files at the end of dBASE Tutorial 5 for the names of the index files you'll need to solve these Case Problems.

1. Biggs and Hang Investment Company

Do the following:

1. You will find a file named INDUSTRY.DBF stored on your data diskette. Open this file in work area 1.

2. Print the file structure.

3. Create an index file named INDX using IND_CODE as the index key.

4. Print the INDUSTRY file.

5. Open JAPAN.DBF in work area 2.

6. Link the JAPAN and the INDUSTRY database files. JAPAN is the source database.

7. Print a list of companies. In your listing include the company name, the industry name, sales, and profits.

8. Create a view file named JAPANIND.

2.   Medi-Source Inc.

Do the following:

1. You will find a file named TYPENAME.DBF stored on your data diskette. Open this file in work area 1.

2. Print the file structure.

3. Create an index file named TYPEX using TYPE as the index key.

4. Print the TYPENAME file.

5. Open ACCTREC.DBF in work area 2.

6. Link the ACCTREC and the TYPENAME database files. ACCTREC is the source database.

7. Print a list of companies. In your listing include the company name, the industry title, and the balance owed.

8. Create a view file named ACCTYPE.

3.   Appleton and Drake Electrical Supply Company

Do the following:

1. You will find a file named DEPARTMT.DBF stored on your data diskette. Open this file in work area 1.

2. Print the file structure.

3. Create an index file named DEPTX using DEPT as the index key.

4. Print the DEPARTMT file.

5. Open EMPLOYEE.DBF in work area 2.

6. Link the EMPLOYEE and the DEPARTMT database files. EMPLOYEE is the source database.

7. Print a list of employees. In your listing include the employee's last name, the full department name, and the employee's annual salary.

8. Create a view file named EMPDEPT.

4.   National Basketball Association

Do the following:

1. You will find a file named TEAMS.DBF stored on your data diskette. Open this file in work area 1.

2. Print the file structure.

3. Create an index file named TEAMX using TEAM as the index key.

4. Print the TEAMS file.

5. Open NBA.DBF in work area 2.

6. Link the NBA and the TEAMS database files. NBA is the source database.

7. Print a list of players. In your listing include each player's last name, the full team name, and each player's annual salary.

8. Print a second list of players, this time in alphabetical order. In your listing include each player's last name, the full team name, and each player's salary. *Hint:* Open the source file with the index file NBAINDX1.NDX.

9. Create a view file named NBATEAM.

Additional Cases

Additional Case 1: Dexter Bicycles

Dexter Bicycles, a growing manufacturer of custom-made, hand-assembled bicycles, is planning to open a new manufacturing facility. The new facility will use robots and computer systems to improve manufacturing processes. A team of technically trained people will be hired to custom-design road, racing, and mountain bicycles.

Dexter's executive managers want to open this new facility in a city that has a high-quality, low-cost employee pool. The managers asked Joanne Buconi, a corporate planner, to set up a database to contain information about the cities they are considering. In her research Joanne has identified several factors that she feels are important. She's compiled the data for 15 cities (Figure 1 on the next page)*.

OBJECTIVES

■ These Additional Cases are designed to challenge students. They do not guide students as much as do the Case Problems that appear at the end of each tutorial. For example, the Additional Cases do not provide the students with the file structures for the database files they must design. In addition, when students are asked to arrange data in a certain order, they are not told to use a certain index file and, in some cases, they must create an index file.

■ The Additional Cases' problems are keyed to each tutorial, so that they can be assigned as the student works through this textbook.

City	Region	Population (1990)	Pop. Growth (1990–1995) (%)	Unemployment (1989) (%)	Average SAT Score	Average Salary (Mfg.)
Atlanta	S	2872062	13	5.1	900	25795
Sacramento	W	1460724	14	4.9	960	25513
Austin	W	787360	12	5.4	983	25884
Columbus	N	1357997	6	4.8	1002	27509
Dallas	W	3923388	10	5.5	963	27450
Phoenix	W	2130850	14	4.3	992	26475
Jacksonville	S	941485	12	5.7	901	22083
Albany	E	856466	2	4.2	1056	25219
Baltimore	E	2389385	5	4.0	945	27369
Boston	E	2848981	0	3.4	998	28176
Buffalo	N	949293	-3	5.8	969	26814
Charlotte	S	1147343	8	3.2	865	21177
Cincinnati	N	1469493	3	4.5	896	29857
Denver	W	1656279	3	5.4	976	29660
Houston	W	3260646	2	5.9	955	30795

Figure 1   *Adapted from *Fortune*, "The Best Cities for Business," October 22, 1990, pp. 48ff.

Case Problems for Tutorial 2

1. Create the database file and name it CITIES. Select a name for each field and determine the data type, the width, and the number of decimal places.

2. Print the structure of the CITIES database file.

Case Problems for Tutorial 3

3. Add all the data in Figure 1 to your database file.

4. Print all the data for all the cities.

5. Change the average SAT score for Cincinnati from 896 to 996.

Case Problems for Tutorial 4

6. Print the name of the city, the population, the average salary, and the average SAT score for all cities.

7. Print the name of the city, the population, the average salary, and the average SAT score for cities with a population over 1 million.

8. Print the name of the city, the region, the population, the population growth, and the unemployment rate for all cities in the South (region code = S) and the West (region code = W).

9. Print the name of the city, the population, the average SAT score, and the average salary for all cities with an average SAT score above 975 and an average salary below $26,000.

10. Use the SUM, AVERAGE, and COUNT commands to fill in the following table:

Region	Number of Cities	Total Population	Average SAT Score	Average Salary
North				
West				
South				
East				

Case Problems for Tutorial 5

11. Sort the cities in alphabetical order. Name the sorted file CITSORT1.

12. Use CITSORT1 to print a list of cities in alphabetical order. Include city name, population, and population growth.

13. Sort the cities in descending order by population. Name the sorted file CITSORT2. Print the cities in order by population. Include all fields for cities with a population under 1 million.

14. Sort the cities by region and within region by average salary with highest average salary first. Name the sorted file CITSORT3.

15. Use CITSORT3 to print a listing by region. Include city name, region, population, and average salary.

16. Use CITIES.DBF to create an index file named CITINDX1 using city name as the indexing field.

17. Print a list of all cities with an average salary below $26,000 in alphabetical order by city name. Include city name, region, population, and population growth.

Case Problems for Tutorial 6

18. Use the report layout sheet in Figure 2 on the next page and the CITIES database to create a report format file. Name the report format file CITY1.

Complete Problems 19 and 20 using the report format file CITY1.

19. Print CITY1 in alphabetical order by city.

20. Print CITY1 for all cities with a population over 1 million ordered by region.

21. Use the report layout sheet in Figure 3 on the next page to create a report format file. Name the report format file CITY2.

22. Use CITY2 to print the cities by region.

```
Page #
Date
                              Leading Cities
                                by Region

        City            Region        Population        Average      Average
                                                           SAT        Salary
                                                          Score
      ─────────────────────────────────────────────────────────────────────
      X---------X          X         XXXXXXXXXX           XXXX        XXXXX
      X---------X          X         XXXXXXXXXX           XXXX        XXXXX
            .              .              .                 .           .
            .              .              .                 .           .
            .              .              .                 .           .
      Total                          XXXXXXXXXX
```

Figure 2

```
Page #
Date
                              Leading Cities
                                By Region

        City           Population        Average       Average
                                           SAT          Salary
                                          Score
      ─────────────────────────────────────────────────────────────
      Region <region>                       .
        X---------X      XXXXXXXXXX         XXXX         XXXXX
        X---------X      XXXXXXXXXX         XXXX         XXXXX
              .                .              .            .
              .                .              .            .
              .                .              .            .
      Subtotal           XXXXXXXXXX

      Region <region>
        X---------X      XXXXXXXXXX         XXXX         XXXXX
        X---------X      XXXXXXXXXX         XXXX         XXXXX
              .                .              .            .
              .                .              .            .
              .                .              .            .
      Subtotal           XXXXXXXXXX

      Total              XXXXXXXXXX
```

Figure 3

Case Problems for Tutorial 7

23. Create a second database file and name it REGIONS. The file will store the following data:

Region Code	Region Name
S	South
E	East
W	West
N	North

24. Print the file structure of REGIONS.DBF.

25. Create an index file named REGIONX. Use region code as the indexing field.

26. Print the REGIONS file.

27. If CITIES.DBF is open, make this file the active database file. If CITIES.DBF is not open, open this file in work area 2. Link the CITIES and REGIONS database files. CITIES is the source database.

28. Print a list of cities ordered by region. Include region name, city name, population, unemployment rate, and average salary.

Additional Case 2:
Off-Campus Housing at Ashland University

David Abelson is a sophomore at Ashland University. He works in the University's housing office, where he maintains a manual system for tracking the availability of off-campus housing. When landlords have vacancies, they call or come by the housing office to list their rental properties with David. University students also come in to seek off-campus housing. With the current system, students look through the housing office's book of available off-campus housing units to try to find units that match their needs.

Although students do find available rentals, the system doesn't work very smoothly. David has found that the system has several flaws. One problem is that too few copies of the housing book are available to meet student demands. In addition housing units that have been rented remain in the book after they are no longer available. Also students can't get a listing of housing units that meet their specific criteria, and they are forced to read *every* listing to find what they want. It would be helpful if students could specify their needs, such as maximum monthly rent, number of bedrooms, and distance from campus, and then have access to a list of units that meet those needs.

David has recently completed a computer course, and he believes that the housing office system is a perfect application for computerization. He suggests to his manager that the housing office create a database of available off-campus housing. Students would then be able to get listings of available units based on their specific needs.

Case Problems for Tutorial 2

1. Prepare a file layout based on the case description and the sample Off-Campus Housing Form in Figure 1.

2. Create the database file and name it HOUSING.

3. Add the data from the first filled-out form (Figure 2) immediately after you create the database structure.

4. Print the structure of the HOUSING database file.

AVAILABLE OFF-CAMPUS HOUSING FORM

1. Rental Address: _____

   _____
   Street Address

   _____
   City   State   Zip

2. Indicate name and phone numbers of owner of rental property

   _____

   Last Name   First Name

   _____
   Home Phone #   Work Phone #

3. Type of rental unit available (check one)
   ( ) House   ( ) Apartment

4. # of bedrooms: ___

5. How many miles is unit from campus? _____

6. Length of lease required (in months)? _____

7. Rent per month? _____

8. Date Available?   __/__/__

9. Please check all amenities that your rental unit features:
   ( ) Utilities included   ( ) Washer/dryer
   ( ) Furnished bedroom(s)   ( ) Dishwasher
   ( ) On bus line   ( ) Pets allowed
   ( ) Wheelchair accessible   ( ) Children allowed

Figure 1

AVAILABLE OFF-CAMPUS HOUSING FORM

1. Rental Address:

   39 Rippling Road
   _____
   Street Address

   Narragansett   RI   02894
   _____
   City   State   Zip

2. Indicate name and phone numbers of owner of rental property

   Panza   Ronald
   _____

   Last Name   First Name

   (401) 555-9912
   _____
   Home Phone #   Work Phone #

3. Type of rental unit available (check one)
   (X) House   ( ) Apartment

4. # of bedrooms: 3

5. How many miles is unit from campus? 8

6. Length of lease required (in months)? 9

7. Rent per month? 510

8. Date Available?   9/01/92

9. Please check all amenities that your rental unit features:
   ( ) Utilities included   ( ) Washer/dryer
   (X) Furnished bedroom(s)   ( ) Dishwasher
   ( ) On bus line   (X) Pets allowed
   ( ) Wheelchair accessible   (X) Children allowed

Figure 2

Case Problems for Tutorial 3

5. Add the data in Figures 3 through 13 to the database.

6. Change the rent per month from $510 to $550 for the property owned by Ronald Panza. It was entered incorrectly.

7. Correct the work telephone number for Janine Kinyo, owner of the rental property at 92 Worden Pond Road, Kingston. The correct number is (401) 555-5637.

AVAILABLE OFF-CAMPUS HOUSING FORM

1. Rental Address:

   28 Main Street
   Street Address

   Wakefield _____ RI _____ 02893
   City   State   Zip

2. Indicate name and phone numbers of owner of rental property

   Scalia _____ Vinnie _____
   Last Name   First Name

   (401) 555-8923 _____ (401) 555-4444 _____
   Home Phone #   Work Phone #

3. Type of rental unit available (check one)
   (X) House   ( ) Apartment

4. # of bedrooms: 4

5. How many miles is unit from campus? 7

6. Length of lease required (in months)? 6

7. Rent per month? 500

8. Date Available? 9 /03/ 92

9. Please check all amenities that your rental unit features:
   ( ) Utilities included   (X) Washer/dryer
   (X) Furnished bedroom(s)   ( ) Dishwasher
   (X) On bus line   ( ) Pets allowed
   ( ) Wheelchair accessible   (X) Children allowed

Figure 3

AVAILABLE OFF-CAMPUS HOUSING FORM

1. Rental Address:

   1 High Street
   Street Address

   Narragansett _____ RI _____ 02893
   City   State   Zip

2. Indicate name and phone numbers of owner of rental property

   Margolis _____ Jeanne _____
   Last Name   First Name

   (401) 555-2109 _____
   Home Phone #   Work Phone #

3. Type of rental unit available (check one)
   ( ) House   (X) Apartment

4. # of bedrooms: 1

5. How many miles is unit from campus? 7

6. Length of lease required (in months)? 3

7. Rent per month? 350

8. Date Available? 9 03 92

9. Please check all amenities that your rental unit features:
   (X) Utilities included   ( ) Washer/dryer
   (X) Furnished bedroom(s)   ( ) Dishwasher
   ( ) On bus line   ( ) Pets allowed
   ( ) Wheelchair accessible   ( ) Children allowed

Figure 4

AVAILABLE OFF-CAMPUS HOUSING FORM

1. Rental Address:

   61 Cheery Drive
   Street Address

   Narragansett _____ RI _____ 02882
   City   State   Zip

2. Indicate name and phone numbers of owner of rental property

   Ross _____ Maude _____
   Last Name   First Name

   (401) 555-9822 _____ (401) 555-2291 _____
   Home Phone #   Work Phone #

3. Type of rental unit available (check one)
   (X) House   ( ) Apartment

4. # of bedrooms: 4

5. How many miles is unit from campus? 8

6. Length of lease required (in months)? 9

7. Rent per month? 600

8. Date Available? 9/05/92

9. Please check all amenities that your rental unit features:
   ( ) Utilities included   ( ) Washer/dryer
   ( ) Furnished bedroom(s)   (X) Dishwasher
   (X) On bus line   ( ) Pets allowed
   (X) Wheelchair accessible   (X) Children allowed

Figure 5

AVAILABLE OFF-CAMPUS HOUSING FORM

1. Rental Address:

   915 Maple Street
   Street Address

   Wakefield _____ RI _____ 02894
   City   State   Zip

2. Indicate name and phone numbers of owner of rental property

   Glass _____ Fred _____
   Last Name   First Name

   (401) 555-9345 _____
   Home Phone #   Work Phone #

3. Type of rental unit available (check one)
   ( ) House   (X) Apartment

4. # of bedrooms: 1

5. How many miles is unit from campus? 7

6. Length of lease required (in months)? 3

7. Rent per month? 400

8. Date Available? 9/03/92

9. Please check all amenities that your rental unit features:
   (X) Utilities included   (X) Washer/dryer
   (X) Furnished bedroom(s)   (X) Dishwasher
   (X) On bus line   ( ) Pets allowed
   (X) Wheelchair accessible   ( ) Children allowed

Figure 6

AVAILABLE OFF-CAMPUS HOUSING FORM

1. Rental Address:

   Crossways Apartments
   Street Address

   Wakefield _____ RI _____ 02879
   City   State   Zip

2. Indicate name and phone numbers of owner of rental property

   Howard _____ Frank
   Last Name   First Name

   (401) 555-9821 _____ (401) 555-0982
   Home Phone #   Work Phone #

3. Type of rental unit available (check one)
   ( ) House   (X) Apartment

4. # of bedrooms: 1

5. How many miles is unit from campus? 1

6. Length of lease required (in months)? 9

7. Rent per month? 350

8. Date Available? 10/01/92

9. Please check all amenities that your rental unit features:

   (X) Utilities included   ( ) Washer/dryer

   (X) Furnished bedroom(s)   ( ) Dishwasher

   ( ) On bus line   ( ) Pets allowed

   ( ) Wheelchair accessible   ( ) Children allowed

Figure 7

AVAILABLE OFF-CAMPUS HOUSING FORM

1. Rental Address:

   50 Yankee Drive
   Street Address

   Narragansett _____ RI _____ 02882
   City   State   Zip

2. Indicate name and phone numbers of owner of rental property

   Mason _____ Jake
   Last Name   First Name

   (401) 555-1983
   Home Phone #   Work Phone #

3. Type of rental unit available (check one)
   (X) House   ( ) Apartment

4. # of bedrooms: 1

5. How many miles is unit from campus? 7

6. Length of lease required (in months)? 9

7. Rent per month? 475

8. Date Available? 9/01/92

9. Please check all amenities that your rental unit features:

   (X) Utilities included   ( ) Washer/dryer

   ( ) Furnished bedroom(s)   ( ) Dishwasher

   ( ) On bus line   ( ) Pets allowed

   ( ) Wheelchair accessible   ( ) Children allowed

Figure 8

AVAILABLE OFF-CAMPUS HOUSING FORM

1. Rental Address:

   92 Worden Pond Road
   Street Address

   Kingston _____ RI _____ 02881
   City   State   Zip

2. Indicate name and phone numbers of owner of rental property

   Kinyo _____ Janine
   Last Name   First Name

   (401) 555-1195 _____ (401) 555-5367
   Home Phone #   Work Phone #

3. Type of rental unit available (check one)
   ( ) House   (X) Apartment

4. # of bedrooms: 2

5. How many miles is unit from campus? 2

6. Length of lease required (in months)? 9

7. Rent per month? 425

8. Date Available? 9/01/92

9. Please check all amenities that your rental unit features:

   (X) Utilities included   (X) Washer/dryer

   (X) Furnished bedroom(s)   ( ) Dishwasher

   (X) On bus line   (X) Pets allowed

   ( ) Wheelchair accessible   ( ) Children allowed

Figure 9

AVAILABLE OFF-CAMPUS HOUSING FORM

1. Rental Address:

   100 Point Judith Road
   Street Address

   Narragansett _____ RI _____ 02882
   City   State   Zip

2. Indicate name and phone numbers of owner of rental property

   Franconi _____ Joe
   Last Name   First Name

   (401) 555-9921 _____ (401) 555-1239
   Home Phone #   Work Phone #

3. Type of rental unit available (check one)
   ( ) House   (X) Apartment

4. # of bedrooms: 2

5. How many miles is unit from campus? 8

6. Length of lease required (in months)? 9

7. Rent per month? 400

8. Date Available? 01/01/93

9. Please check all amenities that your rental unit features:

   ( ) Utilities included   ( ) Washer/dryer

   (X) Furnished bedroom(s)   ( ) Dishwasher

   (X) On bus line   ( ) Pets allowed

   ( ) Wheelchair accessible   ( ) Children allowed

Figure 10

AVAILABLE OFF-CAMPUS HOUSING FORM

1. Rental Address:

968 Ocean Drive
Street Address

Narragansett _____ RI ____ 02882
City   State   Zip

2. Indicate name and phone numbers of owner of rental property

Marks   Heather
Last Name   First Name

(401) 555-9973
Home Phone #   Work Phone #

3. Type of rental unit available (check one)
    (X) House   ( ) Apartment

4. # of bedrooms: 3

5. How many miles is unit from campus? 10

6. Length of lease required (in months)? 9

7. Rent per month? 650

8. Date Available? 9/10/92

9. Please check all amenities that your rental unit features:
    ( ) Utilities included   (X) Washer/dryer
    ( ) Furnished bedroom(s)   ( ) Dishwasher
    (X) On bus line   ( ) Pets allowed
    ( ) Wheelchair accessible   (X) Children allowed

Figure 11

AVAILABLE OFF-CAMPUS HOUSING FORM

1. Rental Address:

1 Goat Island Circle
Street Address

Narragansett _____ RI ____ 02882
City   State   Zip

2. Indicate name and phone numbers of owner of rental property

Razor   Charles
Last Name   First Name

(203) 555-9357   (203) 555-9111
Home Phone #   Work Phone #

3. Type of rental unit available (check one)
    (X) House   ( ) Apartment

4. # of bedrooms: 4

5. How many miles is unit from campus? 8

6. Length of lease required (in months)? 9

7. Rent per month? 700

8. Date Available? 09/01/92

9. Please check all amenities that your rental unit features:
    ( ) Utilities included   (X) Washer/dryer
    ( ) Furnished bedroom(s)   ( ) Dishwasher
    ( ) On bus line   ( ) Pets allowed
    ( ) Wheelchair accessible   (X) Children allowed

Figure 12

---

8.   List owner, rent per month, and home and work phone number of all housing units. Send your output to the printer.

9.   Jeanne Margolis's rental property was rented. Mark the record for deletion.

10. List the addresses of all rental properties. Send the output to the printer.

11. Jeanne Margolis called to tell you the prospective tenant for her rental property backed out. She asks you to continue listing the property. Take the appropriate action.

12. List the addresses of all rental properties. Send the output to the printer.

AVAILABLE OFF-CAMPUS HOUSING FORM

1. Rental Address:

12 Wooded Lane
Street Address

Kingston _____ RI ____ 02881
City   State   Zip

2. Indicate name and phone numbers of owner of rental property

Johnston   Evan
Last Name   First Name

(401) 555-1357   (401) 555-4131
Home Phone #   Work Phone #

3. Type of rental unit available (check one)
    ( ) House   (X) Apartment

4. # of bedrooms: 1

5. How many miles is unit from campus? 1

6. Length of lease required (in months)? 12

7. Rent per month? 425

8. Date Available? 01/01/93

9. Please check all amenities that your rental unit features:
    (X) Utilities included   ( ) Washer/dryer
    (X) Furnished bedroom(s)   ( ) Dishwasher
    ( ) On bus line   ( ) Pets allowed
    (X) Wheelchair accessible   ( ) Children allowed

Figure 13

Case Problems for Tutorial 4

For Problems 13 through 18, you decide on the appropriate fields. Send the output to the printer.

13. Include all rental properties.

14. Include all rental properties in Narragansett.

15. Include all rental properties with monthly rent below $600.

16. Include all rental properties with three or four bedrooms.

17. Include all rental properties that are furnished apartments.

18. Fill in the following table:

	Houses	Apartments
Number		
Average rent		

Case Problems for Tutorial 5

19. Sort the records by city. Name the sorted file HSESORT1.

20. Print the name of owner and the address (street address, city, state, zip) of all rental properties using the sorted file.

21. Sort the HOUSING file by type of rental property and within type of rental property by city. Name the sorted file HSESORT2.

22. Print the type of rental property, name of owner, and the address (street address, city, state, zip) of all rental properties using the sorted file HSESORT2.

23. Create an index file named HSEINDX1 using the HOUSING file. Use the owner's last name as the indexing field.

24. Print the HOUSING file in alphabetical order by owner's name. Also include home and work phone numbers.

Case Problems for Tutorial 6

25. Use the report layout sheet in Figure 14 to create a report format file. Name the report format file HSERPT1.

Page #
Date

Off-Campus Housing Report

Rental Street	Town/ City	Type	Rent	# of Bedrooms
X-------X	X-----X	X	XXXX	X
X-------X	X-----X	X	XXXX	X

Figure 14

26. Use your report format file to print a list of housing units ordered by town.

27. Print a list of housing units ordered by type of housing unit.

Case Problems for Tutorial 7

28. Create a second database file and name it RENTTYPE. The file will store the following data:

Unit Type	Description
H	House
A	Apartment

29. Print the file structure.

30. Create an index file named UNIT. Use unit type as the index key.

31. Print the RENTTYPE.DBF file.

32. Open HOUSING.DBF in work area 2.

33. Link the HOUSING and RENTTYPE database files. HOUSING is the source database.

34. Print a list of rental units. Include the description of the unit, the city where the unit is located, and the rent for the unit.

35. Create a view file named HOUSTYPE.

Index

Note: Symbols listed below are indexed alphabetically by the name given.

→ (arrow symbol). *See* arrow (→) symbol

, comma. *See* comma (,)

- hyphen. *See* hyphen (-)

- minus sign. *See* minus (−) sign

. period. *See* period (.)

/ slash. *See* slash (/)

& ampersand. *See* ampersand (&)

' apostrophe. *See* apostrophe (')

* asterisk. *See* asterisk (*)

@ at sign. *See* at (@) sign

\ backslash. *See* backslash (\)

{} braces. *See* braces ({})

[ ] brackets. *See* brackets ([])

∧ caret. *See* caret (∧)

$ dollar sign. *See* dollar ($) sign

= equal sign. *See* equal (=) sign

> (greater than). *See* greater than (>)

>= (greater than or equal to). *See* greater than or equal to (>=)

< (less than). *See* less than (<)

<= (less than or equal to). See less than or equal to (<=)

<> (not equal to). *See* not equal to (<>)

( ) parentheses. *See* parentheses ( )

% percent sign. *See* percent (%) sign

+ plus sign. *See* plus (+) sign

pound sign. *See* pound (#) sign

? question mark. *See* question (?) mark

" quote sign. *See* quote (") sign

~ tilde sign. *See* tilde (~) sign

_ underscore. *See* underscore (_)

A

absolute cell references (Lotus) 415, 416, 420-26

Access menu (Lotus) 481-82, 506

access time 17

action lines (dBASE) 604

active files (dBASE) 787

active index (dBASE) 728

add-in cards 12

adding
    dBASE
        fields 635-38
        group headings 770-71
        records 654-57

Lotus
    axis titles, graphs 491
    legends, graphs 489-90
    multiple variables, graphs 486-87
    titles, pie charts 498-99

WordPerfect
    new footnotes 284-85

address, cell. *See* cell address

address labels (WP)
    creating labels document 322-26
    creating primary file 321
    merging primary file w/address list 321-22
    printing 326-27

aligning (Lotus)
    labels 396-98
    numbers 389, 390, 439

ALL, as command word (dBASE) 701

alphanumeric sort (WP) 317

[Alt] (Lotus) 565

Alt macros (WP) 273, 275, 276-77, 279

[Alt] (WP) 96

[Alt][=] (WP) 93, 94, 132

[Alt][F1] (Thesaurus) (WP) 164

[Alt][F2] (Replace) (WP) 186, 187

[Alt][F2] (Step) (Lotus) 574

[Alt][F3] (Reveal codes) (WP) 146

[Alt][F3] (Run) (Lotus) 565, 566, 569, 572, 574

[Alt][F4] (Block) (WP) 193, 195

[Alt][F4] (Undo) (Lotus) 367, 453

[Alt][F5] (Learn) (Lotus) 570, 571

[Alt][F6] (Flush Right) (WP) 182, 183

[Alt][F7] (Columns/Table) (WP) 237, 239, 242

[Alt][F8] (Style) (WP) 232, 235

[Alt][F10] (Macro) (WP) 273

ampersand (&) (Lotus) 359

anchoring ranges with period (.) sign (Lotus) 370, 418

.AND. logical operator (dBASE) 696-97, 698

apostrophe (') (Lotus) 353, 396, 563

APPEND command (dBASE) 729

Append option (dBASE) 654

applications software 19-20

Arabic numerals (WP) 257

arguments of a function (Lotus) 386, 420

arrow (→) symbol
    dBASE 797
    WordPerfect 185

arrow keys. *See also* cursor-movement keys
    dBASE 628, 700
    Lotus 350-51, 357-58
    WordPerfect 93, 103, 116, 133-35, 239

ascending sort order
    dBASE 713
    Lotus 526-27
    WordPerfect 320

Photography Credits